The Fate of Man

BY CRANE BRINTON

A History of Western Morals (1959)
The Anatomy of Revolution (1957)
Modern Civilization (1957)
Portable Age of Reason Reader (1956)
History of Civilization (1955)
The World of History (1954)
The Shaping of the Modern Mind (1954)
The Temper of Western Europe (1953)
English Political Thought in the Nineteenth Century (1950)
Ideas and Men (1950)
The United States and Britain (1948)
From Many One (1948)
Nietzsche (1941)
The Lives of Talleyrand (1936)
French Revolutionary Legislation on Illegitimacy (1936)
A Decade of Revolution (1935)
The Jacobins (1930)
Political Ideas of the English Romanticists (1926)

THE
FATE
OF
MAN

Edited with Introductions
and Postscript by
CRANE BRINTON

GEORGE BRAZILLER
NEW YORK 1961

Acknowledgments

The editor and publisher have made every effort to determine and credit the holders of copyright of the selections in this book. Any errors or omissions may be rectified in future volumes. For permission to use these selections, the editor and publisher make grateful acknowledgment to the following authors, publishers and agents, who reserve all rights for the matter reprinted:

From THE FUTURE OF UNBELIEF by Gerhard Szczesny. Translated by Edward B. Garside. Copyright © 1961 by George Braziller, Inc. By permission of George Braziller, Inc.

From THE NAVAHO by Clyde Kluckhohn and Dorothea Leighton. Copyright, 1946, by the President and Fellows of Harvard College. By permission of Harvard University Press.

From PROCESS AND REALITY by Alfred North Whitehead. Copyright 1929 by The Macmillan Company, copyright renewed 1957. By permission of The Macmillan Company.

From OF STARS AND MEN by Harlow Shapley. Copyright, ©, 1958, by Harlow Shapley. By permission of Beacon Press and Elek Books Limited.

From ARISTOTLE by John Herman Randall, Jr. Copyright © Columbia University Press, New York. By permission of Columbia University Press.

From A COMPANION TO THE SUMMA, Vol. IV, by Walter Farrell, O. P. Copyright, 1942 by Sheed & Ward. By permission of Sheed & Ward, Inc.

From SKETCH FOR A HISTORICAL PICTURE OF THE HUMAN MIND by the Marquis de Condorcet. Translated by Jane Barraclough. By permission of The Noonday Press; Library of Ideas and Weidenfeld and Nicolson Ltd.

From THE MARXIAN THEORY OF THE STATE by Sherman H. M. Chang. Copyright 1931 by the Author. By permission of University of Pennsylvania Press.

From ETHICS AND LANGUAGE by Charles L. Stevenson. © 1944 By Yale University Press, Inc. By permission of Yale University Press.

From A MODERN THEORY OF ETHICS by Olaf Stapledon. By permission of Methuen & Co. Ltd. and the Executrix of the Estate of Olaf Stapledon.

From THE PERENNIAL PHILOSOPHY by Aldous Huxley. Copyright 1944, 1945 by Aldous Huxley. By permission of Harper & Brothers and Chatto and Windus Ltd.

From MEISTER ECKHART, a modern translation by Raymond B. Blakney. Copyright 1941 by Harper & Brothers. By permission of Harper & Brothers.

From BLAISE PASCAL by Ernest Mortimer. Copyright © 1959 by Ernest Mortimer. By permission of Harper & Brothers and Methuen & Co. Ltd.

From THE ANTIGONE OF SOPHOCLES. Translated by John Jay Chapman. Copyright, 1930, by John Jay Chapman. By permission of Houghton Mifflin Company.

From THE MAXIMS OF LA ROCHEFOUCAULD. Translated by Louis Kronenberger. © Copyright 1959 by Random House, Inc. By permission of Random House, Inc.

From THE LICHTENBERG READER. Edited and Translated by Franz H. Mautner and Henry Hatfield. By permission of Beacon Press, Inc.

From HUMAN NATURE AND THE HUMAN CONDITION by Joseph Wood Krutch. © Copyright 1959 by Joseph Wood Krutch. By permission of Random House, Inc.

From IN SEARCH OF HUMANITY by Alfred Cobban. © Alfred Cobban 1960. By permission of George Braziller, Inc. and Jonathan Cape Ltd.

From ISSUES OF FREEDOM by Herbert J. Muller. Copyright © 1960 by Herbert J. Muller. By permission of Harper & Brothers.

From THE CONFESSIONS OF SAINT AUGUSTINE. Translated by F. J. Sheed. Copyright, 1943, by Sheed & Ward, Inc. By permission of Sheed & Ward, Inc. and Sheed & Ward Ltd.

From BENJAMIN FRANKLIN: THE AUTOBIOGRAPHY AND SELECTIONS FROM HIS OTHER WRITINGS. Farrand edition. Copyright, 1949, by University of California Press. By permission of University of California Press.

From THE TWO CULTURES AND THE SCIENTIFIC REVOLUTION by C. P. Snow. © C. P. Snow, 1959. By permission of Cambridge University Press.

From THE INTELLECTUALS edited by George B. de Huszar: *America's Post-Radical Critics* by Harold Rosenberg. (Originally published in *The Tradition of the New* by Harold Rosenberg, Horizon Press, 1959-60.) Copyright © 1960 by The Free Press, a Corporation. By permission of The Free Press, Horizon Press, and Harold Rosenberg.

From WORDS AND THINGS by Ernest Gellner. © 1959 by Ernest Gellner. By permission of Beacon Press and Victor Gollancz, Ltd.

From THE WAY THINGS ARE by P. W. Bridgman. Copyright 1959 by the President and Fellows of Harvard College. By permission of Harvard University Press.

From SOCIALISM: UTOPIAN AND SCIENTIFIC by Frederick Engels. Translated by Edward Aveling. Copyright, 1935, by International Publishers Co., Inc. By permission of International Publishers.

From THE PATTERN OF THE PAST: CAN WE DETERMINE IT? by Pieter Geyl, Arnold J. Toynbee, and Pitirim Sorokin. Copyright, 1949, The Beacon Press. By permission of Beacon Press and Uitgeverij F. G. Kroonder.

From THE FUTURE AS HISTORY by Robert Heilbroner. Copyright © 1959, 1960, by Robert L. Heilbroner. By permission of Harper & Brothers and William Morris Agency, Inc.

From THE RECOVERY OF BELIEF by C. E. M. Joad. By permission of Faber and Faber Ltd.

From AN OUTLINE OF MAN'S KNOWLEDGE OF THE MODERN WORLD edited by Lyman Bryson: *The Search for Answers* by Clarence H. Faust. Copyright © 1960 by Catherine McGrattan Bryson, Executrix of the estate of Lyman Bryson. By permission of Doubleday & Company, Inc., and published by McGraw-Hill Book Company, Inc.

From THE WAY OF ZEN by Alan W. Watts. Copyright © 1957 by Pantheon Books, Inc. By permission of Pantheon Books, Inc. and Thames and Hudson Ltd.

From THE STANDARD EDITION OF THE COMPLETE PSYCHOLOGICAL WORKS OF SIGMUND FREUD. Translated and edited by James Strachey and Anna Freud. Translation © James Strachey 1959. By permission of Hogarth Press Ltd., Encyclopaedia Britannica, and Sigmund Freud Copyrights Ltd.

From THE NEW AGE OF FAITH by John Langdon-Davies. Copyright, 1925, by The Viking Press, Inc., 1953 by John Langdon-Davies. By permission of The Viking Press, Inc.

From MAN THE UNKNOWN by Alexis Carrel. Copyright 1935 by Harper & Brothers. By permission of Harper & Brothers.

From ACCENT ON FORM by Lancelot Law Whyte. Copyright 1954 by Lancelot Law Whyte. By permission of Harper & Brothers and Routledge & Kegan Paul Ltd.

From SCIENCE AND THE HUMAN TEMPERAMENT by Erwin Schrödinger. Copyright © by Erwin Schrödinger 1935. (Copyright © by Dover Publications, Inc. 1957 under the title SCIENCE THEORY AND MAN.) By permission of George Allen & Unwin Ltd.

From WHAT SCIENCE STANDS FOR by Orr, Hill, Philip, Gregory, Hall and Hogben. By permission of George Allen & Unwin Ltd.

From MIRAGE OF HEALTH by René Dubos. Copyright © 1959 by René Dubos. By permission of Harper & Brothers and George Allen & Unwin Ltd.

From THE FOREST AND THE SEA by Marston Bates. © Copyright 1960 by Marston Bates. By permission of Random House, Inc. and Museum Press Ltd.

From THE NEXT MILLION YEARS by Charles Galton Darwin. Copyright 1952 by Charles Galton Darwin. By permission of Doubleday & Company, Inc. and Rupert Hart-Davis Ltd.

From POSTHISTORIC MAN by Roderick Seidenberg. Copyright 1950 by the University of North Carolina Press. By permission of The University of North Carolina Press.

From *Encounter,* May 1960: "Inventing the Future" by Dennis Gabor. © 1960 by Encounter Ltd. By permission of *Encounter.*

I wish to thank the many authors and publishers who have made it possible for me to include in this book so much contemporary writing. In particular, I am grateful to Henry Murray, whose provocative Phi Beta Kappa address at Harvard in 1959 set my mind running on several different tacks, one of which ended—for the moment—with this book. My gratitude may seem at first sight paradoxically near ingratitude, since one of my purposes has been to demonstrate how hard it will be, on these matters of the condition of man, to achieve the refreshing meeting of minds Dr. Murray wants. But I take it that we both believe that disagreement must precede agreement in our kind of society. The professional ethics of that singular vocation, book publishing, will not permit me to single out by name the members of the Braziller staff who have done so much to make this book. I am sure they know how grateful I am. Finally, and once more, I wish to thank my secretary, Miss Elizabeth F. Hoxie, for invaluable help with typescript and proofs.

CRANE BRINTON

Cambridge, November 15, 1960

Table of Contents

PART I

SETTING
THE
PROBLEM

I

Setting the Problem

THE VERY DISPARATE WRITINGS GATHERED IN THIS BOOK ARE THERE FOR a purpose. They are part—a very small part indeed—of what an interested mid-twentieth-century American might use to help locate himself in the bewildering world of twentieth-century thought on the great questions we still call *philosophical*. The book is frankly and unashamedly didactic. It is one of a genre that, lowly though it be in the hierarchy of literary genres, is surely indispensable in our democracy: the do-it-yourself book. Make, if you must and can, your own world-view.

I shall shortly attempt to explain more fully what might be done with the materials here collected. But first, in fairness to the prospective reader, I must make clear what this anthology is not. It is not a collection of excerpts from the best books, the greatest books, the books everyone ought to read. It is not a chronologically arranged book of readings in formal philosophy or in the now fashionable history of ideas, designed to accompany a systematic textbook in these subjects. It is not a collection of "primary" source materials in original forms. Indeed, I have not hesitated to use "secondary" materials, good clear expositions of one man's ideas by another man, especially when the original is gracelessly written, very technical, difficult, as, for example, the writings of Aristotle in the form we have received them. This book is not, though a sampling of its later pages might make it appear so, a collection of essays on contemporary "problems," a collection designed to elicit thoughtful and literate compositions from freshman English classes. It is not a collection of pieces that I like, or agree with, or even find always very interesting. But it is, I hope, a useful and only very roughly systematic assemblage of a wide range of human thinking about man's place in the universe. It is meant for the relatively few who feel a need to do such thinking for themselves.

Are they indeed in our mid-twentieth-century world few? We encounter at the very start of our enterprise one of the most difficult and controversial aspects of the basic problem of man's fate as it seems to men today. Are men—Western men, men of the free world at least—in unusually large numbers puzzled, disturbed, adrift—"alienated," as the psychologist likes to put it? I give later in this introductory section a firm statement that ours is indeed an age of—I put it mildly—spiritual confusion, and that we need badly to clear that confusion up. But let me cite now two passages from contemporary writers, both trained psychologists, which put clearly and succinctly the opinion, widespread among the articulate few, that the less-articulate many are today in a state of intellectual and emotional crisis, are, in fact, "alienated." First, here is the distinguished psychoanalyst Bruno Bettelheim[1]:

We are in great haste to send and receive messages from outer space. But so hectic and often so tedious are our days, that many of us have nothing of importance to communicate to those close to us.

Never before have so many had it so good; no longer do we tremble in fear of sickness or hunger, of hidden evils in the dark, of the spell of witches. The burden of killing toil has been lifted from us, and machines, not the labor of our hands, will soon provide us with nearly all we need, and much that we don't really need. We have inherited freedoms man has striven after for centuries. Because of all this and much more we should be living in a dawn of great promise. But now that we are freer to enjoy life, we are deeply frustrated in our disappointment that the freedom and comfort, sought with such deep desire, do not give meaning and purpose to our lives.

With so much at hand that generations have striven for, how bewildering that the meaning of life should evade us. Freedoms we have, broader than ever before. But more than ever before most of us yearn for a self realization that eludes us, while we abide restless in the midst of plenty. As we achieve freedom, we are frightened by social forces that seem to suffocate us, seem to move in on us from all parts of an ever contracting world.

The tedium and dissatisfaction with life are becoming so great that many are getting ready to let freedom slip out of their hands. They feel it is all too complicated, too difficult to hold on to it, and to themselves. If meaning has gone out of their lives, then at least they wish not to be responsible for it, to let society carry the burden of failure and guilt.

Just how to achieve self realization, to preserve freedom, and adapt society to both, seems increasingly harder to know; it is felt as a central, overwhelming problem of our days.

From finding security in a repetition of sameness, of only slight and slow variations, we are having to live with a very different kind of security; one that must rest on achieving the good life, with very little chance to predict the outcome of our actions in a fast changing world.

To manage such a feat, heart and reason can no longer be kept in their separate places. Work and art, family and society, can no longer develop in isolation from each other. The daring heart must invade reason with its own living warmth, even if the symmetry of reason must give way to admit love and the pulsation of life.

No longer can we be satisfied with a life where the heart has its reasons, which reason cannot know. Our hearts must know the world of reason, and reason must be guided by an informed heart.

[1] Bruno Bettelheim, *The Informed Heart* (Glencoe, Ill.: The Free Press, 1960), pp. vii-viii. This interesting and controversial book deals centrally with Dr. Bettelheim's own direct experience of Nazi Germany, including a year in the concentration camps of Dachau and Buchenwald. It is also a tract for the times, worried but not alarmist. The reader will find a stimulating discussion of the meaning of attitudes revealed in the *Diary of Anne Frank*, pp. 252-254.

Second, here is a much more worried passage from a young Harvard psychologist, Kenneth Keniston[2]:

This is an age that inspires little enthusiasm. In the industrial West, and increasingly now in the uncommitted nations of the East, ardor is lacking; instead men talk of their growing distance from one another, from their social order, from their work and play, and even from the values that in a perhaps romanticized past seem to have given their lives cohesiveness and direction. Horatio Alger is replaced by Timon, Napoleon by Ishmael, and even Lincoln now seems pallid before the defiant images of "hoods" and "beats." The vocabulary of social commentary is dominated by terms that characterize this distance: alienation, estrangement, separation, withdrawal, indifference, disaffection, apathy, noninvolvement, neutralism—all these words describe the increasing distance between men and their former objects of love, commitment, loyalty, devotion and reverence. Alienation, once seen as the consequence of a cruel (but changeable) economic order, has become for many the central fact of human existence, characterizing man's "thrown-ness" into a world in which he has no inherent place. Formerly imposed *upon* men by the world around them, estrangement increasingly is chosen *by* them as their dominant reaction to the world.

Dr. Keniston's recital of woe must not be confused with what the historian of Western thought knows is never quite absent from the record—that is, the complaints of the bright young men—and those not so young but still bright—against the ways of their less-gifted fellow men. The now fashionable phrase, "alienation of the intellectuals," if it is taken to mean no more than the discontent of sensitive, high-minded, imaginatively inventive and adventurous persons, expressed in particular over the behavior of the rest of the human race, may be said almost to describe a constant of history. You can find such alienation in the writers of ages that now look most golden and happy, in Plato, in Shakespeare, in almost all the writers of that "Century of Hope," the nineteenth. Here is an example from yesterday:

Why have you Bloomers and Women's Rights Men, and strong-minded women, and Mormons, and anti-renters, and "vote myself a farm" men, Millerites, and Spiritual Rappers, and Shakers, and Widow Wakemanites, and Agrarians, and Grahamites, and a thousand other superstitious and infidel Isms at the North? Why is there faith in nothing, speculation about everything? Why is this unsettled, half-demented, state of the human mind co-extensive in time and space, with free society? Why is Western Europe now starving? and why has it been fighting and starving for seventy years? Why all this, except that free society is a failure? Slave society needs no defense till some other permanently practicable form of society has been discovered. Nobody at the North who reads my book will attempt to reply to it; for all the learned abolitionists had unconsciously discovered and proclaimed the failure of free society long before I did.[3]

Perhaps one might say that Fitzhugh, a Southern journalist who wrote

[2] Kenneth Keniston, "Alienation and the Decline of Utopia," *American Scholar*, 29, Number 2 (Spring, 1960), p. 1.

[3] Letter from George Fitzhugh to A. Hogeboom, 14 January 1856, quoted in the John Harvard Library edition of Fitzhugh's *Cannibals All*, ed. C. Vann Woodward (Cambridge: Harvard University Press, 1960), p. xxvii.

in defense of slavery, meant by "unsettled, half-demented" substantially what Dr. Keniston means by "alienated"? And a hundred years ago apparently there were those who were aware of the unconscious. This brief paragraph deserves careful analysis, for some of it drives home the eternal alienation—at least in what Fitzhugh calls "free society"—of the intellectual; it reminds us that "multanimity"[4] among men is not just of today; and it exhibits one of the weaknesses of these fighters with words, namely their disregard for facts. Surely Western Europe did not starve in those marvelous seventy years of Progress, 1786-1856?

But the alienation of our intellectuals today, if Henry Murray, Gerhard Szczesny, Kenneth Keniston, and a host of others are right, is something more than indignant impatience with the imperfections of human institutions and human "nature." Our intellectuals are discontented with themselves as well as with the universe and their fellows, are prey to an existentialist whistling in the dark, are above all uncertain as to whether they really know, can really plan, let alone achieve, a better way of life here on earth. In fine simple terms: they lack what may well be an essential of human existence, a confident sense that they understand their place in the universe; they lack a firm metaphysics, a firm teleology, a firm cosmology; perhaps we might as well say they lack a firm, consoling, yet duly stimulating *religion*.

Now the above is put with some exaggeration. Historians in the future, with a perspective we cannot gain, may find our twentieth century a fertile and creative time, no more disturbed than seems necessary if we are to grow, or at least, change. Certainly our leading intellectuals are not resigned, defeated, apathetic; they may be bewildered, but they are also indignant, and very, very articulate. I quite deliberately did not write above that they lack a firm ethics, for they clearly do not have any such lack. Their standards of right and wrong are not very different from those of their grandparents, nor, except in manners rather than in morals, is their behavior very different. I feel sure that no one who knows the ways of American intellectuals—teachers, preachers, writers, artists, yes, scientists, for they too are intellectuals—can fairly maintain that as a group they are less well behaved than the rest of Americans. Their spiritual troubles, which are real, have not for the most part undermined their moral sense. I say this firmly, in part just because of recent T.V. quiz scandals.

But how about the rest of our country or, indeed, of the West, for the problem is by no means peculiarly American? Is this alienation of the intellectuals also an alienation of the nonintellectuals? Are the many spiritually disoriented, disturbed, and, if so, are the moral consequences of such widespread popular alienation likely to be a danger to the very

---

[4] I find it hard to believe that I have coined so obvious and useful a word as "multanimity," but I confess I have not found it in any of the three unabridged dictionaries I have consulted.—C. B.

existence of the free world? These are enormous questions, to which the wisest of our spiritual guides and the ablest of our social scientists cannot give the kind of answer we should all like to have. I should not dream of attempting such an answer, but I should like, in order to clarify to the reader just what I expect of him, to set down very briefly indeed a few propositions on this subject, propositions which I trust will encourage the fit reader to go on, and encourage the unfit reader (who may well be very fit indeed for other things, indeed, for other reading) to refrain from going on.

First, though probably all human beings save for the very feeble-minded do have what I shall call "metaphysical concern," do have "ideas" about religion, philosophy, man's condition and man's fate, only a few "think" about such matters; probably only a few *can* think about such matters. I realize that this is a very controversial statement, and one that can hardly be verified experimentally, at least not in the present state of the appropriate social sciences. Yet the range or spectrum of individual human differences in readily assessed external or "physical" capacities and achievements is great and obvious even to the most democratically inspired. We do not usually expect most people to be, or even to become, platinum blondes, possessors of absolute pitch, .300 hitters, or heroic mountain climbers; notably, we do not expect football linemen to serve also as coxswains of eight-oared shells; and—though the ardent democratic egalitarians take this hard—we are resigned to the apparent fact that the male and female of the human species are not quite interchangeable in all respects.

I think it clear that not all human beings can think. Of course I use that word snobbishly, imprecisely—and usefully—to mean a *particular kind of thinking,* the kind of manipulation of "abstractions" you and I are now indulging ourselves in, thinking "philosophically." This kind of thinking is also, for the person doing it, in a sense deserving of those nice adjectives "original" and "creative" even though it results in nothing that has not been thought and said many many times before. Thinking, like loving, is for the individual always a unique and pristine adventure. At this point, I face great temptations to digression and amplification. Let me content myself with noting that our Western tradition, if somewhat ambivalent toward this kind of thinking, on the whole has held it to be a form of privileged, that is, aristocratic, excellence, which is one reason why so many Americans would like to believe that everyone can and ought to indulge in it. In a variant form, still essentially philosophical, which is now called scientific, thinking is today held in high esteem by most Americans.

Second, though probably all mentally normal persons from infancy on do think in concrete daily matters of problem-solving in ways by no means wholly unlike the ways of philosophic or scientific or abstract or analytical thought, it seems likely that their opinions in actual philosophy, religion, ethics and the like are pretty painlessly acquired by a kind of cultural inheritance and training; or at any rate that, once acquired, these opinions are held comfortably, firmly, consciously, of course, but not proddingly. They are part of the ritual regularities of life. Conservative social thinkers—Burke, Le Play, Pareto—have long recognized the importance of these "inherited" and consoling beliefs; hopelessly unrealistic thinkers—like a John Stuart Mill—themselves always thinking, thinking, have wholly misunderstood them, even to the point of maintaining that the unhappy holders actually find their treasured beliefs ("dogmas," horrid word) a burden.

Now I am at least unconvinced that the alienation of the intellectuals in our modern West has spread very far among the non-intellectual (though not stupid) many. Enlightened secularists, numerous among intellectuals, certainly exaggerate the extent to which the fundamentals of our Judaeo-Christian religious inheritance no longer hold the many. Needless to say, this Judaeo-Christian tradition can give a very firm, and very consoling, grasp on its ultimates. Moreover, most of the surrogates for Christianity, and even a Christianity watered down with doubts as to possible transcendence of the this-world of science, can and do for many in our world fend off the cosmic worries that show up in alienation. Indeed, even what I like to call, not secular religion, but the religion of the Enlightment, once it is stripped of its expectation of an immediate First Coming of Happiness on this earth, can be and for many is a consoling faith, suitably prophylactic against the ills of doubt and despair.

Third, however, I should indeed agree with Messrs. Murray, Szczesny, Keniston and many others—some of whom I have included in later sections of this book—that the state of mind diagnosed by them as "alienation" is real, important, and to be fought against, even though it is probably limited to the intellectual few. Let me make here three final comments.

First, though we do not by any means understand, for complex societies such as those of the West, the relations between the intellectual few and the rest of the society, the two groups are not mutually isolated, nor necessarily mutually hostile. Somehow, what the few do does seep down among the many, does affect their beliefs and hence their conduct. Again I brush lightly against an enormous subject. To be summary: I do not think we can have many bright young men in the state of mind Dr. Keniston depicts without a serious corruption of our whole national will to live.

Second, the plight of the alienated intellectuals, though it is certainly due to many complex and interrelated factors, is in part at least, or so it must seem to a historian, due to their fine American ignorance of the past—even of our own past. They, as grandchildren of the eighteenth-century Enlightment, really were brought up to believe that man's normal condition on earth is the *successful* pursuit of happiness. As Robert Heilbroner puts it very succinctly in his recent *The Future As History,* they believed in the "inevitability of progress," moral as well as material; they were optimists, indeed Utopians. And they ran up against a catalogue of horrors, from Sarajevo to Auschwitz and Hiroshima.

Third, and put very briefly: although *relatively* few in the billions of humanity, these troubled intellectuals are *absolutely* numerous indeed, and very important.

I shall attempt further reflections on these matters at the end of this book. Here let me note that I have shaped this anthology above all for the now unhappy few who feel the need of thinking about man's fate and their own, and who have begun to realize that neither their scholastic education, with its neglect of history for vague and quite unreassuring "social studies" slanted toward the democratic pieties, nor their family training with its excessive lack of the vein of iron, has prepared them for the task of placing themselves in a world like ours. What I have gathered under section IV from twentieth-century writers might well have filled the whole book, but this would have meant the loss of what is in some respects the most important thing for our troubled seekers to face: simple historical perspective. Literally hundreds of generations of thinkers have had to face the kind of problems we face—yes, even the apocalyptic fears of total destruction of the race and the universe. The problems have not of course been *identical,* and their solutions have varied; it is possible that over the long centuries there has been in these phases of human culture an understandable and explicable process of the kind we understand well enough in biology by a term like "evolution," in technology by terms like "progress" or "greater efficiency." But on this very problem of the nature and existence of a "cultural evolution," we in the West are by no means in agreement today, as can be seen from the foreword by Leslie A. White and the chapters on the Law of Evolutionary Potential in the excellent volume by Sahlens and Service, *Evolution and Culture,* which I refer to on page 427.

Briefly, men—many men—are obviously driven to ask the kind of question, set the kind of problem, we are concerned with in this book. Quite as obviously, they have not succeded in getting answers, solutions, on which all men can agree. They have not got even the kind of agreement which we expect from common sense, from science, and which the Christians must still expect ultimately in religion—the *securus judicat orbis terrarum* of St. Augustine. A twentieth-century school of philosophers we shall meet briefly in section IV—the logical positivists, or logical analysts, or linguistic philosophers—has been taken among popularizers of philosophical thought and hostile philosophers to have maintained that since such problems (metaphysical, theological, ethical, aesthetic problems) cannot be "solved" as, say, the chemist or the mathematician solves problems in his field, such problems are "meaningless" and therefore not really problems. Yet the most determined logical positivist—better, the most naïve convert to what is itself a rather old metaphysical position—clearly faces, and in a sense solves, such problems daily as a citizen, a husband, a father, a professional man, a reader, a viewer of television, a traveler, and even as that puzzling creature, an individual human being.

He may well, in our day, be very greatly troubled over the difficulties and uncertainties he encounters as he faces these interminable problems; he may even be, as Dr. Keniston holds, "alienated," driven to a despairing abandonment of any attempts to improve his spiritual lot. But he need not feel ashamed, need not feel alone, need not feel that he wants something not quite natural. For what he is after—put it as vaguely, if you like, as "a search for the meaning of life"—is as natural a desire, as essential a part of man's condition, as eating, drinking, or making love. Here, in a recent book[5], is a fine concrete statement of this need:

I had spent some years in the intensive study of imaginative and philosophical literature, and was continually brought up against the problem of the contrast between the meaning of a man's work and life for us, the "likeness" we make, and his own image or idea of himself. We generally underestimate the importance in a man's life of his "life-illusion," and I wanted to compensate my own bias by studying autobiography, the record of this illusion.

Personal experiences reinforced, and perhaps in reality prompted, this purpose. I was frequently startled to find that for other people I was a person with definite characteristics, who in given circumstances could be expected to have certain views and to act in certain ways; while I remained in my own eyes rather indefinite and capable of unforeseeable reactions. I came to realise that I was deluding myself in some degree, but felt that the others were deluding themselves about me also. I am not so fixed as I appear to them, and I am not so indeterminate as I assume. Thinking over recent changes in my thoughts and habits, I found it immensely difficult to decide whether they were foreseeable, as the assertion of a deeper trend over less fundamental attitudes, or whether they were something really new. In either case, it seemed curious that I should be so anxious to persuade myself that I was consistent, that this "I" was an identity; for even if something new had emerged, I tried to prove to myself that it grew organically out of the old. As if freedom could mean something to me only if it was destiny, as if a choice was satisfactory only if it imposed itself as my nature.

This intellectual problem presented itself however as an insistent moral pressure. I do not mean concern for the morality of my behavior and thoughts, though old faults and follies of course cause sleepless nights. *I mean a need for meaning* (italics C. B.). I do not believe that an individual life has a religious or transcendental meaning, and I cannot even comfort myself with the metaphysical despair, the *Angst,* of the existentialists. Nor is it enough to prove to myself that I am fulfilling a social purpose in a useful job. The meaning had to be personal, subjective. I did not pitch my hopes extravagantly high, and felt one could be content if one could feel one's self to be consistent, to have developed naturally and organically, to have remained "true to itself," and if within this framework one could order certain intense experiences whose significance defied analysis but which were peculiarly one's own. The terms are vague, and I cannot say where this pressure comes from, but I think I am delineating a state of mind from which autobiography springs.

[5] Roy Pascal, *Design and Truth in Autobiography* (Cambridge, Mass.: 1960), pp. vii-viii.

HENRY A. MURRAY

Beyond Yesterday's Idealisms

Henry Murray (1893–   ) is Professor of Psychology at Harvard. He gave this address, which is in tone and content a model of its kind, before the Harvard Chapter of Phi Beta Kappa during Commencement week of 1959. It sets neatly some of the problems we shall try to set more fully— and more skeptically—in this book. Note that Dr. Murray asks for a "mythology" worthy of our group adulthood, as, he holds, the Judaeo-Christian "mythology" is not worthy; and note that he does not ask for a "religion" worthy of our adulthood. I am afraid that for most human beings when a set of cosmic beliefs is a mythology it is no longer a set of beliefs. It would be nice if "mythology" did the job of "religion"—in which case Dr. Murray's proposed new New and Old Testaments might be, if at all possible, also useful. But religions just aren't mythologies—not at least while they are alive as religions. I may, however, be unfairly quibbling over definitions. The reader who wants to go further can start with a very suggestive collection by trained scholars, Henry A. Murray, ed., Myth and Mythmaking *(New York: George Braziller, Inc., 1960).*

MR. PRESIDENT, LADIES, AND GENTLEMEN: THE LIST OF ORATORS SINCE the first performance of this rite in 1782, the blaze of famous names, was blinding to one who as an undergraduate was never on the Dean's list but often in his office, blinding to one who has been fumbling in the dark for many years, in the underground of mind, well below the level of luminous rationality sustained by members of this elite society. From the parade of annual orations one receives imposing views of the diversity of elevated thinking in America, challenging yet humbling, I would guess, to pretty nearly anyone your President might pick to add another theme to this medley of reflections.

Happily for a man in this predicament there are transfusions of courage to be had from a host of predecessors, especially, as you well know, from those wondrous emanations in 1837 of the Platonic Over-Soul of Ralph Waldo Emerson. To this apostle of self-confidence I attribute whatever stamina is required to speak freely to you today, some hundred and twenty years beyond his yesterday. Here my cue comes from Emerson himself who reminded his enthralled audience that each age "must write its own books." "The books of an older age will not fit this."

Emerson's preoccupation was Man Thinking, or, to be more accurate, Mr. Emerson Thinking, serene and saintly, solitary and aloof, residing in his own aura without envy, lust, or anger, unspotted by the world and impervious to its horrors. My preoccupation will be a little different, a difference that makes all the difference: men and women thinking, privately and publicly, in the teeth of an infernal, lethal threat that will be here as long as our inhuman human race is here.

In the realm of thought, Sigmund Freud—who, on the question of innate, potential evil, concurred with St. Augustine—Freud marks the great divide which separates us irrevocably from the benign atmosphere of the untempted, unhurt, and unmolested sage of Concord. Also separating us from that tall, angular, gentle, blue-eyed mystic, who saw evil at such a distance that he could dismiss it and condone it, and who, in so doing, as his admirer Santayana pointed out, "surrendered the category of the better and the worse, the deepest foundation of life and reason"—separating us incurably from that justly-venerated poet-thinker are the blights and blasts of more than forty lurid years of enormities and abominations perpetrated by our fellow-men on the sensitive bodies and souls of other men. Before the occurrence of this global epidemic of lies, treacheries, and atrocities, most of us Americans were temperamentally with Emerson, strongly inclined to optimism, and so to shun or to deny the fact that human creatures were still capable of surpassing all other species as callous and ferocious torturers and killers of their own kind. But now that we have seen all this, the darker vision of the once-rejected Herman Melville resonates with more veracity in some of us.

Would that I could offer, out of my well of joy, a nicer prospect, more appropriate to this festive week! But were I, with bland, buoyant or urbane ideas to indulge both you and me, I would deserve that label that Melville, on second thought, attached to Emerson—Confidence Man.

You see there is still danger that out of shallowness and the desire to be pleasant at all costs—two of our besetting sins—we may rid consciousness of the unflattering knowledge we have gained, and, by so doing, cancel the possibility of ever reaching the conclusion that the present degree and aim of certain of our dispositions and certain states and aims of our various societies are definitely out of date, unsuitable for survival. It looks to me as if we must transform or fall apart.

The inevitable decision is that the eminent Yankee seer was right: the books of *his* age, his *own* books—imperishable as they surely are—are not in all respects fitting to *this* age. The present age and your coming age must write its own books.

I suppose that most of you, just-honored intellectuals, will necessarily be occupied for the next years in thinking in a differentiated way, thinking as specialists—as lawyers, business-men, doctors, scientists, historians, educators. There is vigor and ample creativity involved in all of these professions. But later, if not sooner, you will be pressured from within or from without to think seriously once more about yourself and your relations with women and with men, to think personally and then impersonally, to ask yourself embarrassing questions—knowledge for what? freedom for what? existence for what?—to think, in other words, as a free-lance philosopher, or generalist, about matters of profound and superordinate concern: ways and ends of being and becoming, morals, religion, the human situation, the world's plight. At such times each of you will be, in Emerson's sense, Man Thinking, and your reflections may beget a book or brace of books fitting to your age. Your capacity to write a book—logical, critical, and substantial —has been accredited by the conferring of the Key, symbolic of the fact that learning and transforming what you learn may be the happiest of activities, and may, with luck on your side, lead to the solution of crucial problems, turn the lock and open the door to new knowledge.

Today the really crucial problems, as I hook them, are all deep, deep in human nature, and in this country with our long preference for appearances, for tangible, material realities, for perceptible facts, acts, and technics, for the processes and conclusions of conscious rationality, and for quick attainments of demonstrable results—with this native and acquired bent for things that one can plainly see, grasp, count, weigh, manipulate, and photograph, the probability of our solving or even seriously grappling with the strategic problems of our time does not appear to be encouragingly high.

Only if this appraisal is somewhere near the truth can I discern a single reason for your President's election of a depth psychologist as orator for this day. What could his reason be except to have the depth dimension stressed, with the accompanying hint that the key to the more perplexing problems might be lying in the dark. Pertinent to this issue is the old story of the London bobby who, in the blackness of one night, came upon a man half-seas-over stumbling in a circle within the lighted zone around a lamppost. "I am looking for my key," the man explained. "Are you sure you dropped it by this light?" the bobby asked. "No," the man replied, "I dropped it out there in the dark, but I can't see out there and I can see here."

What Freud discovered in the dark of the unconscious was what Puritan and Victorian morality suppressed as Sin, spelt with a capital. But now those floodgates are demolished and sexuality is conspicuously in the open, running loose among the young without benefit of form, grace, or dignity; and what is nowadays repressed, if my reading of the signs is not awry, are all the hopes, yearnings, claims, both dependent and aspiring, which down the centuries were comforted and directed by the mythologies and rituals of religion. Here I leave Freud and stand with Dr. Jung.

That a bent for the ideal is latent in the psyches of men and women of your age is not what I've been told by any confiding undergraduate, and it is about the last conclusion that a reader of modern literature would be likely to arrive at. For certainly most of the best poets, playwrights, and novelists, together with many psychoanalysts, behavioral psychologists, social philosophers, existentialists, and some angry others, seem to be conspiring, with peculiar unanimity, to reduce or decompose, to humiliate so far as they can do it, man's image of himself. In one way or another, the impression is conveyed that, in the realm of spirit, all of us are baffled Beats, Beatniks, or dead-beats, unable to cope as persons with the existential situation.

But tell me, what is the underlying meaning of this flood of discontent and self-depreciation? One pertinent answer comes from Emerson himself. "We grant that human life is mean, but how did we find out that it was mean? What is the ground of this uneasiness of ours, of this old discontent? What is the universal sense of want and ignorance but the *fine innuendo by which the soul makes its enormous claim.*" Yes, surely, "its enormous claim," and in the very midst of this American Paradise of material prosperity. The enormous claim of the sensitive, alienated portions of our society—artists, would-be artists, and their followers—comes, as I catch the innuendoes, from want of a kindling and heartening mythology to feel, think, live, and write by. Our eyes and ears are incessantly bombarded by a mythology which breeds greed, envy, pride, lust, and violence, the mythology of our mass media, the mythology of advertising, Hollywood and Madison Avenue. But a mythology that is sufficient to the claim of head and heart is as absent from the American scene as symbolism is absent from the new, straight-edged, bare-faced, glass buildings of New York.

An emotional deficiency disease, a paralysis of the creative imagination, an addiction to superficials—this is the physician's diagnosis I would offer to account for the greater part of the widespread desperation of our time, the enormous claim of people who are living with half a heart and half a lung. Paralysis of the imagination, I suspect, would also account, in part, for the fact that the great majority of us, wedded to comfort so long as we both shall live, are turning our eyes away from the one thing we should be looking at: the possibility or probability of co-extermination.

In his famous speech of acceptance upon the award of the Nobel prize for literature, Albert Camus declared as follows: "Probably every generation sees itself as charged with remaking the world. Mine, however, knows that it will not remake the world. But its task is perhaps even greater, for it consists in keeping the world from destroying itself."

Were this statement to be made before an auditory of our faculty and students—even by Camus himself, speaking with utter candor out of his embattled deeps of agony—I fear it would be met by a respectful, serious, yet stony silence, an *apparent* silence, for, coming from behind the non-committal, uncommitted faces, all would be aware of the almost palpable, familiar throb of Harvard's splendid engines of sophisticated demolition.

We are as sick of being warned of our proximity to hell as were the members of Jonathan Edwards' congregation. Wolf! Wolf! How, in heaven's name, does Camus imagine that a league of artists and philosophers could possibly prevent the destruction of the world? The nearest that he comes to telling us is when he states that his "generation knows that, in a sort of mad race against time, it ought to re-establish among nations a peace not based on slavery, to reconcile labor and culture again, and to reconstruct with all men an Ark of the Covenant." These words—"re-establish," "reconcile," "reconstruct,"—suggest that in his mind the prevention of destruction does, in fact, call for a remaking of the world, the building of a new Ark of the Covenant as basis for re-union.

Here, reason might lead us to infer that Camus was thinking of the institution of world government, which as scores of enlightened men, from Woodrow Wilson to Bertrand Russell, have insisted is the only rational answer to global, social chaos, a central government being the sole means that man has ever found of securing and maintaining order. But framing a constitution for world government, as the competent Mr. Grenville Clark has done, is not in line with the special genius of Camus, and, furthermore, it is apparent that the concept of world government, though absolutely necessary, is gaining little popular or Federal support. Sanity is overmatched: deep, blind, primitive compulsions which by-pass consciousness are towing us with a cable we have no knife to cut and driving us nearer and nearer to the verge of death.

At such a time, when hidden passions are deciding things, a legal scheme, no matter how commonsensical and logical, is not a magnet to large numbers of men and women: it chills them, leaves them frigid, uninvolved. Nor, at such a time, could something like Plato's plan for a Republic guided by philosophers arouse enthusiasm. But when Plato, envious of Homer's enormous influence in Greece, banished poets and myth-makers from his Republic, he deprived it of the springs of charismatic power, and so, when it came to a show-down with the masses, his beautifully reasoned books were ploughed under by the passionate myths and images of the poet-authors of the Bible. The Bible proved to be *the* fitting book not only for that century but for many centuries to come. It seems highly significant to me that Camus, a firm opponent of the theism of Judaeo-Christianity, should have reached into the fathomless well of the Old Testament to gain a potent image for his hope—Ark of the Covenant. It is there, among those images, that one can find the moulds that shaped the deepest passions of the Western World, including Russia.

At this juncture I shall seize, with your permission, the remaining minutes of this proffered opportunity, with its cherished privilege of free speech, to submit a micro-sketch of a hypothetical book that I would write if I had been vouchsafed the necessary genius and resources. This hypothetical book would also be a sketch, though a far larger and more detailed sketch, of a book to come composed by other authors, a super-personal book, a book of books, that might be termed a testament, a world testament.

Before submitting this micro-sketch of a macro-sketch of a book for a new age, I should warn you that this imagined testament will carry us beyond the mythology of dependent and compliant childhood, the same as that of the dependent childhood of our society in colonial days, that is, the authoritarian father-son mythology of the religion we inherited, and also beyond the mythology of adolescence, the same as that of the adolescence of our Nation, the mythology of protest, rebellion, independence, rugged individualism. Both of these mythologies are still operative. In fact, the mythology of adolescence, stressing freedom without qualifications or conditions, constitutes our national religion. Please understand and hold in mind that in looking forward to a future that has moved beyond these idealisms of today and yesterday, I am not forsaking them. There is a helpless, suffering child and a frustrated, rebellious adolescent in every one of us, and always will be. I would say, there is a time and place for authority and the founding of character, and there is a time and place for liberation from authority and the development and expression of a self-reliant personality. But, as I see the human situation, we are in need of a mythology of adulthood, something that is conspicuous by its absence in Western literature, a mythology of interdependence and creation, not only on the level of imaginative love, marriage, and the forming of a family, but on other levels, especially that of imaginative international reciprocities. Have we not pretty nearly reached the age when we can well afford to go beyond the glorification of vanity, pride, and egotism, individual and national?

Well, now, to return to my sketch of a sketch. The essential features of the testament that now occupies my mind would be roughly these: it would be the product of the interdependent judgments and imaginations of numerous composers, drawn from different cultures and from different callings. The initial task of these presumably creative and judicious thinkers would be to select from the vast libraries of the world, arrange, and edit, whatever past and present writings in poetry or prose were suitable to the appointed purpose. Except for more abundant stores from which to draw their substance, a larger scope and longer span of time, these testament-makers would proceed, we may suppose, as did the compilers and editors of the canonical and non-canonical books of the Bible. They would certainly be advantaged by the example of those fore-runners. Like the Old Testament, this new one would contain numerous variations of subject matter and of style: narratives, historical and biographical, stories, parables, legends, and myths, songs and poems, psalms of praise, codes and ordinances, premonitions and philosophical reflections.

Most difficult for the testament-makers would be the task of loosely integrating, as in the Bible, the selected parts in terms of a philosophy of social evolution—cycles of creation, conservation, decay, or induration—tending, in the long run, toward the fulfillment of that dream of human fellowship which centuries of deep and loving people have recommended to our hearts.

This testament would differ radically from the Bible inasmuch as its mythology would be consonant with contemporary science: its personifications would all refer to forces and functions *within* nature, human nature.

Also, it would differ radically from previous testaments of the Near East and West—the Bible, the Koran, and the Testament of Karl Marx—by describing and praising, with even-handed justice, forms of excellence, achieved by each and every culture. There would be no bowing to special claims, made by any single collectivity, of unique superiority, of divine election, of infallible truth, of salvation for its members and damnation for all others. There would be no ovation for the apocalyptic myth, either in its ancient form—Persian or Judaeo-Christian—or in its modern Communistic form; the myth of the inevitable and final Great Encounter between the all-good and the all-evil, resulting in an eternity of bliss for chosen saints or comrades, and death or everlasting torments for the enemy. There would be no acceptance of the necessity of inquisitions, persecutions, brain-washings, or concentration camps.

In a sense, the world testament would be a parable, a parable of parables, expressive of the universal need for peace, for interdependence, for fruitful reciprocations among those manifold units of mankind which are still proud and quarrelsome, still locked in clenched antagonisms. Its symbolisms would commemorate on all levels the settlement of hostilities between opposites, their synthesis, or creative union: man and nature, male and female, reason and passion, understanding and imagination, enjoyable means and enjoyable ends, science and art, management and labor, West and East. Its ultimate, ethical ideal would be the resolution of differences through mutual embracement and subsequent transformation. In the words of Henry James, senior: "It is no doubt very tolerable finite or creaturely love to love one's own in another, to love another for his conformity to one's self: but nothing can be in more flagrant contrast with the creative Love, all whose tenderness *ex vi termini* must be reserved only for what intrinsically is most bitterly hostile and negative to itself." In the judgment of America's most profound philosopher, Charles S. Peirce, this sublime sentence "discloses for the problem of evil its everlasting solution."

Finally, in contrast to the unrelieved sociological language of the outmoded testament of Marx, this world testament, heir to the secret of the Bible's everlasting magic, would consist in its best parts of moving and revealing poetic passages. Some devout Christians overlook the fact that the stirring and sustaining influence of the Book they dream and live by depends on the marvelous words, the vivid imagery and figures of speech with which its wisdom is transmitted. This is one of the chief qualities by which a religion can be distinguished from a moral philosophy or system of ethics. If the New Testament, for example, had been written by a modern social scientist in the jargon of his profession it would have died at birth, and Mithraism, or Manichaeanism, or Mohammedanism would have taken possession of the European mind. A religion is propagated by the alchemy of the aesthetic imagination, in striking parables and metaphors that solace, cheer, or channel our profoundest feelings. A code of morals, on the other hand, can appeal only to our intellects and to a few of our more shallow sentiments.

If, perchance, a world testament with the mythic qualities I have mentioned became an invitation to the feelings and thoughts of men and women, it would gain this influence only through its power to enchant, charm, clarify, edify, and nourish. There would be no agents of sovereign authority with threatened penalties to enforce compliance, and, in contrast to the testaments of our established Churches, it would be always susceptible to revisions, additions, and subtractions.

Everybody, I assume—especially on reaching the accepted age for the retirement of his brain—is entitled to a dream, and this is mine, heretical at certain points, but not so visionary as it sounds. Works of the magnitude of this imagined testament have been composed in the past, notably in India. Much of what is needed has been in printed form for years. Ample energy and genius is available—literary critics, historians, social scientists, philosophers, and poets—in different quarters of the globe. Enough money for the effort is in the keep of men who are aware of humanity's dire strait. A provisional first edition of the testament would not be very long in coming. Translated into all languages it might turn out to be the book this age is waiting for.

A war that no one wants, an utterly disgraceful end to man's long experiment on earth is a possibility we are facing every day. Events are hanging by a thread, depending on an accident, on some finger on a trigger, on a game of wits and tricks, of pride and saving faces. But ours is no momentary problem to be solved by this or that practical expedient. Does a mature nation sacrifice the future for the present? The day will come when small countries will possess enough lethal energy to eliminate a large country. Does a mature nation have the arrogance to believe that it can buy with dollars the permanent good-will and loyalty of other peoples? Has our government a long time-perspective, a philosophy of history, a world-view to guide its day-by-day and year-by-year decisions? If yes, only a few of us have heard of it.

It is such considerations that have pressured the generation of a vision of something which intellectuals like you and other members of the Phi Beta Kappa society might have a hand in shaping. Why not? Many times in the past, the direction of events has been affected by the publication of a single book. At the very least, the composition of this testament would constitute a brave, far-seeing try—no vulgar try—to kindle a little veritable light in a black world.

The one conversion requisite for those who would lose themselves in this demanding enterprise was long ago described in two famous, pithy sentences by a stubborn American patriot, contemporary with Emerson. No doubt many of you have had occasion to saunter down the elm-shaded path in the middle of Commonwealth Avenue and, arriving at the statue of William Lloyd Garrison, stopped to read these words: "My country is the world. My countrymen are all mankind."

GERHARD SZCZESNY

The Future of Unbelief

Gerhard Szczesny (1918–   ) is a German writer and broadcasting expert, Director of Special Programs of Radio Bavaria. His Die Zukunft des Unglaubens *(1958) [translated into English in 1961 as* The Future of Unbelief] *has attracted wide attention in Germany. It is a most discerning study of the relation between Christianity and what the author calls the "ersatz" or "surrogate" religions of our time, religions which I in this book lump together as sects of the "religion of Enlightenment." Dr. Szczesny's diagnosis of our present troubles—our alienation—will admirably supplement Dr. Murray's and help prepare the reader for what follows. The reader will find it profitable to read* The Future of Unbelief *in its entirety.*

THE EVENTS OF THE FIRST HALF OF OUR CENTURY CERTAINLY HAVE NOT led to a renascence of the Christian faith. They have, however, brought about a revival of the secular currency and authority of Christianity. After the failure of recent substitute religions, Christianity again seems like the unassailable treasure house of all human values. The writings of a David Friedrich Strauss, a Ludwig Feuerbach or a Friedrich Nietzsche, if published today, in all likelihood would be greeted as a public scandal and give rise to parliamentary protest by all "Christian" parties. We are faced by the fact, a fact in many respects historically and psychologically explainable, yet on the whole still extraordinary, that the argument with Christianity which began more than a hundred years ago has in recent decades become increasingly taboo.

One of the reasons for this phenomenon is the collapse of the intellectual and moral optimism that was the mark of the century past. As opposed to a simple, pristinely joyous belief in life, Christianity proved itself to be a richer and deeper thing. It knew more of the unavailingness of all human striving and the need always to take this frustration into account. Finally,

From Gerhard Szczesny, *The Future of Unbelief* (New York: George Braziller, Inc., 1961), pp. 11-17, 75-80.

it knew more about man's inclination to turn to the mysteries, to form some notion of what lies beyond the rationally knowable.

This rediscovery and reawakening of Christianity as a universally binding moral institution has not, to be sure, altered the fact that the real content of the Christian doctrine of salvation, for a dominant type of modern man, has become completely unacceptable, indeed, a matter of indifference. Intelligent Christians admit this without hesitation. However, in the face of modern crises and catastrophes the security afforded by a venerable and firmly built structure of belief makes Christianity, as a whole, taboo and hinders open critical analysis of it, even of its now unbelievable metaphysics. Thus, existing Christian dogma, which possesses social currency even while no longer seriously believed, obstructs that looking out and beyond needed to find new answers to the "final questions."

Our inquiry in this direction is not undertaken with any intention of making apostates of Christians. It is rather concerned with those to whom "unbelievingness" has become habitual, and from whom a return to Christianity can no longer be expected. It is aimed at overcoming the illusion that the "godless" man is an inferior creature, a nihilistic form of existence making for the total ruination of all human order—in sum, an utterly devilish sort of apparition the fighting of which with every means at hand demonstrates insight, humanity and adherence to the Christian way. This book is anti-Christian only in its contention that such views are enjoined or promoted, that there is a recognizable proclivity to bring the non-Christian standpoint into disrepute and to put social, moral and political pressure to bear on those who embrace it. Otherwise this book is no more intended to be anti-Christian than anti-Taoist or anti-Anthroposophic. It will defend the freedom of Christians to profess their beliefs and practice their form of worship. But it will equally defend the rights of those who have non-Christian forms of conviction and modes of behavior. And precisely on this account it will repudiate Christian claims to cultural or political dominion.

The sharpness of many ensuing formulations is conditioned not by the subject matter itself, but by the situation surrounding the subject matter. The author is neither a backslider nor a protester, nor any sort of anti- or pro-religionist. He respects Christianity as a world-shaking historical manifestation, which has left its mark for two thousand years. But Christianity as a confession of faith he does not respect. The author is also well aware that many people who cling earnestly and honestly to Christianity are people of good will and good faith. It is not easy for him to wreak injury on his friends among such Christians. But under present circumstances he sees no way of taking up the cause of the "unbelievers" without at the same time putting the patience and open-mindedness of the believers to a severe test. Any reader who considers this to be asking too much may as well lay the book aside at once. But anyone who, as a Christian, decides to hear the author out, might bear in mind that everybody denied the gift of "belief" can hardly, on that account, abandon all thinking about the world and the role he plays in it, and how these are to be understood.

The following observations represent random thoughts on the relationships between Christianity and modern crises in belief, rather than a systematic analysis. They also represent an attempt to characterize the typical content of a post-Christian ideology or world-outlook. Among these random thoughts appear certain remarks on this great family of problems which assume a solution in a certain direction. Yet in no wise are they to be understood as final or comprehensive. Our task is to throw light on the basic, root question of diversity of viewpoint. Certain trains of thought will recur again and again, since they establish a connection between the widely disparate objects of our analysis. Many things in the following pages may appear trivial. But it is the fate of certain truisms that whereas everyone knows them, no one really pays them the least attention. There are commonplaces which, if publicly expressed, arouse resentment. They are allowed to hold good only as long as no one brings them to mind. This is understandable. The bad conscience of our epoch not only makes for complicated illusions, but for downright suppressions as well.

This observer's platform, then, is nothing more than the usual vantage from which the normal man of our times occasionally tries to cast a look at the great context of his life. "Unbelief" is no longer the prerogative of an especially enlightened minority. It is the fate of a contemporary type of Western man who may actually be in the majority, or who at any rate is very frequently encountered. This contemporary normal man is concerned with the old basic questions: Who am I? What is the nature of the world? What can I believe in and what must I do about it? It is hard to find answers to these questions in the field of learning appropriate to their consideration. Without wishing to belittle the significance of modern philosophy, one must recognize the fact that its contributions toward resolving the spiritual crises of our time are small indeed. On the one hand the philosophers wear themselves out making ever more refined interpretations of handed down conceptual. On the other, their voice never reaches beyond a small circle of initiates to those who might profit by philosophy's answers or solutions. Christianity's claim to spiritual leadership, its fear of the "ideological" and the murkiness of its own terminology seal the self-chosen or guilt-born apartness of Western philosophy. The implicit and unsettled conflict with the Christian metaphysic lies like mildew over all the philosophers' effort to show us how the innermost world is made. Also, the way our school philosophers write, their very style has always served more to cloud than to clarify and continues to do so to this day. The European's specific "intellectual gift" is to think and argue. Yet this gift, in all probability, is largely intelligible as nothing more than the product of a centuries-old clash with theology, in the course of which the art of concealment, evasion and deception has been consummately developed.

But a philosophy that can function only under camouflage and proviso eventually loses clarity of insight and impartiality of judgment. In consequence, the day finally arrives when it can produce nothing but the ambiguous and equivocal.

In all events—the average modern man—and by this we mean the average "educated" man—must manage his life, its problems and tragedies, without benefit of advice from our professional thinkers. There is also reason to suspect that as soon as these people have to measure up to the fundamental questions of human existence outside their bookish province, they, too, will behave in a "dilettante" and naïve fashion. Anyone who has ever listened in on a discussion among philosophers, or a discussion in which philosophers took part, will have noted with astonishment that at decisive moments in the debate they abandon the well-traveled paths of their specialized fund of knowledge and, like any other mortal, at best can utter only subjective, perplexed and simple opinions on God and the world. Actually this is a gratifying thing. At the bottom, to philosophize simply means a direct attempt to read meaning into the nature of things, not spinning thoughts about other thoughts and writing another book about other books.

Therefore, since here what we have in mind is a direct interpretation of the modern situation rather than another contribution to academic philosophy, we shall give up all dependence on documents, writings and citable names to prop our argument. Very little or nothing will be taken for granted. For it must be possible to develop out of raw experience a line of thought that will be accessible to everybody, and to develop it in such fashion that everybody can follow it through. What does it profit us to drag in the name of this or that author, however prominent, if we are not in a position to explain the reference we have in mind in our own words? And would it make our thesis any more enlightening or true if we took refuge behind the authority of some philosopher whose authority, meanwhile, was being questioned by still other authorities?

Our deliberations go straight to the heart of the matter. The world in which we find ourselves offers such aspects as these: birth and death, old age and sickness, happiness and misery, the results of man's scientific insight into nature and into himself. Thus a picture of relationships is generated, and a need to interpret the picture. In this manner what is known as a "Weltanschauung," an ideology, a way of looking at the world, comes into being.

As a word and concept "Weltanschauung" has fallen into disrepute since it was taken over by the propagandists of the new German barbarism. Nevertheless, we feel we cannot dispense with it. The word as such stems neither from Marx nor Haeckel nor Hitler. It was discovered by the Romantics and popularized by Wilhelm Dilthey. And no one was ever less materialistic or trite than he. The word "Weltanschauung"—a way of viewing the world intuitively arrived at—in our opinion more intelligibly expresses the common human need for a comprehensive interpretation of all existence, within reason's grasp and beyond it, than does the word "religion." So thoroughly is the term "religion" steeped in Christian notions of faith and Christian emotional values that it has become virtually unusable except to connote a specifically Christian form of man's response to the cosmos. A restoration of the discredited concept of "Weltanschauung" to its original worth seems possible to us. It can be done if "Welt" (world) is understood as containing everything in the cosmos, known and unknown. Beyond this, "Anschauung" (contemplation) must refer to an intuitive as well as a rational apprehension of the aforementioned totality.

Actually everything that will be said in this book could be couched in terms of an interpretation of both concepts, "religion" and "Weltanschauung" (hereafter, in English, world-outlook or ideology). If "religion" seems to us to be something larger, deeper and more inclusive than mere "ideology," at the same time we are aware that we still harbor a secret wish to fashion our own way of regarding the world, and one which will have no connection with what in this country is called "religion." With this the stage is spiritually and psychologically set for our deliberations. . . .

Today the real Christian creed, viewed in the broad, scarcely survives as a vitally creative force. The peoples of the West, as they live out their lives—and this takes into account the majority of those who call themselves Christians—in their thinking and behavior have ceased to pay the least attention to Christianity's idea of God and the hereafter, or the Christian notions of sin and grace. Christianity was once a faith that really pervaded human existence. But it has been supplanted by a kind of indifferent tolerance of that theological phraseology which, every Sunday, resounds from pulpit and loudspeaker. It has come to be accepted as a ritual composed of humanitarian protestations, appeals and activities, pursued by dint of much expensive publicity. We, the inheritors of Western culture, live in the midst of all kinds of testimonials and memories of Christianity, as will many generations to come, and this circumstance still leaves a characteristic mark on our lives. Yet, in this same connection, the bulk of people who busy themselves professionally with the appreciation and evaluation of these Christian memorials are not motivated in truth by religious zeal, but by a mere philological or esthetic interest.

In spite of this epigonal state of affairs it would be false and reprehensible to propagate the destruction of the inherited form and content of the Christian-Occidental culture. For "progress" of this nature would not only disrupt the historical continuum, but at the same time rob the world of the fruits of the past, riches without which neither present nor future can have meaning. Therefore, it is not so much a question of opposing Christianity as such, as of further awakening a consciousness of the spiritual condition of mankind outside the framework of inherited conviction.

Looking back over the years, we are certainly justified in concluding that none of the ersatz religions—either those tried and found wanting or those still extant, from materialism to psychologism to sociologism—can ever contain reality's plenum of being. At the same time these one-sided and counterfeit movements can be validly adjudged symptomatic of a basic change in the Western-European consciousness. There is no fault to be found with these experiments in the sense that they represent an attempt to bring man and the world into a system based on demonstrable truth. But where they are naïve and false is in their assumption that any new correlation of reality must take, by all means available to the human intellect, the form of a reduction to a common denominator, an ultimate formula acceptable to all. As a matter of fact, in our own times it has been realized that to fill with rational material the "religious" void left by the overthrow of the Christian metaphysic is an impossible task. It is this discovery which holds us in irons, and which has led to a revival of all kinds of antirationalism and subjectivism.

In whatever direction we look, toward philosophy, the arts, literature or science, everywhere minds are hard at work laying bare to view the background and the underground of life, exposing the metaphysical and metapsychical, the magical, the unreal and the beyond-the-real. These analysts, having cut reality ignominiously open on their dissecting table, try to breathe new meaning and mystery into the corpse. Meanwhile, in defensive reaction to this proces, others adjure us to open our eyes to this vain and foolish "flight from God," and again seek refuge and safety in the true faith. The whole history of European enlightenment, these people say, is nothing more than a great heresy, a dangerous illusion and overevaluation of man's intelligence. It behooves us, henceforth, to restore Christ's message of redemption to its rightful supremacy, since from this message alone true knowledge and release can come. None but Christ's teachings can control reason's arrogant claims and again commit mankind to lost moral and spiritual values.

Our conviction is quite opposite. It is our belief that the process of transforming and widening the Western consciousness has been a necessary thing, and cannot be reversed. Within this development there may be errors in need of correction. But this does not hold true for the development as such. Not all the results of scientific study can be suddenly judged false simply because certain credulous men of science happen to draw unwarranted inferences from them.

Western man's emancipation from the spiritualistic and dualistic Christian metaphysic is basically characterized by a discovery of the unity of all being, which revelation has spilled over into the general awareness. As the struggle to get to the bottom of all things is pressed farther and farther, the seeking mind comes hard up against the fact that man and all the forces which motivate him and constitute him are part of the continuum of reality. The world cannot be divided into a life on earth and a hereafter. Actually everything contains a "this side" and a "that side."

The "this side" turns out merely to be that part of world unity which is accessible to the senses, and "that side" the part of the whole which remains in the dark. The absolute dualism of the Christian concept of the world and the concept of deity linked to it, in this view have been done away with. What remains is the relative dualism of the knowable and unknowable. This simply indicates that a portion of the world lies outside human experience, but "not outside the world."

Today we are witnessing an inescapable breakdown of all forms of speculation and myth derivative from ignorance of reality's true relationships. Meanwhile a need has arisen to project a kind of metaphysic that will go beyond the accumulated facts of experience, yet still be rooted in experience. We find ourselves today in a period where the old and new outlooks overlap. On the one hand we see an attempt to force inductive truth into traditional doctrine; on the other, a need to formulate a system of belief resting easily and naturally on these same demonstrable truths.

Even where Catholicism is still deeply rooted, as in such rural and backward parts of Europe as Spain, or in Latin America, places in which Catholicism is still a state religion seemingly in possession of unlimited power over men's souls, it is doubtful whether oncoming generations will spontaneously accept the Christian tradition and carry it forward in time. And in the highly civilized, dominantly Protestant countries—above all in the United States, the nation which henceforth will lead the Western World—in these countries, where Christianity still holds uncontested sway over the cultural façade, the Christian idea has degenerated into trivial moralism, which has no religious superstructure left at all, and in lieu of it projects the Babbitt ideal, of the man who is in all ways healthy, normal and satisfied with himself, the world and providence. The settlers of the "New World" soon found themselves in a situation not unlike that of the Continental peoples at the time of their encounter with Christianity. There was a great urge to create a new way of life. Indeed, this had to be done. This impulse merged with the individualistic, activist and missionary ideology of Christianity, without, however, greatly exciting any desire to think seriously about the religious and philosophical motivation of this ethic. It is fairly obvious, in this general connection, that the pioneer spirit, as linked with Christian individualism, played an essential part in spreading practical humanitarianism and the democratic way of life. But it is only a half-century ago that the problem of finding an ontologically sound and reasonable foundation for ethic and being began to be discussed in America, whereas in the Old World thinking people had been wrestling with the problem for centuries.

As soon as man begins to live consciously, as soon as he ceases to be guided by imported norms and instead conceives a desire to do and strive, wish and want in terms of his own insight, so that he may bring his life, as he feels, into an intelligible relationship with all reality—when this happens any lack of harmony between motive and deed, idea and configuration, the believed and the known tends to become intolerable. Having arrived

at this stage, man must either find new motives while continuing to act
as before, or new forms of action while retaining his old motives. That is,
he must either find a new way to accommodate his existence to the Christian idea of faith, or rebuild his existence on a non-Christian basis. In the
end there is nothing left for him to do but to bring everything that he does,
hopes or wishes into harmony with what he has come to believe is the
nature of the whole.

Though modern "unbelief" is a deep-reaching, collective phenomenon,
the process from which it results is still immature, which in turn limits
individual apostasy. It is a gradual thing. The transformation of a "believer" into an "unbeliever" does not threaten to upset the individual's
psychic equilibrium, as a rule, since it comes about insensibly from a
gradual widening of the consciousness. This process is occurring everywhere. The facts which make for doubt and which force human beings to
think things over and form new ideas are reaching out into the remotest
villages. These facts come into purview, too, without any special outside
assistance. Whether remotely situated people respond to these forces, or let
them pass in indifference depends, of course, on their relative intellectual
and psychological development. The spirit listeth where it will, but bears
fruit only on fertile ground. If a genuine desire for enlightenment obtains,
contemporary man has only to reach out his hand to satisfy it. If this
desire is lacking, better then that he remain secure in his old faith.

As far as prognosis is possible, it seems almost certain that among immediately ensuing generations the structure of consciousness will suffer a
fundamental change. This change will occur even among populations still
living on the periphery of civilization. The thinking of erstwhile backward
and primitive peoples will tend more and more toward the objective. The
same prognosis also applies to the peoples of Asia and Africa, though
here the collision between enlightenment and traditional religious beliefs,
in accordance with the tremendous variety of the latter, very likely will
give rise to motley results and bring all sorts of divers consequences to a
head. Not only Buddhism but Islam as well contains metaphysical postulates which might very well prove quite serviceable as a superstructure for
advancing scientific thought. We have already indicated the compatibility of
the Buddhistic world-idea and rational knowledge. Mohammed's message,
too, is anti-miraculous, and is characterized by a strong incentive, liable
at any moment to be quickened, to make use of man's God-given powers
of understanding in praise of creation. Both religions could have a great
deal of appeal in the West, if they were skillfully maneuvered. The great
conflict among the world's three principal religions has yet to come. There
could be a phase of de-Christianization in which Buddhism and Islam
might come to be regarded as acceptable substitutes. For men driven to
despair will tend first to seek a new meaning for existence in already great
and recognized systems of belief.

PART II

THE WAY
THINGS ARE

II

The Way Things Are

I HAVE GROUPED IN THIS SECTION EXAMPLES OF APPROACHES TO PROBLEMS of what until quite recently everyone would call "philosophy." As philosophy became a professional academic discipline a few centuries ago, however, its followers naturally enough became more exclusive. They not only rejected the old folk-sense in which anybody might have a "philosophical" outlook or interest or temperament; they also rejected that less vague but still unprofessional range of thinking about man's condition of which the Kluckhohn and Leighton analysis of the Navaho "view of life" (p. 37) or the Marxist eschatology (p. 121) are examples. Nonetheless I shall unashamedly, though with protective punctuation, call this section "philosophy."

The subdivisions by no means include all aspects of philosophy. Notably I have been obliged to omit political philosophy, epistemology (theory of knowledge), logic, and a good deal else. But I have tried to give a wide if unsystematic range of subject matter. I begin suitably with what is a fine example of the human need to understand the universe as a system, as something that has a beginning and may have an end, that may once have been *chaos,* but now has *order*—in short, a cosmology. I have chosen to end this series of cosmologies with that of a contemporary astronomer, Harlow Shapley, to emphasize the fact that, though as a good Enlightened humanist he might not wholly accept the analogy, he, like the authors of Genesis, is composing a cosmology. Don't let him fool you with his "cosmographies"; he too is inventing a universe, as indeed is Whitehead. To Dr. Shapley, at least, his is quite clearly a consoling invention.

The second subheading should give no trouble. Teleology, the knowledge of design, and eschatology, the knowledge of ends, final ends, not just current purposes, are both ten-dollar words, but both are worth the money. Here too the sequence from Plato to Marx seems to me at least to be obvious, and not at all rigged. The "classless society" is a heaven, a Utopia, an eschatology in short. Perhaps for many in the democracies of the free West this phase of a world-view is somewhat vague, remote, and certainly not apocalyptic. But I believe it is there, a less pressingly optimis-

tic version of Condorcet's Utopia, to which has been added a dose of
Evolution as seen by T. H. Huxley and Herbert Spencer. It is not only
Americans who believe that "prosperity is just around the corner." Indeed,
the whole world has begun to believe that it ought to be there, or even
closer.

Ethics is a branch of philosophy we all recognize. I have of course by
no means "covered the field," which is almost limitless, but I have again
attempted to present samples of ethical thinking which can bring home
both the range of such thinking and the persistence within our Western
tradition of that range.

Finally, I must apologize for the somewhat nebulous title I have given the
final subdivision of this section—"Transcendence: The Mystic Experience."
What I am trying to bring before the reader here is that range of human
experience indicated by such colorless words as "mysticism," "quietism,"
and, in political thought, "non-violent non-resistance." By temperament (a
question-begging phrase if there ever was one) I suppose I am as incapable
of understanding the mystical experience as the tone-deaf man is incapable
of understanding music. But no tone-deaf man ought to announce that music
is a fake, a wicked fake at that. Something very strong in Western intellectual—and emotional—habits resists Mr. Huxley's "perennial philosophy,"
though Westerners have long been addicted to somewhat simpler forms of
transcendence achieved by alcohol or other drugs. At any rate, here too
I have given the reader a sampling. There is much, much more available
in any library—for the mystic, transcend what these stand for though he
may, simply has to make use of the stained and worldly counters of communication we call words, has indeed to put them together by the worldly
devices we call grammar and rhetoric.

A
Order: Cosmologies,
Cosmogonies, Cosmographies

GENESIS

Perhaps the cosmogony of Genesis should be taken as it comes. But I have followed the dominant opinion of modern biblical scholarship that there are in the story of the creation as it appears in Genesis two different accounts, one older and more naïve or "primitive," the other later and closer to developed Jewish monotheism. I have therefore put the older account first. The two are of course so well put together by the Jewish scholars who edited them that it was only in the last few centuries that the linguistic and historical scholarship of the "higher criticism" was able to discern the fact of editing.

THE EARLIER ACCOUNT OF CREATION

Chapter 2

4 ¶ These *are* the generations of the heavens and of the earth when they were created, in the day that the LORD God made the earth and the heavens.

5 And every plant of the field before it was in the earth, and every herb of the field before it grew: for the LORD God had not caused it to rain upon the earth, and *there was* not a man to till the ground.

6 But there went up a mist from the earth, and watered the whole face of the ground.

7 And the LORD God formed man *of* the dust of the ground, and breathed into his nostrils the breath of life; and man became a living soul.

8 ¶ And the LORD God planted a garden eastward in Eden; and there he put the man whom he had formed.

9 And out of the ground made the LORD God to grow every tree that is pleasant to the sight, and good for food; the tree of life also in the midst of the garden, and the tree of knowledge of good and evil.

10 And a river went out of Eden to water the garden; and from thence it was parted, and became into four heads. . . .

15 And the LORD God took the man, and put him into the garden of Eden to dress it and to keep it.

16 And the LORD God commanded the man, saying, Of every tree of the garden thou mayest freely eat:

17 But of the tree of the knowledge of good and evil, thou shalt not eat of it: for in the day that thou eatest thereof thou shalt surely die.

18 ¶ And the LORD God said, *It is* not good that the man should be alone; I will make him an help meet for him.

19 And out of the ground the LORD God formed every beast of the field, and every fowl of the air; and brought *them* unto Adam to see what he would call them: and whatsoever Adam called every living creature, that *was* the name thereof.

20 And Adam gave names to all cattle, and to the fowl of the air, and to every beast of the field; but for Adam there was not found an help meet for him.

21 And the LORD God caused a deep sleep to fall upon Adam, and he slept: and he took one of his ribs, and closed up the flesh instead thereof;

22 And the rib, which the LORD God had taken from man, made he a woman, and brought her unto the man.

23 And Adam said, This *is* now bone of my bones, and flesh of my flesh: she shall be called Woman, because she was taken out of Man.

24 Therefore shall a man leave his father and his mother, and shall cleave unto his wife: and they shall be one flesh.

25 And they were both naked, the man and his wife, and were not ashamed.

Chapter 3

Now the serpent was more subtil than any beast of the field which the LORD God had made. And he said unto the woman, Yea, hath God said, Ye shall not eat of every tree of the garden?

2 And the woman said unto the serpent, We may eat of the fruit of the trees of the garden:

3 But of the fruit of the tree which *is* in the midst of the garden, God hath said, Ye shall not eat of it, neither shall ye touch it, lest ye die.

4 And the serpent said unto the woman, Ye shall not surely die:

5 For God doth know that in the day ye eat thereof, then your eyes shall be opened, and ye shall be as gods, knowing good and evil.

6 And when the woman saw that the tree *was* good for food, and that it *was* pleasant to the eyes, and a tree to be desired to make *one* wise, she took of the fruit thereof, and did eat, and gave also unto her husband with her; and he did eat.

7 And the eyes of them both were opened, and they knew that they *were* naked; and they sewed fig leaves together, and made themselves aprons.

8 And they heard the voice of the LORD God walking in the garden in the cool of the day: and Adam and his wife hid themselves from the presence of the LORD God amongst the trees of the garden.

9 And the LORD God called unto Adam, and said unto him, Where *art* thou?

10 And he said, I heard thy voice in the garden, and I was afraid, because I *was* naked; and I hid myself.

11 And he said, Who told thee that thou *wast* naked? Hast thou eaten of the tree, whereof I commanded thee that thou shouldest not eat?

12 And the man said, The woman whom thou gavest *to be* with me, she gave me of the tree, and I did eat.

13 And the LORD God said unto the woman, What *is* this *that* thou hast done? And the woman said, The serpent beguiled me, and I did eat.

14 And the LORD God said unto the serpent, Because thou hast done this thou *art* cursed above all cattle, and above every beast of the field; upon thy belly shalt thou go, and dust shalt thou eat all the days of thy life:

15 And I will put enmity between thee and the woman, and between thy seed and her seed; it shall bruise thy head, and thou shalt bruise his heel.

16 Unto the woman he said, I will greatly multiply thy sorrow and thy conception; in sorrow thou shalt bring forth children; and thy desire *shall be* to thy husband, and he shall rule over thee.

17 And unto Adam he said, Because thou hast hearkened unto the voice of thy wife, and hast eaten of the tree, of which I commanded thee, saying, Thou shalt not eat of it: cursed *is* the ground for thy sake; in sorrow shalt thou eat *of* it all the days of thy life;

18 Thorns also and thistles shall it bring forth to thee; and thou shalt eat the herb of the field;

19 In the sweat of thy face shalt thou eat bread, till thou return unto the ground; for out of it wast thou taken: for dust thou *art,* and unto dust shalt thou return.

20 And Adam called his wife's name Eve; because she was the mother of all living.

21 Unto Adam also and to his wife did the LORD God make coats of skins, and clothed them.

22 ¶ And the LORD God said, Behold, the man is become as one of us, to know good and evil; and now, lest he put forth his hand, and take also of the tree of life, and eat, and live for ever:

23 Therefore the LORD God sent him forth from the garden of Eden, to till the ground from whence he was taken.

24 So he drove out the man; and he placed at the east of the garden of Eden Cherubims, and a flaming sword which turned every way, to keep the way of the tree of life.

THE LATER ACCOUNT

Chapter 1

In the beginning God created the heaven and the earth.

2 And the earth was without form, and void; and darkness *was* upon

the face of the deep. And the Spirit of God moved upon the face of the waters.

3 ¶ And God said, Let there be light: and there was light.

4 And God saw the light, that *it was* good: and God divided the light from the darkness.

5 And God called the light Day, and the darkness he called Night. And the evening and the morning were the first day.

6 ¶ And God said, Let there be a firmament in the midst of the waters, and let it divide the waters from the waters.

7 And God made the firmament, and divided the waters which *were* under the firmament from the waters which *were* above the firmament: and it was so.

8 And God called the firmament Heaven. And the evening and the morning were the second day.

9 ¶ And God said, Let the waters under the heaven be gathered together unto one place, and let the dry *land* appear: and it was so.

10 And God called the dry *land* Earth; and the gathering together of the waters called he Seas: and God saw that *it was* good.

11 And God said, Let the earth bring forth grass, the herb yielding seed, *and* the fruit tree yielding fruit after his kind, whose seed *is* in itself, upon the earth: and it was so.

12 And the earth brought forth grass, *and* herb yielding seed after his kind, and the tree yielding fruit, whose seed *was* in itself, after his kind: and God saw that *it was* good.

13 And the evening and the morning were the third day.

14 ¶ And God said, Let there be lights in the firmament of the heaven to divide the day from the night; and let them be for signs, and for seasons, and for days, and years:

15 And let them be for lights in the firmament of the heaven to give light upon the earth: and it was so.

16 And God made two great lights; the greater light to rule the day, and the lesser light to rule the night: *he made* the stars also.

17 And God set them in the firmament of the heaven to give light upon the earth.

18 And to rule over the day and over the night, and to divide the light from the darkness: and God saw that *it was* good.

19 And the evening and the morning were the fourth day.

20 And God said, Let the waters bring forth abundantly the moving creature that hath life, and fowl *that* may fly above the earth in the open firmament of heaven.

21 And God created great whales, and every living creature that moveth, which the waters brought forth abundantly, after their kind, and every winged fowl after his kind: and God saw that *it was* good.

22 And God blessed them, saying, Be fruitful, and multiply, and fill the waters in the seas, and let fowl multiply in the earth.

23 And the evening and the morning were the fifth day.

24 ¶ And God said, Let the earth bring forth the living creature after his kind, cattle, and creeping thing, and beast of the earth after his kind: and it was so.

25 And God made the beast of the earth after his kind, and cattle after their kind, and every thing that creepeth upon the earth after his kind: and God saw that *it was* good.

26 ¶ And God said, Let us make man in our image, after our likeness: and let them have dominion over the fish of the sea, and over the fowl of the air, and over the cattle, and over all the earth, and over every creeping thing that creepeth upon the earth.

27 So God created man in his *own* image, in the image of God created he him; male and female created he them.

28 And God blessed them, and God said unto them, Be fruitful, and multiply, and replenish the earth, and subdue it: and have dominion over the fish of the sea, and over the fowl of the air, and over every living thing that moveth upon the earth.

29 ¶ And God said, Behold, I have given you every herb bearing seed, which *is* upon the face of all the earth, and every tree, in the which *is* the fruit of a tree yielding seed; to you it shall be for meat.

30 And to every beast of the earth, and to every fowl of the air, and to every thing that creepeth upon the earth, wherein *there is* life, *I have given* every green herb for meat: and it was so.

31 And God saw every thing that he had made, and behold, *it was* very good. And the evening and the morning were the sixth day.

Chapter 2

Thus the heavens and the earth were finished, and all the host of them.

2 And on the seventh day God ended his work which he had made; and he rested on the seventh day from all his work which he had made.

3 And God blessed the seventh day, and sanctified it: because that in it he had rested from all his work which God created and made.

CLYDE KLUCKHOHN
and
DOROTHEA LEIGHTON

The Navaho View of Life

The late Clyde Kluckhohn (1905–1960) was Professor of Anthropology at Harvard. Dorothea Leighton, his collaborator, is the wife of Alexander Leighton, a distinguished psychologist and sociologist. Both Professor Kluckhohn and Mrs. Leighton display a first-hand familiarity with the Navaho. This analysis of the Navaho "view of life" should bring home the universality of such "views." The anthropologist can, of course, supply examples of them in a very great variety. Almost all of them contain some sort of "creation-myth," a phase not here emphasized by our authors. A surprising number have stories of a total flood.

SOME PREMISES OF NAVAHO LIFE AND THOUGHT

To understand fully the Navaho "philosophy of life" one must dig deeper. The very fact that The People find it necessary to talk about their "ethical principles" and their values suggests that not everybody lives up to them (any more than is the case in white society). But many characteristically Navaho doings and sayings make sense only if they are related to certain basic convictions about the nature of human life and experience, convictions so deep-going that no Navaho bothers to talk about them in so many words. These unstated assumptions are so completely taken for granted that The People take their views of life as an ineradicable part of human nature and find it hard to understand that normal persons could possibly conceive life in other terms.

Premise One. Life Is Very, Very Dangerous

This premise is of course distinctive only in its intensity and its phrasing. All sensible human beings realize that there are many hazards in living; but

From Clyde Kluckhohn and Dorothea Leighton, *The Navaho* (Cambridge: Harvard University Press, 1946), pp. 223-232.

to many whites, Navahos seem morbid in the variety of threats from this world and from the world of the supernatural which they fear and name. Of course this is largely a point of view. To some detached observers it might seem more healthy to worry about witches than about what you will live on when you are old or about the dreadful consequences of picking up some germ. Whites also tend to personify evil forces. They found relief in "discovering" that World War I was all due to J. P. Morgan. All human beings doubtless have the tendency to simplify complex matters because this gives the gratifying illusion of understanding them and of the possibility of doing something about them.

However, while this is clearly not a matter of black or white, The People do have a more overwhelming preoccupation than whites with the uncertainty of life and the many threats to personal security. The great emphasis laid upon "taking care of things," upon the industry and skills necessary for survival, and upon the ceremonial techniques bear witness to this. There are five main formulas for safety.

Formula 1: Maintain orderliness in those sectors of life which are little subject to human control. By seeming to bring the areas of actual ignorance, error, and accident under the control of minutely prescribed ritual formulas, The People create a compensatory mechanism. . . . these prescriptions are partially negative and partially positive. The Navaho conceives safety either as restoration of the individual to the harmonies of the natural, human, and supernatural world or, secondarily, as restoration of an equilibrium among nonhuman forces.

This is achieved by the compulsive force of order and reiteration in ritual words and acts. The essence of even ceremonial drama is not sharp climax (as whites have it) so much as fixed rhythms. The keynote of all ritual poetry is compulsion through orderly repetition. Take this song which the Singer of a Night Way uses to "waken" the mask of each supernatural supposed to participate in the rite.

> He stirs, he stirs, he stirs, he stirs.
> Among the lands of dawning, he stirs, he stirs;
> The pollen of the dawning, he stirs, he stirs;
> Now in old age wandering, he stirs, he stirs;
> Now on the trail of beauty, he stirs, he stirs.
> He stirs, he stirs, he stirs, he stirs.
>
> He stirs, he stirs, he stirs, he stirs.
> Among the lands of evening, he stirs, he stirs;
> The pollen of the evening, he stirs, he stirs;
> Now in old age wandering, he stirs, he stirs;
> Now on the trail of beauty, he stirs, he stirs.
> He stirs, he stirs, he stirs, he stirs.
>
> He stirs, he stirs, he stirs, he stirs.
> Now Talking God, he stirs, he stirs;
> Now his white robe of buckskin, he stirs, he stirs;

Now in old age wandering, he stirs, he stirs;
Now on the trail of beauty, he stirs, he stirs.
He stirs, he stirs, he stirs, he stirs.[1]

The song goes on like this for many verses. To white people it has a monotonous quality, but infinite repetitions in an expected sequence seem to lull the Navaho into a sense of security.

Formula 2: Be wary of non-relatives. This is, to some extent, the obverse of the centering of trust and affection upon relatives. If one feels thoroughly at home and at ease when surrounded by one's kin, it is natural that one should distrust strangers. In white society (and probably in all others) there is a distrust of strangers, members of the "out-group." But the Navaho fears also the other members of his own people who are not related to him. Hence antiwitchcraft protection must always be carried to a "squaw dance" or any other large gathering. This tendency to be ill at ease when beyond the circle of one's relatives is a truly "primitive" quality and is characteristic, to varying degrees, of most nonliterate folk societies.

This formula is closely related to the preceding one; if one wins security by reducing the uncharted areas of the nonhuman universe to familiar patterns, it is natural that unfamiliar human beings should be regarded as threats.

Formula 3: Avoid excesses. Very few activities are wrong in and of themselves, but excess in the practice of any is dangerous. This is in marked contrast to the puritanical concept of immorality. To Navahos such things as sex and gambling are not "wrong" at all but will bring trouble if indulged in "too much." Even such everyday tasks as weaving must be done only in moderation. Many women will not weave more than about two hours at a stretch; in the old days unmarried girls were not allowed to weave for fear they would overdo, and there is a folk rite for curing the results of excess in this activity. Closely related is the fear of completely finishing anything: as a "spirit outlet," the basketmaker leaves an opening in the design; the weaver leaves a small slit between the threads; the Navaho who copies a sandpainting for a white man always leaves out something, however trivial; the Singer never tells his pupil quite all the details of the ceremony lest he "go dry." Singers also systematically leave out transitions in relating myths.

This fear of excess is reflected also in various characteristic attitudes toward individuals. There is, for example, a folk saying: "If a child gets too smart, it will die young." The distrust of the very wealthy and very powerful and the sanctions and economic practices which tend to keep men at the level of their fellows have already been mentioned.

Formula 4: When in a new and dangerous situation, do nothing. If a threat is not to be dealt with by ritual canons, it is safest to remain inactive. If a Navaho finds himself in a secular situation where custom does not tell him how to behave, he is usually ill at ease and worried. The white Ameri-

---

[1] Washington Matthews, *The Night Chant, a Navaho Ceremony,* Memoirs of the American Museum of Natural History, VI (1902), 110-111.

can under these circumstances will most often overcompensate by putting on a self-confidence he does not in fact have. The American tradition says, "When danger threatens, *do* something." The Navaho tradition says, "Sit tight and perhaps in that way you may escape evil."

Formula 5: Escape. This is an alternative response to Formula 4, which The People select with increasing frequency when pressure becomes too intense. Doing nothing is not enough: safety lies in flight. This flight may take the form of leaving the field in the sheer physical sense. Navahos have discovered that they don't get very far by trying to resist the white man actively; so they scatter. The white man then cannot deal with them as a group—he can't even locate and exhort or admonish or punish them as individuals. Escape may be this sort of passive resistance or it may be simple evasion, as when a Navaho woman, who was otherwise fairly happy in a government hospital, left it rather than ask for one kind of food which she desperately missed. Had she asked, it would have been given her, but she found it simpler to leave. Flight also takes the even more unrealistic form of addiction to alcohol or of indiscriminate sexuality. In effect, the Navaho says, "My only security is in escape from my difficulties."

These types of behavior in the face of danger are documented by the following episode related by a fifth-grader in one of the boarding schools.

We look down to the river, we saw a lot of cows at the river. My brother said, "I am not scared of those cows that are at the river." Soon the cows were going back up the hill. We just climb up on a big tall tree and sit there. The cows come in closer and closer. We stay on the tree. Soon they come under the tree. My brother and I were so scared that we just sit there and not move. Soon my brother start crying. When the cows go away we laugh and laugh. My brother said, "The cows were scared of me." I said, "They are not scared of you." We say that over and over. Soon my brother got angry, then we fight in the sand. After we fight we go home.

Premise Two. Nature Is More Powerful Than Man

Navahos accept nature and adapt themselves to her demands as best they can, but they are not utterly passive, not completely the pawns of nature. They do a great many things that are designed to control nature physically and to repair damage caused by the elements. But they do not even hope to master nature. For the most part The People try to influence her with various songs and rituals, but they feel that the forces of nature, rather than anything that man does, determine success or failure of crops, plagues of grasshoppers, increase of arroyos, and decrease of grass. If a flood comes and washes out a formerly fertile valley, one does not try to dam the stream and replace the soil; instead one moves to a floodless spot. One may try to utilize what nature furnishes, such as by leading water from a spring or stream to his fields, but no man can master the wind and the weather. This is similar to the attitude toward sex, which is viewed as part of nature, something to reckon with, but not a thing to be denied.

Many white people have the opposite view; namely, that nature is a malignant force with useful aspects that must be harnessed, and useless, harmful ones that must be shorn of their power. They spend their energies adapting nature to their purposes, instead of themselves to her demands. They destroy pests of crops and men, they build dykes and great dams to avert floods, and they level hills in one spot and pile them up in another. Their premise is that nature will destroy them unless they prevent it; the Navahos' is that nature will take care of them if they behave as they should and do as she directs.

In addition to all the other forces which make the acceptance of the current program of soil erosion control and limitation of livestock slow and painful, this premise plays an important and fundamental part. To most Navahos it seems silly or presumptuous to interfere with the workings of nature to the extent that they are being told to do. Besides, they believe it won't bring the benefits the white people promise. If anything is wrong these days, it is that The People are forgetting their ways and their stories, so of course anyone would know that there would be hard times. It has nothing to do with too many sheep.

Premise Three. The Personality Is a Whole

This assumption also must be made explicit because white people so generally think of "mind" and body" as separable units. The whole Navaho system of curing clearly takes it for granted that you cannot treat a man's "body" without treating his "mind," and vice versa. In this respect Navahos are many generations ahead of white Americans, who are only now beginning to realize that it is the patient, not the disease, which must be treated. Successful physicians who understood "human nature" have acted on this premise always, but it has found verbal expression and acceptance only recently; at present it is receiving the most publicity in the specialty known as "psychosomatic medicine."

Premise Four. Respect the Integrity of the Individual

While the individual is always seen as a member of a larger group, still he is never completely submerged in that group. There is an area of rigidity where what any given person may and may not do is inexorably fixed, but there is likewise a large periphery of freedom. This is not the "romantic individualism" of white tradition, but in many respects the Navaho has more autonomy, more opportunity for genuine spontaneity than is the case in white society. Rights of individuals, including children, over their immediately personal property, are respected to the fullest degree, even when their wishes run counter to the obvious interests of the family or extended family. White people seeking to purchase a bow and arrow that they see in a hogan are surprised to have the adults refer the question to the five-year-old who owns the toy and whose decision is final. If a youngster unequivocally says he does not want to go to school or to the hospital, that is, in most families, the end of it. Husbands and wives make no attempt to control every aspect of the behavior of the spouse. Although individuals are not regarded as equal in capacity or in all features of the treatment that should be accorded them, still the integrity of every individual is protected from violation at the hands of more powerful people.

Where survival is held to depend on coöperation, the subordination of the individual to the group is rigorously demanded. Such interdependence is felt to exist in all sorts of ways that are not, from the white point of view, realistic. Success in hunting is thought to depend as much upon the faithful observance of taboos by the wife at home as upon the husband's skill or luck in stalking game. The individualism which expresses itself in social innovation is disapproved as strongly as is that which expresses itself in too obtrusive leadership. The following quotation (which, incidentally, is also a nice illustration of Navaho logic) brings out the Navaho feeling exactly.

You must be careful about introducing things into ceremonies. One chanter thought that he could do this. He held a Night Chant. He wanted more old people so he had the dancers cough and dance as old people. He also wanted an abundance of potatoes so he painted potatoes on the dancers' bodies. He desired that there should be a great deal of food so he had the dancers break wind and vomit through their masks to make believe that they had eaten a great deal. They surely got their reward. Through the coughing act a great many of the people got whooping cough and died. In the second change many of the people got spots on their bodies like potatoes only they were measles, sores, and smallpox. In the part, where they asked for all kinds of food, a lot died of diarrhea, vomiting and stomach aches. This chanter thought that he had the power to change things but everyone found out that he was wrong. It was the wrong thing to do and today no one will try to start any new ceremonies. Today we do not add anything.[2]

On the other hand, where autonomy does not seem to threaten the security of established practices or the needful coöperative undertakings, individuality is not only permitted but encouraged. Men and women feel free to vary their costumes to suit their temperaments, to experiment with variations in house style and other technological products, to break the day's routine with trips and other diversions spontaneously decided upon, while displays of jewelry, saddles, and horses bring admiration more than disapproval. He who makes up a new secular song or coins a new pun or quip wins many plaudits. Unity in diversity is the Navaho motto.

Premise Five. Everything Exists in Two Parts, the Male and the Female, Which Belong Together and Complete Each Other

With the Navaho this premise applies to much more than biology. The clear, deep, robins-egg-blue turquoise they call male, and the stone of a greenish hue they call female. The turbulent San Juan River is "male water," the placid Rio Grande "female water." The mountains of the north where harsh, cold winds blow are "male country," the warm open lands of the south "female country." There are male rains and female rains, the one

[2] Willard W. Hill, "Stability in Culture and Pattern," *American Anthropologist*, XLI (1939), 260.

hard and sudden, the other gentle; there are male and female chants; male and female plants are distinguished on the basis of appearance, the male always being the larger. The supernaturals, as seen in the sandpaintings or mentioned in the songs and prayers, are nearly always paired, so that if Corn Boy appears, one can be sure that Corn Girl will soon follow.

Premise Six. Human Nature Is Neither Good Nor Evil—Both Qualities Are Blended in All Persons From Birth On

The notion of "original sin" still lurks in white thinking. But the premise that children are "born bad" and have to be beaten into shape seems completely absent from the Navaho view. On the other hand, white "liberals" act upon the assumption that human beings can be educated into almost complete perfection, that if ignorance is removed people will act in full enlightenment. Similarly, at least some Christian groups hold that "grace" can permanently transform the wayward into paragons of virtue. The Navaho assumption is that no amount of knowledge and no amount of "religious" zeal can do more than alter somewhat the relative proportions of "bad" and "good" in any given individual.

Premise Seven. Like Produces Like and the Part Stands for the Whole

These are two "laws of thought" almost as basic to Navaho thinking as the so-called Aristotelian "laws of thought" have been in European intellectual history since the Middle Ages. Of course, *similia similibus curantur* has been important in the thinking of most human groups since the Old Stone Age or earlier; but among whites this principle is now largely relegated to the realm of folk belief, whereas among The People it still dominates the thought of the most sophisticated members of the society.

Let a few examples do for many. Because the juice of the milkweed resembles milk it is held to be useful in treating a mother who cannot nurse her infant. Since the eagle can see long distances, the diviner who does star-gazing must rub a preparation which includes water from an eagle's eye under his own eyelids. Witchcraft performed over a few hairs from an individual is as effective against the owner of the hairs as if done upon his whole person. In chants small mounds of earth stand for whole mountains.

Premise Eight. What Is Said Is to Be Taken Literally

. . . the easy ambiguities, the fluidities of English speech are foreign to the Navaho. There is little "reading between the lines," little exercise of the imagination in interpreting utterances. A student was asking about a girl who was said by a white person to be feeble-minded. He asked, "Can so-and-so's daughter speak?" The Navaho replied very positively, "Yes." Observation showed that the girl uttered only unintelligible sounds. When this was later thrown back at the original informant he countered, "Well, she *does* speak—but no one can understand her." And this was said without a smile or even a twinkle in the eye.

Similarly, a Navaho will seldom take it upon himself to attribute thoughts or sentiments to others in the absence of very explicit statements on their part. White workers among The People find it irritating when they ask, "What does your wife (or brother, etc.) think about this?" and get the reply, "I don't know. I didn't ask her." Their supposition is that spouses or close relatives or intimate friends have enough general knowledge of each other's opinions to answer such questions with reasonable accuracy even if there has been no discussion of this precise point. But the Navahos do not see it this way.

Premise Nine. This Life Is What Counts

Because the Christian tradition is so prevalent in white society, it is necessary to bring this premise out explicitly. The People have no sense whatsoever that this life is a "preparation" for another existence. Indeed, except for the (by no means universally accepted) view that witches and suicides live apart in the afterworld, there is no belief that the way one lives on this earth has anything to do with his fate after death. This is one reason why morality is practical rather than categorical. While the Navaho feels very keenly that life is *hard,* his outlook is quite foreign to that of "Life is real, life is earnest, and the grave is not the goal." White life is so permeated with the tradition of Puritanism, of "the Protestant ethic," that much Navaho behavior looks amoral or shiftless.

Another reason would seem to be that Navahos do not need to orient themselves in terms of principles of abstract morality. They get their orientations from face-to-face contacts with the same small group of people with whom they deal from birth to death. In a large, complex society like modern America where people come and go and where business and other dealings must be carried on by people who never see each other, it is functionally necessary to have abstract standards which transcend an immediate concrete situation in which two or more persons are interacting.

J. J. M. de GROOT

The Tao or Order of the Universe

*The original or "primary" Chinese texts which correspond in a sense to
our book of Genesis—the cosmological basis of Chinese religion—are really
quite unreadable, even when nicely annotated, by most Westerners. I have
therefore chosen a brief secondary account by a competent older Western
Sinologist, the Dutchman J. J. M. de Groot (1854–1921) who was Professor
of Sinology at the University of Berlin in 1911 when he wrote the popular
lectures that make up his Religion in China. In this account the central
and most important cosmological concept of Yin and Yang seems to me
well presented.*

UNIVERSISM IS TAOISM. INDEED, ITS STARTING-POINT IS THE TAO, WHICH
means the Road or Way, that is to say, the Road or Way in which the
Universe moves, its methods and its processes, its conduct and operation,
the complex of phenomena regularly recurring in it, in short, the Order of
the World, Nature, or Natural Order. It actually is in the main the annual
rotation of the seasons producing the process of growth, or renovation and
decay; it may accordingly be called Time, the creator and destroyer.

Man through obscure ages has mused on Nature's awful power, and
realised his absolute dependence on it. Thus the conviction has ripened in
him that to exist and to live in a happy state, he should comport himself,
as perfectly as possible, in accordance with the universe. Should his acts
disagree with that almighty Tao, a conflict must necessarily ensue, in which
he as the immensely weaker party must inevitably succumb. Such meditations have led him into the path of philosophy—to the study and discovery
of the characteristics of the Tao, of the means of acquiring these for himself, and of framing his conduct upon them; in other words, Man, conceiving
the Universe as an animated Universe, which imposed its will imperiously
and irresistibly, tried to learn this will, to submit to it humbly, and to obey
it implicitly.

From J. J. M. de Groot, *Religion in China. Universism: A Key to the Study of
Taoism and Confucianism.* American Lectures on the History of Religions, Series of
1910-1911 (New York: G. P. Putnam's Sons, 1912), pp. 6-20.

It is evident that this was a catholic system, calculated to embrace the whole sphere of human life and action. It stands before us, in fact, as a system of discipline and ethics based upon observation, divination, and imitation of Nature, and giving birth to a vast compound of private, domestic, and social rules of conduct, extending even to political institutions and laws, everything in which was directed to this one aim: to attract Nature's beneficial influences to the people and its government and to avert its detrimental influences. A principal sub-division of that system was the worship of the Universe, that is to say, the propitiation of a host of gods, which being components of the Universe in visible or invisible shape, manifest themselves in its ways and works.

The Chinese themselves, from a remote antiquity, have called the system the *Jen Tao,* or "Tao of Man," in contradistinction to the Tao of the Universe, which it pretends to copy. And this universal Tao is divided by them into two parts, namely the *T'ien Tao,* or "Tao of Heaven," and the *T'i Tao,* or "Tao of the Earth." It goes without saying (as the Chinese themselves hold) that the Tao of Heaven is paramount in power to the Tao of the Earth, as it is in fact through Heaven,—through its warmth and rains—that the annual process of creation is performed. Heaven, accordingly, is the highest god which the Chinese possess. There is, indeed, in the Chinese system no god beyond the Cosmos, no maker of it, no Yahweh, no Allah. Creation is simply the yearly renovation of Nature, the spontaneous work of Heaven and Earth, repeating itself in every revolution of the Tao.

The name Taoism, which we are wont to give to the system, is, as we see, correctly chosen, and there is no reason to banish it from our science of religions. In fact, the Chinese themselves employ the terms *Tao kiao,* "Doctrine of the Tao," and *Tao mun,* "School of the Tao."

Contemplation of the Universe and study of its laws did not, in China, develop into a correct science of Nature, dethroning the gods who were its parts and phenomena. Universism has outlived all ages, especially in the conservative classical form, which we know as Confucianism. I have stated that its pristine principles are contained in the Classics, which are the holy bibles of Confucianism and Taoism. The holiest of these books is the *Yih king,* esteemed holiest because it divulges the first principles of the system. Its third Appendix, entitled *Hi-ts'zĕ* or "Appended Explanations," the authorship of which many Chinese scholars and critics attribute to Confucius, describes the Universe as a living machine or organism, which it calls *Tái-Kih* or "Supreme Apex," or "Most Ultimate." This produced the "two Regulating Powers" or *Liang I,* which are cosmic souls or breaths, called *Yang* and *Yin.* These souls represent the male and the female parts of the Universe, assimilated respectively with the fructifying heaven and the earth which it fructifies, as also with warmth and cold, and light and darkness. "There is," as the Appended Explanations state, "in the system of mutations [of Nature] the Most Ultimate which produced the two Regulating Powers, which produce the four shapes [or seasons]." It is these two powers which constitute the Tao, for the Appended Explanations add explicitly "that the universal Yin and the universal Yang are the Tao"; indeed the process of Nature or Universal Order is the annual mixture, in various degrees, of cold and warmth, by which the seasons are produced and the processes of birth and decay are carried out. These processes are called *yih,* "changes or mutations"; "the processes of birth and re-birth, or of production of life, are the *yih,*" say the Appended Explanations. Hence the title of the *Yih king,* "holy Book of the Mutations." These mutations being the manifestation of the Tao, and thus actually the Tao itself, Chinese scholars frequently describe the Tao as "the revolving mutations of the *Yin* and *Yang,*" or "the annual revolution of changes produced by the *Yin* and *Yang,*" or "the changes which the *Yin* and *Yang* produce."

Ancient and modern authors are wont to define the Tao of the Universe as "the way of the road of the *Yin* and *Yang.*" The *Yin* is assimilated with the Earth, which is cold and dark, and the *Yang* with Heaven, which is warm and luminous; they are respectively the female and the male of the soul of the Cosmos, its Anima and its Animus.

I have said that the Tao of Man is a line of conduct, which pretends to be an imitation of the Tao of Heaven and Earth, calculated to make him happy. It is prescribed by his absolute dependence on the Universe for his birth and life. This dependence is emphasised by the classical dogma that Man borrows his own vital spirits from the dual soul of the Universe, and thus actually is a product of these powers, as also by the fact that his material body is shaped out of the same elements which constitute the Universe. Indeed in the *Li ki,* the most voluminous collection of classical books, we read, "Man is a product of the beneficial operations of Heaven and Earth, or of the copulation of the Yin and the Yang, and the union of a *kwei* with a *shen;* he consists of the finest breath which the five elements contain."[1] Thus ancient philosophy described Man as a compound of a *kwei* and a *shen,* two souls respectively related, as the context of this passage suggests, with the *Yin, or* terrestrial matter, and with the *Yang,* or immaterial celestial substance.

In the same great classic, which has to the present day narrowly confined Chinese thought within the limits of its doctrines, we do not search in vain for more dogmatic teaching about the nature of Man's dual soul and its relation with the Universe. It states that,

Tsai Ngo said, "I have heard the words *kwei* and *shen,* but I do not know their meaning"; and that Confucius thereupon said to him: "The *khi,* or *breath* is the full manifestation of the *shen,* and the *p'oh* is the full manifestation of the *kwei;* the union of the *kwei* with the *shen* is the highest of all doctrines. Living beings must all die, and the soul which must then return to earth is that which is called *kwei.* But while the bones and the flesh moulder in the ground and imperceptibly become the earth of the fields, the *khi* or breath departs to move on high as a shining light."[2]

[1] The book called *Li yun,* III.
[2] The book called *Tsi i,* II.

This instructive paragraph is the fundamental dogma of Taoist and Con
fucianist psychology. It teaches that the universal *Yang* and *Yin* are divided
into an indefinite number of souls or spirits, respectively called *shen* and
kwei; the *shen* represent light, warmth, productivity, life, which are the
special qualities of the *Yang;* and the *kwei* darkness, cold, sterility, death,
which are the attributes of the *Yin*. The soul of Man, like that of any living
being, consists of a *shen* and a *kwei* or *p'oh;* his birth is an infusion of these
souls, his death is their departure, the *shen* returning to the *Yang* or Heaven,
the *kwei* to the *Yin* or Earth. His body is, like Heaven and Earth, composed of the five elements. Accordingly, Man is an intrinsic part of the
Universe, a microcosm, born spontaneously from and in the macrocosm.
His *shen* is, of course, his principal soul, constituting his intelligence and
life; his *kwei* represents his qualities of the opposite kind.

This classical system of Universistic psychology, beside which no other
ever arose in China, defines the Yang as a supreme, universal *shen,* living,
creating, which divides itself into an infinite number of *shen* and deposits
them in the various beings of the world; and the Yin as an universal *kwei,*
likewise divisible into myriads of particles, each of which, in an individual,
may form his other soul. Accordingly, creation is a continuous emanation
or effusion of parts of the Yang and the Yin, and destruction of life is a
re-absorption of such parts. This process is the principal and highest manifestation of the Tao. It is achieved by the particles themselves, the Tao
doing its work spontaneously. Those particles, the *shen* and the *kwei,* are
innumerable. The Universe is crowded with them in all its parts; they animate every being,—everything, even the things which are wont to be called
dead objects. A *shen*, being a part of the Yang or the beatific half of the
Universe, is considered to be in general a good spirit or a god; and a *kwei,*
belonging to the Yin, is as a rule a spirit of evil, a spectre, devil or demon.
As there is no power beyond the Tao, there is no good in Nature but that
which comes from the *shen,* no evil but that which the *kwei* cause or inflict.
It is the *Yih king* which testifies to the prevalence of these conceptions in
ancient China, and therefore has established to this hour their authority as
holy dogmas of the highest order.

The *shen* are omnipresent; it is they which perform the unfathomable work
of the Yang and the Yin. These two vital breaths [of the Universe] create the
beings; their peregrinating *hwun* (or *shen*) are the causes of the changes [in
Nature], from which, accordingly, we may learn the actions and manners of the
kwei and the *shen*.[3]

According to one of the classics, the omnipresence of the *shen* and the
kwei, and their activity in the process of creation and production overawed
Confucius not less than it must have overawed every thinker of his time.

"How bountiful," exclaimed he, "is the beatific work of the *kwei* and the
shen! We look for them, but we do not see them; we listen for them, but do
not hear them; they incorporate themselves in every being and everything,

[3] *Hi-ts'zĕ,* I.

without exception. They cause all people under heaven to fast and purify themselves and to array themselves in full ceremonial dress, and then, when they thus offer their sacrifices, they, like an ocean, seem to be over their heads and to their left and right."[4]

With these dogmas before us, we may now say that the old groundwork of the Chinese system of religion is an Universistic Animism. The Universe being in all its parts crowded with *shen* and *kwei* the system is, moreover, polytheistic and polydemonistic. The gods are such *shen* as animate heaven, the sun and the moon, the stars, wind, rain, clouds, thunder, fire, the earth, seas, mountains, rivers, rocks, stones, animals, plants, objects of any kind; in particular also the gods are the *shen* of deceased men. And as to the demon-world, nowhere on the earth is it so populous as in China. *Kwei* swarm everywhere. No place exists where man is safe from them. They are especially dangerous during the night, when the power of the *yin* part of the Universe, to which demons belong, is strongest. They snatch the souls out of living men, so that these become ill or die. They strike or touch men, so that dangerous boils or tumours appear on their bodies. Ghosts of the ill-buried dead haunt dwellings with injurious effect, and are not laid until the dead are reburied decently. Hosts of demons not seldom set whole towns and countries in commotion, and utterly demoralise the people. Armies of spectral soldiers, on foot and horse, move through the sky, especially at night, kidnapping children, smiting people with disease and death, even compelling men to defend themselves with noise of gongs and drums, with bows, swords and spears, flaming torches, and fires. They steal the pigtails of inoffensive people. . . . Literature in China abounds with demon-tales—which are no stories in Chinese eyes, but undeniable facts.

Confucius himself divided the demons into three classes, living respectively in mountains and forests, in the water, and in the ground. The mountain-demons may by their mere presence cause drought and, as a consequence, the destruction of crops, hunger, famine—which means in China the death of thousands, nay millions; they have harassed China like chronic plagues in all times and ages.

Water-demons, most of which are souls of drowned men, cunningly cause people to tumble into the water or to sink away in mud flats; or they paralyse swimmers. Demons which inhabit the ground are disturbed by people who dig in the ground or who move heavy objects, and they then take revenge by disturbing the embryo in the womb of woman.

A very large contingent is contributed to the demon kingdom by animals. China has its werewolves, but especially its tiger-demons, ravening in the shape of men. Foxes and vixens in particular, but also wolves, dogs, and snakes are notorious for insinuating themselves into human society for immoral purposes, disguised as charming, handsome youths or female beauties; and not seldom they devour the victims of their lust, and, at all events, make them ill, delirious, insane. Evil is regularly inflicted upon men

---

[4] *Chung yung*, 16.

by all sorts of animals, even by birds, fishes, and insects, especially after assuming human shape. Those endless changes of men into beasts and beasts into men, in order to play their tricks as devils, are the best illustrations of the sway exerted upon the Chinese mind by the system of Universism, which teaches the animation of all beings, men and animals equally, by the same Yang and Yin that constitute the Order of the Universe. As a consequence of this same doctrine, trees, shrubs, herbs, and objects are believed to send out their souls, in order to inflict evil on men.

We thus see the Chinese people living in a world which is crowded on all sides with dangerous evil spirits. That belief is not banished to the domain of superstition or nursery tales. It is a cornerstone of China's Universistic religion, held to be as true as the existence of the Yin, as true, indeed, as the existence of Tao or Order of the World. As the demons act in that Order as distributers of evil (because they represent the Yin, or its cold and dark half), they exercise a dominant influence over human fate, as do, in like manner, the *shen,* the spirits or gods of the Yang, who are the distributers of blessing. But the Yang is as high above the Yin as Heaven (which is the Yang) is above the Earth. Heaven, therefore, is the chief *shen* or god, who rules and controls all evil spirits and their actions. And so Chinese theology has this great dogma, that no demons harm man without the authorisation of Heaven, or at least without its silent consent. This dogma is eminently classical, being laid down in the *Shu king* and the *Yih king.* We there read, "It is Heaven's Tao to give felicity to the good, and to bring misfortune upon the bad;[5] the *kwei* harm the arrogant; the *shen* render the modest happy."[6]

[5] *Shu King,* the book called *T'ang kao.*
[6] *Yih king,* the appendix called *T'wan,* I.

LUCRETIUS

The Formation of the World

The Roman poet T. Lucretius Carus (99?–55? B.C.) is indeed for many admirers a culture-hero, inevitable in any list of the world's great writers. His long philosophical poem, Of *the Nature of Things, was designed to teach to Romans the system of the Greek philosopher Epicurus (342? –271? B.C.). The poem could hardly be further in spirit from what has for two millennia been the vulgar notion of Epicureanism, a notion long ago put neatly, if ironically, by Horace as "a hog from Epicurus' sty." But Lucretius almost certainly was true to the spirit of his hero Epicurus, of whose work we have only fragments. I shall cite Lucretius again, for he has always appealed to what I may call the existentialist temperament. Here below is his creation myth, austerely "materialistic," God or gods strikingly absent; but the myth is somehow consolingly orderly in its final results, presenting a cosmology, inhuman indeed, but happily understandable by enlightened human beings. Lucretius' famous phrase with which our second excerpt concludes,* tantum religio potuit suadere malorum *(such are the crimes to which religion leads), has long been a favorite with the Enlightened, who, like Lucretius himself one may guess, fondly imagine that they are without a religion. I have chosen the late William Ellery Leonard's metrical translation, though I was tempted to use the literal and clear prose translation of Rouse.*

> But in what modes that conflux of first-stuff
> Did found the multitudinous universe
> Of earth, and sky, and the unfathomed deeps
> Of ocean, and courses of the sun and moon,
> I'll now in order tell. For of a truth
> Neither by counsel did the primal germs
> 'Stablish themselves, as by keen act of mind,
> Each in its proper place; nor did they make,

From Lucretius, *Of the Nature of Things.* Translated by William Ellery Leonard (New York: E. P. Dutton & Co., 1957), pp. 204-208, 4-6.

51

Forsooth, a compact how each germ should move;
But, lo, because primordials of things,
Many in many modes, astir by blows
From immemorial aeons, in motion too
By their own weights, have evermore been wont
To be so borne along and in all modes
To meet together and to try all sorts
Which, by combining one with other, they
Are powerful to create: because of *this*
It comes to pass that those primordials,
Diffusèd far and wide through mighty aeons,
The while they unions try, and motions too,
Of every kind, meet at the last amain,
And so become oft the commencements fit
Of mighty things—earth, sea, and sky, and race
Of living creatures.
                              In that long-ago
The wheel of the sun could nowhere be discerned
Flying far up with its abounding blaze,
Nor constellations of the mighty world,
Nor ocean, nor heaven, nor even earth nor air.
Nor aught of things like unto things of ours
Could then be seen—but only some strange storm
And a prodigious hurly-burly mass
Compounded of all kinds of primal germs,
Whose battling discords in disorder kept
Interstices, and paths, coherencies,
And weights, and blows, encounterings, and motions,
Because, by reason of their forms unlike
And varied shapes, they could not all thuswise
Remain conjoinèd nor harmoniously
Have interplay of movements. But from there
Portions began to fly asunder, and like
With like to join, and to block out a world,
And to divide its members and dispose
Its mightier parts—that is, to set secure
The lofty heavens from the lands, and cause
The sea to spread with waters separate,
And fires of ether separate and pure
Likewise to congregate apart.
                              For, lo,
First came together the earthy particles
(As being heavy and intertangled) there
In the mid-region, and all began to take
The lowest abodes; and ever the more they got

One with another intertangled, the more
They pressed from out their mass those particles
Which were to form the sea, the stars, the sun,
And moon, and ramparts of the mighty world—
For these consist of seeds more smooth and round
And of much smaller elements than earth.
And thus it was that ether, fraught with fire,
First broke away from out the earthen parts,
Athrough the innumerable pores of earth,
And raised itself aloft, and with itself
Bore lightly off the many starry fires;
And not far otherwise we often see

. . . . . .

And the still lakes and the perennial streams
Exhale a mist, and even as earth herself
Is seen at times to smoke, when first at dawn
The light of the sun, the many-rayed, begins
To redden into gold, over the grass
Begemmed with dew. When all of these are brought
Together overhead, the clouds on high
With now concreted body weave a cover
Beneath the heavens. And thuswise ether too,
Light and diffusive, with concreted body
On all sides spread, on all sides bent itself
Into a dome, and, far and wide diffused
On unto every region on all sides,
Thus hedged all else within its greedy clasp.
Hard upon ether came the origins
Of sun and moon, whose globes revolve in air
Midway between the earth and mightiest ether,—
For neither took them, since they weighed too little
To sink and settle, but too much to glide
Along the upmost shores; and yet they are
In such a wise midway between the twain
As ever to whirl their living bodies round,
And ever to dure as parts of the wide Whole;
In the same fashion as certain members may
In us remain at rest, whilst others move.
When, then, these substances had been withdrawn,
Amain the earth, where now extend the vast
Cerulean zones of all the level seas,
Caved in, and down along the hollows poured
The whirlpools of her brine; and day by day
The more the tides of ether and rays of sun

On every side constrained into one mass
The earth by lashing it again, again,
Upon its outer edges (so that then,
Being thus beat upon, 'twas all condensed
About its proper centre), ever the more
The salty sweat, from out its body squeezed,
Augmented ocean and the fields of foam
By seeping through its frame, and all the more
Those many particles of heat and air
Escaping, began to fly aloft, and form,
By condensation there afar from earth,
The high refulgent circuits of the heavens.
The plains began to sink, and windy slopes
Of the high mountains to increase; for rocks
Could not subside, nor all the parts of ground
Settle alike to one same level there.

  Thus, then, the massy weight of earth stood firm
With now concreted body, when (as 'twere)
All of the slime of the world, heavy and gross,
Had run together and settled at the bottom,
Like lees or bilge. Then ocean, then the air,
Then ether herself, the fraught-with-fire, were all
Left with their liquid bodies pure and free,
And each more lighter than the next below;
And ether, most light and liquid of the three,
Floats on above the long aerial winds,
Nor with the brawling of the winds of air
Mingles its liquid body. It doth leave
All there—those under-realms below her heights—
There to be overset in whirlwind wild,—
Doth leave all there to brawl in wayward gusts,
Whilst, gliding with a fixèd impulse still,
Itself it bears its fires along. For, lo,
That ether can flow thus steadily on, on,
With one unaltered urge, the Pontus proves—
That sea which floweth forth with fixèd tides,
Keeping one onward tenor as it glides. . . .

                              Whilst human kind
Throughout the lands lay miserably crushed
Before all eyes beneath Religion—who
Would show her head along the region skies,
Glowering on mortals with her hideous face—
A Greek it was who first opposing dared

Raise mortal eyes that terror to withstand,
Whom nor the fame of Gods nor lightning's stroke
Nor threatening thunder of the ominous sky
Abashed; but rather chafed to angry zest
His dauntless heart to be the first to rend
The crossbars at the gates of Nature old.
And thus his will and hardy wisdom won;
And forward thus he fared afar, beyond
The flaming ramparts of the world, until
He wandered the unmeasurable All.
Whence he to us, a conqueror, reports
What things can rise to being, what cannot,
And by what law to each its scope prescribed,
Its boundary stone that clings so deep in Time.
Wherefore religion now is under foot,
And us his victory now exalts to heaven.
   I know how hard it is in Latian verse
To tell the dark discoveries of the Greeks,
Chiefly because our pauper speech must find
Strange terms to fit the strangeness of the thing;
Yet worth of thine and the expected joy
Of thy sweet friendship do persuade me on
To bear all toil and wake the clear nights through,
Seeking with what of words and what of song
I may at last most gloriously uncloud
For thee the light beyond, wherewith to view
The core of being at the centre hid.
And for the rest, summon to judgments true,
Unbusied ears and singleness of mind
Withdrawn from cares; lest these my gifts, arranged
For thee with eager service, thou disdain
Before thou comprehendest: since for thee
I prove the súpreme law of Gods and sky,
And the primordial germs of things unfold,
Whence Nature all creates, and multiplies
And fosters all, and whither she resolves
Each in the end when each is overthrown.
This ultimate stock we have devised to name
Procreant atoms, matter, seeds of things,
Or primal bodies, as primal to the world.

   I fear perhaps thou deemest that we fare
An impious road to realms of thought profane;
But 'tis that same religion oftener far
Hath bred the foul impieties of men:

As once at Aulis, the elected chiefs,
Foremost of heroes, Danaan counsellors,
Defiled Diana's altar, virgin queen,
With Agamemnon's daughter, foully slain.
She felt the chaplet round her maiden locks
And fillets, fluttering down on either cheek,
And at the altar marked her grieving sire,
The priests beside him who concealed the knife,
And all the folk in tears at sight of her.
With a dumb terror and a sinking knee
She dropped; nor might avail her now that first
'Twas she who gave the king a father's name.
They raised her up, they bore the trembling girl
On to the altar—hither led not now
With solemn rites and hymeneal choir,
But sinless woman, sinfully foredone,
A parent felled her on her bridal day,
Making his child a sacrificial beast
To give the ships auspicious winds for Troy:
Such are the crimes to which religion leads.

ST. AUGUSTINE

The Cosmology of Genesis

St. Augustine (354–430), bishop of Hippo in North Africa, was the great-est of the Latin fathers, and a major influence in setting the orthodox doctrines of Roman Catholic theology. Here in a brief selection from his City of God *is Augustine's explanation of the cosmology of* Genesis. *Note that this is far from naïve or fundamentalist thinking. To Augustine, the "days" of the creation are a mystery, if not a symbol.*

That the world is neither without beginning, nor yet created by a new decree of God, by which He afterwards willed what He had not before willed

OF ALL VISIBLE THINGS, THE WORLD IS THE GREATEST; OF ALL INVISIBLE, the greatest is God. But, that the world is, we see; that God is, we believe. That God made the world, we can believe from no one more safely than from God himself. But where have we heard Him? Nowhere more dis-tinctly than in the Holy Scriptures, where His prophet said, "In the be-ginning God created the heavens and the earth."[1] Was the prophet present when God made the heavens and the earth? No; but the wisdom of God, by whom all things were made, was there,[2] and wisdom insinuates itself into holy souls, and makes them the friends of God and His prophets, and noiselessly informs them of His works. They are taught also by the angels of God, who always behold the face of the Father,[3] and announce His will to whom it befits. Of these prophets was he who said and wrote, "In the beginning God created the heavens and the earth." And so fit a witness was he of God, that the same Spirit of God, who revealed these things to him, enabled him also so long before to predict that our faith also would be forthcoming.

But why did God choose then to create the heavens and earth which up

From Saint Augustine, *The City of God.* Translated by Marcus Dods (New York: The Modern Library, 1950), pp. 347-352.

[1] Gen. i. 1.
[2] Prov. viii. 27.
[3] Matt. xviii. 10.

57

to that time He had not made?[4] If they who put this question wish to make
out that the world is eternal and without beginning, and that consequently
it has not been made by God, they are strangely deceived, and rave in
the incurable madness of impiety. For, though the voices of the prophets
were silent, the world itself, by its well-ordered changes and movements,
and by the fair appearance of all visible things, bears a testimony of its
own, both that it has been created, and also that it could not have been
created save by God, whose greatness and beauty are unutterable and
invisible. As for those[5] who own, indeed, that it was made by God, and
yet ascribe to it not a temporal but only a creational beginning, so that in
some scarcely intelligible way the world should always have existed a
created world, they make an assertion which seems to them to defend God
from the charge of arbitrary hastiness, or of suddenly conceiving the idea
of creating the world as a quite new idea, or of casually changing His will,
though He be unchangeable. But I do not see how this supposition of
theirs can stand in other respects, and chiefly in respect of the soul; for if
they contend that it is co-eternal with God, they will be quite at a loss
to explain whence there has accrued to it new misery, which through a
previous eternity had not existed. For if they said that its happiness and
misery ceaselessly alternate, they must say, further, that this alternation
will continue for ever; whence will result this absurdity, that, though the
soul is called blessed, it is not so in this, that it foresees its own misery
and disgrace. And yet, if it does not foresee it, and supposes that it will be
neither disgraced nor wretched, but always blessed, then it is blessed because it is deceived; and a more foolish statement one cannot make. But
if their idea is that the soul's misery has alternated with its bliss during
the ages of the past eternity, but that now, when once the soul has been
set free, it will return henceforth no more to misery, they are nevertheless
of opinion that it has never been truly blessed before, but begins at last
to enjoy a new and uncertain happiness; that is to say, they must
acknowledge that some new thing, and that an important and signal thing,
happens to the soul which never in a whole past eternity happened to it
before. And if they deny that God's eternal purpose included this new
experience of the soul, they deny that He is the Author of its blessedness,
which is unspeakable impiety. If, on the other hand, they say that the
future blessedness of the soul is the result of a new decree of God, how
will they show that God is not chargeable with that mutability which dis-
pleases them? Further, if they acknowledge that it was created in time,
but will never perish in time—that it has, like number,[6] a beginning but
no end—and that, therefore, having once made trial of misery, and been
delivered from it, it will never again return thereto, they will certainly

---

[4] A common question among the Epicureans; urged by Velleius in Cic. *De Nat.
Deor.* i. 9; adopted by the Manichæans and spoken to by Augustine in the *Conf.*
xi. 10, 12, also in *De Gen. contra Man.* i. 3.

[5] The Neo-Platonists.

[6] Number begins at one, but runs on infinitely.

admit that this takes place without any violation of the immutable counsel of God. Let them, then, in like manner believe regarding the world that it too could be made in time, and yet that God, in making it, did not alter His eternal design.

That we ought not to seek to comprehend the infinite ages of time before the world, nor the infinite realms of space

Next, we must see what reply can be made to those who agree that God is the Creator of the world, but have difficulties about the time of its creation, and what reply, also, they can make to difficulties we might raise about the place of its creation. For, as they demand why the world was created then and no sooner, we may ask why it was created just here where it is, and not elsewhere. For if they imagine infinite spaces of time before the world, during which God could not have been idle, in like manner they may conceive outside the world infinite realms of space, in which, if any one says that the Omnipotent cannot hold His hand from working, will it not follow that they must adopt Epicurus' dream of innumerable worlds? with this difference only, that he asserts that they are formed and destroyed by the fortuitous movements of atoms, while they will hold that they are made by God's hand, if they maintain that, throughout the boundless immensity of space, stretching interminably in every direction round the world, God cannot rest, and that the worlds which they suppose Him to make cannot be destroyed. For here the question is with those who, with ourselves, believe that God is spiritual, and the Creator of all existences but Himself. As for others, it is a condescension to dispute with them on a religious question, for they have acquired a reputation only among men who pay divine honours to a number of gods, and have become conspicuous among the other philosophers for no other reason than that, though they are still far from the truth, they are near it in comparison with the rest. While these, then, neither confine in any place, nor limit, nor distribute the divine substance, but, as is worthy of God, own it to be wholly though spiritually present everywhere, will they perchance say that this substance is absent from such immense spaces outside the world, and is occupied in one only, (and that a very little one compared with the infinity beyond,) the one, namely, in which is the world? I think they will not proceed to this absurdity. Since they maintain that there is but one world, of vast material bulk, indeed, yet finite, and in its own determinate position, and that this was made by the working of God, let them give the same account of God's resting in the infinite times before the world as they give of His resting in the infinite spaces outside of it. And as it does not follow that God set the world in the very spot it occupies and no other by accident rather than by divine reason, although no human reason can comprehend why it was so set, and though there was no merit in the spot chosen to give it the precedence of infinite others, so neither does it follow that we should suppose that God was guided by chance when He created the world in that and no earlier time, although previous times had been running by during an infinite past, and though there was no difference by which one time could be chosen in preference to another. But if they say that the thoughts of men are idle when they conceive infinite places, since there is no place beside the world, we reply that, by the same showing, it is vain to conceive of the past times of God's rest, since there is no time before the world.

That the world and time had both one beginning, and the one did not anticipate the other

For if eternity and time are rightly distinguished by this, that time does not exist without some movement and transition, while in eternity there is no change, who does not see that there could have been no time had not some creature been made, which by some motion could give birth to change—the various parts of which motion and change, as they cannot be simultaneous, succeed one another—and thus, in these shorter or longer intervals of duration, time would begin? Since then, God, in whose eternity is no change at all, is the Creator and Ordainer of time, I do not see how He can be said to have created the world after spaces of time had elapsed, unless it be said that prior to the world there was some creature by whose movement time could pass. And if the sacred and infallible Scriptures say that in the beginning God created the heavens and the earth, in order that it may be understood that He had made nothing previously—for if He had made anything before the rest, this thing would rather be said to have been made "in the beginning"—then assuredly the world was made, not in time, but simultaneously with time. For that which is made in time is made both after and before some time—after that which is past, before that which is future. But none could then be past, for there was no creature by whose movements its duration could be measured. But simultaneously with time the world was made, if in the world's creation change and motion were created, as seems evident from the order of the first six or seven days. For in these days the morning and evening are counted, until, on the sixth day, all things which God then made were finished, and on the seventh the rest of God was mysteriously and sublimely signalized. What kind of days these were it is extremely difficult, or perhaps impossible for us to conceive, and how much more to say!

Of the nature of the first days, which are said to have had morning and evening, before there was a sun

We see, indeed, that our ordinary days have no evening but by the setting, and no morning but by the rising, of the sun; but the first three days of all were passed without sun, since it is reported to have been made on the fourth day. And first of all, indeed, light was made by the word of God, and God, we read, separated it from the darkness, and called the light Day, and the darkness Night; but what kind of light that was, and by what periodic movement it made evening and morning, is beyond the reach of our senses; neither can we understand how it was, and yet must unhesitatingly believe it. For either it was some material light, whether proceeding from the upper parts of the world, far removed from our sight, or from the spot where the sun was afterwards kindled; or under the name of light the holy city was signified, composed of holy angels and blessed spirits, the city of which the apostle says, "Jerusalem which is above is our eternal mother in heaven";[7] and in another place, "For ye are all the children of the light, and the children of the day; we are not of the night, nor of darkness."[8] Yet in some respects we may appropriately speak of a morning and evening of this day also. For the knowledge of the creature is, in comparison of the knowledge of the Creator, but a twilight; and so it dawns and breaks into morning when the creature is drawn to the praise and love of the Creator; and night never falls when the Creator is not forsaken through love of the creature. In fine, Scripture, when it would recount those days in order, never mentions the word night. It never says, "Night was," but "The evening and the morning were the first day." So of the second and the rest. And, indeed, the knowledge of created things contemplated by themselves is, so to speak, more colourless than when they are seen in the wisdom of God, as in the art by which they were made. Therefore evening is a more suitable figure than night; and yet, as I said, morning returns when the creature returns to the praise and love of the Creator. When it does so in the knowledge of itself, that is the first day; when in the knowledge of the firmament, which is the name given to the sky between the waters above and those beneath, that is the second day; when in the knowledge of the earth, and the sea, and all things that grow out of the earth, that is the third day; when in the knowledge of the greater and less luminaries, and all the stars, that is the fourth day; when in the knowledge of all animals that swim in the waters and that fly in the air, that is the fifth day; when in the knowledge of all animals that live on the earth, and of man himself, that is the sixth day.[9]

What we are to understand of God's resting on the seventh day, after the six days' work

When it is said that God rested on the seventh day from all His works, and hallowed it, we are not to conceive of this in a childish fashion, as if work were a toil to God, who "spake and it was done"—spake by the spiritual and eternal, not audible and transitory word. But God's rest signifies the rest of those who rest in God, as the joy of a house means the joy of those in the house who rejoice, though not the house, but something else, causes the joy. How much more intelligible is such

[7] Gal. iv. 26.
[8] 1 Thess. v. 5.
[9] Comp. *de Gen. ad lit.* i. and iv.

phraseology, then, if the house itself, by its own beauty, makes the inhabitants joyful! For in this case we not only call it joyful by that figure of speech in which the thing containing is used for the thing contained (as when we say, "The theatres applaud," "The meadows low," meaning that the men in the one applaud, and the oxen in the other low), but also by that figure in which the cause is spoken of as if it were the effect, as when a letter is said to be joyful, because it makes its readers so. Most appropriately, therefore, the sacred narrative states that God rested, meaning thereby that those rest who are in Him, and whom He makes to rest. And this the prophetic narrative promises also to the men to whom it speaks, and for whom it was written, that they themselves, after those good works which God does in and by them, if they have managed by faith to get near to God in this life, shall enjoy in Him eternal rest. This was prefigured to the ancient people of God by the rest enjoined in their sabbath law, of which, in its own place, I shall speak more at large.

ALFRED NORTH WHITEHEAD

God and the World

*Alfred North Whitehead (1861–1947) was a distinguished English mathe-
matician who turned philosopher in his later years and migrated to the
United States. In collaboration with Bertrand Russell he published the
three-volume classic of modern mathematics, the* Principia Mathema-
tica *(1910–1913). Both men, however, had incurably philosophical
minds, though as philosophers their ways were to part. Whitehead used
to say later that he had come to think of "Bertie," who remained in the
empirical tradition and eschewed God, as shallow, while Bertie had come
doubtless to think of him (Whitehead) as fuzzy-minded. Certainly, as the
following passage from Whitehead's major attack on the philosophical
ultimates,* Process and Reality: An Essay in Cosmology *(1929), shows, he
came to use the word "God" quite freely, though not in any orthodox
Christian sense. This God's eye is hardly on the fall of the sparrow, and
there are critics who feel that He is no fit object of worship. But Whitehead is not ashamed of his feelings and he is struggling manfully to avoid
the mechanistic implications of naïve materialism.*

SO LONG AS THE TEMPORAL WORLD IS CONCEIVED AS A SELF-SUFFICIENT
completion of the creative act, explicable by its derivation from an ultimate
principle which is at once eminently real and the unmoved mover, from
this conclusion there is no escape: the best that we can say of the turmoil is, "For so he giveth his beloved—sleep." This is the message of
religions of the Buddhistic type, and in some sense it is true. In this final
discussion we have to ask, whether metaphysical principles impose the
belief that it is the whole truth. The complexity of the world must be
reflected in the answer. It is childish to enter upon thought with the
simple-minded question, What is the world made of? The task of reason
is to fathom the deeper depths of the many-sidedness of things. We must
not expect simple answers to far-reaching questions. However far our
gaze penetrates, there are always heights beyond which block our vision.

From Alfred North Whitehead, *Process and Reality* (New York: The Macmillan
Company, 1929), pp. 519-530.

The notion of God as the "unmoved mover" is derived from Aristotle, at least so far as Western thought is concerned. The notion of God as "eminently real" is a favourite doctrine of Christian theology. The combination of the two into the doctrine of an aboriginal, eminently real, transcendent creator, at whose fiat the world came into being, and whose imposed will it obeys, is the fallacy which has infused tragedy into the histories of Christianity and of Mahometanism.

When the Western world accepted Christianity, Caesar conquered; and the received text of Western theology was edited by his lawyers. The code of Justinian and the theology of Justinian are two volumes expressing one movement of the human spirit. The brief Galilean vision of humility flickered throughout the ages, uncertainly. In the official formulation of the religion it has assumed the trivial form of the mere attribution to the Jews that they cherished a misconception about their Messiah. But the deeper idolatry, of the fashioning of God in the image of the Egyptian, Persian, and Roman imperial rulers, was retained. The Church gave unto God the attributes which belonged exclusively to Caesar.

In the great formative period of theistic philosophy, which ended with the rise of Mahometanism, after a continuance coeval with civilization, three strains of thought emerge which, amid many variations in detail, respectively fashion God in the image of an imperial ruler, God in the image of a personification of moral energy, God in the image of an ultimate philosophical principle. Hume's *Dialogues* criticize unanswerably these modes of explaining the system of the world.

The three schools of thought can be associated respectively with the divine Caesars, the Hebrew prophets, and Aristotle. But Aristotle was antedated by Indian, and Buddhistic, thought; the Hebrew prophets can be paralleled in traces of earlier thought; Mahometanism and the divine Caesars merely represent the most natural, obvious, theistic idolatrous symbolism, at all epochs and places.

The history of theistic philosophy exhibits various stages of combination of these three diverse ways of entertaining the problem. There is, however, in the Galilean origin of Christianity yet another suggestion which does not fit very well with any of the three main strands of thought. It does not emphasize the ruling Caesar, or the ruthless moralist, or the unmoved mover. It dwells upon the tender elements in the world, which slowly and in quietness operate by love; and it finds purpose in the present immediacy of a kingdom not of this world. Love neither rules, nor is it unmoved; also it is a little oblivious as to morals. It does not look to the future; for it finds its own reward in the immediate present.

SECTION II

Apart from any reference to existing religions as they are, or as they ought to be, we must investigate dispassionately what the metaphysical principles, here developed, require on these points, as to the nature of God. There is nothing here in the nature of proof. There is merely the confrontation of the theoretic system with a certain rendering of the facts. But the unsystematized report upon the facts is itself highly controversial, and the system is confessedly inadequate. The deductions from it in this particular sphere of thought cannot be looked upon as more than suggestions as to how the problem is transformed in the light of that system. What follows is merely an attempt to add another speaker to that masterpiece, Hume's *Dialogues Concerning Natural Religion*. Any cogency of argument entirely depends upon elucidation of somewhat exceptional elements in our conscious experience—those elements which may roughly be classed together as religious and moral intuitions.

In the first place, God is not to be treated as an exception to all metaphysical principles, invoked to save their collapse. He is their chief exemplification.

Viewed as primordial, he is the unlimited conceptual realization of the absolute wealth of potentiality. In this aspect, he is not *before* all creation, but *with* all creation. But, as primordial, so far is he from "eminent reality," that in this abstraction he is "deficiently actual"—and this in two ways. His feelings are only conceptual and so lack the fulness of actuality. Secondly, conceptual feelings, apart from complex integration with physical feelings, are devoid of consciousness in their subjective forms.

Thus, when we make a distinction of reason, and consider God in the abstraction of a primordial actuality, we must ascribe to him neither fulness of feeling, nor consciousness. He is the unconditioned actuality of conceptual feeling at the base of things; so that, by reason of this primordial actuality, there is an order in the relevance of eternal objects to the process of creation. His unity of conceptual operations is a free creative act, untrammelled by reference to any particular course of things. It is deflected neither by love, nor by hatred, for what in fact comes to pass. The *particularities* of the actual world presuppose *it*; while *it* merely presupposes the *general* metaphysical character of creative advance, of which it is the primordial exemplification. The primordial nature of God is the acquirement by creativity of a primordial character.

His conceptual actuality at once exemplifies and establishes the categoreal conditions. The conceptual feelings, which compose his primordial nature, exemplify in their subjective forms their mutual sensitivity and their subjective unity of subjective aim. These subjective forms are valuations determining the relative relevance of eternal objects for each occasion of actuality.

He is the lure for feeling, the eternal urge of desire. His particular relevance to each creative act as it arises from its own conditioned standpoint in the world, constitutes him the initial "object of desire" establishing the initial phase of each subjective aim. A quotation from Aristotle's

Metaphysics[1] expresses some analogies to, and some differences from, this line of thought: "And since that which is moved and mover is intermediate, there is a mover which moves without being moved, being eternal, substance, and actuality. And the object of desire and the object of thought are the same. For the apparent good is the object of appetite, and the real good is the primary object of rational desire. But desire is consequent on opinion rather than opinion on desire; for the thinking is the starting point. And thought is moved by the object of thought, and one side of the list of opposites is in itself the object of thought; . . ." Aristotle had not made the distinction between conceptual feelings and the intellectual feelings which alone involve consciousness. But if "conceptual feeling," with its subjective form of valuation, be substituted for "thought," "thinking," and "opinion," in the above quotation, the agreement is exact.

SECTION III

There is another side to the nature of God which cannot be omitted. Throughout this exposition of the philosophy of organism we have been considering the primary action of God on the world. From this point of view, he is the principle of concretion—the principle whereby there is initiated a definite outcome from a situation otherwise riddled with ambiguity. Thus, so far, the primordial side of the nature of God has alone been relevant.

But God, as well as being primordial, is also consequent. He is the beginning and the end. He is not the beginning in the sense of being in the past of all members. He is the presupposed actuality of conceptual operation, in unison of becoming with every other creative act. Thus by reason of the relativity of all things, there is a reaction of the world on God. The completion of God's nature into a fulness of physical feeling is derived from the objectification of the world in God. He shares with every new creation its actual world; and the concrescent creature is objectified in God as a novel element in God's objectification of that actual world. This prehension into God of each creature is directed with the subjective aim, and clothed with the subjective form, wholly derivative from his all-inclusive primordial valuation. God's conceptual nature is unchanged, by reason of its final completeness. But his derivative nature is consequent upon the creative advance of the world.

Thus, analogously to all actual entities, the nature of God is dipolar. He has a primordial nature and a consequent nature. The consequent nature of God is conscious; and it is the realization of the actual world in the unity of his nature, and through the transformation of his wisdom. The primordial nature is conceptual, the consequent nature is the weaving of God's physical feelings upon his primordial concepts.

[1] Cf. *Metaphysics* 1072, trans. by Professor W. D. Ross. My attention was called to the appositeness of this particular quotation by Mr. F. J. Carson.

One side of God's nature is constituted by his conceptual experience. This experience is the primordial fact in the world, limited by no actuality which it presupposes. It is therefore infinite, devoid of all negative prehensions. This side of his nature is free, complete, primordial, eternal, actually deficient, and unconscious. The other side originates with physical experience derived from the temporal world, and then acquires integration with the primordial side. It is determined, incomplete, consequent, "everlasting," fully actual, and conscious. His necessary goodness expresses the determination of his consequent nature.

Conceptual experience can be infinite, but it belongs to the nature of physical experience that it is finite. An actual entity in the temporal world is to be conceived as originated by physical experience with its process of completion motivated by consequent, conceptual experience initially derived from God. God is to be conceived as originated by conceptual experience with his process of completion motivated by consequent, physical experience, initially derived from the temporal world.

SECTION IV

The perfection of God's subjective aim, derived from the completeness of his primordial nature, issues into the character of his consequent nature. In it there is no loss, no obstruction. The world is felt in a unison of immediacy. The property of combining creative advance with the retention of mutual immediacy is what in the previous section is meant by the term "everlasting."

The wisdom of subjective aim prehends every actuality for what it can be in such a perfected system—its sufferings, its sorrows, its failures, its triumphs, its immediacies of joy—woven by rightness of feeling into the harmony of the universal feeling, which is always immediate, always many, always one, always with novel advance, moving onward and never perishing. The revolts of destructive evil, purely self-regarding, are dismissed into their triviality of merely individual facts; and yet the good they did achieve in individual joy, in individual sorrow, in the introduction of needed contrast, is yet saved by its relation to the completed whole. The image—and it is but an image—the image under which this operative growth of God's nature is best conceived, is that of a tender care that nothing be lost.

The consequent nature of God is his judgment on the world. He saves the world as it passes into the immediacy of his own life. It is the judgment of a tenderness which loses nothing that can be saved. It is also the judgment of a wisdom which uses what in the temporal world is mere wreckage.

Another image which is also required to understand his consequent nature, is that of his infinite patience. The universe includes a threefold creative act composed of (i) the one infinite conceptual realization, (ii) the multiple solidarity of free physical realizations in the temporal world, (iii) the ultimate unity of the multiplicity of actual fact with the primordial conceptual fact. If we conceive the first term and the last term in their unity over against the intermediate multiple freedom of physical realizations in the temporal world, we conceive of the patience of God, tenderly saving the turmoil of the intermediate world by the completion of his own nature. The sheer force of things lies in the intermediate physical process: this is the energy of physical production. God's rôle is not the combat of productive force with productive force, of destructive force with destructive force; it lies in the patient operation of the overpowering rationality of his conceptual harmonization. He does not create the world, he saves it: or, more accurately, he is the poet of the world, with tender patience leading it by his vision of truth, beauty, and goodness.

SECTION V

The vicious separation of the flux from the permanence leads to the concept of an entirely static God, with eminent reality, in relation to an entirely fluent world, with deficient reality. But if the opposites, static and fluent, have once been so explained as separately to characterize diverse actualities, the interplay between the thing which is static and the things which are fluent involves contradiction at every step in its explanation. Such philosophies must include the notion of "illusion" as a fundamental principle—the notion of *"mere* appearance." This is the final Platonic problem.

Undoubtedly, the intuitions of Greek, Hebrew, and Christian thought have alike embodied the notions of a static God condescending to the world, and of a world *either* thoroughly fluent, *or* accidentally static, but finally fluent—"heaven and earth shall pass away." In some schools of thought, the fluency of the world is mitigated by the assumption that selected components in the world are exempt from this final fluency, and achieve a static survival. Such components are not separated by any decisive line from analogous components for which the assumption is not made. Further, the survival is construed in terms of a final pair of opposites, happiness for some, torture for others.

Such systems have the common character of starting with a fundamental intuition which we do mean to express, and of entangling themselves in verbal expressions, which carry consequences at variance with the initial intuition of permanence in fluency and of fluency in permanence.

But civilized intuition has always, although obscurely, grasped the problem as double and not as single. There is not the mere problem of fluency *and* permanence. There is the double problem: actuality with permanence, requiring fluency as its completion; and actuality with fluency, requiring permanence as its completion. The first half of the problem concerns the completion of God's primordial nature by the derivation of his consequent nature from the temporal world. The second half of the problem concerns the completion of each fluent actual occasion by its function of objective immortality, devoid of "perpetual perishing," that is to say, "everlasting."

This double problem cannot be separated into two distinct problems. Either side can only be explained in terms of the other. The consequent nature of God is the fluent world become "everlasting" by its objective immortality in God. Also the objective immortality of actual occasions requires the primordial permanence of God, whereby the creative advance ever re-establishes itself endowed with initial subjective aim derived from the relevance of God to the evolving world.

But objective immortality within the temporal world does not solve the problem set by the penetration of the finer religious intuition. "Everlastingness" has been lost; and "everlastingness" is the content of that vision upon which the finer religions are built—the "many" absorbed everlastingly in the final unity. The problems of the fluency of God and of the everlastingness of passing experience are solved by the same factor in the universe. This factor is the temporal world perfected by its reception and its reformation, as a fulfilment of the primordial appetition which is the basis of all order. In this way God is completed by the individual, fluent satisfactions of finite fact, and the temporal occasions are completed by their everlasting union with their transformed selves, purged into conformation with the eternal order which is the final absolute "wisdom." The final summary can only be expressed in terms of a group of antitheses, whose apparent self-contradiction depends on neglect of the diverse categories of existence. In each antithesis there is a shift of meaning which converts the opposition into a contrast.

It is as true to say that God is permanent and the World fluent, as that the World is permanent and God is fluent.

It is as true to say that God is one and the World many, as that the World is one and God many.

It is as true to say that, in comparison with the World, God is actual eminently, as that, in comparison with God, the World is actual eminently.

It is as true to say that the World is immanent in God, as that God is immanent in the World.

It is as true to say that God transcends the World, as that the World transcends God.

It is as true to say that God creates the World, as that the World creates God.

God and the World are the contrasted opposites in terms of which Creativity achieves its supreme task of transforming disjoined multiplicity, with its diversities in opposition, into concrescent unity, with its diversities in contrast. In each actuality these are two concrescent poles of realization—"enjoyment" and "appetition," that is, the "physical" and the "conceptual." For God the conceptual is prior to the physical, for the World the physical poles are prior to the conceptual poles.

A physical pole is in its own nature exclusive, bounded by contradiction: a conceptual pole is in its own nature all-embracing, unbounded by contradiction. The former derives its share of infinity from the infinity of appetition; the latter derives its share of limitation from the exclusiveness of enjoyment. Thus, by reason of his priority of appetition, there can be but one primordial nature for God; and, by reason of their priority of enjoyment, there must be one history of many actualities in the physical world.

God and the World stand over against each other, expressing the final metaphysical truth that appetitive vision and physical enjoyment have equal claim to priority in creation. But no two actualities can be torn apart: each is all in all. Thus each temporal occasion embodies God, and is embodied in God. In God's nature, permanence is primordial and flux is derivative from the World: in the World's nature, flux is primordial and permanence is derivative from God. Also the World's nature is a primordial datum for God; and God's nature is a primordial datum for the World. Creation achieves the reconciliation of permanence and flux when it has reached its final term which is everlastingness—the Apotheosis of the World.

Opposed elements stand to each other in mutual requirement. In their unity, they inhibit or contrast. God and the World stand to each other in this opposed requirement. God is the infinite ground of all mentality, the unity of vision seeking physical multiplicity. The World is the multiplicity of finites, actualities seeking a perfected unity. Neither God, nor the World, reaches static completion. Both are in the grip of the ultimate metaphysical ground, the creative advance into novelty. Either of them, God and the World, is the instrument of novelty for the other.

In every respect God and the World move conversely to each other in respect to their process. God is primordially one, namely, he is the primordial unity of relevance of the many potential forms: in the process he acquires a consequent multiplicity, which the primordial character absorbs into its own unity. The World is primordially many, namely, the many actual occasions with their physical finitude; in the process it acquires a consequent unity, which is a novel occasion and is absorbed into the multiplicity of the primordial character. Thus God is to be conceived as one and as many in the converse sense in which the World is to be conceived as many and as one. The theme of Cosmology, which is the basis of all religions, is the story of the dynamic effort of the World passing into everlasting unity, and of the static majesty of God's vision, accomplishing its purpose of completion by absorption of the World's multiplicity of effort.

HARLOW SHAPLEY

Organization in Nature

Harlow Shapley (1885–   ) is a distinguished American astronomer, Professor emeritus of Astronomy at Harvard, and an active and very successful popularizer of his subject and of the scientist's view of life. His cosmology, which in an effort to dissociate himself from theologians and metaphysicians he calls a "cosmography," is an admirable example of its kind. To the skeptic, Shapley's insistence on dwarfing man in the universe is itself an interesting example of the workings of human emotions—religious emotions—and this cosmology itself a piece of what has been called the "religion of science." One may question whether this dwarfing of man is actually a lesson in humility.

AS AN INITIAL STEP IN THE APPROACH TO THE CENTRAL QUESTIONS ABOUT the universe—that is, to the questions "What, How, and Why"—we shall consider briefly the formal subject of Cosmography. Among other intentions, Cosmography as a research attempts to solve the most intriguing placement problem in the world—the question of the location of man in the universe of space, atoms, and light. Actually the end product of our efforts may be only an approach to knowledge of man's orientation in a complex cosmos, not an arrival. Questions without answers will be a recurrent byproduct.

Again we define Cosmography loosely as the field of study that has the same relation to the cosmos as geography has to the earth.[1] Such a definition requires a prior definition of the cosmos, and that is difficult. We shall see later that cosmos means something more than the physical universe. Nevertheless, even though not sharply defined, Cosmography remains a

From Harlow Shapley, *Of Stars and Men* (Boston: The Beacon Press, 1958), pp. 17-25. Also available in paperback, Washington Square Press (New York: 1959), pp. 15-23.

[1] Cosmogony and cosmology are related words frequently confused with Cosmography, and apparently ambiguous even to the lexicographers; the first, however, generally implies pretensions to knowledge of first origins; the second is commonly defined as a branch of metaphysics.

science—a science with decorations. If at times it sounds a bit like scientific philosophy, or even like a phase of religious teaching, so much the better. It will be no loss for religion and philosophy if they are infiltrated with atoms, stars, and the groping[2] of protozoa.

For the time being at least we shall try to keep our explorations of cosmic content and activity on the descriptive level. Although Cosmography as here presented is an elementary science, it carries a considerable intellectual voltage, enough to charge to full capacity the more sophisticated inquirer, enough to shock the casual and uninitiated.

Whatever else of significance we may later fabricate for life, it early becomes evident that the study of living things can contribute richly to Cosmography. An outstanding example is the direct association of chlorophyll with the age and structure of the sun and stars. This strange association ties the complicated chemical operation of photosynthesis with the internal anatomy of stellar bodies. The primitive plants of the Archeozoic Era, the green algae, were operating the photosynthetic apparatus more than a thousand million years ago; and the complex leaves of the late Carboniferous plants also testify to a sun power that has been essentially constant from then to now. The Paleozoic leaves testify that three hundred million years ago the solar radiation was little if any different from that we now know. The unhurried evolution of stars (at least of one star, the sun) is thus revealed by the Carboniferous ferns. A slow evolution is indicated, but how is it managed? What can be the source of the solar power that radiates energy into space at the rate of more than four million tons a second and yet does not exhaust itself over the millions of years?

The full story is too long for this essay. We simply report that to energize the ancient algae and the tree ferns of the Paleozoic, as well as modern plants, and activate the animals (including us) that are parasites on the plants, the sun transmutes hydrogen into helium and radiation, thus providing abundant energy. Fortunately for us, the radiant energy is issued by a self-regulating power plant.

The collaboration of the various sciences is here nicely shown. Geochemistry, radiology, stratigraphy, atomic physics, and astronomy combine in the clear indication that matter can dissolve into radiation. The fossil plants (and animals), we learn by the way of paleontology, indicate the constancy of the sun's heat and thus, by way of mathematical physics and astrophysics, reveal much about the internal structure of stars.

There are many other tie-ups with biology in the study of the inanimate universe. In the running of ants we can measure an energy flow that is as closely controlled by temperature as the outpouring of energy from distant stars. To study adequately the early climates of this planet we must bring together the methods and facts from a dozen scientific fields, some of them

---

[2] That word "groping" will bear watching. Protozoa are not the only animate gropers!

biological, some physical. When we see that many rules of nature are the same for biological cells and for chemical molecules, and when, as later elaborated, we accept the very impressive probability of millions of planets with highly developed organisms, we must conclude that the world of life should be admitted as a part of the cosmographic program.

Cosmography, when ideally described and studied, involves an extensive and complicated content. It is too comprehensive to be handled thoroughly in brief compass. It appears to be manageable, however, if used chiefly as an instrument in human orientation. In what follows in this chapter we shall report on an attempt to survey sketchily the material universe, with principal emphasis on the basic entities, and on the extent to which the exploration of them and with them appears to pinpoint terrestrial man in the over-all scheme.

Our sense organs are definitely limited in number and power, and our experience in thinking about the cosmos has extended through only a few millennia—scarcely more than a dozen of the revolutions of the outermost planet Pluto. Too much should not be expected of us. We are tyros in the project of cosmic interpretation. Our accomplishments appear to be rather substantial when we look into the past, but have we not unrolled as yet only a fringe of one page of the total Cosmic Writ?

From where we now stand in knowledge of the world it appears that the basic entities of the material universe are . . . the simple-sounding "qualities" or entities of *space, time, matter,* and *energy.* Of the four, we note that matter and energy are two forms of the same thing, tied together with the most popular equation of our times (after $2 + 2 = 4$), namely, $E = Mc^2$. That equation says that to transform mass, M, into energy, E, or energy into mass in a quantitative fashion we simply apply the square of that most fundamental of natural units, c, the velocity of light. By way of the relativity theory, also space and time are now commonly united as space-time. For our present practical approach, however, we shall ignore these postulates of equivalence that arrange our entities in two pairs and consider each one separately. But first, a few remarks on the simple technologies of human understanding.

THE FOUR ELEMENTARY ALPHABETS

History records that the human cultures of the past few millennia have been based to a large extent on the use of some simple aids to communication. These aids we shall call *alphabets,* widening the meaning of that word, since more than the ABC's are involved. Without the alphabets we could not readily ask and answer on a high level or communicate readily from the present to our posterity. Since their invention or emergence, alphabets have enabled men to coordinate better their knowledge and ideas, and to comprehend many phases of the surrounding complex world. They have served to reduce the seeming chaos and to lay the foundation for civilized cooperation among individuals and groups. The alphabets have also enabled men to advance their cultures and build stable societies.

The primitive grunts, squeaks, and gestures that man brought up from the "jungles" did not long suffice for such a mind-evolving primate. He had no marvelous antennae with which to communicate to his fellows, such as those possessed by the ants and used by them in building up their elaborate societies. Evolving man, if he was to survive and grow as a cosmic interpreter, had to devise and use symbols for social communication, and he had to do so more effectively than did the other animals and his own jungle ancestors. For effective communication he had to associate these symbols with sounds and ideas. He needed, and many times did design, tables of symbols to aid in social collaboration. In brief, to build his colonies and eventually his intercolony cultures it became essential to devise and introduce writing, reading, and arithmetic.

A few thousand years ago the elementary alphabets began to appear. They came in the form of ABC's and the 1, 2, 3's. The letters could be formed into words to represent ideas, and in the various isolated cultures the words became standardized. They were formed into phrases, the phrases into sentences, and in some of the higher cultures the sentences were assembled into chapters, books, and libraries.

The number alphabet was basic in primitive economics, and, with the ABC's, eventually produced the business operations of the modern world. The numbers led to our system of weights and measures. Without these alphabets—the letters and the numbers—we would culturally be little advanced beyond the birds, bees, and apes.

Two other elementary alphabets have long existed. One is connected with the entity Time and the other with the entity Space. They are, respectively, the calendars of days, weeks, months, and years, and the maps that record space measures on the face of the earth, that is, record the terrestrial latitudes and longitudes which permit the delimitation of fields, cities, and states.

These elementary alphabets no longer suffice, either in the study of Cosmography, or in any general effort of trying to understand a world that has become enormously rich in information content. They met our needs up to a century or so ago. With the growth in amount of information, however, it has become necessary to supplement the elementary alphabets, and introduce logical classifications. Well-organized, small tabular categories have been set up to facilitate the acquiring of knowledge about stars, atoms, plant varieties, rock series, and the like. These tables, in a way, are minor and specialized alphabets.

To assist further in our study, it is now proposed to construct a major comprehensive alphabet for each of the four entities: time, matter, space, and energy. Through the use of these tabulations we shall simplify the natural complexities arising from so much specific information. Fortunately, two of these basic tabulations are already at hand, perfected and in professional use. They are the periodic table of the elements for matter, and the geological age scale for time. The former concerns matter in its elemental forms; the latter, time in large chunks. . . .

ON THE GOALS OF COSMOGRAPHY

As scientists and dreamers we are curious about our position in the plan of the universe. Curious also about the "planning," and sometimes inclined to talk about the planner. It is a fascinating enterprise. We can have a stimulating and in the end a satisfying experience in contemplating cosmographic facts and speculating on human fate and fancy.

The orientation of man is of course an absorbing subject, in part because he is an awkward and somewhat vain animal, but more because he is, whether he knows it or not, aimed at the stars. However ruthless he may have been in his jungle childhood and during his nonsocial past, he is now instinctively ethical, not so much because virtue may please his tribal gods but because it is good economic and social policy. He is bent also on comprehension. Moreover, to make an anticipatory statement, man now knows that he is participating, at a high and complex level, in a great evolutionary drive; he is going along, for the most part cheerfully, with such companions as the vibrating atoms, the radiating stars, the condensing nebulae, the groping protozoa, and the perennial forests with their aspiring birds and butterflies.

As cosmographers we enjoy the decipherment of some of the rules of the cosmic game. We salute the biological winners when we recognize them, such as the fish and the club mosses which can trace their ancestry of unchanged forms through many geological periods; and we can try to understand the losers, such as the trilobites of the early Paleozoic, the dinosaurs of a hundred million years ago, and Neanderthal Man.

We also occasionally venture to the borders of science to seek deep answers and to discuss our hope of contributing to future ages something more than our fragmented skulls in the fossiliferous rock. Naturally we are proud of the varied beauty of human thought and action, proud of our poetry and song. We are actors in a great cosmic play where the performers include the atoms, the galaxies, and the eternal intangibles.

The prophets of ancient Israel gloried at times in the magnificence of the universe, which of course, in their time, was centered on man. Those days, however, were scientifically very early and chronologically perhaps more than a third of the way back to the beginning of human cultures. What the inquiring mind has since uncovered would have been incredible if revealed to the ancient prophets. Their vision was, we now see, myopic. Our vision is doubtless also deficient, but at least we recognize that we are taking part in a play far grander than foretold in ancient times. The advance notices of two or three millennia ago greatly underestimated the cosmic drama. Reverence then had to be supported with imaginings and superstition. But the accepted facts of now far transcend the fictions of not so long ago. So it seems, at any rate, to those who look downward into atoms and the biological cell and upward to the stars. To be reverent, we now have no need of superstitional aid.

In our cosmic inquiries we may appear boastful with regard to the inadequacies of the ancient philosophies, but we should suffer a healthy pride-shrinking experience in foreseeing that a century hence we, too, may be considered to have been primitives in knowledge and thought. Indeed, two of the present goals of the exploration among galaxies and atoms are the same goals that should prevail in other fields of science, namely, to strengthen the evidence on which we can construct our current understanding and to contribute through research as rapidly as possible to the obsolescence of our presently cherished hypotheses. We hope for greater knowledge and sounder ideas in the future. Deeper thoughts will surely come, wider spread of the senses, fuller appreciation of the functioning of the human brain, higher ambitions for men participating in the greatest operation of nature—an operation of cosmic dimensions that might simply be called Growth.

B

Purpose: Teleologies, Eschatologies

PLATO

Priority of the Soul

With the Athenian philosopher Plato (428–348 B.C.) we come to one of the greatest names in the history of philosophy. Indeed it has often been said that Plato and Aristotle, to whom we come next, between them set the pattern for all Western philosophical thought. This remark is surely a grave over-simplification, but if for a moment you can entertain a sheep-goat dualism of "idealist" and "realist" in the current common-sense use of those last two terms, then Plato is the Master for idealists, Aristotle the Master for realists. I have chosen from the Laws, a work of Plato's old age, a passage of straightforward teleology. But a warning: Plato, though I think that in his depths he was an "idealist," a transcendentalist, a distruster of the this-world of simple sense-experience, was an Athenian trained in one of the world's great "rationalist" cultures; he had a mind naturally far-ranging and disputatious (perhaps also a tendency to "countervail," to set himself against the current); and finally he used with great skill a literary form, the philosophical dialogue among participants with varied points of view, in which his own position is not always crystal-clear. In the whole body of Plato's writings, then, there is a kind of magnificent showcase of the workings of the philosophic mind and temperament. Yet I repeat, at bottom Plato in any such dualism—William James's oft-quoted one of "tender-minded" and "tough-minded" will do once more—belongs on the tender, other-worldly, transcendental side. It is highly significant that Jefferson in his old age, turning to Plato's Republic, found his Enlightened eighteenth-century mind horrified with "the whimsies, the puerilities, and unintelligible jargon" of the work (see his letter to John Adams, dated July 5, 1814).

Cleinias. It is a matter of no small consequence, in some way or other to prove that there are Gods, and that they are good, and regard justice more than men do. The demonstration of this would be the best and noblest prelude of all our laws. And therefore, without impatience, and

From Plato, *The Dialogues.* Translated by B. Jowett, with an introduction by R. Demos (New York: Random House, 1937), pp. 629-634.

without hurry, let us unreservedly consider the whole matter, summoning up all the power of persuasion which we possess.

Athenian. Seeing you thus in earnest, I would fain offer up a prayer that I may succeed:—but I must proceed at once. Who can be calm when he is called upon to prove the existence of the Gods? Who can avoid hating and abhorring the men who are and have been the cause of this argument; I speak of those who will not believe the tales which they have heard as babes and sucklings from their mothers and nurses, repeated by them both in jest and earnest, like charms, who have also heard them in the sacrificial prayers, and seen sights accompanying them,—sights and sounds delightful to children,—and their parents during the sacrifices showing an intense earnestness on behalf of their children and of themselves, and with eager interest talking to the Gods, and beseeching them, as though they were firmly convinced of their existence; who likewise see and hear the prostrations and invocations which are made by Hellenes and barbarians at the rising and setting of the sun and moon, in all the vicissitudes of life, not as if they thought that there were no Gods, but as if there could be no doubt of their existence, and no suspicion of their non-existence; when men, knowing all these things, despise them on no real grounds, as would be admitted by all who have any particle of intelligence, and when they force us to say what we are now saying, how can any one in gentle terms remonstrate with the like of them, when he has to begin by proving to them the very existence of the Gods? Yet the attempt must be made; for it would be unseemly that one half of mankind should go mad in their lust of pleasure, and the other half in their indignation at such persons. Our address to these lost and perverted natures should not be spoken in passion; let us suppose ourselves to select some one of them, and gently reason with him, smothering our anger:—O my son, we will say to him, you are young, and the advance of time will make you reverse many of the opinions which you now hold. Wait awhile, and do not attempt to judge at present of the highest things; and that is the highest of which you now think nothing—to know the Gods rightly and to live accordingly. And in the first place let me indicate to you one point which is of great importance, and about which I cannot be deceived:—You and your friends are not the first who have held this opinion about the Gods. There have always been persons more or less numerous who have had the same disorder. I have known many of them, and can tell you, that no one who had taken up in youth this opinion, that the Gods do not exist, ever continued in the same until he was old; the two other notions certainly do continue in some cases, but not in many; the notion, I mean, that the Gods exist, but take no heed of human things, and the other notion that they do take heed of them, but are easily propitiated with sacrifices and prayers. As to the opinion about the Gods which may some day become clear to you, I advise you go wait and consider if it be true or not; ask of others, and above all of the legislator. In the meantime take care that you do not offend against the Gods. For the duty of the legislator is and always will be to teach you the truth of these matters.

Cle. Our address, Stranger, thus far, is excellent.

Ath. Quite true, Megillus and Cleinias, but I am afraid that we have unconsciously lighted on a strange doctrine.

Cle. What doctrine do you mean?

Ath. The wisest of all doctrines, in the opinion of many.

Cle. I wish that you would speak plainer.

Ath. The doctrine that all things do become, have become, and will become, some by nature, some by art, and some by chance.

Cle. Is not that true?

Ath. Well, philosophers are probably right; at any rate we may as well follow in their track, and examine what is the meaning of them and their disciples.

Cle. By all means.

Ath. They say that the greatest and fairest things are the work of nature and of chance, the lesser of art, which, receiving from nature the greater and primeval creations, moulds and fashions all those lesser works which are generally termed artificial.

Cle. How is that?

Ath. I will explain my meaning still more clearly. They say that fire and water, and earth and air, all exist by nature and chance, and none of them by art, and that as to the bodies which come next in order,—earth, and sun, and moon, and stars,—they have been created by means of these absolutely inanimate existences. The elements are severally moved by chance and some inherent force according to certain affinities among them—of hot with cold, or of dry with moist, or of soft with hard, and according to all the other accidental admixtures of opposites which have been formed by necessity. And after this fashion and in this manner the whole heaven has been created, and all that is in the heaven, as well as animals and all plants, and all the seasons come from these elements, not by the action of mind, as they say, or of any God, or from art, but as I was saying, by nature and chance only. Art sprang up afterwards and out of these, mortal and of mortal birth, and produced in play certain images and very partial imitations of the truth, having an affinity to one another, such as music and painting create and their companion arts. And there are other arts which have a serious purpose, and these co-operate with nature, such, for example, as medicine, and husbandry, and gymnastic. And they say that politics co-operate with nature, but in a less degree, and have more of art; also that legislation is entirely a work of art, and is based on assumptions which are not true.

Cle. How do you mean?

Ath. In the first place, my dear friend, these people would say that the Gods exist not by nature, but by art, and by the laws of states, which are different in different places, according to the agreement of those who make them; and that the honourable is one thing by nature and another thing by law, and that the principles of justice have no existence at all in nature, but that mankind are always disputing about them and altering them; and that the alterations which are made by art and by law have no basis in nature, but are of authority for the moment and at the time at which they are made.—These, my friends, are the sayings of wise men, poets and prose writers, which find a way into the minds of youth. They are told by them that the highest right is might, and in this way the young fall into impieties, under the idea that the Gods are not such as the law bids them imagine; and hence arise factions, these philosophers inviting them to lead a true life according to nature, that is, to live in real dominion over others, and not in legal subjection to them.

Cle. What a dreadful picture, Stranger, have you given, and how great is the injury which is thus inflicted on young men to the ruin both of states and families!

Ath. True, Cleinias; but then what should the lawgiver do when this evil is of long standing? should he only rise up in the state and threaten all mankind, proclaiming that if they will not say and think that the Gods are such as the law ordains (and this may be extended generally to the honourable, the just, and to all the highest things, and to all that relates to virtue and vice), and if they will not make their actions conform to the copy which the law gives them, then he who refuses to obey the law shall die, or suffer stripes and bonds, or privation of citizenship, or in some cases be punished by loss of property and exile? Should he not rather, when he is making laws for men, at the same time infuse the spirit of persuasion into his words, and mitigate the severity of them as far as he can?

Cle. Why, Stranger, if such persuasion be at all possible, then a legislator who has anything in him ought never to weary of persuading men; he ought to leave nothing unsaid in support of the ancient opinion that there are Gods, and of all those other truths which you were just now mentioning; he ought to support the law and also art, and acknowledge that both alike exist by nature, and no less than nature, if they are the creations of mind in accordance with right reason, as you appear to me to maintain, and I am disposed to agree with you in thinking.

Ath. Yes, my enthusiastic Cleinias; but are not these things when spoken to a multitude hard to be understood, not to mention that they take up a dismal length of time?

Cle. Why, Stranger, shall we, whose patience failed not when drinking or music were the themes of discourse, weary now of discoursing about the Gods, and about divine things? And the greatest help to rational legislation is that the laws when once written down are always at rest; they can be put to the test at any future time, and therefore, if on first hearing they seem difficult, there is no reason for apprehension about them, because any man however dull can go over them and consider them again and again; nor if they are tedious but useful, is there any reason or religion, as it seems to me, in any man refusing to maintain the principles of them to the utmost of his power.

Megillus. Stranger, I like what Cleinias is saying.

Ath. Yes, Megillus, and we should do as he proposes; for if impious discourses were not scattered, as I may say, throughout the world, there would have been no need for any vindication of the existence of the Gods—but seeing that they are spread far and wide, such arguments are needed; and who should come to the rescue of the greatest laws, when they are being undermined by bad men, but the legislator himself?

Meg. There is no more proper champion of them.

Ath. Well, then, tell me, Cleinias,—for I must ask you to be my partner, —does not he who talks in this way conceive fire and water and earth and air to be the first elements of all things? these he calls nature, and out of these he supposes the soul to be formed afterwards; and this is not a mere conjecture of ours about his meaning, but is what he really means.

Cle. Very true.

Ath. Then, by Heaven, we have discovered the source of this vain opinion of all those physical investigators; and I would have you examine their arguments with the utmost care, for their impiety is a very serious matter; they not only make a bad and mistaken use of argument, but they lead away the minds of others: that is my opinion of them.

Cle. You are right; but I should like to know how this happens.

Ath. I fear that the argument may seem singular.

Cle. Do not hestitate, Stranger; I see that you are afraid of such a discussion carrying you beyond the limits of legislation. But if there be no other way of showing our agreement in the belief that there are Gods, of whom the law is said now to approve, let us take this way, my good sir.

Ath. Then I suppose that I must repeat the singular argument of those who manufacture the soul according to their own impious notions; they affirm that which is the first cause of the generation and destruction of all things, to be not first, but last, and that which is last to be first, and hence they have fallen into error about the true nature of the Gods.

Cle. Still I do not understand you.

Ath. Nearly all of them, my friends, seem to be ignorant of the nature and power of the soul, especially in what relates to her origin: they do not know that she is among the first of things, and before all bodies, and is the chief author of their changes and transpositions. And if this is true, and if the soul is older than the body, must not the things which are of the soul's kindred be of necessity prior to those which appertain to the body?

Cle. Certainly.

Ath. Then thought and attention and mind and art and law will be prior to that which is hard and soft and heavy and light; and the great and primitive works and actions will be works of art; they will be the first, and after them will come nature and works of nature, which however is a wrong term for men to apply to them; these will follow, and will be under the government of art and mind.

Cle. But why is the word "nature" wrong?

Ath. Because those who use the term mean to say that nature is the first creative power; but if the soul turn out to be the primeval element, and not fire or air, then in the truest sense and beyond other things the soul may be said to exist by nature; and this would be true if you proved that the soul is older than the body, but not otherwise.

ARISTOTLE

The Order of Being

Among philosophers in the narrower sense—as contrasted with men of let-ters, humanists—Aristotle (384–322 B.C.) has until the last few centuries been simply the philosopher. His "realism" is in a sense a foil to Plato's "idealism," and he very definitely attacks some of Plato's ideas. But in the modern sense of "scientific materialism" or "mechanism" or "logical positivism," Aristotle was practically as much a transcendentalist as was Plato. His range, which includes writings on subjects we now call the "natural sciences," is greater than Plato's. Many scholars hold that we do not have Aristotle's own writings, but a rather full set of notes on his lec-tures taken by various hands. For his work totally lacks the literary graces; it is highly technical, and for a modern American, hard reading even in the best translation. I have therefore used the excellent recent exposition of Aristotle's position by J. H. Randall, Jr. This, too, requires concentration from the reader, but if he can penetrate Aristotle's mind he will have learned a great deal about the Western philosophical tradition. In particu-lar, the famous "four causes" have for two millennia bridged for many the gap between such concepts as "cause-and-effect" and "moral purpose."

FIRST PHILOSOPHY

Ousia as a Subject of Discourse

Being, *to on,* is said in many ways, as is set forth in detail in the *Categories.* Now of all these senses which the term "being" has, it is clear that "first being is the 'what' (*to ti estin*) which denotes the *ousia,* and all other things are said to 'be' because they are either quantities or qualities or affections or some other such thing, of such a being." For when we describe the quality of a particular thing, we say that it is good or bad, and not five feet high, or a man; but when we describe "what" it is, we say not that it is white

From **John Herman** Randall, Jr., *Aristotle* (New York: Columbia University Press, 1960), pp. 116-125.

or hot or five feet high, but that it is "a man" or "a god." None of these other things that can be said about a thing has by nature an independent existence, or can be separated from the thing it is said about. But the thing they are said about can be said to "be" in its own right (*kath' hauto*); and such things seem to "be" more truly, because as subjects of discourse (*to hypokeimenon*) they provide something definite (*horismenon*) and determinate. "Hence that which 'is' primarily, not in a qualified sense but just as 'being' (*on haplōs*), will be *ousia*."

"First" or "primary" is said in many ways. But *ousia* is first in all these senses, in definition, in knowledge, and in time. Hence for Aristotle the inquiry into the criteria of what it means to "be" anything is transformed into the inquiry into the character possessed by *ousia*. "Indeed, the question which was raised long ago, is still raised today and always will be asked, and which always baffles us, What is being? (*ti to on?*) is the same as the question, What is *ousia*? (*tis hē ousia?*)."

Ousia is said in four main senses, as the essence (*to ti ēn einai*), the universal (*to katholou*), the genus (*to genos*), and the subject (*to hypokeimenon*). The subject, or the subject matter, is that of which the other three, like all predicates, are said, while it is not itself said of anything else. Hence the primary subject matter or subject seems to be *ousia* in the truest sense. *Ousia* Aristotle thus defines in his First Philosophy, as in the *Categories,* as the subject of discourse.

What, then, is involved in *ousia* as a subject of discourse? I ask, "What is this thing, this *ousia?*" (*ti esti?*). The answer will be "what it is": "This thing is a table." But just what is it that is a "table"? What is the "what it is," the *ti esti,* of this thing?

1) Is "what this thing is" to be identified with "what it is made out of"? Is it enough to say, "It is wood"? Is the thing to be identified with its "material," its *hylē?* Is it just "wood"? No; for this thing is clearly more than just "wood"—it is "this here wood," to indicate which we can only point. The material of this thing alone has no individual character, and is ultimately unstatable in words, and thus unintelligible. This thing is, to be sure, "this here wood," a *tode ti,* a "this here thing." But to say that alone is not an adequate statement of what it is. Well, then,

2) Is "what the thing is" its "form," its *eidos?* Is it a "classroom table," something to put books and papers and watches upon? Is it a "such," a *toionde?* No; "form" or "character" alone does not tell us what this individual thing really is. "Classroom table" is what we can truly *say* this thing is. But "this thing" is not merely "classroom table," it is not merely "such," *toionde;* that alone is not an adequate statement of "what it is." "Classroom table" in general does not exist, "such's" do not exist. We can say and think "such's"; but no "such's" exist as individual, concrete things we can point to and talk about. You cannot point to, look at, observe, experiment with, "such's," with "classroom table." What exists is always "this here thing," "this here classroom table."

In the discussion in Book Zeta so far paraphrased and illustrated, Aristotle has clearly a twofold interest. On the one hand, he wants to take account of the insights of the Platonists. What *logos* grasps and states really "is"—it is *ousia*. We have a genuine knowledge of the real structure of things, and its formulation in scientific statements, like the definition of the essence (*to ti ēn einai*) of a thing, in which, as set forth in the *Posterior Analytics,* science culminates, does give us an intellectual grasp of that structure. Things are what they can be said to be.

On the other hand, the formulations of discourse are not themselves "what is," they are not *ousiai,* they are not "separate" and "individual." The Platonists fell into confusion in hypostatizing forms, objects of mathematics, universals, genera, and such other formulations of *logos.* They are not "things," *ousiai.* Neither the universal nor the genus is an *ousia.* They are not concrete, particular things: they are predicates common to many things. The same holds of the Platonic forms.

But the "essence" of a thing, what it is to be that thing (*to ti ēn einai*), since it is not common to anything else, and since in a sense it is identical with the thing itself, can be said to be the *ousia* of that thing. The *ousia* of an individual thing is peculiar to it and belongs to nothing else. And it is just this character we mean by "what it is to be that thing" (*to ti ēn einai*), and call its "essence." It is this "essence" we express in a formula (*logos*) when we state what that thing is. The "essence" of each thing is that which it is said to be in itself (*kath' hauto*) and in accordance with its own nature (*kata physin*). Hence the essence is one and the same thing with the particular thing,

for it is when we know its essence that we have knowledge of a thing. . . . It follows that each individual thing is one and the same with its essence, and not merely incidentally, because to have knowledge of the individual is to have knowledge of its essence; so that it is evident that both must be identical.

"Essence" is thus defined as what is knowable and statable about an *ousia,* what the definition of a kind will formulate. It is not the formula (*logos*) or the definition (*horismos*) that is identical with the concrete thing, or can properly be said to be an *ousia,* it is what the *logos* formulates, the intelligible structure or make-up of the thing, what we know and state when we know the thing.

Aristotle is wrestling with the attempt to state the same problem as Spinoza, who tries to maintain that the "idea" of the circle is one and the same thing with the circle itself. In an obvious sense, the geometrical circle is different from its algebraic formula or "idea," $a^2 + b^2 = r^2$. Yet in another sense they are two alternative expressions of the same thing. In Spinoza's language, it is possible for him to say, it is the same circle conceived under two different "attributes." Aristotle puts it: in one sense the essence is identical with the individual, in another it is obviously not.

For Aristotle, the difficulty arises because so far he has been dealing with the questions *logikōs,* confining himself within the circle of linguistic analysis. He has raised the question, What is the relation between what language formulates, and that of which it is the formulable aspect? What is the relation of the "such's" we can truly say things are, to the things themselves, that actually exist to point to and look at? Such questions, of the relation between discourse and its subject matter, cannot be answered in terms of the distinctions we can draw within discourse alone. We must have some other way of getting at the subject matter besides talking about it: we must look at it and do things with it. We are taken beyond discourse itself, beyond talking, beyond the talking of the *logikōs,* who, to judge by the long and very painstaking analysis of his problems and mistakes in Book Zeta, must have been talking for quite a while and to no very good purpose before Aristotle came upon the scene to set him straight.

Aristotle takes us to the functional setting of discourse, to the processes by which things are produced and brought into existence, whether they be processes occurring "by nature," or, as in the case of our table, occurring "by art." At this point we are forced to ask, "Just how did this here thing come into existence?" Well, a cabinetmaker took some oak planks, and made them into a "classroom table." He took a this here stuff, a *tode ti,* "some oak wood," and made it into a "such," a *toionde:* he made "some oak wood" into a "classroom table."

3) So this thing, this *ousia,* is really a "this here such." It is a *tode toionde,* "this here classroom table." It is a union of a "this here stuff," of "this here wood," which is its material (*hylē*), and of a "such," a *toionde,* its "form" or *eidos.* It is a "from both" (*to ek touton*), a "composite" (*synolon*).

An individual *ousia,* the particular thing we have been talking about, is the object itself in its "intelligible make-up" or "essence." This *ousia* is not adequately stated as just "some wood," nor yet as merely "something to put books, papers, and watches upon." It is "this here wooden classroom table."

This particular thing *is* of course what it can be correctly defined to be, what it can be truly said to be, a "wooden classroom table." But it is really more than that. It is "this here wooden classroom table." And to be precise, we cannot omit the "this-ness." That is, existing things, *ousiai,* are clearly more than their definitions alone, they are more than what they can be truly said to be. Such concrete things can never be exhausted by what we can say about them. We can never exhaustively "define" any particular and individual *ousia,* we can never say everything that is true about it.

What is involved in *ousia* expressed in discourse, can be stated in another way. Things "are" what they can be said to be, if the saying, the definition, is the outcome of successful inquiry. But *being* what they are is clearly not the same as *saying* what they are. Discourse can state what things are. But things are not discourse. Things can be said to possess a "discursive" or "logical" character or aspect, and this is precisely what we state and express, when we state what they are. This logical or discursive character of things, which Dewey preferred to call their "logiscible" character, is precisely what we state and express when we say what things are, when we state their *"ousia,"* their structure or "essence."[1] But things are not their character, their "essence," alone. They are not exhausted by discourse. Discourse can truly state that "essence" or character: it can state what is "essential" to being that specific kind of thing. But discourse cannot say or state the concrete thing itself. This can be put into Latin: "We can state in words the 'essence' of things, but we cannot state in words their 'existence.' "

These concrete things, that cannot be stated about anything else, that are always subjects of discourse, always what we are talking about, but never predicates, never what we are saying, are things or existences, *ousiai,* in "the first and best sense." They are primary things, primary *ousiai,* "primary substances," the ultimate subject matter of discourse. Their character, what they can be said to be, is their *ousia* put into words. It is what we call *the ousia, the* "substance," or *the* "essence" *of* that kind of thing. Such an *"ousia* expressed" is *ousia* as a predicate, not a subject. Thus when we say 1) "This table is thus and so," we are using "table" to designate a subject, a primary *ousia,* a primary substance. When we say 2) "This is a table," we are using "table" to designate a predicate, a secondary *ousia,* a secondary substance or essence. This distinction between "primary" and "secondary *ousiai"* or "substances" occurs only in the *Categories,* but it clarifies Aristotle's pretty consistent usage of the same term to denote two quite different notions. *Ousia* as subject matter, "primary *ousia,*" exhibits something that cannot be stated in words, but only denoted by pointing: *ho tis anthropos,* "this here man." This is its material or *hylē,* its "matter": what makes it a *tode ti.*

Aristotle's conclusion may be stated: Whatever is can be expressed in words and discourse. There is nothing that cannot be talked about, nothing wholly inaccessible to discourse, nothing "ineffable." But discourse is not its own subject matter—unless the talking is about language itself. Discourse is "about" something that is not itself discourse; though what it is about—its subject matter—has a discursive or logical character, and that character, that intelligible structure, is just what discourse can express and state. Whatever is can be known. There is nothing that is unknowable. But knowledge is of and about something that is not itself knowledge, it is of *ta onta,* the things that are; though what *ta onta* are is precisely what *nous* grasps in its knowing: their *ti esti,* their "what," their "form" or "essence," their knowable aspect.

[1] It must be realized that no single term corresponding to the Latin *essentia,* "essence," occurs in Aristotle. Aristotle uses at least half a dozen terms which can all be translated, in some contexts, as "essence." What complicates the matter is that they can all be translated in certain other contexts as definitely not meaning "essence." *Ousia* is the most troublesome and misleading of these ambiguous terms.

Aristotle's careful distinctions so painstakingly—and so painfully—worked out in Books Zeta and Eta were necessary to clarify the confusions about talking and its relations to what is talked about into which several generations of Greek garrulity seem to have gotten the Greeks. They are still pertinent today: they could, for example, have saved F. H. Bradley several decades of a futile attempt to get literally everything into words.

Ousia as the Outcome of a Process

What is involved in *ousia* as something that changes, that is the outcome of a process? What is involved in the classroom table that was once part of a tree, and that will end in a bonfire? Change in the most general sense, becoming, *metabolē,* and process, "movement" or *kinēsis,* is a fundamental fact of our experienced world, the world "we see." "Only a vegetable would try to deny it," Aristotle remarks rather scornfully of the Eleatics. How is this fact to be expressed, understood, and made intelligible? Things, *ousiai,* are always changing into something else. Materials are always taking on new forms. "This such's" are always becoming "other such's." Of things taken as undergoing such change, as subjects of processes, *kinēseis,* we can ask four different kinds of questions, and get four different kinds of answer, four kinds of *aitia. Aition* means literally the answer or response to a question; it meant in Greek what could be held "answerable" or "responsible" in a law court. Aristotle's four *aitia* are the four different factors "responsible" for a process, the four "necessary conditions" of any process, four *dioti's* or "reasons why," four "wherefores." Since Cicero translated them into Latin as the four *causae,* they have been known in the Western tradition as the "four causes."

1) What is it?	*ti esti?*	*to ti esti*	The What	*Formal Cause*
2) Out of what is it made?	*ex hou?*	*to ex hou*	The From What	*Material Cause*
3) By what agent?	*hypo tinos?*	*to hypo tinos*	The By What	*Efficient Cause*
4) For what end?	*hou heneka?*	*to hou heneka*	The For What	*Final Cause*

Thus we can ask, What is it? It is a flag. Out of what is it made? Bunting. By what was it made? The firm of Rosenkranz and Guildenstern. For what was it made? To serve as a patriotic symbol.

These are four kinds of reason, four kinds of answer, four necessary conditions—necessary for understanding the process: we need to know all four if we are to find it intelligible. Only one of the four, the By What, the agent, the efficient cause, is a "cause" in the popular sense today—if "cause" have any clear meaning in our ordinary language. The unfortunate neglect of the other three has been due to the dominance of mechanical thinking since the day of Newton, complicated by the popular heritage of Hume and John Stuart Mill. It is worth noting, incidentally, that the empiricist notion of causation as constant succession, of "cause" as the invariable antecedent of its effect, is wholly lacking in Aristotle. Cause and effect are always for him simultaneous, *hama.*

All four are factors discoverable in any process. Every process or *kinēsis* is something being made out of some material by some agent or mechanism for some end. This is obvious in processes that take place "by art," *apo technēs,* in human production. But in natural production, processes that take place "by nature," *physei,* or "in accordance with nature," *kata physin,* the situation seems different. And such processes are significantly different. In the first place, in them there is no intelligent maker or craftsman. Secondly, in them there is no "purpose," no consciously foreseen end. Aristotle's "For What," *to hou heneka,* is "end," *telos,* or "final cause"; it is incorrect and very misleading to translate it as "purpose," which in English means "foresight" and "intention." For Aristotle, human purposes do display foresight and intention, and they do form one subdivision of "final causes" or "ends." But whatever may have happened later in the religious adaptations of Aristotelian thought in the Middle Ages, when the operations of nature were identified with the Divine Providence, Aristotle himself finds such "purposes" and "intentions" only in the processes by art, in human production. For Aristotle, there are no purposes in the world outside human actions and makings. Final causes, *telē,* are for him a much broader class than the subclass of "purposes." That broad class includes not only human purposes, but also all natural ends and outcomes in the processes that take place by nature.

For although for Aristotle nature, apart from human arts, exhibits no discoverable purposes, it *does* exhibit natural ends or *telē.* Nature is the scene of productive enterprises, that are not to be understood as mere mixings and unmixings of elements. Events do not merely "happen," they have consequences, they achieve results, they exhibit a pattern of reaching outcomes that is repeated over and over again, that is "always or for the most part." Clouds form, rain falls, seeds sprout, plants grow, with a structure of natural teleology, a fixed order of stages of development. Nature is indisputably teleological; its processes are full of ends, *telē,* that are achieved, of conclusions that are reached over and over. Only in human life are these ends and conclusions consciously intended, only in men are purposes found. For Aristotle, even God has no purpose, only man!

LUCRETIUS

The Universe Not Designed for Man

*Here is Lucretius again, in a passage which sets the tone for the scientist's
apparent denial of cosmic purpose. The universe is not designed for
man, and Lucretius puts the gods so far away they hardly exist. Yet, to repeat, there is order in the universe, a not uninteresting order, and man's
mind is not out of place in it. I feel sure the net effect of Lucretius over the
ages has been tonic rather than depressive.*

             And walking now
In his own foot-prints, I do follow through
His reasonings, and with pronouncements teach
The covenant whereby all things are framed,
How under that covenant they must abide
Nor ever prevail to abrogate the aeons'
Inexorable decrees,—how (as we've found),
In class of mortal objects, o'er all else,
The mind exists of earth-born frame create
And impotent unscathèd to abide
Across the mighty aeons, and how come
In sleep those idol-apparitiòns
That so befool intelligence when we
Do seem to view a man whom life has left.
Thus far we've gone; the order of my plan
Hath brought me now unto the point where I
Must make report how, too, the universe
Consists of mortal body, born in time,
And in what modes that congregated stuff
Establishèd itself as earth and sky,
Ocean, and stars, and sun, and ball of moon;
And then what living creatures rose from out

From Lucretius, *Of the Nature of Things*. Translated by William Ellery Leonard
(New York: E. P. Dutton & Co., 1957), pp. 189-194.

The old telluric places, and what ones
Were never born at all; and in what mode
The human race began to name its things
And use the varied speech from man to man;
And in what modes hath bosomed in their breasts
That awe of gods, which halloweth in all lands
Fanes, altars, groves, lakes, idols of the gods.
Also I shall untangle by what power
The steersman nature guides the sun's courses,
And the meanderings of the moon, lest we,
Percase, should fancy that of own free will
They circle their perennial courses round,
Timing their motions for increase of crops
And living creatures, or lest we should think
They roll along by any plan of gods.
For even *those* men who have learned full well
That godheads lead a long life free of care,
If yet meanwhile they wonder by what plan
Things can go on (and chiefly yon high things
Observed o'erhead on the ethereal coasts),
Again are hurried back unto the fears
Of old religion and adopt again
Harsh masters, deemed almighty,—wretched men,
Unwitting what can be and what cannot,
And by what law to each its scope prescribed,
Its boundary stone that clings so deep in Time.

But for the rest,—lest we delay thee here
Longer by empty promises—behold,
Before all else, the seas, the lands, the sky:
O Memmius, their threefold nature, lo,
Their bodies three, three aspects so unlike,
Three frames so vast, a single day shall give
Unto annihilation! Then shall crash
That massive form and fabric of the world
Sustained so many aeons! Nor do I
Fail to perceive how strange and marvellous
This fact must strike the intellect of man,—
Annihilation of the sky and earth
That is to be,—and with what toil of words
'Tis mine to prove the same; as happens oft
When once ye offer to man's listening ears
Something before unheard of, but may not
Subject it to the view of eyes for him
Nor put it into hand—the sight and touch,

Whereby the opened highways of belief
Lead most directly into human breast
And regions of intelligence. But yet
I will speak out. The fact itself, perchance,
Will force belief in these my words, and thou
Mayst see, in little time, tremendously
With risen commotions of the lands all things
Quaking to pieces—which afar from us
May she, the steersman Nature, guide: and may
Reason, O rather than the fact itself,
Persuade us that all things can be o'erthrown
And sink with awful-sounding breakage down!

But ere on this I take a step to utter
Oracles holier and soundlier based
Than ever the Pythian pronounced for men
From out the tripod and the Delphian laurel,
I will unfold for thee with learnèd words
Many a consolation, lest perchance,
Still bridled by religion, thou suppose
Lands, sun, and sky, sea, constellations, moon,
Must dure forever, as of frame divine—
And so conclude that it is just that those,
(After the manner of the Giants), should all
Pay the huge penalties for monstrous crime,
Who by their reasonings do overshake
The ramparts of the universe and wish
There to put out the splendid sun of heaven,
Branding with mortal talk immortal things—
Though these same things are even so far removed
From any touch of deity and seem
So far unworthy of numbering with the gods,
That well they may be thought to furnish rather
A goodly instance of the sort of things
That lack the living motion, living sense.
For sure 'tis quite beside the mark to think
That judgment and the nature of the mind
In any kind of body can exist—
Just as in ether can't exist a tree,
Nor clouds in the salt sea, nor in the fields
Can fishes live, nor blood in timber be,
Nor sap in boulders; fixèd and arranged
Where everything may grow and have its place.
Thus nature of mind cannot arise alone
Without the body, nor have its being far

From thews and blood. Yet if 'twere possible?—
Much rather might this very power of mind
Be in the head, the shoulders, or the heels,
And, born in any part soever, yet
In the same man, in the same vessel abide
But since within this body even of ours
Stands fixèd and appears arrangèd sure
Where soul and mind can each exist and grow,
Deny we must the more that they can dure
Outside the body and the breathing form
In rotting clods of earth, in the sun's fire,
In water, or in ether's skiey coasts.
Therefore these things no whit are furnishèd
With sense divine, since never can they be
With life-force quickened.

                      Likewise, thou canst ne'er
Believe the sacred seats of gods are here
In any regions of this mundane world;
Indeed, the nature of the gods, so subtle,
So far removed from these our senses, scarce
Is seen even by intelligence of mind.
And since they've ever eluded touch and thrust
Of human hands, they cannot reach to grasp
Aught tangible to us. For what may not
Itself be touched in turn can never touch.
Wherefore, besides, also their seats must be
Unlike these seats of ours,—even subtle too,
As meet for subtle essence—as I'll prove
Hereafter unto thee with large discourse.
Further, to say that for the sake of men
They willed to prepare this world's magnificence,
And that 'tis therefore duty and behoof
To praise the work of gods as worthy praise,
And that 'tis sacrilege for men to shake
Ever by any force from out their seats
What hath been stablished by the Forethought old
To everlasting for races of mankind,
And that 'tis sacrilege to assault by words
And overtopple all from base to beam,—
Memmius, such notions to concoct and pile,
Is verily—to dote. Our gratefulness,
O what emoluments could it confer
Upon Immortals and upon the Blessèd
That they should take a step to manage aught
For sake of us? Or what new factor could,

After so long a time, inveigle them—
The hitherto reposeful—to desire
To change their former life? For rather he
Whom old things chafe seems likely to rejoice
At new; but one that in fore-passèd time
Hath chanced upon no ill, through goodly years,
O what could ever enkindle in such an one
Passion for strange experiment? Or what
The evil for us, if we had ne'er been born?—

ST. THOMAS AQUINAS

The End of Life

St. Thomas Aquinas (c. 1225–1274), Italian born, was the Doctor Angelicus, and the leading scholastic philosopher. His system, embodied in his Summa Theologica and many other writings, as Thomism (or neo-Thomism) is very much alive today and is the philosophical system most favored among Roman Catholics. The Summa is by no means difficult reading in the same way Aristotle is, but it is long, detailed, leisurely, and cast in forms strange to Americans today. I have preferred to choose a piece of Thomas's mind as faithfully put into a contemporary mold by Father Walter Farrell. Here is Thomas on the end of life—end in both the literal and the teleological sense—the Christian eschatology, heaven, and the afterlife.

WHATEVER HAPPENS TO THE WORLD, ALL MEN WILL RISE AGAIN FROM the dead, good and bad, young and old. They will rise at the sound of a trumpet; not that ears long dead, turned to dust, and blown about the face of the earth will be tuned to that note. Lazarus, dead for four days, was hardly on tiptoe waiting for the voice of Christ which, nevertheless, he promptly answered. Rather, the sound of the trumpet will be an instrument of divinity, as the voice of the priest in the consecration of the Mass is a divine instrument; surely, the bread is not listening for those sacred words, impatient to be changed into the body of Christ. The model and exemplar of this last resurrection was the first resurrection, that of Christ on Easter Sunday; its cause must, of course, be divinity. The humanity of Christ, in this and the other divine works of Christ, is always the instrument of the Godhead.

Thomas has a pleasant statement of the part the angels will play in the resurrection of men. It is not to be a necessary part but rather a share thoughtfully provided by God much as a mother allows a child to pay

From Walter Farrell, *A Companion to the Summa,* Vol. IV—*The Way of Life* (Corresponding to the *Summa Theologica IIIA* and Supplement). (New York: Sheed & Ward, 1942), pp. 429-434.

street-car fare or to carry a package along a busy street. The angels have been working with men from the beginning; guiding, guarding, teaching, helping them. It is only fitting that they should have a part in this last climax of human life. Thomas says that they will "prepare the material for the resurrection"; though it is no doubt an exaggeration to picture them as scurrying to the ends of the earth, gathering the dust of men's bodies, assorting it, arranging it in piles, and waiting for the divine word.

Thomas follows this up with a phrase as to the time of the resurrection, a phrase notable in the beauty of its simplicity. He says it will come "when the work of the angels is finished." This is their last work for men; when that is over, both they and their wards can rest, rest forever. Thomas does not try to determine the time of the resurrection; Christ Himself had put an end to that speculation when He said that this was known only to the Father. Granted the secrecy of the time, as secret as the end of the world with which it will coincide, Thomas says that it will probably take place suddenly—since divine power works in an instant—when the work of the angels is finished.

It will be at dawn, conforming to the model of Christ's own resurrection. It will be as though the turn of the wheel of time had just been completed. At creation, which was time's beginning, the day started off at its beginning; not at the siesta hour, not in time for a late dinner, but at dawn with the sun in the east and the moon in the west; so it will be at the resurrection. At that last moment, the world will look as it did long, long ago, when time itself was just starting; in a real sense, time will start again, for men will begin to live again, men, understand, not souls, not a new race of men but the same men, body and soul, as first inhabited the earth.

The resurrection is necessary if men are to live eternally. Yet, there is no point to it if each soul has a body different from its original one; for then not the same, but a different person lives. It is to its same, identical body that the soul has its inclination; this is the body that has merited its share in reward and punishment; this is the body that should be judged. There would be a thoroughly justified grumpiness, for example, in a wrestler who received the body of a chorus girl because of a mixed-up resurrection. It is not enough to retain the same sex and general contours of the original body; the risen body must not only be similar, it must be numerically identical or we have not the same person; it has not been a resurrection but a constitution of a new creature.

This point, reasonable as it is, has been the source of much amusement to scoffers. Perhaps that is why God, in a kind of divine contempt, while assuring us of the fact gave us no information of the manner in which it will be accomplished. Objections have been offered which were meant to be devastating but actually turn out to be amusing. There is the famous case of the cannibal. The difficulty is offered not on the grounds of the bones he picks—after all this was not a bone-eating cannibal—but from the side of the cannibal himself. When he comes to die, there will be nothing

in his body that was not taken from the meat and marrow of other human
bodies; someone will have to go unresurrected, probably the cannibal.
Really to make the point it is aiming at, this objection should maintain that
the cannibal started his meat diet in the first days of his mother's preg-
nancy; a thing of extreme difficulty, even for a cannibal. If the objector is
willing to accept this, he should have no difficulty accepting anything, even
the resurrection of worms. The whole thing arises from a confusion of a
man's body with the whole mass of material that a man possesses in the
course of his whole life; as a matter of fact, some of us can do without a
great deal of that right now. What is demanded for the resurrection is that
some of the identical material go into the risen body, actual defect of material being made up by divine power. After all, if a child dies at seven and
is to rise at thirty, or a man born with one ear is to be perfect in the resurrection, some material must be added; but the bodies will still be identical.

The same objection is given scientific form when it is said that the resurrection is an impossibility because, obviously, human bodies return to their
chemical constituents after death, to enter into the make-up of vegetables,
flowers, animals, and ultimately, no doubt, bodies of other men. The
answer, however, does not change. The resurrection does not pose God the
problem of spreading five pounds of flesh over a big frame; after all, the
original material had its source in a divine command. God does not need
a whole mass of the material; but not even God can make the same body
from totally different materials.

Men, then, will be the same men, but much improved. They will be
integrally perfect, that is, they will have all that pertains to the integrity
of the human body. Specifically, Thomas mentions fingernails and hair, not
primarily for the comfort of the bald, but because there might be some
slight doubt about these superfluities. If, through accident, disease, or con-
genital defect, anything is missing at death, it will be supplied in the resurrection.

Thomas thinks that men will rise at the age at which their development
and perfection reached their height and before they have started to deteriorate. He thought thirty would be about right. And all men and women
will rise at the same age, so that a mother can really be young with her
daughter, and with her grandmother for that matter; perhaps it is only
then that we shall get to know our ancestors. Of course there will be
mothers and grandmothers there, for not all arise in the same sex; they
must, you see, be the same persons. Clearly a strangely bearded grandmother would not be the same grandmother we had known on this earth;
moreover, the diversity of sex is a part of the perfection of the species.

While all will be the same age, they will not all be the same size. There
is no particularly perfect size for a human being. Some will be big, some
small, some tall and some short; but all with the defects of nature corrected, that is no one will be too big, too small, too tall, or too short. In a
word, there will be a pleasant variety, as great a variety, in fact, as there is

now; for there will be exactly the same individuals with the rough spots smoothed off. Yet, with all this physical perfection, there will be none of the operations of animal life; there is simply no point to this activity. Man remains a rational animal, but with his animality totally spiritualized; even the damned will forego all animal life.

In the just, the bodies will be examples of matter completely dominated by spirit. By nature, man is a creature of reason in whom spirit was made to command; in glory, the submission of body to soul far surpasses nature. Four instances of this domination of the soul over the body have been singled out by theologians and called the gifts of the glorified body. The body is said to be "impassable," that is, not subject to injury in any sense, even in that delicate sense of suffering in the very exercise of sense faculties. The soul will dominate the body both as its form and as its mover: in the first case, the result is the gift of "subtlety" which subjects the organic character of the body to the soul; in the second, it is the gift of "agility" which enables the body to move with something of the speed of thought. Finally, just as the body will hinder no operation of the soul, so neither will it cloud or veil the soul's beauty; this is the gift of "clarity" which allows the splendor of the soul to shine through the body, thus making the spiritual beauty as visible as physical beauty is to us in this life.

The bodies of the damned will have none of this supernatural perfection. Since they will have all that nature demands, they will be free from all defects and deformities; but they will have no more than that except for the immortality which keeps them incorruptible, not immune to injury, but rather guaranteed an eternity of punishment. When all men have risen equipped with bodies for eternity, they are prepared for that last great drama in the history of mankind, the drama that strikes such terror to our hearts, principally because we look at it sentimentally rather than rationally; the last judgment.

To put the fundamental reason for general judgment in simple language, it would be enough to say that it takes away from men for all time any grounds for that comforting activity we call grumbling; no sinner will make his way back to hell mumbling "we were robbed." In more dignified language, the general judgment is the ultimate vindication of the justice and mercy of God. Man, after all, is more than an individual, he is a citizen; he is a member of the great family of humanity. He is judged, justly and finally, as an individual immediately after death and there will be no change in that sentence; as a citizen, he stands before the whole world on the day of general judgment that all might know the wonder of God's ways and the complete justice of the original sentence. There will be no grounds for such a gossip's wonder and speculation as "What is that one doing in hell, she seemed such a grand person?" or "Look at Johnny Smith in heaven! Wait a few centuries till they find him out."

The original sentence is final. The just, then, can suffer no unhappiness; a revelation of their sins to the world is an emphasis on their courage and penance in getting rid of sin, not a cause for terror and shame but of wondering gratitude at the mercy of God. Today in heaven, Magdalen feels no shame at the public recitation of her crimes in the Divine Office; nor do those reciting the tale revel in an unholy exultation at uncovering the weakness of another. Rather, like Mary herself, they find these things an occasion for wondering at the goodness of God.

It is quite another thing for the damned. All excuses are made impossible; they are shown plainly in their perversity, their pettiness, their stupidity, with no reason for anything but shame in their sins. It will be, this judgment, a public vindication of Christ the Judge and of those who took Him at His word, taking up their crosses to follow Him. Such complete justice is impossible in this world, or even in the particular judgment; here, the whole person, body as well as soul, is finally rewarded or punished.

MARQUIS de CONDORCET

The Doctrine of Natural Salvation

Antoine Nicolas de Caritat, Marquis de Condorcet (1743–1794) was a French philosophe, deputy to the National Convention during the great French Revolution. As a Girondin to the moderate Right of the triumphant Mountain at the height of the Terror, he was proscribed and went into hiding, where he wrote without benefit of research library his sweeping survey of history, the Esquisse d'un tableau des progrès de l'esprit humain *—literally,* Sketch for a picture of the progresses of the human mind. *There is hardly a better example of the characteristic teleology of the Enlightenment, familiar to us all as the doctrine of Progress. Indeed in Condorcet it is a teleology of human perfectibility that turns in the end—in the last half-dozen paragraphs below—into an Enlightened surrogate for the Christian eschatology of immortal life and final judgment. Condorcet at least hints that the span of human life in this body on this earth has no necessary limits. This is the doctrine of "natural salvation"—physical immortality of the individual here on earth. If you would like to test your ability to face the evidence in the matter of "multanimity," try reading right after this bit of Condorcet the passage from Sir Charles Galton Darwin beginning on page 491.*

IF MAN CAN, WITH ALMOST COMPLETE ASSURANCE, PREDICT PHENOMENA when he knows their laws, and if, even when he does not, he can still, with great expectation of success, forecast the future on the basis of his experience of the past, why, then, should it be regarded as a fantastic undertaking to sketch, with some pretence to truth, the future destiny of man on the basis of his history? The sole foundation for belief in the natural sciences is this idea, that the general laws directing the phenomena of the universe, known or unknown, are necessary and constant. Why should this principle be any less true for the development of the intellectual and moral faculties of man than for the other operations of nature? Since beliefs founded on

From Crane Brinton, ed., *Age of Reason Reader* (New York: The Viking Press, 1956), pp. 220-239.

past experience of like conditions provide the only rule of conduct for the wisest of men, why should the philosopher be forbidden to base his conjectures on these same foundations, so long as he does not attribute to them a certainty superior to that warranted by the number, the constancy, and the accuracy of his observations?

Our hopes for the future condition of the human race can be subsumed under three important heads: the abolition of inequality between nations, the progress of equality within each nation, and the true perfection of mankind. Will all nations one day attain that state of civilization which the most enlightened, the freest and the least burdened by prejudices, such as the French and the Anglo-Americans, have attained already? Will the vast gulf that separates these peoples from the slavery of nations under the rule of monarchs, from the barbarism of African tribes, from the ignorance of savages, little by little disappear?

Is there on the face of the earth a nation whose inhabitants have been debarred by nature herself from the enjoyment of freedom and the exercise of reason?

Are those differences which have hitherto been seen in every civilized country in respect of the enlightenment, the resources, and the wealth enjoyed by the different classes into which it is divided, is that inequality between men which was aggravated or perhaps produced by the earliest progress of society, are these part of civilization itself, or are they due to the present imperfections of the social art? Will they necessarily decrease and ultimately make way for a real equality, the final end of the social art, in which even the effects of the natural differences between men will be mitigated and the only kind of inequality to persist will be that which is in the interests of all and which favours the progress of civilization, of education, and of industry, without entailing either poverty, humiliation, or dependence? In other words, will men approach a condition in which everyone will have the knowledge necessary to conduct himself in the ordinary affairs of life, according to the light of his own reason, to preserve his mind free from prejudice, to understand his rights and to exercise them in accordance with his conscience and his creed; in which everyone will become able, through the development of his faculties, to find the means of providing for his needs; and in which at last misery and folly will be the exception, and no longer the habitual lot of a section of society?

Is the human race to better itself, either by discoveries in the sciences and the arts, and so in the means to individual welfare and general prosperity; or by progress in the principles of conduct or practical morality; or by a true perfection of the intellectual, moral, or physical faculties of man, an improvement which may result from a perfection either of the instruments used to heighten the intensity of these faculties and to direct their use or of the natural constitution of man?

In answering these three questions we shall find in the experience of the past, in the observation of the progress that the sciences and civilization have already made, in the analysis of the progress of the human mind and of the development of its faculties, the strongest reasons for believing that nature has set no limit to the realization of our hopes.

If we glance at the state of the world today we see first of all that in Europe the principles of the French Constitution are already those of all enlightened men. We see them too widely propagated, too seriously professed, for priests and despots to prevent their gradual penetration even into the hovels of their slaves; there they will soon awaken in these slaves the remnants of their common sense and inspire them with that smouldering indignation which not even constant humiliation and fear can smother in the soul of the oppressed.

As we move from nation to nation, we can see in each what special obstacles impede this revolution and what attitudes of mind favour it. We can distinguish the nations where we may expect it to be introduced gently by the perhaps belated wisdom of their governments, and those nations where its violence intensified by their resistance must involve all alike in a swift and terrible convulsion.

Can we doubt that either common sense or the senseless discords of European nations will add to the effects of the slow but inexorable progress of their colonies, and will soon bring about the independence of the New World? And then will not the European population in these colonies, spreading rapidly over that enormous land, either civilize or peacefully remove the savage nations who still inhabit vast tracts of its land?

Survey the history of our settlements and commercial undertakings in Africa or in Asia, and you will see how our trade monopolies, our treachery, our murderous contempt for men of another colour or creed, the insolence of our usurpations, the intrigues or the exaggerated proselytic zeal of our priests, have destroyed the respect and goodwill that the superiority of our knowledge and the benefits of our commerce at first won for us in the eyes of the inhabitants. But doubtless the moment approaches when, no longer presenting ourselves as always either tyrants or corrupters, we shall become for them the beneficent instruments of their freedom.

The sugar industry, establishing itself throughout the immense continent of Africa, will destroy the shameful exploitation which has corrupted and depopulated that continent for the last two centuries.

Already in Great Britain, friends of humanity have set us an example; and if the Machiavellian government of that country has been restrained by public opinion from offering any opposition, what may we not expect of this same spirit, once the reform of a servile and venal constitution has led to a government worthy of a humane and generous nation? Will not France hasten to imitate such undertakings dictated by philanthropy and the true self-interest of Europe alike? Trading stations have been set up in the French islands, in Guiana and in some English possessions, and soon we shall see the downfall of the monopoly that the Dutch have sustained with so much treachery, persecution and crime. The nations of Europe will finally learn that monopolistic companies are nothing more than a tax imposed upon them in order to provide their governments with a new instrument of tyranny.

So the peoples of Europe, confining themselves to free trade, understanding their own rights too well to show contempt for those of other peoples, will respect this independence, which until now they have so insolently violated. Their settlements, no longer filled with government hirelings hastening, under the cloak of place or privilege, to amass treasure by brigandry and deceit, so as to be able to return to Europe and purchase titles and honour, will now be peopled with men of industrious habit, seeking in these propitious climates the wealth that eluded them at home. The love of freedom will retain them there, ambition will no longer recall them, and what have been no better than the counting houses of brigands will become colonies of citizens propagating throughout Africa and Asia the principles and the practice of liberty, knowledge and reason, that they have brought from Europe. We shall see the monks who brought only shameful superstition to these peoples, and aroused their antagonism by the threat of yet another tyranny, replaced by men occupied in propagating amongst them the truths that will promote their happiness and in teaching them about their interests and their rights. Zeal for the truth is also one of the passions, and it will turn its efforts to distant lands, once there are no longer at home any crass prejudices to combat, any shameful errors to dissipate. . . .

The progress of these peoples is likely to be more rapid and certain than our own because they can receive from us everything that we have had to find out for ourselves, and in order to understand those simple truths and infallible methods which we have acquired only after long error, all that they need to do is to follow the expositions and proofs that appear in our speeches and writings. If the progress of the Greeks was lost to later nations, this was because of the absence of any form of communication between the different peoples, and for this we must blame the tyrannical domination of the Romans. But when mutual needs have brought all men together, and the great powers have established equality among societies as well as among individuals and have raised respect for the independence of weak states and sympathy for ignorance and misery to the rank of political principles, when maxims that favour action and energy have ousted those which would compress the province of human faculties, will it then be possible to fear that there are still places in the world inaccessible to enlightenment, or that despotism in its pride can raise barriers against truth that are insurmountable for long?

The time will therefore come when the sun will shine only on free men who know no other master but their reason; when tyrants and slaves, priests and their stupid or hypocritical instruments, will exist only in works of history and on the stage; and when we shall think of them only to pity their victims and their dupes; to maintain ourselves in a state of vigilance by thinking on their excesses; and to learn how to recognize and so to destroy, by force of reason, the first seeds of tyranny and superstition, should they ever dare to reappear amongst us.

In looking at the history of societies we shall have had occasion to observe that there is often a great difference between the rights that the law allows its citizens and the rights that they actually enjoy, and, again, between the equality established by political codes and that which in fact exists amongst individuals: and we shall have noticed that these differences were one of the principal causes of the destruction of freedom in the ancient republics, of the storms that troubled them, and of the weakness that delivered them over to foreign tyrants.

These differences have three main causes: inequality in wealth; inequality in status between the man whose means of subsistence are hereditary and the man whose means are dependent on the length of his life, or, rather, on that part of his life in which he is capable of work; and, finally, inequality in education.

We therefore need to show that these three sorts of real inequality must constantly diminish without, however, disappearing altogether: for they are the result of natural and necessary causes, which it would be foolish and dangerous to wish to eradicate; and one could not even attempt to bring about the entire disappearance of their effects without introducing even more fecund sources of inequality, without striking more direct and more fatal blows at the rights of man.

It is easy to prove that wealth has a natural tendency to equality, and that any excessive disproportion could not exist, or at least would rapidly disappear, if civil laws did not provide artificial ways of perpetuating and uniting fortunes; if free trade and industry were allowed to remove the advantages that accrued wealth derives from any restrictive law or fiscal privilege; if taxes on covenants, the restrictions placed on their free employment, their subjection to tiresome formalities, and the uncertainty and inevitable expense involved in implementing them did not hamper the activity of the poor man and swallow up his meagre capital; if the administration of the country did not afford some men ways of making their fortune that were closed to other citizens; if prejudice and avarice, so common in old age, did not preside over the making of marriages; and if, in a society enjoying simpler manners and more sensible institutions, wealth ceased to be a means of satisfying vanity and ambition, and if the equally misguided notions of austerity, which condemn spending money in the cultivation of the more delicate pleasures, no longer insisted on the hoarding of all one's earnings.

Let us turn to the enlightened nations of Europe, and observe the size of their present populations in relation to the size of their territories. Let us consider, in agriculture and industry, the proportion that holds between labour and the means of subsistence, and we shall see that it would be impossible for those means to be kept at their present level, and consequently for the population to be kept at its present size, if a great number of individuals were not almost entirely dependent for the maintenance of themselves and their family either on their own labour or on the interest from capital invested so as to make their labour more productive. Now both these sources of income depend on the life and even on the health of the head of the family. They provide what is rather like a life annuity, save that it is more dependent on chance; and in consequence there is a very real difference between people living like this and those whose resources are not at all subject to the same risks, who live either on revenue from land, or on the interest on capital, which is almost independent of their own labour.

Here then is a necessary cause of inequality, of dependence and even of misery, which ceaselessly threatens the most numerous and most active class in our society.

We shall point out how it can be in great part eradicated by guaranteeing people in old age a means of livelihood produced partly by their own savings and partly by the savings of others who make the same outlay, but who die before they need to reap the reward; or, again, on the same principle of compensation, by securing for widows and orphans an income which is the same and costs the same for those families which suffer an early loss and for those which suffer it later; or again by providing all children with the capital necessary for the full use of their labour, available at the age when they start work and found a family, a capital which increases at the expense of those whom premature death prevents from reaching this age. It is to the application of the calculus to the probabilities of life and the investment of money that we owe the idea of these methods which have already been successful, although they have not been applied in a sufficiently comprehensive and exhaustive fashion to render them really useful, not merely to a few individuals, but to society as a whole, by making it possible to prevent those periodic disasters which strike at so many families and which are such a recurrent source of misery and suffering.

We shall point out that schemes of this nature, which can be organized in the name of the social authority and become one of its greatest benefits, can also be the work of private associations, which will be formed without any real risk, once the principles for the proper working of these schemes have been widely diffused and the mistakes which have been the undoing of a large number of these associations no longer hold terrors for us. . . .

So we might say that a well-directed system of education rectifies natural inequality in ability instead of strengthening it, just as good laws remedy natural inequality in the means of subsistence, and just as in societies where laws have brought about this same equality, liberty, though subject to a regular constitution, will be more widespread, more complete, than in the total independence of savage life. Then the social art will have fulfilled its aim, that of assuring and extending to all men enjoyment of the common rights to which they are called by nature.

The real advantages that should result from this progress, of which we can entertain a hope that is almost a certainty, can have no other term than that of the absolute perfection of the human race; since, as the various kinds of equality come to work in its favour by producing ampler sources of supply, more extensive education, more complete liberty, so equality will be more real and will embrace everything which is really of importance for the happiness of human beings.

It is therefore only by examining the progress and the laws of this perfection that we shall be able to understand the extent or the limits of our hopes.

No one has ever believed that the mind can gain knowledge of all the facts of nature or attain the ultimate means of precision in the measurement, or in the analysis of the facts of nature, the relations between objects and all the possible combinations of ideas. Even the relations between magnitudes, the mere notion of quantity or extension, taken in its fullest comprehension, gives rise to a system so vast that it will never be mastered by the human mind in its entirety, that there will always be a part of it, always indeed the larger part of it, that will remain forever unknown. People have believed that man can never know more than a part of the objects that the nature of his intelligence allows him to understand, and that he must in the end arrive at a point where the number and complexity of the objects that he already knows have absorbed all his strength so that any further progress must be completely impossible.

But since, as the number of known facts increases, the human mind learns how to classify them and to subsume them under more general facts, and, at the same time, the instruments and methods employed in their observation and their exact measurement acquire a new precision; since, as more relations between various objects become known, man is able to reduce them to more general relations, to express them more simply, and to present them in such a way that it is possible to grasp a greater number of them with the same degree of intellectual ability and the same amount of application; since, as the mind learns to understand more complicated combinations of ideas, simpler formulae soon reduce their complexity; so truths that were discovered only by great effort, that could at first only be understood by men capable of profound thought, are soon developed and proved by methods that are not beyond the reach of common intelligence. If the methods which have led to these new combinations of ideas are ever exhausted, if their application to hitherto unsolved questions should demand exertions greater than either the time or the capacity of the learned would permit, some method of a greater generality or simplicity will be found so that genius can continue undisturbed on its path. The strength and the limits of man's intelligence may remain unaltered; and yet the instruments that he uses will increase and improve, the language that fixes and determines his ideas will acquire greater breadth and precision, and, unlike mechanics, where an increase of force means a decrease of speed, the methods that lead genius to the discovery of truth increase at once the force and the speed of its operations.

Therefore, since these developments are themselves the necessary consequences of progress in detailed knowledge, and since the need for new methods in fact only arises in circumstances that give rise to new methods, it is evident that, within the body of the sciences of observation, calculation and experiment, the actual number of truths may always increase, and that every part of this body may develop, and yet man's faculties be of the same strength, activity and extent.

If we apply these general reflections to the various sciences, we can find in each of them examples of progressive improvement that will remove any doubts about what we may expect for the future. We shall point out in particular the progress that is both likely and imminent in those sciences which prejudice regards as all but exhausted. We shall give examples of the manner and extent of the precision and unity which could accrue to the whole system of human knowledge as the result of a more general and philosophical application of the sciences of calculation to the various branches of knowledge. We shall show how favourable to our hopes would be a more universal system of education by giving a greater number of people the elementary knowledge which could awaken their interest in a particular branch of study, and by providing conditions favourable to their progress in it; and how these hopes would be further raised if more men possessed the means to devote themselves to these studies, for at present even in the most enlightened countries scarcely one in fifty of the people who have natural talents receives the necessary education to develop them; and how, if this were done, there would be a proportionate increase in the number of men destined by their discoveries to extend the boundaries of science. . . .

A very small amount of ground will be able to produce a great quantity of supplies of greater utility or higher quality; more goods will be obtained for a smaller outlay; the manufacture of articles will be achieved with less wastage in raw materials and will make better use of them. Every type of soil will produce those things which satisfy the greatest number of needs; of several alternative ways of satisfying needs of the same order, that will be chosen which satisfies the greatest number of people and which requires least labour and least expenditure. So, without the need for sacrifice, methods of preservation and economy in expenditure will improve in the wake of progress in the arts of producing and preparing supplies and making articles from them.

So not only will the same amount of ground support more people, but everyone will have less work to do, will produce more, and satisfy his wants more fully.

With all this progress in industry and welfare, which establishes a happier proportion between men's talents and their needs, each successive generation will have larger possessions, either as a result of this progress or through the preservation of the products of industry; and so, as a consequence of the physical constitution of the human race, the number of people will increase. Might there not then come a moment when these necessary laws begin to work in a contrary direction; when, the number of people in the world finally exceeding the means of subsistence, there will in consequence ensue a continual diminution of happiness and population, a true retrogression, or at best an oscillation between good and bad? In societies that have reached this stage, will not this oscillation be a perennial source of more or less periodic disaster? Will it not show that a point has been attained beyond which all further improvement is impossible, that the perfectibility of the human race has after long years arrived at a term beyond which it may never go?

There is doubtless no one who does not think that such a time is still very far from us; but will it ever arrive? It is impossible to pronounce about the likelihood of an event that will occur only when the human species will have necessarily acquired a degree of knowledge of which we can have no inkling. And who would take it upon himself to predict the condition to which the art of converting the elements to the use of man may in time be brought?

But even if we agree that the limit will one day arrive, nothing follows from it that is in the least alarming as far as either the happiness of the human race or its indefinite perfectibility is concerned. If we consider that, before all this comes to pass, the progress of reason will have kept pace with that of the sciences, and that the absurd prejudices of superstition will have ceased to corrupt and degrade the moral code by its harsh doctrines instead of purifying and elevating it, we can assume that by then men will know that, if they have a duty towards those who are not yet born, that duty is not to give them existence but to give them happiness; their aim should be to promote the general welfare of the human race or of the society in which they live or of the family to which they belong, rather than foolishly to encumber the world with useless and wretched beings. It is, then, possible that there should be a limit to the amount of food that can be produced, and, consequently, to the size of the population of the world, without this involving that untimely destruction of some of those creatures who have been given life, which is so contrary to nature and to social prosperity. . . .

Organic perfectibility or deterioration amongst the various strains in the vegetable and animal kingdom can be regarded as one of the general laws of nature. This law also applies to the human race. No one can doubt that, as preventive medicine improves and food and housing become healthier, as a way of life is established that develops our physical powers by exercise without ruining them by excess, as the two most virulent causes of deterioration, misery and excessive wealth, are eliminated, the average length of human life will be increased and a better health and a stronger physical constitution will be ensured. The improvement of medical practice, which will become more efficacious with the progress of reason and of the social order, will mean the end of infectious and hereditary diseases and illnesses brought on by climate, food, or working conditions. It is reasonable to hope that all other diseases may likewise disappear as their distant causes are discovered. Would it be absurd, then, to suppose that this perfection of the human species might be capable of indefinite progress; that the day will come when death will be due only to extraordinary accidents or to the decay of the vital forces, and that ultimately the average span between birth and decay will have no assignable value? Certainly man will not become immortal, but will not the interval between the first breath that he draws and the time when in the natural course of events, without disease or accident, he expires, increase indefinitely? Since we are now speaking of a progress than can be represented with some accuracy in figures or on a graph, we shall take this opportunity of explaining the two meanings that can be attached to the word *indefinite*.

In truth, this average span of life, which we suppose will increase indefinitely as time passes, may grow in conformity either with a law such that it continually approaches a limitless length but without ever reaching it, or with a law such that through the centuries it reaches a length greater than any determinate quantity that we may assign to it as its limit. In the latter case such an increase is truly indefinite in the strictest sense of the word, since there is no term on this side of which it must of necessity stop. In the former case it is equally indefinite in relation to us if we cannot fix the limit it always approaches without ever reaching, and particularly if, knowing only that it will never stop, we are ignorant in which of the two senses the term *indefinite* can be applied to it. Such is the present condition of our knowledge as far as the perfectibility of the human race is concerned; such is the sense in which we may call it indefinite.

So, in the example under consideration, we are bound to believe that the average length of human life will forever increase unless this is prevented by physical revolutions; we do not know what the limit is which it can never exceed. We cannot tell even whether the general laws of nature have determined such a limit or not.

But are not our physical faculties and the strength, dexterity and acuteness of our senses, to be numbered among the qualities whose perfection in the individual may be transmitted? Observation of the various breeds of domestic animals inclines us to believe that they are, and we can confirm this by direct observation of the human race.

Finally may we not extend such hopes to the intellectual and moral faculties? May not our parents, who transmit to us the benefits or disadvantages of their constitution, and from whom we receive our shape and features, as well as our tendencies to certain physical affections, hand on to us also that part of the physical organization which determines the intellect, the power of the brain, the ardour of the soul or the moral sensibility? Is it not probable that education, in perfecting these qualities, will at the same time influence, modify and perfect the organization itself? Analogy, investigation of the human faculties and the study of certain facts, all seem to give substance to such conjectures, which would further push back the boundaries of our hopes.

These are the questions with which we shall conclude this final stage. How consoling for the philosopher, who laments the errors, the crimes, the injustices which still pollute the earth, and of which he is often the victim, is this view of the human race, emancipated from its shackles, released from the empire of fate and from that of the enemies of its progress, advancing with a firm and sure step along the path of truth, virtue and happiness! It is the contemplation of this prospect that rewards him for all his efforts to assist the progress of reason and the defence of liberty. He dares to regard these strivings as part of the eternal chain of human destiny; and in this persuasion he is filled with the true delight of virtue and the pleasure of having done some lasting good, which fate can never destroy by a sinister stroke of revenge, by calling back the reign of slavery and prejudice. Such contemplation is for him an asylum, in which the memory of his persecutors cannot pursue him; there he lives in thought with man restored to his natural rights and dignity, forgets man tormented and corrupted by greed, fear, or envy; there he lives with his peers in an Elysium created by reason and graced by the purest pleasures known to the love of mankind.

(Translation by June Barraclough)

HERBERT SPENCER

Reconciliation of Science and Religion

Herbert Spencer (1820–1903) was an English engineer turned philosopher, who, like St. Thomas, also wrote a summa, *though he would have hated that title. Spencer is a better sampling of the modern belief in Progress as cosmic (and human) purpose than Condorcet, for Darwin's work had given the Englishman an explanation of the way change (Progress) came about, an explanation the eighteenth-century French philosophes never satisfactorily arrived at. Rather than choosing one of Spencer's numerous direct expositions of the teleological doctrine of Evolution-Progress, I have chosen a passage on one of the great nineteenth-century topics, the warfare between Religion and Science—a warfare Spencer thought he had settled. Note that Spencer cannot quite rid his mind of a godhead, even though, duly capitalizing, he refers to Him as The Unknowable.*

HERE THEN IS THAT BASIS OF AGREEMENT WE SET OUT TO SEEK. THIS conclusion which objective science illustrates, and subjective science shows to be unavoidable—this conclusion which, while it in the main expresses the doctrine of the English school of philosophy, recognizes also a soul of truth in the doctrine of the antagonist German school—this conclusion which brings the results of speculation into harmony with those of common sense, is also the conclusion which reconciles Religion with Science. Common Sense asserts the existence of a reality; Objective Science proves that this reality cannot be what we think it; Subjective Science shows why we cannot think of it as it is, and yet are compelled to think of it as existing; and in this assertion of a Reality utterly inscrutable in nature, Religion finds an assertion essentially coinciding with her own. We are obliged to regard every phenomenon as a manifestation of some Power by which we are acted upon; though Omnipresence is unthinkable, yet, as experience discloses no bounds to the diffusion of phenomena, we are unable to think of limits to the presence of this Power; while the criticisms of Science teach

From Herbert Spencer, *First Principles* (New York: H. M. Caldwell Co., n.d.). (Fourth edition, Preface dated 1880), pp. 82-90, 93-95.

us that this Power is incomprehensible. And this consciousness of an Incomprehensible Power, called Omnipresent from inability to assign its limits, is just that consciousness on which Religion dwells.

To understand fully how real is the reconciliation thus reached, it will be needful to look at the receptive attitudes that Religion and Science have all along maintained toward this conclusion. We must observe how, all along, the imperfections of each have been undergoing correction by the other; and how the final outcome of their mutual criticisms can be nothing else than an entire agreement on this deepest and widest of all truths.

In Religion let us recognize the high merit that from the beginning it has dimly discerned the ultimate verity, and has never ceased to insist upon it. In its earliest and crudest forms it manifested, however vaguely and inconsistently, an intuition forming the germ of this highest belief in which all philosophies finally unite. The consciousness of a mystery is traceable in the rudest fetishism. Each higher religious creed, rejecting those definite and simple interpretations of Nature previously given, has become more religious by doing this. As the quite concrete and conceivable agencies alleged as the causes of things have been replaced by agencies less concrete and conceivable, the element of mystery has of necessity become more predominant. Through all its successive phases the disappearance of those positive dogmas by which the mystery was made unmysterious, has formed the essential change delineated in religious history. And so Religion has ever been approximating toward that complete recognition of this mystery which is its goal.

For its essentially valid belief, Religion has constantly done battle. Gross as were the disguises under which it first espoused this belief, and cherishing this belief though it still is, under disfiguring vestments, it has never ceased to maintain and defend it. It has everywhere established and propagated one or other modification of the doctrine that all things are manifestations of a Power that transcends our knowledge. Though from age to age, Science has continually defeated it wherever they have come in collision, and has obliged it to relinquish one or more of its positions, it has still held the remaining ones with undiminished tenacity. No exposure of the logical inconsistency of its conclusions—no proof that each of its particular dogmas was absurd, has been able to weaken its allegiance to that ultimate verity for which it stands. After criticism has abolished all its arguments and reduced it to silence, there has still remained with it the indestructible consciousness of a truth which, however faulty the mode in which it had been expressed, was yet a truth beyond cavil. To this conviction its adherence has been substantially sincere. And for the guardianship and diffusion of it Humanity has ever been, and must ever be, its debtor.

But while, from the beginning, Religion has had the all-essential office of preventing men from being wholly absorbed in the relative or immediate, and of awakening them to a consciousness of something beyond it, this office has been but very imperfectly discharged. Religion has ever been more or less irreligious; and it continues to be partially irreligious even now. In the first place, as implied above, it has all along professed to have some knowledge of that which transcends knowledge; and has so contradicted its own teachings. While with one breath it has asserted that the Cause of all things passes understanding, it has, with the next breath, asserted that the Cause of all things possesses such or such attributes— can be in so far understood. In the second place, while in great part sincere in its fealty to the great truth it has had to uphold, it has often been insincere, and consequently irreligious, in maintaining the untenable doctrines by which it has obscured this great truth. Each assertion respecting the nature, acts, or motives of that Power which the Universe manifests to us, has been repeatedly called in question, and proved to be inconsistent with itself, or with accompanying assertions. Yet each of them has been age after age insisted on, in spite of a secret consciousness that it would not bear examination. Just as though unaware that its central position was impregnable, Religion has obstinately held every outpost long after it was obviously indefensible. And this naturally introduces us to the third and most serious form of irreligion which Religion has displayed; namely, an imperfect belief in that which it especially professes to believe. How truly its central position *is* impregnable, Religion has never adequately realized. In the devoutest faith as we habitually see it, there lies hidden an innermost core of scepticism; and it is this scepticism which causes that dread of inquiry displayed by Religion when face to face with Science. Obliged to abandon one by one the superstitions it once tenaciously held, and daily finding its cherished beliefs more and more shaken, Religion shows a secret fear that all things may some day be explained; and thus itself betrays a lurking doubt whether that Incomprehensible Cause of which it is conscious is really incomprehensible.

Of Religion, then, we must always remember, that amid its many errors and corruptions it has asserted and diffused a supreme verity. From the first, the recognition of this supreme verity, in however imperfect a manner, has been its vital element; and its various defects, once extreme but gradually diminishing, have been so many failures to recognize in full that which it recognized in part. The truly religious element of Religion has always been good; that which has proved untenable in doctrine and vicious in practice has been its irreligious element; and from this it has been ever undergoing purification.

And now observe that, all along, the agent which has effected the purification has been Science. We habitually overlook the fact that this has been one of its functions. Religion ignores its immense debt to Science; and Science is scarcely at all conscious how much Religion owes it. Yet it is demonstrable that every step by which Religion has progressed from its first low conception to the comparatively high one it has now reached, Science has helped it, or rather forced it, to take; and that even now, Science is urging further steps in the same direction.

Using the word Science in its true sense, as comprehending all positive and definite knowledge of the order existing among surrounding phenomena, it becomes manifest that from the outset the discovery of an established order has modified that conception of disorder, or undetermined order, which underlies every superstition. As fast as experience proves that certain familiar changes always happen in the same sequence, there begins to fade from the mind the conception of a special personality to whose variable will they were before ascribed. And when, step by step, accumulating observations do the like with the less familiar changes, a similar modification of belief takes place with respect to them.

While this process seems to those who effect, and those who undergo it, an anti-religious one, it is really the reverse. Instead of the specific comprehensible agency before assigned, there is substituted a less specific and less comprehensible agency; and though this, standing in opposition to the previous one, cannot at first call forth the same feeling, yet, as being less comprehensible, it must eventually call forth this feeling more fully. Take an instance. Of old the Sun was regarded as the chariot of a god, drawn by horses. How far the idea thus grossly expressed, was idealized, we need not inquire. It suffices to remark that this accounting for the apparent motion of the Sun by an agency like certain visible terrestrial agencies, reduced a daily wonder to the level of the commonest intellect. When, many centuries after, Kepler discovered that the planets moved round the Sun in ellipses and described equal areas in equal times, he concluded that in each planet there must exist a spirit to guide its movements. Here we see that with the progress of Science, there had disappeared the idea of a gross mechanical traction, such as was first assigned in the case of the Sun; but that while for this there was substituted an indefinite and less easily conceivable force, it was still thought needful to assume a special personal agent as a cause of the regular irregularity of motion. When, finally, it was proved that these planetary revolutions, with all their variations and disturbances, conformed to one universal law—when the presiding spirits which Kepler conceived were set aside, and the force of gravitation put in their place—the change was really the abolition of an imaginable agency, and the substitution of an unimaginable one. For though the *law* of gravitation is within our mental grasp, it is impossible to realize in thought the *force* of gravitation. Newton himself confessed the force of gravitation to be incomprehensible without the intermediation of an ether; and, as we have already seen, the assumption of an ether does not in the least help us. Thus it is with Science in general. Its progress in grouping particular relations of phenomena under laws, and these special laws under laws more and more general, is of necessity a progress to causes that are more and more abstract. And causes more and more abstract are of necessity causes less and less conceivable; since the formation of an abstract conception involves the dropping of certain concrete elements of thought. Hence the most abstract conception, to which Science is ever slowly approaching, is one that merges into the inconceivable or unthinkable, by the dropping of all concreted elements of thought. And so is justified the assertion, that the beliefs which Science has forced upon Religion have been intrinsically more religious than those which they supplanted.

Science however, like Religion, has but very incompletely fulfilled its office. As Religion has fallen short of its function in so far as it has been irreligious, so has Science fallen short of its function in so far as it has been unscientific. Let us note the several parallelisms. In its earlier stages, Science, while it began to teach the constant relations of phenomena, and so discredited the belief in separate personalities as the causes of them, itself substituted the belief in causal agencies which, if not personal, were yet concrete. When certain facts were said to show "Nature's abhorrence of a vacuum," when the properties of gold were explained as due to some entity called "aureity," and when the phenomena of life were attributed to "a vital principle," there was set up a mode of interpreting the facts, which, while antagonistic to the religious mode, because assigning other agencies, was also unscientific, because it professed to know that about which nothing was known. Having abandoned these metaphysical agencies—having seen that they were not independent existences, but merely special combinations of general causes, Science has more recently ascribed extensive groups of phenomena to electricity, chemical affinity, and other like general powers. But in speaking of these as ultimate and independent entities, Science has preserved substantially the same attitude as before. Accounting thus for all phenomena, those of Life and Thought included, it has not only maintained its seeming antagonism to Religion, by alleging agencies of a radically unlike kind; but, in so far as it has tacitly assumed a knowledge of these agencies, it has continued unscientific. At the present time, however, the most advanced men of science are abandoning these later conceptions, as their predecessors abandoned the earlier ones. Magnetism, heat, light, etc., which were a while since spoken of as so many distinct imponderables, physicists are now beginning to regard as different modes of manifestation of some one universal force; and in so doing are ceasing to think of this force as comprehensible. In each phase of its progress, Science has thus stopped short with superficial solutions—has unscientifically neglected to ask what was the nature of the agents it so familiarly invoked. Though in each succeeding phase it has gone a little deeper, and merged its supposed agents in more general and abstract ones, it has still, as before, rested content with these as if they were ascertained realities. And this, which has all along been the unscientific characteristic of Science, has all along been a part cause of its conflict with Religion.

We see then that, from the first, the faults of both Religion and Science have been the faults of imperfect development. Originally a mere rudiment, each has been growing into a more complete form; the vice of each has in all times been its incompleteness; the disagreements between them have throughout been nothing more than the consequences of their incompleteness; and as they reach their final forms, they come into entire harmony.

The progress of intelligence has throughout been dual. Though it has not seemed so to those who made it, every step in advance has been a step toward both the natural and the supernatural. The better interpretation of each phenomenon has been, on the one hand, the rejection of a cause that was relatively conceivable in its nature but unknown in the order of its actions, and, on the other hand, the adoption of a cause that was known in the order of its actions but relatively inconceivable in its nature. The first advance out of universal fetishism manifestly involved the conception of agencies less assimilable to the familiar agencies of men and animals, and therefore less understood; while at the same time, such newly conceived agencies, in so far as they were distinguished by their uniform effects, were better understood than those they replaced. All subsequent advances display the same double result. Every deeper and more general power arrived at as a cause of phenomena has been at once less comprehensible than the special ones it superseded, in the sense of being less definitely representable in thought; while it has been more comprehensible in the sense that its actions have been more completely predicable. The progress has thus been as much toward the establishment of a positively unknown as toward the establishment of a positively known. Though as knowledge approaches its culmination, every unaccountable and seemingly supernatural fact is brought into the category of facts that are accountable or natural; yet, at the same time, all accountable or natural facts are proved to be in their ultimate genesis unaccountable and supernatural. And so there arise two antithetical states of mind, answering to the opposite sides of that existence about which we think. While our consciousness of Nature under the one aspect constitutes Science, our consciousness of it under the other aspect constitutes Religion.

Otherwise contemplating the facts, we may say that Religion and Science have been undergoing a slow differentiation; and that their ceaseless conflicts have been due to the imperfect separation of their spheres and functions. Religion has, from the first, struggled to unite more or less science with its nescience; Science has, from the first, kept hold of more or less nescience as though it were a part of science. Each has been obliged gradually to relinquish that territory which it wrongly claimed, while it has gained from the other that to which it had a right; and the antagonism between them has been an inevitable accompaniment of this process. A more specific statement will make this clear. Religion, though at the outset it asserted a mystery, also made numerous definite assertions respecting this mystery —professed to know its nature in the minutest detail, and in so far as it claimed positive knowledge, it trespassed upon the province of Science. From the times of early mythologies, when such intimate acquaintance with the mystery was alleged, down to our own days, when but a few abstract and vague propositions are maintained, Religion has been compelled by Science to give up one after another of its dogmas—those assumed cognitions which it could not substantiate. In the mean time, Science substituted for the personalities to which Religion ascribed phenomena, certain metaphysical entities; and in doing this it trespassed on the province of Religion; since it classed among the things which it comprehended certain forms of the incomprehensible. Partly by the criticisms of Religion, which has occasionally called in question its assumptions, and partly as a consequence of spontaneous growth, Science has been obliged to abandon these attempts to include within the boundaries of knowledge that which cannot be known; and has so yielded up to Religion that which of right belonged to it. So long as this process of differentiation is incomplete, more or less of antagonism must continue. Gradually as the limits of possible cognition are established, the causes of conflict will diminish. And a permanent peace will be reached when Science becomes fully convinced that its explanations are proximate and relative; while Religion becomes fully convinced that the mystery it contemplates is ultimate and absolute.

Religion and Science are therefore necessary correlatives. As already hinted, they stand respectively for those two antithetical modes of consciousness which cannot exist asunder. A known cannot be thought of apart from an unknown; nor can an unknown be thought of apart from a known. And by consequence neither can become more distinct without giving greater distinctness to the other. To carry further a metaphor before used—they are the positive and negative poles of thought; of which neither can gain in intensity without increasing the intensity of the other. . . .

Volumes might be written upon the impiety of the pious. Through the printed and spoken thoughts of religious teachers may almost everywhere be traced a professed familiarity with the ultimate mystery of things, which, to say the least of it, seems anything but congruous with the accompanying expressions of humility. And surprisingly enough, those tenets which most clearly display this familiarity are those insisted upon as forming the vital elements of religious belief. The attitude thus assumed can be fitly represented only by further developing a simile long current in theological controversies—the simile of the watch. If for a moment we made the grotesque supposition that the tickings and other movements of a watch constituted a kind of consciousness; and that a watch possessed of such a consciousness insisted on regarding the watchmaker's actions as determined like its own by springs and escapements; we should simply complete a parallel of which religious teachers think much. And were we to suppose that a watch not only formulated the cause of its existence in these mechanical terms but held that watches were bound out of reverence so to formulate this cause, and even vituperated, as atheistic watches, any that did not venture so to formulate it; we should merely illustrate the presumption of theologians by carrying their own argument a step further. A few extracts will bring home to the reader the justice of this comparison. We are told, for example, by one of high repute among religious thinkers, that the Universe is "the manifestation and abode of a Free Mind, like our own; embodying His personal thought in its adjustments, realizing His own ideal in its phenomena, just as we express our inner faculty and character through the natural language of an external life. In this view, we interpret Nature by Humanity; we find the key to her aspects in such purposes and affections as our own consciousness enables us to conceive; we look everywhere for physical signals of an ever-living Will; and decipher the universe as the autobiography of an Infinite Spirit, repeating itself in miniature within our Finite Spirit." The same writer goes still further. He not only thus parallels the assimilation of the watchmaker to the watch—he not only thinks the created can "decipher" "the autobiography" of the Creating; but he asserts that the necessary limits of the one are necessary limits of the other. The primary qualities of bodies, he says, "belong eternally to the material datum objective to God" and control his acts; while the secondary ones are "products of pure Inventive Reason and Determining Will"—constitute "the realm of Divine originality." . . . "While on this Secondary field His Mind and ours are thus contrasted, they meet in resemblance again upon the Primary; for the evolutions of deductive Reason there is but one track possible to all intelligences; no *merum arbitrium* can interchange the false and true, or make more than one geometry, one scheme of pure Physics, for all worlds; and the Omnipotent Architect Himself, in realizing the Cosmical conception, in shaping the orbits out of immensity and determining seasons out of eternity, could but follow the laws of curvature, measure and proportion. That is to say, the Ultimate Cause is like a human mechanic, not only as 'shaping' the 'material datum objective to' Him, but also as being obliged to conform to the necessary properties of that datum." Nor is this all. There follows some account of "the Divine psychology," to the extent of saying that we learn "the character of God—the order of affections in Him" from "the distribution of authority in the hierarchy of our impulses." In other words, it is alleged that the Ultimate Cause has desires that are to be classed as higher and lower like our own.* Every one has heard of the king who wished he had been present at the creation of the world, that he might have given good advice. He was humble, however, compared with those who profess to understand not only the relation of the Creating to the created, but also how the Creating is constituted. And yet this transcendent audacity, which claims to penetrate the secrets of the Power manifested to us through all existence—nay even to stand behind that Power and note the conditions to its action—this it is which

---

* These extracts are from an article entitled "Nature and God," published in the *National Review* for October, 1860.

passes current as piety! May we not without hesitation affirm that a sincere recognition of the truth that our own and all other existence is a mystery absolutely and forever beyond our comprehension, contains more of true religion than all the dogmatic theology ever written?

Meanwhile let us recognize whatever of permanent good there is in these persistent attempts to frame conceptions of that which cannot be conceived. From the beginning it has been only through the successive failures of such conceptions to satisfy the mind, that higher and higher ones have been gradually reached; and doubtless, the conceptions now current are indispensable as transitional modes of thought. Even more than this may be willingly conceded. It is possible, nay probable, that under their most abstract forms, ideas of this order will always continue to occupy the background of our consciousness. Very likely there will ever remain a need to give shape to that indefinite sense of an Ultimate Existence, which forms the basis of our intelligence. We shall always be under the necessity of contemplating it as *some* mode of being, that is, of representing it to ourselves in *some* form of thought, however vague. And we shall not err in doing this so long as we treat every notion we thus frame as merely a symbol, utterly without resemblance to that for which it stands. Perhaps the constant formation of such symbols and constant rejection of them as inadequate may be hereafter, as it has hitherto been, a means of discipline. Perpetually to construct ideas requiring the utmost stretch of our faculties, and perpetually to find that such ideas must be abandoned as futile imaginations, may realize to us, more fully than any other course, the greatness of that which we vainly strive to grasp. Such efforts and failures may serve to maintain in our minds a due sense of the incommensurable difference between the Conditioned and the Unconditioned. By continually seeking to know and being continually thrown back with a deepened conviction of the impossibility of knowing, we may keep alive the consciousness that it is alike our highest wisdom and our highest duty to regard that through which all things exist as The Unknowable.

SHERMAN H. M. CHANG

The Stateless-Communistic Society of Marxism

I am repeating a commonplace when I list the Marxist doctrine of the "classless society" as an eschatological doctrine. But Marx, Engels, and their successors, though they were filled with moral purpose, thought of themselves as scientists; and modern natural scientists, revolting against Aristotelian and other formal teleologies, have been very much afraid of teleological language. Many of them smuggled purpose in, of course, but like all smugglers, they were self-consciously furtive. It is not surprising that the Marxist literature is much, much less explicit about their heaven than the Christian is about theirs. Engels' well-known pamphlet Socialism: Utopian and Scientific, *which I shall cite later, has a few suitable passages. But I have decided to take a radical step, and use in an anthology something from a doctoral thesis. Dr. Chang's work has most of the stigmata of the thesis for the Ph.D., including long footnotes many of which I have had to omit. But in good American, it "covers the ground." Here is the Utopia of the Marx-Engels for whom "Utopia" was the silly doctrine of Owen, Fourier, and the like, in contrast to their own Scientific Socialism. If this be Science, they have surely made the most of it.*

AS WE HAVE DESCRIBED THE THEORY OF THE WITHERING-AWAY OF THE proletarian State in detail, we shall proceed further to examine the stateless-communistic society . . .

There are five outstanding features of the stateless-communistic society which are interesting as well as romantic. One obvious feature is anarchy, namely, that there is no government, since the State will have disappeared. Society will then be a vast association for production, wherein all work will be performed voluntarily by every one as a habit. Every one is to be so accustomed to observing the rules of life that even the simplest manag-

From Sherman H, M. Chang, *The Marxian Theory of the State* (Philadelphia: University of Pennsylvania, Ph.D. thesis, 1931), pp. 133-139.

ing functions such as "bookkeeping and control" (in the sense of "watching, recording and issuing receipts") will become unnecessary.

In order to carry out the common economic plan, there may exist, however, some "counting-houses and statistical bureaus":

> The principal work of administering will be done in various counting-houses and statistical bureaus. From these places the whole field of production will be surveyed, and the quantity of goods required will be ascertained. It will also be learned where the number of workers should be increased and where decreased, and how long their working day should be. . . . There will be no necessity for having Ministers for special departments, and no need for policemen, prisons, laws, etc. As in an orchestra all the performers take their cue from the conductor, so all members of society will read the instructions of the bureaus and arrange their work accordingly. . . . In the bureaus there will be one set of workers to-day, and another set to-morrow.[1]

In other words, the functions of these bureaus are, to use Engels's language, "administration of things" rather than "government of persons" and they are not *special* functions of a special class.

The second feature of the stateless-communistic society is the absence of class distinctions, which, as we have seen, is the fundamental reason for the disappearance of the State. We are constantly told by Marx and Engels that in the new society there will be no class antagonisms and no classes, the abolition of which is the ultimate aim of Scientific Socialism. Hence we read in "A B C of Communism":

> In the Communist society . . . there will be no landowners, no capitalists, no wage workers; there will be simply human beings, comrades. There will be no classes, no class war, no class organizations.[2]

The third feature of the stateless-communistic society is the disappearance of the division of labor, which division, according to Engels, "lies at the basis of the division into classes." He characterizes this feature of the new society as follows:

> . . . on the one hand, no single individual will be able to shift his share in productive labor, in providing the essentials of human existence, upon another, and on the other hand productive labor instead of being a means of slavery will be a means toward human freedom, in that *it offers an opportunity to every one to develop his full powers, physical and intellectual, in every direction and to exercise them so that it makes a pleasure out of a burden.*[3]

Hence one result of the disappearance of the division of labor is an all-round development of the faculties of the individual. According to Marx, there will no longer be any distinction between manual and intellectual labor. Intellect will be absorbed into the masses; the bourgeois intellectual class, abolished; and the system of the specialists, destroyed. "The new communistic society strives after unity in production, unity in mental life, in science." Culture will be "general, many-sided"; "it

---

[1] Bukharin and Preobraschensky, *A.B.C. of Communism,* pp. 59-60.
[2] Ibid., p. 59.
[3] Engels, *Landmarks of Scientific Socialism,* pp. 240-241; italics ours.

will be a really human culture, and not a class one." This abolition of intellectuals as a class is also known as "the socialization of intellect and culture."

Another result of the disappearance of the division of labor is the abolition of the distinction between town and country, since this distinction is "the first great division of labor." One of the measures advocated in *the Communist Manifesto* is:

Combination of agriculture with manufacturing industries; gradual abolition of the distinction between town and country by a more equal distribution of population over the country.[4]

Certainly this will have been accomplished by the time the State withers away. The reason for this certainty is given by Engels as follows:

The abolition of the antagonism between town and country is not only possible, it has become an absolute necessity for industrial production itself. It has also become a necessity for agricultural production, and is, above all, essential to the maintenance of the public health. Only through the amalgamation of city and country can the present poisoning of air, water, and localities, be put at an end and the waste filth of the cities be used for the cultivation of vegetation rather than the spreading of disease.[5]

Engels re-assures us:

The abolition of the separation between town and country is no Utopia, it is an essential condition of the proportionate distribution of the greater industry throughout the country. Civilization has left us a number of large cities, as an inheritance, which it will take much time and trouble to abolish. But they must and will be done away with, however much time and trouble it may take.[6]

Thus, in the stateless-communistic society city and country are amalgamated. There will be vegetable gardens in cities and industrial workshops in villages. No more crowded towns, but everywhere "garden cities."

The fourth feature of the stateless-communistic society is abundance of wealth, which makes that society possible. As pointed out by Marx, the formula, "From each according to his ability, to each according to his needs," can be realized "when, with the development of all the faculties of the individual, the productive forces have correspondingly increased and all the springs of social wealth flow more abundantly." Lenin further explains this:

The State will be able to wither away completely when Society has realized the formula: "From each according to his ability; to each according to his needs"; that is, when people have become accustomed to observe the fundamental principles of social life, and their labor is so productive, that they will voluntarily work *according to their abilities*. . . . There will then be no need for an exact calculation by Society of the quantity of products to be distributed to each of its members; each will take freely "according to his needs."[7]

[4] *The Communist Manifesto*, p. 42.
[5] Engels, *Landmarks of Scientific Socialism*, pp. 243-244.
[6] Ibid., p. 244.
[7] Lenin, *The State and Revolution*, p. 102; italics his.

Therefore, in the opinion of Marx and Lenin, abundance is a very important condition in the new society. Engels, too, is fully aware of this. He points out clearly that the division of society into classes was based upon scarcity and that the abolition of classes presupposes abundance. But Engels believes that this abundance is a possibility not far from now:

The possibility of securing for every member of society, by means of socialized production, an existence not only fully sufficient materially, and becoming day by day more full, but an existence guaranteeing to all the free development and exercise of their physical and mental faculties—this possibility is now for the first time here, but *it is here*.[8]

According to Bukharin and Preobraschensky, this possibility will be realized in the new society for three reasons:

First, a great mass of human energy will be set free which was formerly consumed in the class struggle. . . . Second, the energy and wealth which are used up and destroyed in competition, crises and wars, will be devoted to social purposes. . . . Third, organization not only prevents waste; it also makes possible the improvement of technical production . . .[9]

Such being the case, in the stateless-communistic society, then, "there will be an abundance of all things required." "Poverty and scarcity will be unknown."

The fifth feature of the stateless-communistic society is a change in human nature, which makes that society durable and endurable. As we have seen, a new habit will be formed that will make the State wither away, and the new society belongs to the new generations grown up under new conditions. But that habit is so new that it is nothing less than a change in human nature. Hence there will be no one in the new society like "the present unthinking 'man in the street.' " Each will work according to his ability and take according to his needs. In other words, human nature is to be so radically modified by the new environment that all conflicts will cease. There will be a harmony of interests.

In short, a society with the above five features is what is expected in Marxism. Only then, the dialectics of social evolution ceases to work; social revolutions become a history of the past. Only then, man will become really free; man will control nature, instead of being controlled by nature. As Engels depicts the beginning of the new society:

Then for the first time, man, in a certain sense, is finally marked off from the rest of the animal kingdom, and emerges from mere animal conditions of existence into really human ones. The whole sphere of the conditions of life which environ man, and which have hitherto ruled man, now comes under the dominion and control of man, who for the first time becomes the real, conscious lord of Nature, because he has now become master of his own social organization. The laws of his own social action, hitherto standing face to face with man as laws of Nature foreign to, and dominating, him, will then be used with full

---

[8] Cf. Engels, *Socialism, Utopian and Scientific*, p. 133; italics his.
[9] Bukharin and Preobraschensky, op. cit., p. 61.

understanding, and so mastered by him. Man's own social organization, hitherto confronting him as a necessity imposed by Nature and history, now becomes the result of his own free action. The extraneous objective forces that have hitherto governed history, pass under the control of man himself. Only from that time will man himself, more and more consciously, make his own history— only from that time will the social causes set in movement by him have, in the main and in a constantly growing measure, the results intended by him. *It is the ascent of man from the kingdom of necessity to the kingdom of freedom.*[10]

Thus Engels concludes: "Man, at last the master of his own form of social organization, becomes at the same time the lord over Nature, his own master—free."[11]

[10] Engels, *Socialism, Utopian and Scientific,* pp. 134-135; italics ours.
[11] Ibid., p. 139.

C

Right and Wrong:
Ethics

THE OLD AND NEW TESTAMENTS

The Ten Commandments

The Ten Commandments of the Old Testament, the Sermon on the Mount of the New, are the most familiar ethical writings of our culture. Of course the tone of these two is quite different. Yet it is a mistake to set the Ten Commandments and, in particular, the Beatitudes which begin the Sermon on the Mount, in opposition, the first as harsh authoritarianism, the second as gentle philosophical anarchism. The two are merged in common Christian tradition, which is ethically at bottom a surprisingly Whiggish—even Hellenic—one of avoidance of extremes.

EXODUS

Chapter 19

14 ¶ And Moses went down from the mount unto the people, and sanctified the people, and they washed their clothes.

15 And he said unto the people, Be ready against the third day: come not at *your* wives.

16 ¶ And it came to pass on the third day in the morning, that there were thunders and lightnings, and a thick cloud upon the mount, and the voice of the trumpet exceeding loud; so that all the people that *was* in the camp trembled.

17 And Moses brought forth the people out of the camp to meet with God; and they stood at the nether part of the mount.

18 And mount Sinai was altogether on a smoke, because the LORD descended upon it in fire: and the smoke thereof ascended as the smoke of a furnace, and the whole mount quaked greatly.

19 And when the voice of the trumpet sounded long, and waxed louder and louder, Moses spake, and God answered him by a voice.

20 And the LORD came down upon mount Sinai, on the top of the mount: and the LORD called Moses *up* to the top of the mount; and Moses went up.

21 And the LORD said unto Moses, Go down, charge the people, lest they break through unto the LORD to gaze, and many of them perish.

22 And let the priests also, which come near to the LORD, sanctify themselves, lest the LORD break forth upon them.

23 And Moses said unto the LORD, The people cannot come up to mount Sinai: for thou chargedst us, saying, Set bounds about the mount, and sanctify it.

24 And the LORD said unto him, Away, get thee down, and thou shalt come up, thou, and Aaron with thee: but let not the priests and the people break through to come up unto the LORD, lest he break forth upon them.

25 So Moses went down unto the people, and spake unto them.

Chapter 20

And God spake all these words, saying,

2 I *am* the LORD thy God, which have brought thee out of the land of Egypt, out of the house of bondage.

3 Thou shalt have no other gods before me.

4 Thou shalt not make unto thee any graven image, or any likeness *of any thing* that *is* in heaven above, or that *is* in the earth beneath, or that *is* in the water under the earth:

5 Thou shalt not bow down thyself to them, nor serve them: for I the LORD thy God *am* a jealous God, visiting the iniquity of the fathers upon the children unto the third and fourth *generation* of them that hate me;

6 And shewing mercy unto thousands of them that love me, and keep my commandments.

7 Thou shalt not take the name of the LORD thy God in vain; for the LORD will not hold him guiltless that taketh his name in vain.

8 Remember the sabbath day, to keep it holy.

9 Six days shalt thou labour, and do all thy work:

10 But the seventh day *is* the sabbath of the LORD thy God; *in it* thou shalt not do any work, thou, nor thy son, nor thy daughter, thy manservant, nor thy maidservant, nor thy cattle, nor thy stranger that *is* within thy gates:

11 For *in* six days the LORD made heaven and earth, the sea, and all that in them *is,* and rested the seventh day: wherefore the LORD blessed the sabbath day, and hallowed it.

12 ¶ Honour thy father and thy mother: that thy days may be long upon the land which the LORD thy God giveth thee.

13 Thou shalt not kill.

14 Thou shalt not commit adultery.

15 Thou shalt not steal.

16 Thou shalt not bear false witness against thy neighbour.

17 Thou shalt not covet thy neighbour's house, thou shalt not covet thy neighbour's wife, nor his manservant, nor his maidservant, nor his ox, nor his ass, nor any thing that *is* thy neighbour's.

18 ¶ And all the people saw the thunderings, and the lightnings, and the noise of the trumpet, and the mountain smoking: and when the people saw *it,* they removed, and stood afar off.

19 And they said unto Moses, Speak thou with us, and we will hear: but let not God speak with us, lest we die.

20 And Moses said unto the people, Fear not: for God is come to prove you, and that his fear may be before your faces, that ye sin not.

21 And the people stood afar off, and Moses drew near unto the thick darkness where God *was*.

The Sermon on the Mount

MATTHEW

Chapter 5

And seeing the multitudes, he went up into a mountain: and when he was set, his disciples came unto him:

2 And he opened his mouth, and taught them, saying,

3 Blessed *are* the poor in spirit: for theirs is the kingdom of heaven.

4 Blessed *are* they that mourn: for they shall be comforted.

5 Blessed *are* the meek: for they shall inherit the earth.

6 Blessed *are* they which do hunger and thirst after righteousness: for they shall be filled.

7 Blessed *are* the merciful: for they shall obtain mercy.

8 Blessed *are* the pure in heart: for they shall see God.

9 Blessed *are* the peacemakers: for they shall be called the children of God.

10 Blessed *are* they which are persecuted for righteousness' sake: for theirs is the kingdom of heaven.

11 Blessed are ye, when *men* shall revile you, and persecute *you,* and shall say all manner of evil against you falsely, for my sake.

12 Rejoice, and be exceeding glad: for great *is* your reward in heaven: for so persecuted they the prophets which were before you.

13 ¶ Ye are the salt of the earth: but if the salt have lost his savour, wherewith shall it be salted? it is thenceforth good for nothing, but to be cast out, and to be trodden under foot of men.

14 Ye are the light of the world. A city that is set on an hill cannot be hid.

15 Neither do men light a candle, and put it under a bushel, but on a candlestick; and it giveth light unto all that are in the house.

16 Let your light so shine before men, that they may see your good works, and glorify your Father which is in heaven.

17 ¶ Think not that I am come to destroy the law, or the prophets: I am not come to destroy, but to fulfil.

18 For verily I say unto you, Till heaven and earth pass, one jot or one tittle shall in no wise pass from the law, till all be fulfilled.

19 Whosoever therefore shall break one of these least commandments, and shall teach men so, he shall be called the least in the kingdom of heaven: but whosoever shall do and teach *them,* the same shall be called great in the kingdom of heaven.

20 For I say unto you, That except your righteousness shall exceed *the righteousness* of the scribes and Pharisees, ye shall in no case enter into the kingdom of heaven.

PLATO

The Natural Appetites

It is hard indeed to show the range of Plato's ethical thought. I have chosen to emphasize in what I cite below what one might call his basic "Puritanism" —that is, distrust of the "natural appetites" of ordinary men. But this was an ambivalent Puritanism, because Plato had the artist's fascination with what art can do to arouse emotions close to such appetites. He would banish poetry from his Utopian Republic, but he feels he has to apologize for so radical a step.

I DO NOT THINK THAT WE HAVE ADEQUATELY DETERMINED THE NATURE and number of the appetites, and until this is accomplished the inquiry will always be confused.

Well, he said, it is not too late to supply the omission.

Very true, I said; and observe the point which I want to understand: Certain of the unnecessary pleasures and appetites I conceive to be unlawful; every one appears to have them, but in some persons they are controlled by the laws and by reason, and the better desires prevail over them—either they are wholly banished or they become few and weak; while in the case of others they are stronger, and there are more of them.

Which appetites do you mean?

I mean those which are awake when the reasoning and human and ruling power is asleep; then the wild beast within us, gorged with meat or drink, starts up and having shaken off sleep, goes forth to satisfy his desires; and there is no conceivable folly or crime—not excepting incest or any other unnatural union, or parricide, or the eating of forbidden food—which at such a time, when he has parted company with all shame and sense, a man may not be ready to commit.

Most true, he said.

But when a man's pulse is healthy and temperate, and when before going to sleep he has awakened his rational powers, and fed them on noble

From Plato, *The Republic.* Translated by B. Jowett (New York: Charles Scribner's Sons, 1956), pp. 354-355, 406-413 (The Modern Student's Library).

thoughts and inquiries, collecting himself in meditation; after having first indulged his appetites neither too much nor too little, but just enough to lay them to sleep, and prevent them and their enjoyments and pains from interfering with the higher principle—which he leaves in the solitude of pure abstraction, free to contemplate and aspire to the knowledge of the unknown, whether in past, present, or future: when again he has allayed the passionate element, if he has a quarrel against any one—I say, when, after pacifying the two irrational principles, he rouses up the third, which is reason, before he takes his rest, then, as you know, he attains truth most nearly, and is least likely to be the sport of fantastic and lawless visions.

I quite agree.

In saying that I have been running into a digression; but the point which I desire to note is that in all of us, even in good men, there is a lawless wild-beast nature, which peers out in sleep. . . .

And now since we have reverted to the subject of poetry, let this our defence serve to show the reasonableness of our former judgement in sending away out of our State an art having the tendencies which we have described; for reason constrained us. But that she may not impute to us any harshness or want of politeness, let us tell her that there is an ancient quarrel between philosophy and poetry; of which there are many proofs, such as the saying of "the yelping hound howling at her lord," or of one "mighty in the vain talk of fools," and "the mob of sages circumventing Zeus," and the "subtle thinkers who are beggars after all"; and there are innumerable other signs of ancient enmity between them. Notwithstanding this, let us assure our sweet friend and the sister arts of imitation, that if she will only prove her title to exist in a well-ordered State we shall be delighted to receive her—we are very conscious of her charms; but we may not on that account betray the truth. I dare say, Glaucon, that you are as much charmed by her as I am, especially when she appears in Homer?

Yes, indeed, I am greatly charmed.

Shall I propose, then, that she be allowed to return from exile, but upon this condition only—that she makes a defence of herself in lyrical or some other metre?

Certainly.

And we may further grant to those of her defenders who are lovers of poetry and yet not poets the permission to speak in prose on her behalf: let them show not only that she is pleasant but also useful to States and to human life, and we will listen in a kindly spirit; for if this can be proved we shall surely be the gainers—I mean, if there is a use in poetry as well as a delight?

Certainly, he said, we shall be the gainers.

If her defence fails, then, my dear friend, like other persons who are enamoured of something, but put a restraint upon themselves when they think their desires are opposed to their interests, so too must we after the manner of lovers give her up, though not without a struggle. We too are inspired by that love of poetry which the education of noble States has implanted in us, and therefore we would have her appear at her best and truest; but so long as she is unable to make good her defence, this argument of ours shall be a charm to us, which we will repeat to ourselves while we listen to her strains; that we may not fall away into the childish love of her which captivates the many. At all events we are well aware that poetry being such as we have described is not to be regarded seriously as attaining to the truth; and he who listens to her, fearing for the safety of the city which is within him, should be on his guard against her seductions and make our words his law.

Yes, he said, I quite agree with you.

Yes, I said, my dear Glaucon, for great is the issue at stake, greater than appears, whether a man is to be good or bad. And what will any one be profited if under the influence of honour or money or power, aye, or under the excitement of poetry, he neglect justice and virtue?

Yes, he said; I have been convinced by the argument, as I believe that any one else would have been.

And yet no mention has been made of the greatest prizes and rewards which await virtue.

What, are there any greater still? If there are, they must be of an inconceivable greatness.

Why, I said, what was ever great in a short time? The whole period of threescore years and ten is surely but a little thing in comparison with eternity?

Say rather "nothing," he replied.

And should an immortal being seriously think of this little space rather than of the whole?

Of the whole, certainly. But why do you ask?

Are you not aware, I said, that the soul of man is immortal and imperishable?

He looked at me in astonishment, and said: No, by heaven: And are you really prepared to maintain this?

Yes, I said, I ought to be, and you too—there is no difficulty in proving it.

I see a great difficulty; but I should like to hear you state this argument of which you make so light.

Listen then.

I am attending.

There is a thing which you call good and another which you call evil?

Yes, he replied.

Would you agree with me in thinking that the corrupting and destroying element is the evil, and the saving and improving element the good?

Yes.

And you admit that every thing has a good and also an evil; as ophthalmia is the evil of the eyes and disease of the whole body; as mildew is of corn, and rot of timber, or rust of copper and iron: in everything, or in almost everything, there is an inherent evil and disease?

Yes, he said.

And anything which is infected by any of these evils is made evil, and at last wholly dissolves and dies?

True.

The vice and evil which is inherent in each is the destruction of each; and if this does not destroy them there is nothing else that will; for good certainly will not destroy them, nor again, that which is neither good nor evil.

Certainly not.

If, then, we find any nature which having this inherent corruption cannot be dissolved or destroyed, we may be certain that of such a nature there is no destruction?

That may be assumed.

Well, I said, and is there no evil which corrupts the soul?

Yes, he said, there are all the evils which we were just now passing in review: unrighteousness, intemperance, cowardice, ignorance.

But does any of these dissolve or destroy her?—and there do not let us fall into the error of supposing that the unjust and foolish man, when he is detected, perishes through his own injustice, which is an evil of the soul. Take the analogy of the body: The evil of the body is a disease which wastes and reduces and annihilates the body; and all the things of which we were just now speaking come to annihilation through their own corruption attaching to them and inhering in them and so destroying them. Is not this true?

Yes.

Consider the soul in like manner. Does the injustice or other evil which exists in the soul waste and consume her? do they by attaching to the soul and inhering in her at last bring her to death, and so separate her from the body?

Certainly not.

And yet, I said, it is unreasonable to suppose that anything can perish from without through affection of external evil which could not be destroyed from within by a corruption of its own?

It is, he replied.

Consider, I said, Glaucon, that even the badness of food, whether staleness, decomposition, or any other bad quality, when confined to the actual food, is not supposed to destroy the body; although, if the badness of food communicates corruption to the body, then we should say that the body has been destroyed by a corruption of itself, which is disease, brought on by this; but that the body, being one thing, can be destroyed by the badness of food, which is another, and which does not engender any natural infection —this we shall absolutely deny?

Very true.

And, on the same principle, unless some bodily evil can produce an evil of the soul, we must not suppose that the soul, which is one thing, can be dissolved by any merely external evil which belongs to another?

Yes, he said, there is reason in that.

Either, then, let us refute this conclusion, or, while it remains unrefuted, let us never say that fever, or any other disease, or the knife put to the throat, or even the cutting up of the whole body into the minutest pieces, can destroy the soul, until she herself is proved to become more unholy or unrighteous in consequence of these things being done to the body; but that the soul, or anything else if not destroyed by an internal evil, can be destroyed by an external one, is not to be affirmed by any man.

And surely, he replied, no one will ever prove that the souls of men become more unjust in consequence of death.

But if some one who would rather not admit the immortality of the soul boldly denies this, and says that the dying do really become more evil and unrighteous, then, if the speaker is right, I suppose that injustice, like disease, must be assumed to be fatal to the unjust, and that those who take this disorder die by the natural inherent power of destruction which evil has, and which kills them sooner or later, but in quite another way from that in which, at present, the wicked receive death at the hands of others as the penalty of their deeds?

Nay, he said, in that case injustice, if fatal to the unjust, will not be so very terrible to him, for he will be delivered from evil. But I rather suspect the opposite to be the truth, and that injustice which, if it have the power, will murder others, keeps the murderer alive—aye, and well awake too; so far removed is her dwelling-place from being a house of death.

True, I said; if the inherent natural vice or evil of the soul is unable to kill or destroy her, hardly will that which is appointed to be the destruction of some other body, destroy a soul or anything else except that of which it was appointed to be the destruction.

Yes, that can hardly be.

But the soul which cannot be destroyed by an evil, whether inherent or external, must exist for ever, and if existing for ever, must be immortal?

Certainly.

That is the conclusion, I said; and, if a true conclusion, then the souls must always be the same, for if none be destroyed they will not diminish in number. Neither will they increase, for the increase of the immortal natures must come from something mortal, and all things would thus end in immortality.

Very true.

But this we cannot believe—reason will not allow us—any more than we can believe the soul, in her truest nature, to be full of variety and difference and dissimilarity.

What do you mean? he said.

The soul, I said, being, as is now proven, immortal, must be the fairest of compositions and cannot be compounded of many elements?

Certainly not.

Her immortality is demonstrated by the previous argument, and there are many other proofs; but to see her as she really is, not as we now behold her, marred by communion with the body and other miseries, you must contemplate her with the eye of reason, in her original purity; and then her beauty will be revealed, and justice and injustice and all the things which we have described will be manifested more clearly. Thus far, we have spoken the truth concerning her as she appears at present, but we must remember also that we have seen her only in a condition which may be compared to that of the sea-god Glaucus, whose original image can hardly be discerned because his natural members are broken off and crushed and damaged by the waves in all sorts of ways, and incrustations have grown over them of seaweed and shells and stones, so that he is more like some monster than he is to his own natural form. And the soul which we behold is in a similar condition disfigured by ten thousand ills. But not there, Glaucon, not there must we look.

Where then?

At her love of wisdom. Let us see whom she affects, and what society and converse she seeks in virtue of her near kindred with the immortal and eternal and divine; also how different she would become if wholly following this superior principle, and borne by a divine impulse out of the ocean in which she now is, and disengaged from the stones and shells and things of earth and rock which in wild variety spring up around her because she feeds upon earth, and is overgrown by the good things of this life as they are termed: then you would see her as she is, and know whether she have one shape only or many, or what her nature is. Of her affections and of the forms which she takes in this present life I think that we have now said enough.

ARISTOTLE

Classification of Virtues

Here again is Aristotle, this time in a very summary form indeed. But this brief passage from an English Aristotelian scholar of the last century does present clearly the central ethical concept of Aristotle (and of the Greek, or at least Athenian, gentleman). This is the celebrated doctrine of the Golden Mean. It has been attacked by logicians, who insist that rashness cannot be "excess" of courage, nor cowardice "too little" of courage—this is not in fact a relation in any kind of continuum. Yet the doctrine has proved extremely attractive to Western common sense, and has by no means been rejected in ordinary Christian practice; nor, indeed, is it rejected in Christian ethical theory, especially after the "reception" of Aristotle in the medieval West. Duns Scotus, by no means a middle-of-the-roader, could write: "For no vice is found but is the shadow of some virtue. Pride is only the perversion of a true sense of power."

CLASSIFICATION OF VIRTUES TO ILLUSTRATE THE LAW OF THE MEAN.

We may now proceed to show how the principle of proportion applies under different circumstances and conditions of the moral life—how virtue is the avoidance of all extravagance and inconsistency of life, and how the vices are the perversions of what is "fitting" both in feeling and in conduct.

We may use the Diagram of the Virtues and Vices for the purpose of our illustration.

From Walter M. Hatch, ed., *The Moral Philosophy of Aristotle* (London: John Murray, 1879), pp. 70-71.

(A) Self-Regarding Virtues.

	EXCESS	MEAN.	DEFECT.
i. In questions of pleasure and pain ...... } 1. *Avoidance of pain.*			
(a) *In confidence* ...	Rashness.	Courage	Cowardice.
(b) *In fear*	Cowardice.	Courage	Rashness.
2. *Pursuit of pleasure.*	Sensualism.	Temperance ...	Asceticism.
ii. In giving and receiving of money ..... } 1. *Ordinarily.*			
(a) In giving	Prodigality	Liberality	Meanness.
(b) In receiving ..	Meanness	Liberality	Prodigality.
2. In great wealth ...	{ Ostentation and want of taste. }	Magnificence ...	Stinginess.
iii. In seeking honour ..			
1. In great honour ...	Vain-glory	Magnanimity .	{ Littleness of soul.
2. In small honour ..	Ambition ...... [	]	Unambition.

(B) Virtues Relating to Society.

	EXCESS	MEAN.	DEFECT.
i. In regulation of temper	Passionateness ..	Good temper .	{ Listlessness. Indifference
ii. In intercourse of society .... } 1. Regarding truth .... }	Boastfulness	Truthfulness	Dissimulation.
2. Regarding agreeableness.			
(a) In recreation ...	Buffoonery	Politeness	Boorishness.
(b) In business ...	{ Adulation .... Sycophancy .. }	Friendship	Churlishness.

(C) Semi-Virtues.

	EXCESS	MEAN.	DEFECT.
i. In the emotions of shame .... }	Dumbfounded ..	Modest	Shameless.
ii. In contemplating the fortunes of others .. }	Envious	{ Righteously indignant. }	Spiteful.

PRACTICAL CONSIDERATIONS FOR DETERMINING THE MEAN.

i. In comparing the various states of "excess" and "defect" with their proper ideal, we note that they are all mutually opposed the one to the other.

But the following points may be noted in reference to the degrees of opposition which are found among them:

1. The "mean" man in steering his course clear of all extremes, pleases neither of the extremes: each of them call him by the name of the other. The temperate man, for instance, seems an ascetic in the eyes of the sensualist, and a sensualist in the eyes of the ascetic.

2. The extremes are wider apart from one another than either from the mean. Between the mean and either of the extremes there is a kind of affinity and some elements in common, but the extremes are utterly dissimilar and at variance with one another.

3. The mean is more opposed to one extreme than to the other. There is a twofold reason why this should be so: (a) In the nature of the case there is a greater correspondence between one extreme and the mean, than between the other—the natural affinities being greater. (β) From our own

susceptibilities: we are more *prone* to one thing than to another; and that extreme is the worst towards which we are the more easily led.

ii. We have now said enough to show what is implied in the dictum that Virtue is a "mean state": it is an ideal standard by which all conduct and all feeling might be made to assume the noblest conceivable form.

But in delineating this perfect conception of our actual life we have implied that it is a difficult task to realize it. The beauty of life is so easily marred: the estimate of times and means which give the exact turn to action, is so easily mistaken, that it is difficult indeed to be virtuous after this ideal pattern.

We may, however, suggest a few simple rules which may serve for our guidance in the effort to attain to the perfect "fitness" of virtue.

1. Avoid the worst extreme:—though you should rebound to the other extreme, choose the least of evils.

2. Avoid your besetting sin: set yourself resolutely against that form of evil to which your own tendencies incline you most easily.

3. Avoid pleasure above all things: admire and praise the charms which pleasure can afford, but dismiss it from your aims as the Greek counsellors voted to dismiss Helen.

Still rules are for the most part futile: no system of casuistry can anticipate the infinite complications of circumstance. The varied shapes and combinations of circumstance must be judged separately, as each new phase arises. The only sure index is the Moral Sense of the agent. [To train and educate that Moral Sense until it becomes an unerring instinct, or Conscience, is the work of life, and requires very favourable conditions of discipline and experience.] The Moral Sense must take an instantaneous survey of what has to be done under the conditions of the moment, and its judgment, when fully educated, will be infallibly right.

EPICTETUS

The Practice of Stoicism

*Epictetus (about 100 A.D.) was a Greek slave who became a famous phi-
losopher and teacher. He was a Stoic, a follower of a philosophy of life
which served the ruling classes of the imperial Graeco-Roman world as a
religion of high-minded duty. Stoicism put the gods quite as far from men as
did the Epicureanism of Lucretius. It came close, as indeed did Aristotle
himself in his doctrine of* theoria, *to setting up an ideal of complete detachment from the world of the flesh, an almost Buddhist* nirvana. *This is the
Stoic doctrine of* ataraxia, *impassiveness (reflected characteristically in our
contemporary culture by one of the new tranquillizers, marketed as* Atarax).
*But in practice Stoicism was no more than another form of the eternal West-
ern Puritanism, disciplining but not wholly denying the flesh, and—in Epictetus at least—by no means without a wry and practical sense of humor. We
do not have Epictetus' own works, but instead a very full account of his
teachings by a pupil, Arrian. In his main work, Arrian goes into lively and
concrete detail; but he made a less lively summary of the master's work,
known as the Handbook (Encheiridion) which, if not quite so interesting, is
a very good survey, from which I quote at some length.*

OF ALL EXISTING THINGS SOME ARE IN OUR POWER, AND OTHERS ARE NOT
in our power. In our power are thought, impulse, will to get and will to
avoid, and, in a word, everything which is our own doing. Things not in our
power include the body, property, reputation, office, and, in a word, everything which is not our own doing. Things in our power are by nature free,
unhindered, untrammelled; things not in our power are weak, servile, subject
to hindrance, dependent on others. Remember then that if you imagine
that what is naturally slavish is free, and what is naturally another's is your
own, you will be hampered, you will mourn, you will be put to confusion,
you will blame gods and men; but if you think that only your own belongs

From Epictetus, *The Discourses and Manual.* Translated with Introduction and
Notes by P. E. Matheson, Vol. II (Oxford: The Clarendon Press, 1916), pp. 213-
219, 234.

to you, and that what is another's is indeed another's, no one will ever put compulsion or hindrance on you, you will blame none, you will accuse none, you will do nothing against your will, no one will harm you, you will have no enemy, for no harm can touch you.

Aiming then at these high matters, you must remember that to attain them requires more than ordinary effort; you will have to give up some things entirely, and put off others for the moment. And if you would have these also—office and wealth—it may be that you will fail to get them, just because your desire is set on the former, and you will certainly fail to attain those things which alone bring freedom and happiness.

Make it your study then to confront every harsh impression with the words, "You are but an impression, and not at all what you seem to be." Then test it by those rules that you possess; and first by this—the chief test of all—"Is it concerned with what is in our power or with what is not in our power?" And if it is concerned with what is not in our power, be ready with the answer that it is nothing to you.

Remember that the will to get promises attainment of what you will, and the will to avoid promises escape from what you avoid; and he who fails to get what he wills is unfortunate, and he who does not escape what he wills to avoid is miserable. If then you try to avoid only what is unnatural in the region within your control, you will escape from all that you avoid; but if you try to avoid disease or death or poverty you will be miserable.

Therefore let your will to avoid have no concern with what is not in man's power; direct it only to things in man's power that are contrary to nature. But for the moment you must utterly remove the will to get; for if you will to get something not in man's power you are bound to be unfortunate; while none of the things in man's power that you could honourably will to get is yet within your reach. Impulse to act and not to act, these are your concern; yet exercise them gently and without strain, and provisionally.

When anything, from the meanest thing upwards, is attractive or serviceable or an object of affection, remember always to say to yourself, "What is its nature?" If you are fond of a jug, say you are fond of a jug; then you will not be disturbed if it be broken. If you kiss your child or your wife, say to yourself that you are kissing a human being, for then if death strikes it you will not be disturbed.

When you are about to take something in hand, remind yourself what manner of thing it is. If you are going to bathe put before your mind what happens in the bath—water pouring over some, others being jostled, some reviling, others stealing; and you will set to work more securely if you say to yourself at once: "I want to bathe, and I want to keep my will in harmony with nature," and so in each thing you do; for in this way, if anything turns up to hinder you in your bathing, you will be ready to say, "I did not want only to bathe, but to keep my will in harmony with nature, and I shall not so keep it, if I lose my temper at what happens."

What disturbs men's minds is not events but their judgements on events. For instance, death is nothing dreadful, or else Socrates would have thought it so. No, the only dreadful thing about it is men's judgement that it is dreadful. And so when we are hindered, or disturbed, or distressed, let us never lay the blame on others, but on ourselves, that is on our own judgements. To accuse others for one's own misfortunes is a sign of want of education; to accuse oneself shows that one's education has begun; to accuse neither oneself nor others shows that one's education is complete.

Be not elated at an excellence which is not your own. If the horse in his pride were to say, "I am handsome," we could bear with it. But when you say with pride, "I have a handsome horse," know that the good horse is the ground of your pride. You ask then what you can call your own. The answer is—the way you deal with your impressions. Therefore when you deal with your impressions in accord with nature, then you may be proud indeed, for your pride will be in a good which is your own.

When you are on a voyage, and your ship is at anchorage, and you disembark to get fresh water, you may pick up a small shellfish or a truffle by the way, but you must keep your attention fixed on the ship, and keep looking towards it constantly, to see if the Helmsman calls you; and if he does, you have to leave everything, or be bundled on board with your legs tied like a sheep. So it is in life. If you have a dear wife or child given you, they are like the shellfish or the truffle, they are very well in their way. Only, if the Helmsman call, run back to your ship, leave all else, and do not look behind you. And if you are old, never go far from the ship, so that when you are called you may not fail to appear.

Ask not that events should happen as you will, but let your will be that events should happen as they do, and you shall have peace.

Sickness is a hindrance to the body, but not to the will, unless the will consent. Lameness is a hindrance to the leg, but not to the will. Say this to yourself at each event that happens, for you shall find that though it hinders something else it will not hinder you.

When anything happens to you, always remember to turn to yourself and ask what faculty you have to deal with it. If you see a beautiful boy or a beautiful woman, you will find continence the faculty to exercise there; if trouble is laid on you, you will find endurance; if ribaldry, you will find patience. And if you train yourself in this habit your impressions will not carry you away.

Never say of anything, "I lost it," but say, "I gave it back." Has your child died? It was given back. Has your wife died? She was given back. Has your estate been taken from you? Was not this also given back? But you say, "He who took it from me is wicked." What does it matter to you through whom the Giver asked it back? As long as He gives it you, take care of it, but not as your own; treat it as passers-by treat an inn. . . .

Remember that you must behave in life as you would at a banquet. A dish is handed round and comes to you; put out your hand and take it politely. It passes you; do not stop it. It has not reached you; do not be impatient to get it, but wait till your turn comes. Bear yourself thus towards children, wife, office, wealth, and one day you will be worthy to banquet with the gods. But if when they are set before you, you do not take them but despise them, then you shall not only share the gods' banquet, but shall share their rule. For by so doing Diogenes and Heraclitus and men like them were called divine and deserved the name.

When you see a man shedding tears in sorrow for a child abroad or dead, or for loss of property, beware that you are not carried away by the impression that it is outward ills that make him miserable. Keep this thought by you: "What distresses him is not the event, for that does not distress another, but his judgement on the event." Therefore do not hesitate to sympathize with him so far as words go, and if it so chance, even to groan with him; but take heed that you do not also groan in your inner being.

Remember that you are an actor in a play, and the Playwright chooses the manner of it: if he wants it short, it is short; if long, it is long. If he wants you to act a poor man you must act the part with all your powers; and so if your part be a cripple or a magistrate or a plain man. For your business is to act the character that is given you and act it well; the choice of the cast is Another's.

On no occasion call yourself a philosopher, nor talk at large of your principles among the multitude, but act on your principles. For instance, at a banquet do not say how one ought to eat, but eat as you ought. Remember that Socrates had so completely got rid of the thought of display that when men came and wanted an introduction to philosophers he took them to be introduced; so patient of neglect was he. And if a discussion arise among the multitude on some principle, keep silent for the most part; for you are in great danger of blurting out some undigested thought. And when some one says to you, "You know nothing," and you do not let it provoke you, then know that you are really on the right road. For sheep do not bring grass to their shepherds and show them how much they have eaten, but they digest their fodder and then produce it in the form of wool and milk. Do the same yourself; instead of displaying your principles to the multitude, show them the results of the principles you have digested.

ST. AUGUSTINE

Christian vs. Pagan Ethics

This passage from St. Augustine's City of God *is particularly useful for its contrast of the Christian and the pagan ethical attitudes as they seem to St. Augustine. The work of Marcus Varro to which he refers is lost. Some commentators might feel that Varro's 288 "sects" is an underestimate.*

1. *That Varro has made out that two hundred and eighty-eight different sects of philosophy might be formed by the various opinions regarding the supreme good*

AS I SEE THAT I HAVE STILL TO DISCUSS THE FIT DESTINIES OF THE TWO cities, the earthly and the heavenly, I must first explain, so far as the limits of this work allow me, the reasonings by which men have attempted to make for themselves a happiness in this unhappy life, in order that it may be evident, not only from divine authority, but also from such reasons as can be adduced to unbelievers, how the empty dreams of the philosophers differ from the hope which God gives to us, and from the substantial fulfilment of it which He will give us as our blessedness. Philosophers have expressed a great variety of diverse opinions regarding the ends of goods and of evils, and this question they have eagerly canvassed, that they might, if possible, discover what makes a man happy. For the end of our good is that for the sake of which other things are to be desired, while it is to be desired for its own sake; and the end of evil is that on account of which other things are to be shunned, while it is avoided on its own account. Thus, by the *end of good*, we at present mean, not that by which good is destroyed, so that it no longer exists, but that by which it is finished, so that it becomes complete; and by the *end of evil* we mean, not that which abolishes it, but that which completes its development. These two ends, therefore, are the supreme good and the supreme evil; and, as I have said, those who have in this vain life

From Saint Augustine, *The City of God*. Translated by Marcus Dods (New York: The Modern Library, 1950), pp. 669-679.

professed the study of wisdom have been at great pains to discover these
ends, and to obtain the supreme good and avoid the supreme evil in this
life. And although they erred in a variety of ways, yet natural insight has
prevented them from wandering from the truth so far that they have not
placed the supreme good and evil, some in the soul, some in the body,
and some in both. From this tripartite distribution of the sects of
philosophy, Marcus Varro, in his book *De Philosophia,*[1] has drawn so
large a variety of opinions, that, by a subtle and minute analysis of distinctions, he numbers without difficulty as many as 288 sects—not that
these have actually existed, but sects which are possible.

To illustrate briefly what he means, I must begin with his own introductory statement in the above-mentioned book, that there are four
things which men desire, as it were by nature without a master, without
the help of any instruction, without industry or the art of living which
is called virtue, and which is certainly learned:[2] either pleasure, which
is an agreeable stirring of the bodily sense; or repose, which excludes
every bodily inconvenience; or both these, which Epicurus calls by
the one name, pleasure; or the primary objects of nature,[3] which comprehend the things already named and other things, either bodily, such
as health, and safety, and integrity of the members, or spiritual, such as
the greater and less mental gifts that are found in men. Now these
four things—pleasure, repose, the two combined, and the primary objects of nature—exist in us in such sort that we must either desire virtue
on their account, or them for the sake of virtue, or both for their own
sake; and consequently there arise from this distinction twelve sects,
for each is by this consideration tripled. I will illustrate this in one instance,
and, having done so, it will not be difficult to understand the others. According, then, as bodily pleasure is subjected, preferred, or united to virtue,
there are three sects. It is subjected to virtue when it is chosen as sub-
servient to virtue. Thus it is a duty of virtue to live for one's country, and
for its sake to beget children, neither of which can be done without bodily
pleasure. For there is pleasure in eating and drinking, pleasure also in
sexual intercourse. But when it is preferred to virtue, it is desired for its
own sake, and virtue is chosen only for its sake, and to effect nothing else
than the attainment or preservation of bodily pleasure. And this, indeed,
is to make life hideous; for where virtue is the slave of pleasure it no
longer deserves the name of virtue. Yet even this disgraceful distortion
has found some philosophers to patronize and defend it. Then virtue is
united to pleasure when neither is desired for the other's sake, but both
for their own. And therefore, as pleasure, according as it is subjected,
preferred, or united to virtue, makes three sects, so also do repose, pleasure and repose combined, and the prime natural blessings, make their

---

[1] Not extant.
[2] Alluding to the vexed question whether virtue could be taught.
[3] The *prima naturæ*, or πρῶτα χατὰ Φύδιν of the Stoics.

three sects each. For as men's opinions vary, and these four things are sometimes subjected, sometimes preferred, and sometimes united to virtue, there are produced twelve sects. But this number again is doubled by the addition of one difference, viz. the social life; for whoever attaches himself to any of these sects does so either for his own sake alone, or for the sake of a companion, for whom he ought to wish what he desires for himself. And thus there will be twelve of those who think some one of these opinions should be held for their own sakes, and other twelve who decide that they ought to follow this or that philosophy not for their own sakes only, but also for the sake of others whose good they desire as their own. These twenty-four sects again are doubled, and become forty-eight by adding a difference taken from the New Academy. For each of these four and twenty sects can hold and defend their opinion as certain, as the Stoics defended the position that the supreme good of man consisted solely in virtue; or they can be held as probable, but not certain, as the New Academics did. There are, therefore, twenty-four who hold their philosophy as certainly true, other twenty-four who hold their opinions as probable, but not certain. Again, as each person who attaches himself to any of these sects may adopt the mode of life either of the Cynics or of the other philosophers, this distinction will double the number, and so make ninety-six sects. Then, lastly, as each of these sects may be adhered to either by men who love a life of ease, as those who have through choice or necessity addicted themselves to study, or by men who love a busy life, as those who, while philosophizing, have been much occupied with state affairs and public business, or by men who choose a mixed life, in imitation of those who have apportioned their time partly to erudite leisure, partly to necessary business: by these differences the number of the sects is tripled, and becomes 288.

I have thus, as briefly and lucidly as I could, given in my own words the opinions which Varro expresses in his book. But how he refutes all the rest of these sects, and chooses one, the Old Academy, instituted by Plato, and continuing to Polemo, the fourth teacher of that school of philosophy which held that their system was certain; and how on this ground he distinguishes it from the New Academy,[4] which began with Polemo's successor Arcesilaus, and held that all things are uncertain; and how he seeks to establish that the Old Academy was as free from error as from doubt—all this, I say, were too long to enter upon in detail, and yet I must not altogether pass it by in silence. Varro then rejects, as a first step, all those differences which have multiplied the number of sects; and the ground on which he does so is that they are not differences about the supreme good. He maintains that in philosophy a sect is created only by its having an opinion of its own different from other schools on the point of the ends-in-chief. For man has no other reason for philosophizing than that he may be happy; but that which makes him happy is itself the

[4] Frequently called the Middle Academy; the New beginning with Carneades.

supreme good. In other words, the supreme good is the reason for philosophizing; and therefore that cannot be called a sect of philosophy which
pursues no way of its own towards the supreme good. Thus, when it is
asked whether a wise man will adopt the social life, and desire and be
interested in the supreme good of his friend as in his own, or will, on the
contrary, do all that he does merely for his own sake, there is no question here about the supreme good, but only about the propriety of associating or not associating a friend in its participation: whether the wise
man will do this not for his own sake, but for the sake of his friend in
whose good he delights as in his own. So, too, when it is asked whether
all things about which philosophy is concerned are to be considered uncertain, as by the New Academy, or certain, as the other philosophers maintain, the question here is not what end should be pursued, but whether or
not we are to believe in the substantial existence of that end; or, to put it
more plainly, whether he who pursues the supreme good must maintain
that it is a true good, or only that it appears to him to be true, though
possibly it may be delusive—both pursuing one and the same good. The
distinction, too, which is founded on the dress and manners of the Cynics,
does not touch the question of the chief good, but only the question
whether he who pursues that good which seems to himself true should
live as do the Cynics. There were, in fact, men who, though they pursued
different things as the supreme good, some choosing pleasure, others
virtue, yet adopted that mode of life which gave the Cynics their name.
Thus, whatever it is which distinguishes the Cynics from other philosophers,
this has no bearing on the choice and pursuit of that good which constitutes happiness. For if it had any such bearing, then the same habits of
life would necessitate the pursuit of the same chief good, and diverse
habits would necessitate the pursuit of different ends.

2. *How Varro, by removing all the differences which do not form sects, but are
merely secondary questions, reaches three definitions of the chief good, of
which we must choose one*

The same may be said of those three kinds of life, the life of studious
leisure and search after truth, the life of easy engagement in affairs, and
the life in which both these are mingled. When it is asked, which of these
should be adopted, this involves no controversy about the end of good,
but inquires which of these three puts a man in the best position for finding and retaining the supreme good. For this good, as soon as a man finds
it, makes him happy; but lettered leisure, or public business, or the alternation of these, do not necessarily constitute happiness. Many, in fact, find
it possible to adopt one or other of these modes of life, and yet to miss
what makes a man happy. The question, therefore, regarding the supreme
good and the supreme evil, and which distinguishes sects of philosophy,
is one; and these questions concerning the social life, the doubt of the
Academy, the dress and food of the Cynics, the three modes of life—

the active, the contemplative, and the mixed—these are different questions, into none of which the question of the chief good enters. And therefore, as Marcus Varro multiplied the sects to the number 288 (or whatever
large number he chose) by introducing these four differences derived from
the social life, the New Academy, the Cynics, and the threefold form of
life, so, by removing these differences as having no bearing on the supreme
good, and as therefore not constituting what can properly be called sects,
he returns to those twelve schools which concern themselves with inquiring
what that good is which makes man happy, and he shows that one of
these is true, the rest false. In other words, he dismisses the distinction
founded on the threefold mode of life, and so decreases the whole number
by two-thirds, reducing the sects to ninety-six. Then, putting aside the
Cynic peculiarities, the number decreases by a half, to forty-eight. Taking
away next the distinction occasioned by the hesitancy of the New Academy,
the number is again halved, and reduced to twenty-four. Treating in a
similar way the diversity introduced by the consideration of the social life,
there are left but twelve, which this difference had doubled to twenty-four.
Regarding these twelve, no reason can be assigned why they should not
be called sects. For in them the sole inquiry is regarding the supreme good
and the ultimate evil—that is to say, regarding the supreme good, for this
being found, the opposite evil is thereby found. Now, to make these
twelve sects, he multiplies by three these four things—pleasure, repose,
pleasure and repose combined, and the primary objects of nature which
Varro calls *primigenia*. For as these four things are sometimes subordinated
to virtue, so that they seem to be desired not for their own sake, but for
virtue's sake; sometimes preferred to it, so that virtue seems to be necessary
not on its own account, but in order to attain these things; sometimes joined
with it, so that both they and virtue are desired for their own sakes—we
must multiply the four by three, and thus we get twelve sects. But from
those four things Varro eliminates three—pleasure, repose, pleasure and
repose combined—not because he thinks these are not worthy of the
place assigned them, but because they are included in the primary objects
of nature. And what need is there, at any rate, to make a threefold division out of these two ends, pleasure and repose, taking them first severally
and then conjunctly, since both they, and many other things besides, are
comprehended in the primary objects of nature? Which of the three remaining sects must be chosen? This is the question that Varro dwells
upon. For whether one of these three or some other be chosen, reason
forbids that more than one be true. This we shall afterwards see; but meanwhile let us explain as briefly and distinctly as we can how Varro makes
his selection from these three, that is, from the sects which severally hold
that the primary objects of nature are to be desired for virtue's sake, that
virtue is to be desired for their sake, and that virtue and these objects are
to be desired each for their own sake.

3. *Which of the three leading opinions regarding the chief good should be preferred, according to Varro, who follows Antiochus and the Old Academy*

Which of these three is true and to be adopted he attempts to show in the following manner. As it is the supreme good, not of a tree, or of a beast, or of a god, but of man, that philosophy is in quest of, he thinks that, first of all, we must define man. He is of opinion that there are two parts in human nature, body and soul, and makes no doubt that of these two the soul is the better and by far the more worthy part. But whether the soul alone is the man, so that the body holds the same relation to it as a horse to the horseman, this he thinks has to be ascertained. The horseman is not a horse and a man, but only a man, yet he is called a horseman, because he is in some relation to the horse. Again, is the body alone the man, having a relation to the soul such as the cup has to the drink? For it is not the cup and the drink it contains which are called the cup, but the cup alone; yet it is so called because it is made to hold the drink. Or, lastly, is it neither the soul alone nor the body alone, but both together, which are man, the body and the soul being each a part, but the whole man being both together, as we call two horses yoked together a pair, of which pair the near and the off horse is each a part, but we do not call either of them, no matter how connected with the other, a pair, but only both together? Of these three alternatives, then, Varro chooses the third, that man is neither the body alone, nor the soul alone, but both together. And therefore the highest good, in which lies the happiness of man, is composed of goods of both kinds, both bodily and spiritual. And consequently he thinks that the primary objects of nature are to be sought for their own sake, and that virtue, which is the art of living, and can be communicated by instruction, is the most excellent of spiritual goods. This virtue, then, or art of regulating life, when it has received these primary objects of nature which existed independently of it, and prior to any instruction, seeks them all, and itself also, for its own sake; and it uses them, as it also uses itself, that from them all it may derive profit and enjoyment, greater or less, according as they are themselves greater or less; and while it takes pleasure in all of them, it despises the less that it may obtain or retain the greater when occasion demands. Now, of all goods, spiritual or bodily, there is none at all to compare with virtue. For virtue makes a good use both of itself and of all other goods in which lies man's happiness; and where it is absent, no matter how many good things a man has, they are not for his good, and consequently should not be called good things while they belong to one who makes them useless by using them badly. The life of man, then, is called happy when it enjoys virtue and these other spiritual and bodily good things without which virtue is impossible. It is called happier if it enjoys some or many other good things which are not essential to virtue; and happiest of all, if it lacks not one of the good things which pertain to the body and the soul. For life is not the same thing as virtue, since not every life, but a wisely regulated life, is virtue; and yet, while there can be life of some kind without virtue, there cannot be virtue without life. This I might apply to memory and reason, and such mental faculties; for these exist prior to instruction, and without them there cannot be any instruction, and consequently no virtue, since virtue is learned. But bodily advantages, such as swiftness of foot, beauty, or strength, are not essential to virtue, neither is virtue essential to them, and yet they are good things; and, according to our philosophers, even these advantages are desired by virtue for its own sake, and are used and enjoyed by it in a becoming manner.

They say that this happy life is also social, and loves the advantages of its friends as its own, and for their sake wishes for them what it desires for itself, whether these friends live in the same family, as a wife, children, domestics; or in the locality where one's home is, as the citizens of the same town; or in the world at large, as the nations bound in common human brotherhood; or in the universe itself, comprehended in the heavens and the earth, as those whom they call gods, and provide as friends for the wise man, and whom we more familiarly call angels. Moreover, they say that, regarding the supreme good and evil, there is no room for doubt, and that they therefore differ from the New Academy in this respect, and they are not concerned whether a philosopher pursues those ends which they think true in the Cynic dress and manner of life or in some other. And, lastly, in regard to the three modes of life, the contemplative, the active, and the composite, they declare in favour of the third. That these were the opinions and doctrines of the Old Academy, Varro asserts on the authority of Antiochus, Cicero's master and his own, though Cicero makes him out to have been more frequently in accordance with the Stoics than with the Old Academy. But of what importance is this to us, who ought to judge the matter on its own merits, rather than to understand accurately what different men have thought about it?

4. *What the Christians believe regarding the supreme good and evil, in opposition to the philosophers, who have maintained that the supreme good is in themselves*

If, then, we be asked what the city of God has to say upon these points, and, in the first place, what its opinion regarding the supreme good and evil is, it will reply that life eternal is the supreme good, death eternal the supreme evil, and that to obtain the one and escape the other we must live rightly. And thus it is written, "The just lives by faith,"[5] for we do not as yet see our good, and must therefore live by faith; neither have we in ourselves power to live rightly, but can do so only if He who has given us faith to believe in His help do help us when we believe and pray. As for those who have supposed that the sovereign good and evil are to be found in this life, and have placed it either in the soul or the body, or in both, or, to speak more explicitly, either in pleasure or in virtue, or in

[5] Hab. ii. 4.

both; in repose or in virtue, or in both; in pleasure and repose, or in virtue, or in all combined; in the primary objects of nature, or in virtue, or in both—all these have, with a marvellous shallowness, sought to find their blessedness in this life and in themselves. Contempt has been poured upon such ideas by the Truth, saying by the prophet, "The Lord knoweth the thoughts of men" (or, as the Apostle Paul cites the passage, "The Lord knoweth the thoughts of the *wise*") "that they are vain."[6]

For what flood of eloquence can suffice to detail the miseries of this life? Cicero, in the *Consolation* on the death of his daughter, has spent all his ability in lamentation; but how inadequate was even his ability here? For when, where, how, in this life can these primary objects of nature be possessed so that they may not be assailed by unforeseen accident? Is the body of the wise man exempt from any pain which may dispel pleasure, from any disquietude which may banish repose? The amputation or decay of the members of the body puts an end to its integrity, deformity blights its beauty, weakness its health, lassitude its vigour, sleepiness or sluggishness its activity—and which of these is it that may not assail the flesh of the wise man? Comely and fitting attitudes and movements of the body are numbered among the prime natural blessings; but what if some sickness makes the members tremble? what if a man suffers from curvature of the spine to such an extent that his hands reach the ground, and he goes upon all fours like a quadruped? Does not this destroy all beauty and grace in the body, whether at rest or in motion? What shall I say of the fundamental blessings of the soul, sense and intellect, of which the one is given for the perception, and the other for the comprehension of truth? But what kind of sense is it that remains when a man becomes deaf and blind? where are reason and intellect when disease makes a man delirious? We can scarcely, or not at all, refrain from tears, when we think of or see the actions and words of such frantic persons, and consider how different from and even opposed to their own sober judgment and ordinary conduct their present demeanour is. And what shall I say of those who suffer from demoniacal possession? Where is their own intelligence hiddden and buried while the malignant spirit is using their body and soul according to his own will? And who is quite sure that no such thing can happen to the wise man in this life? Then, as to the perception of truth, what can we hope for even in this way while in the body, as we read in the true book of Wisdom, "The corruptible body weigheth down the soul, and the earthly tabernacle presseth down the mind that museth upon many things?"[7] And eagerness, or desire of action, if this is the right meaning to put upon the Greek ὁρμή, is also reckoned among the primary advantages of nature; and yet is it not this which produces those pitiable movements of the insane, and those actions which we shudder to see, when sense is deceived and reason deranged?

[6] Ps. xciv. 11, and 1 Cor. iii. 20.
[7] Wisdom ix. 15.

In fine, virtue itself, which is not among the primary objects of nature, but succeeds to them as the result of learning, though it holds the highest place among human good things, what is its occupation save to wage perpetual war with vices—not those that are outside of us, but within; not other men's, but our own—a war which is waged especially by that virtue which the Greeks call σωφροσύνη, and we temperance,[8] and which bridles carnal lusts, and prevents them from winning the consent of the spirit to wicked deeds? For we must not fancy that there is no vice in us, when, as the apostle says, "The flesh lusteth against the spirit";[9] for to this vice there is a contrary virtue, when, as the same writer says, "The spirit lusteth against the flesh." "For these two," he says, "are contrary one to the other, so that you cannot do the things which you would." But what is it we wish to do when we seek to attain the supreme good, unless that the flesh should cease to lust against the spirit, and that there be no vice in us against which the spirit may lust? And as we cannot attain to this in the present life, however ardently we desire it, let us by God's help accomplish at least this, to preserve the soul from succumbing and yielding to the flesh that lusts against it, and to refuse our consent to the perpetration of sin. Far be it from us, then, to fancy that while we are still engaged in this intestine war, we have already found the happiness which we seek to reach by victory. And who is there so wise that he has no conflict at all to maintain against his vices?

What shall I say of that virtue which is called prudence? Is not all its vigilance spent in the discernment of good from evil things, so that no mistake may be admitted about what we should desire and what avoid? And thus it is itself a proof that we are in the midst of evils, or that evils are in us; for it teaches us that it is an evil to consent to sin, and a good to refuse this consent. And yet this evil, to which prudence teaches and temperance enables us not to consent, is removed from this life neither by prudence nor by temperance. And justice, whose office it is to render to every man his due, whereby there is in man himself a certain just order of nature, so that the soul is subjected to God, and the flesh to the soul, and consequently both soul and flesh to God—does not this virtue demonstrate that it is as yet rather labouring towards its end than resting in its finished work? For the soul is so much the less subjected to God as it is less occupied with the thought of God; and the flesh is so much the less subjected to the spirit as it lusts more vehemently against the spirit. So long, therefore, as we are beset by this weakness, this plague, this disease, how shall we dare to say that we are safe? and if not safe, then how can we be already enjoying our final beatitude? Then that virtue which goes by the name of fortitude is the plainest proof of the ills of life, for it is these ills which it is compelled to bear patiently. And this holds good, no matter though the ripest wisdom co-exists with it. And I am at a loss to

[8] Cicero, *Tusc. Quæst.* iii. 8.
[9] Gal. v. 17.

understand how the Stoic philosophers can presume to say that these are no ills, though at the same time they allow the wise man to commit suicide and pass out of this life if they became so grievous that he cannot or ought not to endure them. But such is the stupid pride of these men who fancy that the supreme good can be found in this life, and that they can become happy by their own resources, that their wise man, or at least the man whom they fancifully depict as such, is always happy, even though he become blind, deaf, dumb, mutilated, racked with pains, or suffer any conceivable calamity such as may compel him to make away with himself; and they are not ashamed to call the life that is beset with these evils happy. O happy life, which seeks the aid of death to end it! If it is happy, let the wise man remain in it; but if these ills drive him out of it, in what sense is it happy? Or how can they say that these are not evils which conquer the virtue of fortitude, and force it not only to yield, but so to rave that it in one breath calls life happy and recommends it to be given up? For who is so blind as not to see that if it were happy it would not be fled from? And if they say we should flee from it on account of the infirmities that beset it, why then do they not lower their pride and acknowledge that it is miserable? Was it, I would ask, fortitude or weakness which prompted Cato to kill himself? for he would not have done so had he not been too weak to endure Cæsar's victory. Where, then, in his fortitude? It has yielded, it has succumbed, it has been so thoroughly overcome as to abandon, forsake, flee this happy life. Or was it no longer happy? Then it was miserable. How, then, were these not evils which made life miserable, and a thing to be escaped from?

IMMANUEL KANT

The Metaphysics of Morality

It is quite a leap in time from St. Augustine to Kant, but I cannot spare the space for Abelard, or St. Thomas Aquinas, or for such remarkable early modern ethical thinkers as Spinoza, who actually wrote an Ethics Mathematically Demonstrated. *Kant (1724–1804), however, is a must in any attempt to present a sampling of Western writing on ethics. I shall quote for the reader a much better introduction to Kant's famous "categorical imperative" than any I could devise. Here is Nietzsche commenting in his* Beyond Good and Evil:[1]

It seems to me that there is everywhere an attempt at present to divert attention from the actual influence which Kant exercised on German philosophy, and especially to ignore prudently the value which he set upon himself. Kant was first and foremost proud of his Table of Categories; with it in his hand he said: "This is the most difficult thing that could ever be undertaken on behalf of metaphysics." Let us only understand this "could be"! He was proud of having *discovered* a new faculty in man, the faculty of synthetic judgment *a priori.* Granting that he deceived himself in this matter; the development and rapid flourishing of German philosophy depended nevertheless on his pride, and on the eager rivalry of the younger generation to discover if possible something—at all events "new faculties"—of which to be still prouder!—But let us reflect for a moment—it is high time to do so. "How are synthetic judgments *a priori possible?*" Kant asks himself—and what is really his answer? *"By means of a means* (faculty)"—but unfortunately not in five words, but so circumstantially, imposingly, and with such display of German profundity and verbal flourishes, that one altogether loses sight of the comical *niaiserie allemande* involved in such an answer. People were beside themselves with delight over this new faculty, and the jubilation reached its climax when Kant further discovered a moral faculty in man—for at that time Germans were still moral, not yet dabbling in the "Politics of hard fact." Then came the honeymoon of German philosophy. All the young theologians of the Tübingen institution went immediately into the groves—all seeking for "faculties." And what did they not find—in that innocent, rich, and still youthful period of the German spirit, to which Romanticism, the malicious fairy, piped and sang, when one could not yet distinguish between "finding" and "inventing"! Above all a faculty for the "transcendental"; Schelling christened it, intellectual intuition, and thereby

[1] Friedrich Nietzsche, *Beyond Good and Evil.* Translated by Helen Zimmern (New York: The Macmillan Company, 1924), S. 11.

155

gratified the most earnest longings of the naturally pious-inclined Germans. One can do no greater wrong to the whole of this exuberant and eccentric movement (which was really youthfulness, notwithstanding that it disguised itself so boldly in hoary and senile conceptions), than to take it seriously, or even treat it with moral indignation. Enough, however—the world grew older, and the dream vanished. A time came when people rubbed their foreheads, and they still rub them to-day. People had been dreaming, and first and foremost—old Kant. "By means of a means (faculty)"—he had said, or at least meant to say. But, is that—an answer? An explanation? Or is it not rather merely a repetition of the question? How does opium induce sleep? "By means of a means (faculty)," namely the *virtus dormitiva,* replies the doctor in Molière,

> *Quia est in eo virtus dormitiva,*
> *Cujus est natura sensus assoupire.*[2]

But such replies belong to the realm of comedy, and it is high time to replace the Kantian question, "How are synthetic judgments *a priori* possible?" by another question, "Why is belief in such judgments *necessary?*"—in effect, it is high time that we should understand that such judgments must be *believed* to be true, for the sake of the preservation of creatures like ourselves; though they still might naturally be *false* judgments! Or, more plainly spoken, and roughly and readily—synthetic judgments *a priori* should not "be possible" at all; we have no right to them; in our mouths they are nothing but false judgments. Only, of course, the belief in their truth is necessary, as plausible belief and ocular evidence belonging to the perspective view of life. And finally, to call to mind the enormous influence which "German philosophy"—I hope you understand its right to inverted commas (goosefeet)?—has exercised throughout the whole of Europe, there is no doubt that a certain *virtus dormitiva* had a share in it; thanks to German philosophy, it was a delight to the noble idlers, the virtuous, the mystics, the artists, the three-fourths Christians, and the political obscurantists of all nations, to find an antidote to the still overwhelming sensualism which overflowed from the last century into this, in short—*"sensus assoupire."* . . .

Nietzsche is of course unfair to Kant. But it is one of the facts of the intellectual life that in our many-minded Western culture there are a good many people at all times—yes, even in the Middle Ages—among whom the kind of thinking Kant exemplifies almost too neatly arouses intense dislike and indignation—moral indignation. To the morally hard-boiled, the morally soft-boiled are quite simply immoral.

THERE IS THEREFORE BUT ONE CATEGORICAL IMPERATIVE, WHICH MAY be thus stated: *Act in conformity with that maxim, and that maxim only, which you can at the same time will to be a universal law.*

Now, if from this single imperative, as from their principle, all imperatives of duty can be derived, we shall at least be able to indicate what we mean by the categorical imperative and what the conception of it

From John Watson, translator and editor, *The Philosophy of Kant* (New York: Macmillan & Co., 1888), pp. 241-246, 248-250.
[2] Because there is in it a sleep-making virtue, the nature of which is to deaden the senses.—C. B.

implies, although we shall not be able to say whether the conception of duty may not itself be empty.

The universality of the law which governs the succession of events, is what we mean by *nature,* in the most general sense, that is, the existence of things, in so far as their existence is determined in conformity with universal laws. The universal imperative of duty might therefore be put in this way: *Act as if the maxim from which you act were to become through your will a universal law of nature.*

If we attend to what goes on in ourselves in every transgression of a duty, we find, that we do not will that our maxim should become a universal law. We find it in fact impossible to do so, and we really will that the opposite of our maxim should remain a universal law, at the same time that we assume the liberty of making an exception in favour of natural inclination in our own case, or perhaps only for this particular occasion. Hence, if we looked at all cases from the same point of view, that is, from the point of view of reason, we should see that there was here a contradiction in our will. The contradiction is, that a certain principle is admitted to be necessary objectively or as a universal law, and yet is held not to be universal subjectively, but to admit of exceptions. What we do is, to consider our action at one time from the point of view of a will that is in perfect conformity with reason, and at another time from the point of view of a will that is under the influence of natural inclination. There is, therefore, here no real contradiction, but merely an antagonism of inclination to the command of reason. The universality of the principle is changed into a mere generality, in order that the practical principle of reason may meet the maxim half way. Not only is this limitation condemned by our own impartial judgment, but it proves that we actually recognize the validity of the categorical imperative, and merely allow ourselves to make a few exceptions in our own favour which we try to consider as of no importance, or as a necessary concession to circumstances.

This much at least we have learned, that if the idea of duty is to have any meaning and to lay down the laws of our actions, it must be expressed in categorical and not in hypothetical imperatives. We have also obtained a clear and distinct conception (a very important thing), of what is implied in a categorical imperative which contains the principle of duty for all cases, granting such an imperative to be possible at all. But we have not yet been able to prove *a priori,* that there actually is such an imperative; that there is a practical law which commands absolutely on its own authority, and is independent of all sensuous impulses; and that duty consists in obedience to this law.

In seeking to reach this point, it is of the greatest importance to observe, that the reality of this principle cannot possibly be derived from the *peculiar constitution of human nature.* For by duty is meant the practically unconditioned necessity of an act, and hence we can show that duty is a law for the will of all human beings, only by showing that it is applicable to all rational beings, or rather to all rational beings to whom an imperative applies at all.

The question, then, is this: Is it a necessary law *for all rational beings,* that they must always estimate the value of their actions by asking whether they can will that their maxims should serve as universal laws? If there is such a law, it must be possible to prove entirely *a priori,* that it is bound up with the very idea of the will of a rational being. To show that there is such a connection we must, however reluctantly, take a step into the realm of metaphysic; not, however, into the realm of speculative philosophy, but into the metaphysic of morality. For we have here to deal with objective practical laws, and therefore with the relation of the will to itself, in so far as it is determined purely by reason. All relation of the will to what is empirical is excluded as a matter of course, for if reason determines the relation *entirely by itself,* it must necessarily do so *a priori.*

Will is conceived of as a faculty of determining itself to action *in accordance with the idea of certain laws.* Such a faculty can belong only to a rational being. Now that which serves as an objective principle for the self-determination of the will is an *end,* and if this end is given purely by reason, it must hold for all rational beings. On the other hand, that which is merely the condition of the possibility of an action the effect of which is the end, is called the *means.* The subjective ground of desire is natural inclination, the objective ground of volition is a motive; hence there is a distinction between subjective ends, which depend upon natural inclination, and objective ends, which are connected with motives that hold for every rational being. Practical principles that abstract from all subjective ends are *formal;* those that presuppose subjective ends, and therefore natural inclinations, are *material.* The ends which a rational being arbitrarily sets before himself as material ends to be produced by his actions, are all merely relative; for that which gives to them their value is simply their relation to the peculiar susceptibility of the subject. They can therefore yield no universal and necessary principles, or practical laws, applicable to all rational beings, and binding upon every will. Upon such relative ends, therefore, only hypothetical imperatives can be based.

Suppose, however, that there is something the existence of which has in itself an absolute value, something which, *as an end in itself,* can be a ground of definite laws; then, there would lie in that, and only in that, the ground of a possible categorical imperative or practical law.

Now, I say, that man, and indeed every rational being as such, *exists* as an end in himself, *not merely as a means* to be made use of by this or that will, and therefore man in all his actions, whether these are directed towards himself or towards other rational beings, must always be regarded as an end. No object of natural desire has more than a conditioned value; for if the natural desires, and the wants to which they give rise, did not exist, the object to which they are directed would have no value at all. So far are the natural desires and wants from having an absolute value, so far are they from being sought simply for themselves that every rational being must wish to be entirely free from their influence. The value of every object which human action is the means of obtaining, is, therefore, always conditioned. And even beings whose existence depends upon nature, not upon our will, if they are without reason, have only the relative value of means, and are therefore called *things*. Rational beings, on the other hand, are called *persons,* because their very nature shows them to be ends in themselves, that is, something which cannot be made use of simply as a means. A person being thus an object of respect, a certain limit is placed upon arbitrary will. Persons are not purely subjective ends, whose existence has a value *for us* as the effect of our actions, but they are objective ends, or things whose existence is an end in itself, for which no other end can be substituted. If all value were conditioned, and therefore contingent, it would be impossible to show that there is any supreme practical principle whatever.

If, then, there is a supreme practical principle, a principle which in relation to the human will is a categorical imperative, it must be an *objective* principle of the will, and must be able to serve as a universal practical law. For, such a principle must be derived from the idea of that which is necessarily an end for every one because it is an *end in itself*. Its foundation is this, that *rational nature exists as an end in itself.* Man necessarily conceives of his own existence in this way, and so far this is a *subjective* principle of human action. But in this way also every other rational being conceives of his own existence, and for the very same reason; hence the principle is also *objective,* and from it, as the highest practical ground, all laws of the will must be capable of being derived. The practical imperative will therefore be this: *Act so as to use humanity, whether in your own person or in the person of another, always as an end, never as merely a means. . . .*

All rational beings stand under the law, that each should treat himself and others, *never simply as means,* but always as *at the same time ends in themselves*. Thus there arises a systematic combination of rational beings through the medium of common objective laws. This may well be called a kingdom of ends, because the object of those laws is just to relate all rational beings to one another as ends and means. Of course this kingdom of ends is merely an ideal.

Morality, then, consists in the relation of all action to the system of laws which alone makes possible a kingdom of ends. These laws must belong to the nature of every rational being, and must proceed from his own will. The principle of the will, therefore, is, that no action should be done from any other maxim than one which is consistent with a universal law. This may be expressed in the formula: *Act so that the will may regard itself as in its maxims laying down universal laws.* Now, if the maxims of rational beings are not by their very nature in harmony with this objective principle, the principle of a universal system of laws, the necessity of acting in conformity with that principle is called practical obligation or *duty*. No doubt duty does not apply to the sovereign will in the kingdom of ends, but it applies to every member of it, and to all in equal measure. *Autonomy* is thus the foundation of the moral value of man and of every other rational being.

The three ways in which the principle of morality has been formulated are at bottom simply different statements of the same law, and each implies the other two.

An absolutely good will, then, the principle of which must be a categorical imperative, will be undetermined as regards all objects, and will contain merely the *form of volition* in general, a form which rests upon the *autonomy* of the will. The one law which the will of every rational being imposes upon itself, and imposes without reference to any natural impulse or any interest, is, that the maxims of every good will must be capable of being made a universal law.

How *such an a priori synthetic practical proposition is possible,* and why it is necessary, is a problem which it is not the task of a metaphysic of morality to solve. We have not even affirmed it to be true, much less have we attempted to prove its truth. To prove that practical reason is capable of being employed synthetically, and that morality is not a mere fiction of the brain, requires us to enter upon a criticism of the faculty of practical reason itself.

JEREMY BENTHAM

The Principle of Utility

Jeremy Bentham (1748–1833) was an English philosopher—indeed a phi-
losopher in the old-fashioned sense used on the vaudeville stage, absent-
minded, eccentric, pleasantly pompous, full of ideas, some of which were
practical enough, but never himself engaged in practical affairs. He coined
many phrases and words, of which "international" has proved indispensa-
ble. His ethical position is known as "hedonism," from a Greek root mean-
ing "pleasure," and is a constant of Western ethical thought from the
Epicureans on. But it is significant that Bentham, and his English Utilitarian
followers like J. S. Mill, in this respect like Epicurus and Lucretius, were
far from meaning by "pleasure" what Babbitt, Hollywood, and Mrs.
Grundy mean by pleasure, that is, somewhat disreputable self-indulgence
in the varied delights of the flesh. No, these hedonistic philosophers usually
set specific ethical standards close to Stoic and Christian self-discipline,
and even austerity. I should not for a moment deny, however, that the
"principle of utility" outlined in the famous and very Benthamite passage
below has been used to defend far less altruistic and high-minded standards
than those we associate with Christian ethics.

I. NATURE HAS PLACED MANKIND UNDER THE GOVERNANCE OF TWO
sovereign masters, *pain* and *pleasure*. It is for them alone to point out what
we ought to do, as well as to determine what we shall do. On the one
hand the standard of right and wrong, on the other the chain of causes and
effects, are fastened to their throne. They govern us in all we do, in all we
say, in all we think: every effort we can make to throw off our subjection,
will serve but to demonstrate and confirm it. In words a man may pretend
to abjure their empire: but in reality he will remain subject to it all the
while. The *principle of utility* recognizes this subjection, and assumes it for
the foundation of that system, the object of which is to rear the fabric of
felicity by the hands of reason and of law. Systems which attempt to ques-

From Crane Brinton, ed., *Age of Reason Reader* (New York: The Viking Press, 1956), pp. 93-97.

tion it deal in sounds instead of sense, in caprice instead of reason, in darkness instead of light.

But enough of metaphor and declamation: it is not by such means that moral science is to be improved.

II. The principle of utility is the foundation of the present work: it will be proper therefore at the outset to give an explicit and determinate account of what is meant by it. By the principle of utility is meant that principle which approves or disapproves of every action whatsoever, according to the tendency which it appears to have to augment or diminish the happiness of the party whose interest is in question: or, what is the same thing in other words, to promote or to oppose that happiness. I say of every action whatsoever; and therefore not only of every action of a private individual, but of every measure of government.

III. By utility is meant that property in any object, whereby it tends to produce benefit, advantage, pleasure, good, or happiness, (all this in the present case comes to the same thing) or (what comes again to the same thing) to prevent the happening of mischief, pain, evil, or unhappiness to the party whose interest is considered: if that party be the community in general, then the happiness of the community: if a particular individual, then the happiness of that individual.

IV. The interest of the community is one of the most general expressions that can occur in the phraseology of morals: no wonder that the meaning of it is often lost. When it has a meaning it is this. The community is a fictitious *body,* composed of the individual persons who are considered as constituting as it were its *members.* The interest of the community then is, what?—the sum of the interests of the several members who compose it.

V. It is in vain to talk of the interest of the community, without understanding what is the interest of the individual. A thing is said to promote the interest, or to be *for* the interest, of an individual, when it tends to add to the sum total of his pleasures: or, what comes to the same thing, to diminish the sum total of his pains.

VI. An action then may be said to be conformable to the principle of utility, or, for shortness' sake, to utility, (meaning with respect to the community at large) when the tendency it has to augment the happiness of the community is greater than any it has to diminish it.

VII. A measure of government (which is but a particular kind of action, performed by a particular person or persons) may be said to be conformable to or dictated by the principle of utility, when in like manner the tendency which it has to augment the happiness of the community is greater than any which it has to diminish it.

VIII. When an action, or in particular a measure of government, is supposed by a man to be conformable to the principle of utility, it may be convenient, for the purposes of discourse, to imagine a kind of law or dictate, called a law or dictate of utility: and to speak of the action in question, as being conformable to such law or dictate.

IX. A man may be said to be a partisan of the principle of utility, when the approbation or disapprobation he annexes to any action, or to any measure, is determined by and proportioned to the tendency which he conceives it to have to augment or to diminish the happiness of the community: or in other words, to its conformity or unconformity to the laws or dictates of utility.

X. Of an action that is conformable to the principle of utility one may always say either that it is one that ought to be done, or at least that it is not one that ought not to be done. One may say also, that it is right it should be done; at least that it is not wrong it should be done: that it is a right action; at least that it is not a wrong action. When thus interpreted, the words *ought,* and *right* and *wrong,* and others of that stamp, have a meaning: when otherwise, they have none.

XI. Has the rectitude of this principle been ever formally contested? It should seem that it had, by those who have not known what they have been meaning. Is it susceptible of any direct proof? it should seem not: for that which is used to prove everything else, cannot itself be proved: a chain of proofs must have their commencement somewhere. To give such proof is as impossible as it is needless.

XII. Not that there is or ever has been that human creature breathing, however stupid or perverse, who has not on many, perhaps on most occasions of his life, deferred to it. By the natural constitution of the human frame, on most occasions of their lives men in general embrace this principle, without thinking of it: if not for the ordering of their own actions, yet for the trying of their own actions, as well as of those of other men. There have been, at the same time, not many, perhaps, even of the most intelligent, who have been disposed to embrace it purely and without reserve. There are even few who have not taken some occasion or other to quarrel with it, either on account of their not understanding always how to apply it, or on account of some prejudice or other which they were afraid to examine into, or could not bear to part with. For such is the stuff that man is made of: in principle and and in practice, in a right track and in a wrong one, the rarest of all human qualities is consistency.

XIII. When a man attempts to combat the principle of utility, it is with reasons drawn, without his being aware of it, from that very principle itself. His arguments, if they prove anything, prove not that the principle is *wrong,* but that, according to the applications he supposes to be made of it, is is *misapplied.* Is it possible for a man to move the earth? Yes; but he must first find out another earth to stand upon.

CHARLES L. STEVENSON

The Semantic Approach

Quite as typical a philosophical approach to ethics in our day is that exemplified by the following passage. Charles L. Stevenson (1908–   ) is Professor of Philosophy at the University of Michigan. His Ethics and Language *is a moderate and tentative application to the field of ethics of the approach variously known as semantic, or analytical, or (mostly by opponents) as "linguistic philosophy." The close relation of this approach to the psychological one should be obvious. Professor Stevenson in his introduction states clearly that he is not writing a full treatise on the whole of ethics, but an essay on a narrowly specialized part of it.*

OUR FIRST QUESTION, THOUGH SEEMINGLY PERIPHERAL, WILL PROVE TO be of central importance:

What is the nature of ethical *agreement* and *disagreement?* Is it parallel to that found in the natural sciences, differing only with regard to the relevant subject matter; or is it of some broadly different sort?

If we can answer the question, we shall obtain a general understanding of what constitutes a normative *problem;* and our study of terms and methods, which must explain how this kind of problem becomes articulate and how it is open to argument or inquiry, will be properly oriented. There are certain normative problems, of course, to which the question is not directly relevant—those which arise in personal deliberation, rather than in interpersonal discourse, and which involve not disagreement or agreement but simply uncertainty or growing conviction. But we shall later find that the question is indirectly relevant even to them; and meanwhile there is a convenience in looking chiefly to the interpersonal problems, where the use of terms and methods is most clearly evidenced.

For simplicity let us limit our explicit attention to "disagreement," treating the positive term by implication. And let us begin by distinguishing two broad kinds of disagreement. We can do this in a wholly general

From Charles L. Stevenson, *Ethics and Language* (New Haven: Yale University Press, 1944), pp. 2-8, 11-12.

way, temporarily suspending any decision about which kind is most typical of normative ethics, and drawing our examples from other fields.

The disagreements that occur in science, history, biography, and their counterparts in everyday life, will require only brief attention. Questions about the nature of light-transmission, the voyages of Leif Ericsson, and the date on which Jones was last in to tea, are all similar in that they may involve an opposition that is primarily of beliefs. (The term "beliefs" must not, at least for the moment, include reference to ethical convictions; for whether or not the latter are "beliefs" in the present sense is largely the point that is to be discussed.) In such cases one man believes that p is the answer, and another that not-p, or some proposition incompatible with p, is the answer; and in the course of discussion each tries to give some manner of proof for his view, or revise it in the light of further information. Let us call this "disagreement in belief."

There are other cases, differing sharply from these, which may yet be called "disagreements" with equal propriety. They involve an opposition, sometimes tentative and gentle, sometime strong, which is not of beliefs, but rather of attitudes—that is to say, an opposition of purposes, aspirations, wants, preferences, desires, and so on.[1] Since it is tempting to over-intellectualize these situations, giving too much attention to beliefs, it will be helpful to examine them with care.

Suppose that two people have decided to dine together. One suggests a restaurant where there is music; another expresses his disinclination to hear music, and suggests some other restaurant. It may then happen, as we commonly put it, that they "cannot easily agree on which restaurant to choose." The disagreement springs more from divergent preferences than from divergent beliefs, and will end when they both *wish* to go to the same place. It will be a mild, temporary disagreement for this simple case —a disagreement in miniature; yet it will be a "disagreement" in a wholly familiar sense.

Further examples are easily found. Mrs. A has social aspirations, and wants to move with the elite. Mr. A is easy-going, and loyal to his old friends. They accordingly disagree about what guests they will invite to their party. The curator of the museum wants to buy pictures by contemporary artists; some of his advisers prefer the purchase of old masters. They disagree. John's mother is concerned about the dangers of playing football, and doesn't want him to play. John, even though he agrees (in belief) about the dangers, wants to play anyhow. Again, they disagree. These examples, like the previous one, involve an opposition of attitudes, and differ only in that the attitudes in question are a little stronger, and are likely to be defended more seriously. Let us refer to disagreement of

[1] The term "attitude" is here used in much the same broad sense that R. B. Perry gives to "interest." See his *General Theory of Value* (Longmans, Green, 1926), particularly p. 115.

this sort as "disagreement in attitude."[2] Two men will be said to disagree in attitude when they have opposed attitudes to the same object—one approving of it, for instance, and the other disapproving of it—and when at least one of them has a motive for altering or calling into question the attitude of the other. Let us be careful to observe, however, that when one man is seeking to alter another's attitudes, he may at the same time be preparing to alter his own attitudes in the light of what the other may say. Disagreement in attitude, like disagreement in belief, need not be an occasion for forensic rivalry; it may be an occasion for an interchange of aims, with a reciprocal influence that both parties find to be beneficial.

The two kinds of disagreement differ mainly in this respect: the former is concerned with how matters are truthfully to be described and explained; the latter is concerned with how they are to be favored or disfavored, and hence with how they are to be shaped by human efforts.

Let us apply the distinction to a case that will sharpen it. Suppose Mr. Nearthewind maintains that most voters favor a certain bill, and Mr. Closerstill maintains that most of them are against it. It is clear that the two men disagree, and that their disagreement concerns *attitudes*—namely, the attitudes they believe the voters to have. But are Nearthewind and Closerstill disagreeing in attitude? Clearly not. So far as their above contentions show, they are disagreeing in *belief about* attitudes, and need not be disagreeing *in* attitude at all. Disagreement in belief about attitudes is simply a special sort of disagreement in belief, differing from disagreement in belief about head colds only with regard to subject matter. It implies not an opposition of the attitudes of the speakers, but only an opposition of certain of their beliefs that refer to attitudes. Disagreement *in* attitude, however, implies an opposition of the very attitudes of the speakers. Nearthewind and Closerstill may have opposing beliefs about attitudes without having opposing attitudes, just as they may have opposing beliefs about head colds without having opposing head colds. In so far as they are seeking detached descriptions of the state of human attitudes, they are disagreeing in belief; for attitudes enter only as a topic for cognitive study.

A parallel distinction holds for the positive term, "agreement," which may designate either convergent beliefs or convergent attitudes. And agreement in belief must still be distinguished from agreement in attitude, even when the beliefs are about attitudes. It will be convenient to use "agreement," whether in belief or in attitude, as the logical contrary of "disagreement," rather than as its full contradictory. People may neither agree nor disagree—as will happen when they are in a state of mutual indecision or irresolution, or when they simply "differ," having divergent beliefs or attitudes without a sufficient motive for making them alike.

Let us continue to preserve expository economy by giving explicit at-

[2] In all of the examples given there may be a *latent* disagreement in belief, in addition to the disagreement in attitude. This is likely to be true of any example that is not painfully artificial; but the present examples are serviceable enough for their introductory purpose.

tention to "disagreement," treating "agreement" mainly by implication. The opposite procedure, which perhaps would seem more natural, has not been adopted for this simple reason: Our distinctions will subsequently be carried over to ethical *methodology*. For this special purpose disagreement requires closer scrutiny than agreement; for although the norms which are generally accepted, and embodied in the mores of any given society, are undoubtedly more numerous than the controversial ones, the latter present instances where methods of reasoning are more overtly employed, and more readily available for illustration and study.

We must now see how the two sorts of disagreement are related, still illustrating our conclusions by examples that are not (or at least not obviously) ethical.

It is by no means the case that every argument represents one sort of disagreement to the exclusion of the other. There is often disagreement of both sorts. This is to say little more than that our beliefs and attitudes must not be compartmentalized. Our attitudes, as many have pointed out, often affect our beliefs, not only by causing us to indulge in wishful thinking, but also by leading us to develop and check such beliefs as point out the means of getting what we want. And conversely, our beliefs often affect our attitudes; for we may alter our form of approval of something when we change our beliefs about its nature. The causal connection between beliefs and attitudes is usually not only intimate but reciprocal. To ask whether beliefs in general direct attitudes in general, or whether the causal connection goes rather in the opposite direction, is simply a misleading question. It is like asking, "Do popular writers influence public taste, or does public taste influence them?" Any implication that the alternatives are mutually exclusive can only be rejected. The influence goes both ways, although at times only one direction of influence may predominate.

There is accordingly a close relationship between the sorts of disagreement that have been distinguished. Indeed, in some cases the existence of one may wholly depend on the existence of the other. Suppose that A and B have convergent attitudes toward the *kind* of thing that X *actually* is, but indicate divergent attitudes to X itself simply because A has erroneous beliefs about it, whereas B has not. Discussion or inquiry, correcting A's errors, may resolve the disagreement in belief; and this in turn may be sufficient to resolve the disagreement in attitude. X was an occasion for the latter sort of disagreement *only* because it was an occasion for the former.

In cases of this sort one might be inclined to reject the expression, "Both kinds of disagreement were initially present, the one depending on the other," and say instead, "Only disagreement in belief was initially present, the disagreement in attitude with regard to X being simply apparent." If X was designated without ambiguity, however, so that the same X could be *recognized* by both parties regardless of their divergent beliefs about it, then the latter idiom would be seriously misleading. One man was definitely striving for X, and the other definitely striving to oppose it; and if this involved ignorance, where one of the men was acting to defeat his broader aims, it remains altogether appropriate to say that the initial divergence in attitude, so far as X was concerned, was genuine. It is convenient to restrict the term "apparent" disagreement to cases which involve ambiguity —to cases where the term that seems to designate X for both parties actually designates Y for one of them.

The relationship between the two sorts of disagreement, whenever it occurs, is always factual, never logical. So far as the logical possibilities are concerned, there may be disagreement in belief without disagreement in attitude; for even if an argument must always be motivated, and to that extent involve attitudes, it does not follow that the attitudes which attend opposed beliefs must themselves be opposed. People may share the ideals and aims which guide their scientific theorizing, for instance, and still reach divergent beliefs. Similarly, there may be disagreement in attitude without disagreement in belief. Perhaps every attitude must be accompanied by some belief about its object; but the beliefs which attend opposed attitudes need not be incompatible. A and B may both believe that X has Q, for instance, and have divergent attitudes to X *on that very account,* A approving of objects that have Q and B disapproving of them. Since it may also happen that both sorts of disagreement occur conjointly, or that neither should occur, the logical possibilities are all open. Hence one must appeal to experience to determine which of the possibilities, in any given case or class of cases, is in fact realized. But experience clearly shows, as we shall later see in detail, that the cases which involve *both* sorts of disagreement (or agreement) are extremely numerous.

We have now seen how the sorts of disagreement can be distinguished, and how (in a very broad way) they are related. There is only one further point, among these preliminary considerations, that deserves mention. Our distinction between the sorts of disagreement has presupposed a more general one—that between beliefs and attitudes. Like so many psychological distinctions, the latter is not easily made clear. Would further analysis serve to undermine it? Does any sharp separation reflect an antiquated school of thought, in which beliefs are so many mental photographs, the product of a special cognitive faculty, whereas attitudes stand apart as the drives or forces of a totally different faculty?

A moment's consideration will show that the distinction can be preserved in a much more legitimate manner. It is possible, for instance, to accept the pragmatic contention that beliefs and attitudes must both be analyzed, partly at least, with reference to dispositions to action. Such a view in no way suggests that beliefs and attitudes are "identical," so long as it is soberly understood. It shows that they are more alike than the older psychologists suspected, but it does not make them alike in every respect. The common genus does not obliterate all differentiae.

If it is difficult to specify just *how* beliefs and attitudes differ, it remains the case that for practical purposes we do and must make such a distinction every day. A chess expert, playing with a novice, uses an opening that appears very weak. An onlooker wonders, "Does he make the move because he *believes* that it is a strong one, or because, out of charity to his opponent, he doesn't *want* to make a strong one?" The distinction here between a belief and a want (attitude) is certainly beyond any practical objection. One can imagine the expert, with constant beliefs about the opening, using it or not in accordance with his changing desires to win; or one can imagine him, with constant desires to win, using it or not in accordance with his changing beliefs. If in imagining this independent variation of the "causal factors" involved one is tempted to hypostatize either "belief" or "attitude," the fault must be corrected not by dispensing with the terms in favor of purely *generic* talk about action, but rather by coming to understand the full complexity of reference that lies behind the convenient simplicity of language. To say that beliefs and attitudes are distinguishable factors, and that an action which they determine will vary with a variation in either one, is to use a familiar English idiom, which makes good sense so long as it is not pressed into some artificially simple mold. It is parallel to the statement that the selectivity and sensitivity of a radio are distinguishable factors, and that the quality of reception which they determine will vary with a variation in either one. Such a statement need not make "selectivity" and "sensitivity" designate hypostatic "parts" of the radio; nor does the parallel statement about beliefs and attitudes require a hypostatic psychology.

In the example of the chess player, it may be added, there is no lack of empirical criteria by which the onlooker may determine *which* attitudes and *which* beliefs determine the expert's play. No matter where the onlooker's inferences may lead him, he must *begin* by observing the expert's behavior, and can find there all the evidence that a practical decision requires. The behavior that enables him to decide this is endlessly more complicated than the simple move of the pawn. . . .

When ethical issues become controversial, they involve disagreement that is of a *dual* nature. There is almost inevitably disagreement in belief, which requires detailed, sensitive attention; but there is also disagreement in attitude. An analysis which seeks a full picture of ethics, in touch with practice, must be careful to recognize both factors, neither emphasizing the former to the exclusion of the latter, nor the latter to the exclusion of the former. Only by this means can it reveal the varied functions of the ethical terms, and make clear how the methods of ethics compare with those of the natural sciences. Only by this means, indeed, can it envisage its proper task; for the central problem of ethical analysis—one might almost say "the" problem—is one of showing in detail how beliefs and attitudes are related.

If we examine the concrete ethical problems that arise in daily life, we shall easily see that they have much to do with beliefs. Unless an object is to be evaluated in ignorance, it must be viewed in its living, factual context. Disagreement in belief about this context, which may in turn occasion divergent evaluations of the object, must accordingly be recognized as an important source of ethical controversy.

The beliefs that are relevant to determining the value of an object may be extremely complicated—no less so than the network of causes and effects in which the object lies. There can be no thought of marking off certain beliefs as ethically relevant, and certain others as ethically irrelevant. Potentially, *any* belief has a bearing on ethics. This is a point which many theorists have been careful to recognize; but they have too often recognized it only for certain aspects of ethics—and aspects which are commonly thought to be of little philosophical interest. When an issue is concerned with the value of something as a means to further ends, then (so the familiar contention runs) a great many beliefs, dealing with means-ends relationships, quite obviously become relevant. But when issues concern ultimate ends—and these issues are taken to be of central philosophical importance—then the relevant beliefs become much less diversified. The beliefs that are then involved are thought to be limited, perhaps, to special divisions of psychology or biology; or perhaps to some peculiarly ethical field that lies beyond the scope of scientific investigation. Such views are not the only ones that can be found in the philosophical tradition, but they are sufficiently prevalent to deserve attention.

Now the present work, diverging from these views, will endeavor to show that the full range of men's beliefs, in all their variety, are no less relevant in establishing ends than they are in establishing means. This conclusion will be based upon a logical and psychological analysis of how means and ends are related—an analysis that is not dissimilar, in its broad outlines, to that found in the ethical writings of John Dewey. The details of such an analysis become somewhat technical, and cannot profitably be developed at present, even in cursory form. . . . But it has been necessary to anticipate their general purport, . . . for they will show that beliefs may be relevant throughout the whole structure of ethics, and that any effort to minimize their variety can only result in grievous oversimplifications.

OLAF STAPLEDON

Moral Zeal, Disillusion, and Ecstasy

W. Olaf Stapledon (1886–1950) was an English writer known chiefly for some very philosophical science-fiction, such as Last and First Men, Odd John, *and* Sirius. *His treatise on ethics is not well known, but I find it suggestive, and at any rate it is a good example—as its subtitle,* A Study of the Relations of Ethics and Psychology, *indicates—of one of the relatively new directions formal writing on ethics has taken in the twentieth century.*

THERE SEEM TO BE AT LEAST THREE MOODS WHICH THE MIND MAY experience with regard to good and evil. I will call them the mood of moral zeal, the mood of disillusion, and the mood of ecstasy. It is ecstasy that I will venture to discuss; but, first, it will be well to distinguish the three moods from one another. They do not necessarily exclude one another. It is possible to have various blends of them in which now one and now another is more prominent. Or perhaps I should rather say that we may attend at once to those diverse aspects of experience which conduce to each of these three moods, and that we may be concerned now chiefly with one, now with another aspect. The mood of ecstasy, indeed, seems in some sense to involve and to transform both the others.

In our customary daily life we seldom experience any of these moods, for we are too closely engaged by the successive strokes of the game of living, to contemplate it as a whole. With little thought as to what it really is that we are doing, we fulfil our private needs and the habitually recognized claims of our neighbours; or we brood upon our defeats, or build castles in the air. Now and again, however, the mind is shocked into a poignant realization of the stark difference between good and bad, and perhaps into some gesture of allegiance to the good.

This mood of moral zeal may sometimes spring from an unusually intense and indignant experience of private need, or from a self-forgetful espousal of the needs of another, or others, or from the spectacle of animal

From Olaf Stapledon, *A Modern Theory of Ethics: A Study of the Relations of Ethics and Psychology* (London: Methuen & Co. Ltd., 1929), pp. 241-251.

171

suffering. Or, again, it may arise from the discovery of some inconsistency
or insincerity in oneself or another. But whatever the origin of the moral
mood, it consists in a white-hot indignation against all that is conceived
as bad, and in particular against all that is conceived as conflicting with
the free activities of human beings and perhaps of animals, or (as some
would put it) against all that is thought of as "contrary to the will of God."
The universe is regarded single-mindedly in relation to the ethical distinction, the great struggle between the powers of light and the powers of
darkness, or between life and death, or spirit's activity and the inertia of
matter. We are so impressed by the urgent needs of living things, and perhaps by the needs of a world regarded as itself alive, that the ethical distinction seems to be an absolute distinction between characters of the real
itself, and no mere accidental result of our sensitivity. If the stars are indifferent to this vast crusade for the good, so much the worse for them.
If they be not themselves alive or seats of life, we may ignore them; unless
indeed they can be made somehow instrumental to the achievement of the
ideal. If, as some believe, the great enterprise of life on this planet must
sooner or later end in defeat, then the universe is contemptible, a brute-
mother devouring her divine foster-child. For nothing, in this mood, matters but the abolition of evils and the achievement of goods.

From this zealous mood we may fall into disillusion.[1] This is experienced
as a definite contraction of the spirit, or a collapse from a more alive to a
less alive mode of being. Our headlong ethical enthusiasm is perhaps suddenly and mysteriously checked, as though by a change of weather. As
though by spongy ground, we are reduced suddenly from a gallop to a
hang-dog walk. Perhaps we have been exhausted by some hidden physiological change, and have projected our jaundiced mood upon the environment.
Perhaps, on the other hand, it is mere thought that has fatigued us and
projected its pale cast upon the world.

Anyhow, from whatever cause, we find ourselves disillusioned about
all values, save probably the fierce negative value of sensory pain. The
normal mind seldom sinks so far as to be *disillusioned* about the badness of
pain stimuli. It may indeed transcend their badness, rise to some degree of
emancipation from their tyranny, through the experience of higher values;
but this transcendence is no mere disillusionment. In disillusion all values
above the sensory level simply escape our apprehension. No longer is the
world a theatre of intense personal dramas, or of the cosmical epic of
good and evil; it is just a tedious and chaotic accident, a foul tangle of
thorns and marshes wherein one has somehow to find a tolerable resting
place. Of course there are sweets, a few rare berries to be captured now

[1] The word "disillusion" may either mean literally the process of admitting
cherished illusions to be in fact only illusions, together with the emotional attitude
of bored disappointment, which such a discovery usually evokes; or it may mean
the disappointed emotional attitude alone, whether it happens to be justified by the
situation or not. Here I use it in the latter sense, namely, to mean the emotional
attitude. It is possible to have an illusory disillusion.

and then. But mostly they turn sour in the mouth, and always after them comes colic. The prudent man takes as little as possible of the hostile world into his system. He loves as mildly and as rarely as possible. He eschews all loyalties. He exerts his will only to keep reality at arm's length. For life, in this mood, seems a long and sleepless night in an uncomfortable bed. We toss and yawn, and stop our ears against the clamour of the world, and construct a defence of pleasant fantasies, or hypnotize ourselves with mildly laborious and aimless antics, to entice sleep.

When we succeed to some extent in this attempt to keep ourselves from being implicated in the world that is over against us, our disillusion may achieve a certain cynical complacency of triumph. And this may sometimes be so intense that, buttressed by a little confused thinking, it may persuade us that we have attained a sublime detachment from ephemeral values and have found the goal that transcends good and evil. When, on the other hand, the demands of the body, or of other persons to whose needs we happen to be sensitive, are so insistent that we cannot disengage ourselves from them, or again when we contemplate the insecurity of all our defences, we may taste abject terror on account of our vulnerability. And this terror, so long as it is experienced only in imagination, may sometimes exalt itself into a kind of pseudo-tragic ecstasy. For we are all capable of masochism—at a safe distance from the actual.

But these moods of triumph and terror are in truth mere phases of the disillusioned flight from the enticing and wounding object of experience. And in defence of this withdrawal we may construct or accept all sorts of theories, the gist of which is always that the difference between good and bad is illusory, and that obligation is a meaningless concept; and indeed that the preference for pleasure rather than pain is itself a fortuitous and crazy bias, which the prudent man will seek to escape as far as possible.

THE RISE TO ECSTASY

The third mood, which I venture to call "ecstasy," is less easy to describe. Some would perhaps identify it with the more triumphant kind of disillusion; for in some sense it certainly involves both triumph and detachment from all desire. Others may refuse to distinguish it from disillusion of the more tortured type; for it is not wholly unlike masochism. Some may claim that it is essentially moral, though it is emancipated from every particular moral bias and every moral code; for certainly it is an experience in which a supreme duty seems to be fulfilled by the stripped and cleansed spirit. Others may think of it as the highest reach of that kind of experience which we call aesthetic; for they perhaps know it best in contemplation of works of art. Some, however, would insist that what is under discussion is simply the religious experience, since it is essentially the contemplation of supreme excellence, and the spiritual gesture which we call worship.

Many, of course, would simply deny that there is any such experience as that which I wish to describe. They suspect that anyone who thinks he has, or did have, such experiences is merely mistaken. Some precious dogma or other (they suggest) demands that there should be the possibility of intuitive apprehension of occult reality, or of value other than teleological values; and so in certain moods of zest a believer may persuade himself that he is face to face with the supreme excellence, when, as a matter of fact, he is merely rather excited. It is so easy to believe that an experience has the character that we want it to have, and even easier is it to assume that a past experience did have the desired character.

In all these spheres there is indeed grave danger of self-deception and faulty introspection. But in the last resort it is only by more rigorous introspection that our error is to be discovered. We cannot afford to discard introspection altogether merely because it sometimes fails us. No doubt many have deceived themselves into believing that they have had definitely super-normal experience. Possibly others, however, really have had such experience, and have been unable to describe it intelligibly to the mystically blind. Indeed, the literature of mysticism is so vast and detailed, and so much in agreement, that the existence, as opposed to the interpretation, of unique mystical experiences may be considered publicly established by the testimony of many persons who, claming to have had it, have established also their own honesty and their accuracy of introspection. But, alas, it is almost impossible to disentangle their data from their interpretations. The professed mystics may have seen the truth, but they fail to describe it intelligibly, and their interpretations are often naïve.

Here, however, I am concerned with something less remote than the experience of the great mystics, namely, a mood which may happen to very many of us if not to all. Perhaps I am not entitled to use the term "ecstasy" to signify experiences which, it may be, are wholly unlike the alleged mystical ecstasy. Yet I adopt this magniloquent word to mark the fact that the experience under discussion is strikingly different from all our ordinary value-experiences, and that it involves a sense of exaltation; and further, that the excellence which it claims to apprehend is conceived as the attribute not of a part but of the whole universe, or of the whole universe as it is presented to the individual. It is an experience which, though it may occur but rarely in the life of any particular person, is not properly called super-normal. I would hazard the guess that, though many might disown the experience entirely, they have as a matter of fact had it, but have failed to distinguish it from other experiences somewhat like it, or have perhaps simply failed to notice it when it has occurred. For it is an experience which must be very carefully introspected if we would neither overlook it entirely nor mistake it for something else. To careful introspection it appears to be neither an enjoyment of teleological fulfilment nor a mystical apprehension of the reality behind familiar appearances. It is essentially, I should say, the appreciation of an unfamiliar and surpassing excellence in the total object of familiar experience. It is not insight into the "reality" behind "appearances," but discovery of a hitherto unappreciated excellence of the familiar world itself.

As with disillusion, so also the mood which I have called ecstasy is very possibly conditioned by the state of the body. As in the one case certain physiological changes seem to diminish our capacity for intuiting value, so in the other case it may well be that other physiological changes induce in us a more delicate sensitivity, or a shrewder percipience. However this be, the mood comes to us with an enjoyment of intensified physical activity, a kind of unusual wide-awakeness. This, perhaps, means simply that we find ourselves at grips with a more stimulating, more vivid, or more complex objective field than usual; or, since this much is also characteristic of the intense ethical zeal, it were better to say that in the mood that I am describing we seem to discover in the urgent struggle between goods and bads a more serene and hitherto neglected aspect. We glimpse the same reality from a fresh angle. Or, to use an imperfect but perhaps helpful image, from seeing things single-mindedly, with monocular ethical vision we pass to a stereoscopic, binocular, or argus-eyed vision, in which the ethical is but one factor. What we see is what we saw before, but we see it solid. Whereas before we could appreciate only the good of victory, now we salute a higher kind of excellence which embraces impartially both victory and defeat.

Very diverse situations may afford occasion for this enlightenment, situations so diverse that it seems at first impossible to find any feature common to them all. Fleeting sense-objects are sometimes potent symbols that evoke the experience. A breath of fresh air may be enough, or an odour, or a clash of colours or of sounds, or such more complex objects as a gesture or the curve of a limb. On the other hand, objects of a very different kind may effect the change in us, for instance, a supreme work of art, especially if it be tragic, or a subtle matter of intellectual study which taxes our powers of comprehension and affords the illusion of emancipating us from our human limitations.

In fact, almost any kind of object may afford the stimulus for this mood of ecstasy, or on the other hand may never do so. One kind of situation, however, is perhaps peculiarly significant for an understanding of the experience. Grave personal danger, or conviction of final defeat in some most cherished enterprise, or the danger or final downfall of some dearest object of loyalty—it is perhaps in these situations that the precise content of the mood is best seen.

It is possible, for instance, to be on the verge of panic, to be reduced to quivering incapacity and terror, and yet all the while to be an exultant onlooker, rapt in observation of the spectacle, yet in a queer way aloof. It is possible even in the compulsive reaction to pain in one's own flesh, and even while helplessly watching a beloved's pain, to be, precisely, in the very act of frantic revulsion, coldly, brilliantly, enlightened, not as to the excellence of pain, but as to the excellence of the universe.

There seem to be two factors common to these experiences. They all involve the vigorous espousal of some need or other, great or small; and they are all experiences of the defeat of the espoused need. They are all occasions of intense psychical activity, and all occasions of defeat. From unusually intense and thwarted desire we seem to wake, without any disillusionment from the ends at stake, into apprehension of value or excellence of an entirely different order. Not that we pierce beyond illusory appearances to reality itself, or contemptuously turn from the shadow to the substance, but rather, as I have said, we appreciate something that was presented before but was hitherto beyond our appreciation. Not even that we "re-value"; for re-valuation implies some denial of the urgency of former values. Rather we prize these even more than formerly; and, just because of this new apprehension, just because experience of this other order of excellence irradiates even the familiar valuations that it transcends, we may be even more active in their defence than we were before our enlightenment. For, paradoxically, the familiar values, even with their new poignancy, are perceived as members in that higher excellence which does indeed both eclipse them and enhance them.

EMANCIPATION FROM TELEOLOGY

Well may we call this mood ecstasy, even though perhaps it is profoundly different from the ecstasy of the mystics. For it is essentially a standing outside oneself, and an aloofness from all the familiar objects of the will, a detachment not merely from the private person but equally from the world and its claims, not indeed to deny them, but to appreciate them with a new serenity. To speak almost in the same breath of detachment and of enhanced appreciativeness may seem inconsistent. But anyone who has ever attempted any work of art must understand this description. For it is only when we stand aloof from our work, that we most justly and most keenly appreciate whatever is good in it. Immersed no longer in the technical labour, with all its incidental but engrossing defeats and victories, we can value without distraction (and therefore with closer attention, and therefore more sharply), the aesthetic whole that we have devised.

I do not mean merely that in ecstasy our private desires may come to be regarded as unimportant and contemptible compared with the needs (say) of mankind as a community of interdependent minds; somewhat as, within the individual's private economy, momentary impulses may be regarded as less worthy of consideration than permanent and deep-seated dispositions. It is not this comparative evaluation of needs and their fulfilments that is in question. In this mood of ecstasy we *seem* in some manner to pass beyond the whole cramping, limiting distinction between good and bad; we may even contemplate with a kind of cold fervour of acquiescence the possibility even that the whole enterprise of mind in the cosmos should fail, that the richest capacity of the universal active substance should never achieve expression in the supreme level of organism, and that all that has hitherto been achieved should be lost. For in this mood not only victory but also defeat, even final catastrophe, is experienced as good. We seem to stand above the battle in which we ourselves are eager and hard-pressed fighters, and to admire it as a work of divine art, in which tragic aesthetic excellence overwhelmingly vindicates all the defeat and pain even of those who may never have access to this vision.

Evidently if this account of ecstasy be true, we have come upon a very serious difficulty for an ethical theory according to which we *mean* by "good" simply fulfilment of activity or tendency. For if by "good" we *mean* fulfillment, it is meaningless even to ask of a certain instance of "good" whether it is an instance of fulfilment or not. Let us, however, put aside this difficulty for the present, and pursue our empirical investigation of ecstasy. It is this radical difference between the familiar values and the value glimpsed in ecstasy that leads some to suppose that in ecstasy the distinction between good and bad is seen to be abolished. This I believe to be an error. Detachment from lower values for the sake of higher is mistaken for emancipation from value itself. There is, no doubt, a sense in which the spiritual life involves a "disintoxication" from the influence of all values,[2] an aloofness even in the most exalted delights. But these negative phrases describe only the process of emancipation, not the end for the sake of which emancipation is attempted. And even so they mis-describe; for there is nothing in them to distinguish ecstasy from disillusion, the somnolent failure to value at all from the awakening into a new mode of valuation and a new sphere of values, unnoticed in familiar moods. It is true that in ecstasy we have peace, and that we are indeed emancipated from all desire, and can accept whatever befalls. This, however, does not imply that we have transcended value, but rather that we have discovered, or seem to have discovered, that whatever befalls is good. We *admire* the issue of fate; we are not indifferent to it. Those who claim that the "spiritual life" consists in an emancipation from value, admit that to the imperfectly spiritual the goal of spirituality constitutes a value, and the supreme value; but, they argue, the goal itself is a state in which value is seen to be illusory. In the spiritual view it matters not whether anyone attains to spirituality, still less whether the world's enterprises succeed or fail. Therefore, we are told, in the spiritual view value is altogether escaped. But this is to overlook the fact, insisted upon often by the mystics them-selves, and even by those who claim that value is transcended, that the spiritual life has its joys. It may be in a sense emancipated from desire, but only in the sense that it possesses what is most desirable, and has no occasion to desire more.

This dispute evidently does not turn on the propriety of the use of the words "good" and "value" with reference beyond the familiar plane of teleology. Rather the question is as to whether the experience is or is not

[2] G. Santayana, *Platonism and the Spiritual Life*, p. 30.

affectively toned, and conatively active. Is it *mere* detachment, *mere* disintoxication, or is it definitely "ecstatic" in the familiar sense? Surely it comes to us as essentially the contemplation of an object *as good,* though as good in a manner very different from the familiar manner. It is not mere contemplation, but admiring contemplation. There is a judgment, implicit or explicit, that the object of contemplation *ought to be,* that it is an end in itself and for itself, and further that when it is delivered to our contemplation we ought to salute it with that gesture of the spirit which we call admiration or worship. If anyone should ask what meaning there is in saying that an object is an end in and for itself, we must answer that in the final ethical analysis it turns out that in *all* value-judgments, an objective situation, such as organic fulfilment or personal fulfilment, is simply judged good in and for itself. We cannot analyse the experience further.

D

Transcendence:
The Mystic Dimension

ALDOUS HUXLEY

The Perennial Flight

Aldous Huxley (1894–   ), English-born but long resident in southern California, hardly needs introduction to anyone interested in twentieth-century intellectual life. Novelist of ideas and essayist, he has always been fascinated by what one may call vulgarly intoxication, from that induced by drugs to that induced by God. The introduction to the anthology of recorded mystical experiences and writings on mystical life which he calls The Perennial Philosophy *can serve us here as an admirable introduction to this section of our study. Critics have often noted the contrast between Huxley's admirably clear, sophisticated, often epigrammatic (dare one say, rationalistic?) prose style and the depths he is trying to sound, depths that usually echo to a very different rhetoric.*

PHILOSOPHIA PERENNIS—THE PHRASE WAS COINED BY LEIBNIZ; BUT THE thing—the metaphysic that recognizes a divine Reality substantial to the world of things and lives and minds; the psychology that finds in the soul something similar to, or even identical with, divine Reality; the ethic that places man's final end in the knowledge of the immanent and transcendent Ground of all being—the thing is immemorial and universal. Rudiments of the Perennial Philosophy may be found among the traditionary lore of primitive peoples in every region of the world, and in its fully developed forms it has a place in every one of the higher religions. A version of this Highest Common Factor in all preceding and subsequent theologies was first committed to writing more than twenty-five centuries ago, and since that time the inexhaustible theme has been treated again and again, from the standpoint of every religious tradition and in all the principal languages of Asia and Europe. In the pages that follow I have brought together a number of selections from these writings, chosen mainly for their significance—because they effectively illustrated some particular point in the general system of the Perennial Philosophy—but also for their intrinsic

From Aldous Huxley, *The Perennial Philosophy* (New York: Harper & Brothers, 1944-45), pp. VII-XI.

beauty and memorableness. These selections are arranged under various heads and embedded, so to speak, in a commentary of my own, designed to illustrate and connect, to develop and, where necessary, to elucidate.

Knowledge is a function of being. When there is a change in the being of the knower, there is a corresponding change in the nature and amount of knowing. For example, the being of a child is transformed by growth and education into that of a man; among the results of this transformation is a revolutionary change in the way of knowing and the amount and character of the things known. As the individual grows up, his knowledge becomes more conceptual and systematic in form, and its factual, utilitarian content is enormously increased. But these gains are offset by a certain deterioration in the quality of immediate apprehension, a blunting and a loss of intuitive power. Or consider the change in his being which the scientist is able to induce mechanically by means of his instruments. Equipped with a spectroscope and a sixty-inch reflector an astronomer becomes, so far as eyesight is concerned, a superhuman creature; and, as we should naturally expect, the knowledge possessed by this superhuman creature is very different, both in quantity and quality, from that which can be acquired by a star-gazer with unmodified, merely human eyes.

Nor are changes in the knower's physiological or intellectual being the only ones to affect his knowledge. What we know depends also on what, as moral beings, we choose to make ourselves. "Practice," in the words of William James, "may change our theoretical horizon, and this in a twofold way: it may lead into new worlds and secure new powers. Knowledge we could never attain, remaining what we are, may be attainable in consequences of higher powers and a higher life, which we may morally achieve." To put the matter more succinctly, "Blessed are the pure in heart, for they shall see God." And the same idea has been expressed by the Sufi poet, Jalal-uddin Rumi, in terms of a scientific metaphor: "The astrolabe of the mysteries of God is love."

This book, I repeat, is an anthology of the Perennial Philosophy; but, though an anthology, it contains but few extracts from the writings of professional men of letters and, though illustrating a philosophy, hardly anything from the professional philosophers. The reason for this is very simple. The Perennial Philosophy is primarily concerned with the one, divine Reality substantial to the manifold world of things and lives and minds. But the nature of this one Reality is such that it cannot be directly and immediately apprehended except by those who have chosen to fulfil certain conditions, making themselves loving, pure in heart, and poor in spirit. Why should this be so? We do not know. It is just one of those facts which we have to accept, whether we like them or not and however implausible and unlikely they may seem. Nothing in our everyday experience gives us any reason for supposing that water is made up of hydrogen and oxygen; and yet when we subject water to certain rather drastic treatments, the nature of its constituent elements becomes manifest. Similarly, nothing in our everyday experience gives us much reason for supposing that the mind of the average sensual man has, as one of its constituents, something resembling, or identical with, the Reality substantial to the manifold world; and yet, when that mind is subjected to certain rather drastic treatments, the divine element, of which it is in part at least composed, becomes manifest, not only to the mind itself, but also, by its reflection in external behaviour, to other minds. It is only by making physical experiments that we can discover the intimate nature of matter and its potentialities. And it is only by making psychological and moral experiments that we can discover the intimate nature of mind and its potentialities. In the ordinary circumstances of average sensual life these potentialities of the mind remain latent and unmanifested. If we would realize them, we must fulfil certain conditions and obey certain rules, which experience has shown empirically to be valid.

In regard to few professional philosophers and men of letters is there any evidence that they did very much in the way of fulfilling the necessary conditions of direct spiritual knowledge. When poets or metaphysicians talk about the subject matter of the Perennial Philosophy, it is generally at second hand. But in every age there have been some men and women who chose to fulfil the conditions upon which alone, as a matter of brute empirical fact, such immediate knowledge can be had; and of these a few have left accounts of the Reality they were thus enabled to apprehend and have tried to relate, in one comprehensive system of thought, the given facts of this experience with the given facts of their other experiences. To such first-hand exponents of the Perennial Philosophy those who knew them have generally given the name of "saint" or "prophet," "sage" or "enlightened one." And it is mainly to these, because there is good reason for supposing that they knew what they were talking about, and not to the professional philosophers or men of letters, that I have gone for my selections.

In India two classes of scripture are recognized: the Shruti, or inspired writings which are their own authority, since they are the product of immediate insight into ultimate Reality; and the Smriti, which are based upon the Shruti and from them derive such authority as they have. "The Shruti," in Shankara's words, "depends upon direct perception. The Smriti plays a part analogous to induction, since, like induction, it derives its authority from an authority other than itself." This book, then, is an anthology, with explanatory comments, of passages drawn from the Shruti and Smriti of many times and places. Unfortunately, familiarity with traditionally hallowed writings tends to breed, not indeed contempt, but something which, for practical purposes, is almost as bad—namely a kind of reverential insensibility, a stupor of the spirit, an inward deafness to the meaning of the sacred words. For this reason, when selecting material to illustrate the doctrines of the Perennial Philosophy, as they were formulated in the West, I have gone almost always to sources other than the Bible. This Christian Smriti, from which I have drawn, is based upon the Shruti of the canonical books, but has the great advantage of being less well known and therefore more vivid and, so to say, more audible than they are. Moreover much of this Smriti is the work of genuinely saintly men and women, who have qualified themselves to know at first hand what they are talking about. Consequently it may be regarded as being itself a form of inspired and self-validating Shruti—and this in a much higher degree than many of the writings now included in the Biblical canon.

In recent years a number of attempts have been made to work out a system of empirical theology. But in spite of the subtlety and intellectual power of such writers as Sorley, Oman and Tennant, the effort has met with only a partial success. Even in the hands of its ablest exponents empirical theology is not particularly convincing. The reason, it seems to me, must be sought in the fact that the empirical theologians have confined their attention more or less exclusively to the experience of those whom the theologians of an older school called "the unregenerate"—that is to say, the experience of people who have not gone very far in fulfilling the necessary conditions of spiritual knowledge. But it is a fact, confirmed and re-confirmed during two or three thousand years of religious history, that the ultimate Reality is not clearly and immediately apprehended, except by those who have made themselves loving, pure in heart and poor in spirit. This being so, it is hardly surprising that a theology based upon the experience of nice, ordinary, unregenerate people should carry so little conviction. This kind of empirical theology is on precisely the same footing as an empirical astronomy, based upon the experience of naked-eye observers. With the unaided eye a small, faint smudge can be detected in the constellation of Orion, and doubtless an imposing cosmological theory could be based upon the observation of this smudge. But no amount of such theorizing, however ingenious, could ever tell us as much about the galactic and extra-galactic nebulae as can direct acquaintance by means of a good telescope, camera and spectroscope. Analogously, no amount of theorizing about such hints as may be darkly glimpsed within the ordinary, unregenerate experience of the manifold world can tell us as much about divine Reality as can be directly apprehended by a mind in a state of detachment, charity and humility. Natural science is empirical; but it does not confine itself to the experience of human beings in their merely human and unmodified condition. Why empirical theologians should feel themselves obliged to submit to this handicap, goodness only knows. And of course, so long as they confine empirical experience within these all too human limits, they are doomed to the perpetual stultification of their best efforts. From the material they have chosen to consider, no mind, however brilliantly gifted, can infer more than a set of possibilities or, at the very best, specious probabilities. The self-validating certainty of direct awareness cannot in the very nature of things be achieved except by those equipped with the moral "astrolabe of God's mysteries." If one is not oneself a sage or saint, the best thing one can do, in the field of metaphysics, is to study the works of those who were, and who, because they had modified their merely human mode of being were capable of a more than merely human kind and amount of knowledge.

ST. JOHN OF THE CROSS

Practical Advice to the Religious

St. John of the Cross (1542–1591), a Spanish Carmelite, is well known for his mystical writings, but like his contemporary, St. Teresa, whom he knew well and with whom he collaborated, he was also an active religious reformer, and a thorn in the side of conservatives. His "Cautions" are practical advice to the religious who wish to attain a state which here sounds very much like Aristotelian theoria, Stoic ataraxia, Buddhist nirvana. For, in spite of analogies one can make between this mystical experience and more fleshly forms of ecstasy, the great preachers of mysticism (I put the matter unfairly when I use the word "preacher") do come out at something very austere, very unfleshly, yes, very unemotional in the Hollywood sense of emotional—a sort of untroubled Puritanism that has won the "civil war in the breast." They can apparently forget, rather than condemn, the world, and can sometimes continue to try to reform it.

CAUTIONS

which any who would be a true religious and would quickly attain to perfection must needs bear ever in mind. Addressed to the Carmelite Nuns of Beas.

The religious who desires to attain quickly to holy recollection, silence, spiritual detachment and poverty of spirit, wherein is enjoyed the peaceful refreshment of the Holy Spirit and whereby the soul reaches union with God, and is freed from the hindrances of all creatures of this world, and is defended from the wiles and deceits of the devil and is disencumbered of itself, must needs practise the following instructions.

With habitual care and with no further labour or other kind of exercise, failing not of his own part to do that which his state enjoins on him, he will progress very quickly to great perfection, gaining all the virtues together and attaining to holy peace.

From Saint John of the Cross, *Complete Works*. Translated from the critical edition of P. Silverio de Santa Teresa, C.D., and edited by E. Allison Peers, Vol. III (London: Burns Oates & Washbourne Ltd., 1935), pp. 220–226.

To this end it must first be noted that the evils which the soul receives come from the enemies aforementioned—namely, the world, the devil and the flesh. The world is the least difficult enemy. The devil is the hardest to understand. The flesh is the most tenacious of all and its assaults continue for so long as the old man exists.

In order to conquer any of these three enemies, it is necessary to conquer them all three; and, if one is weakened, the other two are weakened: and, when all three are conquered, no more war remains in the soul.

AGAINST THE WORLD

In order to free thyself perfectly from the evil which the world can do to thee, thou shalt use three cautions.

Caution the First

The first caution is that for all persons thou shalt have equal love and equal forgetfulness, whether they be thy relatives or no; withdrawing thy heart from these as much as from those; more so, indeed, in some ways, from thy kinsmen, lest flesh and blood quicken with natural love, which is ever alive among kinsfolk, the which thou must ever mortify for spiritual perfection. Hold them all as strangers to thee; in this way thou dost serve them better than by setting upon them the affection which thou owest to God. Love not one person better than another or thou shall go astray, for he whom God loves best is worthy to be loved best, and thou knowest not who it is that God best loveth. But if thou are equally forgetful of them all, as befits thee for holy recollection, thou shalt free thyself from going astray with respect to them, whether little or much. Think not of them at all, neither good things nor evil things; flee from them in so far as thou fairly canst. And, if thou observe not this, thou hast not learned to be a religious, neither shalt be able to attain to holy recollection, nor to free thyself from the imperfections that come to thee hereby. And if in this matter thou desire to allow thyself a certain licence, the devil will deceive thee in one way or in another, or thou wilt deceive thyself, under some colour of good or of evil. In doing that which has been described lies security, for in no other way canst thou free thyself from the imperfections and evils which the soul obtains from creatures.

Caution the Second

The second caution against the world is with respect to temporal blessings. Herein it is needful, if thou wouldst truly free thyself from this kind of evil and moderate the excesses of thine appetite, to abhor all kinds of possession and to have no care for them—neither as to food, nor clothing, nor any other created thing, nor as to the morrow. Thou must direct this care to something higher, namely, to seeking the kingdom of God—that is, to not failing God—and the rest, as His Majesty says, shall be added unto us. For He that cares for the beasts will not be forgetful of thee. In this way shalt thou attain silence and peace in the senses.

Caution the Third

The third caution is very necessary if thou art to learn to guard thyself in the convent from all evil with respect to the religious. Many, through not observing it, have not only lost the peace and blessing of their souls, but have fallen, and habitually fall, into many evils and sins. This caution is that thou shouldst keep thyself with all diligence from setting thy thoughts upon what happens in the community, and still more from speaking of it. This may concern, or may have concerned, some religious in particular: thou shalt say naught of his character, or of his manner of life, or of any of his business, however grave it be, either under pretext of zeal or of desire to remedy matters, save to that person to whom it is right that thou shouldst speak of it, and this at its proper time. Nor shouldst thou ever be shocked or marvel at aught that thou seest or hearest, but shouldst strive to keep thy soul in forgetfulness of it all.

For if thou desirest to consider any of these things, even though thou live among angels, many of them will seem to thee to be amiss, since thou wilt not understand the substance of them. Take thou here for an example Lot's wife, who, because she was troubled at the perdition of the Sodomites and looked backward to see what was happening, was punished by God, who turned her into a pillar of salt. By this understand that, even though thou live among devils, God wills thee to live among them in such a way that thou look not back in thy thought at their business, but abandon them wholly, striving to keep thy soul pure and sincere with God, undisturbed by thoughts either of one thing or of another. Thou mayest take it for certain that convents and communities will never be without some occasion of stumbling, since there are never wanting devils who strive to overthrow the saints, and God permits this in order to exercise them and prove them. And if thou keep not thyself, as has been said, as though thou wert not in the house, thus canst never be a religious, however much thou doest, nor attain to holy detachment and recollection, nor free thyself from the evils that lie herein. For, if thou do not this, however good may be thy intention and however great thy zeal, the devil will entrap thee either in one place or in another, and thou art already securely entrapped when thou dost permit thy soul to be distracted in any of these ways. Remember that which is said by the apostle S. James: If any man thinketh himself to be religious and bridleth not his tongue, that man's religion is vain. This is to be understood no less of inward speech than of outward.

AGAINST THE DEVIL

These three cautions should be used by him that aspires to perfection, in order to free himself from the devil, his second enemy. To this end it must be noted that, among the many wiles used by the devil to deceive spiritual persons, the most ordinary is that of deceiving them under an appearance of what is good and not under an appearance of what is evil; for he knows that if they recognize evil they will scarcely touch it. And thus thou must ever have misgivings concerning that which seems good, when it is not commanded thee by obedience. Security and success in this matter come from taking proper counsel in it.

Caution the First

Let the first caution, then, be that, save when thou art so commanded by obligation, thou be moved to nothing, however good and full of charity it may seem, whether it be for thyself or for anyone within or without the house, without being ordered by obedience. In observing this thou gainest merit and security. Avoid attachment and thou shalt flee from the devil and from evils of which thou knowest not, but whereof God shall call for an account of thee in His time. And if thou observe not this caution, both in little things and in great, however successful thou seem to be, thou canst not fail, either to a small or to a great degree, to be deceived by the devil. And, although thou do no worse than fail to be ruled in all things by obedience, thou strayest and art therefore to be blamed; for God prefers obedience to sacrifice, and the actions of a religious are not his own but belong to obedience, and if thou withdraw them from obedience, thou wilt have to account them as lost.

Caution the Second

Let the second caution be that thou never consider thy superior as less than if he were God, be the superior who he may, for to thee he stands in the place of God. And observe that the devil, the enemy of humility, meddles herein greatly. If thou consider thy superior as has been said, thou gainest and profitest greatly, but otherwise thy loss and harm are great. Keep thyself, therefore, with great vigilance from considering his character, his ways or his habits or any of his other characteristics, for, if thou do this, thou wilt do thyself the harm of exchanging Divine obedience for human, by being moved, or not being moved, only by the visible characteristics of thy superior, instead of by the invisible God Whom thou servest in his person. And thy obedience will be vain, or will be the more unfruitful, if thou take offence at any unpleasing characteristic in thy superior, or rejoice when thou findest him good and pleasant. For I tell thee that the devil has ruined the perfection of a great multitude of religious by causing them to consider these characteristics, and their obedience is of very little worth in the eyes of God, because they have considered these things and not paid sole respect to obedience. If thou strive not until thou come to regard no one superior as of more importance than another, in so far as thine own feelings are concerned, thou canst in no wise become a spiritual person nor keep thy vows well.

Caution the Third

The third caution aimed directly against the devil is that thou strive ever to humble thy heart in word and in deed, rejoicing at the good of others as at thine own, and desiring that others be preferred to thyself in all things, and this with all thy heart. And in this way shalt thou overcome evil with good and shalt cast the devil far from thee and shalt have joy of heart; and strive thou to practise this most with respect to those who least attract thee. And know that, if thou practise it not thus, thou shalt not attain to true charity neither shalt make progress therein. And love ever to be taught by all men rather than to desire to teach him that is least of all.

AGAINST THE FLESH

Three further cautions should be observed by him that desires to conquer himself and his sensual nature, which is his third enemy.

Caution the First

The first caution is that thou shouldst understand that thou hast come to the convent only that all may fashion thee and try thee. And thus, in order to free thyself from the imperfections and disturbances that may arise from the temperaments and habits of the religious, and to pluck advantage from every happening, thou must think that all who are in the convent are workmen who are to try thee, as in truth they are. For some have to fashion thee in thy words, others in thy deeds and others in thy thoughts; and thou must be subject to them in all things even as an image is subject to him that fashions it and to him that paints it and to him that gilds it. And, if thou observe not this, thou shalt not be able to overcome thy sensual nature and thy feelings, neither shalt thou be able to conduct thyself well in the convent with the religious, nor shall attain holy peace nor free thyself from many evils and occasions of stumbling.

Caution the Second

The second caution is that thou never fail to perform any good works because of the lack of pleasure or sweetness that thou findest therein, if it be fit that they should be done in the service of Our Lord; neither perform thou them only for the sweetness and pleasure that they give thee. On the contrary, it behooves thee equally to perform these and others that are distasteful to thee, for otherwise it is impossible for thee to gain constancy and overcome thy weakness.

Caution the Third

Let the third caution be that the spiritual man must never in his exercises set his eyes upon that which is delectable in them and thence derive attachment to them, and perform them for this reason only; neither must he flee from that which is displeasing to him in them, but rather he must seek that which is toilsome and distasteful. In this way he bridles his sensual nature; and if thou do otherwise thou wilt neither lose the love of thyself, nor wilt win and attain the love of God.

MEISTER ECKHART

Idealism

Johannes Eckhart, called Meister Eckhart (c. 1260–c. 1328), was a German Dominican mystic and philosopher whose work has seemed to some anti-Germans to be one of the roots of the persistent Germanic philosophical "idealism" they so dislike. The fragments here cited are probably authentic enough. Of course they don't sound much like Benjamin Franklin. But that's the way mystics are.

FRAGMENTS

MEISTER ECKHART ALSO SAID: HUMILITY EXALTS GOD AND THE MORE I have it, the more he is exalted and the more gently and sweetly his divine influence and gifts flow into me.

That God is exalted by humility, I argue thus: The more I abase myself the higher God rises above me. Humility is like a well. The deeper the well the higher he will stand who stands on the top. Similarly, the deeper I dig down into humility the more exalted God becomes and the more gently and sweetly his divine influence pours into me. That is why I must exalt God by humility.

Meister Eckhart said: We should contrive not to need to pray to God, asking for his grace and divine goodness . . . but take it without asking. . . .

The question has been raised as to whether it is possible to make the senses obey the mind.

Meister Eckhart answered it by saying: If the mind is fixed on God and continues so, the senses will obey it. It is like hanging a needle on a magnet and then another needle onto that, and so on. It might even be possible to suspend four needles from the magnet in this way. As long as the first

From *Meister Eckhart*, translated by Raymond B. Blakney (New York: Harper Torchbooks, 1957), pp. 234-247, 251.

needle hangs onto the magnet, the rest will hang onto it, but if the first drops off, it will lose the rest. And so, as long as the mind is firmly fixed on God, the senses will obey it but when the mind drops away from God, the senses drop off from the mind and are unruly.

I much prefer a person who can love God enough to take a handout of bread, to a person who can give a hundred dollars for God's sake. How do I explain that? Like this. It is the common opinion of all authorities that honor is worth more than any fleeting good. To give a hundred dollars for God's sake is therefore to make a big profit in honor and glory on the money; for the giver, offering the money with one hand, takes in more and better than he gave with the other; but when the poor man extends his hand to beg the bread, he trades his honor in exchange. The giver buys the honor the receiver sells.

There is more to it than that. The poor man, by taking the handout, gets closer to God than he who gave the one hundred dollars for God's sake. The giver is glad to be so good-natured and is proud of it but the taker has to subdue his feelings and despise his status. The giver is much courted for his gifts whereas the beggar is despised and rejected for being a taker. . . .

Meister Eckhart said: Grace comes only with the Holy Spirit. It carries the Holy Spirit on its back. Grace is not a stationary thing; it is always found in a Becoming. It can only flow out of God and then only immediately. The function of grace is to transform and reconvey [the soul] to God. Grace makes the soul godlike. God, the core of the soul, and grace belong together.

In limpid souls God beholds his own image; he rests in them and they in him.

As I have often said, I like best those things in which I see most clearly the likeness of God. Nothing in all creation is so like God as stillness.

It is God's nature to be without a nature. To think of his goodness, or wisdom, or power is to hide the essence of him, to obscure it with thoughts about him. Even one single thought or consideration will cover it up. Such is the divine order of things, and when God finds this order in a soul he begets his Son, and the soul bursts into light with all its energy and from that energy, that light, there leaps a flame. That is love; and the soul, with all its energy, has penetrated to the divine order.

When I pray for something, I do not pray; when I pray for nothing, I really pray. . . . To pray for anything except God might be called idolatry or injustice. Right prayer is prayer in spirit and in truth. When I pray for some person such as Henry or Conrad, I pray least, but when I pray for no one in particular, I pray most of all. Really to pray, one must want nothing, for as far as God is concerned there is neither Henry nor Conrad. When one prays for what God is not, there is something wrong and faithless about the prayer and it is a sign of immaturity. As I said not long ago, when one puts something before God, he makes God nothing, and nothing, God.

When God laughs at the soul and the soul laughs back at God, the persons of the Trinity are begotten. To speak in hyperbole, when the Father laughs to the Son and the Son laughs back to the Father, that laughter gives pleasure, that pleasure gives joy, that joy gives love, and love gives the persons [of the Trinity] of which the Holy Spirit is one.

I have spoken at times of a light in the soul that is uncreated, a light that is not arbitrarily turned on. I am accustomed to hint at it frequently in my sermons, for it refers to the immediacy of God, as undisguised and naked as he is by himself and to the [divine] act of begetting. Thus I may truthfully say that this light is rather to be identified with God than with any [perceptive] power of the soul, even though it is essentially the same. You must know that within my psyche this light takes no precedence over the least and coarsest of my faculties, such as hearing, or vision, or any other that can be influenced by heat or cold, hunger or thirst. This is due to the essential uniformity of the soul. Thus, if one refers the soul's agents back to the soul's essence, the agents are alike and of equal rank, but if the agents are referred to their functions, then some do rank above the others.

Therefore, I say that to the extent a person can deny himself and turn away from created things, he will find his unity and blessing in that little spark in the soul, which neither space nor time touches. The spark is averse to creatures, and favorable only to pure God as he is in himself. It is not satisfied with the Father, nor the Son, nor the Holy Spirit, nor with all three persons together, as long as their several properties are preserved. To tell the truth, this light is not satisfied with the unity of this fruitful conception of the divine nature, but I shall go further and say what must sound strange —though I am really speaking the truth—that this light is not satisfied by the simple, still, motionless essence of the divine being that neither gives nor takes. It is more interested in knowing where this essence came from. It wants to penetrate the simple core, the still desert, into which no distinction ever crept—neither the Father, the Son, nor the Holy Spirit. It wants to get into the secret, to which no man is privy, where it is satisfied by a Light whose unity is greater than its own. This core is a simple stillness,

which is unmoved itself but by whose immobility all things are moved and
all receive life, that is to say, all people who live by reason and have their
center within themselves. That we, too, may live so intelligently, may God
help us. Amen.

LEGEND

Meister Eckhart met a beautiful naked boy.
He asked him where he came from.
He said: "I come from God."
Where did you leave him?
"In virtuous hearts."
Where are you going?
"To God."
Where do you find him?
"Where I part with all creatures."
Who are you?
"A king."
Where is your kingdom?
"In my heart."
Take care that no one divide it with you!
"I shall."
Then he led him to his cell.
Take whichever coat you will.
"Then I should be no king!"
And he disappeared.
For it was God himself—
Who was having a bit of fun.

BLAISE PASCAL

Renunciation

Blaise Pascal (1623–1662) was a French mathematician, scientist, religious polemicist, author of an unfinished apologia for Christianity known as the Pensées. *He had in 1654 a mystical experience—call it mildly conversion —which he recorded in a fascinating document known as the Memorial. I give the Memorial as translated with comments and explanation, in a sympathetic recent life of Pascal by an English clergyman, Ernest Mortimer. Mr. Mortimer subtitles his book* The Life and Work of a Realist, *a use of "realist" which should suggest to the reader how far indeed we Westerners are from the kind of basic agreement on ultimates Professor Murray asks for in his Phi Beta Kappa address.*

PASCAL'S MEMORIAL

WHILE HE SO THOUGHT AND PRAYED THERE WAS GIVEN HIM THAT TIMELESS eternal moment (he meticulously timed it afterwards; it lasted two hours) which some are allowed. During that space or on that level (our language is not competent for this matter) common experience loses its opacity. It is still there and still real, indeed still visible as is the window through which a man looks; but he is no longer looking upon it. No secular event, no earthly thing, can give or take away that which is seen and which is equally and eternally there whether it is seen or not; and the man who has seen is now permanently aware that pain, injustice, the defilements of guilt, the corrosion of time, failure, the brevity of life, all the *lachrymae rerum,* are indeed still present; sorrow can still move him, temptation can still assail; but they can never again assume their appearance of finality or their power to crush the spirit.

On emerging from the vision Pascal seized a paper and wrote at headlong speed an account, copying it afterwards on to a piece of parchment. Both were found after his death, sewn into his doublet. The parchment has been

From Ernest Mortimer, *Blaise Pascal: The Life and Work of a Realist* (New York: Harper & Brothers, 1959), pp. 123–125, 224–225.

lost; the paper original survives among the Pascal MSS together with a careful copy made by Blaise's nephew, the Abbé Louis Périer.

The year of grace, 1654.
Monday, 23rd. November, Feast of S. Clement, Pope and Martyr,
and of others in the Martyrology
Vigil of S. Chrysogonus, Martyr, and others,
From about half-past ten in the evening until about half-
past twelve

FIRE

God of Abraham, God of Isaac, God of Jacob, not of the
philosophers and savants
Certitude. Certitude. Feeling. Joy. Peace.
God of Jesus Christ.
My God and Thy God
"Thy God shall be my God"
Forgetfulness of the world and of everything except God
He is to be found only in the ways taught in the Gospel
Grandeur of the human soul
Righteous Father, the world hath not known Thee, but I have
known Thee
Joy, joy, joy, tears of joy
I have fallen from Him
"They have forsaken Me, the Fountain of living waters"
My God, wilt Thou forsake me?
May I not fall from Him for ever
This is life eternal, that they might know Thee, the only
true God, and Jesus Christ Whom Thou has sent
Jesus Christ
Jesus Christ
I have fallen away: I have fled from Him, denied Him crucified
Him
May I not fall from Him for ever
We hold Him only by the ways taught in the Gospel
Renunciation total and sweet
Total submission to Jesus Christ and to my director
Eternally in joy for a day's exercise on earth
I will not forget Thy word. Amen.*

* L'an de grâce 1654
lundi 23 novembre jour de St Clément pape et martyr
et autres au martyrologe
Veille de St Chrysogone martyr et autres
Depuis environ dix heures et demie du soir jusques
environ minuit et demi

Feu

Dieu d'Abraham, Dieu d'Isaac, Dieu de Jacob.
Non des philosophes et des savants

Men have discussed and will continue to discuss the psychological clues afforded by this document. Aldous Huxley has remarked on the curious alternation of devotional and philosophical statements (in Pascalian terms, the alternation of *l'esprit* and *le cœur*). Others have hesitated over the orthodoxy of the phrase "God of Jesus Christ," or over Pascal's reasons for dismissing the "philosophers and savants." Strowski (who gives a beautiful analysis of the whole Memorial), noting the accuracy and fullness of the Biblical quotations, observes, "Pascal has not lost his *sang-froid*." Men have picked out and dwelt upon the characteristic and significant words: *Feu, certitude, joye, grandeur de l'âme humaine*. They have asked whether the Fire is a metaphor or an actual perception, and if a perception whether present to the senses or only to the mind. They have pondered over the meaning, for Pascal, of *"renonciation totale et douce."*

All this is well and just and necessary. It is the duty of a biographer to scan and analyse the documents which throw light on his human subject, and the Memorial is an incomparable human document. Nothing else that he wrote reveals him to us as this single page does. But its main interest does not lie there.

How shall we pose this main point? If Pascal was in fact alone in that room that night, then the interest and importance of his particular thoughts and personal reactions dwindle considerably, since they were based on some sort of illusion. If in fact Pascal was not alone there that night, then again the interest of his personal reactions dwindles to vanishing point, in the presence of a more compelling interest.

Men put pen to paper for many reasons and with many effects. Among the writings of men there are some which convey a sort of claim, or conviction, or impression, that the writer as well as the pen has been used as an instrument. It is a tenable suggestion that such writings are, on the whole,

---

Certitude, certitude, sentiment, joie, paix.
    Dieu de Jésus-Christ
    Deum meum et deum vestrum
    Ton Dieu sera mon Dieu.
Oubli du monde et de tout hormis Dieu
Il ne se trouve que par les voies enseignées
    dans l'évangile
    Grandeur de l'âme humaine.
Père juste le monde ne t'a point connu mais
    je t'ai connu.
    Joie joie joie pleurs de joie
    Je m'en suis séparé
Dereliquerunt me fontem aquae vivae
    Mon Dieu me quitterez-vous?
Que je n'en sois pas séparé éternellement
Cette est la vie éternelle qu'ils te connaissent
Seul vrai Dieu et Celui que tu as envoyé, Jésus-Christ
      Jésus-Christ
      Jésus-Christ
Je m'en suis séparé; je l'ai fui, renoncé, crucifié,
    Que je n'en sois jamais séparé.
Il ne se conserve que par les voies enseignées dans l'Evangile
    Renonciation totale et douce etc.

those which should command our attention above all others, for they may be evidential.

Outside Holy Writ is there, in any language of any age, any extant writing which conveys this impression with more immediacy than Pascal's Memorial?

PART III

THE WAY MEN ARE

III

The Way Men Are

IN THIS SECTION WE ESCAPE FROM FORMAL PHILOSOPHY AND THEOLOGY, and enter literature. It is a section that could embrace the content of whole libraries, whole lists of some publishing houses, for "human nature" has been the inexhaustible concern of poet, dramatist, novelist, essayist, has indeed made the stuff of all the literary genres. Such discussion has the imprecision, the concreteness and the universal interest of another great human topic, the weather. All I dare attempt here, once more, is to show some of the range or spectrum of opinion on this pressing topic. I omit entirely currently popular semantic assertions that the phrase "human nature" is meaningless, has no "referent." I need refer only in passing to the richness of the field in folk-wisdom and stereotypes, of which one familiar example is the statement, infuriating to most intellectuals, that "you can't change human nature." And—this requires a more apologetic note—I have had to omit all scientific, or "social-scientific" attacks on the problem of human nature, from phrenology and physiognomy through more respectable attempts at characterology by anthropologists like Sheldon (endomorphs, mesomorphs, ectomorphs) to the very useful achievements of modern psychology. (Freud I have to come to later, but not to him primarily for his views on human nature.) It would be sheer obscurantism to question the very real achievements of modern social scientists in the study of man. I give in my list of further reading suggestions at the end of this book titles with which the reader may begin to appreciate this work. These social sciences are new indeed, however, and one of my main purposes here is to give a long time-dimension to these problems of man's condition.

For such a purpose there is nothing like our literary heritage, in which is to be found a very great deal of wisdom about the human stuff, not formulated according to the canons of scientific method, but scattered, loaded with words that have most unscientific overtones, biased, only partly true—and sometimes only partly wise. Even with this material, I must leave much out—the novel, the drama, history, biography, all very rich indeed. I have begun with two ancient outbursts on man's nature, followed this with samples of early modern estimates of human nature, including perhaps proportionately an undue amount from that fascinating genre, the aphorism or maxim, which probably is in the balance too rough on us poor mortals. I then give three contemporary estimates, and end with four samplings of the single richest genre of all for our purposes, autobiographical writings. Reading autobiographies may not let us see ourselves as others see us, for as Lichtenberg says in an aphorism I cite later (p. 229.) "A book is a mirror: when a monkey looks in, no apostle can look out"; but autobiographies can give us firsthand experience of what many different kinds of men would like us to think they are like.

SOPHOCLES

"What a Thing Is Man!"

The Greek tragic poet Sophocles (496–406 B.C.) has left us in this great chorus from the Antigone *lines which have long been a* sursum corda *for "humanists" who find the Judaeo-Christian estimate of man's condition somewhat depressing and unduly pessimistic. The careful reader will note, however, that these lines are by no means the Chamber of Commerce kind of boosting optimism. Sophocles' old men come in their last verses to chide this marvelous creature man for his perversity. The word which Chapman and most others translate as "wonder" in the first two lines comes from a root,* dein, *which originally had overtones of "fear" in the sense of a portent, an act of the gods, something remarkable but not humanly very comfortable. The full implication is that man is a* fearsome *wonder.*

> What a thing is man! Among all wonders
> The wonder of the world is man himself.
> He scuds the angry pallor of the seas
> Upon the blast and chariot of the storm,
> Cutting a pathway through the drownéd waste.
> He stirs and wears the unweariable Earth—
> The eldest of his gods—with shuttling ploughs
> And teams that toil and turn from year to year.
>
> Man the Contriver! Man the master-mind
> That with his casting-nets
> Of woven cunning snares the light-wit birds;
> And savage brutes; and sea-swarms of the deep;
> Yea, every wary beast that roams the hills
> Hath he subdued through excellence of wit.
> Beneath his eye the horse accepts the yoke
> And the mad mountain bullock seeks his stall.

From Sophocles, *Antigone*. Translated by John Jay Chapman (Boston and New York: Houghton Mifflin Co., 1930), pp. 18–19.

Man the Householder, the Resourceful,
Safe from the drench of the arrowy rain
And the chill of the frozen sky;—
The Inventor of speech and soaring thought,
A match for all things, competent, victorious—
Against Death only shall he call for aid,
          And call in vain.

Yea, wondrous is man's Sagacity:
Through this he climbeth on high,
Through this also he falleth.
In the confidence of his power he stumbleth;
In the stubborness of his will he goeth down.

While he honoreth the laws of the land
And that Justice which he hath sworn to maintain,
          Proudly stands his city.
But when rash counsels have mastered him, he dwells with perversity:
          Such a man hath no city.
Never may he share my hearth, never think my thoughts,
     who doeth such things.

ECCLESIASTES

Ecclesiastes, or The Preacher, *is one of the so-called "wisdom books" of the Old Testament about which, as usual, scholars dispute a good deal. It is certainly no paean of joy, but neither, as these concluding chapters suggest, is it unrelieved pessimism, lightly cynical or heavy-handedly despairing. This kind of eloquent folk-pessimism is common enough—in the Greek Hesiod, for instance—among a folk who never knew* The Affluent Society. *I suspect it has a kind of morally antiseptic value rather greater than that of the complaining of our currently alienated intellectuals. But moral antiseptics, though no doubt highly ethical drugs, can't be manufactured.*

Chapter 11

Cast thy bread upon the waters: for thou shalt find it after many days.

2 Give a portion to seven, and also to eight; for thou knowest not what evil shall be upon the earth.

3 If the clouds be full of rain, they empty *themselves* upon the earth: and if the tree fall toward the south, or toward the north, in the place where the tree falleth, there it shall be.

4 He that observeth the wind shall not sow; and he that regardeth the clouds shall not reap.

5 As thou knowest not what *is* the way of the spirit, *nor* how the bones *do grow* in the womb of her that is with child: even so thou knowest not the works of God who maketh all.

6 In the morning sow thy seed, and in the evening withhold not thine hand: for thou knowest not whether shall prosper, either this or that, or whether they both *shall be* alike good.

7 ¶ Truly the light *is* sweet, and a pleasant *thing it is* for the eyes to behold the sun:

8 But if a man live many years, *and* rejoice in them all; yet let him remember the days of darkness; for they shall be many. All that cometh *is* vanity.

9 ¶ Rejoice, O young man, in thy youth; and let thy heart cheer thee in the days of thy youth, and walk in the ways of thine heart, and in the sight of thine eyes: but know thou, that for all these *things* God will bring thee into judgment.

10 Therefore remove sorrow from thy heart, and put away evil from thy flesh: for childhood and youth *are* vanity.

Chapter 12

Remember now thy Creator in the days of thy youth, while the evil days come not, nor the years draw nigh, when thou shalt say, I have no pleasure in them;

2 While the sun, or the light, or the moon, or the stars, be not darkened, nor the clouds return after the rain:

3 In the day when the keepers of the house shall tremble, and the strong men shall bow themselves, and the grinders cease because they are few, and those that look out of the windows be darkened,

4 And the doors shall be shut in the streets, when the sound of the grinding is low, and he shall rise up at the voice of the bird, and all the daughters of musick shall be brought low;

5 Also *when* they shall be afraid of *that which is* high, and fears *shall be* in the way, and the almond tree shall flourish, and the grasshopper shall be a burden, and desire shall fail: because man goeth to his long home, and the mourners go about the streets:

6 Or ever the silver cord be loosed, or the golden bowl be broken, or the pitcher be broken at the fountain, or the wheel broken at the cistern.

7 Then shall the dust return to the earth as it was: and the spirit shall return unto God who gave it.

8 ¶ Vanity of vanities, saith the preacher; all *is* vanity.

9 And moreover, because the preacher was wise, he still taught the people knowledge; yea, he gave good heed, and sought out, *and* set in order many proverbs.

10 The preacher sought to find out acceptable words: and *that which was* written *was* upright, *even* words of truth.

11 The words of the wise *are* as goads, and as nails fastened *by* the masters of assemblies, *which* are given from one shepherd.

12 And further, by these, my son, be admonished: of making many books *there is* no end; and much study *is* a weariness of the flesh.

13 ¶ Let us hear the conclusion of the whole matter: Fear God, and keep his commandments: for this *is* the whole *duty* of man.

14 For God shall bring every work into judgment, with every secret thing, whether *it be* good, or whether *it be* evil.

FRANÇOIS,
DUC de LA ROCHEFOUCAULD

Aphorisms

François, duc de La Rochefoucauld (1613–1680) is one of the greatest of aphorists. The aphorism is a favorite genre of the moralist, and especially so among the French. No doubt the aphorist, like the satirist, has to be cleverer than the rest of us; he has to try to show us the extent of the gap between what we think we are—what we hope we are—and what we actually are. No doubt the best aphorists, like La Rochefoucauld, are by no means without malice. I should not maintain that La Rochefoucauld, Lichtenberg, or Nietzsche reports human behavior with the coolness and objectivity of a trained naturalist recounting his observations of animal behavior. I should maintain that they often lift a corner of a concealing cover and show us something underneath: that something is not by any means always nasty, and at any rate really is there. La Rochefoucauld himself was a nobleman who got involved in the confused civil war known as the Fronde, ended his political career with the failure of the revolt, and retired to compose his famous maxims. But his work is not explicable as compensation for balked ambition. These grapes are not sour—most of us find them pleasantly tart.

¶ *6:* Passion often turns the cleverest men into idiots and makes the greatest blockheads clever.

¶ *19:* We all have strength enough to endure the misfortunes of others.

¶ *25:* It takes greater character to carry off good fortune than bad.

¶ *26:* We cannot look squarely at either death or the sun.

From La Rochefoucauld, *Maxims*. Translated by Louis Kronenberger (New York: Random House, Modern Library Paperbacks, 1959), *passim*.

207

¶ *35:* Pride exists equally in all men; the only difference lies in what ways they manifest it.

¶ *43:* We think we lead when we are being led, and while making for one goal with our minds, are unconsciously drawn toward another by our hearts.

¶ *68:* It is difficult to define love: in the soul, it is a thirst for mastery; in the mind, a harmony of thought; in the body, nothing but a delicately hidden desire to possess, after many mysteries, whatsoever one loves.

¶ *87:* Men would not get on for long in society if they did not fool one another.

¶ *102:* The mind is always the dupe of the heart.

¶ *111:* The more one loves one's mistress, the closer one is to hating her.

¶ *460:* We far from realize all that our passions make us do.

¶ *481:* Nothing is rarer than real kindliness; even those who think they have it are in general only obliging or weak.

¶ *504:* After discussing the falsity of so many seeming virtues, it seems proper to say something about how false is our scorn of death. I mean that scorn of death which unbelievers boast of acquiring through their own inner strength, without hope of a life to come. There is a difference between meeting death bravely and scorning it. The first is usual enough, but I doubt whether the second is ever sincere. Yet men have done their best to persuade us that death is no evil, and the greatest weaklings among them no less than the heroes have produced a thousand famous examples to bear out their contention. But I doubt whether any sensible person has ever believed it, and the trouble men take to persuade themselves and others that it is true shows how difficult it is to accept. We may have many reasons for being disgusted with life, we never have any for despising death. Even those who choose to kill themselves do not hold it cheap, and are as shocked and resistant as the rest of us when it advances toward them in some other form than they have chosen. The varying degrees of courage that we note in all sorts of brave men derive from the varying ways in which death strikes their imagination, and strikes it more forcibly at one time than at another. Thus, after scorning what they are ignorant of they at length become frightened of what they know. If we would not judge death the worst of all misfortunes, we must avoid facing it in all its dire complexity. The bravest and most resourceful men are those who use the soundest pretexts to avoid facing it, but every man who can see it exactly as it is finds it appalling. The certainty of death produced all the strong-

mindedness of the old philosophers: they deemed it best to go uncomplain-
ingly where they could not avoid going; unable to immortalize their lives,
they did all they could to immortalize their reputations, and to save from
shipwreck as much as might be salvaged. Let us be content, for the sake
of appearances, with not even telling ourselves all we think of death, and
put more faith in our temperaments than in those feeble arguments which
would convince us that we can face death unconcernedly. The distinction
of dying bravely, the hope of being remembered fondly, the wish to leave
an honored name, the certainty of shedding all life's ills and of being no
longer buffeted by fortune, are consolations not to be rejected; but neither
are they to be supposed unfailing helps. They offer much the same reassur-
ance as a mere hedge can offer soldiers under fire: at a distance it seems
ample protection, but close at hand provides almost useless shelter. We
delude ourselves if we suppose that death, when imminent, is as we
imagined it when remote, and that our feelings, shaky as they really are,
are so finely tempered as to stand up under the severest of all trials. We
also misjudge the force of self-love if we think it will help us set at naught
the very thing that will destroy it; and reason, which we count on as so
resourceful, is at such a time too weak to provide the strength of mind we
desire. Indeed, it is our minds which at such moments oftenest desert us
and, instead of inspiring us with scorn of death, make clear how fearful
and terrible it is. All they can do for us is bid us look away and contemplate
other things. Cato and Brutus chose noble visions; a lackey, some time
since, was content to dance on the scaffold when he was about to be broken
in pieces. Thus, though the motives may differ, the effects are the same, so
that whatever the disparity between great men and ordinary ones, on a
thousand occasions we see one sort meeting death like the other. But
always with this distinction: when great men show scorn for death, it is
a love of glory that distracts their minds from the truth; when ordinary men
do so, it is because their lack of understanding shields them from the
gravity of their plight, and leaves them free to think of other things.

¶ 505: God has put as differing talents in man as trees in Nature; and
each talent, like each tree, has its own special character and aspect. The
finest pear tree in the world cannot produce the most ordinary apple, the
most splendid talent cannot duplicate the effect of the homeliest skill. Hence
to wish to make maxims while lacking the proper touch is as absurd as
expecting tulips to bloom where not even onions have been planted.

¶ 516: We should not be offended that other people conceal the truth
from us, seeing how often we conceal it from ourselves.

¶ 519: Evil results from good, and good from evil.

¶ 563: Self-love is love of self and of everything for the self's sake: it
makes men worship themselves and tyrannize, whenever the means are

to hand, over others. It finds no rest outside itself and only pauses among outside things as do bees among flowers, to feed upon them. Nothing is so impetuous as its desires, so deep-dyed as its schemes, so guileful as its maneuvers; its twisting and turning is beyond words, its altered looks surpass the chameleon's, its subtle blendings outdo the chemist's. There is no plumbing the depths or piercing the darkness of its abysses; darting in and out of them it escapes the sharpest eye and is often invisible even to itself. All unknowingly it breeds, nourishes, rears a variety of affections and hatreds, some of them so monstrous that when it has brought them to light it fails to recognize or refuses to acknowledge them. Very strange are some of the night-begotten notions it has of itself, while these in turn breed error, ignorance, coarse feelings and silly thoughts on the subject. The next step is for self-love to think its feelings dead when they are merely dormant; to think it would run no longer as soon as it stops to rest; to think it has lost its taste when it has satisfied its craving. But the heavy veil that hides it from itself never prevents its seeing clearly what lies outside; in this it resembles our eyesight, which can see everything but our eyes. Indeed, in its most vital interests and concerns, where the violence of its desires exacts its whole attention, it sees and hears, feels and imagines, suspects, detects and guesses everything, enough to inspire the thought that each of its passions exerts a magic all its own. Nothing equals the tightness of its bonds, which it tries vainly to break on observing the disasters that threaten it. Yet it achieves on occasion, in short space and with no effort, what with all its resources it could not do over a period of years. It would thus seem that the desires of self-love are kindled, not by the glow or worth of what attracts it, but by its own efforts; that its own cravings create value and add embellishment; that what it pursues is itself, and that it is pleasing itself in seeking the things it finds pleasant. It is a mass of opposites: imperious and submissive, sincere and deceitful, compassionate and cruel, timid and bold. Its inclinations alter as do the moods that shape it, that incite it now toward glory, again toward wealth, yet again toward pleasure. Its inclinations alter with age, station, experience of life; but it cares not a whit whether they are single or many since, at need or at will, it can attend to all or concentrate on one. It is fickle and, quite beyond changes wrought from without, there are countless ones created from within; it is fickle from mere fickleness, from shallowness, from weariness, from love of novelty, from disgust; it is capricious, struggling at times with vast zeal and boundless effort to obtain things of no use to it, indeed of positive harm, but which it is driven to by desire. It is eccentric, and often turns itself inside out for trifles, exulting in the most insipid of them, proudest of the most contemptible. Living everywhere, off anything, off nothing, it is part of every aspect and circumstance of life; it adjusts to what it finds or what it fails to. It even joins the enemy army, enters into their plans and—amazingly—hates itself as they do, plots and helps perpetrate its own destruction. It wants, in brief, only to exist and so long as it does is content to be its own enemy. No wonder then that it often acquires and, to its own ruin, wears in public a self-fortifying look, for in the act of destroying itself in one place it restores itself in another. When it seems to have foresworn pleasure it has only deferred or redirected it, and even when beaten and apparently quite undone, it arises triumphant from its own defeat. There you have the portrait of self-love, whose whole life is an unflagging turmoil. The sea may be fairly compared to it, in the tireless ebb and flow of whose waves self-love finds an accurate image of its own seething thoughts and its eternal restlessness.

ANTHONY, EARL OF SHAFTESBURY

Concerning Enthusiasm

The third Earl of Shaftesbury (1671–1713) was an English moralist, whose Characteristics of Men, Manners, Opinions, and Times *was a very popular book in the eighteenth century. Shaftesbury is usually listed in the textbooks as a sentimental optimist about human nature, and certainly he rarely sounds like a La Rochefoucauld. But he is no simple-minded believer in the natural goodness of man. He distrusts "enthusiasm" as did most of his Augustan colleagues. His is a kind of common-sense cheerfulness about the possibilities of life on this earth if only we don't worry too much about another life.*

IF THE KNOWING WELL HOW TO EXPOSE ANY INFIRMITY OR VICE WERE A sufficient security for the virtue which is contrary, how excellent an age might we be presumed to live in! Never was there in our nation a time known, when folly and extravagance of every kind were more sharply inspected or more wittily ridiculed. And one might hope at least from this good symptom, that our age was in no declining state, since whatever our distempers are, we stand so well affected to our remedies. To bear the being told of faults, is in private persons the best token of amendment. It is seldom that a public is thus disposed. For where jealousy of state, or the ill lives of the great people, or any other cause, is powerful enough to restrain the freedom of censure in any part, it in effect destroys the benefit of it in the whole. There can be no impartial and free censure of manners where any peculiar custom or national opinion is set apart, and not only exempted from criticism, but even flattered with the highest art. It is only in a free nation, such as ours, that imposture has no privilege and that neither the credit of a court, the power of a nobility, nor the awfulness of a Church, can give her protection, or hinder her from being arraigned in every shape

From Anthony, Earl of Shaftesbury, *Characteristics of Men, Manners, Opinions, and Times*. Rev. Walter M. Hatch, ed., Vol. I (London: Longmans, Green, 1870), pp. 10-25.

and appearance. It is true, this liberty may seem to run too far. We may perhaps be said to make ill use of it.——So every one will say, when he himself is touched, and his opinion freely examined. But who shall be judge of *what* may be freely examined, and *what* may not? *where* liberty may be used, and *where* it may not? What remedy shall we prescribe to this in general? Can there be a better than from that liberty itself which is complained of? If men are vicious, petulant, or abusive, the magistrate may correct them; but if they reason ill, it is reason still must teach them to do better. Justness of thought and style, refinement in manners, good-breeding, and politeness of every kind, can come only from the trial and experience of what is best. Let but the search go freely on and the right measure of every thing will soon be found. Whatever humour has got the start, if it be unnatural, it cannot hold; and the ridicule, if ill placed at first, will certainly fall at last where it deserves.

I have often wondered to see men of sense so mightily alarmed at the approach of any thing like ridicule on certain subjects, as if they mistrusted their own judgment. For what ridicule can lie against reason? Or how can any one of the least justness of thought endure a ridicule wrong placed? Nothing is more ridiculous than this itself. The vulgar, indeed, may swallow any sordid jest, any mere drollery or buffoonery; but it must be a finer and truer wit which takes with the men of sense and breeding. How comes it to pass, then, that we appear such cowards in reasoning, and are so afraid to stand the test of ridicule?—O! say we, the subjects are too grave. —Perhaps so. But let us see first whether they are *really* grave or no; for in the manner we may conceive them, they may peradventure be very grave and weighty in our imagination, but very ridiculous and impertinent in their own nature. Gravity is of the very essence of imposture. It does not only make us mistake other things, but is apt perpetually almost to mistake itself. For even in common behaviour, how hard is it for the grave character to keep long out of the limits of the formal one? We can never be too grave, if we can be assured we are really what we suppose. And we can never too much honour or revere any thing for grave, if we are assured the thing is grave, as we apprehend it. The main point is, to know always true gravity from the false. And this can only be, by carrying the rule constantly with us, and freely applying it not only to the things about us, but to ourselves. For if unhappily we lose the measure in ourselves, we shall soon lose it in every thing besides. Now, what rule or measure is there in the world, except in the considering of the real temper of things, to find which are truly serious, and what ridiculous? And how can this be done, unless by applying the ridicule, to see whether it will bear? But if we fear to apply this rule in *any* thing, what security can we have against the imposture of formality in *all* things? We have allowed ourselves to be formalists in one point; and the same formality may rule as it pleases in all other.

It is not in every disposition that we are capacitated to judge of things. We must beforehand judge of our own temper, and accordingly of other things which fall under our judgment. But we must never more pretend to judge of things, or of our own temper in judging them, when we have given up our preliminary right of judgment, and, under a presumption of gravity, have allowed ourselves to be most ridiculous, and to admire profoundly the most ridiculous things in nature, at least for aught we know; for having resolved never to try, we can never be sure.

Ridiculum acri
Fortius et melius magnas plerumque secat res.[1]

This, my Lord, I may safely aver, is so true in itself, and so well known for truth by the cunning formalists of the age, that they can better bear to have their impostures railed at, with all the bitterness and vehemence imaginable, than to have them touched ever so gently in this other way. They know very well that as modes and fashions, so opinions, though ever so ridiculous, are kept up by solemnity, and that those formal notions, which grew up probably in an ill mood, and have been conceived in sober sadness, are never to be removed but in a sober kind of cheerfulness, and by a more easy and pleasant way of thought. There is *a melancholy* which accompanies all enthusiasm.[2] Be it love or religion (for there are enthusiasms in both), nothing can put a stop to the growing mischief of either, till the melancholy be removed, and the mind at liberty to hear what can be said against the ridiculousness of an extreme in either way.

It was heretofore the wisdom of some wise nations to let people be fools as much as they pleased, and never to punish seriously what deserved only to be laughed at, and was, after all, best cured by that innocent remedy. There are certain humours in mankind which, of necessity, must have vent. The human mind and body are both of them naturally subject to commotions; and as there are strange ferments in the blood, which in many bodies occasion an extraordinary discharge, so in reason, too, there are heterogeneous particles which must be thrown off by fermentation. Should physicians endeavour absolutely to allay those ferments of the body, and strike in the humours which discover themselves in such eruptions, they might, instead of making a cure, bid fair perhaps to raise a plague, and turn a spring ague, or an autumn surfeit, into an epidemical malignant fever. They are certainly as ill physicians in the *body-politic,* who would needs be tampering with these mental eruptions, and, under the specious pretence of healing this itch of superstition, and saving souls from the contagion of enthusiasm, should set all nature in an uproar, and turn a few innocent carbuncles into an inflammation and mortal gangrene.

We read in history, that Pan, when he accompanied Bacchus in an expedition to the Indies, found means to strike a terror through a host of enemies, by the help of a small company, whose clamours he managed to

---

[1] The light touch often solves knotty problems better and more forcefully than the heavy. Horace, *Satires,* I, x, 14.

[2] It must be borne in mind that Shaftesbury is using "enthusiasm" in a bad sense, as a form of a disordered imagination.

good advantage among the echoing rocks and caverns of a woody vale. The hoarse bellowing of the caves, joined to the hideous aspect of such dark and desert places, raised such a horror in the enemy, that in this state their imagination helped them to hear voices, and doubtless to see forms too, which were more than human, whilst the uncertainty of what they feared made their fear yet greater, and spread it faster by implicit looks than any narration could convey it. And this was what in after times men called *a panic*. The story indeed gives a good hint of the nature of this passion, which can hardly be without some mixture of enthusiasm, and horrors of a superstitious kind.

One may, with good reason, call every passion *panic* which is raised in a multitude, and conveyed by aspect, or, as it were, by contact or sympathy. Thus, popular fury may be called panic, when the rage of the people, as we have sometimes known, has put them beyond themselves especially where religion has had to do. And, in this state, their very looks are infectious. The fury flies from face to face, and the disease is no sooner seen than caught. They who, in a better situation of mind, have beheld a multitude under the power of this passion, have owned that they saw in the countenances of men something more ghastly and terrible than at other times is expressed on the most passionate occasions. Such force has society, in ill as well as in good passions, and so much stronger any affection is for being social and communicative.

Thus, my Lord, there are many panics in mankind, besides merely that of fear. And thus is religion also panic, when enthusiasm of any kind gets up, as oft, on melancholy occasions, it will; for vapours naturally rise, and in bad times especially, when the spirits of men are low, as either in public calamities, or during the unwholesomeness of air or diet, or when convulsions happen in nature, storms, earthquakes, or other amazing prodigies: at this season the panic must needs run high, and the magistrate of necessity give way to it. For, to apply a serious remedy, and bring the sword, or *fasces,* as a cure, must make the case more melancholy, and increase the very cause of the distemper. To forbid men's natural fears, and to endeavour the overpowering them by other fears, must needs be a most unnatural method. The magistrate, if he be any artist, should have a gentler hand, and instead of caustics, incisions, and amputations, should be using the softest balms, and, with a kind sympathy, entering into the concern of the people, and taking, as it were, their passion upon him, should, when he has soothed and satisfied it, endeavour, by cheerful ways, to divert and heal it.

This was ancient policy; and hence, as a notable author of our nation expresses it, it is necessary a people should have a *public leading* in Religion. For to deny the magistrate a worship, or take away a National Church, is as mere enthusiasm as the notion which sets up persecution. For why should there not be public walks as well as private gardens? Why not public libraries as well as private education and home-tutors? But to prescribe bounds to fancy and speculation, to regulate men's apprehensions, and religious beliefs or fears, to suppress by violence the natural passion of enthusiasm, or to endeavour to ascertain it, or reduce it to one species, or bring it under any one modification, is in truth no better sense, nor deserves a better character, than what the comedian declares of the like project in the affair of love—

> Nihilo plus agas
> Quam si des operam, ut cum ratione insanias.[3]

Not only the visionaries and enthusiasts of all kinds were tolerated, your Lordship knows, by the ancients, but, on the other side, philosophy had as free a course, and was permitted as a balance against superstition; and whilst some sects, such as the Pythagorean and latter Platonic, joined in with the superstition and enthusiasm of the times, the Epicurean, the Academic, and others, were allowed to use all the force of wit and raillery against it. And thus matters were happily balanced. Reason had fair play; learning and science flourished. Wonderful was the harmony and temper which arose from all these contrarieties. Thus superstition and enthusiasm were mildly treated, and being let alone, they never rose to that degree as to occasion bloodshed, wars, persecutions, and devastations in the world. But a new sort of policy, which extends itself to another world, and considers the future lives and happiness of men rather than the present, has made us leap the bounds of natural humanity, and, out of a supernatural charity, has taught us the way of plaguing one another most devoutly. It has raised an antipathy which no temporal interest could ever do, and entailed upon us a mutual hatred to all eternity; and now *uniformity in opinion* (a hopeful project!) is looked on as the only expedient against this evil. The *saving of souls* is now the heroic passion of exalted spirits, and is become in a manner the chief care of the magistrate, and the very end of government itself.

If magistracy should vouchsafe to interpose thus much in other sciences, I am afraid we should have as bad logic, as bad mathematics, and in every kind as bad philosophy, as we often have divinity in countries where a precise orthodoxy is settled by law. It is a hard matter for a government to settle wit. If it does but keep us sober and honest, it is likely we shall have as much ability in our spiritual as in our temporal affairs; and, if we can but be trusted, we shall have wit enough to save ourselves, when no prejudice lies in the way. But if honesty and wit be insufficient for this *saving* work, it is in vain for the magistrate to meddle with it, since, if he be ever so virtuous or wise, he may be as soon mistaken as another man. I am sure the only way to save men's sense, or preserve wit at all in the world, is to give liberty to wit. Now wit can never have its liberty, where the freedom of raillery is taken away; for against serious extravagancies, and splenetic humours, there is no other remedy than this.

[3] You will no more succeed than if you sought to go sensibly mad. Terence, *Eunuch,* Act I, scene i.

We have indeed full power over all other modifications of spleen. We may treat other enthusiasms as we please. We may ridicule love or gallantry, or knight errantry, to the utmost; and we find that, in these latter days of wit, the humour of this kind, which was once so prevalent, is pretty well declined. The Crusades, the rescuing of Holy Lands, and such devout gallantries, are in less request than formerly. But, if something of this militant religion, something of this soul-rescuing spirit and saint-errantry prevails still, we need not wonder, when we consider in how solemn a manner we treat this distemper, and how preposterously we go about to cure enthusiasm.

I can hardly forbear fancying, that if we had a sort of inquisition, or formal court of judicature, with grave officers and judges, erected to restrain poetical licence, and in general to suppress that fancy and humour of versification, but in particular that most extravagant passion of love, as it is set out by poets, in its heathenish dress of Venuses and Cupids; if the poets, as ringleaders and teachers of this heresy, were, under grievous penalties, forbid to enchant the people by the vein of rhyming; and if the people, on the other side, were, under proportionable penalties, forbid to hearken to any such charm, or lend their attention to any love-tale, so much as in a play, a novel, or a ballad, we might perhaps see a new Arcadia arising out of this heavy persecution: old people and young would be seized with a versifying spirit: we should have field-conventicles of lovers and poets: forests would be filled with romantic shepherds and shepherdesses, and rocks resound with echoes of hymns and praises offered to the powers of love. We might indeed have a fair chance, by this management, to bring back the whole train of heathen gods, and set our cold northern island burning with as many altars to Venus and Apollo, as were formerly in Cyprus, Delos, or any of those warmer Grecian climates.

BERNARD MANDEVILLE

Private Vices, Public Honor

Bernard Mandeville (c. 1670–1733), a Dutchman by birth, trained in medicine at Leyden University, emigrated to England and made his career there. His Fable of the Bees *(1714) was a* succès *de scandale, declared a nuisance by a Middlesex grand jury. Its thesis is well indicated by its subtitle,* Private Vices, Public Benefits. *The "view of life" reflected in the book is not unlike that of Machiavelli's* Prince *as generally interpreted: our high ethical standards are a false front, which conceals in most of us even from ourselves our solid and useful immoral practice. Mandeville's tone is often insufferably bright, omniscient, and patronizing. I do not think it can be maintained, as it can be for Machiavelli, that he was really an "inverted idealist," a moralist outraged by what should outrage us all. At bottom, his stance reminds me of the late H. L. Mencken's: men are boobs . . . thank God!*

NOTHING WAS MORE INSTRUMENTAL IN FORWARDING THE REFORMATION, than the sloth and stupidity of the *Roman* clergy; yet the same Reformation has roused them from the laziness and ignorance they then laboured under, and the followers of *Luther, Calvin,* and others, may be said to have reformed not only those whom they drew in to their sentiments, but likewise those who remained their greatest opposers. The clergy of *England* by being severe upon the Schismatics, and upbraiding them with want of learning, have raised themselves such formidable enemies as are not easily answered; and again, the dissenters by prying into the lives, and diligently watching all the actions of their powerful antagonists, render those of the established church more cautious of giving offence, than in all probability they would, if they had no malicious overlookers to fear. It is very much owing to the great number of *Huguenots* that have always been in *France,* since the late utter extirpation of them, that that kingdom has a less dissolute and more learned clergy to boast of than any other *Roman Catholic* country. The clergy of that church are nowhere more sovereign than in

From Bernard Mandeville, *The Fable of the Bees,* Douglas Garman, ed. (London: Wishart, 1934), pp. 81–85, 103–106.

Italy, and therefore nowhere more debauched; nor anywhere more ignorant than they are in *Spain,* because their doctrine is nowhere less opposed.

Who would imagine, that virtuous women, unknowingly should be instrumental in promoting the advantage of prostitutes? Or (what still seems the greater paradox) that incontinence should be made serviceable to the preservation of chastity? And yet nothing is more true. A vicious young fellow, after having been an hour or two at church, a ball, or any other assembly, where there is a great parcel of handsome women dressed to the best advantage, will have his imagination more fired than if he had the same time been poling at *Guildhall,* or walking in the country among a flock of sheep. The consequence of this is, that he will strive to satisfy the appetite that is raised in him; and when he finds honest women obstinate and uncomatable, it is very natural to think, that he will hasten to others that are more compliable. Who would so much as surmise, that this is the fault of the virtuous women? They have no thoughts of men in dressing themselves, poor souls, and endeavour only to appear clean and decent, everyone according to her quality.

I am far from encouraging vice, and think it would be an unspeakable felicity to a state, if the sin of uncleanness could be utterly banished from it; but I am afraid it is impossible: the passions of some people are too violent to be curbed by any law or precept; and it is wisdom in all governments to bear with lesser inconveniencies to prevent greater. If courtesans and strumpets were to be prosecuted with as much rigour as some silly people would have it, what locks or bars would be sufficient to preserve the honour of our wives and daughters? For it is not only that the women in general would meet with far greater temptations, and the attempts to ensnare the innocence of virgins would seem more excusable even to the sober part of mankind than they do now: but some men would grow outrageous, and ravishing would become a common crime. Where six or seven thousand sailors arrive at once, as it often happens at *Amsterdam,* that have seen none but their own sex for many months together, how is it to be supposed that honest women should walk the streets unmolested, if there were no harlots to be had at reasonable prices? For which reason the wise rulers of that well-ordered city always tolerate an uncertain number of houses, in which women are hired as publicly as horses at a livery stable; and there being in this toleration a great deal of prudence and economy to be seen, a short account of it will be no tiresome digression.

In the first place the houses I speak of are allowed to be nowhere but in the most slovenly and unpolished part of the town, where seamen and strangers of no repute chiefly lodge and resort. The street in which most of them stand is counted scandalous, and the infamy is extended to all the neighbourhood round it. In the second, they are only places to meet and bargain in, to make appointments, in order to promote interviews of greater secrecy, and no manner of lewdness is ever suffered to be transacted in them; which order is so strictly observed, that bar the ill-manners and

noise of the company that frequent them, you will meet with no more
indecency, and generally less lasciviousness there, than with us are to be
seen at a playhouse. Thirdly, the female traders that come to these evening
exchanges are always the scum of the people, and generally such as in the
daytime carry fruit and other eatables about in wheelbarrows. The habits
indeed they appear in at night are very different from their ordinary ones;
yet they are commonly so ridiculously gay, that they look more like the
Roman dresses of strolling actresses than gentlewomen's clothes; if to this
you add the awkwardness, the hard hands, and coarse breeding of the
damsels that wear them, there is no great reason to fear, that many of the
better sort of people will be tempted by them.

The music in these temples of *Venus* is performed by organs, not out
of respect to the Deity that is worshipped in them, but the frugality of the
owners, whose business it is to procure as much found for as little money
as they can, and the policy of the government, which endeavours as little
as is possible, to encourage the breed of pipers and scrapers. All seafaring
men, especially the *Dutch,* are like the element they belong to, much given
to loudness and roaring, and the noise of half-a-dozen of them, when they
call themselves merry, is sufficient to drown twice the number of flutes or
violins; whereas with one pair of organs they can make the whole house
ring, and are at no other charge than the keeping of one scurvy musician,
which can cost them but little; yet notwithstanding the good rules and strict
discipline that are observed in these markets of love, the *Schout* and his
officers are always vexing, mulcting, and upon the least complaint removing the miserable keepers of them: which policy is of two great uses;
first it gives an opportunity to a large parcel of officers, the magistrates
make use of on many occasions and which they could not be without, to
squeeze a living out of the immoderate gains accruing from the worst
of employments, and at the same time punish those necessary profligates,
the bawds and panders, which, though they abominate, they desire yet not
wholly to destroy. Secondly, as on several accounts it might be dangerous
to let the multitude into the secret, that those houses and the trade that
is drove in them are connived at, so by this means appearing unblameable,
the wary magistrates preserve themselves in the good opinion of the weaker
sort of people, who imagine that the government is always endeavouring,
though unable, to suppress what it actually tolerates: whereas if they
had a mind to rout them out, their power in the administration of justice
is so sovereign and extensive, and they know so well how to have it ex-
ecuted, that one week, nay one night, might send them all a packing.

In *Italy* the toleration of strumpets is yet more barefaced, as is evident
from their public stews. At *Venice* and *Naples* impurity is a kind of mer-
chandize and traffic; the *Courtesans* at *Rome,* and the *Cantoneras* in *Spain,*
compose a body in the state, and are under a legal tax and impost. It is
well known, that the reason why so many good politicians as these tolerate
lewd houses, is not their irreligion, but to prevent a worse evil, an impurity

of a more execrable kind, and to provide for the safety of women of honour. *About two hundred and fifty years ago,* says Monsieur *de St. Didier,* Venice *being in want of courtesans, the Republic was obliged to procure a great number from foreign parts. Doglioni,* who has written the memorable affairs of *Venice,* highly extols the wisdom of the Republic in this point, which secured the chastity of women of honour daily exposed to public violences, the churches and consecrated places not being a sufficient asylum for their chastity.

Our universities in *England* are much belied if in some colleges there was not a monthly allowance *ad expurgandos Renes;* and time was when the monks and priests in *Germany* were allowed concubines on paying a certain yearly duty to their Prelate. *It is generally believed,* says Monsieur *Bayle* (to whom I owe the last paragraph) *that Avarice was the cause of this shameful indulgence; but it is more probable their design was to prevent their tempting modest women, and to quiet the uneasiness of husbands, whose resentments the clergy do well to avoid.* From what has been said it is manifest, that there is a necessity of sacrificing one part of woman-kind to preserve the other, and prevent a filthiness of a more heinous na-ture. From whence I think I may justly conclude (what was the seeming paradox I went about to prove) that chastity may be supported by inconti-nence, and the best of virtues want the assistance of the worst of vices. . . .

Clothes were originally made for two ends, to hide our nakedness, and to fence our bodies against the weather, and other outward injuries: to these our boundless pride has added a third, which is ornament; for what else but an excess of stupid vanity, could have prevailed upon our reason to fancy that ornamental, which must continually put us in mind of our wants and misery, beyond all other animals that are ready clothed by nature herself? It is indeed to be admired how so sensible a creature as man, that pretends to so many fine qualities of his own, should condescend to value himself upon what is robbed from so innocent and defenceless an animal as a sheep, or what he is beholden for to the most insignificant thing upon earth, a dying worm; yet whilst he is proud of such trifling depredations, he has the folly to laugh at the hottentots on the furthest promontory of *Africk,* who adorn themselves with the guts of their dead enemies, without considering that they are the ensigns of their valour those barbarians are fine with, the true *spolia opima,* and that if their pride be more savage than ours, it is certainly less ridiculous, because they wear the spoils of the more noble animal.

But whatever reflections may be made on this head, the world has long since decided the matter; handsome apparel is a main point, fine feathers make fine birds, and people where they are not known, are generally honoured according to their clothes and other accoutrements they have about them; from the richness of them we judge of their wealth, and by their ordering of them we guess at their understanding. It is this which encourages everybody, who is conscious of his little merit, if he is anyways able to wear clothes above his rank, especially in large and populous cities, where obscure men may hourly meet with fifty strangers to one acquaintance, and consequently have the pleasure of being esteemed by a vast majority, not as what they are, but what they appear to be; which is a greater temptation than most people want to be vain.

Whoever takes delight in viewing the various scenes of low life, may on Easter, Whitsuntide, and other great holidays, meet with scores of people, especially women, of almost the lowest rank, that wear good and fashionable clothes: if coming to talk with them, you treat them more courteously and with greater respect than what they are conscious they deserve, they will commonly be ashamed of owning what they are; and often you may, if you are a little inquisitive, discover in them a most anxious care to conceal the business they follow, and the places they live in. The reason is plain; whilst they receive those civilities that are not usually paid them, and which they think only due to their betters, they have the satisfaction to imagine, that they appear what they would be, which to weak minds is a pleasure almost as substantial as they could reap from the very accomplishments of their wishes. This golden dream they are unwilling to be disturbed in, and being sure that the meanness of their condition, if it is known, must sink them very low in your opinion, they hug themselves in their disguise, and take all imaginable precaution not to forfeit by a useless discovery the esteem which they flatter themselves that their good clothes have drawn from you.

Though everybody allows, that as to apparel and manner of living, we ought to behave ourselves suitable to our conditions, and follow the examples of the most sensible and prudent among our equals in rank and fortune: yet how few, that are not either miserably covetous, or else proud of singularity, have this discretion to boast of? We all look above ourselves, and, as fast as we can, strive to imitate those, that some way or other are superior to us.

The poorest labourer's wife in the parish, who scorns to wear a strong, wholesome frieze, as she might, will half-starve herself and her husband to purchase a secondhand gown and petticoat, that cannot do her half the service; because, forsooth, it is more genteel. The weaver, the shoemaker, the tailor, the barber, and every mean, working fellow, that can set up with little, has the impudence with the first money he gets, to dress himself like a tradesman of substance: the ordinary retailer in the clothing of his wife, takes pattern from his neighbour, that deals in the same commodity by wholesale, and the reason he gives for it, is, that twelve years ago the other had not a bigger shop than himself. The druggist, mercer, draper and other creditable shopkeepers can find no difference between themselves and merchants, and therefore dress and live like them. The merchant's lady, who cannot bear the assurance of those mechanics, flies for refuge to the other end of the town, and scorns to follow any fashion but what she takes from thence. This haughtiness alarms the court, the women of quality are frightened to see merchants' wives and daughters dressed like themselves; this impudence of the city, they cry, is intolerable; mantua-makers are sent for, and the contrivance of fashions becomes all their study, that they may have always new modes ready to take up, as soon as those saucy cits shall begin to imitate those in being. The same emulation is continued through the several degrees of quality to an incredible expense, till at last the prince's great favourites and those of the first rank of all, having nothing else left to outstrip some of their inferiors, are forced to lay out vast estates in pompous equipages, magnificent furniture, sumptuous gardens and princely palaces.

To this emulation and continual striving to outdo one another it is owing, that after so many various shiftings and changings of modes, in trumping up new ones and renewing of old ones, there is still a *plus ultra* for the ingenious; it is this, or at least the consequence of it that sets the poor to work, adds spurs to industry, and encourages the skilful artificer to search after further improvements.

JEAN de LA BRUYÈRE

Varieties of Character

Jean de La Bruyère (1645–1696) was a French moralist whose Les caractères, *constantly expanded during his life, was undertaken in imitation of the work of Theophrastus, a Greek pioneer in characterology. La Bruyère's work is essentially aphoristic, and his estimate of human nature rather more amused and amusing than indignant. Still, he is clearly a* moraliste *in the great French tradition.*

LET US NOT BE ANGRY WITH MEN WHEN WE SEE THEM CRUEL, UNGRATEFUL, unjust, proud, egotists, and forgetful of others; they are made so; it is their nature; we might just as well quarrel with a stone for falling to the ground, or with a fire when the flames ascend.

In one sense men are not fickle, or only in trifles; they change their habits, language, outward appearance, their rules of propriety, and sometimes their taste; but they always preserve their bad morals, and adhere tenaciously to what is ill and to their indifference for virtue.

Stoicism is a mere fancy, a fiction, like Plato's Republic. The Stoics pretend a man may laugh at poverty; not feel insults, ingratitude, loss of property, relatives, and friends; look unconcernedly on death, and regard it as a matter of indifference which ought neither to make him merry nor melancholy; not let pleasure or pain conquer him; be wounded or burned without breathing the slightest sigh or shedding a single tear; and this phantasm of courage and imaginary firmness they are pleased to call a philosopher. They have left man with the same faults they found in him, and did not blame his smallest foible. Instead of depicting vice as something terrible or ridiculous, which might have corrected him, they have limned an idea of perfection and heroism of which man is not capable, and they exhorted him to aim at what is impossible. Thus, the philosopher that is to be, but will

Jean de La Bruyère, *The "Characters."* Translated by Henri Van Laun (London: John C. Nimmo, 1885), pp. 271-273, 282-288.

never exist except in imagination, finds himself naturally, and without any exertions of his own, above all events and all ills; the most excruciating fit of the gout, the most severe attack of colic, cannot draw from him the least complaint; Heaven and earth may be overturned, without dragging him along in their downfall; and he remains calm and collected amidst the ruins of the universe, whilst a man really beside himself utters loud exclamations, despairs, looks fierce, and is in an agony for the loss of a dog or for a China dish broken into pieces.

Restlessness of mind, inequality of temper, fickleness of affections, and instability of conduct, are all vices of the mind, but they are all different; and, in spite of their appearing analogous, are not always found in one and the same subject.

It is difficult to decide whether irresolution makes a man more unfortunate than contemptible, or even whether it is always a greater disadvantage to take a wrong step than to take none at all.

A man of variable mind is not one man, but several men in one; he multiplies himself as often as he changes his taste and manners; he is not this minute what he was the last, and will not be the next what he is now; he is his own successor. Do not ask what is his nature, but what are his proclivities; nor what mood he is in, but how many sorts of moods he has. Are you not mistaken, and is it Eutichrates whom you accost? To-day he is cool to you, but yesterday he was anxious to see you, and was so demonstrative that his friends were jealous of you. Surely he does not remember you; tell him your name. . . .

Impoliteness is not a vice of the mind, but the consequence of several vices; of foolish vanity, of ignorance of one's duties, of idleness, of stupidity, of absence of mind, of contempt for others, and of jealousy. Though it only shows itself outwardly, it is not the less odious, because it is a fault which is always visible and manifest; however, it gives more or less offence, according as the motives for displaying it are more or less offensive.

If we say of an angry, captious, quarrelsome, melancholy, formal, capricious person, that it is all owing to his temper, it is not to find an excuse for him, whatever people may think, but an involuntary acknowledgment that such great faults admit of no remedy.

What we call good temper is a thing too much neglected among men; they ought to understand that they should not alone be good, but also appear to be so, at least if they are inclined to be sociable and disposed to friendly intercourse; in other words, if they would be men. We do not require wicked men to be gentle and urbane; in these qualities they are never wanting, for they employ them to ensnare the simple, and to find a larger field for their operations; but we wish kind-hearted men always to be tractable, accessible, and courteous; so that there should no longer be any reason for saying that wicked men do harm and that good men make others uncomfortable.

The generality of men proceed from anger to insults; others act differently, for they first give offence and then grow angry; our surprise at such behaviour always supersedes resentment.

Men do not sufficiently take advantage of every opportunity for pleasing other people. When a person accepts a certain post, it seems that he intends to acquire the power of obliging others without using it; nothing is quicker and more readily given than a refusal, whilst nothing is ever granted until after mature reflection.

Know exactly what you are to expect from men in general, and from each of them in particular, and then mix with the people around you.

If poverty is the mother of all crimes, lack of intelligence is their father.

A knave can hardly be a very intelligent man; a clear and far-seeing mind leads to regularity, honesty, and virtue; it is want of sense and penetration which begets obstinacy in wickedness as well as in duplicity; in vain we endeavour to correct such a man by satire; it may describe him to others, but he himself will not know his own picture; it is like scolding a deaf man. It would be well, please gentlemen of sense and culture, and avenge everybody, if a rogue were not so constituted as to be without any feeling whatever.

There are some vices for which we are indebted to none but ourselves, which are innate in us, and are strengthened by habit; there are others we contract which are foreign to us. Sometimes men are naturally inclined to yield without much difficulty, to be urbane, and to desire to please; but by the treatment they meet from those whom they frequent and on whom they depend, they soon lose all moderation, and even change their disposition; they grow melancholy and peevish to a degree ere this unknown to them; their temper is completely changed, and they are themselves astonished at their being rude and tetchy.

Some people ask why the whole bulk of mankind does not constitute one nation, and does not like to speak the same language, obey the same laws, and agree among themselves to adopt the same customs and the same worship? For my part, observing how greatly minds, tastes, and sentiments differ, I am astonished to see seven or eight persons, living under the same roof and within the same walls, constitute one family.

There are some extraordinary fathers, who seem, during the whole course of their lives, to be preparing reasons for their children for being consoled at their deaths.

Everything is strange in the dispositions, morals, and manners of men: one person who during his whole lifetime has been melancholy, passionate, avaricious, fawning, submissive, laborious, and egotistical, was born lively, peaceable, indolent, ostentatious, and with lofty feelings, abhorring anything base; want, circumstances, and dire necessity have compelled him and caused such a great change. Such a man's inmost feelings can really not be described, for too many external things have altered, changed, and upset him, so that he is not exactly what he thinks he is himself or what he appears to be.

Life is short and tedious, and is wholly spent in wishing; we trust to find rest and enjoyment at some future time, often at an age when our best blessings, youth and health, have already left us. When at last that time has arrived, it surprises us in the midst of fresh desires; we have got no farther when we are attacked by a fever which kills us; if we had been cured, it would only have been to give us more time for other desires.

A man requesting a favour from another, surrenders himself at discretion to the personage from whom he expects it, but when he is quite sure it will be granted, he temporises, parleys, and capitulates.

It is so usual for men not to be happy, and so essential for every blessing to be acquired with infinite trouble, that what is obtained easily is looked upon with suspicion. We can hardly understand how anything which costs us so little can be greatly to our advantage, or how by strictly honest means we can so easily obtain what we want; we may think we deserve our success, but we ought very seldom to depend on it.

A man who says he is not born happy may at least become so by the happiness his friends and relatives enjoy, but envy deprives him even of this last resource.

Whatever I may somewhere have said, it is, perhaps, wrong to be dejected. Men seem born to misfortune, pain, and poverty, and as few escape this, and as every kind of calamity seems to befall them, they ought to be prepared for every misfortune.

Men find it so very difficult to make business arrangements, they are so very touchy where their smallest interests are concerned, they are so bristling over with difficulties, so willing to deceive and so unwilling to be deceived, they place so high a value on what belongs to themselves, and are so apt to undervalue what belongs to others, that I admit I cannot understand how and in what way marriages, contracts, acquisitions, conventions, truces, treaties, and alliances are brought about.

Among some people arrogance supplies the place of grandeur, inhumanity of decision, and roguery of intelligence.

Knaves easily believe others as bad as themselves; there is no deceiving them, neither do they long deceive.

I would rather at any time be considered a fool than a rogue.

We never deceive people to benefit them, for knavery is a compound of wickedness and falsehood. . . .

Suppose men were to live for ever in this world, I do not think I could discover what more they could do than they do at present.

If life be wretched, it is hard to bear it; if it be happy, it is horrible to lose it; both come to the same thing.

There is nothing men are so anxious to keep, and yet are so careless about, as life.

GEORG CHRISTOPH LICHTENBERG

More Aphorisms

Georg Christoph Lichtenberg (1742–1799), in his own day known chiefly as a distinguished scientist, a professor at the University of Göttingen, has long been familiar to Germans as one of their greatest aphorists and satirists. One of the advantages of the aphoristic form for a certain kind of mind is that it permits all kinds of shots in all directions, some of which hit lightly targets which others can establish more solidly afterward. I begin my list from Lichtenberg with an amazing "anticipation" of Freud. But Lichtenberg also "anticipates" a good deal of contemporary logical positivism. He deserves to be better known in this country. Incidentally, in his own day he was one of the severest critics of a then fashionable attempt to systematize "scientifically" our knowledge of human nature, the science of physiognomy of the Swiss Lavater.

MANY CONCLUSIONS ABOUT MEN'S CHARACTERS COULD PERHAPS BE DRAWN from their dreams, if they would report them exactly. But quite a few would be needed, not just one.

I commend dreams again; we live and feel as much dreaming as waking and are the one as much as the other. It is one of the superiorities of man that he dreams *and knows it*. We have hardly made the right use of this yet. Dream is a life which, combined with the rest of us, makes up what we call human life. Dreams gradually merge into our waking; we cannot say where man's waking state begins.

We often strive to subdue some vicious emotion, and try at the same time to preserve all of our good ones. This comes from our method of describing man: we fail to see his character as a very neatly constructed totality, which can be rearranged only by changing the relative position of its various parts. Rather, we regard his emotions as adhesive beauty-patches,

From *The Lichtenberg Reader*. Translated, edited, and introduced by Franz H. Mautner and Henry Hatfield (Boston: The Beacon Press, 1959), pp. 43-100 *passim*.

which we may shift or throw away at will. Many such errors derive from the languages indispensable in describing the emotions. Thus we always think of the most ordinary meaning the moment we neglect, to the slightest degree, the particular association. Therefore, if a general system of characterization is to be invented, a proper language must first be found.

Everyone should study at least enough philosophy and *belles lettres* to make his sexual experience more delectable.

If an angel were to tell us about his philosophy, I believe many of his statements might well sound like "$2 \times 2 = 13$."

With voluptuous anxiety.

What is a "German character"? What? Tobacco-smoking and honesty, didn't you say? O you simple dolts! Listen: be good enough to tell me what the weather is like in America. Shall I tell instead of you? All right. It lightens, it hails, it's muddy, it's sultry, it's unbearable, it's snowing, freezing, windy, and the sun is shining.

Truth has to overcome a thousand obstacles to get on paper undamaged, and back from the paper to the mind. Liars are its weakest enemies. The star-gazing writer, who holds forth about all matters and views all matters as other honest people do when they have had a drop too much; the super-subtle, affected "judge of human nature," who sees and wants to see a man's whole life mirrored in each of his acts; the good, pious man who believes in every instance because he is respectful, who examines none of the things he learned before his fifteenth year and builds up the little bit he has examined of an unexamined base—these are enemies of truth.

Because of his obscure sense of his own perfectibility, man still thinks himself far from the goal even when he has reached it; and reason does not sufficiently enlighten him. What he finds easy, he thinks bad, and so he strains from the bad to the good, and from the good to a type of the bad which he thinks better than good.

The progress of the good and the purposeful in the world. If, for instance, it is rooted in human nature that ultimately the Christian religion will perish again some day, it will happen whether people oppose this or not. Going against the stream and obstructing it for a little while makes only an infinitely small bend in the line. Only it is too bad that *we* have to be the spectators and not some other generation; no one can blame us for working as hard as we can to shape our times according to our own minds.

I always think that we on this sphere serve a purpose whose fulfillment a conspiracy of the whole human race cannot prevent. In just the same way a good book will go down to posterity even if all the critical judges should combine to cast suspicion on it—not by satire but with the mien of the innocent lamb and the accent of the lover of truth—even if they should keep absolute silence about it. If it contains a dozen new truths, stated well and vigorously, if the expert in human nature appears in the rest of the work, then a legion of witty magazine writers will be as little able to block its course to eternity as I could fan back the storm or the rising flood with a playing card. *A* man can condemn a good book through envy, lack of judgment, or foolishness, but Man cannot.

A on his lips; and non-A in his heart.

It would be worth-while to investigate whether it isn't harmful to devote too much care to bringing up children. We don't yet know man well enough to relieve chance completely of this function. I believe that if our pedagogues succeed in their intention—I mean, if they bring it about that the children are shaped completely by their influence—there won't be a single really great man produced from now on.

A book is a mirror: when a monkey looks in, no apostle can look out.

The reason that people can retain so little of what they read is that they think so little themselves. When a person knows how to repeat sensibly what others have said, he has usually thought a great deal himself—unless his mind is a mere pedometer.

What they call "heart" is located far lower than the fourth vest button.

If a later generation were to reconstruct the man of today from our sentimental writings, they would believe he had been a heart with testicles.

Just as one says someone "holds an office," while actually the office holds him.

I am convinced that a person doesn't only love himself in others; he also hates himself in others.

Materialism is the asymptote of psychology.

In a machine as complicated as this world, we are all, I think, gambling in a lottery as far as the essentials are concerned, even though we may have a slight part in determining events.

As soon as people know that someone is blind, they think they can tell it from behind.

We don't devour each other; we merely slaughter each other.

I and *me*. *I* feel *me*—that makes two objects. Our false philosophy is embodied in the language as a whole: one might say that we can't reason without reasoning wrong. People don't bear in mind that speaking, no matter about what, is a philosophy. Everyone who speaks is a folk-philosopher, and our academic philosophy consists of qualifications of the popular brand. All our philosophy is an improving of linguistic usage; that is, an improving of a philosophy—of the most common of all, in fact. But the ordinary philosophy has the advantage of possessing declensions and conjugations. Thus we always teach true philosophy in the language of the false one. Defining words is no help; for by using explanations, I don't change the pronouns and their declensions.

There is something in every person's character that cannot be broken— the bony structure of his character. Wanting to change it is the same as teaching a sheep to retrieve.

The myths of the physicists.

Sense is order; and order is, in the last analysis, harmony with our own nature. When we speak reasonably, we speak only from our essence and our nature. In order to incorporate something in our memory, therefore, we always try to supply sense or another sort of ordering. Therefore *genera* and *species* among plants and animals, as well as other similarities, including rhyme. In just that category, our hypotheses also belong; we must have some, because otherwise we could not remember things. This has been said very long ago, but one comes back to it again from all directions.

Thus we try to bring sense into the physical world. But the question is whether we can really make sense of everything. Certainly, by much testing and reflection, a meaning can be brought into something which is not sensible for us, or not sensible at all. Thus one sees in the sand faces, landscapes, etc., which certainly are not the intention of these patterns. Symmetry belongs here too; silhouette in the blot of ink, etc. Also the scale in the range of creatures—all that is *not in the things but in us*. Generally one forgets too easily that when we observe nature, we always observe only ourselves, especially our orderings.

Just as the supporters of Herr Kant always reproach their opponents for not understanding him, it seems that some others believe that Herr Kant is right *because* they understand him.

I've thought for a long time that Philosophy will yet devour herself. Metaphysics has already partially devoured herself.

Man is a creature who searches for causes; he could be named the cause-searcher within the hierarchy of minds. Other minds perhaps conceive things under other categories, incomprehensible to us.

In nature we see not words but always the initial letters of words only, and if we then try to read, we discover that the new so-called words are again only the initials of others.

Just let governments of the people take over everywhere: then presumably other conditions will ensue as unpalatable to Reason as the present ones. For that the republican system should be quite free of all harm is a dream, a mere notion. What would it be like if it should become reality? I believe, without wanting to set myself up as a judge, that society will be hurled by revolutions forever and ever from one system to another, and that the duration of each will depend on the virtue of the subjects at the time.

Probably no invention came more easily to man than inventing Heaven.

Is it really so absolutely certain that our reason can know nothing metaphysical? Might man not be able to weave his ideas of God with just as much purpose as the spider weaves his net to catch flies? Or, in other words: might not beings exist who admire us as much for our ideas of God and immortality as we admire the spider and the silk worm?

FRIEDRICH WILHELM NIETZSCHE

Human, All Too Human

Friedrich Wilhelm Nietzsche (1844–1900) usually gets catalogued as a philosopher, perhaps because he was a German. But he never produced the kind of systematic treatise a philosopher is expected to produce, nor, after his early writings in defense of Wagner and in attack on German philistinism, did he write connected essays. He wrote extended aphorisms, loosely tied together, given unity only by his temperament, which was by no means simple, monolithic. Indeed the aphorism as a literary form pulls a writer in two quite opposite directions. It commits him, if only in competition with his predecessors, to epigrammatic brevity, carefully polished sentences, meticulous choice of words, long hours of revision; and yet it also permits him to avoid systematic planning of a whole carefully articulated work, lets him take the lazy man's way out of tossing off his bright ideas as they come, regardless of how they fit together. Nietzsche's work is a fine example of both these contrary pulls.

Nietzsche had an immense influence on the generation of 1900, not only in Germany, but throughout the West. As to what he meant to do with the words he used so skillfully there has long been great debate: to some he is the more-than-Christian idealist, a gentle, fighting soul; to others, a proto-Nazi, a hater of human beings, a neurotic intellectual overcompensating for his physical defects by preaching the need for a new aristocracy of the strong. We cannot here attempt to go into the Nietzsche question. I cite passages from one of his earlier aphoristic books, the relatively cheerful Human, All Too Human.

ADVANTAGES OF PSYCHOLOGICAL OBSERVATION

THAT REFLECTION REGARDING THE HUMAN, ALL-TOO-HUMAN—OR AS THE learned jargon is: psychological observation—is among the means whereby the burden of life can be made lighter, that practice in this art affords

From Friedrich Nietzsche, *Human, All Too Human.* Translated by Alexander Harvey (Chicago: Charles H. Kerr & Company, 1908), pp. 77–100 *passim*.

presence of mind in difficult situations and entertainment amid a weari-
some environment, aye, that maxims may be culled in the thorniest and
least pleasing paths of life and invigoration thereby obtained: this much
was believed was known—in former centuries. Why was this forgotten
in our own century, during which, at least in Germany, yes in Europe,
poverty as regards psychological observation would have been manifest
in many ways had there been anyone to whom this poverty could have
manifested itself. Not only in the novel, in the romance, in philosophical
standpoints—these are the works of exceptional men; still more in the
state of opinion regarding public events and personages; above all in
general society, which says much about men but nothing whatever about
man, there is totally lacking the art of psychological analysis and synthesis. But why is the richest and most harmless source of entertainment
thus allowed to run to waste? Why is the greatest master of the psychological maxim no longer read?—for, with no exaggeration whatever be
it said: the educated person in Europe who has read La Rochefoucauld
and his intellectual and artistic affinities is very hard to find; still harder,
the person who knows them and does not disparage them. Apparently,
too, this unusual reader takes far less pleasure in them than the form
adopted by these artists should afford him: for the subtlest mind cannot
adequately appreciate the art of maxim-making unless it has had training
in it, unless it has competed in it. Without such practical acquaintance,
one is apt to look upon this making and forming as a much easier thing
than it really is, one is not keenly enough alive to the felicity and the
charm of success. Hence present day readers of maxims have but a
moderate, tempered pleasure in them, scarcely, indeed, a true perception
of their merit, so that their experiences are about the same as those of
the average beholder of cameos: people who praise because they cannot
appreciate, and are very ready to admire and still readier to turn away.

OBJECTION.—Or is there a counter-proposition to the dictum that psychological observation is one of the means of consoling, lightening, charming existence? Have enough of the unpleasant effects of this art been
experienced to justify the person striving for culture in turning his regard
away from it? In all truth, a certain blind faith in the goodness of human
nature, an implanted distaste for any disparagement of human concerns,
a sort of shamefacedness at the nakedness of the soul, may be far more
desirable things in the general happiness of a man, than this only occasionally advantageous quality of psychological sharpsightedness; and perhaps belief in the good, in virtuous men and actions, in a plenitude of
disinterested benevolence has been more productive of good in the world
of men in so far as it has made men less distrustful. If Plutarch's heroes
are enthusiastically imitated and a reluctance is experienced to looking
too critically into the motives of their actions, not the knowledge but the
welfare of human society is promoted thereby: psychological error and

above all obtuseness in regard to it, help human nature forward, whereas knowledge of the truth is more promoted by means of the stimulating strength of a hypothesis; as La Rochefoucauld in the first edition of his "Sentences and Moral Maxims" has expressed it: "What the world calls virtue is ordinarily but a phantom created by the passions, and to which we give a good name in order to do whatever we please with impunity." La Rochefoucauld and those other French masters of soul-searching (to the number of whom has lately been added a German, the author of "Psychological Observations") are like expert marksmen who again and again hit the black spot—but it is the black spot in human nature. Their art inspires amazement, but finally some spectator, inspired, not by the scientific spirit but by a humanitarian feeling, execrates an art that seems to implant in the soul a taste for belittling and impeaching mankind.

NEVERTHELESS.—The matter therefore, as regards pro and con, stands thus: in the present state of philosophy an awakening of the moral observation is essential. The repulsive aspect of psychological dissection, with the knife and tweezers entailed by the process, can no longer be spared humanity. Such is the imperative duty of any science that investigates the origin and history of the so-called moral feelings and which, in its progress is called upon to posit and to solve advanced social problems:—The older philosophy does not recognize the newer at all and, through paltry evasions, has always gone astray in the investigation of the origin and history of human estimates (Werthschatzungen). With what results may now be very clearly perceived, since it has been shown by many examples, how the errors of the greatest philosophers have their origin in a false explanation of certain human actions and feelings; how upon the foundation of an erroneous analysis (for example, of the so called disinterested actions), a false ethic is reared, to support which religion and like mythological monstrosities are called in, until finally the shades of these troubled spirits collapse in physics and in the comprehensive world point of view. But if it be established that superficiality of psychological observation has heretofore set the most dangerous snares for human judgment and deduction, and will continue to do so, all the greater need is there of that steady continuance of labor that never wearies putting stone upon stone, little stone upon little stone; all the greater need is there of a courage that is not ashamed of such humble labor and that will oppose persistence to all contempt. It is, finally, also true that countless single observations concerning the human, all-too-human, have been first made and uttered in circles accustomed, not to furnish matter for scientific knowledge, but for intellectual pleasure-seeking; and the original home atmosphere—a very seductive atmosphere—of the moral maxim has almost inextricably interpenetrated the entire species, so that the scientific man involuntarily manifests a sort of mistrust of this species and of its seriousness. But it is sufficient to point to the consequences: for already it is becoming evident that events of the most portentous nature are developing in the domain of psychological observation. What is the leading conclusion arrived at by one of the subtlest and calmest of thinkers, the author of the work "Concerning the Origin of the Moral Feelings," as a result of his thorough and incisive analysis of human conduct? "The moral man," he says, "stands no nearer the knowable (metaphysical) world than the physical man." This dictum, grown hard and cutting beneath the hammer-blow of historical knowledge, can some day, perhaps, in some future or other, serve as the axe that will be laid to the root of the "metaphysical necessities" of men—whether more to the blessing than to the banning of universal well being who can say?—but in any event a dictum fraught with the most momentous consequences, fruitful and fearful at once, and confronting the world in the two faced way characteristic of all great facts.

To What Extent Useful.—Therefore, whether psychological observation is more an advantage than a disadvantage to mankind may always remain undetermined: but there is no doubt that it is necessary, because science can no longer dispense with it. Science, however, recognizes no considerations of ultimate goals or ends any more than nature does; but as the latter duly matures things of the highest fitness for certain ends without any intention of doing it, so will true science, doing with ideas what nature does with matter, promote the purposes and the welfare of humanity, (as occasion may afford, and in many ways) and attain fitness [to ends]—but likewise without having intended it.

He to whom the atmospheric conditions of such a prospect are too wintry, has too little fire in him: let him look about him, and he will become sensible of maladies requiring an icy air, and of people who are so "kneaded together" out of ardor and intellect that they can scarcely find anywhere an atmosphere too cold and cutting for them. Moreover: as too serious individuals and nations stand in need of trivial relaxations; as others, too volatile and excitable require onerous, weighty ordeals to render them entirely healthy: should not we, the more intellectual men of this age, which is swept more and more by conflagrations, catch up every cooling and extinguishing appliance we can find that we may always remain as self contained, steady and calm as we are now, and thereby perhaps serve this age as its mirror and self reflector, when the occasion arises? . . .

Above Animal.—The beast in us must be wheedled: ethic is necessary, that we may not be torn to pieces. Without the errors involved in the assumptions of ethics, man would have remained an animal. Thus has he taken himself as something higher and imposed rigid laws upon himself. He feels hatred, consequently, for states approximating the animal: whence the former contempt for the slave as a not-yet-man, as a thing, is to be explained. . . .

SYMPATHY GREATER THAN SUFFERING.—There are circumstances in which sympathy is stronger than the suffering itself. We feel more pain, for instance, when one of our friends becomes guilty of a reprehensible action than if we had done the deed ourselves. We once, that is, had more faith in the purity of his character than he had himself. Hence our love for him, (apparently because of this very faith) is stronger than is his own love for himself. If, indeed, his egoism really suffers more, as a result, than our egoism, inasmuch as he must take the consequences of his fault to a greater extent than ourselves, nevertheless, the unegoistic —this word is not to be taken too strictly, but simply as a modified form of expression—in us is more affected by his guilt than the unegoistic in him.

HYPOCHONDRIA.—There are people who, from sympathy and anxiety for others become hypochrondiacal. The resulting form of compassion is nothing else than sickness. So, also, is there a Christian hypochondria, from which those singular, religiously agitated people suffer who place always before their eyes the suffering and death of Christ. . . .

THE DESIRE TO INSPIRE COMPASSION.—La Rochefoucauld, in the most notable part of his self portraiture (first printed 1658) reaches the vital spot of truth when he warns all those endowed with reason to be on their guard against compassion, when he advises that this sentiment be left to men of the masses who stand in need of the promptings of the emotions (since they are not guided by reason) to induce them to give aid to the suffering and to be of service in misfortune: whereas compassion, in his (and Plato's) view, deprives the heart of strength. To be sure, sympathy should be manifested but men should take care not to feel it; for the unfortunate are rendered so dull that the manifestation of sympathy affords them the greatest happiness in the world.—Perhaps a more effectual warning against this compassion can be given if this need of the unfortunate be considered not simply as stupidity and intellectual weakness, not as a sort of distraction of the spirit entailed by misfortune itself (and thus, indeed, does La Rochefoucauld seem to view it) but as something quite different and more momentous. Let note be taken of children who cry and scream in order to be compassionated and who, therefore, await the moment when their condition will be observed; come into contact with the sick and the oppressed in spirit and try to ascertain if the wailing and sighing, the posturing and posing of misfortune do not have as end and aim the causing of pain to the beholder: the sympathy which each beholder manifests is a consolation to the weak and suffering only in as much as they are made to perceive that at least they have the power, notwithstanding all their weakness, to inflict pain. The unfortunate experiences a species of joy in the sense of superiority which the manifestation of sympathy entails; his imagination is exalted; he is always strong enough, then, to cause the world pain. Thus is the thirst for sympathy a thirst for self enjoyment and at the expense of one's fellow creatures: it shows man in the whole ruthlessness of his own dear self: not in his mere "dullness" as La Rochefoucauld thinks.—In social conversation three fourths of all the questions are asked, and three fourths of all the replies are made in order to inflict some little pain; that is why so many people crave social intercourse: it gives them a sense of their power. In these countless but very small doses in which the quality of badness is administered it proves a potent stimulant of life: to the same extent that well wishing—(Wohl-wollen) distributed through the world in like manner, is one of the ever ready restoratives.—But will many honorable people be found to admit that there is any pleasure in administering pain? that entertainment—and rare entertainment—is not seldom found in causing others, at least in thought, some pain, and in raking them with the small shot of wickedness? The majority are too ignoble and a few are too good to know anything of this *pudendum*: the latter may, consequently, be prompt to deny that Prosper Mérimée is right when he says: "Know, also, that nothing is more common than to do wrong for the pleasure of doing it."

How Appearance Becomes Reality.—The actor cannot, at last, refrain, even in moments of the deepest pain, from thinking of the effect produced by his deportment and by his surroundings—for example, even at the funeral of his own child: he will weep at his own sorrow and its manifestations as though he were his own audience. The hypocrite who always plays one and the same part, finally ceases to be a hypocrite; as in the case of priests who, when young men, are always, either consciously or unconsciously, hypocrites, and finally become naturally and then really, without affectation, mere priests: or if the father does not carry it to this extent, the son, who inherits his father's calling and gets the advantage of the paternal progress, does. When anyone, during a long period, and persistently, wishes to appear something, it will at last prove difficult for him to be anything else. The calling of almost every man, even of the artist, begins with hypocrisy, with an imitation of deportment, with a copying of the effective in manner. He who always wears the mask of a friendly man must at last gain a power over friendliness of disposition, without which the expression itself of friendliness is not to be gained—and finally friendliness of disposition gains the ascendancy over him—he *is* benevolent.

The Point of Honor in Deception.—In all great deceivers one characteristic is prominent, to which they owe their power. In the very act of deception, amid all the accompaniments, the agitation in the voice, the expression, the bearing, in the crisis of the scene, there comes over them a belief in themselves; this it is that acts so effectively and irresistibly upon the beholders. Founders of religions differ from such great deceivers in that they never come out of this state of self deception, or

else they have, very rarely, a few moments of enlightenment in which
they are overcome by doubt; generally, however, they soothe themselves by ascribing such moments of enlightenment to the evil adversary.
Self-deception must exist that both classes of deceivers may attain far
reaching results. For men believe in the truth of all that is manifestly
believed with due implicitness by others. . . .

ABILITY TO WAIT.—Ability to wait is so hard to acquire that great
poets have not disdained to make inability to wait the central motive of
their poems. So Shakespeare in Othello, Sophocles in Ajax, whose suicide
would not have seemed to him so imperative had he only been able to
cool his ardor for a day, as the oracle foreboded: apparently he would
then have repulsed somewhat the fearful whispers of distracted thought
and have said to himself: Who has not already, in my situation, mistaken
a sheep for a hero? is it so extraordinary a thing? On the contrary it is
something universally human: Ajax should thus have soothed himself.
Passion will not wait: the tragic element in the lives of great men does
not generally consist in their conflict with time and the inferiority of
their fellowmen but in their inability to put off their work a year or two:
they cannot wait.—In all duels, the friends who advise have but to ascertain if the principals can wait: if this be not possible, a duel is rational
inasmuch as each of the combatants may say: "either I continue to live
and the other dies instantly, or vice versa." To wait in such circumstances would be equivalent to the frightful martyrdom of enduring dishonor in the presence of him responsible for the dishonor: and this can
easily cost more anguish than life is worth.

GLUTTING REVENGE.—Coarse men, who feel a sense of injury, are
in the habit of rating the extent of their injury as high as possible and
of stating the occasion of it in greatly exaggerated language, in order to
be able to feast themselves on the sentiments of hatred and revenge thus
aroused.

VALUE OF DISPARAGEMENT.—Not a few, perhaps the majority of men,
find it necessary, in order to retain their self esteem and a certain uprightness in conduct, to mentally disparage and belittle all the people they
know. But as the inferior natures are in the majority and as a great deal
depends upon whether they retain or lose this uprightness, so—

THE MAN IN A RAGE.—We should be on our guard against the man
who is enraged against us, as against one who has attempted our life, for
the fact that we still live consists solely in the inability to kill: were looks
sufficient, it would have been all up with us long since. To reduce anyone
to silence by physical manifestations of savagery or by a terrorizing process
is a relic of under civilization. So, too, that cold look which great per-

sonages cast upon their servitors is a remnant of the caste distinction between man and man; a specimen of rude antiquity: women, the conservers of the old, have maintained this survival, too, more perfectly than men. . . .

GENERAL STANDARD.—One will rarely err if extreme actions be ascribed to vanity, ordinary actions to habit and mean actions to fear.

MISUNDERSTANDING OF VIRTUE.—Whoever has obtained his experience of vice in connection with pleasure, as in the case of one with a youth of wild oats behind him, comes to the conclusion that virtue must be connected with self denial. Whoever, on the other hand, has been very much plagued by his passions and vices, longs to find in virtue the rest and peace of the soul. That is why it is possible for two virtuous people to misunderstand one another wholly.

THE ASCETIC.—The ascetic makes out of virtue a slavery. . . .

AMBITION A SUBSTITUTE FOR MORAL FEELING.—Moral feeling should never become extinct in natures that are destitute of ambition. The ambitious can get along without moral feeling just as well as with it.— Hence the sons of retired, ambitionless families, generally become by a series of rapid gradations, when they lose moral feeling, the most absolute lunkheads. . . .

THE SOUL'S SKIN.—As the bones, flesh, entrails and blood vessels are enclosed by a skin that renders the aspect of men endurable, so the impulses and passions of the soul are enclosed by vanity: it is the skin of the soul.

SLEEP OF VIRTUE.—If virtue goes to sleep, it will be more vigorous when it awakes.

SUBTLETY OF SHAME.—Men are not ashamed of obscene thoughts, but they are ashamed when they suspect that obscene thoughts are attributed to them.

NAUGHTINESS IS RARE.—Most people are too much absorbed in themselves to be bad.

THE MITE IN THE BALANCE.—We are praised or blamed, as the one or the other may be expedient, for displaying to advantage our power of discernment.

LUKE 18, 14 IMPROVED.—He that humbleth himself wisheth to be exalted.

JOSEPH WOOD KRUTCH

The Conditioned Man

Joseph Wood Krutch (1893–   ) is an American writer who has had a varied career as Professor of English at Columbia, dramatic critic, and naturalist—the last in the Thoreauvian sense, not in that of formal biological scientific research. He is, clearly, essentially a moralist. I give here at length a characteristic estimate of human capacities by a representative contemporary American intellectual. Mr. Krutch seems to me to display clearly one of the sources of the "alienation" of his kind with which we began this book: he doesn't think very highly of his fellowmen and is certainly not very charitable towards them; he inclines to the hope that they are by nature not as bad as they are now in condition in the United States in the 1960's; he seems to hold that "something" has gone wrong, something in the environment (the human condition); and yet he has no clear notion of how to lift the many out of the bad environment into a better, seems indeed at times to feel that the human stuff really is hopelessly corrupt. Can a good democrat hold a low opinion of the human stuff?

NO OFFHAND SAYING IS MORE FAMILIAR THAN "YOU CAN'T CHANGE human nature." Nevertheless, we are today much more likely to proceed upon the assumption that you can; and the whole of the prevalent, Marxist-tinged social philosophy takes it for granted that "human nature," far from being a constant, is nothing but a determined and predictable reaction to "society."

Moreover, that old-fashioned minority which says and really means, "You can't change human nature," is generally dismissed as reactionary and cynical. What they are usually assumed to mean (and what they very often do mean) is merely that man is incurably self-centered, selfish, envious, grasping, combative, greedy, mischievous, and cruel.

The possibly encouraging aspects of the assumption that there is

From Joseph Wood Krutch, *Human Nature and the Human Condition* (New York: Random House, 1959), pp. 169-190.

something permanent about human nature and that it is changeable only within limits, is curiously overlooked. If man is incurably this or that unamiable thing he may also be, incurably, this or that admirable or even noble thing. When liberals consider what the Nazi and Communist totalitarians have made the condition of millions to be and when they assume that this condition will prove intolerable in the end, they sometimes say that "sooner or later human nature will rebel." But it won't and it can't unless human nature is, indeed, an independent reality, not merely a product.

Even in the United States the same unanswered question arises in a milder form, because all proponents of a completely "planned society" also go on the assumption that human nature can be made to become whatever the social, political, and economic organization are designed to make it. To say to them that "you can't change human nature" *may* mean, as it often does, that you cannot condition man to the abandonment of all desire for personal profit, personal possessions, "status," and all the other prizes given to excellence. But it may also mean, perhaps, that you cannot make him the pure conformist and pure materialist which many "planned societies" seem to want to make him.

Considered thus, "You can't change human nature" may be an expression of the last best hope for an age which has lost faith in man as, in any sense, the captain of his soul. And since it does seem to suggest such a hope, then surely there is good reason to re-examine the so generally neglected assumption that there is, after all, some such thing as human nature, or to put it in another way, that what we are born with is not a completely blank slate.

One had best begin by remembering that just such a re-examination of the theory was made during the eighteenth century for exactly the same reason that we would like to make it, and also that those who, for a time, did confidently reassert the reality of human nature were worsted a few generations later by that new wave of destructive criticism of which so much of today's thinking is a part.

The nihilistic conclusions which inevitably follow from the Hobbesian premise had been drawn by Hobbes himself and eagerly embraced by the intellectuals of his time, who felt themselves emancipated from the traditions of a sobered generation much as those of the nineteen twenties felt themselves emancipated from Victorianism. But after hardly more than a generation of exuberant Hobbesism the early eighteenth century began to put up its own fight against the nihilism to which, like us, it could no longer oppose traditional religious assumptions.

Its answer to the question, "To what shall we turn for guidance now that we no longer have God's revealed word?" was the concepts of nature and of right reason.

If, so it argued, the good cannot be defined as "that which is in accord with God's will" it is at least "that which is in accord with nature." And it proposed a simple criterion by which it thought that nature might be distinguished from custom or mere fashion. Whatever tastes, customs, or convictions vary radically from time to time and from place to place were recognized as mere matters of fashion. Whatever all men tended to agree upon was accepted as "in accord with nature."

The *Iliad,* for example, exemplified the natural laws of aesthetics because all men who had ever known it found it admirable. Because a belief in God seemed to be a universal characteristic of all societies this belief must also be natural, though none of the theological creeds which are so wildly variable and inconsistent are. Thus nature (including human nature) was presumed to set up its own absolutes.

What men should do was not, to them, whatever men do do, but rather what men have always thought they *should* do. Education was not, as we now think it should be, an "adjustment" to the prevailing or fashionable mores but to a life "in accordance with that right reason which understands and accepts the laws of nature." The best literature or music was not, as we now tend to think, whatever is at the moment preferred by the greatest number of people but what, in the long run, nature is seen to be striving toward.

Unfortunately, perhaps, this fight against the nihilistic implications of the blank slate and the relativism which follows logically from it turned out to be only a delaying action. Presently, the concept of nature was criticized out of existence just as that of God had been. There simply is not, said its critics, *anything* in religion, or morals, or art upon which, in actual fact, all men, or even nearly all men, have agreed.

The support and factual amplification of this criticism became one of the chief tasks of anthropology and sociology during the nineteenth and twentieth centuries. Before the first of these centuries was over, William Lecky in his very influential *History of European Morals* could write that there is no act which cannot be shown to have been forbidden as a sin at one time and place and enjoined as a duty at some other. And so, after the heroic struggle of the eighteenth century Lecky brought us back once more to the conviction that morals are merely mores; that neither God nor any permanent human nature gives sanction to one system of ethics rather than another. We were, in other words, given back the blank slate upon which anything can be written, and, on the whole, the twentieth century has accepted it.

Professor Leo Strauss, a present-day defender of the now usually discredited concept of natural right, has recently pointed out that the collapse of the eighteenth-century argument based upon "general consent" does not logically invalidate the concept itself:

" 'Consent of all mankind,' " he writes, "is by no means a necessary condition of the existence of natural right. Some of the greatest natural right teachers have argued that, precisely if natural right is rational, its discovery presupposes the cultivation of reason, and therefore natural right will not be known universally: one ought not even expect any real knowledge of natural right among savages."

This defense is applicable, not only to the concept of natural right, but equally to all the other phases of the more general concept of the natural as some sort of reality. But it is not likely to be very effective with most contemporary relativists because it assumes that reason, as distinct from rationalization, is possible and because it rules out as irrelevant the opinions and practices of the savage, the uncultivated, and the stupid upon which the relativists lean so heavily in drawing their conclusions concerning what is "natural" and "normal"!

Neverthless, the fact remains that in a world which has so definitely rejected all transcendental sanctions for either codes of behavior or standards of value, "nature" and "human nature" seem to be the only possible place to look for a norm which is not merely an average or a concept of an "ought" which is more than a description of usual conduct. The question whether or not there is such a thing as human nature therefore remains for us the grandest of all living questions and makes it necessary for us to ask whether the usual negative answer really is justifiable and permanent or whether we shall some day swing again in a different direction and discover evidence now neglected that human nature really is something in itself and does provide certain absolutes, valid at least in the human realm.

Have the anthropologists been so preoccupied with the collection of materials to demonstrate the enormous *differences* between cultures that they have overlooked some things which really are common to them all? Have the experimental psychologists been so busy conditioning both animals and men that they have paid little attention to the resistance to conditioning which both can put up?

One little straw blowing in the winds of psychological doctrine seems to point in that direction. Some skeptics have begun to wonder whether instinct on the one hand and the conditioned reflex on the other really can account for all the behavior of living organisms. A brain which carries written upon it even a system of instincts is far from being a blank slate. But that is by no means all. Certain other sufficiently obvious facts have recently been emphasized: (1) Birds know by instinct how to fly and do not have to be taught. (2) Seals do not know instinctively how to swim but are very easily taught by their mothers to do so. (3) You would have a very hard time indeed teaching most songbirds to swim.

There are, in other words, not just two classes of animal behavior (inborn and learned) but also a third—that which is not inborn though the ability to learn it easily is.

Some to whom these facts have come home have begun to wonder whether the same may not be true, not only of skills, but throughout the whole psychic realm of beliefs, tastes, and motives. The thesis of the moral relativists is—to take an extreme case—that since no one was born with the "innate idea" that dishonesty and treachery are evil, then the conviction that they are evil can be nothing but the result of social education. The opposite, so they say, could just as easily be taught. Value judgments are therefore merely the rationalized prejudices of a given culture.

May not, in actual fact, the contrary be true, namely, that certain ideas are more *easily learned* than others; that what the eighteenth century called natural law, natural taste, and the rest is real and consists in those beliefs and tastes which are most readily learned and also most productive of health and happiness?

Perhaps you can condition an individual or a society to think and behave "unnaturally" just as you might possibly teach a robin to swim. But men who have been conditioned to think or behave unnaturally are as unhappy and as inefficient as swimming robins. As the biochemist Roger J. Williams puts it, "There are blanks and blanks. The blank brain of the child is capable as time goes on of accepting, digesting (perceiving), and acting upon a multitude of impressions that the brain of a rat is quite incapable of handling."

Is this belaboring the obvious? At least it is not anything so obvious that the implications have not been for long disregarded by those who preferred to disregard them. Perhaps no ideas are innate; but if the capacity to entertain readily some ideas and not others is innate, then it all comes down to much the same thing. Professor Williams has led us back by a new route to the eighteenth century and to one of the most discredited exponents of its ideas. "Nature affords at least a glimm'ring light;/The lines, tho' touch'd but faintly, are drawn right."

What Pope thought of as a metaphor may be an accurate biological statement. On the not quite blank slate the lines are touched too faintly to constitute an automatic instinct. They are much like the latent image on a photographic plate—imperceptible until developed. But what development will reveal already exists. There is such a thing as human nature. What we are born with is not a blank slate but a film bearing already a latent image.

No doubt—as Pope went on to say elsewhere, as experimental psychologists prove in the laboratory, and as educators as well as dictators have all too often demonstrated—the lines may be "o'er laid," and the unnatural cease to seem a creature of hideous mien. But the conditioners have to work at it—hard. Men believe in, for instance, the reality of good and evil much more readily than they can be made to accept cultural relativism.

Such an assumption is at least one which no valid science forbids, and if we make it we are saved from the nihilism of present-day cultural and moral relativism as the eighteenth century was saved from the nihilism of

Hobbes. In a sense, God—or at least a useful substitute for Him—exists. We have again some point of reference now lacking in every inquiry which sets out to determine what kind of society, or education, or culture would be best for us. One thing is no longer as good as another provided only it can be shown, or made, to exist. We need no longer talk only about what can be *done to* men or what we might be able to *make* them into. We can talk again about what, in themselves, they *are*.

That involves what is certainly no easy inquiry. One of the most terrifying of Pascal's *Pensées* seems to range him with the enemy: "They say that habit is second nature; perhaps nature is only first habit." To distinguish correctly between the one and the other is one of the most difficult tasks we could set ourselves. But perhaps it is also the most important.

More than two thousand years ago when Herodotus was inventing cultural anthropology he noted a fact which anthropologists still make much of. Inquiring about funeral customs, he discovered that those who burned their dead were shocked when told that some peoples buried theirs and that the latter were no less shocked to learn that other human beings were so impious as to consign human bodies to the flames. On the basis of this fact Herodotus was already almost prepared to conclude what the nineteenth century hailed as a great and novel discovery, namely that morals are, after all, only mores. When in Rome you should do as the Romans do—not merely because that is the courteous way to behave but because the customs of the Romans are, in that latitude, what is truly right, seemly, and proper.

Does this necessarily follow in any such unqualified and unlimited sense? True, history may give us no reason to suppose that burying one's dead is more in accord with human nature than burning or that burning is more in accord with it than burying. But there is, nevertheless, a fact which neither Herodotus nor most recent cultural and moral relativists seem to have noticed: There is a good deal of evidence to support the contention that an enduring characteristic of the nature of man does bid him dispose of human remains in *some* traditional and ritual fashion. Burial customs of one kind or another appear so early in human prehistory that their existence may be one of the criteria for distinguishing between men and mere half-men, and some sort of respect for his dead may have been part of the nature of man for as long as there has been man to have a nature.

All such imperatives (if there are any) as originate in human nature itself must be, like that which bids man pay respect to his dead, highly generalized rather than specific. But even such highly generalized imperatives can have important consequences. The pure relativist who denies the existence of *anything* permanent in human nature and who then finds himself shocked by, let us say, the "atrocities" committed against the dead by Nazi authorities is logically bound to tell himself that he is merely reacting according to a prejudice unworthy of one who has come to understand intellectually that custom is never more than custom and that there is no reason why, for instance, corpses should not always be made into useful soap—as they were in Germany during the second world war.

But such "mere prejudices" may not be prejudices at all. They may be rather a revulsion against a practice which violates something fundamental in human nature, namely, that something which does not require burial rather than cremation or cremation rather than burial but does require ritual respect for the dead. Similarly, other Nazi attitudes toward, say, the victims of genocide may not be merely part of the unfamilar mores of another race but one of the clear signs that Nazism consists of a whole complex of principles and practices repugnant not merely to "prevalent ideas of right and wrong" but to the nature of man himself. Perhaps, indeed, the fundamental horror of Nazism may be just that it follows further than we have yet followed the implications of the relativism we profess without yet having so consistently implemented them.

If it is true that human nature does require some ceremonial respect for the bodies of the dead as a testimony of respect and an expression of awe in the face of death, then that fact will suggest another generalization. It may be true that cultures exhibit such a bewildering variety of actions and attitudes as to give a superficial air of probability to the conclusion that *all* moral ideas and all ideas of what constitutes propriety are no more than what limitlessly variable custom has established. Yet men almost invariably believe that *some* beliefs and *some* customs are right. However diverse and irreconcilable specific moral judgments are and have been, moral judgment itself has been a constantly continuing activity of the human mind. What no society has ever been able to believe for long is precisely the doctrine which ours has embraced—namely, that morals are no more than mores.

A sense that right and wrong (however difficult to determine) are nevertheless both real and tremendously important seems to be part of fundamental human nature. In simple societies no sanction other than custom may be needed to justify what is done or what is not done, because custom itself is naïvely accepted as the final arbiter and is not regarded as "mere" custom. The more intellectually sophisticated a society becomes, the more complicated the questions involved are seen to be, the more subtly they are investigated, and the less clear the answers.

But the conviction that the difference between right and wrong is tremendously important persists and has hardly been got rid of even in those societies which profess the most unqualified relativism. To state the proposition in the most general possible terms, it comes down to this: An obvious characteristic of the nature of man is his inveterate habit of making value judgments. Perhaps he is the only animal who can give rational form to his preferences or is capable of calling them by such names as The Good and The Beautiful. But he cannot be better defined than by saying that he is the animal which *can do* and *does insist upon doing* just that.

Yet this is the fact which the cultural relativists most strangely overlook, both when they profess to be purely objective and when, as has often been the case, they draw lessons or "morals" of their own. They point out how irreconcilable different sets of customs and different sets of values can be. What is "good" in one primitive tribe is "bad" in another. They bid us therefore recognize the relativity of all such judgments and then, in the light of our understanding, divest ourselves of the "prejudices" of our own culture.

What they fail to notice is the most striking fact of all: that no enduring society ever has been "unprejudiced" in that sense. Even if they insist upon denying what is here maintained—namely, that to have "prejudices" is a necessary consequence of the nature of man—they should at least admit that such "prejudices" obviously have a tremendous "survival value."

A current college textbook of psychology gives a conveniently simple statement of the relativist position. "Moral conduct," so it says, "is conduct of which a given society approves," and by the absoluteness of its state- ment it clearly implies that "moral conduct" is also "nothing but" just that. If the author is convinced that this is a truth which it is his duty as a scientist to promulgate, he should at least add also the simple warning: "Undeniable as this fact is, no society which limited itself to this definition has ever endured for long." To try to live without "moral prejudices" (i.e., without making value judgments) is to try to live in a condition so funda- mentally repugnant to our nature that it cannot long continue.

Unless we admit that man is a creature to whom moral judgments are "natural," we cannot ask a great many meaningful questions such as, for example, what is the good life, as distinguished from a "high standard of living." We cannot ask them because they can be asked only in connec- tion with some conviction concerning what kind of life it is in the nature of man to lead. And it is because we cannot discuss the good life that it has not become either so unqualified or so accessible as our mastery of the physical environment should make it.

We can ask what are the "needs of industry." We can debate the relative merits of laissez faire, socialism, and any economic system in between— but only so long as we confine ourselves to the question which of them most successfully promotes abundant production, not which makes a good life most accessible. We can also ask what laws and what system of education best meet the needs of either technology or pure science. But we cannot ask *what would best meet the needs of man* or consider the question whether or not, in any specific instance, the "needs of industry" (or even the needs of science) may require some modification in the in- terests of the possibly conflicting needs of man. We cannot ask any such questions because we have ceased to believe that man has any nature and believe instead that, since he has no needs of his own, he will "adapt" or "adjust" to whatever conditions are most favorable to industry, technology or science, or what not.

The only categorical imperative we accept, almost the only inescapable obligation we feel, is the obligation to realize all the potentialities inherent in technology. Whenever the possibility of moving faster, of producing more, or of exercising any increased power presents itself we accept the duty of moving faster and of wielding more power. What can be done must be done. But we feel no such responsibility toward the potentialities of human nature and we cannot do so as long as we continue to assume that such potentialities do not exist except in so far as they consist in an almost limitless adaptability to the conditions which the nonhuman can create.

That eighteenth century which believed so confidently in the law of nature and appealed so frequently to it fell often into a folly the opposite of ours. Instead of denying that the "natural" or "normal" had any meaning, it was very ready to proclaim that almost any attitude or custom with which it was thoroughly familiar and sympathetic was "in accord with nature" and any conflicting attitude or custom "contrary to nature." It was insufficiently aware—as we certainly are not—that to distinguish between the natural and the merely customary is often extremely difficult, perhaps sometimes impossible.

Against their sometimes fatuous pronouncements "cultural relativism" is in part a protest. Yet the difficulty was never really forgotten even when the reality of the distinction was most unquestioningly accepted. That habit is "second nature" is an idea so old that it fills our literature and John Donne can refer to "that demi-nature custom" without implying that custom is more than a simulacrum. Most certainly it behooves those of us who undertake to assert again that man does have a nature to be fully aware of the difficulties. The nature of man is something which may be inferred, not directly demonstrated, and the more specific any alleged characteristic of that nature is, the less certain it will be that it actually is "nature" and not what Donne called "demi."

We must begin with the minimum assertion that human nature, though enormously variable and exceedingly plastic, is not infinitely so; that though men readily believe and want and do a great variety of different things, they are not readily or very often conditioned to believe or want or do certain others; and that though the discoverable traits of their nature can generally be described only in very general terms our history is sufficiently well known to support the inference that some of the generalities can be stated.

One such probably permanent characteristic of the nature of man has already been mentioned: namely, the persistence with which he makes value judgments of some kind and thus persistently raises the very questions which relativists dismiss as either demonstrably unanswerable or radically meaningless. He insists upon believing that right and wrong are real, that justice and injustice do exist, even though he is not certain what any of them are.

Even if we could get no further than that, we would have already gone a long way. We would have demonstrated that "cultural and moral relativism" is a doctrine repugnant to the nature of man and that the attempt to build a society upon such relativism is certain to reduce him to a condition which he can come to accept comfortably only in so far as he succeeds in dehumanizing himself. Anxiety, tension, and the other forms of malaise whose prevalence so many have observed with alarm are in part the penalty paid by those who have not been completely conditioned into accepting comfortably their condition. The mass-man is the creature who has to some extent escaped the malaise by ceasing to be a man at all.

About the nature of man we shall perhaps never have much detailed knowledge. The very fact that habit can imitate nature so cunningly may forever prevent the development of any body of positive, detailed knowledge comparable to that which has accumulated around other subjects in themselves less important. Perhaps there can never be a real science of man, however much those who are trying to dehumanize him may believe that they have already founded it. The objectivity of science is possible only because it does involve a subject (man) and an object (the external world). But a science of man proposes that the subject—call him the observer, if you like—should be also the object; and that is impossible. Man can observe other men "objectively" only in so far as he excludes from his observation the fact that they are men like himself. Therefore what is nowadays called the science of man is, in actual fact, only the science of man-considered-as-something-less-than-man.

We shall never see ourselves other than through a glass, darkly. For that and for other reasons there will always be disputes over the question whether or not some specific law or custom is or is not "in accord with nature." But to say that is to say only that right and wrong or the beautiful and the ugly must continue to be, as they have always been, to some degree outside the scope of positive knowledge. Yet no matter how inconclusive any discussion which involves them may be, the very fact that the discussion does take place is sufficient to set any society which takes the discussion seriously significantly apart from any society which tends, as our own does, to consider it not worth engaging in. No disagreement concerning *what* is right or wrong is so fundamental as that between those who believe that *some* value judgment is valid and those who believe that none is more valid than any other. Similarly, on a lower level, no two societies can differ so greatly because of what they consider "good manners" as either differs from a society in which no such thing as "good manners" exists.

The appeal to nature will, then, never settle the dispute between the big-endians and the little-endians in any Lilliput. Perhaps, for instance, monogamy is not "natural" and polygamy "unnatural," any more than burial of the dead is the one and cremation the other. But again it may well be true nevertheless that it is "natural" to accept *some* code rather than none at all governing the relations of the sexes—just as it is natural to feel that some ceremonial disposition of the dead is "right and proper."

Should we, however, ever come again to believe that the question whether or not something is "in accord with human nature" is a meaningful—perhaps the most meaningful—question, we shall want to explore this permanent human nature in many directions and test the extent to which it is possible to determine, with some degree of probability at least, characteristics of that nature somewhat more specific than any so far suggested. Are there any which seem pretty obvious in the light of what we already know about the histories of cultures?

I myself should confidently say, "Yes, at least one other"; and it is this: Man is not by nature a pure materialist or satisfied with what are called common-sense value judgments. One of the most evident constants of human nature is the desire for Goods other than the material, and the vast majority of cultures have put something else first. They have sought God as the ancient Hebrews did, or, like the Greeks, beauty and wisdom. Below those levels they have sometimes put the highest value on glory, courage, personal prowess, or military success and believed that comfort as well as security were well sacrificed for them. Even the belief that a large collection of shrunken human heads is the thing most to be desired testifies to the fact that to believe something more worth having than material wealth is as nearly universal as the belief that some things are good and some evil. A society which, like ours, defines the good life as identical with the high standard of living is running contrary to a fundamental characteristic of the nature of man.

In *Notes from Underground,* Dostoevsky asked: "Does not man, perhaps, love something besides well-being?" and then he half-answered his own question with, "Perhaps he is just as fond of suffering." This answer is no doubt an exaggeration—even what we are fond of calling a "neurotic exaggeration." But perhaps it is only an overstatement of the true reply. Perhaps the animals do not desire anything except well-being. That we cannot know. But that man does desire something else is part of his humanity. Call it perversity or call it the determination to transcend the most obvious Goods. In either case it exists and is important, so important that we might well hesitate before trying to "condition" him out of it. Should we succeed, we might find that we had turned man back into an animal again.

Could we at this moment get no further than the two statements already made, namely, that man is (1) inveterately a maker of value judgments and (2) not by nature a pure materialist or utilitarian, we should already have called attention to the fact that in at least these two important respects the present condition of man is one to which he cannot "adjust" without violating his nature.

Thus the ideal of the welfare state has its dangers unless we are willing to raise seriously the question, "In what does total welfare for a human being consist?" And that question cannot very well be raised without some concept of "normality." Why could we not follow the lead of Shaw's oculist and recognize that the criterion should be what an eye (or a man) *can be* rather than what either most often is? By any such definition a "normal human being" is some kind of individual, while the "average human being" is little more than a mass-man. Today we are obsessed with origins and must stretch a point to consider even potentialities. Perhaps we shall have again to recognize the meaning of entelechy—to ask, that is to say, not merely what was the origin but also what is the destiny of man; not merely what is he but what is he striving to become?

From the two statements already made about normal human nature one might well proceed to raise at least two questions—not to be answered confidently, but upon which would in turn depend the answer to the question whether or not, in two other respects, our society is organized upon "unnatural" assumptions.

Do men naturally desire justice as well as believe that it is a reality? The ancient philosophers thought they did, whereas we moderns have decided that what they desire is only their individual or their class interest instead. Should it turn out that the ancients were even partly right, that might make a great difference in our way of dealing with our fellows—beginning even in the nursery and the kindergarten.

Some child psychologists insist that what children need is "uncritical love" and that they should be made to feel that they can count upon it no matter how "naughty" they may be. Yet it is a common observation that what the unsympathetic call "spoiled" children seem very often extremely unhappy. Can that be because the expectation—the desire, even —that acts should have consequences and that the way one is treated should depend to some extent upon the way one behaves is latent on the not quite blank slate and constitutes the most primitive form of that idea of justice which, in some way and to some extent, all "normal" men do love. Perhaps a world which violently disappoints this expectation is seriously disturbing even to a child. Perhaps the best way to deal with delinquency and crime would be not to assume as we now tend to do that "society" is wholly to blame, but to mix some justice with "understanding." Perhaps if we did so both the delinquent and the criminal would be less "mixed up" just because he found himself in a society which, to that extent, met one of the expectations of normal human nature.

The second question would be whether the technology which has made the environment of most men who live in every "developed" country one almost wholly man-made has not placed them in what seems to fundamental human nature an abnormal environment. Perhaps the natural context for the human being is the context of the natural world. Once he was surrounded by other living things and his most intimate relations were with other men, with animals, and with plants. Now his most usual and intimate business is with machines. Does that tend to make him machinelike? Is it ultimately responsible for the fact that he has become a mechanist as well as a materialist and thus tries to believe things contrary to his nature?

Both the behavior of man and the condition of man have been exhaustively investigated in our century. Any attempt to investigate his nature would certainly involve such questions as those we have just been raising and they cannot be answered so easily as questions concerning his condition (What proportion of homes has a telephone?) or his behavior (What is the average number of hours he spends in watching television?). But they are more significant. The attempt to study the nature of man would involve both what, on the evidence of history and anthropology, seem to be the constants and perhaps also an attempt to apply that reason which, as Professor Strauss pointed out, may be more important than "common consent" in any successful attempt to discover what "the natural" really is.

Neither method will be easy for us to apply. The first will not be easy because of the inherent difficulty in distinguishing between the habitual and the natural; the second because it must assume the validity of reason despite the fact that of all the faiths which modern man has lost the most disastrous may well be his loss of faith in reason itself. When the eighteenth century ceased to believe in revelation it proclaimed its faith in reason. We dismiss reason as no more than the rationalization of individual interests, class interests, and the prejudices of a particular culture. Unless the lost faith is to some degree recovered no true humanism is possible.

ALFRED COBBAN

The Decline in Ethical Judgment

Alfred Cobban (1901–   ) is Professor of History in the University of London. He is an authority on the eighteenth century in the West, and has a special interest in the Enlightenment and its consequences. These passages from his In Search of Humanity *show a thoughtful, open-minded believer in the world-view first fully stated and widely disseminated in our modern Western world in the late seventeenth and in the eighteenth centuries. This book is a good clear exposition of the world view—or religion—of Enlightenment, but an exposition motivated at least in part, like the address of Professor Murray with which we began this book, by an awareness that what has gone on so far in the twentieth century has for many persons weakened the hold this world-view has on them. Professor Cobban is clearly and firmly on the side of the angels . . . of Enlightenment. But like all sensible believers of his kind today, he shares the feeling that there is something lacking in this world-view, that something needs to be done to modify and strengthen it. Like Professor Murray, he asks us to think more, and think better—a perfectly suitable suggestion, for the Enlightenment is nothing if it is not a form of rationalism.*

But Professor Cobban does throw us right back on the problem. The question "How rational is the human stuff?" is surely not answered—perhaps not even answerable—in the sense the engineer can answer a problem as to the strength of given materials.

EACH AGE HAS MANY PROBLEMS, BUT AMONG THEM ONE OR ANOTHER seems in turn to take precedence and to present the major threat to society, or to civilized life, if it is not eliminated. In fact—and this is encouraging—such problems seldom are solved: most often they are transmuted by time, fade into the general mass of difficulties that beset every generation, and under the influence of some obsessive new threat are seen to be no longer as fundamental as was once thought. Boom and slump, inflation and

From Alfred Cobban, *In Search of Humanity* (New York: George Braziller, Inc., 1960), pp. 11-13, 242-245.

deflation, mass unemployment, over-production and under-production, economic crisis in all its forms, presented the basic problem of the 'twenties and 'thirties of this century. In the 'thirties the economic problem became also a political problem, assuming the menacing shape of totalitarianism. This in turn merged into total war, which in the period since the Second World War has mushroomed into the ultimate threat of the atomic or hydrogen cloud. As we look back on these several crises they melt into one another and are seen to be less separable than we may have thought at the time, as well as less novel. Economic distress, political tyranny, war—though now on a large scale than ever before—are not new. Basic to them all are not the changing though calculable objective facts but the changeless and incalculable human behaviour that can at any moment give urgency to a perennial danger.

To admit so much is to perform the opening gambit in the familiar manœuvre which begins with a platitude and ends with Original Sin, the most convenient, indubitable and compendious of explanations for all human evils. It has many advantages. Since it came about once for all, and so long ago, we ourselves need not feel more than a vicarious responsibility for it. At the same time, since it is now an integral part of human nature, we can hardly be expected to change it, at least in other people, who make up the majority of the human race. Original Sin, as such or secularized as simple human nature, is the perfect scapegoat for all the ills of society.

If, however, we concentrate our attention on human behaviour rather than human nature, the whole argument changes, for human behaviour has frequently been altered in the past and therefore presumably can be altered again. Thinking in terms of behaviour, and forgetting that elusive thing human nature, we may be less willing to seek salvation only by plunging into those mystic depths in which all remedial action is sunk without trace, and more prepared to concieve the possibility of positive effort to counter current evils. It is not unreasonable to approach our problems from this direction. Economic crises, totalitarianism, war, may or may not be the inevitable consequences of human nature. They may be the product of good or bad, noble or ignoble motives. They may be calculated, or unintended, results of our actions. But at any rate they are all aspects of human behaviour, and we deplore them not because of their varying and suppositious motivation, but because of the effects that flow from them. From this point of view they can fairly be considered together, for not only are they bound together historically but their results are fundamentally the same. Economic crisis meant declining standards of life, destitution, and a kind of suspended animation for masses of the people; totalitarianism meant inter alia the murder, torture, exile, or use as slave labour, of incalculable numbers of human beings; and we should have a fair idea what total war in the form of the hydrogen bomb means. All these add up to the deliberate infliction of pain or death on such a colossal scale that it numbs the imagination. Yet it is only the monstrous proportions that prevent us from recognizing what we dislike in all this as a very simple and common thing. On a smaller scale it would be called cruelty. There may be other reasons for objecting to economic distress, totalitarianism and war, but the major reason why we regard them as such great evils is, I suggest, because they are inseparable from the infliction on a colossal scale of otherwise avoidable pain, suffering and death. This may be a mere emotional reaction, but it is a widespread and influential one and it is probably the determining factor in the identification of our major problems; because if we did not have this reaction we should not necessarily have found these forms of behaviour objectionable, or not objectionable in the particular way in which we do. It may be said that such a supposition is inconceivable; but it would only be so if the feeling of revulsion against cruelty is as much to be taken for granted as we are apt to suppose.

That this assumption needs further consideration could easily be demonstrated from the contemporary world. It was brought to my mind during a short pleasure trip along one of London's canals, when the helmsman pointed out a family of ducks—a mother and six or seven ducklings scuttling through the water in the prettiest way. There were nine or ten to begin with, he said, and she will be lucky if she rears two of them. He added, apart from those that will die from cold nights and natural enemies, the boys kill them by stoning. It seemed a pity, but for one's mind to veer to Belsen and Buchenwald was perhaps rather inconsequent. Between killing a baby duckling for pleasure and the murder of six, eight or ten million human beings, the difference is so great that it seems almost indecent to mention them in the same breath. Yet boys, or men and women, have done, or do, both; and one has only to look at popular fiction or films to suspect that many people, even those who would not easily bring themselves to do cruel things, enjoy reading about them or seeing them represented. . . .

It is possible to return now to the problem with which this inquiry began, that of the increasing re-brutalization of contemporary life, particularly, though by no means exclusively, manifested in its politics. In international relations, it may be said, an assertion of moral standards that the twentieth century has deserted is necessary not only for the survival of civilized life but for the survival of human life itself. This is the practical issue, and the first and simplest solution is obviously inadequate. Regimes which violently conflict with the ethical standards we have inherited can be, and have been, resisted and overthrown by force; but recent history shows that force by itself is not enough. Those who begin by opposing mere force to force, are liable to end by finding themselves copying the methods of their enemies.

It is evident, secondly, that an appeal to the conscience of the individual is also not an adequate solution, for this evidently varies from individual to individual and even more from society to society. It is a mistake to suppose that the followers of Hitler, like those of Stalin, had—or have— no moral principles. In a sense they had more than their enemies, for they were prepared to kill and torture millions to uphold them. Similarly, the dropping of two atomic bombs on Japan, and in fact all the bombing of civilian populations, might be presented as a profoundly moral decision. It was one of which Western Europe in the eighteenth century would hardly have been capable. The point is not that some individuals or societies are moral and others are not, but that different ones have different moral principles, and the problem is to choose between them.

Thirdly, the easiest solution is to refuse to see that there is a problem at all. There are traditional standards, it may be said, which were good enough for our fathers and are all the stronger for having religious convictions behind them: all we need to do is to return to them. It would be foolish to disregard the sanction that religion can add to a social ethic. The trouble is that any system that depends on the unquestioned acceptance of the decrees of a superhuman authority—apart from objections on philosophical grounds—can only function successfully so long as the authority does in fact remain unquestioned. Moreover, it has been shown that it is remarkably easy to replace one absolute authority by another, and the habit of accepting ethical standards because they are laid down by authority is easily transferred. An examination of the recent history of, say, Italy, Spain, Germany and Russia, countries in which religious authority appeared to be particularly strong, must lead to some doubts whether the religious sanction is an adequate barrier against the rise of ideologies which promote, justify and institutionalize systems of terror and torture. A further difficulty is that traditional systems of ethics are apt to include features which were perhaps appropriate to earlier social situations, but which in a new situation may have lost their ethical content and have sometimes even become repulsive to contemporary morality.

A fourth alternative, which has already been mentioned, is the appeal to science. There are intimate connections between the rise of science and moral progress. The scientific and empirical spirit of the seventeenth and eighteenth centuries provided an essential element in the ethical achievements of enlightened thought. One might have supposed that the further progress of the scientific outlook, and in particular its application in the field of social and political life, would have promoted, for example, a progressive decline in irrational cruelties. This has not proved so, and the reason, as has been suggested above, is that science by itself is a form of knowledge, not a stimulus to action. It can help us to adapt the means we employ to the ends we wish to achieve, it cannot choose those ends for us. This is why the great growth in scientific knowledge has proved no barrier to the decay of ethical thought. Indeed, the social sciences, as they have grown in stature, have endeavoured to assimilate the ethical indifference of the physical sciences.

This series of negative answers seems to leave us with only one recourse. The effective stimulus to social morality, I suggest, can only come directly from developments of the ethical judgment, such as took place in the Enlightenment of the eighteenth century. Fifth-century Greece witnessed a comparable wave of ethical thought, which continued in some respects up to the first century of the Christian era. In both these ages the process was set off by a great increase of interest in the problems of ethics. Correspondingly, the decline in standards in recent times was preceded and accompanied by a decline in the discussion of public and political behaviour in ethical terms.

In the absence of rational and ethical discussion of the ends of society, political theory has tended to turn into either the analysis of mere power relations, with no attempt at judgment on them, or else the repetition of shibboleths, words like "peace" and "democracy" which may mean anything or nothing, but which because of their former ethical connotation can be employed as substitutes for the discussion of practical ethical issues. They have become at best mere classificatory symbols like the old school tie, which can be used alike by those who are and by those who are not entitled to them. Their hollowness is the measure of the problem before us.

The apparent inadequacy of other solutions, however, does not mean that we are thrown back on a simple recapitulation of the ideas of the Enlightenment. It would be a mistake to suppose that they would necessarily mean to us what they did to their creators. The principles of the Enlightenment, to which we now cling largely out of sheer force of habit when we condemn the things in the contemporary world that we generally do condemn, may or may not be capable of resuscitation in the form in which they were originally stated. Codes of moral behaviour and ideals are necessarily related to circumstances; they may become irrelevant not only because of moral progress or regression, but also as a result of changes in the facts to which they are related. The Enlightenment can only be a starting-point. It represents the achievements of the last stage of vigorous ethical discussion in the history of Western civilization; and it is not difficult to see that we can profitably take up the argument where it was dropped then. Though we may hope to reach a minimum of ethical agreement, such as is needed to restore some sense of purpose to civilization and has always been necessary for the survival of a community, the actual discussion is more important than arriving at particular conclusions, which will, as always, have their limitations and their transient features. A genuine and widespread discussion of the problems of society and government, considered as moral issues, has the virtue that whatever conclusions are reached will not be arbitrary ones, created to fit the terms of an hypothesis: they will be framed by positive conditions and dictated by the needs of the age. The twentieth century is belatedly becoming aware that something is missing, though it hardly as yet knows what that is. The more "advanced" the country, the more this gap is felt. It is the price that is paid for the creation of a technological society, which devotes endless energy to the problem of how to do things, but little thought to whether they are worth doing. Serious ethical and political discussion was the first victim; there are signs, where the devotion to technology has reached its height, that science may be the next. This is more or less speculative, but the results of the decline of moral and political theory have been patent in the world at large. They have naturally been most pronounced in countries where the ethical influence of the Enlightenment was most superficial, but it would be simple self-deceit to suppose that they are confined to them. Even if we condemn, for example, the monstrous cruelties of the contemporary world, the conflict between the behaviour which we condemn, and the moral consciousness which leads us to condemn it, is an unequal struggle so long as, while the behaviour is concrete enough, the moral consciousness remains merely an historical memory, a repetition of clichés with no active thought behind it. The object of this study has been to raise questions rather than to provide answers. But the thing we perhaps most need to learn is the importance of asking these questions. We have inherited everything else from the Enlightenment and only forgotten the thing that was essential.

HERBERT J. MULLER

The Nature of Man

Herbert J. Muller (1905–   ) is Professor of English and Government at Indiana University, author of two remarkable surveys of Western history, The Uses of the Past *and* The Loom of History. *Professor Muller's view of human nature is considerably more serene and balanced than that of Joseph Wood Krutch, and, I should maintain, much nearer that held by most thoughtful Americans today.*

THE POWER TO CHOOSE AND CARRY OUT HIS OWN PURPOSES MAY BE HELD the essential condition of man's claim to peculiar dignity and worth. This is a disputable claim, especially in view of the use he has made of this power in recent times. It raises further questions. Is man actually free to choose his own purposes? If so, is he fit for freedom? Does he really want to be independent? Such questions in turn force a broader, more fundamental one: What is the essential nature of man? Implicit in all ethical and political theory, as in all the higher religions, is some conception of human nature. Any serious thought about what is good for man logically requires some idea of what he is good for. And here is the beginning of a deeper confusion.

In our own tradition the oldest, most persistent definition of man— older than Plato—has split him in two, conceiving him as an immortal soul somehow imprisoned in flesh. Christian thought intensified this dualism, magnifying both the beast and the angel in man. He was a fallen creature, a cesspool of natural depravity; and he was nevertheless potentially fit for an eternity of bliss with his Heavenly Father, in whose image he had been created. Secular thinkers then seized upon either of his dual aspects as the fundamental truth about him. To Hobbes he was incorrigibly selfish and aggressive, always lusting after power, and could be made obedient only by fear. To the philosophers of the Enlightenment he was naturally good and potentially still better, perfectible by virtue

From Herbert J. Muller, *Issues of Freedom* (New York: Harper & Brothers, 1960), pp. 21-36.

of being a rational animal, and therefore deserving of freedom. In the last century he was studied much more intensively as history became a major interest and the new sciences of man got under way—psychology, sociology, anthropology. As a result we now have an immense body of knowledge, and a profounder confusion than ever before. Having gone through the mill of Darwin, Nietzsche, Marx, Freud, Pareto, and Dewey, looked into the mirror of Zola, Dostoyevsky, D. H. Lawrence, Joyce, Kafka, and Sartre, modern man may be forgiven some uncertainty about his being. And these radically different conceptions of human nature not only have as different theoretical consequences for the good life and the good society, but make some difference in man's actual behavior. Although the ordinary man has a certain toughness of spirit that enables him to resist his mentors, he wants to be "natural," and his common sense is a tissue of more or less unconscious theory about his nature. He may violently resent criticism of his self-image.

The confusion is not hopeless, however. Much of it is due to an insistence on strictly undemonstrable assumptions, such as man's possession of an immortal soul, and more especially to an arbitrary selection of some one potentiality of human nature as its "essence." The fact remains that we do have an immense body of reliable knowledge, in particular the advantage of historical and anthropological perspectives that make it fairly easy to discount the many oversimplified definitions of man. It is possible, I think, to reach an agreement upon some broad generalizations —not broad enough to include all the ideal possibilities cherished by many men, but adequate as premises for a study of human freedom, and even surprisingly helpful in avoiding common confusion. I am accordingly stating as objective truths, not mere hypotheses or articles of faith, the premises that man is a social animal, an animal with unique powers of mind, and therefore a culture-building animal. Through the development of culture, which long tended to obscure the individual, he eventually realized that he was also an animal with a distinctive capacity for individuality, or personality.

That he is an animal I take it is unquestioned. This is the body, the flesh, the beast in him that believers in his immortal destiny are the first to emphasize. With other animals he shares such basic drives as hunger and sex, such basic emotions as fear and rage, and all the physical limits on freedom. He can also enjoy sensations of physical well-being, take pleasure in his kinship with other forms of life, feel at home in the natural world. Everyone knows these elemental pleasures and pains of the flesh, the beginnings of good and evil, but lofty thinkers tend to slight them. They have often sought a freedom from all bodily desire, under the aegis of disembodied reason or spirit. Gratified by the thought that man cannot live on bread alone, they may forget that man cannot live without it, that untold millions have died for want of it, and that today most of the world's population still have to live without enough of it. They may see nothing very bad in bodily suffering, or even view health with some suspicion.

That man is a social animal should be as plain. In this respect he is still akin to the many other animals who live in flocks, herds, swarms, and schools, not to mention the highly developed insect societies. The "state of nature" is for man a social state if only because of the prolonged helplessness of the human infant. As far back as we can see him, in prehistoric caves, we find him living in groups; and as he emerges more clearly we see him differing from other animals in that he takes care not only of his young but his old, even his dead. Nowhere do we see the anarchic individualism, the endless war of all against all, that Hobbes pictured as his natural state, and Schopenhauer assumed was his most natural tendency. Looking to the unformed child—the little savage in our midst—we see him eager to learn all kinds of rules, and indeed to make them up.

Even so, many "realists" still assume that man is essentially an anti-social animal, an egotist whose oldest, deepest instincts are hostile to law and order. Such assumptions grew out of the traditional emphasis on the natural depravity of man, and grew more plausible in a highly competitive society devoted to the pursuit of wealth and power. They took on the appearance of scientific authority from evolutionary thought, with its early emphasis on the constant struggle for survival. They were confirmed by Freud, who saw a blind self-seeking and mutual antagonism as the primal drive in the unconscious, described conscience as "merely the dread of society," and regarded civilization as a ceaseless struggle against the state of nature. And there is plainly some truth in such views, which in complacent periods may be the truth that most needs to be said. Any parent knows that the human child is not a born angel, trailing clouds of glory, and that he likes to break rules too. The best friends of man have always known that he has selfish, egotistical, unsocial tendencies. From their different point of view champions of individual freedom have likewise assumed a basic hostility between the individual and society.

Yet the historical evidence overwhelmingly confirms the natural sociality of man. Almost all societies, from the most primitive to the most civilized, have emphasized duties much more than rights or liberties, and almost all their members have accepted these duties without protest. The inconstant creature feared by political philosophers has generally been constant in obedience, often submitting to what may strike us as wholly arbitrary, unnecessary constraints on his selfish interests. From the evolutionary point of view, the struggle for survival has been primarily a struggle between species, not individuals, and man has succeeded primarily by co-operating, not fighting with his fellows. Today we overlook the extraordinary extent of his co-operative behavior—co-operation required by organized competition—because it is less conspicuous and dramatic than competitive, aggressive behavior, or simply because we have come to take it for granted. If men are naturally antagonistic, as Freud believed, they have none the less succeeded so well in living together that the "abnormal" individual is the one who does not accept the constraints of the group. As for the champions of individual freedom, they are a rare type historically, and have rarely been popular. Their ardor testifies that the impulse to accept and obey is much stronger than the impulse to rebel.

To define man as a social animal is therefore no more idealistic than to call a bee a social insect. His sociality does indeed provide a natural basis for idealism, in that his "selfish" interests always include the interests of some other selves, the need of warmth and affection. It involves a natural sympathy and natural piety, as in the care of his dead, which may flower in ideals of our common humanity, or of "natural rights"; it is not based primarily on anything so uncertain as enlightened self-interest. But this is also to say that it is generally unreasoned. Another word for man's constancy is inertia, another word for sociality is herd instinct. Today the common word for it is conformism. It can be said that most men are not intelligent enough to pursue their own interests, not courageous enough to have self-esteem. It cannot be said that sociality means simple fraternity. Men have never loved their neighbors as themselves, still less all other men. Their natural loyalty to their own group has always tended to make them suspicious of outsiders, hostile to other groups. Societies have most clearly exhibited the selfishness and aggressiveness that have been attributed to the anti-social nature of man, and conflicts between them have been fiercer because their members have usually been willing to sacrifice their personal interests to the cause, even to die for the group.

Hence "realists" may still find sufficient propensity to evil, or, if they prefer, Original Sin. My point is merely that it is not realistic to describe man as an animal who has been driven into society in defiance of his natural instincts, and who can be held there only by force or through fear. The life of the lone wolf is no more natural to him than the life of the hermit. In the tensions of our own society, which has set up an ideal of individualism, encouraged competition in education and recreation as well as business, demanded an unprecedented extent of co-operation, achieved an unprecedented degree of organization, and provided an unprecedented wealth of opportunity for self-realization and for maladjustment, it is both more tempting and more misleading to assume an inveterate hostility between the individual and society. The rugged individualism that alarms some critics and the lack of individuality that depresses others are alike social products. Today, as in the past, society dominates the great majority of its members. From its domination arise the major issues of freedom.

Also beyond dispute, and a source of incessant dispute, are the powers of mind that most clearly distinguish man from all other animals. In physiological terms, he has by all odds the most complex, elaborate ner-

vous system, centered in the brain, which gives him abilities different
not only in degree but in kind from the intelligence displayed by other
"higher" animals. Some animals can solve problems, and many—down
to chickens, fish, and cockroaches—can learn from experience after a
fashion; only man can consciously remember what he learns, concep-
tualize it, put it into words, teach it to his young. With his power of
reasoning he has as distinctive capacities of imagination, sensibility, and
insight. His consciousness is a stream of perceptions, intuitions, feelings,
fantasies, impulses, thoughts unimaginably different from whatever goes
on in an animal's mind. As Dewey observed, the idiomatic meanings of
mind give a more comprehensive, just idea of its nature than do the
formal definitions of logicians and most psychologists. I have states of
of mind, good and bad; I make up or change my mind; I keep things
on it, and put it on matters; I may lose it, though without losing my
consciousness or my nervous system; I may be of two minds or half a
mind; I mind my step, mind my own business; I mind my children and
make them mind me; I mind if I am deprived of my freedom. Ultimately
mind involves the vague but real power of the "human spirit," which
seeks the good, the true, and the beautiful, and inspires the exalted idea
of soul. Immediately it also involves less agreeable possibilities. Because
man can make conscious choices, he may make unintelligent, ridiculous,
even fatal choices. No other animal is so stupid as a human fool.

Only with drastic qualifications, then, can man be defined as a "rational
animal." His experience is much broader and richer, untidier and wilder,
than a pure rationalist would have it. His basic impulses—to eat, to make
love, to rest, or simply to go on living—are all non-rational; his behavior
is often positively irrational, more "brutal" than the purely instinctive
behavior of brutes. Still, this is to judge him by rational standards, and
finally to emphasize his capacity for rational thought and behavior. The
capacity is most apparent in the practical activities by which he has
gained power over the natural environment, but it is also implicit in his
co-operation with his fellows. In every known society he has recognized
the principle of *ought* by assuming responsibilities, committing himself
to duties at the expense of his own sweet pleasure. In every society he is
held responsible, punished when he does what he ought not to do. In
civilized societies those who insist on the basic irrationality of man still
lay down the law for him and insist that he obey it, stay in his place.
Such demands on him are grounds for the assumption that he ought to
be treated as potentially a rational animal, not a brute. If thought does
not make the whole dignity of man, as Pascal declared, his capacity for
thought in the broadest sense remains the clearest index of his humanity,
the basis of his claims to dignity and worth—and so to the right of
freedom.

Together with his sociality, it has made him a culture-building animal.
Whereas every generation of apes begins and ends where the last genera-

tion did, without benefit of the wisdom of their ancestors, the children of men begin by acquiring the knowledge, skills, and arts accumulated over the countless generations before them. With these they absorb the whole way of life of the fathers. And here the most pertinent fact is the most conspicuous one in an anthropological and historical view—the extraordinary diversity of the world's cultures. It makes plain what is never plain to men in any given society. Man lives primarily in a symbolical world, a world of his own creation. Always set in a natural environment, always compelled to deal with natural forces, he gets from his society all his ruling ideas about the nature of the world and how to deal with it. His basic "reality" is not physical but cultural, spiritual. He begins learning metaphysics in his cradle. If he becomes a professional metaphysician, he is more likely to lose sight of the cultural facts of life.

So we might pause to consider the familiar term *nature,* which is as ambiguous and confusing as any in the language. His mentors have often told man to live "in accordance with Nature," finding in Nature the source of his duties and more recently of his rights. So capitalized, the word means something like God and enjoins some ethical code, but it only veils the mystery of the nature and the will of God; what code it enjoins will depend upon the speaker and his culture. Another common meaning of *nature,* the unbaptized universe and everything in it, is no more helpful; in this sense nothing can be contrary to nature, whatever man chooses to do is a natural event in the universal show. In the more common sense of the external world, everything in the universe apart from man, *nature* becomes more misleading. It may now mean a bountiful provider, a haven from care, a playfield, a bloody battleground, a constant menace, an enemy of all man's works—a spectacle beautiful or grim, serene or wild, majestic or awful; but if the familiar counsel to "follow nature" means to follow instincts, live like other animals, it is positively inhuman so far as it is feasible at all. At best, the simple idea of going back to nature simply obscures the real problem, the ultimate concern of all philosophy and religion—the problem of what is the good life for man, a creature for whom all kinds of behavior, from loving to killing, are on the face of it "natural."

Immediately it obscures the basic fact that "human" nature is a second nature—largely made by man, not simply born in him. Whatever instincts he is born with may be cultivated, blended, modified, diverted, or suppressed in so many different ways that they appear to be bare potentialities, raw materials for the unconscious artistry of culture. The ruling drive in one society may be a matter of indifference to another, a positive abnormality to still another. Hence when men grew self-conscious and sophisticated enough to inquire into their nature, their culture suggested the answers; and the endless confusion began. In the Western world the answers grew more diverse as society grew more complex and unsettled, but the confusion was intensified by the nature of thinkers—their common craving for simplicity, the One instead of the Many. Bent on reducing the many apparent motives to a single ruling motive, they have variously defined it as self-interest, the will to power, sexual drive, the craving for freedom, the craving for security. Today many still overlook the plain implications of the diversity of human culture, the radically different ways of life that alike seem natural to men brought up in them. The most solemn injunctions about the needs of Man usually spring from the parochial needs of some contemporaries.

We can still make out basic uniformities, however, else we could not speak of *man* at all. Men everywhere have a common structure, common needs and desires, common capacities; everywhere they have to cope with the same exigencies of birth, growth, sex, toil, suffering, and death. Their common mortality is the strongest reminder that their common humanity is not a mere ideal, but a fact. Hence even the apparent artificialities of culture are to some extent natural outgrowths of common potentialities. A man might think it patently unnatural for women to paint their fingernails and toenails—were it not that women have always been doing such things, as far back as we can see; and men have seemed no less interested in improving on God's or nature's handiwork. The universal vanity involves the common possession of an aesthetic sense. The rise of civilization brought ways of life that would seem still more artificial, except that all along the most natural behavior for man was evidently not to follow nature but to master it, adapt it to his own purposes. Finally, in the Greek world, there emerged the ideal of culture in the high sense of the word, the conscious cultivation of human nature and its capacities for the pursuit of truth, goodness, and beauty. With this emerged the choicest and the most troublesome product of civilization—the self-conscious individual. The dignity of man, wrote G. H. Mead, consists in the fact that when he calls upon himself he finds himself at home.

In the Western world this fortunate caller has dared as never before, dared even to stand alone. He has made extreme claims for himself. He has demanded political freedom, to participate in the determination of the group purposes, the means to the common good; individual freedom within the state to carry out his private purposes, realize his own good; freedom against the state, to assure his inalienable rights. He has proclaimed the supreme value of personality, even when he no longer identifies it with an immortal soul. He has declared that the individual must be regarded as an end in himself—the state exists only to serve him.

He is therefore apt to forget that he is a parvenu in history. Whatever consciousness other animals may have is certainly not self-consciousness. If man in primitive societies ever thinks of calling upon himself, he seldom finds his *self;* he has little consciousness of individuality apart from his group, and less of rights against it. In most civilizations it never occurred to men to think of consciousness as intrinsically individual, or of individuality as the quintessence of human nature. Hence, too, this parvenu has been liable to extravagance. His rise in the world has inspired an atomic individualism that represents society as a kind of artificial bond, created by self-conscious individuals for the sake of enlightened self-interest, with the policeman on the corner to keep watch on the unenlightened; a rugged individualism that makes self-interest a moral principle, and tends to narrow and impoverish individuality by an exclusive devotion to economic ends; a romantic individualism, or cult of genius, that conceives individuality as the sum or essence of what distinguishes or separates a man from his fellows, excluding all that unites them. It becomes necessary to repeat the commonplace that man is a social animal. His very consciousness is a social product; he becomes aware of himself only through his relations with other selves. Likewise his individuality can be realized only in a society, and a rich one achieved only in a highly developed society. The gospel of individualism is itself a product of a free society.

Today, however, students of society are most likely to ignore the individual or to deny his importance. Anthropologists have generally treated him as a mere carrier of culture, which has its own laws and seems to carry on by itself. Historians concentrate on the deep, involuntary processes of social change, and in reacting against the Hero theories of history they often explicitly minimize the role of individuals. Sociologists likewise concentrate on impersonal processes that may appear to be automatic. Some have declared that the individual is only a cell in the social organism, and that as a creature having an independent reality he is a "discredited hypothesis"; more have buried him in statistical abstractions like the "average man"— a monster who has 2½ children. Many students of the life and work of even the great men of the past study them primarily as products of their age or examples of major tendencies. It appears that the deepest meaning of a play by Shakespeare or Racine must be the thought or feeling of most ordinary men of their time.

I therefore judge that what most needs to be stressed today is the reality and the unique importance of the individual. Physiologically, man is the most highly individualized of animals, and as he developed his latent powers of mind he would naturally become more so. Individual differences have made a great deal of difference, even if during most of his history man has put little stock in any except military prowess; for whatever progress he has made must ultimately be traced to them. Knowing nothing about the origins of culture, we can still be confident that it was a very gradual, unplanned growth, not the conscious creation of farsighted individuals; yet it did depend upon the discoveries and inventions of exceptional individuals. "Society" did not dream up the idea of pots and looms and wheels. With the rise of civilization came a massive growth that may look involuntary and certainly was beyond the understanding and control of the individual; yet it involved more conscious doing and making, in which gifted individuals had freer play for creative achievement. If society now made possible a Socrates, a Confucius, an Archimedes, a Christ, it still cannot claim full credit for their greatness—it produced chiefly ordinary men. And as we begin to trace the growth of freedom, it becomes more necessary to keep an eye on the individual. Whether or not we regard him as an end in himself, the freedom of a society is meaningful only as it is exercised by individuals, and can be observed only in their behavior.

A more debatable issue, however, is raised by the democratic tradition that has made so much of the individual and done so much for him. Eighteenth-century philosophers who helped to shape this tradition commonly assumed that man is a rational animal who has not only a natural right to freedom but a natural passion for it. History hardly supports this congenial idea: until recently the masses of men have not demanded such a right or displayed such a passion. History suggests rather that Dostoyevsky's Grand Inquisitor may have been right. For the great majority of man, he said, the freedom of choice offered by Christ is an intolerable burden; what they want and need first of all is bread, and then "miracle, mystery, and authority." Now psychologists and sociologists are asserting that the ruling passion of man is for security. Hitler may have been sincere when he proclaimed himself an emancipator: "Providence has ordained that I should be the greatest liberator of humanity. I am freeing man from the demands of a freedom and personal independence that only a few can sustain."

ST. AUGUSTINE

Confession

St. Augustine, whom we have already met in these pages, has left in his
Confessions *one of the most remarkable, and in a sense historically the
earliest, of true autobiographies. The book was, like everything else he
wrote, part of a great* apologia *for the Christian faith. But it is not "propaganda" in the bad modern sense that word has acquired. Augustine is
trying very hard to get inside himself, to see himself as God made him.*

GIVE ME LEAVE, O MY GOD, TO SPEAK OF MY MIND, YOUR GIFT, AND OF
the follies in which I wasted it. It chanced that a task was set me, a task
which I did not like but had to do. There was the promise of glory if I
won, the fear of ignominy, and a flogging as well, if I lost. It was to declaim
the words uttered by Juno in her rage and grief when she could not keep
the Trojan prince from coming to Italy. I had learnt that Juno had never
said these words, but we were compelled to err in the footsteps of the
poet who had invented them: and it was our duty to paraphrase in prose
what he had said in verse. In this exercise that boy won most applause in
whom the passions of grief and rage were expressed most powerfully and in
the language most adequate to the majesty of the personage represented.

What could all this mean to me, O My true Life, My God? Why was
there more applause for the performance I gave than for so many class-
mates of my own age? Was not the whole business so much smoke and
wind? Surely some other matter could have been found to exercise mind
and tongue. Thy praises, Lord, might have upheld the fresh young shoot of
my heart, so that it might not have been whirled away by empty trifles,
defiled, a prey to the spirits of the air. For there is more than one way of
sacrificing to the fallen angels.

Yet it was no wonder that I fell away into vanity and went so far from
Thee, My God, seeing that men were held up as models for my imitation

From Saint Augustine, *The Confessions*. Translated by F. J. Sheed (New York:
Sheed & Ward, 1942), Book I, sections XVII-XX.

who were covered with shame if, in relating some act of theirs in no way evil, they fell into some barbarism or grammatical solecism: yet were praised, and delighted to be praised, when they told of their lusts, provided they did so in correct words correctly arranged. All these things Thou seest, O Lord, and art silent: for Thou art patient and plenteous in mercy and truth. But wilt Thou always stay silent? Even now Thou dost draw out of this pit of horror the soul that seeks Thee and thirsts for Thy joys, *the heart that says to Thee I have sought Thy face: Thy face, Lord, will I still seek:* for to be darkened in heart is to be far from Thy face. It is not on our feet or by movement in space that we go from Thee or return to Thee: Thy prodigal son did not charter horses or chariots or ships, or fly with wings or journey on his two feet to that far country where he wasted in luxurious living what Thou as a loving father hadst given him on his departure—loving when Thou didst give, more loving still to Thy son when he returned, all poor and stripped. To be lustful, that is darkened, in heart, is to be far from Thy face.

Behold, O Lord My God, and, seeing, see patiently, with what anxious care the sons of men observe the rules of letters and syllables taught by the speakers of our tongue before us, while they neglect the eternal rules of everlasting salvation taught by You. The learner or teacher of the established rules of pronunciation is held more contemptible if he drops an 'h' and speaks of a 'uman being[1]—thus breaking a law of language—than if he hates a human being—thus breaking a law of God. It is strange that we should not realise that no enemy could be more dangerous to us than the hatred with which we hate him, and that by our efforts against him we do less damage to our enemy than is wrought in our own heart. Obviously the knowledge of letters is not more deeply engraved in us than the law of conscience against doing to another what one would not bear if done to oneself. How hidden art Thou, O God the only great, dwelling in silence in the high places, and by Thy untiring law sending blindness as the punishment for unlawful lusts. A man seeking the fame of eloquence —before a judge who is also a man, with a multitude of men standing about—inveighs against his adversary with inhuman hatred. Such a man will be most vigilantly on guard lest by a slip of the tongue he drop an 'h' and murder the word "human": yet worries not at all that by the fury of his mind he may murder a real human.

These were the ways of the world upon whose threshold I stood as a boy, and such was the arena for which I was training—more concerned to avoid committing a grammatical error than to be void of envy in case I did commit one and another did not. This I say and confess to Thee, O My God: and in this I was praised by those whom my one idea of success was to please. I did not see the whirl of vileness into which I had been cast away from Thy eyes: for what was more unclean than I, seeing that I did

[1] Thus neatly does Dr. Pusey represent the man who for "hominem" says "ominem."

not win the approval even of my own kind: I told endless lies to my tutors, my masters and my parents: all for the love of games, the craving for stage shows, and a restlessness to do what I saw done in these shows.

I stole from my parents' cellar and table, sometimes because I was gluttonous myself, sometimes to have something to give other boys in exchange for implements of play which they were prepared to sell although they loved them as much as I. Even in games, when I was clearly outplayed I tried to win by cheating, from the vain desire for first place. At the same time I was indignant and argued furiously when I caught anyone doing the very things that I had done to others. When I was caught myself, I would fly into a rage rather than give way.

Is this boyhood innocence? It is not, Lord. I cry Thy mercy, O My God. Yet as we leave behind tutors and masters and nuts and balls and birds and come to deal with prefects and kings and the getting of gold and estates and slaves, these are the qualities which pass on with us, one stage of life taking the place of another as the greater punishments of the law take the place of the schoolmaster's cane. Therefore, O God our King, when you said "of such is the Kingdom of Heaven," it could only have been humility as symbolised by the low stature of childhood that you were commending.

Yet, Lord I should have owed thanks to You, My God and the most excellent Creator and Ruler of the Universe, even if it had been Your will that I should not live beyond boyhood. For even then I was; I lived: I felt: even so early I had an instinct for the care of my own being, a trace in me of that most profound Unity whence my being was derived; in my interior sense I kept guard over the integrity of my outward sense perception, and in my small thoughts upon small matters I had come to delight in the truth. I hated to be wrong, had a vigorous memory, was well trained in speech, delighted in friendship, shunned pain, meanness and ignorance. In so small a creature was not all this admirable and reason for praise? Yet all these were the gifts of my God, for I did not give them to myself. All these were good and all these were I. Therefore He Who made me is good and He is my Good: and in Him I shall exult for all the good qualities that even as a boy I had. But in this lay my sin: that I sought pleasure, nobility, and truth not in God but in the beings He had created, myself and others. Thus I fell into sorrow and confusion and error. Thanks be to Thee, my Joy and my Glory and my Hope and my God: thanks be to Thee for Thy gifts: but do Thou preserve them in me. Thus Thou wilt preserve me, and the things Thou hast given me will increase and be made perfect, and I shall be with Thee: because even that I exist is Thy gift.

FRANÇOIS,
DUC de LA ROCHEFOUCAULD

Self-Portrait

La Rochefoucauld's "Portrait of Himself" is no full autobiography, but a mere sketch that seems to have been originally written for reading in literary salons. But it is an interesting example of a genre which is of particular value to the student of human nature, and even to the professional psychologist.

I AM OF MEDIUM BUILD, BROAD AND WELL-PROPORTIONED. MY COM-plexion is dark, but fairly uniform; my forehead is high and reasonably wide, my eyes are black, small, deep-set, with brows that though black and thick are well-formed. I find it hard to give a proper description of my nose, for it is neither flat, nor aquiline, nor thick, nor pointed—or so at least it seems to me. All I can say is that it is on the large rather than the small side, and that it is perhaps a trifle too long. I have a big mouth and my lips, which are usually rather red, are neither well nor ill shaped. My teeth are white and passably regular. In the old days I used to be told that I had too much chin: I have just felt it, and also looked in the glass to see if this is so, and I really cannot say whether it is true or not. As for the shape of my face, it is either squarish or oval: I should find it hard to be sure which. My hair is black, curls naturally, and is sufficiently long and thick for me to be able to claim a fine head of hair. My expression has something of gloom and also of pride to it: this has led most people to assume that I am contemptuous of them, though no assumption could be further from the truth. I move with ease and perhaps slightly too much, to the extent that I gesticulate a great deal when talking. That is my frank opinion of my appearance, and it will be found, I think, that this description is not far removed from the truth. I shall be equally honest in the remaining part of this self-portrait; for I have studied myself enough to know

From La Rochefoucauld, *Maxims*. Translated by Constantine FitzGibbon (London: Allen Wingate, 1957), pp. 24-30.

myself well, and I have both sufficient self-assurance to be able to speak openly of those good qualities I may possess and enough sincerity to admit to my defects.

In the first place, my prevailing humour may be described as melancholic, to the extent that in these last three or four years I have hardly been known to laugh more than three or four times. Nevertheless it seems to me that my melancholia would be sufficiently bearable and gentle were it derived solely from my temperament: but I have been afflicted with so many extraneous causes for sadness, which have so filled my imagination and preoccupied my mind, that I usually sit in silence, lost in thought, or when I do speak it is in an abstracted fashion. I am extremely reserved with strangers, and I am not even very open with most of the people whom I know. This is a defect, as I am well aware, and I shall spare no pains to rid myself of it: but since my somewhat gloomy expression tends to make me appear even more reserved than I actually am, and since it is not within our power to alter a disagreeable appearance which is due to nature's arrangement of our features, I fear that though I may correct the internal causes of the impression I make, the displeasing external marks of this failing will remain with me, do what I may.

I am witty,[1] and I do not blush to say so; why put up any pretence in the matter? Endless shilly-shallyings and apologetics before stating one's advantages seem to me to smack of vanity hidden beneath a show of modesty: it is a very skilful means of persuading others to think even more highly of oneself than one allegedly wishes them to do. For myself I have no desire that I should be thought finer than I say I am, nor better tempered than I paint myself as being, nor wittier and cleverer than my own description of myself. So, once again, I have wit,[1] but it is tainted with melancholy: for though I can express myself well, have a useful memory and can think without confusion, I am nevertheless so preoccupied with my own chagrins that I often, in fact, put my meaning across rather badly.

One of the pleasures I value most highly is well-bred conversation; I like it to be serious, and to deal largely with moral questions. Nevertheless I am quite able to appreciate flippancy as well; and if I do not often myself make remarks intended to raise a laugh, it is not at all that I do not enjoy a well-turned witticism, and I find those amusing interchanges, at which certain relaxed and quick minds are so adept, highly entertaining.

I write well in prose, and also in verse; and if I were to attach more importance to the glory that comes from such accomplishments I believe that I could, with a little effort, achieve quite a considerable reputation as a writer. I like reading, my favourite books being those which help to form the mind and fortify the soul. Above all, I derive an extreme satisfaction from reading aloud, with a clever companion; for when so doing one will be constantly reflecting upon the written word; and the reflexions

___

[1] More literally "I have a good mind."—C.B.

thus made constitute the most agreeable sort of conversation in the world, and the most useful.

When my opinion is asked I am a fairly good judge of works in verse or in prose; but I am inclined to express my views on them somewhat too freely. Another mistake I make is my tendency to be overfastidious and too harsh in my criticism. It does not distress me when others argue, and I will even on occasion join in quite voluntarily; but I usually advance my own opinions with undue heat; and when the wrong cause is being upheld against me, I will sometimes become so passionate an advocate of reason as to grow wellnigh unreasonable myself.

My sentiments are virtuous, my intentions good, and so great is my desire to be a perfect gentleman and honourable man-of-the-world that my friends can cause me no greater pleasure than by frankly pointing out to me when I am at fault. Those persons who know me fairly well, and who have been good enough on occasion to advise me in this fashion, will admit that I have always listened to them with the utmost gratification and with all the humility of mind that can be desired.

All my passions are rather gentle and well under my control: I have hardly ever been observed in a temper, and I have never hated anyone. This does not mean that I am incapable of exacting vengeance, particularly if I have been offended in a matter that touches my honour and which I therefore cannot ignore. On the contrary, I am sure that my sense of duty towards myself will, at such times, so well replace the emotion of hatred that in my search for vengeance I will display even greater energy than other men.

I am not troubled by ambition. There are few things which frighten me, death least of any. I am scarcely susceptible to pity, and would wish not to feel it at all. On the other hand there are no lengths to which I will not go in order to alleviate the afflictions of others; and I really believe that in such cases one should do everything, even to the extent of showing a great deal of compassion for them in their misfortunes; but I also believe that one should be satisfied with the display and avoid, most carefully, the true feeling. For pity is an emotion which is quite useless in a well-formed soul; it serves only to enfeeble the heart; and it should be left to the common people who, since they never behave according to the dictates of reason, must be stirred by emotion.

I am fond of my friends, so fond of them that I should not hesitate for a moment if it were a question of sacrificing my interests for theirs; I am tolerant, will patiently endure their bad moods, and will readily make excuses for them. But I am not particularly demonstrative as a friend, nor am I much put out if I do not see them for considerable periods of time.

I am by nature poorly endowed with curiosity concerning most of those matters which others find of such absorbing interest. I am very discreet and have less difficulty than most in keeping a secret that has been entrusted to me. I am extremely reliable: I never break my word, no matter what the results of keeping it may be, and that is a rule of conduct to which I have adhered with the utmost rigour throughout my whole life.

With women I am meticulously polite, and I do not believe that I have ever behaved, in the presence of a woman, in such a way as to cause her distress. When they have good minds, I prefer their conversation to that of men; their talk has a sort of gentleness which is never to be met with in ours, and, apart from that, it seems to me that they can express themselves more neatly and can give a pleasanter turn to what they say.

As for love, in the past I have gone in for it a little; at present I do so no longer, although I am still young. I have given up flirting, and it is a source of astonishment to me that so many honest people should still indulge in it.

I have the greatest respect for fine passions, which are the mark of great souls; and although the disquiet they engender is in some ways antagonistic to strict wisdom, they are so easily linked to the most austere virtues that I do not believe they can be justly condemned. Knowing well all the delicacy and strength of great passion, I do believe that should I myself ever fall in love, it will be in this manner; but being made the way I am, I very much doubt whether this knowledge of mine will ever be transferred from the head to the heart.

JEAN JACQUES ROUSSEAU

One Confession Out of Many

Jean Jacques Rousseau (1712–1778), Protean man of letters, tagged as father of the romantic movement, has left in his Confessions *one of the most famous of autobiographies. The book can hardly shock our generation by its frankness on the author's sex life; indeed, it can hardly seem frank to us on such matters. But the moralist can still be shocked by Rousseau's self-righteousness, the conservative can still be sure that Rousseau's defiance of convention is unsound anarchism, his individualism ruinous to the individual. I give below his justification of his relations with Thérèse le Vasseur, with whom he lived for years, and who bore him children. The "Mamma" to whom Rousseau refers was Madame de Warens, an older woman of higher social status who had taken him in after he ran away from his Genevan home, and had been rather more than a mother to him. If you can summon detachment enough, you will find this an illuminating episode in the human comedy.*

I HAVE ALWAYS CONSIDERED THE DAY WHICH UNITED ME TO MY THÉRÈSE as that which determined my moral being. I needed an attachment, since that which should have sufficed me had been so cruelly broken. The thirst for happiness is never quenched in man's heart. Mamma was growing old and degraded. It was clear to me that she could never again be happy in this world. Thus, the only thing left for me was to seek for a happiness which should be my own, since I had for ever lost all hope of sharing hers. I drifted for some time from one idea, from one plan, to another. My voyage to Venice would have plunged me into public affairs, if the man with whom I was to be connected had been possessed of common sense. I am easily discouraged, especially in difficult and long-winded undertakings. My ill-success in this disgusted me with all others; and since, in accordance with my old maxim, I looked upon distant objects as decoys for fools, I determined to live henceforth without any fixed plan, as I no longer saw anything in life which might have tempted me to exert myself.

From Jean Jacques Rousseau, *Confessions* (New York: The Modern Library, n.d.), pp. 426-435.

It was just at that time that we became acquainted. The gentle character of this good girl appeared to me so well suited to my own, that I united myself to her by means of an attachment which neither time nor wrongs have been able to lessen, and everything which ought to have broken it has only increased it. The strength of this attachment will be seen in the sequel, when I lay bare the wounds and pangs with which she has rent my heart during the height of my misery, without a word of complaint to anyone ever escaping me, until the moment when I am writing these lines.

When it becomes known that, after having done all and braved everything, to avoid being separated from her, after having lived with her for twenty-five years, in spite of destiny and mankind, I finally married her in my old age, without any expectation or solicitation on her part, without any engagement or promise on my own, it will be believed that a mad love, which turned my head from the first day, gradually led me on to the last extravagance; and it will be the more readily believed, when the special and weighty reasons, which should have prevented me from ever doing such a thing, also become known. What then will the reader think, when I declare to him, in all the sincerity which he must now recognise as part of my character, that, from the first moment when I saw her up to this day, I never felt the least spark of love for her; that I no more desired her possession than that of Madame de Warens, and that the sensual needs, which I satisfied in her person, were only for me those of sexual impulse, without being in any way connected with the individual? He will perhaps believe that, being constituted differently from other men, I was incapable of feeling love, since it did not enter into the feelings which attached me to those women who have been most dear to me. Patience, reader! the fatal moment is approaching, when you will be only too rudely undeceived.

I repeat myself; I know it; but it is unavoidable. The first, the greatest, the most powerful, the most irrepressible of all my needs was entirely in my heart; it was the need of a companionship as intimate as was possible; it was for that purpose especially that I needed a woman rather than a man, a female rather than a male friend. This singular want was such, that the most intimate corporal union had been unable to satisfy it; I should have wanted two souls in the same body; without that, I was always conscious of a void. I thought that the moment had come, when I should feel it no longer. This young person, amiable by reason of a thousand excellent qualities, and, at that time, even by her personal appearance, which was without a trace of unnaturalness or coquetry, would have confined my whole existence in herself, if I had been able to confine hers to me, as I had hoped. I had nothing to fear from men; I am certain that I am the only man she ever truly loved, and her passions were so cool, that she rarely felt the want of other men, even when I had ceased to be one to her in this respect. I had no family; she had one; and this family, the members of which were all of a far different character from herself, was not such that I could ever have regarded it as my own. This was the first cause of my unhappiness. What would I not have given to have been able to make myself her mother's child! I tried all I could to do so, but never succeeded. It was useless for me to attempt to unite all our interests; it was impossible. She always created interests different from mine, set them in opposition to mine, and even to those of her daughter, which were already identical with them. She and her other children and grandchildren became so many leeches, and the least injury they did to Thérèse was that of robbing her. The poor girl, who was accustomed to give in, even to her nieces, allowed herself to be robbed and ruled without saying a word; and it pained me to see that, while I exhausted my money and good advice in vain, I could do nothing to assist her. I tried to get her away from her mother; but she always opposed it. I respected her opposition, and esteemed her the more for it; but this refusal was none the less prejudicial to her interests and my own. Devoted to her mother and the rest of her family, she belonged more to them than to me, even more than to herself. Their greed was not so ruinous to her as their advice was pernicious; in short, if, thanks to her love for me and her naturally good disposition, she was not completely their slave, she was sufficiently so to prevent, in great part, the effect of the good principles which I endeavoured to instil into her, and to cause us always to remain two, in spite of all my efforts to the contrary.

Thus it came to pass that, notwithstanding a sincere and mutual attachment, upon which I had bestowed all the tenderness of my heart, the void in this heart was never completely filled. Children, who might have effected this, were born to us; but this only made matters worse. I shuddered at the thought of handing them over to the care of this badly brought up family, to be brought up even worse. The risks of bringing up at the Foundling Hospital were far less. This reason for the resolution which I took, stronger than all those which I stated in my letter to Madame de Francueil, was, however, the only one which I did not venture to tell her. I preferred to remain not completely cleared from so grave a reproach, in order to square the family of a person whom I loved. But it may be judged, from the behaviour of her miserable brother, whether, in spite of anything that may be said about it, I should have been justified in exposing my children to the risk of receiving a similar education to his.

Being unable to enjoy to the full this intimate intercourse of which I felt the need, I sought to supplement it in a manner which, although it did not completely fill the void, caused me to feel it less. For want of a friend, who should be entirely devoted to me, I needed friends whose impulse might overcome my indolence. For this reason I cultivated and strengthened my relations with Diderot and the Abbé de Condillac, entered into fresh and still closer relations with Grimm, and, in the end, owing to the unlucky Essay, the history of which I have related, I found myself thrown back, without any idea of it, upon literature, which I thought I had abandoned for ever.

My first appearance led me by a new path into another intellectual world, the simple and lofty economy of which I was unable to look upon without enthusiasm. My continued attention to it soon convinced me, that there was nothing but error and folly in the doctrine of our philosophers, and misery and oppression in our social arrangements. Deluded by my foolish pride, I thought that I was born to destroy all these illusions, and, believing that, in order to gain a hearing, it was necessary for my manner of life to harmonize with my principles, I adopted the singular course which I have not been permitted to continue, in which I set an example for which my pretended friends have never forgiven me, which at first made me ridiculous, and would have ended by making me respectable, if it had been possible for me to persevere in it.

Hitherto I had been good; from that moment I became virtuous, or, at least, intoxicated with virtue. This intoxication had commenced in my head, but had passed on into my heart. The noblest pride sprang up therein on the ruins of uprooted vanity. I pretended nothing; I became really what I seemed; and, for the four years at least, during which this state of effervescence lasted in all its force, there was nothing great or beautiful, which a man's heart could contain, of which I was not capable between heaven and myself. This was the origin of my sudden eloquence, of the truly celestial fire which inflamed me and spread over my first writings, and which for forty years had not emitted the least spark, since it was not yet kindled.

I was truly transformed; my friends and acquaintances no longer recognised me. I was no longer the shy, bashful rather than modest man, who did not venture to show himself or utter a word, whom a playful remark disconcerted, whom a woman's glance caused to blush. Audacious, proud, undaunted, I carried with me everywhere a confidence, which was firmer in proportion to its simplicity, and had its abode rather in my soul than in my outward demeanour. The contempt for the manners, principles, and prejudices of my age, with which my deep meditations had inspired me, rendered me insensible to the raillery of those who possessed them, and I pulverised their trifling witticisms with my maxims, as I should have crushed an insect between my fingers. What a change! All Paris repeated the penetrating and biting sarcasms of the man who, two years before and ten years afterwards, never knew how to find the thing he ought to say, nor the expression he ought to use. Anyone who endeavours to find the condition of all others most contrary to my nature will find it in this. If he desires to recall one of those brief moments in my life during which I ceased to be myself, and became another, he will find it again in the time of which I speak; but, instead of lasting six days or six weeks, it lasted nearly six years, and would, perhaps, have lasted until now, had it not been for the special circumstances which put an end to it, and restored me to Nature, above which I had attempted to elevate myself.

This change began as soon as I had left Paris and the sight of the vices of the great city ceased to keep up the indignation with which it had inspired me. As soon as I lost sight of men, I ceased to despise them; as soon as I lost sight of the wicked, I ceased to hate them. My heart, little adapted for hatred, only caused me to deplore their wretchedness, from which it did not distinguish their wickedness. This gentler, but far less lofty, frame of mind soon dulled the burning enthusiasm which had so long carried me away, and, without anyone perceiving it, even without perceiving it myself, I became again shy, courteous, and timid; in a word, the same Jean Jacques as I had been before.

If this revolution had merely restored me to myself, and had gone no further, all would have been well; but, unfortunately, it went much further, and carried me away rapidly to the other extreme. From that time my soul, in a state of agitation, no longer kept its centre of gravity, and its oscillations, ever renewed, always destroyed it. I must describe at some length this second revolution—the terrible and fatal epoch of a destiny without example among mankind.

As we were only a party of three in our retreat, leisure and solitude naturally increased the intimacy of our intercourse. This was what occurred in the case of Thérèse and myself. We spent some delightful hours together under the shady trees, more delightful than any I had ever enjoyed before. She herself appeared to appreciate it more than she had hitherto done. She opened her heart to me without reserve, and told me things about her mother and her family, which she had been strong-minded enough to conceal from me for a long time. Both had received from Madame Dupin a number of presents intended for me, which the cunning old woman, to save me annoyance, had appropriated for herself and her other children, without leaving any for Thérèse, whom she strictly forbade to say anything to me about them—a command which the poor girl obeyed with an obedience which is almost incredible.

A thing which surprised me still more, was the discovery that, besides the secret conversations which Diderot and Grimm had frequently held with both, in order to estrange them from me, but which had failed in their object owing to the opposition of Thérèse, both of them had since then held frequent secret conferences with her mother, without her knowing anything of what was brewing between them. She only knew that sundry little presents played a part in it; that there were little journeys to and fro, which they attempted to conceal from her, of the reason of which she was completely ignorant. At the time when we left Paris, Madame le Vasseur had long been in the habit of calling upon Grimm two or three times a month, and spending some time there with him in private conversation, on which occasions even his servant was always sent out of the room.

I judged that the motive of all this was no other than the same scheme into which they had attempted to make the daughter enter, by promising to procure for them, through Madame d'Epinay's influence, a licence to retail salt, or a tobacco-shop; in a word, by tempting them with the prospect of gain. They had represented to these women that, as I was not in a position to do anything for them, I could not do anything for myself either, on account of them. As I saw nothing in all this but good intentions, I was not absolutely annoyed with them. Only the secrecy revolted me, especially on the part of the old woman, who, in addition, daily showed herself more toadying and wheedling in her manner towards me, which, however, did not prevent her from incessantly reproaching her daughter in private with being too fond of me and telling me everything, saying that she was a fool, and would find herself taken in the end.

This woman possessed in the highest degree the art of killing two birds with one stone, of concealing from one what she received from another, and from me, what she received from all. I might have pardoned her for her avarice, but I could not forgive her dissimulation. What could she have to conceal from me—from me, whose happiness she so well knew depended almost entirely upon her daughter's happiness and her own? What I had done for her daughter, I had done for myself, but what I had done for her deserved some acknowledgment on her part; she at least should have been grateful to her daughter for it, and should have loved me also out of love for her who loved me. I had rescued her from utter misery; from me she received the means of existence, to me she owed all those acquaintances whom she so well knew how to make use of. Thérèse had long supported her by her own exertions, and was now supporting her with bread supplied by me. She owed all to this daughter, for whom she had done nothing, while her other children, on whom she had bestowed marriage portions, and for whom she had ruined herself, far from helping to support her, devoured her substance and my own. It seemed that, under these circumstances, she should have regarded me as her only friend, as her most reliable protector, and, far from keeping me in the dark as to my own affairs, far from joining in a plot against me in my own house, should have faithfully informed me of everything that might concern me when she learned it sooner than I did. In what light, then, could I regard her deceitful and mysterious conduct? Above all, what was I to think of the sentiments with which she endeavoured to inspire her daughter? What monstrous ingratitude must have been the mother's, when she sought to instil it into the daughter!

All these considerations finally alienated my heart so completely from this woman, that I could no longer look upon her without contempt. However, I never ceased to treat the mother of the partner of my life with respect, and to show her in everything almost the consideration and esteem of a son; but I must admit that I never cared to remain long in her company, and I am ill able to put restraint upon myself.

This, again, is one of the brief moments of my life, in which I have been almost within sight of happiness, without being able to attain to it, although through no fault of my own. If this woman had been of good character, we should, all three, have been happy to the end of our days; the last survivor would alone have deserved pity. Instead of this, the reader will see the development of events, and be able to judge whether I could have altered it.

Madame le Vasseur, seeing that I had gained ground in her daughter's heart while she had lost it, endeavoured to recover it; and, instead of regaining my esteem through the daughter, attempted to alienate her from me altogether. One of the means that she employed was to invoke the assistance of her family. I had begged Thérèse not to invite any of them to the Hermitage, and she had promised not to do so. They were invited in my absence, without consulting her, and they then made her promise to say nothing to me about it. When the first step was taken, the rest was easy. When a person once keeps anything secret from one whom he loves, he soon feels no scruple about concealing everything from him. As soon as I was at La Chevrette, the Hermitage was full of people, who enjoyed themselves tolerably well. A mother has always great influence over a daughter of good disposition; nevertheless, in spite of all her efforts, the old woman could never induce Thérèse to enter into her views, or persuade her to join the conspiracy against me. As for herself, she made up her mind irrevocably. As she saw, on the one side, her daughter and myself, at whose house she could live and that was all; and, on the other, Diderot, Grimm, d'Holbach, and Madame d'Epinay, who promised much and gave something, it never entered her head that she could possibly be in the wrong in company with a farmer-general's wife and a Baron. If I had been more observant, I should have seen, from that moment, that I was nourishing a serpent in my bosom; but my blind confidence, which nothing had as yet diminished, was such that it never even occurred to me, that anyone could wish to injure a person who deserved to be loved. While I saw a thousand conspiracies formed around me, all I could complain of was the tyranny of those whom I called my friends, and whose only object, as I imagined, was to force me to be happy in their own fashion rather than in my own.

Although Thérèse refused to enter into the conspiracy with her mother, she again kept her secret. Her motive was praiseworthy; I will not undertake to decide whether she did well or ill. Two women who have secrets are fond of chattering together about them. This brought them closer together; and Thérèse, by dividing her attentions, sometimes caused me to feel that I was alone, for I could no longer regard as a society the relations between us three. Then it was that I felt keenly the mistake which I had committed, at the beginning of our connection, in not having taken advantage of the pliability which was the result of her affection, to improve her mind and furnish her with a store of knowledge, which by drawing us closer together in our retirement, would have filled up her time and my own agreeably, and prevented us from ever noticing the length of a *tête-à-tête*. Not that our conversation ever flagged, or that she showed any signs of weariness during our walks; but we had not a sufficient number of ideas in common to make a great stock. We could no longer speak incessantly of our plans, which henceforth were limited to plans of enjoyment. The objects around us inspired me with reflections which were beyond her comprehension. An attachment of twelve years had no longer need of words; we knew each other too well to be able to find anything fresh. The only resource left was gossip, scandal, and feeble jokes. It is in solitude especially that one feels the advantage of living with someone who knows how to think. I had no need of this resource to amuse myself in her society; but she would have needed it, in order to be able always to amuse herself in mine. The worst thing was, that we were obliged to hold our interviews secretly; her mother, who had become a nuisance to me, forced me to look out for opportunities. I felt under restraint in my own house—this is saying everything. The atmosphere of love ruined simple friendship. We enjoyed an intimate intercourse without living in intimacy.

As soon as I thought I observed that Thérèse sometimes sought excuses to avoid the walks which I proposed to her, I ceased to propose them, without being annoyed with her for not finding as much pleasure in them as myself. Pleasure does not depend upon the will. I was sure of her affection, and that was enough for me. As long as my pleasures were hers, I enjoyed them with her; when this was not the case, I preferred her contentment to my own.

Thus it happened that, half deceived in my expectation, leading a life after my own inclination, in a spot which I had chosen for myself, with a person who was dear to me, I nevertheless at length found myself almost isolated. What I still lacked prevented me from enjoying what I possessed. In the matter of happiness and enjoyment, I must have all or nothing.

BENJAMIN FRANKLIN

Moral Perfection

Benjamin Franklin (1706–1790), a contemporary of Rousseau's, seems here a good balance, if not an antidote, to the volatile Genevan. Franklin's "bold and arduous project of arriving at moral perfection," as here recounted, is a good example of one of the characteristics of autobiographies. Written usually in old age, they show the author intimately aware of time, process, growth, of that interaction between the persona *and the environment, cultural as well as material, which produces a personality, itself never absolutely fixed. Franklin is amused at his youthful hope of moral perfection, which he knows he did not attain; but the young man who made that very eighteenth-century list of virtues still survives in the wise old man.*

I regret that I cannot, in this section on how men have estimated human capabilities and human performance, make a wider and more representative choice of such autobiographical writings. I suspect many readers will like to go further on their own. For them I suggest as a convenient guide the recent Design and Truth in Autobiography *by Roy Pascal (Cambridge, Mass., 1960) which gives on pp. 196–200 a very good representative list of autobiographies from Abelard's to Stefan Zweig's.*

IT WAS ABOUT THIS TIME I CONCEIVED THE BOLD AND ARDUOUS PROJECT of arriving at moral perfection. I wished to live without committing any fault at any time; I would conquer all that either natural inclination, custom, or company might lead me into. As I knew, or thought I knew, what was right and wrong, I did not see why I might not *always* do the one and avoid the other. But I soon found I had undertaken a task of more difficulty than I had imagined. While my attention was taken up and care employed in guarding against one fault, I was often surprised by another. Habit took the advantage of inattention. Inclination was sometimes too strong for reason. I concluded at length that the mere speculative conviction that it was our interest to be completely virtuous was not sufficient to prevent our

From Benjamin Franklin, *Autobiography*. Edited, with an Introduction by Herbert W. Schneider (New York: The Liberal Arts Press, 1952), pp. 80-84, 90-92.

slipping, and that the contrary habits must be broken and good ones acquired and established before we can have any dependence on a steady, uniform rectitude of conduct. For this purpose I therefore contrived the following method:

In the various enumerations of the moral virtues I had met with in my reading, I found the catalogue more or less numerous, as different writers included more or fewer ideas under the same name. Temperance, for example, was by some confined to eating and drinking, while by others it was extended to mean the moderating every other pleasure, appetite, inclination, or passion—bodily or mental, even to our avarice and ambition. I proposed to myself, for the sake of clearness, to use rather more names with fewer ideas annexed to each than a few names with more ideas; and I included under thirteen names of virtues all that at that time occurred to me as necessary or desirable, and annexed to each a short precept which fully expressed the extent I gave to its meaning.

These names of virtues with their precepts were:

1. Temperance

Eat not to dullness. Drink not to elevation.

2. Silence

Speak not but what may benefit others or yourself. Avoid trifling conversation.

3. Order

Let all your things have their places. Let each part of your business have its time.

4. Resolution

Resolve to perform what you ought. Perform without fail what you resolve.

5. Frugality

Make no expense but to do good to others or yourself; i.e., waste nothing.

6. Industry

Lose no time. Be always employed in something useful. Cut off all unnecessary actions.

7. Sincerity

Use no hurtful deceit. Think innocently and justly; and, if you speak, speak accordingly.

8. Justice

Wrong none by doing injuries or omitting the benefits that are your duty.

9. Moderation

Avoid extremes. Forbear resenting injuries so much as you think they deserve.

10. Cleanliness

Tolerate no uncleanliness in body, clothes, or habitation.

11. Tranquillity

Be not disturbed at trifles or at accidents common or unavoidable.

12. Chastity

Rarely use venery but for health or offspring—never to dullness, weakness, or the injury of your own or another's peace or reputation.

13. Humility

Imitate Jesus and Socrates.

My intention being to acquire the *habitude* of all these virtues, I judged it would be well not to distract my attention by attempting the whole at once but to fix it on one of them at a time, and when I should be master of that, then to proceed to another, and so on till I should have gone through the thirteen. And as the previous acquisition of some might facilitate the acquisition of certain others, I arranged them with that view as they stand above. *Temperance* first, as it tends to procure that coolness and clearness of head, which is so necessary where constant vigilance was to be kept up, and guard maintained, against the unremitting attraction of ancient habits and the force of perpetual temptations. This being acquired and established, *Silence* would be more easy; and my desire being to gain knowledge at the same time that I improved in virtue, and considering that in conversation it was obtained rather by the use of the ear than of the tongue, and therefore wishing to break a habit I was getting into of prattling, punning, and joking, which only made me acceptable to trifling company, I gave *Silence* the second place. This and the next, *Order,* I expected would allow me more time for attending to my project and my studies. *Resolution,* once become habitual, would keep me firm in my endeavors to obtain all the subsequent virtues; *Frugality* and *Industry,* freeing me from my remaining debt and, producing affluence and independence, would make more easy the practice of *Sincerity* and *Justice,* etc., etc. Conceiving then that agreeable to the advice of Pythagoras in his golden verses, daily examination would be necessary, I contrived the following method for conducting that examination.

I made a little book in which I allotted a page for each of the virtues. I ruled each page with red ink so as to have seven columns, one for each day

of the week, marking each column with a letter for the day. I crossed these
columns with thirteen red lines, marking the beginning of each line with
the first letter of one of the virtues, on which line and in its proper column
I might mark by a little black spot every fault I found upon examination
to have been committed respecting that virtue upon that day.

I determined to give a week's strict attention to each of the virtues
successively. Thus in the first week my great guard was to avoid even the
least offense against temperance, leaving the other virtues to their ordinary
chance, only marking every evening the faults of the day. Thus if in the
first week I could keep my first line marked "T." clear of spots, I supposed the habit of that virtue so much strengthened and its opposite
weakened that I might venture extending my attention to include the next,
and for the following week keep both lines clear of spots. Proceeding thus
to the last, I could go through a course complete in thirteen weeks, and
four courses in a year. And like him who, having a garden to weed, does
not attempt to eradicate all the bad herbs at once, which would exceed
his reach and his strength, but works on one of the beds at a time, and
having accomplished the first, proceeds to a second; so I should have (I
hoped) the encouraging pleasure of seeing on my pages the progress I
made in virtue by clearing successively my lines of their spots, till in the
end by a number of courses, I should be happy in viewing a clean book
after a thirteen weeks' daily examination. . . .

It will be remarked that, though my scheme was not wholly without
religion, there was in it no mark of any of the distinguishing tenets of any
particular sect. I had purposely avoided them; for being fully persuaded of
the utility and excellence of my method, and that it might be serviceable
to people in all religions, and intending sometime or other to publish it, I
would not have anything in it that should prejudice anyone of any sect
against it. I purposed writing a little comment on each virtue, in which I
would have shown the advantages of possessing it and the mischiefs attending its opposite vice; I should have called my book *The Art of Virtue*[1]
because it would have shown the means and manner of obtaining virtue,
which would have distinguished it from the mere exhortation to be good,
that does not instruct and indicate the means, but is like the apostle's man
of verbal charity, who only, without showing to the naked and hungry how
or where they might get clothes or victuals, exhorted them to be fed and
clothed (*James* II: 15, 16).

But it so happened that my intention of writing and publishing this comment was never fulfilled. I did, indeed, from time to time put down short
hints of the sentiments, reasonings, etc., to be made use of in it, some of
which I have still by me; but the necessary close attention to private business in the earlier part of life and public business since have occasioned
my postponing it. For it being connected in my mind with *a great and ex-*

[1] Nothing so likely to make a man's fortune as virtue. [marg. note]

tensive project that required the whole man to execute, and which an unforeseen succession of employs prevented my attending to, it has hitherto
remained unfinished.

In this piece it was my design to explain and enforce this doctrine: That
vicious actions are not hurtful because they are forbidden, but forbidden
because they are hurtful, the nature of man alone considered; that it was
therefore everyone's interest to be virtuous who wished to be happy even in
this world. And I should from this circumstance, there being always in the
world a number of rich merchants, nobility, states, and princes who have
need of honest instruments for the management of their affairs, and such
being so rare, have endeavored to convince young persons that no qualities
are so likely to make a poor man's fortune as those of probity and integrity.

My list of virtues contained at first but twelve. But a Quaker friend
having kindly informed me that I was generally thought proud, that my
pride showed itself frequently in conversation, that I was not content with
being in the right when discussing any point, but was overbearing and rather
insolent—of which he convinced me by mentioning several instances—I
determined endeavoring to cure myself if I could of this vice or folly
among the rest, and I added *Humility* to my list, giving an extensive meaning to the word. I cannot boast of much success in acquiring the *reality*
of this virtue, but I had a good deal with regard to the *appearance* of it. I
made it a rule to forbear all direct contradiction to the sentiments of others
and all positive assertion of my own. I even forbade myself, agreeable to
the old laws of our Junto, the use of every word of expression in the
language that imported a fixed opinion, such as "certainly," "undoubtedly,"
etc.; and I adopted instead of them, "I conceive," "I apprehend," or "I
imagine" a thing to be so or so, or "It so appears to me at present." When
another asserted something that I thought an error, I denied myself the
pleasure of contradicting him abruptly and of showing immediately some
absurdity in his proposition; and in answering I began by observing that
in certain cases or circumstances his opinion would be right, but that in the
present case there "appeared" or "seemed to me" some difference, etc. I
soon found the advantage of this change in my manners: The conversations
I engaged in went on more pleasantly; the modest way in which I proposed
my opinions procured them a readier reception and less contradiction; I
had less mortification when I was found to be in the wrong, and I more
easily prevailed with others to give up their mistakes and join with me
when I happened to be in the right. And this mode, which I at first put on
with some violence to natural inclination, became at length so easy and so
habitual to me that perhaps for these fifty years past no one has ever heard
a dogmatical expression escape me. And to this habit (after my character
of integrity) I think it principally owing that I had early so much weight
with my fellow citizens when I proposed new institutions, or alterations in
the old, and so much influence in public councils when I became a member.
For I was but a bad speaker, never eloquent, subject to much hesitation

in my choice of words, hardly correct in language, and yet I generally carried my point.

In reality there is perhaps no one of our natural passions so hard to subdue as *pride;* disguise it, struggle with it, beat it down, stifle it, mortify it as much as one pleases, it is still alive and will every now and then peep out and show itself. You will see it perhaps often in this history. For even if I could conceive that I had completely overcome it, I should probably be proud of my humility.

PART IV

THE TWENTIETH CENTURY: SEA OF TROUBLES

IV

The Twentieth Century: Sea of Troubles

FOR THIS SECTION I CAN MAKE NO CLAIM EVEN OF REPRESENTATIVE RANGE. Most of it might be classified as "Whither Mankind?" writing, a very characteristic form of our time. All I have tried to do here is to illustrate part of the range of our worries. The subdivisions in particular have given me difficulty, and perhaps I should merely have arranged these pieces alphabetically by author. Yet I suppose I have been guided by a desire to illustrate above all the characteristic, indeed in perfectly defensible senses the *new,* forms these old questions take in our time. I begin with the "alienation of the intellectuals," already almost an old chestnut, but unavoidable here. I then go very briefly to the linguistic or analytical philosophy, the characteristic formal philosophical fashion of our time, a fashion never, of course, universally followed, and possibly now on the wane—though certainly it is hard to discern a successor. I have omitted existentialism, not because it is of negligible importance, but because it has so little new in it. I then follow with a subdivision on historicism, very characteristic indeed of our time, and of major importance in the history of ideas, if not in the history of philosophy. There was long preparation for our modern use of history, in a sense from St. Augustine, but specifically from the eighteenth century, through the nineteenth-century evolutionists and the Marxists right on to Spengler, the first widely read contemporary historicist. Indeed, if you feel you have to give up a Christian or other supernaturalist cosmology, and yet must make sense out of the universe, you can today hardly avoid falling back on history; physics will no longer do.

The Christian view of life and the universe is of course far from dead; and there are other and varied modern views the holders of which are not, as are most of our Enlightened, unwilling to call themselves religious. A subsection "Back to Religion" could hardly be omitted from a work of this sort. Once more, I have by no means, in my five choices, "covered the field." Next, the characteristic Enlightened effort to find in science a guide to life, a wholly satisfactory substitute for "religion," still continues in our day, and I for one can discern no real retreat on a large scale from what I like to call this religion of Enlightenment.

I have taken from a lively article by Dennis Gabor in the English magazine *Encounter* the title for my final subdivision. This is a kind of writing very fashionable indeed today—the attempt to describe a very distant future. Now there are certainly elements in these works of something very old in our culture, the Utopian or apocalyptical work, the prophecy. The invention of the future, like most shattering human inventions, took place long ago in prehistoric times. But our contemporary prophets are neither Cassandras nor Jeremiahs, certainly not Thomas Mores or Campanellas. They are contemporary historicists attempting under the influence of natural science to extrapolate on a long time-scale, attempting to understand the universe, attempting to answer the great questions of man's fate. How clearly they belong in this book should be evident from a moment's consideration of the vulgar questions: what *good* will it do anybody to know what's going to happen in the "next million years"? what is likely to happen in the next few years may be worth modest efforts at extrapolation, but can anybody now *do* anything in the twenty-first century? These questions are unanswerable in a frame of reference of common-sense, practical, everyday concerns. But we ask them, for the answers help give us the kind of satisfaction any believed-in cosmology can give. And the answers do affect our present, however little they have to do with any real future. Most of the current answers, especially those I here cite, help reconcile us with the failure of the twentieth century to achieve what the eighteenth (read your Condorcet) thought to be just around the corner.

A
The Alienation of the Intellectuals

C. P. SNOW

The Literati and the Scientists

C. P. Snow (1905–   ) is a most successful English novelist who began as a physicist, and has kept close links with the world of scientists. The thesis he sets out so firmly below is put with characteristic self-assurance. Whether or not the gap between scientists and humanists is as great as he contends it is, there can be no doubt that intellectuals today on both sides are greatly worried over it. The passage below is from the Rede lecture, delivered at the University of Cambridge in 1959. It has a good many topical allusions, but should give the American reader no serious difficulty.

I BELIEVE THE INTELLECTUAL LIFE OF THE WHOLE OF WESTERN SOCIETY is increasingly being split into two polar groups. When I say the intellectual life, I mean to include also a large part of our practical life, because I should be the last person to suggest the two can at the deepest level be distinguished. I shall come back to the practical life a little later. Two polar groups: at one pole we have the literary intellectuals, who incidentally while no one was looking took to referring to themselves as "intellectuals" as though there were no others. I remember G. H. Hardy once remarking to me in mild puzzlement, some time in the 1930's: "Have you noticed how the word 'intellectual' is used nowadays? There seems to be a new definition which certainly doesn't include Rutherford or Eddington or Dirac or Adrian or me. It does seem rather odd, don't y' know."[1]

Literary intellectuals at one pole—at the other scientists, and as the most representative, the physical scientists. Between the two a gulf of mutual incomprehension—sometimes (particularly among the young) hostility and dislike, but most of all lack of understanding. They have a curious distorted

From C. P. Snow, *The Two Cultures and the Scientific Revolution* (New York: Cambridge University Press, 1959), pp. 4-19.

[1] This lecture was delivered to a Cambridge audience, and so I used some points of reference which I did not need to explain. G. H. Hardy, 1877-1947, was one of the most distinguished pure mathematicians of his time, and a picturesque figure in Cambridge both as a young don and on his return in 1931 to the Sadleirian Chair of Mathematics.

image of each other. Their attitudes are so different that, even on the level of emotion, they can't find much common ground. Non-scientists tend to think of scientists as brash and boastful. They hear Mr. T. S. Eliot, who just for these illustrations we can take as an archetypal figure, saying about his attempts to revive verse-drama, that we can hope for very little, but that he would feel content if he and his co-workers could prepare the ground for a new Kyd or a new Greene. That is the tone, restricted and constrained, with which literary intellectuals are at home: it is the subdued voice of their culture. Then they hear a much louder voice, that of another archetypal figure, Rutherford, trumpeting: "This is the heroic age of science! This is the Elizabethan age!" Many of us heard that, and a good many other statements beside which that was mild; and we weren't left in any doubt whom Rutherford was casting for the role of Shakespeare. What is hard for the literary intellectuals to understand, imaginatively or intellectually, is that he was absolutely right.

And compare "this is the way the world ends, not with a bang but a whimper"—incidentally, one of the least likely scientific prophecies ever made—compare that with Rutherford's famous repartee, "Lucky fellow, Rutherford, always on the crest of the wave." "Well, I made the wave, didn't I?"

The non-scientists have a rooted impression that the scientists are shallowly optimistic, unaware of man's condition. On the other hand, the scientists believe that the literary intellectuals are totally lacking in foresight, peculiarly unconcerned with their brother men, in a deep sense anti-intellectual, anxious to restrict both art and thought to the existential moment. And so on. Anyone with a mild talent for invective could produce plenty of this kind of subterranean back-chat. On each side there is some of it which is not entirely baseless. It is all destructive. Much of it rests on misinterpretations which are dangerous. I should like to deal with two of the most profound of these now, one on each side.

First, about the scientists' optimism. This is an accusation which has been made so often that it has become a platitude. It has been made by some of the acutest non-scientific minds of the day. But it depends upon a confusion between the individual experience and the social experience, between the individual condition of man and his social condition. Most of the scientists I have known well have felt—just as deeply as the non-scientists I have known well—that the individual condition of each of us is tragic. Each of us is alone: sometimes we escape from solitariness, through love or affection or perhaps creative moments, but those triumphs of life are pools of light we make for ourselves while the edge of the road is black: each of us dies alone. Some scientists I have known have had faith in revealed religion. Perhaps with them the sense of the tragic condition is not so strong. I don't know. With most people of deep feeling, however high-spirited and happy they are, sometimes most with those who are happiest and most high-spirited, it seems to be right in the fibres, part of the weight of life. That is as true of the scientists I have known best as of anyone at all.

But nearly all of them—and this is where the colour of hope genuinely comes in—would see no reason why, just because the individual condition is tragic, so must the social condition be. Each of us is solitary: each of us dies alone: all right, that's a fate against which we can't struggle—but there is plenty in our condition which is not fate, and against which we are less than human unless we do struggle.

Most of our fellow human beings, for instance, are underfed and die before their time. In the crudest terms, *that* is the social condition. There is a moral trap which comes through the insight into man's loneliness: it tempts one to sit back, complacent in one's unique tragedy, and let the others go without a meal.

As a group, the scientists fall into that trap less than others. They are inclined to be impatient to see if something can be done: and inclined to think that it can be done, until it's proved otherwise. That is their real optimism, and it's an optimism that the rest of us badly need.

In reverse, the same spirit, tough and good and determined to fight it out at the side of their brother men, has made scientists regard the other culture's social attitudes as contemptible. That is too facile: some of them are, but they are a temporary phase and not to be taken as representative.

I remember being cross-examined by a scientist of distinction. "Why do most writers take on social opinions which would have been thought distinctly uncivilised and démodé at the time of the Plantagenets? Wasn't that true of most of the famous twentieth-century writers? Yeats, Pound, Wyndham Lewis, nine out of ten of those who have dominated literary sensibility in our time—weren't they not only politically silly, but politically wicked? Didn't the influence of all they represent bring Auschwitz that much nearer?"

I thought at the time, and I still think, that the correct answer was not to defend the indefensible. It was no use saying that Yeats, according to friends whose judgment I trust, was a man of singular magnanimity of character, as well as a great poet. It was no use denying the facts, which are broadly true. The honest answer was that there is, in fact, a connection, which literary persons were culpably slow to see, between some kinds of early twentieth-century art and the most imbecile expressions of anti-social feeling.[2] That was one reason, among many, why some of us turned our backs on the art and tried to hack out a new or different way for ourselves.[3]

But though many of those writers dominated literary sensibility for a generation, that is no longer so, or at least to nothing like the same extent.

[2] I said a little more about this connection in *The Times Literary Supplement*, "Challenge to the Intellect," 15 August 1958. I hope some day to carry the analysis further.

[3] It would be more accurate to say that, for literary reasons, we felt the prevailing literary modes were useless to us. We were, however, reinforced in that feeling when it occurred to us that those prevailing modes went hand in hand with social attitudes either wicked, or absurd, or both.

Literature changes more slowly than science. It hasn't the same automatic corrective, and so its misguided periods are longer. But it is ill-considered of scientists to judge writers on the evidence of the period 1914–50.

Those are two of the misunderstandings between the two cultures. I should say, since I began to talk about them—the two cultures, that is—I have had some criticism. Most of my scientific acquaintances think that there is something in it, and so do most of the practising artists I know. But I have been argued with by non-scientists of strong down-to-earth interests. Their view is that it is an over-simplification, and that if one is going to talk in these terms there ought to be at least three cultures. They argue that, though they are not scientists themselves, they would share a good deal of the scientific feeling. They would have as little use—perhaps, since they knew more about it, even less use—for the recent literary culture as the scientists themselves. J. H. Plumb, Alan Bullock and some of my American sociological friends have said that they vigorously refuse to be corralled in a cultural box with people they wouldn't be seen dead with, or to be regarded as helping to produce a climate which would not permit of social hope.

I respect those arguments. The number 2 is a very dangerous number: that is why the dialectic is a dangerous process. Attempts to divide anything into two ought to be regarded with much suspicion. I have thought a long time about going in for further refinements: but in the end I have decided against. I was searching for something a little more than a dashing metaphor, a good deal less than a cultural map: and for those purposes the two cultures is about right, and subtilising any more would bring more disadvantages than it's worth.

At one pole, the scientific culture really is a culture, not only in an intellectual but also in an anthropological sense. That is, its members need not, and of course often do not, always completely understand each other; biologists more often than not will have a pretty hazy idea of contemporary physics; but there are common attitudes, common standards and patterns of behaviour, common approaches and assumptions. This goes surprisingly wide and deep. It cuts across other mental patterns, such as those of religion or politics or class.

Statistically, I suppose slightly more scientists are in religious terms unbelievers, compared with the rest of the intellectual world—though there are plenty who are religious, and that seems to be increasingly so among the young. Statistically also, slightly more scientists are on the Left in open politics—though again, plenty always have called themselves conservatives, and that also seems to be more common among the young. Compared with the rest of the intellectual world, considerably more scientists in this country and probably in the U.S. come from poor families.[4] Yet, over a whole range of thought and behaviour, none of that matters very much. In their

---

[4] An analysis of the schools from which Fellows of the Royal Society come tells its own story. The distribution is markedly different from that of, for example, members of the Foreign Service or Queen's Counsel.

working, and in much of their emotional life, their attitudes are closer to other scientists than to non-scientists who in religion or politics or class have the same labels as themselves. If I were to risk a piece of shorthand, I should say that naturally they had the future in their bones.

They may or may not like it, but they have it. That was as true of the conservatives J. J. Thomson and Lindemann as of the radicals Einstein or Blackett: as true of the Christian A. H. Compton as of the materialist Bernal: of the aristocrats Broglie or Russell as of the proletarian Faraday: of those born rich, like Thomas Merton or Victor Rothschild, as of Ruther-ford, who was the son of an odd-job handyman. Without thinking about it, they respond alike. That is what a culture means.

At the other pole, the spread of attitudes is wider. It is obvious that between the two, as one moves through intellectual society from the physi-cists to the literary intellectuals, there are all kinds of tones of feeling on the way. But I believe the pole of total incomprehension of science radiates its influence on all the rest. That total incomprehension gives, much more pervasively than we realise, living in it, an unscientific flavour to the whole "traditional" culture, and that unscientific flavour is often, much more than we admit, on the point of turning anti-scientific. The feelings of one pole become the anti-feelings of the other. If the scientists have the future in their bones, then the traditional culture responds by wishing the future did not exist.[5] It is the traditional culture, to an extent remarkably little diminished by the emergence of the scientific one, which manages the west-ern world.

This polarisation is sheer loss to us all. To us as people, and to our society. It is at the same time practical and intellectual and creative loss, and I repeat that it is false to imagine that those three considerations are clearly separable. But for a moment I want to concentrate on the intellectual loss.

The degree of incomprehension on both sides is the kind of joke which has gone sour. There are about fifty thousand working scientists in the country and about eighty thousand professional engineers or applied scientists. During the war and in the years since, my colleagues and I have had to interview somewhere between thirty to forty thousand of these—that is, about 25 per cent. The number is large enough to give us a fair sample, though of the men we talked to most would still be under forty. We were able to find out a certain amount of what they read and thought about. I confess that even I, who am fond of them and respect them, was a bit shaken. We hadn't quite expected that the links with the traditional culture should be so tenuous, nothing more than a formal touch of the cap.

As one would expect, some of the very best scientists had and have plenty of energy and interest to spare, and we came across several who

---

[5] Compare George Orwell's *1984*, which is the strongest possible wish that the future should not exist, with J. D. Bernal's *World Without War*.

had read everything that literary people talk about. But that's very rare. Most of the rest, when one tried to probe for what books they had read, would modestly confess, "Well, I've *tried* a bit of Dickens," rather as though Dickens were an extraordinarily esoteric, tangled and dubiously rewarding writer, something like Rainer Maria Rilke. In fact that is exactly how they do regard him: we thought that discovery, that Dickens had been transformed into the type-specimen of literary incomprehensibility, was one of the oddest results of the whole exercise.

But of course, in reading him, in reading almost any writer whom we should value, they are just touching their caps to the traditional culture. They have their own culture, intensive, rigorous, and constantly in action. This culture contains a great deal of argument, usually much more rigorous, and almost always at a higher conceptual level, than literary persons' arguments—even though the scientists do cheerfully use words in senses which literary persons don't recognise, the senses are exact ones, and when they talk about "subjective," "objective", "philosophy" or "progressive",[6] they know what they mean, even though it isn't what one is accustomed to expect.

Remember, these are very intelligent men. Their culture is in many ways an exacting and admirable one. It doesn't contain much art, with the exception, an important exception, of music. Verbal exchange, insistent argument. Long-playing records. Colour-photography. The ear, to some extent the eye. Books, very little, though perhaps not many would go so far as one hero, who perhaps I should admit was further down the scientific ladder than the people I've been talking about—who, when asked what books he read, replied firmly and confidently: "Books? I prefer to use my books as tools." It was very hard not to let the mind wander—what sort of tool would a book make? Perhaps a hammer? A primitive digging instrument?

Of books, though, very little. And of the books which to most literary persons are bread and butter, novels, history, poetry, plays, almost nothing at all. It isn't that they're not interested in the psychological or moral or social life. In the social life, they certainly are, more than most of us. In the moral, they are by and large the soundest group of intellectuals we have; there is a moral component right in the grain of science itself, and almost all scientists form their own judgments of the moral life. In the psychological they have as much interest as most of us, though occasionally I fancy they come to it rather late. It isn't that they lack the interests. It is much more that the whole literature of the traditional culture doesn't seem to them relevant to those interests. They are, of course, dead wrong. As a result, their imaginative understanding is less than it could be. They are self-impoverished.

[6] *Subjective,* in contemporary technological jargon, means "divided according to subjects." *Objective* means "directed towards an object." *Philosophy* means "general intellectual approach or attitude" (for example, a scientist's "philosophy of guided weapons" might lead him to propose certain kinds of "objective research"). A "progressive" job means one with possibilities of promotion.

But what about the other side? They are impoverished too—perhaps more seriously, because they are vainer about it. They still like to pretend that the traditional culture is the whole of "culture", as though the natural order didn't exist. As though the exploration of the natural order was of no interest either in its own value or its consequences. As though the scientific edifice of the physical world was not, in its intellectual depth, complexity and articulation, the most beautiful and wonderful collective work of the mind of man. Yet most non-scientists have no conception of that edifice at all. Even if they want to have it, they can't. It is rather as though, over an immense range of intellectual experience, a whole group was tone-deaf. Except that this tone-deafness doesn't come by nature, but by training, or rather the absence of training.

As with the tone-deaf, they don't know what they miss. They give a pitying chuckle at the news of scientists who have never read a major work of English literature. They dismiss them as ignorant specialists. Yet their own ignorance and their own specialisation is just as startling. A good many times I have been present at gatherings of people who, by the standards of the traditional culture, are thought highly educated and who have with considerable gusto been expressing their incredulity at the illiteracy of scientists. Once or twice I have been provoked and have asked the company how many of them could describe the Second Law of Thermodynamics. The response was cold: it was also negative. Yet I was asking something which is about the scientific equivalent of: *Have you read a work of Shakespeare's?*

I now believe that if I had asked an even simpler question—such as, What do you mean by mass, or acceleration, which is the scientific equivalent of saying, *Can you read?*—not more than one in ten of the highly educated would have felt that I was speaking the same language. So the great edifice of modern physics goes up, and the majority of the cleverest people in the western world have about as much insight into it as their neolithic ancestors would have had.

Just one more of those questions, that my non-scientific friends regard as being in the worst of taste. Cambridge is a university where scientists and non-scientists meet every night at dinner.[7] About two years ago, one of the most astonishing experiments in the whole history of science was brought off. I don't mean the sputnik—that was admirable for quite different reasons, as a feat of organisation and a triumphant use of existing knowledge. No, I mean the experiment at Columbia by Yang and Lee. It is an experiment of the greatest beauty and originality, but the result is so startling that one forgets how beautiful the experiment is. It makes us think again about some of the fundamentals of the physical world. Intuition, common sense—they are neatly stood on their heads. The result is usually known as the contradiction of parity. If there were any serious communica-

---

[7] Almost all college High Tables contain Fellows in both scientific and non-scientific subjects.

tion between the two cultures, this experiment would have been talked about at every High Table in Cambridge. Was it? I wasn't here: but I should like to ask the question.

There seems then to be no place where the cultures meet. I am not going to waste time saying that this is a pity. It is much worse than that. Soon I shall come to some practical consequences. But at the heart of thought and creation we are letting some of our best chances go by default. The clashing point of two subjects, two disciplines, two cultures—of two galaxies, so far as that goes—ought to produce creative chances. In the history of mental activity that has been where some of the breakthroughs came. The chances are there now. But they are there, as it were, in a vacuum, because those in the two cultures can't talk to each other. It is bizarre how very little of twentieth-century science has been assimilated into twentieth-century art. Now and then one used to find poets conscientiously using scientific expressions, and getting them wrong—there was a time when "refraction" kept cropping up in verse in a mystifying fashion, and when "polarised light" was used as though writers were under the illusion that it was a specially admirable kind of light.

Of course, that isn't the way that science could be any good to art. It has got to be assimilated along with, and as part and parcel of, the whole of our mental experience, and used as naturally as the rest.

I said earlier that this cultural divide is not just an English phenomenon: it exists all over the western world. But it probably seems at its sharpest in England, for two reasons. One is our fanatical belief in educational specialisation, which is much more deeply ingrained in us than in any country in the world, west or east. The other is our tendency to let our social forms crystallise. This tendency appears to get stronger, not weaker, the more we iron out economic inequalities: and this is specially true in education. It means that once anything like a cultural divide gets established, all the social forces operate to make it not less rigid, but more so.

The two cultures were already dangerously separate sixty years ago; but a prime minister like Lord Salisbury could have his own laboratory at Hatfield, and Arthur Balfour had a somewhat more than amateur interest in natural science. John Anderson did some research in organic chemistry in Würzburg before passing first into the Civil Service, and incidentally took a spread of subjects which is now impossible.[8] None of that degree of interchange at the top of the Establishment is likely, or indeed thinkable, now.[9]

[8] He took the examination in 1905.
[9] It is, however, true to say that the compact nature of the managerial layers of English society—the fact that "everyone knows everyone else"—means that scientists and non-scientists do in fact know each other as people more easily than in most countries. It is also true that a good many leading politicians and administrators keep up lively intellectual and artistic interests to a much greater extent, so far as I can judge, than is the case in the U.S. These are both among our assets.

CRANE BRINTON

On the Discrimination of Anti-Intellectualisms

There is always some awkwardness in including a piece of one's own in an anthology edited by one's self. But so many intellectuals use so carelessly and defensively the term "anti-intellectualism" that I hope I may be pardoned for printing here the English original of an essay translated into Spanish and published under the title "Para la discriminación del anti-intellectualismo" in Imago Mundi *(Buenos Aires), No. 6, a quarterly published under the editorship of José Luis Romero.*

I

FOR THE HISTORIAN OF MODERN WESTERN IDEAS, THE EIGHTEENTH CENtury is the last for which he has a good generally accepted term: the Enlightenment. The historian knows, of course, that the thinkers of the Enlightenment were by no means agreed among themselves; he knows that their two magic words, Nature and Reason, are most complex clusters of ideas, which vary with the nationality, personality, and place in time of thinkers who use them; and he knows that not even in France were the *philosophes* of the Enlightenment unopposed by those who appealed to earlier, indeed to medieval, systems of thought. Nevertheless, when compared with the nineteenth and twentieth centuries, the prevailing systems of thought of the eighteenth century can be fairly easily sorted out and labeled.

Their eyes as usual firmly fastened on their own country, French historians refer to the years from 1789 to the present as "contemporary." The word is, however, useful for us all. It may be that the confusion and even chaos of nineteenth- and twentieth-century thought as it appears to us is simply a result of our immersion in it. It may be that the historian of 2100 will find for our time labels that satisfy him as well as "Medieval," "Renaissance" or "Enlightenment" satisfy us. We can already see that one major strand in contemporary thought is the emphasis on growth, on devel-

304

opment, and hence on history, of the group as well as the individuals; and it is a commonplace that Darwin stands for the nineteenth century as a neat summation, much as Newton does for the eighteenth. Yet "The Age of Historicism" seems a flat, dull and most incomplete phrase to tie together the complex clusters of ideas of our time. Nature as History was even more Protean than Nature as Reason.

One very strong strand in Western thought since the Enlightenment is the subject of this essay. The strand needs the work of the historian of ideas; it needs to be isolated—in analysis only, for in reality it is inseparably interwoven with many others—and to be given, if possible, a generally acceptable name. The present writer, taking his lead from Graham Wallas, who used the word in his *Human Nature in Politics,* first published in 1908, has used for this strand the term "anti-intellectualism." But he is increasingly aware that the strand itself is in fact a cable, composed of several separable strands or ropes, and that the term "anti-intellectualism" is one that arouses opposition in many minds and leads to confusion. In short, the phenomenon, the reality, the thing—for there is something behind the confusion of our terminology—needs the kind of elementary systematic attention the biologist calls taxonomy.

The thing, the cable at its thickest, is quite simply revolt against the belief of the eighteenth-century Enlightenment in Reason, and especially that form of belief in Reason most neatly shown in Condorcet. Men, the belief revolted against runs, using their minds with a magnificent combination of mathematics and common sense, are all capable of thinking the same way, and will shortly think their way into Utopia; human beings are all really potential Descartes, with a happy, and perhaps saving, touch of Benjamin Franklin. It is surely no accident that terms like "anti-intellectualism" or "anti-rationalism" have arisen to describe this revolt, for it was and is a revolt. This is not to say that there is nothing positive in the modern clusters of ideas that have been put against the simple faith of a Condorcet. It is to say that in all these clusters of ideas the notion that Condorcet and his like misunderstood men and the universe, and misled men, is very strong. And no doubt the prefix "anti" holds its strength in part because, in spite of all the misery and suffering that has gone on in the West since Condorcet himself came to so un-Utopian an end, the belief that men are capable of thinking their way into Utopia is still so strong, especially among English-speaking peoples. But it holds its strength in part also because it is hard to get a positive term to describe what thinkers since the eighteenth century have put in place of Reason to hold their universe together. Feeling, self-interest, will, the dialectical process, evolution, *Blut und Boden, le génie latin,* the id, *Angst,* and many more, have all been summoned as masters of, or substitutes for, poor human reason.

If, then, we tentatively continue to use the term "anti-intellectualism" to apply to all these revolts against the rationalism of the Enlightenment, we shall still have a grave problem of semantics on our hands. At the very least, we shall have to follow the lead of a master to whom all historians of ideas owe a great deal, Arthur O. Lovejoy. Working over one historic phase of what we have above called "anti-intellectualism" Professor Lovejoy concluded that even the accepted name for that phase, "romanticism," was in fact a most complex compound or cluster of ideas. He therefore had recourse to the plural, as in the well-known essay "On the Discrimination of Romanticisms," reprinted in his *Essays in the History of Ideas;* and he could write in the same collection a paper on "The Chinese Origin of *a* Romanticism." There is then certainly more than one "anti-intellectualism."

There still remains a residual problem, that of describing and naming each anti-intellectualism. Those of us concerned chiefly with ideas about man's fate, with ideas of thinkers the French call *politiques et moralistes,* must envy the biological taxonomist; but not even in irony can we work on a Linnean system, and refer to *Democratia orientalis var. Lenin* or *Democratia occidentalis var. Jefferson.* We really have but two resources: discriminate among the varieties we seek to separate by applying different adjectives to the old noun; or frankly invent new nouns of our own, or give a quite new sense to the old one. Carlton Hayes in his studies of nationalism has used the first method, distinguishing "liberal" nationalism, "integral" nationalism and others. Pareto with his "residues" and "derivations," Sorokin with his "sensate" and "ideational" used the second method. Perhaps one can generalize and say that historians, with their literary past, tend to prefer the accepted language, and that the sociologists, with their aspirations toward the status of real scientists, tend to prefer the neologisms. But this is an imperfect generalization, which leaves Mr. Arnold Toynbee, who uses old words in his own private senses, in between the historian and the sociologist—which, after all, is perhaps where he belongs.

We shall in this paper try to dodge this residual problem for the moment by a device borrowed from mathematics, and distinguish tentatively by numerical exponent three kinds of anti-intellectualism, anti-intellectualism[1], anti-intellectualism[2], anti-intellectualism[3]. This typographically rather ugly, or perhaps merely unusual, device has been suggested as one possible way of Westernizing Chinese writing. It can serve us for the occasion for lack of a better way. It should go without saying that these three kinds or types of anti-intellectualism can be subdivided into others, and that the whole process is merely one of analysis. In real life these clusters of ideas exist, as do the individual human beings who hold them, in what amounts in common sense to infinite variety.

II

Anti-intellectualism[1] holds the instrument of thought, even in some sense "Reason" as the Enlightenment understood it, to be useful and good, indeed on this earth man's best hope. But the thinkers who can be brought together under this rubric are generally agreed that first, the reasoning process itself is a much more devious and complicated one than most eighteenth-century thinkers seemed to hold it to be. In this connection it is significant that in our day, when anti-intellectualism[1] is certainly of great influence among—the paradox is purely verbal and superficial—intellectuals, Diderot's reputation should have risen so high. For of all the great men of the Enlightenment, not only in France but in the rest of the West, Diderot's notion of how the human mind really works, his "psychology" in short, is most like that most fashionable today—outside Russia, of course, and perhaps, in spite of Marx, even there. Those who hold anti-intellectualism[1] are even more generally agreed on a second point: the instrument of thought, good though it is, is in most men, and especially in the masses, of no great strength, and not capable of any rapid strengthening. The metaphor imposes itself: reason, cerebration, ratiocination, the instrument of thought, which appeared to the eighteenth-century *philosophes* to be a brilliant light burning in all men, hid in the masses of men only by a thick but easily removable cover of ignorance, superstition, and tradition, appears in the light of anti-intellectualism[1] to be a little candle, constantly threatened with extinction, which has to be carefully shielded. But anti-intellectualism[1] does indeed want very much to shield it, to help it grow in brightness; and herein, as will be shortly pointed out, anti-intellectualism[1] differs sharply from anti-intellectualism[2].

The taxonomist of ideas can divide and subdivide the thinkers he classifies under anti-intellectualism[1]. One obvious criterion, which can be roughly estimated for each thinker along a kind of spectrum, is the extent to which a given thinker accepts as a good thing the broad general tradition of Western abstract thought. At one extreme are philosophers like Bergson and William James, or a *politique et moraliste* like Georges Sorel. None of these, though sometimes they are put in a class with the real denigrators of abstract thought, considered himself as an irrationalist, as outside the tradition we date from the Greeks. They did indeed think that the *philosophes* of the eighteenth century were the ones outside the tradition; or rather, that these *philosophes* abused abstract thought, in part by oversimplifying it, but even more by considering it a fixed system which produced absolute and perfect results. James condemned "the viciously privative employment of abstract characters and class names." Whitehead wrote that "thought is abstract and the intolerant use of abstractions is the major vice of the intellect." Richard Humphrey, who quotes both these men in the second chapter of his admirable study of Georges Sorel, points out that according to this kind of anti-intellectualism[1], "if a man is to obtain any meaning from the physical world about him he must rationalize, he must make abstractions, but it is in the *intolerant* use of abstractions that the danger lies." Anti-intellectualism[1] at this extreme, then, is above all against intellectualism of the kind neatly exemplified in Robespierre's "*périssent les colonies plutôt qu'un principe.*" It is not against intellectualism which is respectful of the facts of the physical and the moral world.

At the other extreme in this respect is a thinker like Nietzsche, who often writes as if he really belonged in the category of anti-intellectualism[2], who often seems to tell us that the *Uebermensch* will have far better things to do than thinking. But in much of the *Genealogy of Morals* and *Beyond Good and Evil* it seems possible to call him a devotee of anti-intellectualism[1]. Here he is attacking, not the use of the instrument of thought, but what he regards as its abuse, its mis-appraisal. Pareto, too, though in his characteristic desire to *épater le bourgeois* he sometimes writes as if he agreed with Thomas Hardy that thought is a disease of the flesh, is a very good example of anti-intellectualism[1]. Pareto held that in most men thought is a very feeble candle indeed—though burning pretty bright in himself; but also clearly he held that, as exemplified in the great tradition of natural science, the "logico-experimental" method is the only tool for the better understanding of human behavior.

Freud, however, is one of the clearest, and perhaps the most important, exemplar of anti-intellectualism[1]. In spite of the trials and unhappiness of his later years, in spite, perhaps, of a certain attraction he always felt for the dark world of the death-wish, Freud remained true to the scientific tradition in which he was trained. He believed that men shall know the truth, and the truth shall make them free. Only for Freud the truth was not a series of neat formulas, easily discoverable and communicable, withheld from the masses only by the accumulated bad environment kings, nobles, priests, philosophers and rich men had somehow managed to foist upon them. Truth was very hard indeed for the individual to get at; the human condition itself, birth and infancy, not mere laws and institutions, conspired to hide the truth from him, to make him live at best in a world of makeshift and adjustments, at worst in a world of neurotic maladjustments or sheer insanity. But the long, patient—and disastrously expensive —process of psychoanalysis could, for him who could afford it, let in the light on these dark places, free him for a better life here on earth. Psychoanalysis indeed is a form of rationalism, though Condorcet—and one suspects Kant himself—would hardly have been able to recognize it as such. Like other forms of anti-intellectualism[1], it is a chastened, perhaps even a disillusioned, rationalism, but nonetheless it is clearly a kind of rationalism. The psychoanalyst does *not* want the human world restricted to the free play of libido or id.

Some of the more ardent and less subtle followers of contemporary anti-intellectualism[1] have brought to their belief in a possible newly freed reason so much of the spirit of the *philosophes* of the Enlightenment that they seem to be repeating them. To put it another way, these contemporaries, though they have learned from modern psychology and sociology that men are not quite what Condillac and Condorcet thought them, though they know there are psychological as well as institutional barriers to the attainment of complete understanding and agreement among human beings, still believe they have found at last the real key to Utopia. This key is semantics. A good example of this attitude is the American publicist Stuart Chase. Mr. Chase had embraced many good causes, including the now almost forgotten one of technocracy, which was an American engineer's belated version of St. Simonism. But none had worked. Then in middle age Mr. Chase discovered that men did not agree about the meaning of "democracy" or "justice" or "rights" as they did agree about the meaning of "right-angle triangle." In his *Tyranny of Words* he went so far as to suggest that when tempted to use these doubtful and disputed words we substitute "blah-blah" or some other nonsense word to remind us of our erring ways. Once humanity is thoroughly trained in semantics—the not-so-new version of Right Reason—all will at last be well. In fairness to Mr. Chase it should be noted that he did not consistently maintain his position; he has continued to write books full of nice ambiguous words.

III

Anti-intellectualism[2] does want a human world restricted to the free play of instinct, libido, drives, *Blut und Boden,* at any rate something that does not have to do with the cerebrum. Anti-intellectualism[2] not only commonly regards the instrument of thought as a feeble candle; it wants to blow the candle out. Some of its devotees, who are usually rather excited people, seem to regard the instrument of thought as, at least in many individuals, dangerously strong. For such devotees, it is a false light, the sooner extinguished the better, no matter how hard the task. Since unfortunately language and grammar are inevitably deeply stamped by the instrument of thought, the anti-intellectualist[2] is forced to use some kind of reasoning to attack reasoning. But so too is the religious mystic, whom the anti-intellectualist[2] joins at certain points, certainly in his feeling that language is not enough.

Examples of anti-intellecutalism[2] will occur readily to anyone familiar with contemporary *politiques et moralistes*. Historical romanticism is deeply tinctured with it, and the historian of ideas can summon up a whole series of characteristic romantic aphorisms that exhibit it: *Gefuehl ist alles,* One impulse from a vernal wood, Thought is a disease of the flesh. Fascism—Italian, German, and Spanish—is full of anti-intellectualism[2]. One of its clearest examples, worth standing as a neat summary, is the remark attributed to the falangist General Millán Astray during the trouble over Unamuno at Salamanca: "Abajo la intelligencia y viva la muerte!" "Down with intelligence and hurrah for death!" That is stark enough, if not exactly crystal-clear.

Like anti-intellectualism[1], anti-intellectualism[2] is not a simple category, all of one piece. Within it can be comprehended a considerable range of attitudes toward what is right and good on this earth for men. At the far extreme are the wild men, the Dadaistes, the racists who want men to think with their blood—or their genes—the modern phallic worshipers, some of the anarchists, the primitivists, many of the existentialists. At the other, often very close indeed to anti-intellectualism[1] are the more moderate: Mussolini himself, so far as he was a thinker: the often rather bewildered followers of Nietzsche, such as Ludwig Klages; conservatives in the tradition of Burke, who have never recovered from the French Revolution, which they blame on men's thinking; and some of the less excited existentialists. Many not fairly placed under the rubric of anti-intellectualism[2] have their moments of impatience, doubt, desire, or boredom, and throw off a phrase or two in denigration of the instrument of thought. The simplicities and dogmatism of the less gifted *philosophes*—Helvetius for instance—continue so to frighten the Western intellectual classes that most of us feel obliged to give evidence from time to time that we, too, have our depths. But the real anti-intellectualists[2] are numerous enough in the contemporary world, and their classification presents a serious problem to the taxonomist of ideas.

One special group, quite clearly to be placed among the adherents of anti-intellectualism[1], should be mentioned at this point, for to one not of their own circle they seem to have limited the role and importance of reason so much that they have turned over most of human life to the realm of non-reason, to have given great aid and comfort to the anti-intellectualists[2], to be, therefore, pragmatically classifiable as contributing in this world to the vogue of anti-intellectualism[2]. These are the logical positivists, or analysts, who following leads from P. W. Bridgman and some of the semanticists have decided that reason has a very restricted field indeed, that it must always be tested by an "operation," and that therefore traditional fields in which reason has commonly been used, metaphysics, ethics, political philosophy, theology, and in general most of what concerns human beings on this earth must be turned over to something else in the human consciousness or unconsciousness or subconsciousness. The logical analysts appear to have painted themselves into a corner of the room, where they claim to be comfortable but where they look to the rest of us most cramped. They simply disavow interest in all not in their narrow corner, a disavowal which is an invitation to anti-intellectualism[2] to take possession of most of human living space.

IV

With anti-intellectualism[3] we come to an increasingly common usage of the term which is on a quite different level of application from those just analyzed. Certainly in the United States, and to a certain extent in other parts of Western society, "anti-intellectualism" has come to mean being against, being in opposition to, the conventionally or "liberally" educated classes. The term has therefore come to have not primarily a philosophical meaning, as have anti-intellectualism[1] and anti-intellectualism[2], but primarily a sociological meaning. Indeed, during the recent investigations by the late Senator McCarthy, one of whose chief targets was the universities and the liberal professions, publicists attacking McCarthy almost always accused him of anti-intellectualism. McCarthy, like most born manipulators of men, probably had a low opinion of their intelligence, but he would appear to have had little interest in philosophical problems, and is hardly to be classified under anti-intellectualism[1] or anti-intellectualism[2].

There is certainly a connection between anti-intellectualism[2] and anti-intellectualism[3]. Most forms of fascist or Rightist totalitarianism throw over the whole inheritance of the Enlightenment and deny to ordinary men the free exercise of what "reason" they have. Anti-intellectualism[1] may go either way politically. With Graham Wallas—an extreme case, for he somewhat repented of his earlier anti-intellectualism—it may be on the side of democracy; but most anti-intellectualists[1] are so doubtful about the common man's intelligence that they make rather poor democrats. But at bottom, as we have insisted, anti-intellectualism[1] and anti-intellectualism[2] are concerned with psychological and indeed epistemological matters; anti-intellectualism[3] is concerned with social and political matters, is, in short, a cluster of ideas not indeed unrelated to the two previously analyzed clusters, but applied to quite different human concerns.

Anti-intellectualism[3], then, expresses the opposition, even the hostility, certain groups in contemporary societies feel toward the group, or groups, members of which write, preach, teach, do research, or concern themselves with the fine arts. These are the groups which slang in the United States has successively singled out with the derogatory terms of "highbrow," "longhair" and "egg-head"—which last significantly enough seems to be a literal translation of the Nazi *"Eierkopf,"* which was also a derogatory term used against the liberal opposition. Anti-intellectualism[3] is very obviously no new thing. If we had had nothing left but the dialogues of Plato, we should know that there was class feeling in Athens between the many and the educated few, between the "lowbrows" and the "highbrows." Still, the contemporary forms of this very old form of class struggle are in part new, in part exacerbated by the very great gap between the pure scientist and the research scholar on one hand and the man in the street on the other. Moreover, its forms vary from country to country. It is by no means the same thing in France, where in spite of widespread admiration for the arts and learning it most certainly exists, and in the United States, where there has been since the first emigration from "finished" Europe a very great ambivalence of feeling toward the arts and learning. Americans admired and wanted the distinction cultural achievements in these fields clearly brought with them, and in all fairness it must be said that many immigrants had and retained a genuine love and respect for the traditions of Western literate culture; on the other hand, this culture was associated with decadent Europe, was something to be repudiated by free men who were going to start anew. North Americans, in spite of their great ignorance of what goes on to the south of them, are pretty sure that South America, too, has its own forms of this old class struggle. One wishes that it were easier to penetrate the so-called Iron Curtain, for it seems likely that the Marxists have not exactly exorcised this class struggle.

In this essay we are not directly concerned with the further development and analysis of the content of anti-intellectualism[3]. The subject is of major importance and worth the careful attention of trained minds, which like the mind of the good physician, will not be shocked into blind indignation by the fact that the conditions to be studied exist. Most contemporary writing touching the subject, such as Julien Benda's well-known *Trahison des Clercs,* really does start out with the assumption, surely not at all justified by the facts of life, that the *clercs,* the intellectuals, though responsible leaders, and active ones, ought not to evoke any kind of class struggle.* It is sufficient for our purposes here, however, to note that the general term "anti-intellectualism," already beclouded by the differences we have above analyzed as anti-intellectualism[1] and anti-intellectualism[2], is further obscured by this relatively new and quite different application we have labeled anti-intellectualism[3].

V

It would seem desirable, if it can be done, to find some terminology to differentiate clearly among some, at least, of these meanings of anti-intellectualism. Unlike Professor Lovejoy's "romanticism," which though it has been a call to battle now among critics and the literary generally for over a century, has never really got down to the masses, "anti-intellectualism," especially with the development of the cluster of ideas we have gathered under the exponent[3], has indeed got down among the many, where it joins a whole host of other fighting words. Moreover, there are signs that even among the small group directly interested, the old struggle over "romantic" and "classic" is really dying out. Irving Babbitt, Pierre Lasserre, the Baron Seillère, doughty warriors in the battle, now seem to have been fighting over "old, unhappy, far-off things." We may then talk of "romanticisms," and differentiate one romanticism from another. But we cannot afford the same luxury with anti-intellectualism.

For the vogue of the meaning of anti-intellectualism[3] has made many very intelligent people wholly unable to grant to the word the meaning of anti-intellectualism[1]. The present writer, who has long been using the meaning anti-intellectualism[1], has recently had occasion to refer to Freud as an anti-intellectual in the company of two psychoanalysts, one of them nurtured in the holy city of Vienna itself. Both these disciples of Freud displayed at once a great degree of anger, and denied that Freud was in any sense an anti-intellectual. For both, of course, the term aroused lively connotations of anti-intellectualism[2], probably overlaid with rather vaguer connotations of anti-intellectualism[3]. For both, it was as though Freud had been classed with a Hitler, or worse. Both failed almost entirely to under-

* See Dennis Gabor's remarks on *Trahison des Clercs,* page 517.

stand a careful explanation of the sense in which the term had been used in our conversation.

In the West generally, certainly among the educated classes, and in spite of all that has been said and done since the Enlightenment to discredit abstract thinking, the word "intelligence" and all its derivatives have overtones of praise; they are eulogistic terms. Therefore the term *anti*-intellectual inevitably becomes a dyslogistic term, which is unfortunate if one is trying to use it as a eulogistic term, or as a neutral term. It would be highly desirable if at least for anti-intellectualism[1] some other term could gain general acceptance in the West.

Yet it is extremely difficult to breast the current or popular usage in language. It is not merely that we do not understand how a neologism catches on among the many; it is also that the would-be inventor of a neologism, if he has any feeling for language, can hardly bring himself to do too great violence to something that is part of him. The present writer became convinced some thirty years ago that the French Jacobins and the Russian Bolsheviks behaved in many ways as certain groups of Christians had behaved. Others, such as Bertrand Russell, had most certainly noted the phenomenon also. Yet to write of Jacobinism and Bolshevism as "religions" means to offend—and to impair communication with—many for whom the term religion has to include specific belief in a theistic god, or at the very least in a supernatural force. Jacobins and Bolshevists both repudiated the idea of the supernatural, and that of a personal, theistic god. Yet there seemed to be available to describe their behavior no good word; religion it had to be. "Creed" was a mere evasion, "organized belief" weak and vague, and a complete neologism, such as "revolutionary teleology," barbarous and foolish. "Religion" then it had to be, qualified indeed as "lay religion" or "surrogate religion."

It might indeed be desirable to call anti-intellectualism[1] by a slightly, but significantly, different term, *anti-rationalism.* This might indeed be made positive in the form of "chastened rationalism" or even, perhaps, "relativistic" or "realistic rationalism." Anti-intellectualism[2] of our scheme could then become *irrationalism,* though doubtless not with the consent of the irrationalists. Anti-intellectualism would then be left with no more than the meaning of our *anti-intellectualism[3]*, which in fact has already happened for most North Americans. But these are no doubt a semanticist's dreams. The portentous term will continue for some time at least to be bandied about in all sorts of senses, until we are tempted to agree with the *simpliste* Stuart Chase that "blah-blah" might just as well be substituted for it. The important thing, however, is to try to keep its referents straight in our minds. If Graham Wallas, William James, Freud, Nietzsche, Bergson, Tristan Tzara, Kafka, Alfred Rosenberg, Hitler, Stalin, and the late Senator McCarthy all belong in the same boat, it must be a pretty big boat, with several water-tight, or better, air-tight, compartments.

HAROLD ROSENBERG

America's Post-Radical Critics

*In part to introduce to readers who have not discovered it an anthology
which will give them a thorough introduction to the many phases of this
problem of the alienated intellectual, I cite from George B. de Huszar,*
The Intellectuals: A Controversial Portrait, *a portion of Harold Rosenberg's* The Tradition of the New *(1959) adapted for Mr. de Huszar's
book under the title "America's Post-Radical Critics."*

AMONG THE GRAND METAPHYSICAL THEMES OF THIS PERIOD, THE MOST
persistent and popular has been that of "alienation," the loss by the individual of personal identity through the operation of social processes.
The tone of the post-War imagination was set by Orwell's *1984;* since the
appearance of that work, the victim of "the dehumanized collective that
so haunts our thoughts" (as William H. Whyte, Jr., described it in *The
Organization Man*) has passed from the realm of fiction into the testimony of the sociologist and cultural anthropologist. Riesman's *The
Lonely Crowd,* with its "other-directed" phantoms of automobile show-
rooms and PTA meetings, left no doubt among Americans that the
familiar feeling of being someone else, or "nothing," was not a mere after-
effect of seeing the wrong movie. With Whyte's *The Organization Man,*
Spectorsky's *The Exurbanites,* Mills' *White Collar,* Packard's *Hidden
Persuaders,* filling in details of personnel, locale and genesis, the Creature
Who Lost Himself emerged as a statistical probability from the file cards
of the social analyst. Since then, he has regularly inhabited the unhappy
hunting grounds of beatnik poets, anti-conformist preachers, anti-modern
crisis-philosophers.

In contrast to this figure of the pulverized ego—whom we may nick-
name the Orgman—stands the four-square dynamic individualist of the

From George B. de Huszar, *The Intellectuals: A Controversial Portrait* (Glencoe,
Ill.: The Free Press, 1960), pp. 524-527. Adapted by Rosenberg from *The Tradition
of the New* (1959), pp. 280-285; printed by the permission of the author and the
publisher, Horizon Press, Inc. Title supplied by Rosenberg.

19th century, Riesman's Inner Directed Man, Whyte's Protestant Ethic Person. It is by the measure of this fleshy hero that our contemporaries are seen as mere components of the faceless hordes of "the new middle class."

The effect of its backward-looking is to denude the new social criticism of radical implications, or, for that matter, of any political or moral consequence. Its charge that *all* present-day social behavior tends towards robotization is a more extreme accusation than that of the Leftism that preceded it; it implicates everyone, without distinction as to social class, function or idea, in a single, deepening process of dehumanization. Yet by this very extremism it generates an atmosphere of relaxed acquiescence to a developing totalitarianism from which there can be no escape. Regretting the disappearance of the old, driving, uncomfortable capitalist type. *The Organization Man* places the fate of the new corporation executive, as well as of the beneficiaries of "fringe benefits" farther down the line, in a shadow world where "the demands for his surrender are constant and powerful, and the more he has come to like the organization the more difficult does he find it to resist these demands, or even to recognize them."

But there is more to the conception of the Orgman than regret for an older social type. As the representative of the new post-War employed intelligentsia, the post-radical critic suffers also a nostalgia for himself as an independent individual. For his former abstract sympathy with a nominal working class, the intellectual of this decade has substituted an examination in the mirror of his own social double as insider of The Organization and The Community. It is what he sees there that has caused him to project a morbid image of society compared with which the old "class struggle" America seems not only naïf but as relatively healthy as a war with rifles and cannons.

For in regard to the misery of alienation, who is a greater victim of what Whyte calls the split "between the individual as he is and the role he is called upon to play" than the member of the intellectual caste newly enlisted *en masse* in carrying out society's functions? As writer, artist, social scientist, he is one with his talents and his education for creative work; in playing his part in the service of the organization he must eliminate any thought of functioning for himself. Through his personal inventiveness he has in the past fifteen years achieved prosperity and social prestige; yet he is the most dependent of wage earners and the most anxiously conscious of his dependence—*The Exurbanites* chronicles this dependence and anxiety to the last installment dollar. (Applying itself to the narrower spectrum of the commercialized intellectuals, *The Exurbanites* is the most realistic of the works here mentioned.)

The intellectual employee also accepts a more total identification with his role than other workers, in that the editorial director, the designer, the copywriter, etc., sells himself more completely in terms of both psychic energy expended and number of hours worked. With him the division between work and leisure, discipline and freedom, has truly been erased. If the free artist or the founder of a great enterprise builds his life exclusively out of the substance of his work, today's intellectual unbuilds his life in order to live his job.[1]

Besides being the prime victim and exemplar of self-loss in contemporary society, the "organized" professional cannot escape a conviction of guilt for his part in depriving others of their individuality. He has consented to use his capacities as a tool and to approve in practice the proposition recorded by Whyte that "all the great ideas have already been discovered." His skills tend to relate to human management, e.g., writing, image-making, program-forming; even if his specialty is in engineering or the physical sciences, the results of his work directly augment the force by which society is controlled. The intellectual cannot function as Organization Man without also functioning as Organization-Man moulder; as human object he must also affect others as objects; as manipulated act as manipulator. Thus he cannot help but feel himself to be a betrayer of humanity as of his own mind. Helpless to change anything, he is yet the chief culprit of the alienation drama, the driven "scientist," who directs the undermining of the simple human individual, whether as motivational expert, inventor of personnel tests, or as preacher of despairing acceptance.

Self-displacement through one's acts is the innermost problem of life in America as of that in all civilized countries. The Social Type has always been among us, of course, despite Riesman's and Whyte's efforts to distinguish today's other-directed man from his nineteenth-century ancestor. Tolstoy's Ivan Ilych, who decorated his house entirely according to his own original ideas only to have it turn out exactly like all other houses of his class, is as good an example of automatic "radared" taste-exchanging (Riesman) as can be found in Fairfield County. Tolstoy explicitly insisted that Ilych was a socially made up man, an "object" guided by public opinion, an example of "dead" living.

In the United States, nineteenth-century literature, whether in the popular stage-comedies of manners or in the symbolism of the romantics, centers on society's human abstractions. The hero of Poe's "The Man Who Was Made Up" owed to industry all his movable parts. A contemporary of this invention was the ubiquitous Salesman-Preacher, whom Melville, writing in a less unctuous age than ours, named The Confidence Man. Like Whyte, Spectorsky, and Packard, Melville saw in this professional supplier of things, ideas and feelings the outstanding specimen of man as social artifice, while from the silent recesses of the office files, he

---

[1] The rule quoted by Whyte for corporation executives generally, "You promote the guy who takes his problem home with him," becomes for the intellectual, "You hire the guy who takes his problem to bed with him." His job has a creative side in which his preconscious must also collaborate. Take this into account in computing his average salary, and the difference between the wage-earner of the suburb and of the company town becomes largely a matter of overtime pay. At $2.50 an hour, the totally employed intellectual would earn more than $20,000 a year.

drew forth the white-collared tomb deity, Bartleby. And he too, set up an apposite type; "inner-directed" like Riesman's, morally absolutist like Whyte's "Protestant;" the brooding subjective Indian fighter, paranoiac Ahab of the prairies.

What is new in America is not the socially reflexive person but the presence of a self-conscious intellectual caste whose disillusionment has induced its members to volunteer to serve as tools. The predicament in which these individuals find themselves is what casts a bar sinister over their image of America. The fear-augury that the Orgman will become everyone in a quiet, unopposable totalitarianism is not a conclusion based on social analysis but a projection of the fate the intellectuals have chosen for themselves. The American landscape has by no means been re-made by the "Social Ethic" compression machine into an electrified Eden set out on porcelain grass. Except in the new suburbs, the physical condition of America's cities, towns and villages is of itself proof enough that decay, shiftlessness, egotism and other forms of popular expressionism are more than holding their own against other-direction. Granted that the growth of the supercorporation and the absorption and standardization of small business has changed the independent operator into an agent, at the same time that mechanization has been turning the workman into a technician; granted that Whyte's notation that "the collectivization so visible in the corporation has affected almost every field of work" is indisputable; and that today Orgmen reproduce themselves like fruit flies in whatever is organized, be it a political party or a museum of advanced art—given this groundwork for the conquest of America by this "type", still the contention that the nation is, or even might be, subordinated to such a master is at least as ludicrous as it is alarming. The increasing concentration of control and the standardization of work present well-known alternatives which we need not discuss here; but for the individual, the last voice in the issue of being or not being himself is still his own.

The inhabitant of the sacred groves has, however, surrendered all choices. Having accepted self-alienation in trade for social place, the post-radical intellectual can see nothing ahead but other-direction and a corporately styled personality. For him the Orgworld has closed for good. Within these limits the deploring of "conformity" is simply an expression of self-pity. The strategy (Whyte's) of fighting the organization through secret resistance behind the outershaped mask is, by the measure of the ancient intellectual tradition of denunciation or self-exile, only a dreary professional's ruse for holding on to the best of both worlds. That such a proposal should seem relevant is another proof that the Orgman is, with necessary additions and disguise, none else than the new intellectual talking about himself. Certainly the deft management of the corporate Look which solves things for Whyte would be of no help to the farmer or to the workingman, nor would the boss need to make use of it. The "what to do about it" part of the studies of Whyte and Riesman are clearly sermons for their milieu rather than challenges to history in the name of mankind.

The critics of the new America are disheartened by a revolution won—their revolution, which can go no farther than the ending of the underground life of the American intellectual mass through economic recognition of the services it has to offer. With his own success achieved, the only issue the intellectual can see as remaining for society is "personality". Somehow, this seems unattainable in "the dehumanized collective" in the building of which he is taking a leading part. The result is depression—and it is by the power of the depression it generates, in contrast to the smugness of the old-time boosting, that the present sociology is a force against a more radical and realistic understanding of American life.

B

Meaning Is All:
The Linguistic Philosophy

ERNEST GELLNER

The Mystical Philistines

It is perhaps unfair, but it is also usually illuminating, to let a hostile thinker explain a given philosophical system. I am letting Ernest Gellner (1925–   ), himself a former scholar of Balliol, outline some important aspects of what he calls the typically Oxford "linguistic philosophy."

Gellner's book has roused the kind of tempest such books can rouse, notably in Oxford itself. It clearly does violate some of the canons of scholarly debate as they have developed in England. But this latest Oxford school has perhaps had things too much its own way, and has developed a tender-minded sensitivity to critical attack, a sensitivity the truly tough-minded ought to be able to overcome.

There seems to be no accepted term—accepted even in the sense of "Utilitarianism" for the Benthamites, or "Pragmatism" for the school of William James and John Dewey—we can use for a very strong current of twentieth-century thought which is a phase of what I have called above (pp. 304–313) "anti-intellectualism.¹" The central conception of this current of thinking may be put oversimply as the deliberate limitation of philosophical reasoning to problems that hold promise of being resolved by methods and with results we associate by experience with the achievements of a natural science, say physics, and with mathematical logic. I refer to one of the enthusiastic popularizers of this philosophy, Mr. Stuart Chase, and to his best-selling Tyranny of Words. *Mr. Chase suggests that whenever we are tempted to use great big terms not subject to the close definition and empirical (or operational) checking the natural scientist employs—terms like "rights of man," "democracy," "free enterprise" and many, many more—we discipline ourselves by substituting "blah-blah"; thus, perhaps, saying "life, blah-blah, and the pursuit of blah-blah" (or is "life," after all, so vague a concept that we had better use "blah-blah" for this word, too, in Jefferson's preamble to our Declaration of Independence—or perhaps we should also say, Declaration of Blah-Blah?).*

You can see how readily this latest rationalist current of thought can be run into the ground of ridicule. Mr. Gellner is less unfair than I have been in the last few sentences, but he is still a hostile critic. I shall let Mr.

320

*Bridgman, a very distinguished physicist who has thought hard about
how he goes about thinking, speak from the margins of the school. Its
central figure is probably the Viennese exile in England, Ludwig Wittgenstein, a difficult thinker indeed whom I dare not attempt to use here.
I shall make further suggestions at the end of this book. Meanwhile, I
can perhaps fix the school—or schools—in your mind most clearly if I
say that their central problem is the problem of* meaning, *and communication of meaning, which is called* semantics. *One of the classics—most
readable—of the school is I. A. Richards and C. K. Ogden,* The Meaning of Meaning *(1923). And as a final shot, here is how Bertrand Russell
—by no means an other-worldly, tender or fuzzy-minded anti-scientist—
ends his introduction to Mr. Gellner's book.*

When I was a boy, I had a clock with a pendulum which could be lifted off.
I found that the clock went very much faster without the pendulum. If the main
purpose of a clock is to go, the clock was better for losing its pendulum. True,
it could no longer tell the time, but that did not matter if one could teach oneself
to be indifferent to the passage of time. The linguistic philosophy, which cares
only about language, and not about the world, is like the boy who preferred
the clock without the pendulum because, although it no longer told the time,
it went more easily than before and at a more exhilarating pace.

AN IDEOLOGY

LINGUISTIC PHILOSOPHY IS AN IDEOLOGY. I USE THE TERM "IDEOLOGY"
in a non-pejorative and very general sense. Linguistic Philosophy happens
to be *bad* ideology, but that is not a pleonasm.

An ideology manifests itself simultaneously as a set of ideas or doctrines, a set of practices, and a more or less closely organised, more or
less institutionalised social group. The ideas form a reasonably connected
system, related in part by mutual entailment such that if key ideas are
understood, the others follow, and in part by weaker relationships of similarity and mutual suggestiveness.

There can be no doubt that ideologies in this sense exist "in the air,"
as general ways of going about things, suggesting approaches, facilitating
interpretation and communication, whilst blocking alternative approaches
or interpretations.

So far, in talking of "ideology," I have in effect been defining my use
of the term. I now wish to specify some important characteristics which
are, I think, often displayed by successful ideologies:

(1) A great plausibility, a powerful *click* at some one or more points
which gives it a compulsiveness of a kind.

(2) A great absurdity, a violent intellectual resistance-generating offensiveness at some one or more other points.

From Ernest Gellner, *Words and Things* (Boston: Beacon Press, 1959), pp. 231-
239.

The first of these is a kind of bait. An appealing outlook must some-how account for some striking features of our experience which otherwise remain unaccounted for, or are otherwise less well explained. The second feature, though initially repellent, is what binds the group, what singles out the cluster of idea from the general realm of true ideas. The swallow-ing of an absurdity is, in the acceptance of an ideology, what a painful *rite de passage* is in joining a tribal group—the act of commitment, the investment of emotional capital which ensures that one does not leave it too easily. The intellectually offensive characteristics may even be ob-jectively valid: it is only essential that, at the beginning, and perhaps in some measure always, they should be difficult to accept.

The plausibilities of Linguistic Philosophy are numerous and striking. It seems to account for the sterility of past philosophy, for how philosophy is possible despite the lack of experimentation, etc., on the part of phi-losophers. It appears to follow from the obvious, but nevertheless striking and often neglected, insight that there is such a thing as language, that it has rules like any other non-random activity, that words have meanings which must not be violated if one is to talk sense: it explains why common sense is so often right and justifies our daily reliance on it: it unmasks pretentiousness and vacuity, and diagnoses it. It fits in with the general naturalistic, anti-doctrinaire temper of the time.

Its intellectual offensiveness on the other hand resides in its claim that it denies legitimacy to certain questions, doubts, and a certain kind of ignorance, which in our hearts we know full well to be legitimate: we do *not* know whether others see the same colours as we do, whether other people have feelings, whether we are free to choose our aims, whether induction is legitimate, whether morality is truly binding or merely an illusion, etc. Many or all of these doubts and questions, which Linguistic Philosophy characteristically "cures" as misunderstandings of language, are in fact genuine. Their suppression without real conviction is an accept-ance of an absurdity which binds the adherent to the movement. (This is also what is liable to produce such anger in him when he encounters a doubter of the movement.)

Of its plausibilities, the most important perhaps is that it is positivist—in the sense of allocating the exploration and understanding of nature and things in general to experimental science (whilst nevertheless reserving other functions for itself). It is doubtful whether ideologies which are not positivist in some sense have much chance of success in the modern world. This is due not so much to the existence of plausible epistemological models showing that only experimental science *can* explore the world—such models have always been available, almost since the beginning of thought, and they have not always been felt to be cogent—as to the con-junction of these models with the overwhelming, manifest success of natural science, contrasted with the unprogressive and woolly squabbling in non-scientific fields such as philosophy or theology. This makes some recognition of the place of science essential to an ideology if it is to appeal to modern man. Pure positivism, in the traditional sense, consists *au fond* of recommending that all thinking should emulate the ways of science, whatever they be, or pack up. This particular way out has certain disadvantages, notably that the ways of science (whatever they be) do not provide answers to some pressing questions, or fail to provide definite or intelligible answers, or provide uncomfortable ones. This being so, modern ideologies must, on the one hand, supplement science, and, on the other, make sure that they do not conflict with it and do not appear to trespass on its domain.

Contemporary theological doctrines, for instance, tend to take care to convey by their very tone and style that they are somehow at an altogether different level from scientific or ordinary thinking: gone are the days when the existence of God, the creation of the world and so on were debated between pro-religious and pro-scientific parties on the assumption that the meaning of the issue was clear but its truth was in dispute. In its own domain, the greater reliability of science is no longer seriously in doubt: the question is now how to delimit what its domain is and discover or establish whether other domains exist; and, if so, to indicate their features and the truths to be found in them. (Modern theologians no longer explain strange Revelations about the ordinary world, but tend to seek strange realms in which those Revelations will be ordinary truths.)

But what is true of the adjustment of theology to the hegemony of science is doubly true of those ideologies which actually emerged in the modern world.

SOME COMPARISONS

The striking examples, with which it is illuminating to compare the linguistic tradition in philosophy, are Marxism, psychoanalysis and Existentialism. Of these, the first two claim to be parts of science, but, unlike the big bulk of science, they provide suggestive, all-embracing and immediately striking systems of concepts, implicit guidance and so forth, which fit them, if true, to be orientations for life. The last does not claim to be part of science, but abstains from trespassing on it and contains an implicit explanation of why there is room for Existentialism in a region not open to science. Marxism resembles Linguistic Philosophy in possessing a monolithic theory of error: intellectual delusion will wither away with the State when the class struggle, which is responsible for their emergence, ceases. There are positive affinities in doctrine—the naturalistic view of man, the Third Person view of knowledge *—and in type of ideological device, notably the Two-Tier trick (see above), the custom of explaining away opposition and the associated Revelation complex. There are, of course, far more important and profound differences between the two

* Cf. A. MacIntyre, *Universities and Left Review*, Summer 1958.

outlooks, and it is in a way offensive to Marxism to compare the two. Marxism is about more serious matters and has an incomparably wider appeal, Linguistic Philosophy being of its essence an ivory tower pursuit, which can only make sense in an extremely limited environment.

Psycho-analysis, again, is profoundly possessed by a Revelation complex and the custom of explaining away disagreement in terms of the characteristics of the objector. It, too, has its values camouflaged under the notion of health. It, too, makes a specious claim to neutrality, and pliably insinuates the values of the practitioner. It, too, considers itself primarily a study of pathology, though the insights gained are generalised, and it, too, fails to recognise with sufficient clarity that doctrines and values are presupposed by the very drawing of the line between health and disease. As with Marxism and Linguistic Philosophy, the committing of the Naturalist Fallacy is inherent in it when it is treated as a world-outlook.

The similarities and divergences with Existentialism are of a different kind. Despite the profound divergence in the style and tone of the two movements, there is even a positive similarity in their starting points: both started from the realisation that certain questions are very strange and cannot be answered in ordinary ways. There is even a resemblance in the diagnosis of *why* these questions are strange: because we are inescapably involved in the asking and the matter questioned. To ask a conceptual question is, generally, not to ask something that "the world" can answer, at any rate directly, but is rather to ask something about the manner in which *we* handle things. To ask fundamental religious questions—including sceptical queries *about* religion—is to query the manner in which we look at the world. This is one of the key ideas of Wittgenstein's, just as it is of Kierkegaard's account of the religious quest. There is, of course, a difference: for Wittgenstein it was man the knower, the conceptualiser, the language-user who was inherently too involved in saying things to be able to say what saying things about the world amounted to; whereas, for Kierkegaard, it was man the agent or the chooser who *was* the act or the choice and could not therefore guarantee it by some ratiocination. But this is a difference in the *application* of a similar idea.

There is a further interesting analogy: both sprang from a reaction to pan-logism. Both were born from a rejection of a view that the appearances of this world are a cloak thrown over an underlying structure, which in turn was conceived as a kind of reified version of a current logical theory. It is true that the logical theory in question was quite different in the two cases: in one case, Hegel's dialectic, in the other, modern mathematical logic. A kind of visual concretisation of the former makes some sense with regard to history and society, whilst an interpretation of the latter makes sense for parts of higher mathematics. Neither lends itself to a generalised application as a model outside its home subject, so to speak—if indeed either should be reified at all. But both have been so applied, and in both cases the *reaction* was a doctrine stressing involve-ment (as opposed to reliance on the alleged underlying structure) and the essential-ness of idiosyncrasy (as opposed to placing stress on the alleged underlying homogeneity). In this way, Kierkegaard and Wittgen-stein resemble each other both in the form of their views and in their manner of reaching them.

But from this point onward the two movements cease to be parallel and become almost diametrically opposed mirror-images of each other. Some later Existentialism, just because the question is so strange, makes a positive cult of the act of answering it, and places no taboo on neces-sarily strange talk about the nature and conditions of such *engagé* and unbacked "answering," or rather, deciding. Linguistic Philosophy, on the other hand, either rules out the odd questions and their answers, or (and here it gets closest to Existentialism) makes a mystique of their ineffability, or (and here it comes to differ from it and becomes most characteristic of itself) comes to claim that answers are not merely impermissible but actually redundant.

It is almost tempting to explain the difference in terms of temperament: on the one side, because there can never be a validated or objective answer, a great fuss is made of this and the matter treated with the greatest of reverence as central to life; on the other, for the same reason, the matter is discounted as pathological and as doomed to wither away when the nature of its oddity is fully understood.

On the side of Continental philosophy, a greater and greater cult of paradox and obscurity, an appetite which feeds on what it consumes and, as with a galloping illness, hardly allows the imagination to conceive its end: who can outdo Heidegger? On the other side, a patient diagnosis of paradox, and an equation of philosophy with the recovery of platitude, and the realisation that an unsatisfiable lament *is* pointless . . . a trend to an era of increasing platitude, dullness and vacuity. On the fundamental issue of values, the two doctrines, disregarding idiosyncrasies of expression and the associated meta-philosophy, are identical: both, in effect, main-tain the subjectivity of value as an inescapable feature of the human situa-tion. But one side maintains that, just because it is a necessary fact, it is most deeply tragic or glorious; the other, for the very same reason, main-tains that it must therefore be trivial, no cause for worry, or indeed that it cannot be asserted at all. . . .

Thus Existentialism gives odd answers, or quasi-answers of an odd kind, to odd questions: the linguistic philosopher declines to answer the question because it is odd and because the answer would be odd. Both, as it were, find man in the condemned cell, as imagined by Pascal to convey the human situation: one makes a great fuss because the situation is in-escapable, the other, because it is inescapable, tries to convince himself that there is no fuss to be made. (He might say: "There is no contrast to this situation, the possibility of death, so how can a contrast-less charac-

teristic be usefully asserted, let alone be a matter for sorrow?") On the
one side, a little too much fuss is being made, perhaps; but the nonchalance
on the other side is, indisputably, somewhat affected. . . .

The diagnoses of the oddity of the fundamental question remain similar:
the involvement, the impossibility of transcendence, the cult of the irreducible idiosyncrasy of the concrete situation in which the question arises.

Both styles of thought make use of these features to account for the
fact that they deal with something not covered by science. In both cases,
the essential, inescapable idiosyncrasy of the object investigated accounts
for how science and its systematic and generalising procedure are avoided;
the involvement accounts for the difficulty of any but oblique expression;
whilst the impulse to transcendence and its necessary frustration provide
the problem.

THE NARODNIKS OF NORTH OXFORD

Linguistic Philosophy differs from the other ideologies mentioned by
sometimes affecting a certain modesty. It *can* be preached in a dramatic
or messianic style, and it is very easy to interpret it as being of the utmost
importance (if all past philosophies are wrong, this is no small matter,
especially if one understands *why,* and how to avoid mistakes in the
future); and although its protagonists are messianic in the sense of being
deeply imbued with the conviction of their own rightness, nevertheless it
is extremely modest in one important way—it claims not to interfere with
anything. It not merely does not teach anyone how to make shoes, but
it also claims to abstain from telling anyone how to live, how to find his
soul, how to choose his pictures, how to vote, how or where or whether
to worship, whether or which authority to obey, and even how to think
or talk! Not only does it claim not to do these things, or very seldom (its
prescriptions and prohibitions are only directed at other philosophers,
and are meant to interfere only with philosophising, and with nothing
else), it is extremely proud of this fact, and its practitioners are liable to
begin their works with such emphatic disclaimers of evaluative or prescrip-
tive intent that one feels they protest too much.

Linguistic Philosophy, at long last, provided a philosophic form eminently suitable for gentlemen. Nothing is justified. It is merely explained
that justification is redundant, that the need for it is pathological. The
philosophy is simultaneously esoteric—it is so refined and subtle in its
effects that a prolonged habituation to its practices, and hence leisure, is
necessary before one sees the point—and yet its message is that everything remains as it is, and no technicality is required. No vulgar new
revelation about the world, no guttersnipe demands for reform, no technical specialisms are encouraged.

It is, at the same time, a kind of vindication of the extravert against
the introvert. Those who see the world through the haze of their thoughts

or their feelings are shown up as somehow philosophically mistaken: those who concentrate on inner feelings, or on the other hand see things as instances of abstract characteristics, are shown up as people who are under the sway of a misunderstanding of language which leads them to over-rate and over-value what is in fact trivial.

Those who see things bluntly and straightforwardly—in effect, conventionally—with no room for strange or unusual doubts, are vindicated. "Nothing is hidden."

The arguments of Linguistic Philosophy are really a kind of inverted mystical exercise—they quite avowedly bring no new truth and change nothing, they simply confirm us in our faith in what we knew anyway: it is, indeed, a mysticism of philistinism, but a mysticism none the less, for it does not argue, it initiates. It seeks devices for making fully acceptable truths which it really holds not merely beyond doubt, but beyond argument. It concentrates on bringing out why argument is unnecessary and irrelevant. Now there may be truths which deserve such reverent treatment: but Linguistic Philosophy equates philosophy with this kind of reverent illumination of the allegedly indubitable, and suggests that common sense or the rules of current use have such a status.

In its preference for and vindication of the simple unspoilt popular view against the reasoned subtleties of the ratiocinator, Linguistic Philosophy is a kind of Populism. The folk whose simple but sound folk-culture is being defended and preserved against corruption by specious, theoretical philosophy is the folk of North Oxford, roughly.

P. W. BRIDGMAN

Words and Meanings

P. W. Bridgman (1882–   ), Hollis Professor of Mathematics and Natural History, emeritus, at Harvard, is a practicing physicist who has long been interested in some of the logical, indeed philosophical, implications of his work. His Logic of Modern Physics *(1927) has long been famous. He has recently (1959) gone over the ground again in a book he calls* The Way Things Are, *from which I have chosen a passage which touches on the meaning of integrity. Bridgman approaches this problem not with naïveté, but rather with a freshness, almost an innocence, he could never have had had he undergone a typical classical humanist, or even social-scientific, training.*

THE INADEQUACIES OF OUR TRADITIONAL INTELLECTUAL TOOLS ARE MOST manifest when we deal with the opposition between ourselves and other people as distinguished from the opposition between ourselves and inanimate things.

It is easy to see how things got this way. The infant in his attempt to adjust to his environment *has* to accept the methods employed by his culture. Not only is the infant not developed enough intellectually to be able to subject these methods to a critical examination, but he has time only to acquire as quickly as he can some method which will meet the necessities of the moment. It is thus almost inevitable that he adopt the methods which the people around him use, that is, the methods acceptable to his society and culture. Now the methods which have survived in any society are subject to one control which dominates so overwhelmingly that it casts into eclipse practically all other considerations. This is the control based on the requirement of survival of the society. If the method does not satisfy this requirement the society that uses it gets automatically eliminated, and with it all its component individuals. Now the brute requirement for survival is not a discriminating requirement, so that it comes about that anything goes, so long only as this one need is met. This need is by no means coextensive with the needs of the individuals of which the society is composed, and in fact is often directly opposed to them. It would indeed be a

From P. W. Bridgman, *The Way Things Are* (Cambridge: Harvard University Press, 1959), pp. 316-325.

miracle if there were not an opposition here. Survival of the race requires the survival of the individual up to the time when he has reproduced himself by procreation, but the individual wants to survive longer and furthermore has many other needs. It is true that some of these needs will also be automatically satisfied in society in virtue of the fact that society is the sum of its individuals. If, for example, every individual strives for a higher standard of living it is probable that the standard of living of the society as a whole will be high. It seems to me that most of the needs which are more or less automatically filled by society are on the "material" plane. One reason is that nearly all people feel the same material needs. Having agreed on the need it is usualy not difficult to agree on means for meeting it. Everyone agrees that it is nice to have enough to eat and to have good roads to drive automobiles on, and everyone knows that to get these things land has to be planted to crops and roads bulldozed. Although the individual can regard society in the long run as a pretty effective arrangement for satisfying his material needs, this does not mean by any means that the interests of society and the individual are identical even on the material plane. Wherever there is personal aggrandisement of the individual at the expense of others the conflict of material interests is manifest. The impulse to such personal aggrandisement is one of the commonest human traits, all the way from the bully in school to the tyrant or dictator.

However, it is on the intellectual plane that the mechanism which secures adaptation of society to the needs of its individuals is least effective and where failure to meet the needs of the individuals concerned most serious. The principle reason for this is perhaps the simple fact that so few individuals feel or express such intellectual needs. Perhaps the most pressing intellectual need of the individual is simple integrity. Society, on the other hand, has no need for integrity except insofar as it conduces to social stability. The result is that the individual can have no assurance that the intellectual tools which he has inherited from society are of such a nature that he can use them with integrity, or that he can acquiesce with integrity in the social philosophy which society expects him to accept. Not only is there no *assurance* that the individual can practice his intellectual life with integrity in the context afforded by society, but it seems to me to be a fact of observation that such integrity is well-nigh impossible with the present make-up of society. If the contemporary individual wants to live a life of intellectual integrity he pretty much has to do it on his own. Society as a whole is not interested in this and in fact is often positively hostile. There are so few other individuals interested in it that there is little or no public discussion of how to solve the problems, few books get written on the subject, and there is no cumulative body of practice on which the individual can build. Furthermore, the individual himself usually does not come to a realization of all this until he has matured and relaxed sufficiently from the pressure of making things happen in the material world to be able to devote leisurely thought to it. Contrast this with the situation in physics—where would physics be today if every new physicist had to start by himself from scratch? It will be a long time before the individual fully emancipates himself from his intellectual thralldom to society, and therefore a long time before the individual can effectively emerge. Perhaps the process may be accelerated somewhat as leisure becomes more general, and perhaps, even, this book may help a little.

I now propose to make an explicit list of situations in which it seems to me that the individual will find it difficult to use with integrity the intellectual tools which he receives from society. I shall also list situations in which the social philosophy which he is supposed to accept cannot be acquiesced in with integrity.

It may be well first to attempt to clarify what I mean by "integrity." It is the first place an attribute of the individual, and, as I shall use it as applied to myself and by projection to others, an attribute of which I am conscious. This is not the sense in which it is sometimes said that a "well integrated" person has integrity. The word is also sometimes used in a more impersonal sense, as for instance when a process of logic may be said to have integrity, but this usage is rare and is nearly synonymous with "soundness," and I shall not use the word in this sense. There is a connection with soundness, however. If I were aware that a certain process in logic were not sound and if I continued to use it, I would not be acting with integrity. Because of the implication of awareness it does not make sense to speak of society as having integrity. Although society as such cannot have integrity, nevertheless certain actions by society may have the same effect as would actions which performed by an individual would connote lack of integrity. For me, integrity in the individual implies "intellectual honesty," but it is more than this. It is a frame of mind. Integrity demands that I *want* to know what the facts are and that I *want* to analyze and to understand my mental tools and know what happens when I apply these tools to the facts. The flesh being frail and life short and there being many other things to do I have to make some sort of compromise with the demands of integrity. But there is one thing which I may not do and retain my integrity—if I have a new vision of something which I did not appreciate before, I may not try to put the vision back and pretend that I did not have it and refuse to admit that there may be consequences. Now it is often difficult to think through the consequences of a new vision, and often one simply does not have time. It seems to me that the individual who finds himself in such a situation can only react with diffidence—"humility" is not quite the right word. And it is to be continually kept in mind that new visions do occur, both to the individual and to society. Intellectually the human race is still young, and even without any evolutionary change in its intellectual capacities, it has many new intellectual experiences ahead of it.

Let us now consider in detail some of the characteristics of the mental tools, and this means mostly the verbal tools, which I have received from society which make it difficult for me to practice intellectual integrity. We have discussed many respects in which the traditional tools are imperfect;

each of these imperfections is a potential danger to my integrity to the extent that I have not thought through how best to adapt myself to the imperfection. Some of these imperfections are not due to any "fault" of society, but would appear to be intrinsic in the nature of things, before which society is as powerless as the individual. Furthermore, some of the characteristics of our mental tools which reflect something intrinsic in the nature of things are not to be classed as imperfections at all, at least until someone has a bright new idea. Among such perhaps are to be reckoned the commitment of our speech to the three-dimensionality of space and the forward flow of time. Among the characteristics which perhaps reflect something intrinsic in the nature of things and which we would perhaps be more inclined to rate as imperfections is the inability of language to deal with self-reflexive situations as we would like. Language has to be handled with the greatest circumspection if we are to avoid paradox, as is well known with regard to some of the situations in elementary logic. A special case of the self-reflexive situation is afforded by introspection. There are great difficulties here—I have tried to meet some of them by the device of using certain primarily introspectional words only as "relational" words, but this device does not meet all the demands. For example, we have seen that it is extraordinarily difficult to get into words what I mean by the "quality" of my sensation of red, but there is nevertheless something pretty definite here to which nearly everyone responds. It may well be that we are here trying for something which is intrinsically unobtainable, for we are trying to get into words, which are the instrument of communication, that which cannot be communicated. We are up against it—we cannot talk about it without using some noncommittal word like the "that" of the last sentence, whereas introspection discloses no "that." One of the most serious consequences of this ineptness of words in dealing with introspection is that it makes it so difficult to formulate satisfactorily the fundamental introspectional insight that I cannot get away from myself.

The hand of society is not especially obvious in these various specific ineptnesses of our verbal machinery. But it is not so obvious whether society has or has not played a role in casting our communication and thinking into the mold of words at all. The use of words may perhaps be inevitable because of the construction of the individual brain. Now words have certain characteristics that are so limiting that they may well be called imperfections. For example, words are static as used in language to convey meaning, and a sentence in general has no meaning until it has been completed. But recognizable mental activities occur during the utterance of the sentence, and these activities are very difficult to get into words. It is not now obvious whether in the predawn of history the human race took a fork in the road which committed it to the use of the mechanism of words with their static meanings instead of a fork which might have allowed it to reproduce more faithfully the fluent character of things as they are.

The formative hand of society is no less obvious in the way in which the individual thinks about the future in general, particularly events after his own presumptive death. Society has a continuity which the individual does not, so that society finds a utility in the conventional concept of an objectively existing future which the individual does not. I have not always found it easy to hold myself to a realization that any meaning which I have a right to ascribe to the future is to be found in things which happen to *me, now.* The conventional tool of language is not adapted to make this easier.

Other examples could be given—in fact examples could be drawn from most of the instances discussed in this book in which a conventional concept leaves something to be desired. However, enough has been said to show that the individual has not played a very large role in the development of many of the concepts which he uses, and that these concepts themselves are not particularly well adapted to the needs of the individual. In all these instances the role played by society has been more or less incidental and the final result has been rather in the nature of an artifact of the total situation. There are many situations, however, in which the role played by society is more active, and indeed where the role played by society, if it had been played by an individual, would not have been called innocent. We have seen that the control exerted by the survival motif is so overwhelming that social philosophies get accepted and forced on the individual with no regard to their truth. Such disregard of truth in the behavior of an individual would hardly be said to exemplify integrity. Although the property of integrity can hardly be associated with the action of society as a whole, it must be remembered that the total activity of society is compounded of the actions of its individuals. I cannot believe that society has accepted casuistical arguments in the past without some individuals knowing that they were casuistical and condoning them, it may even be because of considerations of the common good. If there have been such individuals in the past, and history makes it evident that there have been, I cannot concede that they have been acting with integrity.

Let us now look at some of the situations in which society asks the individual to subscribe to a philosophy which he cannot accept with integrity. These often occur in connection with the rationalizations which society asks the individual to accept for its mores and codes of conduct, that is, for its values. It seems to me that one of the most sweeping dicta which society asks the individual to accept is the dictum that in the long run, and from the broad point of view, all things considered, the interests of society and the interests of the individual are identical. This dictum played an appreciable role in my own bringing up. Such a dictum may have been tenable with the assistance of the concept of a future life in which the individual may expect to be rewarded or punished in accordance with the social value of his actions on earth. But without such a supernatural mechanism, the dictum is just plain not true, and anyone would be a simple fool to accept it, to say nothing of integrity. Even if such a crude supernatural mechanism is not used, the importance to society of getting its individuals to accept the values of society is obviously so great that all sorts of pressures are put on the individual to see his own values through the eyes of society. The values of society are presented to the individual as having an absolute quality that for some reason demands their acceptance by the individual. In their social context values thought of simply as *values,* without qualification, forgetting that a value has to be a value *for* someone. Now if anything is obvious to the individual it is that his own values have nothing of the absolute about them, but are continually changing with time, and therefore for this reason alone cannot possibly be identical with the values of society. But this is something that society, for obvious reasons, feels that it cannot let the individual say out loud, and does all in its power to prevent. Integrity in the thinking of the individual demands that he recognize this situation. Whether integrity also demands that he speak his thought out loud is a matter for the individual to decide.

It is not difficult to understand the mechanism by which the values of society acquire a degree of absoluteness. For when I talk about a value of society I am talking about a sort of average or least common denominator of the values of all my fellows. And when my neighbor talks about a value of society he is talking about a similar average, which he obtains by the same sort of process that I did, except that my value appears in his average and his own drops out, whereas in my case the converse happens, my own value dropping out and his appearing. When society consists of many individuals, the two averages, that of my neighbor and myself, are so nearly alike that the differences may be disregarded, and the "value" of society emerges as something absolute in the sense that all individuals come to approximately the same result. Furthermore, a value thus generated has considerable stability in time, a much greater stability than do my own personal values. The reason is simply that the average over the community is the average over all age groups, and the relative numbers in the different age groups have stability, although the individual members of each age group are in a constant state of flux. The values of society thus come to have a certain stability and "objectivity." This is no reason, however, why the individual who thinks about the matter should accept them.

The situation presented by values is typical of the general situation. Society feels that it cannot permit free discussion of many topics, and wherever this occurs the integrity of the individual is threatened. The instances could be multiplied. Perhaps the supreme example of an insight which the individual must be prevented at all costs from saying out loud, and the utterance of which constitutes the supreme *lèse majesté* against society, is that the individual is free to accept or reject in his inmost heart any demand of society. Society will go to any length to prevent people from realizing this—it is my personal opinion that some of the roots of juvenile delinquency may be found here; at least I can see how I might have been forced into delinquency by such treatment.

The institution of nationalism is one that society at present expects the individual to accept without discussion. It is easy to imagine the social furor which would greet a proposal to discuss seriously the question "Why *should* I be patriotic?" The word "subversion" would often be heard in the clamor. Politics within the nation affords many instances. In a country such as ours it is the common opinion that anyone born to be a citizen of the country is by that very fact committed irretrievably to a defense of its political institutions as the best possible. It is regarded as pretty close to treason to suggest that one's own political institutions are capable of improvement. The workings of such a philosophy are particularly obvious in a time like the present. Every one of us in this country should be re-examining our fundamental political suppositions to see how they stand up under the altered technological conditions of our times and to find ways of modifying them if it should appear desirable. Instead of this, because of rivalry with Russia, every citizen of this country is expected to defend the institutions of this country as better in every possible way than those of Russia. The disadvantages of a set-up as inflexible and as frozen as this would seem obvious without argument. So long as this inflexibility remains, the only way in which the human race as a whole and from a long range point of view can be expected to progress is in those few moments of flexibility when an old political system breaks down and is replaced by another. This occurred during our American Revolution. If we are not able to achieve greater flexibility it may happen again to us, in reverse. And if it is Russia that dominates after the next break-up, it will in turn happen to Russia, unless Communism achieves a flexibility of which it gives no present hint. In the meantime, and from the point of view of the individual, it is evident that the political arena is no place for the practice of individual integrity. It seems to be more and more the case that political success is achieved at the cost of personal integrity.

The pressures are hardly less compelling in the field of ethics. It is expected that every individual will esteem the indefinite preservation and welfare of the human race as the supreme good and value for him personally, even if racial survival has to be purchased at the price of not being allowed to use one's mind freely. It is also often assumed that the ideal of service to others or to the race in general is the highest motivation that an individual can have for conduct. The usual rationalizations for these values must, I think, strike the critical individual as pretty crude, but the individual is nevertheless expected to accept them. The difficulty of maintaining integrity in an atmosphere like this is obvious. It is not easy for the individual to be continually questioning and rejecting the consensus of his fellows.

In spite of the generally unfavorable social atmosphere I do not believe that the difficulties of achieving a satisfactory intellectual integrity on the social level are overwhelming, for it is usually pretty clear when a demand made by society fails in intellectual probity. It must be kept in mind that in saying this I do not imply that integrity need be pushed to the point of martyrdom. Some individuals may feel that their integrity demands martyrdom, but such integrity is of another sort, not intellectual integrity. In fact, martyrdom may sometimes be evidence of just the opposite of intellectual integrity, involving a willful refusal to see things as they are.

C

Historical Inevitability

FRIEDRICH ENGELS

Scientific Socialism

The great systematic use of the doctrine of historical inevitability in our time is still the one that stems from Marx and Engels. I give below a classical statement of that doctrine from the pen of Friedrich Engels (1820–1895) the collaborator—more, the chief stay and support—of Karl Marx, without whom, it can be argued, the very great gifts of Marx might have come to nothing.

THIS POINT IS NOW REACHED. THEIR POLITICAL AND INTELLECTUAL bankruptcy is scarcely any longer a secret to the bourgeoisie themselves. Their economic bankruptcy recurs regularly every ten years. In every crisis, society is suffocated beneath the weight of its own productive forces and products, which it cannot use, and stands helpless, face to face with the absurd contradiction that the producers have nothing to consume, because consumers are wanting. The expansive force of the means of production bursts the bonds that the capitalist mode of production had imposed upon them. Their deliverance from these bonds is the one precondition for an unbroken, constantly accelerated development of the productive forces, and therewith for a practically unlimited increase of production itself. Nor is this all. The socialised appropriation of the means of production does away not only with the present artificial restrictions upon production, but also with the positive waste and devastation of productive forces and products that are at the present time the inevitable concomitants of production, and that reach their height in the crises. Further, it sets free for the community at large a mass of means of production and of products, by doing away with the senseless extravagance of the ruling classes of today, and their political representatives. The possibility of securing for every member of society, by means of socialised production, an existence not only fully sufficient materially, and becoming day by day more full, but an existence guaranteeing to all the free development and exercise of their physical and

From Friedrich Engels, *Socialism: Utopian and Scientific.* Translated by Edward Aveling (New York: International Publishers Co., 1935), pp. 71-75.

mental faculties—this possibility is now for the first time here, but *it is here*.*

With the seizing of the means of production by society, production of commodities is done away with, and, simultaneously, the mastery of the product over the producer. Anarchy in social production is replaced by systematic definite organisation. The struggle for individual existence disappears. Then for the first time, man, in a certain sense, is finally marked off from the rest of the animal kingdom, and emerges from mere animal conditions of existence into really human ones. The whole sphere of the conditions of life which environ man, and which have hitherto ruled man, now comes under the dominion and control of man, who for the first time becomes the real, conscious lord of nature, because he has now become master of his own social organisation. The laws of his own social action, hitherto standing face to face with man as laws of nature foreign to and dominating him, will then be used with full understanding, and so mastered by him. Man's own social organisation, hitherto confronting him as a necessity imposed by nature and history, now becomes the result of his own free action. The extraneous objective forces that have hitherto governed history pass under the control of man himself. Only from that time will man himself, more and more consciously, make his own history—only from that time will the social causes set in movement by him have, in the main and in a constantly growing measure, the results intended by him. It is the ascent of man from the kingdom of necessity to the kingdom of freedom.

Let us briefly sum up our sketch of historical evolution.

I. *Mediæval Society*—Individual production on a small scale. Means of production adapted for individual use; hence primitive, ungainly, petty, dwarfed in action. Production for immediate consumption, either of the producer himself or of his feudal lords. Only where an excess of production over this consumption occurs is such excess offered for sale, enters into exchange. Production of commodities, therefore, is only in its infancy. But already it contains within itself, in embryo, *anarchy in the production of society at large*.

II. *Capitalist Revolution*—Transformation of industry, at first by means of simple co-operation and manufacture. Concentration of the means of

---

* A few figures may serve to give an approximate idea of the enormous expansive force of the modern means of production, even under capitalist pressure. According to Mr. Giffen, the total wealth of Great Britain and Ireland amounted, in round numbers, in

1814	to	£2,200,000,000
1865	to	£6,100,000,000
1875	to	£8,500,000,000

As an instance of the squandering of means of production and of products during a crisis, the total loss in the Germany iron industry alone, in the crisis 1873-78, was given at the second German Industrial Congress (Berlin, February 21, 1878) as £22,750,000.

production, hitherto scattered, into great workshops. As a consequence, their transformation from individual to social means of production—a transformation which does not, on the whole, affect the form of exchange. The old forms of appropriation remain in force. The capitalist appears. In his capacity as owner of the means of production, he also appropriates the products and turns them into commodities. Production has become a *social* act. Exchange and appropriation continue to be *individual* acts, the acts of individuals. *The social product is appropriated by the individual capitalist.* Fundamental contradiction, whence arise all the contradictions in which our present day society moves, and which modern industry brings to light.

A. Severance of the producer from the means of production. Condemnation of the worker to wage labour for life. *Antagonism between the proletariat and the bourgeoisie.*

B. Growing predominance and increasing effectiveness of the laws governing the production of commodities. Unbridled competition. *Contradiction between socialized organization in the individual factory and social anarchy in production as a whole.*

C. On the one hand, perfecting of machinery, made by competition compulsory for each individual manufacturer, and complemented by a constantly growing displacement of labourers. *Industrial reserve army.* On the other hand, unlimited extension of production, also compulsory under competition, for every manufacturer. On both sides, unheard of development of productive forces, excess of supply over demand, overproduction, glutting of the markets, crises every ten years, the vicious circle: excess here, of means of production and products—excess there, of labourers, without employment and without means of existence. But these two levers of production and of social well-being are unable to work together because the capitalist form of production prevents the productive forces from working and the products from circulating, unless they are first turned into capital—which their very superabundance prevents. The contradiction has grown into an absurdity. *The mode of production rises in rebellion against the form of exchange.* The bourgeoisie are convicted of incapacity further to manage their own social productive forces.

D. Partial recognition of the social character of the productive forces forced upon the capitalists themselves. Taking over of the great institutions for production and communication, first by joint-stock companies, later on by trusts, then by the state. The bourgeoisie demonstrated to be a superfluous class. All its social functions are now performed by salaried employees.

III. *Proletarian Revolution*—Solution of the contradictions. The proletariat seizes the public power, and by means of this transforms the socialised means of production, slipping from the hands of the bourgeoisie, into public property. By this act, the proletariat frees the means of production from the character of capital they have thus far borne, and gives their socialised character complete freedom to work itself out. Socialised production upon a predetermined plan becomes henceforth possible. The development of production makes the existence of different classes of society thenceforth an anachronism. In proportion as anarchy in social production vanishes, the political authority of the state dies out. Man, at last the master of his own form of social organisation, becomes at the same time the lord over nature, his own master—free.

To accomplish this act of universal emancipation is the historical mission of the modern proletariat. To thoroughly comprehend the historical conditions and thus the very nature of this act, to impart to the now oppressed proletarian class a full knowledge of the conditions and of the meaning of the momentous act it is called upon to accomplish, this is the task of the theoretical expression of the proletarian movement, scientific socialism.

ARNOLD J. TOYNBEE

The Pattern of the Past

One no longer hears quite as much of Arnold Toynbee (1889–   ) as one did in the late forties and early fifties, when D. C. Somervell's abridgment of the immensely long and learned Study of History *(10 volumes, 1934–1956) attained phenomenal success. But his work remains one of the great efforts of our time to build a world-view out of history—history seen, it is true, through the eyes of a convinced Christian theist. Someday I suppose a doctoral thesis will examine with care Toynbee's work in direct comparison with St. Augustine's* City of God—*perhaps this has already been done. The* Study of History, *in the Somervell abridgment, does not lend itself to excerpting. I give therefore a brief summary of Toynbee's central concepts by Pieter Geyl (1887–   ), a distinguished Dutch historian who disagrees with him but does outline him fairly. Indeed, I know no brief analysis of Toynbee as good as this one. I follow with an interesting discussion between Toynbee and Geyl, originally aired over the Third Programme of the British Broadcasting Corporation in 1948.*

CHALLENGE AND RESPONSE

HIS [TOYNBEE'S] WORK IS INTENDED TO BE A COMPARATIVE STUDY OF civilizations as a basis for general conceptions about history. Civilizations are for him the real units of history, not states, which he is wont to indicate contemptuously as "parochial," or nations, whose hypertrophied self-consciousness, under the description "nationalism," he detests.

In the six thousand years of which we have knowledge, he lists twenty-one such civilizations. He enumerates them, fixes their mutual relationships —in so far as they were not self-contained, which is a rare occurrence— and observes that they are all decayed or have perished, with the exception of Western civilization, that is the Latin-Christian civilization, which he represents as having sprung from the Hellenic, in its Roman phase. About

From Pieter Geyl, Arnold J. Toynbee, and Pitirim A. Sorokin, *The Pattern of the Past: Can We Determine It?* (Boston: Beacon Press, 1949), pp. 5-13, 73-89.

the prospects of this, our own civilization, that big swallow-all, Professor Toynbee leaves us in uncertainty; he has already repeatedly touched upon the problem, but only in his twelfth part will he treat it thoroughly. Meanwhile he believes it possible, even at this stage in his investigation, to state rules; sometimes he uses the word *laws,* on other occasions he speaks of *standard patterns of development,* of *tendencies* occurring in certain circumstances.

How do civilizations *come into being?* Not by climate, soil, or situation favoring the process; on the contrary, by overcoming obstacles: thus the shock is administered by which portions of mankind have passed out of the equilibrium of an existence without, or before, civilization, "from the integration of custom to the differentiation of civilization." The author proceeds to examine these adverse conditions at length under a number of headings: "hard countries," "blows," "pressures," "penalizations." "Challenge and response" is the formula in which he summarizes this movement in human history, a rhythm which makes itself felt over the entire field of human action.

Next comes the *growth* of civilizations. There is an increasing command over the environment, in the first place the physical environment; there follows a process of what Toynbee terms "etherealization," in which the physical environment loses its importance, and action shifts from outside to within. Progressive differentiation is and remains typical of the process of growth. Here too we are shown in all stages the action of challenge and response. But the author thinks it possible to be more specific: the growth of a civilization takes place through creative persons or creative minorities, whose action is conditioned by a movement of "withdrawal and return." The larger half of Volume III is taken up by illustrations of this process.

In Volume IV the phenomenon of the *breakdown* of civilization is discussed. The vast majority of civilizations known to us have after a longer or a shorter period been overtaken by this fate. The duration of growth differs greatly. It is not possible therefore to speak of a normal stretch of time from rise to breakdown, and Toynbee expressly denies that the decline is inherent in an iron law of fate such as governs the physical world. The decay proceeds from the doomed civilization itself, but it must be understood as the result of a shortcoming not decreed by any law; it is a human failure, there is no necessity about it.

The volume is mainly devoted to an analysis of the causes of breakdown. Very emphatically he rejects the view that the downfall can be ascribed to forces from the outside. He finds the causes of breakdown in the retarding force which arises from the mechanical element in the "mimesis" of the majority—that very mimesis through which the creative personality or minority can obtain a hold on them; in the "intractability of institutions," giving them a paralyzing or vitiating effect (he mentions very dissimilar instances, like those of democracy and industrialism acting upon "parochial" sovereignty, the effect of "parochialism" on churches, of religion on caste systems); in what he calls "the nemesis of creativity," the stiffening or exhaustion following upon creative action, as exemplified in the "idolization" of an achievement or of an attainment, of an institution, of a technique; under this heading he brings the intoxication of successful violence, militarism, triumph—not only in the military sense, though, for of the historical examples with which he illustrates his argument, none is elaborated at greater length than that of the papacy, which, after having been carried by Gregory VII to the height of power, was ruined by the blind self-conceit of Boniface VIII. (This, by the way, is his method throughout: a large number of particular cases, from antiquity or from modern times, from alien and distant civilizations and from our own, is always adduced to prove the theses presented.)

Breakdown is followed by *disintegration*. This process is studied in Volumes V and VI. Nowhere else in human history has Professor Toynbee found so fixed a regularity. The "creative minority" changes into a "ruling minority," the masses into a "proletariat"—a word by which Toynbee, detaching it from its now usual narrower meaning, understands a group which has no longer any real share in the civilization of its society. This is the "schism," for him the first sign of a civilization's having broken down—a schism into three parts, for besides the ruling minority there emerges "an internal and an external proletariat," which latter clashes against the frontiers of the State or the Empire of the ruling minority. The course of history proceeds by the rhythm of challenge and response; but while a growing society has always been able to find the right answer, and is therefore faced each time by a different challenge, a broken-down society can no longer really succeed; it is at best able to put off the evil day and finds itself after some time confronted again by the same problem. In the souls of men, too, the schism can be observed. Social disharmony creates a feeling of impotence, of sin; the standards of style and of behavior get out of order; ways out of the unbearable present are tried through "archaism"—back to the past, or through "futurism"—a leap into the future; or an attempt is made to detach oneself from society by means of philosophy or of religion. Toynbee here discerns the working of another form of challenge and response, "schism and palingenesis": a higher religion is founded by the proletariat segregating itself from society, although the creation is only apparently due to the majority. The external proletariat reacts through the formation of "war bands" and "heroic poetry." In any case this movement does not touch the now doomed society. Its history is governed by another variant of the rhythm, "rout and rally." The rout takes the form of ever more violent wars between states conscious only of their independence; this is "the Time of Troubles," another sign of a broken-down civilization. The rally materializes in a "universal state," the best creative work of which a ruling minority is capable. But the breathing-space of the *pax oecumenica* is of short duration, the universal state brings in its train only an "Indian summer," soon it is troubled again—

another rout, followed by another rally, until the rout, each time worse than before, can no longer be stayed and leads to dissolution, to ruin. This is not, of course, the end of all things. A new civilization has been preparing itself, chrysalis-like woven into the Universal Church, a creation of the Schismatic Proletariat, and this now unfolds itself.

As for the action of individuals in these circumstances, however brightly the creative spark may glow within them, it is doomed to failure. Professor Toynbee distinguishes four kinds of Saviors of Society—for this is the shape in which the great man now appears: by the sword, by power; by an appeal to the past or to the future—these two are the attempts to save society itself; then there are the two kinds of those who want to save man *from* society: the founders of a philosophy who, however, work only for the ruling minority, and the founders of a religion, whose empire is not of this world.

Professor Toynbee believes he has observed in history that this decline of a civilization after its breakdown follows a much more regular course than the growing process, to which no inescapable limit has been set. He has been so much struck by the uniformity with which the various "institutions" and phases—Time of Troubles, Universal State, Indian Summer, Universal Church, External War Bands and Heroic Age—spring from the body of a disintegrating civilization that he has reduced it all to a table. Stronger still is the similarity of the psychological condition of men in disintegrating civilizations. The general tendency can be characterized by the word "standardization": the result of all this violent movement is therefore exactly the reverse of that in growing civilizations, where it leads to differentiation. And it develops, in rout and rally, sub-rout and sub-rally, down to catastrophe, in three and a half beats.

Here we have the dry bones of a system to which the author gives flesh and life. The idea inspiring him is that of Christianity. It is true that Toynbee at times recalls Spengler, and his view of history is in fact not unrelated to the *Untergang des Abendlandes*. He expressly rejects Spengler's identification of civilizations with animate beings, which are born, are young, grow older, and die; when they break down it is by their own act alone. Similarly, he speaks emphatically against Spengler's connecting civilization with race. But if he insists on the freedom of choice, on the spiritual factor unrelated to blood or to the perishable flesh, he too carries to great lengths the presentation of his civilizations as well-rounded units. Above all, during the centuries-long process of disintegration following upon breakdown, he sees them subjected to a regularity of decay hardly less rigid than Spengler's parallel with the biological process.

In any case, however much he may diverge from Spengler, his system is even more diametrically opposed to historical materialism. He may speak of laws, his mind may be stocked richly with scientific notions, from which his language is ever borrowing terms and images; in reality the

sovereignty and the freedom of the spirit are his main concern and his
Bible texts are more than a mere decoration of his argument, for in them
he finds his profoundest truths foreshadowed and confirmed. God become
man in Christ is to him the veritable sense of history. Of the great con-
structors of systems, St. Augustine is most closely related to him in spirit,
and Professor Toynbee himself, in the preface to his second series, written
in that gloomy year 1939, brings respectful homage to the bishop who completed *De Civitate Dei* while the Vandals were besieging his episcopal
town. Material advantage is nothing in Toynbee's view; it is obstacles
which rouse the spirit to consciousness. Violence he detests, he is a searcher
after "gentleness." He meets history with ethical appreciations. The spirit,
the highly gifted individual, the small group, these are the sources of creative force. Power is an illusion, if not a boomerang. As a civilization grows,
it etherealizes. What exactly does he mean by this? He expresses it in
morphological, in biological, in philosophical, and finally also in religious
terms. No doubt all the rest for him is comprehended in the phrase belonging to the last-named category, according to which etherealization
means: "a conversion of the soul from the World, the Flesh, and the Devil,
to the Kingdom of Heaven."

DISCUSSION BETWEEN
PIETER GEYL AND ARNOLD J. TOYNBEE

Professor Geyl

The six volumes of Toynbee's *Study of History* appeared before the
war, but it is since the war that the book and the author have become
famous. A generation only just recovering from the terrible experiences
of the war and already anxious about the future, is reading the work in the
hope of finding in its pages the answer to its perplexities. It is indeed the
author's claim to discover for us, in the at first sight chaotic and confusing
spectacle of human history, a pattern, a rhythm. . . .

I must come straight to the main features of the system. Has Toynbee
proved that the histories of civilizations fall into these sharply marked
stages of growth and disintegration, separated by breakdown? Has he
proved that the work of the creative minds, or of the creative minorities,
can be successful only in the first stage and that in the second it is doomed
to remain so much fruitless effort?

In my opinion he has not. How do I know that the difference is caused
by the triumphant creator acting in a growing society, and the hopelessly
struggling one in a society in disintegration? I have not been convinced of
the essential difference between the phases of civilization. There are evil
tendencies and there are good tendencies simultaneously present at every
stage of human history, and the human intellect is not sufficiently comprehensive to weigh them off against each other and to tell, before the event,

which is to have the upper hand. As for the theory that the individual leader, or the leading minority, is capable of creative achievement in a growing society only and doomed to disappointment in one that is in disintegration —that theory lapses automatically when the distinction is not admitted in the absolute form in which our author propounds it.

I am glad that you are present here, Toynbee, and going to reply. For this is surely a point of great practical importance. *A Study of History* does not definitely announce ruin as did Spengler's book by its very title. But in more than one passage you give us to understand that Western civilization broke down as long ago as the sixteenth century, as a result of the wars of religion. The last four centuries of our history would thus, according to your system, be one long process of disintegration, with collapse as the inevitable end—except for the miracle of a reconversion to the faith of our fathers.

There is no doubt, when we look around us, a great deal to induce gloom. But I do not see any reason why history should be read so as to deepen our sense of uneasiness into a mood of hopelessness. Earlier generations have also had their troubles and have managed to struggle through. There is nothing in history to shake our confidence that the future lies open before us.

Professor Toynbee

The fate of the world—the destiny of mankind—*is* involved in the issue between us about the nature of history.

In replying to Professor Geyl now, I am going to concentrate on what, to my mind, are his two main lines of attack. One of his general criticisms is: "Toynbee's view of history induces gloom." The other is: "Toynbee has set himself to do something impossible. He is trying to make sense of human history, and that is beyond the capacity of the human mind." I will pay most attention to this second point, because it is, I am sure, by far the more important of the two.

Let me try to dispose of the "gloom" point first. Suppose my view of history did point to a gloomy conclusion, what of it? "Gloomy" and "cheerful" are one thing, "true" and "false" quite another.

Professor Geyl has interpreted me rightly in telling you that I have pretty serious misgivings about the state of the world today. Don't you feel the same misgivings? Doesn't Professor Geyl feel them? That surely goes without saying. But what doesn't go without saying is what we are going to do about it; and here Professor Geyl has been handsome to me in telling you where I stand. He has told you that I disbelieve in predestination and am at the opposite pole, on that supremely important question, from the famous German philosopher Spengler. He has told you that my outlook is the reverse of historical materialism; that, in my view, the process of civilization is one of vanquishing the material problems to grapple with the spiritual ones; that I am a believer in free will; in man's freedom to respond with all his heart and soul and mind when life presents him with a challenge. Well, that is what I do believe. But how, I ask you, can one lift up one's heart and apply one's mind unless one does one's best to find out the relevant facts and to look them in the face?—the formidable facts as well as the encouraging ones.

In the state of the world today, the two really formidable facts, as I see them, are that the other civilizations that we know of have all broken down, and that in our recent history one sees some of those tendencies which, in the histories of the broken-down civilizations, have been the obvious symptoms of breakdown. But what's the moral? Surely not to shy at the facts. Professor Geyl himself admits them. And also, surely, not to be daunted by the "sense of uneasiness" which these formidable facts are bound to give us. "I don't see any reason," said Professor Geyl just now, "why history should be read so as to deepen our sense of uneasiness into a mood of hopelessness." That is a telling criticism of Spengler, who does diagnose that our civilization is doomed, and who has nothing better to suggest than that we should fold our hands and await the inevitable blow of the axe. But that ball doesn't take my wicket, for in my view, as Geyl has told you, uneasiness is a challenging call to action, and not a death sentence to paralyze our wills. Thank goodness we do know the fates of the other civilizations; such knowledge is a chart that warns us of the reefs ahead. Knowledge can be power and salvation if we have the spirit to use it. There is a famous Greek epigram which runs: "I am the tomb of a shipwrecked sailor, but don't let that frighten off you, brother mariner, from setting sail; because, when we went down, the other ships kept afloat."

"There is nothing in history," said Professor Geyl in his closing sentence, "to shake our confidence that the future lies open before us." Those might have been my own words, but I don't quite see what warrant Professor Geyl has for using them. The best comfort Professor Geyl can give us is: "If we take care not to unnerve ourselves by trying to chart the seas, we may be lucky enough to get by without hitting the rocks." No, I haven't painted him quite black enough, for his view is still gloomier than that. "To make a chart of history," he says, "is a sheer impossibility." Professor Geyl's own chart, you see, is the "perfect and absolute blank" of Lewis Carroll's bellman who hunted the snark. Geyl, too, has a chart, like Spengler and me. We all of us have one, whether we own up to it or not, and no chart is more than one man's shot at the truth. But surely, of those three, the blank is the most useless and the most dangerous.

Professor Geyl thinks I am a pessimist because I see a way of escape in a reconversion to the faith of our fathers. "This," says Professor Geyl, "is an unnecessarily gloomy view of our situation"—like the old lady who was advised to leave it to Providence and exclaimed: "Oh dear, has it come to that?"

What was our fathers' chart of history? As they saw it, it was a tale told by God, unfolding itself from the Creation through the Fall and the

Redemption to the Last Judgment. As Professor Geyl says he sees it, it seems like a tale told by an idiot, signifying nothing. You may not agree with our fathers' view that history is a revelation of God's providence; but it is a poor exchange, isn't it, to swap their faith for the view that history makes no sense.

Of course, Professor Geyl is no more singular in his view than I am in mine. What one may call the nonsense view of history has been fashionable among Western historians for the last few generations. The odd thing is that some of the holders of this view—I don't know whether I could count Professor Geyl among the number—defend it principally on the ground that it is scientific. Of course, it is only human that historians should have wanted to be scientific in an age when science has beeen enjoying such prestige. I am, myself, a historian who believes that science has an awful lot to teach us. But how strange to suppose that one is being scientific by despairing of making sense! For what is science? It is only another name for the careful and scrupulous use of the human mind. And, if men despair of reason, they are lost. Nature hasn't given us wings, fur, claws, antennae or elephant's trunks; but she has given us the human intellect—the most effective of all implements, if we are not too timid to use it. And what does this scientific intellect do? It looks at the facts, but it doesn't stop there. It looks at the facts and it tries to make sense of them. It does, you see, the very thing that Professor Geyl takes me to task for trying to do with the facts of history.

Is history really too hard a nut for science to crack? When the human intellect has wrested her secret from physical nature, are we going to sit down under an *ex cathedra* dictum that the ambition to discover the secret of human history will always be bound to end in disappointment? We don't need to be told that Man is a harder—a very much harder—nut than the atom. We have discovered how to split the atom and are in danger of splitting it to our own destruction. By comparison with the science of physics, the science of man is so difficult that our discoveries in the two fields have gone forward at an uneven pace till they have got quite out of step with each other. It is partly this that has got us into our present fix. Is science to shirk trying to do anything about it? "The proper study of mankind is man," says Pope. "The human intellect," sighs Geyl, "is not sufficiently comprehensive."

I say: We can't afford such defeatism; it is unworthy of the greatness of man's mind; and it is refuted by the human mind's past achievements. The mind has won all its great victories by well-judged boldness. And today, before our eyes, science is launching a characteristically bold offensive in what is now the key area of the mental battlefield. Why, she has got her nutcrackers round this nut, this human nut, already. One arm of the pincers is the exciting young science of psychology, which is opening out entirely new mental horizons for us, in the very direction in which we are most in need of longer vistas. The other is the forbidding yet rewarding discipline of statistics. Science has set herself now in good earnest to comprehend human nature, and, through understanding, to show it how to master itself and thereby *to* set itself free. Science, so long preoccupied with the riddles of non-human nature, has now joined in the quests of philosophy and religion, and this diversion of her energies has been timely. There is, indeed, no time to be lost. We are in for a life-and-death struggle. And, at this critical hour, is science to get no support from our professedly scientific historians?

Well, in this "mental fight," I have deliberately risked my neck by putting my own reading of the facts of history on the table. I should never dream of claiming that my particular interpretation is the only one possible. There are, I am sure, many different alternative ways of analyzing history, each of which is true in itself and illuminating as far as it goes, just as, in dissecting an organism, you can throw light on its nature by laying bare either the skeleton or the muscles or the nerves or the circulation of the blood. No single one of these dissections tells the whole truth, but each of them reveals a genuine facet of it. I should be well-content if it turned out that I had laid bare one genuine facet of history, and even then, I should measure my success by the speed with which my own work in my own line was put out of date by further work by other people in the same field. In the short span of one lifetime, the personal contribution of the individual scholar to the great and growing stream of knowledge can't be more than a tiny pailful. But if he could inspire—or provoke—other scholars to pour in their pailfuls too, well, then he could feel that he had really done his job. And this job of making sense of history is one of the crying needs of our day—I beg of you, believe me.

Professor Geyl

Well I must say, Toynbee, that I felt some anxiety while you were pouring out over me this torrent of eloquence, wit and burning conviction, but that was of course what I had to expect from you. And now that is over I'm relieved to feel that I'm still there, and my position untouched.

Professor Toynbee pictures me as one of those men who mistake the courage to see evils for gloom, and who when others sound the call for action take refuge from the dangers of our time in an illusionist optimism. But have I been saying that we are not in danger? And that no action is required? What I have said is that Toynbee's system induces the wrong kind of gloom because it tends to make action seem useless. "But I am a believer in man's free will," Toynbee replies. I know. But nevertheless, his system lays it down that the civilization which has been overtaken by a breakdown is doomed. Now Toynbee has repeatedly suggested that our Western civilization did suffer a breakdown as long ago as the sixteenth century, and that consequently, try as we may, we cannot avoid disaster. Except in one way, except in case we allow ourselves to be reconverted to the faith of our fathers. And here Toynbee exclaims: "You see, I'm not so gloomy after all." Perhaps not. But if one happens to hold a different opinion both of the efficacy and of the likelihood of application of his particular remedy, one cannot help thinking that Toynbee is but offering us cold comfort. He talks as if we cannot advance matters by "so hotly canvassing and loudly advertising," as he contemptuously puts it, "our political and economic maladies." It is the loss of religious faith that is the deadly danger. To most of us this is indeed condemning all our efforts to futility.

Of course, Toynbee, it is only your picturesque way of putting things when you describe me as one of those historians who cling to the nonsense view of history. Because I cannot accept either your methods or your system it does not follow that to my mind history has no meaning. I do not believe that at any time it will be possible to reduce the past to so rigid a pattern as to enable us to forecast the future—granted. Yet to me, as to you, the greatest function of the historian is to interpret the past—to find sense in it, although at the same time it is the least scientific, the most inevitably subjective of his functions.

I am surprised that you class me with those historians who believe that their view of history rests securely on scientific foundations. In fact it is you who claim to be proceeding on the lines of empiricism towards laws of universal validity, while I have been suggesting that these and other scientific terms which you are fond of using have no real meaning in a historical argument. Even just now, didn't you deduce from the conquest of the mystery of the atom the certainty that man's mind will be able to conquer the mystery of the historical process as well? In my opinion these are fundamentally different propositions.

Let me remind you especially of what I have been saying about the uncertain nature of historical events, and the difficulty of detaching them from their contexts. And also of my contention that the cases and instances strewn over your pages have been arbitrarily selected from an infinite number and haven't therefore that value as evidence which you attach to them.

Professor Toynbee

There can be no doubt that you look upon this last point as an important one. . . . I see what you're getting at. I set out to deal with history in terms of civilizations, of which there are, of course, very few specimens, but in the illustrations I give, and the points I make, I don't confine myself to these rare big fellows, I hop about all over the place, bringing up as illustrations of my points events on a much smaller scale, which to you seem to be chosen arbitrarily, because they're just a few taken out of a large number. They also, as you point out, lend themselves to more interpretations than one. Yes, I think that's fair criticism, and quite telling. In answer I'd say two things. I think, as I said a minute or two ago, the same historical event often can be analyzed legitimately in a number of different ways, each of which brings out some aspect of historical truth which is true as far as it goes, though not the whole truth. I have myself sometimes made the same historical event do double or treble duty in this way, and I don't think this is a misleading way of using facts. As I've said before, several different dissections can all be correct, each in its own line.

My second point is that I bring in these illustrations taken from the small change of history, not for their own sake but to throw indirect light on the big units, which I call civilizations, which are my main concern. I helped myself out in this way because, in the very early stage in human history in which our generation happens to be living, the number of civilizations that have come into existence up to date, is still so small—not more than about twenty, as I make it out.

To take up the case of your own country, Holland, now, which I have used to throw light on the rise of the Egyptian and Sumerian civilizations: you challenged my account of Holland's rise to greatness. I found my explanation of it in the stimulus of a hard country. The people of Holland had to wrest the country for the sea and they rose to the occasion. Your criticism is that I've arbitrarily isolated one fact out of several. The Dutch, you say, didn't do it by themselves, they were helped at the start by efficient outsiders, and then the country, when it had been reclaimed, turned out to have a rich soil, as well as a good situation for commerce.

Yes, of course, those are also facts of Dutch history, but my answer is that they're not the key facts. If the outsiders that you have in mind are the Romans, well, the benefits of Roman efficiency were not enjoyed by Holland alone; Belgium, France and England enjoyed them as well. So Holland's Roman apprenticeship won't account for achievements that are special to Holland and that distinguish her from her neighbors. Then the fertile soil and good location: these aren't causes of Holland's great feat of fighting and beating the North Sea, they're effects and rewards of it. It is a case of "to him that hath, shall be given." What the Dutch had, before these other things were given them, was the strength of will to raise their country out of the waters. The terrific challenge of the sea to a country below sea level is surely the unique and distinguishing feature of Dutch history. With all deference to you, Geyl, as a Netherlander and a historian, I still think I'm right in picking out the response of the people of Holland to this challenge as being the key to the greatness of your country. I do also think that the case of Holland throws valuable light on the cases of Egypt and Babylonia, two other places where people have had to fight swamp and sea in order to reclaim land, and where this struggle between man and nature has brought to life two out of the twenty or so civilizations known to us.

Of course if one could lay hands on some more civilizations, one might be able to study history on that scale without having to bother about little bits and pieces like Holland and England. I wish I were in that happy position, and if you now, Geyl, would help me by taking up your archeological spade and unearthing a few more forgotten civilizations for me, I should be vastly obliged to you. But even if you proved yourself a Layard, Schliemann and Arthur Evans rolled into one, you could only raise my present figure of twenty-one known civilizations to twenty-four, and that of course wouldn't help me to reduce my margin of error appreciably.

To turn for a moment to a different point, I want to correct an impression that I think our listeners may have got, of something else that you were saying just now. Anyway, I got the impression myself that you still thought I claimed to be able to foretell the future from the past, that I'd laid it down that our own civilization was doomed. This is a very important point and I want to make my position on it clear beyond all possibility of mistake. So let me repeat: I don't set up to be a prophet, I don't believe history can be used for telling the world's fortune, I think history can perhaps sometimes show one possibilities or even probabilities, but never certainties. With the awful warning of Spengler's dogmatic determinism before my eyes, I always have been and shall be mighty careful, for my part, to treat the future of our own civilization as an open question—not at all because I'm afraid of committing myself, but because I believe as strongly as you do, Geyl, that it *is* an open question.

ROBERT L. HEILBRONER

The Limits of Determinism

Robert L. Heilbroner (1919–   ) is a young American writer trained as an economist. I conclude this subsection on historical inevitability with an excerpt from his thoughtful essay, The Future As History. *Mr. Heilbroner's position is far from that of doctrinaire historical determinism. Indeed, as a historian, I am delighted to be able to cite this measured, sensible little book as evidence that one can accept history as a guide, even a restraint, a limitation, without setting it up as a master. For, of course, in this latter case, it is really the historian who sets himself up as master. Mr. Heilbroner's own "view of life" as it comes out in this book is surely not an example of "alienation," nor of "anti-intellectualism" nor of "existentialism," but rather of what I shall call chastened Enlightenment, Enlightenment without hubris.*

A RECAPITULATION OF THE FUTURE AS HISTORY

IN THE PAST, AS WE KNOW, WE HAVE APPROACHED THE FUTURE WITH THE sustaining beliefs of a philosophy of optimism. That is, we have always conceived of the future in terms of its benignity, its malleability, its compatibility with our hopes and desires. But if our preceding pages have had any purpose, it has been to demonstrate the inadequacy of this belief today. It is no longer possible for America to commit itself trustingly into the hands of a deity of history whose agent forces are comfortably circumscribed and comfortingly familiar. If one thing is certain it is that history's forces have reached a power utterly unlike that of our sheltered past, and that the changes those forces portend are very different from the propitious historic transformations they brought about in our past.

Let us briefly recapitulate what some of those changes are likely to be:

1. As a consequence of the new weapons technology we have not only lost our accustomed military security, but also any possibility of enforcing

From Robert L. Heilbroner, *The Future As History* (New York: Harper & Brothers, 1960), pp. 175-178, 181-184, 193-209.

a military "solution" to the problem of communism. The weapons stalemate has thus magnified the influence of the non-military determinants of the central struggle of our times. The "historic forces" of politics and economics, of technologies and ideologies, are therefore of crucial importance in the resolution of this contest.

2. The trend of these forces is not an encouraging one. In the huge continents to the East and South we have witnessed an explosive awakening of hitherto ignored or abused peoples, who now seek a rapid redress of their age-old grievances. This has led the underdeveloped nations into a desperate effort for economic development—an effort which, in the environment of underdevelopment, turns naturally in the direction of economic collectivism. There are strong possibilities that this collectivism will veer far to the left, whether or not it falls directly under communist hegemony. It is likely as well to discard the frail structures of democracy, and to maintain its morale by an exaggerated nationalism. Finally, we must not ignore the possibility that American economic growth, by widening the gap between the underdeveloped peoples and ourselves, may place America at the focus of the frustration and resentments which economic development is likely at first to generate.

3. At the same time, the drift of Western society is itself away from the traditional forms of capitalism. In all nations, including our own, a framework of "socialist" planning is replacing the unregulated market mechanism. In Europe this drift into planning is made more significant by the fact that European capitalism, unlike American, is not a self-assured and unchallenged social order.

4. However, within our own nation there are strong tendencies which move us away from the traditional, and now perhaps nostalgic idea of American society. One of these is the rampant technological and scientific development which marks our time. This development manifests itself in a proliferation of institutions needed to "support" the increasingly dependent individual, and in the rise of bureaucratic apparatuses needed to control the technological machinery itself. The rise of the welfare state, on the one hand, and of the military bureaucracy, on the other, are instances of the manner in which technology is enforcing a socialization of life.

5. There are also visible other tendencies which are transforming our society, particularly in its economic aspect. There is a strong likelihood that a radical redefinition of the limits of public economic activity will be enforced by the pressure of events. Over the near future this is likely to be provided in disguised form by the enlarging military sector, but in the longer run we shall probably be forced to find civilian outlets to replace the military. Somewhat further ahead lies the still more difficult problem of providing internal economic discipline in a society in which the usual market control mechanisms are increasingly weakened by widespread social abundance.

6. All these collectivist trends are accelerated by our main historic

movement—our growth. The problem then is the degree to which our blind economic momentum makes it impossible to respond effectively to the technological, political, and economic forces which are bringing about a closing-in of our historic future. This is a question to which dogmatic answers cannot be given. But it must be pointed out that an effective control over the historic forces of our times would require changes not only in the structure of power but in the common denominator of values, which do not seem likely to occur, at least for a considerable period. . . .

THE LIMITS OF THE POSSIBLE

Everyone who considers . . . what is "possible" and "impossible" in history—soon comes up against a classic dilemma. This is the dilemma of "free will"—or in terms of the historic process, of determinism versus historic freedom. It is the dilemma of choosing between a world where everything is "possible" and therefore where nothing can be counted on, including the most basic necessities for the continuance of the human community; and a world where nothing is possible, and therefore where nothing can be hoped for except that which is inevitably and immutably fixed and beyond alteration. It is a choice between history as chaos and history as a prison.

This is a dilemma which still exercises philosophers and historians. But the dilemma has more to do with the limitations of abstract thought than with the experience of history itself. For when we turn to the living reality of history, we do not encounter a dilemma, but a *problem*—which is a very different thing. And this problem is not to formulate the meaning of historic freedom in general and forever, but to determine in the light of the actualities of the moment how much of history lies within our grasp and how much lies beyond.

Once we approach the matter in this direct and pragmatic fashion, the idea of what is "possible" in history presents itself intelligibly enough before us. We then find ourselves confronted, as a condition of life, with a situation which may be logically awkward but which is not at all awkward as a fact. This is the coexistence of freedom and necessity in history—the simultaneous existence of its glacial imperturbability, its "laws," its "necessities" on the one hand, and its "freedom," its openness, its amenability to our wills on the other.

The point at which we can divide freedom from necessity also comes to us with reasonable clarity. We all know that there are some historic events —such as, for instance, the internal politics of Soviet rule—which it is virtually impossible for us to affect. We recognize another class of events that lie directly—or at least to an important degree—within the scope of our control and responsibility. The "possibility" of war, for instance, is a matter in which we are quite sure that our free decisions play an immense and probably determinative role—all the more so, since so many aspects of the "historic" situation clearly set the stage for war.

This is, however, only one way of assessing what is historically possible for us. For what we deem to be "historic events" by no means exhausts the aspects of change and development in history. As Karl Popper reminds us, "There is no history of mankind, there is only an indefinite number of histories of all kinds of aspects of human life";[1] and when we turn to those aspects of history with which this book has been primarily concerned —the aspects of social change rather than of immediate political conflict— we find our possibilities of history-making sharply curtailed. In our society, the "history" of technological progress and penetration, or the "history" of political belief and economic development are not facets of human life which we normally subject to "history-making" decisions. In general we allow these aspects of history to follow their autonomous courses, and to evolve by their unguided interactions. Thus we limit our idea of what is possible in history by excluding from our control the forces of history themselves.

This is a very different situation from that which obtains in a more collectivistic society. The enormous national effort of Russian growth or the wholesale alterations in the social structure of China are instances of historic change whose possibility was initially discounted by observers who had in mind the limitations of historic intervention in our own kind of society. The point, then, is that there are no fixed and immutable limits to what is historically possible. Rather, different organizations of society define for themselves the limits of what is and what is not within reach of conscious history-making choice. Authoritarian societies, as a generality, have a much more comprehensive direction of the "forces" of history than open societies. On the other hand, open societies, through their democratic apparatus, retain a wider degree of control over the course of their "heroic" history, i.e., over the policies of their leaders. . . .

THE INERTIA OF HISTORY

Because we live in a time of great change, and because our philosophy of optimism makes us expectant of and receptive to change, we may easily overlook a deeply important aspect of historic development. This is its quality of inertia. It is a quality which is manifest not only in resistance to change—although that is one of its more important aspects—but in the viscosity which is imparted to history because people tend to repeat and continue their ways of life as long as it is possible for them to do so.

We do not usually call inertia to mind when we seek the great molding forces of history. And yet this humble characteristic is responsible for more of "history" than all the campaigns, the movements, the revolutions we readily call to mind. The simple, but quintessential fact that human beings persist in living their lives in familiar ways, which are the only ways they know how, is the very lifeline of social continuity itself.

This inertia which exerts so powerful a drag on history undoubtedly has

[1] *The Open Society* (London, 1952), vol. II, p. 270.

its biological and psychological roots. But it is more than just an "innate" human characteristic. It is also the outcome of the historic social condition of man. For the persistence of habit acts as a protective reflex for the overwhelming majority of men who know very little except that life is a fragile possession, and that tried and true ways, however onerous, have at least proved capable of sustaining it. A mulish perseverance in old ways is not without reason when life is lived at the brink of existence where a small error may spell disaster. An instance in point was provided some years ago when a team of United Nations agricultural experts sought in vain to persuade Turkish farmers to improve their crops by removing the stones from their fields. Finally a few of the younger ones consented— whereupon, to the chagrin of the experts, their yields promptly *declined*. In the arid climate of Turkey, the stones had served the function of help- ing to retain the scanty moisture in the soil.[2]

Inertia shows itself as well in a general reluctance to embrace new social ideas. Reformers throughout history have deplored the tenacity with which the privileged classes have clung to their prerogatives—even when it was no longer in their "best interests" to do so. This is not so surprising when we view the enormous gulf which has normally separated the privileged and the unprivileged. What is far more striking is the difficulty which reformers have had in making even the most miserable and oppressed classes "see" the inequity of their lot, and in persuading them to rise in protest. The fact that our historic glance is easily caught by a few *jacqueries* obscures the fact that revolutions are remarkable in history not for their frequency but for their rarity, even though the "normal" condition of man has always been harsh enough to warrant revolutionary sentiments. We must conclude that whenever it has been possible the human being has *wished* to believe in the rightness and fixity of the situation in which he has found himself.

The inertia of ideologies as well as of institutions is often taken as a lamentable fact. It is the despair of the social engineer, the *bête noir* of the utopian planner. Nonetheless we must remember that there is a con- structive role which this inertia also plays. A society without ideological inertia would live from instant to instant in peril of a fatal turning. The fixity of our voting habits, our customary beliefs, our stubbornly held ideas, even when these are wrong, serves a purpose in protecting and stabilizing the community. The reformer who despairs because people will not listen to reason forgets that it is this same suspicion of change which helps to prevent people from heeding the Pied Pipers for whom society never lacks. We may make progress only by freeing ourselves from the rut of the past, but without this rut an orderly society would hardly be possible in the first place.

This historic undertow of inertia warns us against facile conceptions of "progress" in two respects. In the first place it disabuses us of the notion

[2] *Cultural Patterns and Technical Change,* ed. Margaret Mead (New York, 1955), p. 186.

of the "ease" of social change. For most of the world's peoples, who have known only the changlessness of history, such a stress on the difficulty of change would not be necessary. But for ourselves, whose outlook is conditioned by the extraordinary dynamism of our unique historic experience, it is a needed caution. Contrary to our generally accepted belief, change is not the rule but the exception in life. Whether it is imposed from above or imposes itself from below, change must reckon with the reluctance of humankind to relinquish habits not only of a lifetime, but of life itself. This is the reason why even such enormous transformations as those we have dealt with in this book are slow, stretched out over generations, invisible from one day to the next.

Second, the drag of inertia warns us against the overestimation of the effects of change. The optimistic conception of progress calls our attention to the sweeping improvements which can be brought about by technology or democracy or economic advance. All that is certainly true as far as it goes. No one can doubt the capacity of history's forces to legislate beneficial changes in society. But there is a level of social existence to which these forces penetrate last and least. This is the level at which "society" is visible only as the personal and private encounters of each of us with his fellow man. It is the level at which life is *lived,* rather than the level at which it is abstractly conceived.

Here, at this final level of personal experience, the inertia of history is most apparently manifest. It is here that the revolutionary, having brought about tremendous changes in "society," comes to grips with the petty irritations of inefficient colleagues and apathetic clerks, of the "human factor" which like sand in a machine, has wrecked so many well-planned enterprises. It is not that revolutions, or the more gradual changes of historic evolution, make these daily frictions of life any worse. It is rather that so much of life remains the same, regardless of the new boundaries in which it is contained.

In this grinding persistence of the "human factor" lies the reason for much of the disillusion which so frequently follows a passionate attempt to bring about social progress. As Ignazio Silone has written: "Political regimes come and go; bad habits remain."[3] The underlying sameness of life, the reassertion of old established ways, of "bad habits," is an aspect of history which must not be lost to sight amid the more dramatic changes of the superstructure of society. An appreciation of the fact of human inertia must not lead us to understate the extent to which change is possible in sociey, but it should caution us against identifying this change with the equivalent "progress" of human life at a fundamental level.

THE HERITAGE OF THE HUMAN CONDITION

We have seen that optimism misleads us with respect to the possibilities of "progress" because it tends to underestimate the difficulty and to over-

[3] "The Choice of Comrades," *Voices of Dissent* (New York, 1958), p. 325.

estimate the consequences of historic change. But it compounds that short-coming with a second and perhaps even more important failure. This is its lack of realism as to our starting point in the making of history. It is its failure to confront truthfully and unflinchingly the condition of the human being as it now exists.

Optimism tacitly views that condition in a favorable light. The very assumption that the growth of technical skill, political equality, or economic well-being will automatically lead to "progress"—rather than to increased destructiveness, heightened social disorder, or vulgar opulence—already takes for granted an environment in which rationality, self-control, and dignity are paramount social attributes.

But this is hardly the impression one gets from an examination of the panorama of human existence. If there is such a thing as an average human being, he is to be found among the majority of mankind which lives in the continents of the East and South. The chasm which divides the average life on these continents from our own is so wide that we can barely imagine existence on the other side. To be an Indian villager, a Chinese peasant, an African mine-worker is to be in a human condition whose dark and narrow confines cannot be penetrated by a Western mind.

But life on our side of the chasm is also very far from presenting a heartening vista. In the United States, for example, preventable disease and even deformity are still widespread. Mental aberration identifiably touches a tenth of the population. Criminality, in various social forms from murder to tax evasion, is prevalent among all classes. The urban environment in which life is mainly lived is crowded, often unspeakably ugly, and in its spreading slums, vicious. The average education is barely adequate to allow the population to cope with the technological complexities of the age, and insufficient to allow all but a few to understand them. Large numbers of families do not know or care how to raise their children, as witness the epidemic incidence of juvenile disorders.

The list could be extended without difficulty. But what characterizes many, if not all of these degradations of life, is that they are unnecessary. Most of them could be vastly alleviated by a sustained and wholehearted effort. Yet such an effort—as to whose immense "value" all would agree —seems impossible to undertake. Indeed, the very suggestion that these areas of need should carry an absolutely overriding priority, taking precedence over any and all more "profitable" activities, smacks of a suspicious radicalism. We are simply not concerned, beyond a mild lip-service, with mounting an all-out effort to raise the level of national health or civic virtue, or mass living conditions or average education or upbringing. Looking at some of the institutions we nourish and defend, it would not be difficult to maintain that our society is an immense stamping press for the careless production of under-developed and malformed human beings, and that, whatever it may claim to be, it is not a society fundamentally concerned with moral issues, with serious purposes, or with human dignity.

The point, however, is not to berate ourselves for our obvious failure to produce anything like a "good society." The point is rather that, with all its glaring and inexcusable failures, the United States is still probably the most favored and favorable place on earth for a child to be born and to grow up.

These melancholy facts must assume their rightful place in any evaluation of the prospects for "social progress." For in such a social atmosphere the forces of history do not lead automatically in the direction which optimism assumes. In an atmosphere of neglect and of indifference to human capabilities, it is not at all surprising that technology should result in the trivialization of life and the stultification of work. It is certainly not remarkable that, in the harsh and primitive setting of underdevelopment, popular political aspirations press toward extreme and violent "solutions" to the problems of underdevelopment; nor that, in the more advanced societies, they mold society in the image of the mediocrity of mind and sentiment they represent. Nor, given the prevalence of physical poverty in the backward nations and of psychological poverty in all nations, is the pre-eminence of materialistic drives and goals to be wondered at. In sum, today as in the past, the half-educated, half-emancipated state of human society assures that there will be a long continuation of the violence, the instability, the blatant injustice, which are the most grievous aspects of the human tragedy. This is the true heritage of the human condition, and its bitter legacy.

What is perhaps the most sorrowful aspect of this tragedy is that its victims are chosen arbitrarily and at random. There is no guilt or innocence, no measure of culpability or responsibility in the fate meted out by a world which is still more brute than man. Those who fall in wars do not "start" the wars. The victims of Hitler or Stalin were not those who raised these dictators to power. Nor will there be a fine balancing of accounts when the crimes of South Africa eventually exact their terrible retribution, or when the indignities of the American South work their full damage to the American social fabric. In a world in which conscious morality can be regarded with derision, and reason with suspicion, this random toll of social tragedy cannot be avoided. It is the consequence of a situation in which, as Albert Camus writes in *The Fall:* "We cannot assert the innocence of anyone, whereas we can state with certainty the guilt of all."

To raise these dark thoughts is not to sermonize that man is "wicked" or to avoid the conclusion that some men are much more guilty than others. Neither is it to maintain that there is no hope for a betterment of the human condition. On the contrary, there is today a greater long-term prospect for such betterment than humanity has ever known before. But the heritage of the past is too deep to be overcome in a matter of a few generations. It will be a long while until the human condition has been substantially improved. Not to face up to this fact with compassion and concern is only to cringe before reality. And while this should urge us on with all the strength at our command to support every effort to improve the condition of man, it cannot but chasten us as to the reasonable expectations of the "progress" which that condition will permit.

THE AMBIGUITY OF EVENTS

In the very idea of progress, as we commonly accept it, is contained the notion of goals. We strive for specific objectives, located in the future, and imagine that each objective gained is a recognizable step toward "progress." As a result we find ourselves confounded when, having reached an objective, what we encounter is not the "progress" we anticipated but a new set of problems stemming from the very advance itself.

This disconcerting aspect of experience can be described as the ambiguity of events. By this we mean that every event in history has a Januslike quality—one face which regards the past, and one which looks ahead; one aspect which is the culmination of what has gone before, and another which is the point of departure for what is to follow.

Simplistic ideas of progress see only the near face of events when they look to the future. Hence such views of the future typically underrate its complexities. They do not consider that the solution of one problem is only the formulation of the next. What an awareness of the ambiguity of events thus subtracts from the optimistic view of progress is the luxury of believing that progress is a simple pyramiding of success. The two-sided nature of future events does not deny that our problems may be our opportunities but it asserts with equal conviction that our opportunities may become our problems.

There is no more dramatic example of this than the impact on world history of that most "unambiguous" of all evidences of progress: the development of modern medicine. It is not necessary to spell out the enormous benefits which medical science has brought to mankind. Yet no assessment of the over-all impact of modern medicine on our age can ignore the fact that it has also been the "cause" of an immense amount of additional suffering in the world. By its success in reducing the scourges of mass disease and infant mortality, the "progress" of medical science has crowded the already overpopulated villages and cities of Asia and South America with still more mouths, and has thus aggravated the very human suffering it set out to relieve.

Needless to say, not every instance of progress cancels itself out in so direct and distressing a fashion as this. The point, rather, is that progress does not merely consist in the surmounting of a previous problem, but inherently consists in the emergence of a new problem which, although different, may be quite as grave as the old. In the course of this book, for example, we have seen such new problems emerging from the advance of technology or from the achievement of abundance in our own society. These new problems do not gainsay the advances which technology or economic growth bring us. But it may well be that the consequences of our technological captivity, or the control problems of economic abundance will be just as humanly crushing as the problems of insufficiency or technical inadequacy from whose solution they emerged. There is no reason to believe that the successive problems of "progress" pose easier challenges; indeed it is probable that the overcoming of the "simpler" problems of poverty and disease opens the doors on progressively more profound, elusive, and insoluble human dilemmas.

Marx and Hegel called this ambiguous aspect of progress the dialectic of history. Marx, however, brought his dialectical analysis to a halt with the achievement of communism as the "terminus" of the history of class struggle. Ironically enough, it is probable that there is no aspect of future history which today more desperately needs dialectical clarification than the achievement of the communist—or for the West, the socialist—goal. It is clear that as the "near side" of socialism approaches, it is the "far side" which becomes of ever greater interest and importance. To consider socialism as a "goal" of social history is to fall prey to the optimistic delusion that goals are milestones in history from which the next stage of development promises to be "easier" or unambiguously "better" than the past. To rid oneself of this comforting notion is not to lessen one's ardor to resolve the difficulties of the present, but to arm oneself realistically for the continuance of the human struggle in the future.

THE GRAND DYNAMIC OF HISTORY

Is there then no possibility for progress?

As it must by now be clear, much depends on what one means by the question. If by "progress" we mean a fundamental elevation in the human estate, a noticeable movement of society in the direction of the ideals of Western humanism, a qualitative as well as a quantitative betterment of the condition of man, it is plain that we must put away our ideas of progress over the foreseeable vista of the historic future. For whereas there is no question but that the forces of our time are bringing about momentous and profound changes, it is only optimistic self-deception to anticipate, or even to wish for, the near advent of a perceptibly "better" world as a result. Taking into account the human condition as it now exists, the laggard slowness with which improvements in institutions are followed by improvements in "life," the blurred and ambiguous fashion in which history passes from problem to problem, it is certain enough that the tenor of world history will remain much as it is for a long while to come.

Indeed, from the point of view of the West and especially of America, it may seeem to be deteriorating. As we have seen through the pages of this book, many of the tendencies of world history are likely to manifest themselves to us as a worsening of the outlook. We may well be tempted to interpret this growing intractability of the environment as the metamorphosis of progress into retrogression.

Against this dark horizon it is hardly possible to cling to the sanguine hopes and complacent expectations of the past. And yet if we can lift our gaze beyond the confines of our own situation, it is possible to see that every one of these changes is essential and inescapable if the present condition of humankind is to be surpassed. Until the avoidable evils of society have been redressed, or at least made the target of the wholehearted effort of the organized human community, it is not only premature but presumptuous to talk of "the dignity of the individual." The ugly, obvious, and terrible wounds of mankind must be dressed and allowed to heal before we can begin to know the capacities, much less enlarge the vision, of the human race as a whole.

In the present state of world history the transformations which are everywhere at work are performing this massive and crude surgery. We have dwelt sufficiently in the preceding pages on the violence and cruelty, the humanly deforming aspects of the changes about us. Now we must see that in their ultimate impact on history it is the positive side of these great transformations which must be stressed. However unruly the revolution of the underdeveloped nations, it is nonetheless the commencement of a movement away from the squalor and apathy which three-quarters of the human race still consider to be life. With all its disregard for Western standards of justice and liberty, the forced march of communism is nevertheless retreading the essential, but now forgotten path of early industrial development of the West. Whatever its capacity for the destruction or the diminution of man, the perfection and application of industrial technology is withal the only possible escape from the historic indenture of man. And no matter what its difficulties, the painful evolution beyond present-day capitalism is indispensable if those nations which have gained the benefits of material wealth are now to cope rationally with its administration.

Thus the blind and often brutal impact of the historic forces of our day can still be said to point in the direction of optimism and of progress. Only in our present situation, the West is no longer the spearhead of those forces, but their target. What is at bottom a movement of hope and well-being for the inarticulate and inadequate masses of mankind is a fearful threat to the delicate and now gravely exposed civilization of the articulate and advanced few.

No member of the Western community who loves its great achievements and who has enjoyed the inestimable value of its liberties and values can confront this outlook of history without anguish. Of all those who will feel the blows of the future, none will suffer more than the heirs of the long tradition of Western humanism, and none will more acutely feel the delays and the recession of "progress" as the world endures its protracted ordeal.

More aware than the rising masses of the world of the destination to which their inchoate revolution may hopefully carry them, it is the humanist spirits of the West who will feel most betrayed by the violence and excess which will likely accompany its course. Ever hopeful of the re-entry of the communist nations into the Western community of thought, it is the Western intellectuals and idealists who will bear the full agony of watching for and waiting for signs of change which may be very long in coming. Alive to the immense potential benefits of the technical virtuosity of their age, it is again the guardians of the humanist tradition who will most despair at its continued misapplication; just as it will be they rather than the masses who will wish for a more responsible form of economic society and who will chafe at the continuance of the old order.

This prospect of disappointment and delay may give rise to a tragedy greater than the tragic events of history itself. This would be the disillusion fo Western thought and the abandonment of its hopes for and its distant vision of progress. It would be the surrender of the very ideals of the West before the crushing advent of history, and the adoption of an indifference, or worse, a cynicism before the march of events.

If this tragedy is to be avoided, the West will have need of two qualities: fortitude and understanding. It must come to see that because this is not a time of fulfillment does not mean that it is a time of waste. It is rather a time when the West must take upon itself a new and more difficult role in history than in the past: not that of leading in the van of history's forces under the banner of progress, but that of preserving from the ruthless onslaught of history's forces the integrity of the very idea of progress itself.

Particularly for Americans will this long period of abeyance provide a test of the spirit. Accustomed by our historic training to expect a mastery over events which is no longer possible, we are apt to interpret the intransigence of history as a kind of personal betrayal rather than as a vast and impersonal process of worldwide evolution. Thus there is the danger that we may abandon our optimism for a black and bitter pessimism, or for a kind of "heroic" defiance.

But neither pessimism nor defiance, any more than optimism, will give us the fortitude and understanding we require. For this we need an attitude which accepts the outlook of the historic future without succumbing to false hopes or to an equally false despair; a point of view which sees in the juggernaut of history's forces both the means by which progress painfully made in the past may be trampled underfoot, and the means by which a broader and stronger base for progress in the future may be brought into being.

Such an attitude may retain its kernel of optimism. But more is needed for the display of stoic fortitude than a residual faith in the idea of progress. Above all there is required an understanding of the grand dynamic of history's forces in preparing the way for eventual progress. There is needed a broad and compassionate comprehension of the history-shaking transformations now in mid-career, of their combined work of demolition and construction, of the hope they embody and the price they will exact. Only from such a sense of historic understanding can come the strength to pass through the gauntlet with an integrity of mind and spirit.

What is tragically characteristic of our lives today is an absence of just such an understanding. It is very difficult while America and the West are at bay to feel a sense of positive identification with the forces that are preparing the environment of the future. Less and less are we able to locate our lives meaningfully in the pageant of history. More and more do we find ourselves retreating to the sanctuary of an insulated individualism, sealed off in our private concerns from the larger events which surround us.

Such an historic disorientation and disengagement is a terrible private as well as public deprivation. In an age which no longer waits patiently through this life for the rewards of the next, it is a crushing spiritual blow to lose one's sense of participation in mankind's journey, and to see only a huge milling-around, a collective living-out of lives with no larger purpose than the days which each accumulates. When we estrange ourselves from history we do not enlarge, we diminish ourselves, even as individuals. We subtract from our lives one meaning which they do in fact possess, whether we recognize it or not. We cannot help living in history. We can only fail to be aware of it. If we are to meet, endure, and transcend the trials and defeats of the future—for trials and defeats there are certain to be—it can only be from a point of view which, seeing the future as part of the sweep of history, enables us to establish our place in that immense procession in which is incorporated whatever hope humankind may have.

D

Back to Religion

C. E. M. JOAD

The Plight of the Intellectual

I use here the word "religion" in the sense which excludes the secular religious sects I like to call the religion—or religions—of Enlightenment. Indeed, the return to religion is for us primarily, though not wholly, a return to Christianity. I should not claim that the way traced by the English philosopher and publicist C. E. M. Joad (1891–1953) is typical. But Joad was an Enlightened intellectual, and his way to belief in Christianity is here put with disarming sincerity.

Reason and Faith

THE FOLLOWING BOOK IS AN ACCOUNT OF SOME OF THE REASONS WHICH have converted me to the religious view of the universe in its Christian version. They are predominantly arguments designed to appeal to the intellect.

The intellectual approach to religion is out of fashion today and in this introductory chapter I want to explain why in this book I have adopted it.

There are many to whom faith comes easily. These feel no impulse to justify their beliefs since, for them, justification is unnecessary. That God created the world and sent His Son into it at a certain point of time are to them patent truths which it never occurs to them to doubt. I do not think that the number of such persons is as great as it was, at least among educated people; I, at any rate, am not one of them. Until comparatively late in my life the deliverances of reason no less than the weight of the evidence seemed to me to tell heavily against the religious view of the universe, and faith unsupported by reason seemed to me to be no more than a pious propensity to believe in propositions which there was no reason to think true.

It seems so still. While I admit that intellect cannot go all the way, there can, for me, be no believing which the intellect cannot, so far as its writ runs, defend and justify. I must, as a matter of psychological compulsion, adopt the most rational hypothesis, the most rational being that which

From C. E. M. Joad, *The Recovery of Belief: A Restatement of Christian Philosophy* (London: Faber and Faber Limited, 1952), pp. 13-27.

seems to cover most of the facts and to offer the most plausible explanation of our experience as a whole. The hypothesis in question is that which is known as the religious view of the world, and the following pages are designed to explain why I find it so.

Belief and Will

There has been much discussion in my time of the part played by the will in belief. Men have spoken of "the will to believe," a phrase popularised by William James. But, divorced from reason, the dictates of the will have no authority and carry no conviction. One might just as well will to believe X as will to believe Y. The fact that one does believe X is, on this view, evidence of nothing but the fact that one wills to believe X. The willing of the belief has, then, no bearing upon the truth of that which the belief asserts. Certainly it does not constitute evidence for supposing that the belief is true. Will, in short, neither creates nor destroys the truth of beliefs.

If, in deference to current fashion, I were to try to indicate the part played by will in respect of my own beliefs, I should say that I *will* to believe the hypothesis in whose support the most reasons quantitatively and the most cogent reasons qualitatively can be adduced. If to believe because you want to do so constitutes no evidence in favour of religion, to believe in spite of the fact that you would prefer not to do so constitutes no evidence against it. So far from my own religious belief being the result of what the psychologists call wishful thinking, I am disposed to doubt whether, if my wishes had their way, I should to-day be trying to practise Christianity. For while it is true that my intellect is in the main convinced, my wishes —what I suppose Christianity would call "the natural man"—protest. For the belief that life in this world derives its explanation in the last resort from another cannot but increase the difficulty of living it.

Suppose for a moment that you think that the Christian view of earthly existence as a course of training in moral discipline is correct; then you cannot help but try to act as if you were at school. If the purpose of your existence is not to win personal happiness but to improve your character, much that you would have light-heartedly done on the former assumption will be forbidden to you on the latter. And though, no doubt, it is a bad thing always to be taking one's moral temperature, one is nevertheless constantly driven to put to oneself the questions: "Ought I to have acted as I did?" "Ought I not to resist this desire which I take to be a temptation?" "Could I not behave better than I am now doing?" Now for most of my life I have cheerfully subscribed to Bentham's maxim that if the word "ought" means anything at all it *ought* to be excluded from the dictionary. Thus the adoption of the Christian view of the world has not, to put it mildly, made for greater simplicity and ease of living. On the contrary, it has complicated the problem of conduct by adding to the task of securing happiness the task of conforming to moral obligation.

The Disappointments of Christianity

I do not mean that "duty" has now taken the place of "happiness" as the motive and the test of conduct. Rather the two run in double harness as first one and then the other takes the bit and directs the course. I say "first one and then the other," but truthfulness compels the confession that nine times out of ten it is to obtain happiness rather than to do my duty that I aim. Christianity, as I have been taught, insists that this is a false opposition, since, for it, true happiness is to be found only in conformity to the dictates of moral obligation. Bradley's *Ethical Studies*—which, as a teacher of philosophy, it is my business to expound—teaches the same truth. I do not doubt that those who live better lives than I do can testify from their own experience that this truth is indeed true. I can only say that I have not experienced its truth myself. I am disappointed that this should be so. In fact, the whole endeavour to live the Christian life is a series of disappointments. Faith falters, prayer is intermittent, the consolations of religion seem few and doubtful, the sense of disillusion is at times keen. I hoped to become a better person; I do, indeed, at times try. But on the whole, except in so far as the effort, the usually unsuccessful effort, itself has merit, I must confess that I do not often succeed.

(And yet sometimes I think there is a difference. I am told by Christianity that if I pray to God for His help and try to live so as to deserve it, it will be granted. There have been times . . . when I have believed myself to experience the truth of this assertion.)

I do not love God, or I love Him but little even on the rare occasions when I happen to think of Him; I do not love my neighbour as myself, and emphatically I do not do unto others as I would be done by. My character, therefore, is little improved; the main change is in the ever-increasing consciousness of its need for improvement. Yet while Christianity has made little change in my life, my conviction of its truth grows stronger.

If it is not wishful thinking, if it is not the dictate of an arbitrary will to believe that has brought me to Christianity, I see no alternative to the conclusion that the main impulsion is from the intellect. It is because, as I said above, the religious view of the universe seems to me to cover more of the facts of experience than any other that I have been gradually led to embrace it.

Action and Belief

And this approach is, after all, in line with that traditionally adopted by Christian thinkers, more particularly in the *philosophia perennis* which has some claim to be regarded as the philosophical background of the Christian creed. Christians are no doubt required to practise the precepts laid down by Christ and enjoined by the Church, but belief cannot affect conduct, unless the belief has an intellectual content, for action always presupposes an attitude of mind from which it springs, an attitude which, explicit when the action is first embarked upon, is unconscious by the time it has become an habitual and well-established course of conduct. When I act in a certain manner towards anything, I recognise by implication that it possesses those characteristics which make my conduct appropriate. So, too, with my action in regard to God, which implies some sort of knowledge of Him and His relation to the familiar world and to myself as a creature living in that world. If I cannot find good grounds for my beliefs, I shall certainly not persuade myself to act in conformity with them; thus, if I do not accept the attribution of personality to God I shall not succeed in inducing myself to act towards Him as if He were a Person; that is, I shall not seek to know and to love Him, or to pray to Him. Thought, in other words, precedes action in the religious as in other spheres, and the practical significance of the precepts of religion is not separable from the theoretical content from which they derive. It is, then, because my intellect is on the whole convinced that I make such shift as I can to live conformably with its dictates.

I have tried to indicate the relation between the intellect, faith, will and desire as they co-operate to produce religious belief and the endeavour to act conformably with it. If I am right, intellectual conviction must, at least for educated people, come first. Hence the chapters that follow are concerned to indicate the grounds for that conviction and to remove some of the obstacles which in the contemporary world militate against it. I propose to try to argue that the religious hypothesis is the one that covers more of the facts of experience than any other, among which must be included both the fact of the desire to believe and the fact of moral conflict. Due weight must, I suggest, be given to the significance of both these facts.

Qualifications

Having proceeded so far, I am constrained to realise that my position is by no means so simple as the foregoing statement suggests. To make it accurate and to make it acceptable even to myself I must introduce three qualifications.

First, I have been taught by psychology that the concept of the personality as a bundle of faculties, reason and emotion, instinct, desire, will and so forth, is untenable. There are, I am told, no such separate faculties; all shade off, one into another, by imperceptible gradations. Hence to oppose the intellect to will or to intuition, as if they could be separated in fact even if they may be distinguishable in thought, entails a false dichotomy.

Secondly, since it is nevertheless the case that some distinction of faculties must be assumed for purposes of discussion—the nature of my experience when, parched with thirst, I crave for water, being clearly different in kind from the sort of experience that I have when I am doing a sum in my head or trying to solve a chess problem, and it would be, to say the least of it, inconvenient to have no words at my disposal to indicate the fact of this difference, so that I could speak of "desire" in the first instance and of "reason" in the second—I propose to say a word on the sense in which I am going to use the words "reason" and "intellect." This is broadly the sense in which Plato in *The Republic* conceives the first, the reasoning, "part" of the soul.

There is in Plato no hard and fast distinction between reason and desire regarded as psychological faculties. On the contrary, each of his three "parts" of the soul is informed by its own specific dynamism. I apologise for the vagueness of this word; what I have in mind is that element of passional striving for which psychologists use the term "conation." For this element of "conation" no separate provision is made in the Platonic psychology. Rather each "part" of the soul is infused with its own conation, which expresses itself in the desires and determines the pattern of the characteristic life of that "part." Hence, the distinction which Plato draws between "parts" is referable not to different faculties but to the different kinds of object upon which the characteristic "appetition" of each of the three "parts" is fixed. Thus, the first "part" of the soul is not intellect; it is the soul or personality as a whole, insofar as its appetition is centred upon the ends appropriate to the intellect; that is to say, upon knowledge. Plato adds that only the perfectly "real" can be perfectly known and that in the knowledge of the "real" what we call the intellect is transcended so that it is the whole personality, albeit a personality transfigured by the nature of its quest, that knows the Forms. It is in this sense, the sense of an aspect of our personalities informed by the desire to pursue and to know certain kinds of "object" and to "make after" certain kinds of end, that I wish to use the words "intellect" and "reason."

Thirdly, I am far from wishing to suggest that reason covers all the ground. Much, probably most, of the universe must, I think, remain unknown by the reasons of human beings, at any rate in their present bodily condition. In particular, as I shall argue later, the nature of the spiritual world and, more particularly, the nature of its relation to and intercourse with the familiar order of physical things moving about in space and changing in time must remain unknown by reason. Not only can we not wholly understand—or we understand only formally without realising what it is that we understand—what it means to say that God is a transcendent being, but we cannot understand by what method or by what mode of entry. He enters from time to time into relation with the natural order of events which science studies, interrupting them with a series of mighty acts. Intellect, then, can light up only a small area of the universe. For my part, I should subscribe to the familiar paradox that the more we know, the more we are conscious of our ignorance; the further the distance the intellect has travelled, the smaller it seems relatively to the distance still to be travelled.

Claims for the Intellect

I wish, then, to put the claims of the intellect no higher than the following: (1) The intellect does, indeed, take us part of the way; (2) we have no other mode of conveyance; and (3) in taking us as far as it does, it justifies us in taking the rest on trust. And this, I suppose, is where faith comes in. If, so far as your reason takes you, the religious view of the universe seems to afford the most plausible explanation of your experience, then it seems not unreasonable to follow this same view beyond the point at which it leaves reason behind. If it accounts for the things you know and can understand, then it seems to me not unreasonable to hold that it could also offer an explanation of the things that you do not know and cannot understand—always, of course, provided that it is not positively at variance with the findings of any aspect of your experience and does not positively contradict the conclusions of reason in regard to the things that you do believe yourself to know.

Now in following the religious account of the universe beyond the point at which it leaves reason behind, and trusting to it as an explanation of the many things that pass our understanding, we are accepting on faith conclusions which are not demonstrated by reason. In other words, we are acting as if a hypothesis were true which, at the moment at which we act upon it, is still a hypothesis and not a truth. Nevertheless, it is, I suggest, knowledge, the knowledge which we possess already and which reason has won for us, that makes it reasonable to do so. This, in brief, is my own position. I have what I like to believe is a reasonable assurance in regard to the truth of the religious view of the universe, an assurance which, however, never hardens to the point of absolute conviction. I could wish that it did.

The Plight of Contemporary Intellectuals

I think—perhaps because I wish to think—that a belief in religion comes with a quite special degree of difficulty to persons of my training and equipment living in the middle of the twentieth century. We have been taught to take nothing on trust; to bring everything for judgment to the bar of the intellect. Hence faith, which must be taken on trust, and which gives little or no account of itself at the bar of the intellect, runs counter to our training and habits; faith, in a word, is hard for us, while the simple unreflecting faith of uneducated persons is impossible. But that is only to say that we have the habits and the outlook proper to educated men in all ages who have been trained to rely upon their intellects. If this were all, it would be no great matter, but there is more to it than that. We are the inheritors of a century of religious doubt. This doubt was never so widely spread or so deeply ingrained. In the circles in which I have moved consisting mainly of left wing and left centre politicians, journalists, writers, artists and dons, it is a comparatively rare thing to find an educated man who is also a Christian. It is not merely that only one in ten of the population in contemporary Britain has any continuing connection with any church. More to the point is the fact that the ten per cent includes a very high proportion of elderly persons, particularly of elderly and comparatively uneducated women.

Among my own acquaintances I do not think that I number more than half a dozen who are believing Christians. I could, I know, name well over a hundred who are not. In sum, the findings of the contemporary intellect tell heavily against religion. Moreover, the climate of the time is hostile to it, so hostile that many take it for granted that religion does not deserve serious consideration and the traditional religious explanation both of the universe at large and of particular occurrences within the universe is rejected out of hand.

To take a particular example, where I might cite a hundred, consider the implications of the words I have italicised in the following quotation from an address by Professor D. S. M. Watson, delivered to fellow biologists at Cape Town in December 1943: "Evolution has been accepted by scientists, not because it has been observed to occur or proved by logical coherent evidence to be true, *but because the only alternative, special creation, is clearly unacceptable.*"

I, too, have grown up in this climate and inherit these findings. For most of my life I have been not only an agnostic but a vocal and militant agnostic. I have had all the arguments against the religious hypothesis at my intellectual fingertips, and was ready and apt in their use for the discomfiture of Christian apologists.[1] The habits of a lifetime cannot quickly be outgrown, and although, as I have said, I now believe that the balance of reasoned considerations tells heavily in favour of the religious, even of the Christian view of the world, it is still in terms of balance and plausibility that my thought proceeds. Where I would testify to certain conviction, I must still speak in terms of plausible hypothesis; when I would rely on the support and enjoy the comfort of a firm faith, I must still confess to moments of disbelief, days of doubt and periods of absolute indifference. Moreover, the questioning intellect will not keep quiet. Constantly, continually, it perceives fresh grounds for doubt and poses new, unanswerable questions.

. . . let me here make my one sacrifice to the gods of my past by citing a few examples as evidence of the sort of difficulties with which I must contend.

I will give one example of each kind.

Questions and Doubts

First, as to questions. At the moment of writing there is a great pother about the announcement of a new dogma by the Roman Catholic Church, the dogma of the physical resurrection and present existence in the body of the Virgin Mary. Clergymen of the Church of England complain of another and, as it seems to them, so gratuitous a spoke placed by the Roman Catholics in the wheel of the reunion of the Christian Churches. Nevertheless, they (and I) affirm, in common with all other members of the Anglican Communion, our belief in the Resurrection of the Body. Sunday after Sunday as we do so, I (but not they) wonder what all the

[1] Many of these I have set out at length in the early chapters of my *God and Evil*.

fuss is about. For why, I want to know, do we complain so bitterly of the announcement of this new Catholic dogma that the Virgin's body exists and is resurrected at the very moment that we are professing as an article of faith in regard to *all* human beings who would normally be called dead, either that their bodies exist now, or that they will sooner or later again come into existence in order that they may be resurrected? Is the element of time so important? Granted that we accept the miracle of the Resurrection of the Body, does it so much matter from the point of view of dogma *when* its Resurrection occurs?

The Pain of Animals

Secondly, as to doubts. I was for years baffled by the problem of pain and evil; in fact, it was this problem that for years denied belief in the Christian religion. Now, I think I see the answer, or at least so much of the answer as will suffice to justify me in taking the rest on trust. God did not wish to create a race of virtuous automata, for of what merit is the virtue, if virtue it can be called, of those who have no choice but to desire, to will and to act as they do? Of what value, then, to be praised or loved by such as these? And what joy or merit can there be in loving them in return, even if it were possible to do so? Hence God created beings possessed of free will in order that they might be in a postion to acquire merit by acting rightly *when it was possible for them to act wrongly,* with the result that the amount of virtue in the universe would be increased—of virtue and also of love, since those who acquired virtue by their own efforts as a result of their resistance to temptation and their endurance of suffering would be worthy objects of God's love. Now if they are to be free to choose wrongly, it will follow that some wrong choices will almost certainly be made. The evil in the universe is the consequence of wrong choices or, alternatively, we may say that evil must already be present in the universe in order that it may be chosen. Pain, which is an evil, is also a consequence of wrong choices. Pain, thus comes into the world because men do evil.

So far, so good. The argument is difficult and abstract, but it holds together. Then comes the doubt. What of the pain of the animal kingdom *before* man appeared upon the scene? There has been life upon the planet, according to the biologists, for something like a thousand million years; human life for about a million. During the whole of that vast preliminary period, if the record of the rocks is to be believed, nature was red in tooth and claw. Animals were preying one upon another, going in fear of one another, dying of cold, dying of hunger and wounds. Impossible to believe that they did not suffer; impossible, at least for me, to believe that physical suffering is not evil. Yet this suffering of the animals cannot be explained by the formula to which I have just had resort; it cannot, that is to say, be attributed to the wrong choices of human beings, for human beings did not as yet exist. What, then, are we to say, if we are not to say that God foresaw, permitted and perhaps ordained it? But that, I feel, cannot be. The problem, then—and it is one of many—is for me unresolved. The most familiar way of dealing with it—it is adopted in the writings of N. P. Williams and suggested by C. S. Lewis—is to postulate a cosmic "Fall" as a result of which the whole of life is infected with sin. I find this doctrine hard to credit on common sense grounds, apart from the fact that it seems to me to have the effect, not so much of solving the problem of the evil of animal pain, as of putting back in point of time the problem of the origin of such evil. Nor are such other solutions as I am acquainted with in the least convincing.

More Immediate Difficulties

Thirdly, my mind is assailed with more immediate difficulties arising from the acceptance of the Christian religion. For example, there is the danger to mankind from science or, more precisely, from man's use in war of the results of scientific research. Wars have always occurred in the past and will presumably occur again unless—and of this there is no sign— mankind adopts a system of world government with a monopoly of force which makes war impossible, or unless human nature itself changes. At the time of writing, short of such a system or short of such a change, it seems highly probable that the "cold war" between the U.S.S.R. and the West will become open warfare, so soon as the U.S.S.R. has a sufficient supply of A- and/or H-bombs to enable the Soviet Government to wage war with what it takes to be a reasonable chance of success.

If the war occurs soon and ends in a decisive victory for one side, some vestiges of civilisation might survive it, but if it is long delayed, so rapid is the rate of scientific invention and advance, that the complete destruction of civilisation and reversion to primitive barbarism seem likely, especially if, when war comes, it is prolonged and indecisive.

The End of Human Life

There is a further possibility. Famine due to the destruction of crops by radio-active sprays, pestilence resulting from the practice of bacteriological warfare, may cause the disappearance of human life. Radio-active clouds, drifting round the planet, may disintegrate living tissue everywhere. I do not say that these things are certain or even probable; they are at least possible.

What is the bearing of these possibilities on religion? Does God foresee the possible destruction of the human race? Can He prevent it? Does He perhaps even intend it? There is much in Christian literature which might seem to countenance such an eventuality. There are, for example, the talk of Armageddon, the Apocalyptic writings of the Book of Revelation, the persistent belief of the early Christians in the rapidly approaching end of the world and the second coming of Christ—though early Christian writings always speak of these events as if they were to be brought about by the direct intervention of God; not as if they were to be permitted to occur as the result of the unchecked wickedness of man.

Let us suppose for a moment that ours is the only planet anywhere in the universe on which life like our own exists. The question then arises, can God permit this creature, man, whom He has sent into the world in order that, according to the Christian view, he may increase the amount of virtue in the universe and of objects worthy of God's love—can He, one wonders, permit man to come to so lamentable an end and to destroy himself through misuse of that very gift of intelligence with which God has endowed him? Can God, in other words, permit His experiment to fail? And if not, will He once again intervene with one of His mighty acts to arrest the drift of mankind to self-destruction? May there perhaps be a Second Coming? Certainly the stage seems set for it. Yet how difficult, how almost impossible for a modern intellectual to believe in it as an actually impending historical event.

Birth Control and the Population Problem

Hard on the heels of this question comes another with its attendant difficulties. One of the most probable causes of war is the pressure of ever-increasing populations upon the world's diminishing food supplies. Throughout most of recorded history the human population of the earth has stood at approximately five hundred millions. Fifty years ago it was just under two thousand millions. In 1950 it was two thousand three hundred millions, and by the end of the century it will be three thousand millions. At the moment it is increasing at the rate of over sixty thousand a day. Thereafter the rate of increase, short of the adoption of birth control over most of the globe, must be very rapid. Science is, once again, the main factor in the situation. Science has improved hygiene, has diminished plague, diminished maternal mortality, diminished infant mortality, so much so that, while a hundred years ago the average age at death of the population of this country was under thirty, today it is over sixty. This new-won ability to protect and lengthen human life has still to be used on behalf of the majority of the world's population. Thus, while the death rate in England is ten per thousand, in India it is nearly thirty per thousand. We may look, then, short of birth control, for a far more rapid increase of the numbers of the human race in the future.

Further, it is science or, rather, the misuse of science's gifts which is reducing the world's potential food supply. It is not merely that ever-increasing areas of food-producing land are taken for industrial purposes, for spreading suburbs, roads, factories and aerodromes; more to the point is the fact that science has enabled man to farm in such a way as to impoverish the soil and render it unfit for further food cultivation. Civilisation's most obvious need is, then, in the circumstances in which we find ourselves, the need to control the size of the population. Science, having interfered with the laws governing death, should also, one would have supposed, be permitted to interfere with the laws governing birth, and a world population policy prescribing for each nation its optimum population in the light of the available and prospective food supplies is both dictated by the deliverances of reason and demanded by the counsels of prudence. Yet the Churches in general look with disfavour on birth control by artificial methods, and the Roman Catholic Church in particular officially condemns the use of contraceptives on the ground that it is contrary to the teaching of Christ and the will of God. For who, they ask, is man that he should frustrate the life that God intended and prevent the coming into existence of another immortal soul?

Here, then, is a situation in which it would appear *prima facie* that the Roman Catholic Church[2] is deliberately fostering a policy which will tend to promote the destruction of mankind, by positively encouraging the steps which are calculated to make it more likely and by impeding and forbidding the measures which will make it less likely.

Can God, one wonders, will that his creatures should deliberately compass their own destruction through the agency of his Church? Again, I do not know the answer to this question. I mention the matter only because it affords one more example of the conflict between reason and would-be faith by which the contemporary intellect is beset. It is scarcely necessary to add that my own intellect is not immune.

[2] I hesitate to speak of the official attitude of the Anglican Church, which is wrapped in its all too familiar obscurity.

A. R. ORAGE

Life as Gymnastics

*This little extract may not seem to belong here; its author is not urging a
return to any organized religion, nor at least on the surface, acceptance of
a new one. Yet one of the main functions of a religion, the cure of souls,
clearly does not always come off well among the Enlightened. A. R. Orage
(1873–1934), a very clever Englishman who impressed many Americans
during his stays here in the 1920's, sets out to provide a surrogate—or several of them—for the consoling, counseling labor of the priest or minister.
In particular, he advanced the ideas of a certain G. I. Gurdjieff, who
achieved "psychosynthesis" by means of sacred dances, movements (not
quite gymnastics) that tuned the soul to the universe. On the whole, I have
in this anthology avoided including the "lunatic fringe." We must, however,
have at least a mild sample, first, because the lunatic fringe exists, is perhaps
more numerous in times like ours than in more serene times, and second,
because there is always a movement from these fringes into establishment
and respectability. The trouble is to pick the particular lunacy that is going
to graduate into the fellowship of sober men. Anyway, here is the lively
Mr. Orage, minus, I regret, the dances.*

IN A THOUSAND AND ONE PHRASES WE INDICATE THE IMPORTANCE OF
"right attitude." "I approached it in the wrong attitude"—"his attitude was
all wrong"—"you'll have to change your attitude if you want to get on"—
"a proper attitude" and so on. What do we mean by attitude? We mean the
general state of mind of the person relatively to the object; or, rather, his
emotional state in regard to it. If he feels suspicious of it, his attitude is
one of suspicion. If he feels fear, affection, trust, hope, his attitude corresponds. Whatever the emotion evoked by the object, the attitude is determined by it.

Can we change our attitude towards things? Obviously our attitude can
be changed for us by circumstances. In regard to most objects and persons

From A. R. Orage, *The Active Mind: Adventures in Awareness* (New York:
Hermitage House, 1954), pp. 115-119.

our attitudes, in fact, change almost from day to day. One day we like so-
and-so very much and are disposed, in consequence, to act thus and thus;
but next day, owing to some change in him or in circumstances affecting
ourselves, our attitude has changed, and we are cool where we were warm.
Observation of ourselves will easily show how infinitely changeable we are
in our attitudes, that is to say, in our emotional responses to things. But
the question is: Can we change our attitude voluntarily at our own discretion, without the stimulus of a change in the object? For clearly, if we
could do that, we should be on the way to becoming masters of our fate,
since circumstances can affect us only as we are affectable. If I can adopt
any attitude I choose—that is, have any emotion I like—then anything
whatever that happens is all the same to me. I can feel about it as I please.

Such self-mastery is, of course, far beyond most of us; but there is no
doubt that we do and can begin to attain it. For instance, when we find an
attitude vis-a-vis some situation or person too painful to continue, we try to
change the object, and, failing that, we change our state in regard to it. The
fable of the fox and the grapes is applicable here. Having tried in vain to obtain the grapes, the fox persuaded itself that the grapes were sour. By
imagining the grapes to be sour, the fox induced a different emotion, or attitude in itself. It no longer *felt* about the grapes as it had felt before. The
practical conclusion to be drawn is that imagination is the means by which
our attitude can be controlled. Our emotions are evoked by our imagination;
and to the extent that our imagination is under our control, our emotions
and attitudes are also.

It is clear that the dominant attitude of our lives is our attitude or emotional response towards life itself. This colors everything. As we commonly say, some see everything "through rose-colored glasses"; others have
a "gloomy outlook" on life; others again have a serious or happy-go-lucky
or a religious or a sporting attitude. As many people, so many attitudes;
though all can be reduced to a definite number of groups. And in every
case their dominant attitude is decisive of every subordinate attitude. For
instance, if your characteristic attitude towards life is gloomy, even your
occasional moods of cheerfulness will be affected; they will in all probability
be both intense and brief. Or if your dominant attitude is gay and reckless,
your moments of depression may be profound but not lasting. Practically
all preaching, whether religious or secular, and all teaching, whether institutional or personal, has for its real object the inducement of a changed
attitude towards life. Equally, most of the modern systems of therapy, including Christian Science and Psychoanalysis, aim consciously or unconsciously, at bringing about a change of heart (or attitude) in their pupils
and patients. So all-important has it been found in its effects upon the
organism as a whole, that practically every method aiming at betterment
must begin with correcting the attitude towards life.

Attitude, we have seen, is conditioned by imagination. What you imagine
a thing to be, you needs must feel it to be. If you imagine a coiled rope
lying in the path to be a snake, you will feel and act accordingly. When

you discover your mistake, and have a different view of the rope, your emotional attitude will change.

What is our imagination of life? What do we take it to be? Is it for us a coiled rope or a snake? It may prove in the end impossible to know for certain what life is; but in that case, we are free to imagine it to be what we please; and it is only commonsense to imagine it to be something *useful* to us. All religious and similar systems aim, in short, at inducing in us a *useful* attitude towards life; an attitude, that is, in which we can act freely and usefully as regards our own ends or somebody else's. Some religions and systems, for instance, try to induce an attitude of submission towards life, with the design of making use of us for their own advantage. Others—but very few—aim at evoking an active or creative attitude towards life in us with the object of enlisting our voluntary co-operation. And all alike proceed by a common method, namely, by changing our imagination of life.

We can name a few typical life-pictures, each, be it remembered, drawn to evoke its proper emotions, attitude and consequent conduct. There is the "Puritan" picture which represents life as a hard and narrow school. This evokes the attitude of the nervous schoolboy in the constant presence of the stern dominie. There is the "Pagan" picture of life as an orgy of Greek gods inviting men to drink and feast with them. There is the "Serious" view of life which imagines "God" to be struggling against almost helpless odds for the redemption of matter. The emotion or attitude evoked is one of "helping poor father." There is the "Scientific" view that sees life as an orderly insignificance, all dressed up with nowhere to go. There is the "Aesthetic" view in which life is an artist making and exhibiting works of art, with man as the appreciative witness. And so on; each being designed, as has been said, to evoke an attitude or emotional response useful to somebody or other, either to the preachers or to their congregations.

It may be that each view in turn is useful; but there can be little doubt that for most of us, in the present epoch, the image of life as a gymnasium is a greatly needed tonic. Compare the difference in your attitude (emotional response) on entering a gymnasium and on entering, let us say, a cabaret, or a Y.M.C.A. lecture hall or a house of mourning. Try to realize what and how you actually feel. You are braced up, you have the intention of strengthening yourself, you delight in the difficulties—provided you choose them yourself. In short, you feel at your strongest and getting stronger.

The classic Greek conception of life was just that; and everybody knows that the gymnasium was the most popular institution of Pythagorean Greece. What is not so well known is that the gymnasium was for the Greeks a symbol of life itself. Their God ran this planet as a gymnasium for the exercise of men, and all experiences were to be taken as movements, turns, stretches, exercises in wrestling, running, lifting, and so on. Moderns will find what the ancient Greeks found in this image of life—the evocation of a creative emotion.

It is difficult to see in what other direction we moderns can look for a new image and therefore attitude towards life. We have no longer the possibility of religion in the traditional sense. Ordinary goodness—in the sense of doing what others call good—has no intelligent appeal. And, after the still recent Great War, the belief in world progress is superstition. But the clean, strong idea of life as a field of exercise for the development of all our muscles—physical, emotional and intellectual—has still the unspoiled quality of manly and womanly idealism. And life lived in that attitude would certainly be interesting as well as profitable.

CLARENCE H. FAUST

The Search for Answers

Clarence H. Faust (1901–   ), President of the Fund for the Advancement of Education established by the Ford Foundation, examines in this thoughtful essay, one most congruous with the aims of this anthology, the relation between contemporary psychology and psychiatry on one hand and "religion" on the other.

MAN OUGHT TO FEEL MORE AT HOME IN THE MODERN WORLD. AT LEAST he should feel surer about himself and surer about the world around him than his ancestors did. For as this survey of modern knowledge vividly indicates, we understand ourselves and the processes of the universe today much better than ever before, and we have vastly extended our ability to adapt the forces of the universe to our own purposes. It may well be that we sometimes overstate the facts when we talk about our increasing control of nature. But certainly it is true that in dozens of areas we can now defeat, direct, control, or harness natural forces that our ancestors could only view in helpless awe or terror.

Yet we are not at ease in this Zion of our own making, not at all confident about ourselves and our place in the world. If anything, we are more troubled about these matters than were our ancestors. Day by day we seem to become less certain of our ability to make firm distinctions between what is right and what is wrong, less sure of the meaning and purpose of human life and of society, less assured about the place of humanity in the scheme of things; we are more hesitant about defining our role as individuals or as members of society, about assigning praise and blame to human actions, and about what our responsibilities to ourselves and others may be.

We do understand the processes of nature better, but we are less sure that we understand the sum total of their significance. We know infinitely more about how to manipulate the forces around us, but are inclined to regard these forces as morally neutral. Although we find ourselves capable

From Lyman Bryson, ed., *An Outline of Man's Knowledge of the Modern World* (New York: McGraw-Hill Book Co., 1960), pp. 668-677.

of unlocking the sources of atomic energy, we are fearfully aware that this incredible new power may become the instrument of race suicide, and none of us is deeply certain that the brave talk about harnessing these new powers for productive purposes in the satisfaction of human needs is more than unrealistic idealism or desperate wishful thinking.

This uncertainty afflicts most of us today, including many who adhere to a religious faith. We are often reminded that a larger proportion of our population belongs to some church body now than ever before in American history. And yet, it is certainly true that though millions of people today rely as happily on a church-centered faith as did anyone in the Middle Ages, church members are not exempt from the peculiar uncertainties and anxieties of our time. It is typical of our age that magazines (including religious publications), books, and broadcasting programs regularly present "individual approaches" and "philosophies" that are no more than modifications or interpretations of orthodox creeds. The point of view taken here grows out of the concern common to those who are religiously inclined. It is implicit in this discussion that the solution of the problems which have their roots in these concerns must come, in part at least, from religious leaders who are prepared to fulfill the function they have fulfilled in the past; that is, who will develop a synthesis of our new knowledge, especially of our new scientific knowledge, in relation to the persistent problems and troubles of mankind. But such a solution is by no means inevitable, for it cannot be taken for granted that the necessary relationships and cross interpretations of science, philosophy, and theology will actually take place.

Man's Search for Values

We seem now more than ever before to be trying to discover the source of all principles of what ought to be and all forces that promote the good in human affairs, simply in individual human desires or ideals, or in social decisions.

This attempt to individualize our values is evident in what seems to be a key word, perhaps *the* key word, of modern ethics, namely, responsibility. The highest praise we can give a good citizen is to describe him as a highly responsible person. And one of the most effective ways of attacking an aspirant for high public office is to suggest that he is irresponsible. Yet the word responsibility has for us an almost purely social or individual reference. The terms in which we define responsibility reflect what is either socially desirable or in accordance with individual conscience.

And yet it is obvious that we are troubled about the validity of these terms of reference. We praise and reward a social sense of responsibility, but at the same time we are concerned about the pressures to conformism which this interpretation of responsibility would seem to justify and increase. We admire the independent man, the man of firm perpendicularity, but are worried that what passes for individual conscience and conscientiousness may after all be merely the product of social conditioning.

This same uncertainty is further illustrated in the difficulty our educational institutions have in dealing with what we have come to call "values." The term values is at best ambiguous, for it can mean either that which is in itself truly valuable or that which has merely come to be valued. All of our terms of ultimate reference—"the public good" with respect to society, for example, and "maturity" or "adjustment to society" with respect to the individual—have the same unsatisfactory ultimate point of reference.

Our means of dealing with the problems of ethics, with values, with responsibility—in short, with what *ought* to be—seem all to have the same unhappy lack of reach, to fall short of anything beyond individual or social preference. Applying the most admirable modern refinements of the scientific method to these problems, we achieve descriptive but not normative conclusions. We know more and more about what makes people think and act as they do and about how society operates, but we are less and less sure about the way we ought to behave and what makes a good society. If we assume that these matters are not amenable to scientific investigation but must depend upon some right posture of the emotions, upon some undefined "maturity" which cannot be rationally analyzed or justified but only appropriately appreciated or felt, then we have no way of discriminating ultimately between what is better and worse in human propensities. The feelings of the individual may be shaped by characteristics peculiar to him alone or may be merely culturally conditioned. It is well and good to be able to describe social aims, ideals, and commitments as products of historical processes; but that does not make it any the less difficult to justify them as in any sense right in themselves.

It is for these reasons that modern man, though he knows much more about the universe in which he lives and can mold it much more fully to his purposes, still does not feel at home in it and restlessly alternates between dependence upon individual conscience, which he fears may be merely personal and irresponsible, and conformity to society, which he fears may be no more than the product of historical accidents. Distressed and troubled by all these uncertainties, he at last has to seek some security in force—the force which within society is exerted through the pressures of self-interested advertising and propaganda, and which in the international area depends upon the creation of more and more potent weapons. Security comes to mean power, the power to maintain our status and to pursue our individual and social ends.

The Need for Guiding Principles

There can be no satisfactory or fundamental solution to the problem of ethics, no assurance about the real nature of good and evil, no confidence of ultimate success in the search for answers concerning the significance of man's career on this planet and the nature of his responsibilities to himself or to his society without a sense of the direction of the universe apart from man's desires and choices.

What our age then needs to establish is a sense of direction, not dogmatically but with sufficient confidence to make firm commitments and even sacrifices, some sense that the path laid out is in accord with the constitution and processes of the universe. It is easier to specify the conditions which must be met in a search for answers than to state the answers or even to point out the line of inquiry to be pursued. The conditions themselves are simple. What we need are some conceptions of the universe which hold out hope of a relationship between the human and the non-human, some conception which makes man feel at home in his world—not necessarily at ease in it or with himself but clearly and confidently aware of his successes and failures, or, to use older words, of his virtues and vices.

The kind of answer required in the search we are describing must contain the word "ought." The question is, what direction or directions *ought* the individual and society take? To satisfy this need, the answer must be more than a description of individual desires or wants or of social purposes and commitments. It is this requirement which makes the contemporary term "values" unsatisfactory, for it does not necessarily transcend human wishes and often merely denotes qualities which for some reason—conditioning, social pressure, or historical accident—have come to be valued.

It is for this reason that the search for ethical direction involves the idea of sacrifice. That which is in itself valuable (over and above being merely valued) has the characteristic that it demands in cases of conflict that we override what merely happens to be valued. The course of right action involves the willingness to give up desires in favor of the good, that is, in favor of what is valuable in itself; and right action requires the will to do so when the two are in conflict. In such circumstances sacrifice, or the readiness to sacrifice, becomes a mark of virtue. This is not to say that suffering or pain is itself a good thing or is in itself virtuous. It is a recognition of the fact that it may be painful to give up a desire because of a compelling sense of a purpose rooted in the nature of things, beyond man's wishes and wants.

It is here that modern man finds himself so much at a loss. The admirably effective and productive methods by which he is able to lay hold of some aspects of the nature of things, the methods of the natural sciences, fail him; not because they are inadequate for their primary purpose, but because they do not reveal the basis of ethical choice. They do enable him to predict the sequences in the processes of things. They do provide him with the means of injecting himself into these processes so that he can direct them to satisfy his own desires and wants. But they do *not* tell him what direction he or a society ought to take. In nothing is this more evident than in the triumph of science in releasing atomic energy. The methods which unlocked those secrets provided a knowledge of natural processes and immense capacity for production or destruction. But they have given us no guide to the basic problems of war or peace.

We are at last driven to look inward for guides, to search our own feelings for direction. But here our difficulty is that human beings are patently moved by conflicting forces, that they exhibit aggressive as well as affectionate tendencies. And, as we have said, we find reasons to suppose or to fear that our feelings are either the result of peculiarly individual characteristics or are socially conditioned. Since we are conscious of many uncertainties, the distinctions we do make between right and wrong are set apart from purely factual or descriptive propositions by being called "preference statements" or "emotive language." The term "preference" reveals with even less ambiguity than the term "values" the limitations of our search for answers which would make it possible to discriminate clearly between what we prefer and what is really valuable—which would, in other words, put a moral demand upon us.

Religion, Natural Law, and the Universe

In times past religion provided a conception of man's relation to the universe which gave his life meaning or taught him how to order his life in order to make it meaningful. In one way or another, religion has always attempted to establish a relationship between human purposes and aspirations and the scheme of the universe. By devices which in their primitive form seem naïve, religion has asserted the possibility of establishing a harmonious connection between human intentions and behavior and the universal course of things. If all that exists is under the firm and universal direction of a being who can be called "Father" or "King," there is hope that man's enterprises may be related to, judged, and given at least long-range assurance of success so long as they are compatible with the nonhuman nature and processes of the world. But the growing emphasis on the authority and reliability of the physical and social sciences has made it increasingly difficult for many modern people to accept or to use these terms with any conviction.

In the eighteenth century the concept of natural law, "the law of nature and of nature's god," served the same purpose as religion once did. The conception grew out of or implied the idea that the constitution and course of all things could appropriately be regarded as under laws which were not of man's devising but were written in the nature of things. Such a conception consequently provided a reference point for the appraisal of human organizations, laws, and courses of action. But despite our vastly increased knowledge of the regularity of natural processes, even this concept is no longer convincing to many modern men. The eighteenth century farm boy and the city dwellers alike were constantly reminded of the forces of nature—the succession of the seasons, the processes of generation and growth, the frightful effects of disease. Since it was obvious that all of this was beyond human contrivance, the conception that it was the result of the operation of natural law was persuasive. But we now know that much that was once believed to be immutable in nature can be altered or controlled or directed by man. Modern technology daily performs more

astonishing miracles and daily makes us less dependent upon and more
distant from the processes of nature. Today's children know milk only as
a nourishing liquid that is delivered in cartons, and the hurried modern
businessman spans the continent in a few hours, in an elaborately contrived machine, and is conveyed from plane to city in another shiny piece
of artifice and deposited in an air-conditioned hotel room. It is hardly surprising that natural law is for many people today an archaic concept.

Today we live not by nature but by technology. But there are tremendous, if not insurmountable, difficulties in establishing a new sense of
man's relatedness to the universe, as it is pictured by modern science.
One difficulty is simply the overwhelming sense of its immensity. The
astronomer's universe with its galaxies millions of light years away, each
larger than our own but still an infinitesimal part of an expanding system,
is hardly calculated to make the inhabitant of a small planet in a minor
solar system feel at home in his world. Such a universe is almost beyond
our comprehension. Yet the fundamental difficulty does not, I believe,
depend on size alone. The man of the eighteenth century living in America
on the eastern edge of an as yet unexplored continent also had ample, if
less spectacular, reason to feel relatively insignificant in the world he inhabited.

The real difficulty in feeling at home in the universe, in developing a
sense of relationship to it and deriving therefrom convictions concerning
what is in itself valuable and demanding beyond our immediate wants
and wishes, is conceptual. The world of the modern physicist is conceptually
utterly foreign to most of his contemporaries. Most of us, certainly, cannot
conceive of a fourth dimension, or of particles with negative spin, and to
all but a few the mathematical formulas of modern physics are as unintelligible as the markings on clay tablets made thousands of years ago by
a people whose language has been utterly lost. So alien are these modern
concepts that there are not even workable analogies to convey to us at least
an inkling of what the universe is like and what it intends or at least where
it is tending. We are benumbed by size and defeated by complexity.

The Relationship of Religion and Psychology

Human nature being what it is and its needs being what they are, it would
be astonishing if there were not some groping beginnings and tentative
conceptions of a possible new relation between modern man and his
universe. Surely we are not quite as much at a loss as a contemplation of
the empty niches in which man's older conceptions once stood would indicate. It is reasonable to suppose that somewhere in the burgeoning new
sciences of our time and in the new techniques based upon them there are
emerging fruitful new conceptions of man's relationship to the world
around him and to processes not of his own making or willing.

Though we cannot yet discern their outlines, we can properly assume that
the new conceptions must have some of the characteristics of the older

ones. The concepts by which we once lived clearly established values and standards that existed quite apart from man's desires and choices. They pointed the direction for man's thoughts, feelings, and conduct and indicated the path which he could hope would bring him into harmony with the nature of things. In short, they provided a basis for ethics which was beyond individual and social interests, a foundation deeper than individual and social desires for discriminating between virtue and vice. They put demands upon men. They specified the nature and ground of sacrifice, that is, they established both the reason and the compulsion to forego immediate emotional pressures. As a result they created for man an important kind of relatedness, and while they did not necessarily provide ease and comfort for him, they did make a man feel at home in his world as he might feel at home in a family which he sometimes found demanding and even irksome but in which his relationships and responsibilities were clear.

If we ask where in modern man's thinking about himself and his world such criteria may in a measure be satisfied, we are driven to the conclusion, I think, that it is most likely to be found in the area explored by psychology and psychiatry. Of this, there are many signs. Modern parents read Dr. Spock as Puritan parents conned the Scriptures or the Calvinistic interpretations of them. Not a few individuals in our society relate themselves to a psychiatrist as our forefathers related themselves to a priest or parson. There seems everywhere to be an increasing tendency to believe that many of the physical difficulties with which our medical men deal are ultimately best understood in terms of the psychological stresses of modern life, and that they can be treated most effectively by techniques which see mind and body as interrelated parts of the whole person.

The comparison between the religions and psychological approaches can be carried further. The demonic in human life, which used to be associated with the presence of evil, supernatural beings such as devils and witches, is now located in the realm in which psychology and psychiatry operate. We seem increasingly to suppose that there is an area beyond our immediate perception in the depths of the subconscious which in its functions has supplanted demonic hosts. Freud, Dr. Erik Erikson observes, has "unearthed mankind's daimonic inner world."

Psychology and psychiatry are also being called upon to establish a new foundation and new conceptions of virtue and vice. Moreover, there appears to be an increasing tendency to look for salvation in this area. Thomas Mann wrote prophetically when in *The Magic Mountain* he described the lecture of Dr. Krokowski at the sanitarium at Davos:

It seemed that at the end of his lecture Dr. Krokowski was making propaganda for psychoanalysis: with open arms he summoned all and sundry to come unto him. "Come unto me," he was saying, though not in those words, "Come unto me, all ye who are weary and heavy laden." And he left no doubt of his conviction that all those present *were* weary and heavy laden. He spoke of secret

suffering, of shame and sorrow, of the redeeming power of the analytic. He
advocated the bringing of light into the unconscious mind and explained how
the abnormality was metamorphosed into the conscious emotion; he urged them
to have confidence; he promised relief.

The close relationship between this new approach to the fundamental
questions of life and the answers once supplied by religion is evidenced by
the increasing interest which it arouses in churches and churchmen. In this
connection the report of a conference sponsored by the Group for the Advancement of Psychiatry on "Some Considerations of Early Attempts in
Cooperation Between Religion and Psychiatry" is most illuminating. The
participants at the meeting, which was held in 1957, included Protestant,
Catholic, and Jewish theologians, as well as psychiatrists. Much was made
on both sides of the fundamental differences between religion and psychiatry and between the problems of pastoral service and psychiatric practice. One of the participants took the position that "Religion gives a way
of life; psychiatry is a branch of medicine which, it would appear from
observation and reading, has been accepted by some as a way of life, or at
least as a *Weltanschauung,* and this in spite of the disavowal by Freud of
the possibility." Another, however, outlined a religious role for psychiatry:

The education and spiritual development of man was entirely in the hands
of the Church in the early part of European civilization, and the clergy was,
therefore, in a central position. In the centuries following the Reformation,
personality development became increasingly a matter of education. Humanistic
ideas of development superseded the older religious ideas. With the decline of
religion and humanism at the turn of the century, the psychiatrist has moved
into a unique position. He is now the recognized, scientifically trained expert on
personality development and is expected to fulfill all functions previously
divided among clergymen, educators, parents, and other agencies. If we now
attempt to reestablish a relationship between psychiatry and religion, it must
be recognized that long-range planning is necessary. At this moment of history,
many patients cannot accept what religion has to offer. These individuals consider the psychiatrist to be the only firm reliance in the ocean of emotional
currents. Therefore, the present role of the psychiatrist seems to be to make
it possible for the patient to interact with his social and cultural environment.

What psychiatry presents to modern man is in effect something quite
apart from man's conscious desires and choices. It proposes an insight into
the direction of things which exist outside of conscious impulses and wishes
—an insight which seems to hold out the prospect of becoming a guide to
good and evil in human feelings, thoughts, and conduct. In this sense, the
processes of psychiatry do resemble the processes of religion. They promise
to reveal to distressed and confused people what their feelings or their conduct mean in the light of the nature of things, or rather the substratum of
things, in the human mind and in human association. And like religion,
psychiatry frequently insists upon the critical importance of helping the
individual himself to uncover and understand the hidden sources of behavior and feeling.

There are indeed many similarities between religion and psychiatry. But there are also differences and difficulties, for despite the bridges which are being thrown across the chasm between psychiatry and religion, there are still serious obstacles to communication between the two. Some psychiatrists say that man cannot get on without religion, but such statements seem to many religious leaders to make the unacceptable assumption that any religion will serve the purpose as well as another. Furthermore, the Freudian theory that religion is based largely on the Oedipus complex seems to be a destructive misconception of religion as it is conceived by most religious people. There are many such areas of difference. As Victor von Weizsacker has pointed out in reporting his discussions with Freud about the conflicts of psychoanalysis and religion, "One can no longer evade the question whether psychoanalysis has substituted for religion." Such substitution shocks many thoughtful religious people. Jacques Maritain, in his essay on *Freudianism and Psychoanalysis—A Thomist View*, takes care to distinguish between the method of psychoanalysis, Freudian psychology, and Freudian philosophy, and he sharply states his opinion:

> . . . on the first plane [psychoanalytic method], Freud shows himself to be an investigator of genius. On the third plane [Freudian philosophy], he seems almost like a man obsessed. On the second plane [Freudian psychology], he appears to be an admirably penetrating psychologist, whose ideas, inspired by his astonishing instinct for discovery, are spoiled by a radical empiricism and an erroneous metaphysics that is unaware of itself.

In short, though he acknowledges certain therapeutic values in psychiatry, Maritain rejects its religious and moral implications: "The phenomena that psychotherapy attempts to modify are pathological phenomena and not moral faults. Its end is not to render people virtuous, but to restore them to health."

It would be bold to the point of foolhardiness to predict the course which the relationships of psychiatry and religion will take: whether differences will be sharpened and battle lines fixed; whether different territories will, as suggested by Maritain, be assigned to each; or whether reformulations on both sides will establish a productive peace. Much depends—everything, perhaps—on whether there will emerge a creative intellectual leadership which is capable of opening generally acceptable ways of dealing with the problem. There are reasons to expect that under such leadership fundamental concepts on both sides might be brought into a productive working relationship. For one thing, the growth of religious tolerance, which in America, at least, has been essential to peaceful coexistence of various religions in a united but pluralistic society, has tended to establish and make acceptable the view that there is some truth in every religious position and an element of universality in each. Furthermore, the resolution of the conflicts between science and religion which troubled the nineteenth century, especially after the rise of Darwinism, has left as a legacy the opinion that science does not necessarily threaten religious beliefs. There are, indeed, in our own earlier religious history some encouraging examples of the reconciliation of religion and psychology. The great task of our most original theologian and metaphysician, Jonathan Edwards, was the reinterpretation during the eighteenth century of Calvinistic theology in terms of the powerful new psychological concepts of John Locke, a reinterpretation which proceeded to the point where the process of salvation and even the idea of the Trinity were reformulated in psychological terms.

In the final analysis, the success of efforts to find the terms in which man may have some sense of being at home in his universe depends upon the intellectual and spiritual power of any new religious leadership which may arise. Its intellectual power will be revealed by the depth of its insight into the implications of modern science, including psychology and psychiatry. Its spiritual power must rest upon the development of a view which is not merely contrived to meet the human need and desire for man's understanding of himself in relation to the world, but which also reflects the force of inescapable demands made by the universe on man. The faith, the hope, the ethical criteria of religion require the recognition that inescapable demands are imposed upon man and society, rather than being merely generated by men's problems and desires. In this sense the search for answers in this time of burgeoning scientific knowledge must be a religious search, and its products must have something of the force of revelation.

The search for such answers will, of course, inevitably go on. No matter how impressive our scientific knowledge may become, men will be restless until they can form a satisfactory picture of themselves in the kind of universe which science has revealed. The search will be a long, hard task, as long and hard as were those in the days when religion and philosophy provided a rationale for the evaluation of individual and social behavior. No task could be more vital to the welfare of mankind. The most urgent problem of the twentieth century is whether man today can discover and accept the demands which his conception of the universe puts upon him— the necessity to find his own place and society's place in the scheme of things before he destroys himself by the abuse of the powers which science has given him.

ALAN W. WATTS

"Sitting Quietly, Doing Nothing"

Alan W. Watts (1915–   ) is an American scholar specializing in Asian studies, author of a very successful popular exposition of Zen Buddhism, a faith—a way of life, a religion—which has continued to arouse increasing interest in the West especially since war brought the East so much closer. How far any Oriental faith can get beyond intellectual faddist circles in our West I shouldn't dare pronounce. I should guess Zen Buddhism has not yet got very far beyond such circles. But it is no mere product of a lunatic fringe. Like Taoism it is an old, tried, and successful religion in its Oriental homeland.

IN BOTH LIFE AND ART THE CULTURES OF THE FAR EAST APPRECIATE nothing more highly than spontaneity or naturalness (*tzu-jan*). This is the unmistakable tone of sincerity marking the action which is not studied and contrived. For a man rings like a cracked bell when he thinks and acts with a split mind—one part standing aside to interfere with the other, to control, to condemn, or to admire. But the mind, or the true nature, of man cannot actually be split. According to a *Zenrin* poem, it is

> *Like a sword that cuts, but cannot cut itself;*
> *Like an eye that sees, but cannot see itself.*

The illusion of the split comes from the mind's attempt to be both itself and its idea of itself, from a fatal confusion of fact with symbol. To make an end of the illusion, the mind must stop trying to act upon itself, upon its stream of experiences, from the standpoint of the idea of itself which we call the ego. This is expressed in another *Zenrin* poem as

> *Sitting quietly, doing nothing,*
> *Spring comes, and the grass grows by itself.*

This "by itself" is the mind's and the world's natural way of action, as when the eyes see by themselves, and the ears hear by themselves, and

From Alan W. Watts, *The Way of Zen* (New York: Pantheon Books, 1957), pp. 134-153. Also available in Mentor Books, pp. 133-143, 145-150.

the mouth opens by itself without having to be forced apart by the fingers. As the *Zenrin* says again:

> *The blue mountains are of themselves blue mountains;*
> *The white clouds are of themselves white clouds.*

In its stress upon naturalness, Zen is obviously the inheritor of Taoism, and its view of spontaneous action as "marvelous activity" (*miao-yung*) is precisely what the Taoists meant by the word *te*— "virtue" with an over-tone of magical power. But neither in Taoism nor in Zen does it have any-thing to do with magic in the merely sensational sense of performing super-human "miracles." The "magical" or "marvelous" quality of spontaneous action is, on the contrary, that it is perfectly human, and yet shows no sign of being contrived.

Such a quality is peculiarly subtle (another meaning of *miao*), and extremely hard to put into words. The story is told of a Zen monk who wept upon hearing of the death of a close relative. When one of his fellow students objected that it was most unseemly for a monk to show such personal attachment he replied, "Don't be stupid! I'm weeping be-cause I want to weep." The great Hakuin was deeply disturbed in his early study of Zen when he came across the story of the master Yen-t'ou, who was said to have screamed at the top of his voice when murdered by a robber. Yet this doubt was dissolved at the moment of his *satori,* and in Zen circles his own death is felt to have been especially admirable for its display of human emotion. On the other hand, the abbot Kwaisen and his monks allowed themselves to be burned alive by the soldiers of Oda Nobunaga, sitting calmly in the posture of meditation. Such contradictory "naturalness" seems most mysterious, but perhaps the clue lies in the saying of Yün-men: "In walking, just walk. In sitting, just sit. Above all, don't wobble." For the essential quality of naturalness is the sincerity of the undivided mind which does not dither between alternatives. So when Yen-t'ou screamed, it was such a scream that it was heard for miles around.

But it would be quite wrong to suppose that this natural sincerity comes about by observing such a platitude as "Whatsoever thy hand findeth to do, do it with all thy might." When Yen-t'ou screamed, he was not scream-ing *in order* to be natural, nor did he first make up his mind to scream and then implement the decision with the full energy of his will. There is a total contradiction in planned naturalness and intentional sincerity. This is to overlay, not to discover, the "original mind." Thus to try to be natural is an affectation. To try not to try to be natural is also an affectation. As a *Zenrin* poem says:

> *You cannot get it by taking thought;*
> *You cannot seek it by not taking thought.*

But this absurdly complex and frustrating predicament arises from a simple and elementary mistake in the use of the mind. When this is understood, there is no paradox and no difficulty. Obviously, the mistake arises in the attempt to split the mind against itself, but to understand this clearly we have to enter more deeply into the "cybernetics" of the mind, the basic pattern of its self-correcting action.

It is, of course, part of the very genius of the human mind that it can, as it were, stand aside from life and reflect upon it, that it can be aware of its own existence, and that it can criticize its own processes. For the mind has something resembling a "feed-back" system. This is a term used in communications engineering for one of the basic principles of "automation," of enabling machines to control themselves. Feed-back enables a machine to be informed of the effects of its own action in such a way as to be able to correct its action. Perhaps the most familiar example is the electrical thermostat which regulates the heating of a house. By setting an upper and a lower limit of desired temperature, a thermometer is so connected that it will switch the furnace on when the lower limit is reached, and off when the upper limit is reached. The temperature of the house is thus kept within the desired limits. The thermostat provides the furnace with a kind of sensitive organ—an extremely rudimentary analogy of human self-consciousness.[1]

The proper adjustment of a feed-back system is always a complex mechanical problem. For the original machine, say, the furnace, is adjusted by the feed-back system, but this system in turn needs adjustment. Therefore to make a mechanical system more and more automatic will require the use of a series of feed-back systems—a second to correct the first, a third to correct the second, and so on. But there are obvious limits to such a series, for beyond a certain point the mechanism will be "frustrated" by its own complexity. For example, it might take so long for the information to pass through the series of control systems that it would arrive at the original machine too late to be useful. Similarly, when human beings think too carefully and minutely about an action to be taken, they cannot make up their minds in time to act. In other words, one cannot correct one's means of self-correction indefinitely. There must soon be a source of information at the end of the line which is the final authority. Failure to trust its authority will make it impossible to act, and the system will be paralyzed.

The system can be paralyzed in yet another way. Every feed-back system needs a margin of "lag" or error. If we try to make a thermostat absolutely accurate—that is, if we bring the upper and lower limits of tem-

[1] I do not wish to press the analogy between the human mind and servo-mechanisms to the point of saying that the mind-body is "nothing but" an extremely complicated mechanical automaton. I only want to go so far as to show that feed-back involves some problems which are similar to the problems of self-consciousness and self-control in man. Otherwise, mechanism and organism seem to me to be different in principle—that is, in their actual functioning—since the one is made and the other grown. The fact that one can translate some organic processes into mechanical terms no more implies that organism is mechanism than the translation of commerce into arithmetical terms implies that commerce is arithmetic.

perature very close together in an attempt to hold the temperature at
a constant 70 degrees—the whole system will break down. For to the
extent that the upper and lower limits coincide, the signals for switching off
and switching on will coincide! If 70 degrees is both the lower and upper
limit the "go" sign will also be the "stop" sign; "yes" will imply "no"
and "no" will imply "yes." Whereupon the mechanism will start "trembling," going on and off, on and off, until it shakes itself to pieces. The
system is too sensitive and shows symptoms which are startlingly like
human anxiety. For when a human being is so self-conscious, so self-con-
trolled that he cannot let go of himself, he dithers or wobbles between opposites. This is precisely what is meant in Zen by going round and round
on "the wheel of birth-and-death," for the Buddhist *samsara* is the pro-
totype of all vicious circles.[2]

Now human life consists primarily and originally in action—in living
in the concrete world of "suchness." But we have the power to control
action by reflection, that is, by thinking, by comparing the actual world with
memories or "reflections." Memories are organized in terms of more
or less abstract images—words, signs, simplified shapes, and other symbols
which can be reviewed very rapidly one after another. From such memories,
reflections, and symbols the mind constructs its idea of itself. This corresponds to the thermostat—the source of information about its own past
action by which the system corrects itself. The mind-body must, of course,
trust that information in order to act, for paralysis will soon result from
trying to remember whether we have remembered everything accurately.

But to keep up the supply of information in the memory, the mind-body
must continue to act "on its own." It must not cling too closely to its own
record. There must be a "lag" or distance between the source of information
and the source of action. This does *not* mean that the source of action must
hesitate before it accepts the information. It means that it must not identify
itself with the source of information. We saw that when the furnace responds too closely to the thermostat, it cannot go ahead without also trying
to stop, or stop without also trying to go ahead. This is just what happens
to the human being, to the mind, when the desire for certainty and security
prompts identification between the mind and its own image of itself. It
cannot let go of itself. It feels that it should not do what it is doing, and
that it should do what it is not doing. It feels that it should not be what it
is, and be what it isn't. Furthermore, the effort to remain always "good" or
"happy" is like trying to hold the thermostat to a constant 70 degrees by
making the lower limit the same as the upper.

The identification of the mind with its own image is, therefore, paralyzing because the image is fixed—it is past and finished. But it is a fixed image
of oneself in motion! To cling to it is thus to be in constant contradiction

[2] See the fascinating discussion of analogies between mechanical and logical contradictions and the psychoneuroses by Gregory Bateson in Reusch and Bateson,
Communication: the Social Matrix of Psychiatry, esp. Chap. 8. (Norton: New York,
1950.)

and conflict. Hence Yün-men's saying, "In walking, just walk. In sitting, just sit. Above all, don't wobble." In other words, the mind cannot act without giving up the impossible attempt to control itself beyond a certain point. It must let go of itself both in the sense of trusting its own memory and reflection, and in the sense of acting spontaneously, on its own into the unknown.

This is why Zen often seems to take the side of action as against reflection, and why it describes itself as "no-mind" (*wu-hsin*) or "no-thought" (*wu-nien*), and why the masters demonstrate Zen by giving instantaneous and unpremeditated answers to questions. When Yün-men was asked for the ultimate secret of Buddhism, he replied, "Dumpling!" In the words of the Japanese master Takuan:

When a monk asks, "What is the Buddha?" the master may raise his fist; when he is asked, "What is the ultimate idea of Buddhism?" he may exclaim even before the questioner finishes his sentence, "A blossoming branch of the plum," or "The cypress-tree in the court-yard." The point is that the answering mind does not "stop" anywhere, but responds straightway without giving any thought to the felicity of an answer.

This is allowing the mind to act on its own.

But reflection is also action, and Yün-men might also have said, "In acting, just act. In thinking, just think. Above all, don't wobble." In other words, if one is going to reflect, just reflect—but do not reflect about reflecting. Yet Zen would agree that reflection about reflection is also action—provided that in doing it we do just that, and do not tend to drift off into the infinite regression of trying always to stand above or outside the level upon which we are acting. Thus Zen is also a liberation from the dualism of thought and action, for it thinks as it acts—with the same quality of abandon, commitment, or faith. The attitude of *wu-hsin* is by no means an anti-intellectualist exclusion of thinking. *Wu-hsin* is action on any level whatsoever, physical or psychic, without trying *at the same moment* to observe and check the action from outside. This attempt to act and think about the action simultaneously is precisely the identification of the mind with its idea of itself. It involves the same contradiction as the statement which states something about itself—"This statement is false."

The same is true of the relationship between feeling and action. For feeling blocks action, and blocks itself as a form of action, when it gets caught in this same tendency to observe or feel itself indefinitely—as when, in the midst of enjoying myself, I examine myself to see if I am getting the utmost out of the occasion. Not content with tasting the food, I am also trying to taste my tongue. Not content with feeling happy, I want to feel myself feeling happy—so as to be sure not to miss anything.

Whether trusting our memories or trusting the mind to act on its own, it comes to the same thing: ultimately we must act and think, live and die, from a source beyond all "our" knowledge and control. But this source is ourselves, and when we see that, it no longer stands over against us as a threatening object. No amount of care and hesitancy, no amount of introspection and searching of our motives, can make any ultimate difference to the fact that the mind is

Like an eye that sees, but cannot see itself.

In the end, the only alternative to a shuddering paralysis is to leap into action regardless of the consequences. Action in this spirit may be right or wrong with respect to conventional standards. But our decisions upon the conventional level must be supported by the conviction that whatever we do, and whatever "happens" to us, is ultimately "right." In other words, we must enter into it without "second thought," without *arrière-pensée* of regret, hesitancy, doubt, or self-recrimination. Thus when Yün-men was asked, "What is the Tao?" he answered simply, "Walk on! (*ch'ü*)."

But to act "without second thought," without double-mindedness, is by no means a mere precept for our imitation. For we cannot realize this kind of action until it is clear beyond any shadow of doubt that it is actually impossible to do anything else. In the words of Huang-po:

Men are afraid to forget their own minds, fearing to fall through the void with nothing on to which they can cling. They do not know that the void is not really the void but the real realm of the Dharma. . . . It cannot be looked for or sought, comprehended by wisdom or knowledge, explained in words, contacted materially (i.e., objectively) or reached by meritorious achievement.

Now this impossibility of "grasping the mind with the mind" is, when realized, the non-action (*wu-wei*), the "sitting quietly, doing nothing" whereby "spring comes, and the grass grows by itself." There is no necessity for the mind to try to let go of itself, or to try not to try. This introduces further artificialities. Yet, as a matter of psychological strategy, there is no need for trying to avoid artificialities. In the doctrine of the Japanese master Bankei (1622-1693) the mind which cannot grasp itself is called the "Unborn" (*fusho*), the mind which does not arise or appear in the realm of symbolic knowledge.

A layman asked, "I appreciate very much your instruction about the Unborn, but by force of habit second thoughts [*nien*] keep tending to arise, and being confused by them it is difficult to be in perfect accord with the Unborn. How am I to trust in it entirely?"

Bankei said, "If you make an attempt to stop the second thoughts which arise, then the mind which does the stopping and the mind which is stopped become divided, and there is no occasion for peace of mind. So it is best for you simply to believe that originally there is no (possibility of control by) second thoughts. Yet because of karmic affinity, through what you see and what you hear these thoughts arise and vanish temporarily, but are without substance."

"Brushing off thoughts which arise is just like washing off blood with blood. We remain impure because of being washed with blood, even when the blood that was first there has gone—and if we continue in this way the impurity never departs. This is from ignorance of the mind's unborn, unvanishing, and unconfused nature. If we take second thought for an effective reality, we keep going on and on around the wheel of birth-and-death. You should realize that such thought is just a temporary mental construction, and not try to hold or to reject it. Let it alone just as it occurs and just as it ceases. It is like an image reflected in a mirror. The mirror is clear and reflects anything which comes before it, and yet no image sticks in the mirror. The Buddha mind (i.e., the real, unborn mind) is ten thousand times more clear than a mirror, and more inexpressibly marvelous. In its light all such thoughts vanish without trace. If you put your faith in this way of understanding, however strongly such thoughts may arise, they do no harm."

This is also the doctrine of Huang-po, who says again:

If it is held that there is something to be realized or attained apart from mind, and, thereupon, mind is used to seek it, (that implies) failure to understand that mind and the object of its search are one. Mind cannot be used to seek something from mind for, even after the passage of millions of kalpas, the day of success would never come.

One must not forget the social context of Zen. It is primarily a way of liberation for those who have mastered the disciplines of social convention, of the conditioning of the individual by the group. Zen is a medicine for the ill effects of this conditioning, for the mental paralysis and anxiety which come from excessive self-consciousness. It must be seen against the background of societies regulated by the principles of Confucianism, with their heavy stress on propriety and punctilious ritual. In Japan, too, it must be seen in relation to the rigid schooling required in the training of the *samurai* caste, and the emotional strain to which the *samurai* were exposed in times of constant warfare. As a medicine for these conditions, it does not seek to overthrow the conventions themselves, but, on the contrary, takes them for granted—as is easily seen in such manifestations of Zen as the *cha-no-yu* or "tea ceremony" of Japan. Therefore Zen might be a very dangerous medicine in a social context where convention is weak, or, at the other extreme, where there is a spirit of open revolt against convention ready to exploit Zen for destructive purposes.

With this in mind, we can observe the freedom and naturalness of Zen without loss of perspective. Social conditioning fosters the identification of the mind with a fixed idea of itself as the means of self-control, and as a result man thinks of himself as "I"—the ego. Thereupon the mental center of gravity shifts from the spontaneous or original mind to the ego image. Once this has happened, the very center of our psychic life is identified with the self-controlling mechanism. It then becomes almost impossible to see how "I" can let go of "myself," for I am precisely my habitual effort to hold on to myself. I find myself totally incapable of any mental action which is not intentional, affected, and insincere. Therefore anything I do to give myself up, to let go, will be a disguised form of the habitual effort to hold on. I cannot be intentionally unintentional or purposely spontaneous. As soon as it becomes important for me to be spontaneous, the intention to be so is strengthened; I cannot get rid of it, and yet it is the one thing that stands in the way of its own fulfillment. It is as if someone had given me some medicine with the warning that it will not work if I think of a monkey while taking it.

While I am remembering to forget the monkey, I am in a "double-bind" situation where "to do" is "not to do," and vice versa. "Yes" implies "no," and "go" implies "stop." At this point Zen comes to me and asks, "If you cannot help remembering the monkey, are you doing it on purpose?" In other words, do I have an intention for being intentional, a purpose for being purposive? Suddenly I realize that my very intending is spontaneous, or that my controlling self—the ego—arises from my uncontrolled or natural self. At this moment all the machinations of the ego come to nought; it is annihilated in its own trap. I see that it is actually impossible not to be spontaneous. For what I cannot help doing I am doing spontaneously, but if I am at the same time trying to control it, I interpret it as a compulsion. As a Zen master said, "Nothing is left to you at this moment but to have a good laugh."

In this moment the whole quality of consciousness is changed, and I feel myself in a new world in which, however, it is obvious that I have always been living. As soon as I recognize that my voluntary and purposeful action happens spontaneously "by itself," just like breathing, hearing, and feeling, I am no longer caught in the contradiction of trying to be spontaneous. There is no real contradiction, since "trying" is "spontaneity." Seeing this, the compulsive, blocked, and "tied-up" feeling vanishes. It is just as if I had been absorbed in a tug-of-war between my two hands, and had forgotten that both were mine. No block to spontaneity remains when the trying is seen to be needless. As we saw, the discovery that both the voluntary and involuntary aspects of the mind are alike spontaneous makes an immediate end of the fixed dualism between the mind and the world, the knower and the known. The new world in which I find myself has an extraordinary transparency or freedom from barriers, making it seem that I have somehow become the empty space in which everything is happening. . . .

Zen does not make the mistake of using the experience "all things are of one Suchness" as the premise for an ethic of universal brotherhood. On the contrary, Yüan-wu says:

If you are a real man, you may by all means drive off with the farmer's ox, or grab the food from a starving man.

This is only to say that Zen lies beyond the ethical standpoint, whose sanctions must be found, not in reality itself, but in the mutual agreement of human beings. When we attempt to universalize or absolutize it, the ethical standpoint makes it impossible to exist, for we cannot live for a day without destroying the life of some other creature.

If Zen is regarded as having the same function as a religion in the West, we shall naturally want to find some logical connection between its central experience and the improvement of human relations. But this is actually

putting the cart before the horse. The point is rather that some such experience or way of life as this is the object of improved human relations. In
the culture of the Far East the problems of human relations are the sphere
of Confucianism rather than Zen, but since the Sung dynasty (959-1278)
Zen has consistently fostered Confucianism and was the main source of
the introduction of its principles into Japan. It saw their importance for
creating the type of cultural matrix in which Zen could flourish without
coming into conflict with social order, because the Confucian ethic is
admittedly human and relative, not divine and absolute.

Although profoundly "inconsequential," the Zen experience has consequences in the sense that it may be applied in any direction, to any
conceivable human activity, and that wherever it is so applied it lends an
unmistakable quality to the work. The characteristic notes of the spontaneous life are *mo chih ch'u* or "going ahead without hesitation," and *wu-
shih,* lack of affectation or simplicity.

While the Zen experience does not imply any specific course of action,
since it has no purpose, no motivation, it turns unhesitatingly to anything
that presents itself to be done. *Mo chih ch'u* is the mind functioning without
blocks, without "wobbling" between alternatives, and much of Zen training
consists in confronting the student with dilemmas which he is expected
to handle without stopping to deliberate and "choose." The response to
the situation must follow with the immediacy of sound issuing from the
hands when they are clapped, or sparks from a flint when struck. The student unaccustomed to this type of response will at first be confused, but
as he gains faith in his "original" or spontaneous mind he will not only
respond with ease, but the responses themselves will acquire a startling ap-
propriateness. This is something like the professional comedian's gift of
unprepared wit which is equal to any situation.

The master may begin a conversation with the student by asking a series
of very ordinary questions about trivial matters, to which the student
responds with perfect spontaneity. But suddenly he will say, "When the bath-
water flows down the drain, does it turn clockwise or counter-clockwise?"
As the student stops at the unexpectedness of the question, and perhaps
tries to remember which way it goes, the master shouts, "Don't think!
Act! This way—" and whirls his hand in the air. Or, perhaps less helpfully,
he may say, "So far you've answered my questions quite naturally and
easily, but where's your difficulty now?"

The student, likewise, is free to challenge the master, and one can
imagine that in the days when Zen training was less formal the members
of Zen communities must have had enormous fun laying traps for each
other. To some extent this type of relationship still exists, despite the great
solemnity of the *sanzen* interview in which the *koan* is given and answered.
The late Kozuki Roshi was entertaining two American monks at tea when
he casually asked, "And what do you gentlemen know about Zen?" One
of the monks flung his closed fan straight at the master's face. All in the

same instant the master inclined his head slightly to one side, the fan shot straight through the paper *shoji* behind him, and he burst into a ripple of laughter.

Suzuki has translated a long letter from the Zen master Takuan on the relationship of Zen to the art of fencing, and this is certainly the best literary source of what Zen means by *mo chih ch'u,* by "going straight ahead without stopping." Both Takuan and Bankei stressed the fact that the "original" or "unborn" mind is constantly working miracles even in the most ordinary person. Even though a tree has innumerable leaves, the mind takes them in all at once without being "stopped" by any one of them. Explaining this to a visiting monk, Bankei said, "To prove that your mind is the Buddha mind, notice how all that I say here goes into you without missing a single thing, even though I don't try to push it into you." When heckled by an aggressive Nichiren monk who kept insisting that he couldn't understand a word, Bankei asked him to come closer. The monk stepped forward. "Closer still," said Bankei. The monk came forward again. "How well," said Bankei, "you understand me!" In other words, our natural organism performs the most marvelously complex activities without the least hesitation or deliberation. Conscious thought is itself founded upon its whole system of spontaneous functioning, for which reason there is really no alternative to trusting oneself completely to its working. Oneself *is* its working.

Zen is not merely a cult of impulsive action. The point of *mo chih ch'u* is not to eliminate reflective thought but to eliminate "blocking" in both action and thought, so that the response of the mind is always like a ball in a mountain stream—"one thought after another without hesitation." There is something similar to this in the psychoanalytic practice of free association, employed as a technique to get rid of obstacles to the free flow of thought from the "unconscious." For there is a tendency to confuse "blocking"— a purely obstructive mechanism—with thinking out an answer, but the difference between the two is easily noticed in such a purely "thinking out" process as adding a column of figures. Many people find that at certain combinations of numbers, such as 8 and 5 or 7 and 6, a feeling of resistance comes up which halts the process. Because it is always annoying and disconcerting, one tends also to block at blocking, so that the state turns into the kind of wobbling dither characteristic of the snarled feedback system. The simplest cure is to feel free to block, so that one does not block at blocking. When one feels free to block, the blocking automatically eliminates itself. It is like riding a bicycle. When one starts falling to the left, one does not resist the fall (i.e., the block) by turning to the right. One turns the wheel to the left—and the balance is restored. The principle here is, of course, the same as getting out of the contradiction of "trying to be spontaneous" through accepting the "trying" as "spontaneous," through not resisting the block.

"Blocking" is perhaps the best translation of the Zen term *nien* as it occurs in the phrase *wu-nien,* "no-thought" or, better, "no second thought." Takuan points out that this is the real meaning of "attachment" in Buddhism, as when it is said that a Buddha is free from worldly attachments. It does not mean that he is a "stone Buddha" with no feelings, no emotions, and no sensations of hunger or pain. It means that he does not block at anything. Thus it is typical of Zen that its style of action has the strongest feeling of commitment, of "follow-through." It enters into everything wholeheartedly and freely without having to keep an eye on itself. It does not confuse spirituality with thinking about God while one is peeling potatoes. Zen spirituality is just to peel the potatoes. In the words of Lin-chi:

When it's time to get dressed, put on your clothes. When you must walk, then walk. When you must sit, then sit. Don't have a single thought in your mind about seeking for Buddhahood. . . . You talk about being perfectly disciplined in your six senses and in all your actions, but in my view all this is making *karma.* To seek the Buddha (nature) and to seek the Dharma is at once to make *karma* which leads to the hells. To seek (to be) Bodhisattvas is also making *karma,* and likewise studying the *sutras* and commentaries. Buddhas and Patriarchs are people without such artificialities. . . . It is said everywhere that there is a Tao which must be cultivated and a Dharma which must be realized. What Dharma do you say must be realized, and what Tao cultivated? What do you lack in the way you are functioning right now? What will you add to where you are?

As another *Zenrin* poem says:

> There's nothing equal to wearing clothes and eating food.
> Outside this there are neither Buddhas nor Patriarchs.

This is the quality of *wu-shih,* of naturalness without any contrivances or means for being natural, such as thoughts of Zen, of the Tao, or of the Buddha. One does not exclude such thoughts; they simply fall away when seen to be unnecessary. "He does not linger where the Buddha is, and where there is no Buddha he passes right on."

For as the *Zenrin* says again:

> To be conscious of the original mind, the original nature—
> Just this is the great disease of Zen!

As "the fish swims in the water but is unmindful of the water, the bird flies in the wind but knows not of the wind," so the true life of Zen has no need to "raise waves when no wind is blowing," to drag in religion or spirituality as something over and above life itself. This is why the sage Fa-yung received no more offerings of flowers from the birds after he had had his interview with the Fourth Patriarch, for his holiness no longer "stood out like a sore thumb." Of such a man the *Zenrin* says:

> Entering the forest he moves not the grass;
> Entering the water he makes not a ripple.

No one notices him because he does not notice himself.

It is often said that to be clinging to oneself is like having a thorn in the skin, and that Buddhism is a second thorn to extract the first. When it is out, both thorns are thrown away. But in the moment when Buddhism, when philosophy or religion, becomes another way of clinging to oneself through seeking a spiritual security, the two thorns become one—and how is it to be taken out? This, as Bankei said, is "wiping off blood with blood." Therefore in Zen there is neither self nor Buddha to which one can cling, no good to gain and no evil to be avoided, no thoughts to be eradicated and no mind to be purified, no body to perish and no soul to be saved. At one blow this entire framework of abstractions is shattered to fragments. As the *Zenrin* says:

> *To save life it must be destroyed.*
> *When utterly destroyed, one dwells for the first time in peace.*

> *One word settles heaven and earth;*
> *One sword levels the whole world.*

Of this "one sword" Lin-chi said:

If a man cultivates the Tao, the Tao will not work—on all sides evil conditions will head up competitively. But when the sword of wisdom [*prajna*] comes out there's not one thing left.

The "sword of *prajna*" which cuts away abstraction is that "direct pointing" whereby Zen avoids the entanglements of religiosity and goes straight to the heart. Thus when the Governor of Lang asked Yao-shan, "What is the Tao?" the master pointed upwards to the sky and downwards to a water jug beside him. Asked for an explanation, he replied: "A cloud in the sky and water in the jug."

CARL GUSTAV JUNG

The Modern Spiritual Problem

Carl Gustav Jung (1875–   ) is the famous Swiss psychologist and psychiatrist who long ago broke with his master Freud, in no small part over just the question of the place of religion, the Judaeo-Christian religion, in a modern world-view. Jung is convinced that such a religion is necessary—indeed, true.

THE SPIRITUAL PROBLEM OF MODERN MAN IS ONE OF THOSE QUESTIONS which belong so intimately to the present in which we are living that we cannot judge of them fully. The modern man is a newly formed human being; a modern problem is a question which has just arisen and whose answer lies in the future. In speaking, therefore, of the spiritual problem of modern man we can at most state a question—and we should perhaps put this statement in different terms if we had but the faintest inkling of the answer. The question, moreover, seems rather vague; but the truth is that it has to do with something so universal that it exceeds the grasp of any single human being. We have reason enough, therefore, to approach such a problem with true moderation and with the greatest caution. I am deeply convinced of this, and wish it stressed the more because it is just such problems which tempt us to use high-sounding words—and because I shall myself be forced to say certain things which may sound immoderate and incautious.

To begin at once with an example of such apparent lack of caution, I must say that the man we call modern, the man who is aware of the immediate present, is by no means the average man. He is rather the man who stands upon a peak, or at the very edge of the world, the abyss of the future before him, above him the heavens, and below him the whole of mankind with a history that disappears in primeval mists. The modern man

From C. G. Jung, *Modern Man in Search of a Soul* (New York: Harcourt, Brace Harvest Books, n.d.). Translators' (W. S. Dell and Cary F. Baynes) Preface dated 1933, pp. 226-254.

The author has made some changes in this essay since its publication in German. (*Trans.*)

—or, let us say again, the man of the immediate present—is rarely met with. There are few who live up to the name, for they must be conscious to a superlative degree. Since to be wholly of the present means to be fully conscious of one's existence as a man, it requires the most intensive and extensive consciousness, with a minimum of unconsciousness. It must be clearly understood that the mere fact of living in the present does not make a man modern, for in that case everyone at present alive would be so. He alone is modern who is fully conscious of the present.

The man whom we can with justice call "modern" is solitary. He is so of necessity and at all times, for every step towards a fuller consciousness of the present removes him further from his original *"participation mystique"* with the mass of men—from submersion in a common unconsciousness. Every step forward means an act of tearing himself loose from that all-embracing, pristine unconsciousness which claims the bulk of mankind almost entirely. Even in our civilizations the people who form, psychologically speaking, the lowest stratum, live almost as unconsciously as primitive races. Those of the succeeding stratum manifest a level of consciousness which corresponds to the beginnings of human culture, while those of the highest stratum have a consciousness capable of keeping step with the life of the last few centuries. Only the man who is modern in our meaning of the term really lives in the present; he alone has a present-day consciousness, and he alone finds that the ways of life which correspond to earlier levels pall upon him. The values and strivings of those past worlds no longer interest him save from the historical standpoint. Thus he has become "unhistorical" in the deepest sense and has estranged himself from the mass of men who live entirely within the bounds of tradition. Indeed, he is completely modern only when he has come to the very edge of the world, leaving behind him all that has been discarded and outgrown, and acknowledging that he stands before a void out of which all things may grow.

These words may be thought to be but empty sound, and their meaning reduced to mere banality. Nothing is easier than to affect a consciousness of the present. As a matter of fact, a great horde of worthless people give themselves the air of being modern by overleaping the various stages of development and the tasks of life they represent. They appear suddenly by the side of the truly modern man as uprooted human beings, bloodsucking ghosts, whose emptiness is taken for the unenviable loneliness of the modern man and casts discredit upon him. He and his kind, few in number as they are, are hidden from the undiscerning eyes of mass-men by those clouds of ghosts, the pseudo-moderns. It cannot be helped; the "modern" man is questionable and suspect, and has always been so, even in the past.

An honest profession of modernity means voluntarily declaring bankruptcy, taking the vows of poverty and chastity in a new sense, and—what is still more painful—renouncing the halo which history bestows as a mark of its sanction. To be "unhistorical" is the Promethean sin, and in this sense modern man lives in sin. A higher level of consciousness is like a burden of guilt. But, as I have said, only the man who has outgrown the stages of consciousness belonging to the past and has amply fulfilled the duties appointed for him by his world, can achieve a full consciousness of the present. To do this he must be sound and proficient in the best sense—a man who has achieved as much as other people, and even a little more. It is these qualities which enable him to gain the next highest level of consciousness.

I know that the idea of proficiency is especially repugnant to the pseudo-moderns, for it reminds them unpleasantly of their deceits. This, however, cannot prevent us from taking it as our criterion of the modern man. We are even forced to do so, for unless he is proficient, the man who claims to be modern is nothing but an unscrupulous gambler. He must be proficient in the highest degree, for unless he can atone by creative ability for his break with tradition, he is merely disloyal to the past. It is sheer juggling to look upon a denial of the past as the same thing as consciousness of the present. "Today" stands between "yesterday" and "tomorrow," and forms a link between past and future; it has no other meaning. The present represents a process of transition, and that man may account himself modern who is conscious of it in this sense.

Many people call themselves modern—especially the pseudo-moderns. Therefore the really modern man is often to be found among those who call themselves old-fashioned. He takes this stand for sufficient reasons. On the one hand he emphasizes the past in order to hold the scales against his break with tradition and that effect of guilt of which I have spoken. On the other hand he wishes to avoid being taken for a pseudo-modern.

Every good quality has its bad side, and nothing that is good can come into the world without directly producing a corresponding evil. This is a painful fact. Now there is the danger that consciousness of the present may lead to an elation based upon illusion: the illusion, namely, that we are the culmination of the history of mankind, the fulfilment and the end-product of countless centuries. If we grant this, we should understand that it is no more than the proud acknowledgement of our destitution: we are also the disappointment of the hopes and expectations of the ages. Think of nearly two thousand years of Christian ideals followed, instead of by the return of the Messiah and the heavenly millennium, by the World War among Christian nations and its barbed-wire and poison-gas. What a catastrophe in heaven and on earth!

In the face of such a picture we may well grow humble again. It is true that modern man is a culmination, but tomorrow he will be surpassed; he is indeed the end-product of an age-old development, but he is at the same time the worst conceivable disappointment of the hopes of humankind. The modern man is aware of this. He has seen how beneficent are science, technology and organization, but also how catastrophic they can be. He has likewise seen that well-meaning governments have so thoroughly paved the way for peace on the principle "in time of peace prepare for war," that

Europe has nearly gone to rack and ruin. And as for ideals, the Christian church, the brotherhood of man, international social democracy and the "solidarity" of economic interests have all failed to stand the baptism of fire—the test of reality. Today, fifteen years after the war, we observe once more the same optimism, the same organization, the same political aspirations, the same phrases and catch-words at work. How can we but fear that they will inevitably lead to further catastrophes? Agreements to outlaw war leave us sceptical, even while we wish them all possible success. At bottom, behind every such palliative measure, there is a gnawing doubt. On the whole, I believe I am not exaggerating when I say that modern man has suffered an almost fatal shock, psychologically speaking, and as a result has fallen into profound uncertainty.

These statements, I believe, make it clear enough that my being a physician has coloured my views. A doctor always spies out diseases, and I cannot cease to be a doctor. But it is essential to the physician's art that he should not discover diseases where none exists. I will therefore not make the assertion that the white races in general, and occidental nations in particular, are diseased, or that the Western world is on the verge of collapse. I am in no way competent to pass such a judgement.

It is of course only from my own experience with other persons and with myself that I draw my knowledge of the spiritual problem of modern man. I know something of the intimate psychic life of many hundreds of educated persons, both sick and healthy, coming from every quarter of the civilized, white world; and upon this experience I base my statements. No doubt I can draw only a one-sided picture, for the things I have observed are events of psychic life; they lie within us—on the *inner side,* if I may use the expression. I must point out that this is not always true of psychic life; the psyche is not always and everywhere to be found on the inner side. It is to be found on the *outside* in whole races or periods of history which take no account of psychic life as such. As examples we may choose any of the ancient cultures, but especially that of Egypt with its imposing objectivity and its naïve confession of sins that have not been committed.* We can no more feel the Pyramids and the Apis tombs of Sakkara to be expressions of personal problems or personal emotions, than we can feel this of the music of Bach.

Whenever there is established an external form, be it ritual or spiritual, by which all the yearnings and hopes of the soul are adequately expressed —as for instance in some living religion—then we may say that the psyche is outside, and no spiritual problem, strictly speaking, exists. In consonance with this truth, the development of psychology falls entirely within the last decades, although long before that man was introspective and intelligent enough to recognize the facts that are the subject-matter of psychology.

* According to Egyptian tradition, when the dead man meets his judges in the underworld, he makes a detailed confession of the crimes he has *not* committed, but leaves unmentioned his actual sins. (*Trans.*)

The same was the case with technical knowledge. The Romans were familiar with all the mechanical principles and physical facts on the basis of which they could have constructed the steam-engine, but all that came of it was the toy made by Hero of Alexandria. There was no urgent necessity to go further. It was the division of labour and specialization in the nineteenth century which gave rise to the need to apply all available knowledge. So also a spiritual need has produced in our time our "discovery" of psychology. There has never, of course, been a time when the psyche did not manifest itself, but formerly it attracted no attention—no one noticed it. People got along without heeding it. But today we can no longer get along unless we give our best attention to the ways of the psyche.

It was men of the medical profession who were the first to notice this; for the priest is concerned only to establish an undisturbed functioning of the psyche within a recognized system of belief. As long as this system gives true expression to life, psychology can be nothing but a technical adjuvant to healthy living, and the psyche cannot be regarded as a problem in itself. While man still lives as a herd-being he has no "things of the spirit" of his own; nor does he need any, save the usual belief in the immortality of the soul. But as soon as he has outgrown whatever local form of religion he was born to—as soon as this religion can no longer embrace his life in all its fulness—then the psyche becomes something in its own right which cannot be dealt with by the measures of the Church alone. It is for this reason that we of today have a psychology founded on experience, and not upon articles of faith or the postulates of any philosophical system. The very fact that we have such a psychology is to me symptomatic of a profound convulsion of spiritual life. Disruption in the spiritual life of an age shows the same pattern as radical change in an individual. As long as all goes well and psychic energy finds its application in adequate and well-regulated ways, we are disturbed by nothing from within. No uncertainty or doubt besets us, and we *cannot* be divided against ourselves. But no sooner are one or two of the channels of psychic activity blocked, than we are reminded of a stream that is dammed up. The current flows backward to its source; the inner man wants something which the visible man does not want, and we are at war with ourselves. Only then, in this distress, do we discover the psyche; or, more precisely, we come upon something which thwarts our will, which is strange and even hostile to us, or which is incompatible with our conscious standpoint. Freud's psychoanalytic labours show this process in the clearest way. The very first thing he discovered was the existence of sexually perverse and criminal fantasies which at their face value are wholly incompatible with the conscious outlook of a civilized man. A person who was activated by them would be nothing less than a mutineer, a criminal or a madman.

We cannot suppose that this aspect of the unconscious or of the hinterland of man's mind is something totally new. Probably it has always been there, in every culture. Each culture gave birth to its destructive opposite, but no culture or civilization before our own was ever forced to take these psychic undercurrents in deadly earnest. Psychic life always found expression in a metaphysical system of some sort. But the conscious, modern man, despite his strenuous and dogged efforts to do so, can no longer refrain from acknowledging the might of psychic forces. This distinguishes our time from all others. We can no longer deny that the dark stirrings of the unconscious are effective powers—that psychic forces exist which cannot, for the present at least, be fitted in with our rational world-order. We have even enlarged our study of these forces to a science—one more proof of the earnest attention we bring to them. Previous centuries could throw them aside unnoticed; for us they are a shirt of Nessus which we cannot strip off.

The revolution in our conscious outlook, brought about by the catastrophic results of the World War, shows itself in our inner life by the shattering of our faith in ourselves and our own worth. We used to regard foreigners—the other side—as political and moral reprobates; but the modern man is forced to recognize that he is politically and morally just like anyone else. Whereas I formerly believed it to be my bounden duty to call other persons to order, I now admit that I need calling to order myself. I admit this the more readily because I realize only too well that I am losing my faith in the possibility of a rational organization of the world, that old dream of the millennium, in which peace and harmony should rule, has grown pale. The modern man's scepticism regarding all such matters has chilled his enthusiasm for politics and world-reform; more than that, it does not favour any smooth application of psychic energies to the outer world. Through his scepticism the modern man is thrown back upon himself; his energies flow towards their source and wash to the surface those psychic contents which are at all times there, but lie hidden in the silt as long as the stream flows smoothly in its course. How totally different did the world appear to mediaeval man! For him the earth was eternally fixed and at rest in the centre of the universe, encircled by the course of a sun that solicitously bestowed its warmth. Men were all children of God under the loving care of the Most High, who prepared them for eternal blessedness; and all knew exactly what they should do and how they should conduct themselves in order to rise from a corruptible world to an incorruptible and joyous existence. Such a life no longer seems real to us, even in our dreams. Natural science has long ago torn this lovely veil to shreds. That age lies as far behind as childhood, when one's own father was unquestionably the handsomest and strongest man on earth.

The modern man has lost all the metaphysical certainties of his mediaeval brother, and set up in their place the ideals of material security, general welfare and humaneness. But it takes more than an ordinary dose of optimism to make it appear that these ideals are still unshaken. Material security, even, has gone by the board, for the modern man begins to see that every step in material "progress" adds just so much force to the threat of a more stupendous catastrophe. The very picture terrorizes the imagination.

What are we to imagine when cities today perfect measures of defence against poison-gas attacks and practise them in "dress rehearsals"? We cannot but suppose that such attacks have been planned and provided for —again on the principle "in time of peace prepare for war." Let man but accumulate his materials of destruction and the devil within him will soon be unable to resist putting them to their fated use. It is well known that fire-arms go off of themselves if only enough of them are together.

An intimation of the law that governs blind contingency, which Heraclitus called the rule of *enantiodromia* (conversion into the opposite), now steals upon the modern man through the by-ways of his mind, chilling him with fear and paralysing his faith in the lasting effectiveness of social and political measures in the face of these monstrous forces. If he turns away from the terrifying prospect of a blind world in which building and destroying successively tip the scale, and if he then turns his gaze inward upon the recesses of his own mind, he will discover a chaos and a darkness there which he would gladly ignore. Science has destroyed even the refuge of the inner life. What was once a sheltering haven has become a place of terror.

And yet it is almost a relief for us to come upon so much evil in the depths of our own minds. We are able to believe, at least, that we have discovered the root of the evil in mankind. Even though we are shocked and disillusioned at first, we yet feel, because these things are manifestations of our own minds, that we hold them more or less in our own hands and can therefore correct or at least effectively suppress them. We like to assume that, if we succeeded in this, we should have rooted out some fraction of the evil in the world. We like to think that, on the basis of a widespread knowledge of the unconscious and its ways, no one could be deceived by a statesman who was unaware of his own bad motives; the very newspapers would pull him up: "Please have yourself analysed; you are suffering from a repressed father-complex."

I have purposely chosen this grotesque example to show to what absurdities we are led by the illusion that because something is psychic it is under our control. It is, however, true that much of the evil in the world is due to the fact that man in general is hopelessly unconscious, as it is also true that with increasing insight we can combat this evil at its source in ourselves. As science enables us to deal with injuries inflicted from without, so it helps us to treat those arising from within.

The rapid and world-wide growth of a "psychological" interest over the last two decades shows unmistakably that modern man has to some extent turned his attention from material things to his own subjective processes. Should we call this mere curiosity? At any rate, art has a way of anticipating future changes in man's fundamental outlook, and expressionist art has taken this subjective turn well in advance of the more general change.

This "psychological" interest of the present time shows that man expects something from psychic life which he has not received from the outer world: something which our religions, doubtless, ought to contain, but no longer do contain—at least for the modern man. The various forms of religion no longer appear to the modern man to come from within—to be expressions of his own psychic life; for him they are to be classed with the things of the outer world. He is vouchsafed no revelation of a spirit that is not of this world; but he tries on a number of religions and convictions as if they were Sunday attire, only to lay them aside again like worn-out clothes.

Yet he is somehow fascinated by the almost pathological manifestations of the unconscious mind. We must admit the fact, however difficult it is for us to understand that something which previous ages have discarded should suddenly command our attention. That there is a general interest in these matters is a truth which cannot be denied, their offence to good taste notwithstanding. I am not thinking merely of the interest taken in psychology as a science, or of the still narrower interest in the psychoanalysis of Freud, but of the widespread interest in all sorts of psychic phenomena as manifested in the growth of spiritualism, astrology, theosophy, and so forth. The world has seen nothing like it since the end of the seventeenth century. We can compare it only to the flowering of Gnostic thought in the first and second centuries after Christ. The spiritual currents of the present have, in fact, a deep affinity with Gnosticism. There is even a Gnostic church in France today, and I know of two schools in Germany which openly declare themselves Gnostic. The modern movement which is numerically most impressive is undoubtedly Theosophy, together with its continental sister, Anthroposophy; these are pure Gnosticism in a Hindu dress. Compared with these movements the interest in scientific psychology is negligible. What is striking about Gnostic systems is that they are based exclusively upon the manifestations of the unconscious, and that their moral teachings do not baulk at the shadow-side of life. Even in the form of its European revival, the Hindu *Kundalini-Yoga* shows this clearly. And as every person informed on the subject of occultism will testify, the statement holds true in this field as well.

The passionate interest in these movements arises undoubtedly from psychic energy which can no longer be invested in obsolete forms of religion. For this reason such movements have a truly religious character, even when they pretend to be scientific. It changes nothing when Rudolf Steiner calls his Anthroposophy "spiritual science," or Mrs. Eddy discovers a "Christian Science." These attempts at concealment merely show that religion has grown suspect—almost as suspect as politics and world-reform.

I do not believe that I am going too far when I say that modern man, in contrast to his nineteenth-century brother, turns his attention to the psyche with very great expectations; and that he does so without reference to any traditional creed, but rather in the Gnostic sense of religious experience. We should be wrong in seeing mere caricature or masquerade when the movements already mentioned try to give themselves scientific airs; their doing so is rather an indication that they are actually pursuing "science" or knowledge instead of the *faith* which is the essence of Western religions. The modern man abhors dogmatic postulates taken on faith and the religions based upon them. He holds them valid only in so far as their knowledge-content seems to accord with his own experience of the deeps of psychic life. He wants to know—to experience for himself. Dean Inge of St. Paul's has called attention to a movement in the Anglican Church with similar objectives.

The age of discovery has only just come to a close in our day when no part of the earth remains unexplored; it began when men would no longer *believe* that the Hyperboreans inhabited the land of eternal sunshine, but wanted to find out and to see with their own eyes what existed beyond the boundaries of the known world. Our age is apparently bent on discovering what exists in the psyche outside of consciousness. The question asked in every spiritualistic circle is: What happens when the medium has lost consciousness? Every Theosophist asks: What shall I experience at higher levels of consciousness? The question which every astrologer puts is this: What are the effective forces and determinants of my fate beyond the reach of my conscious intention? And every psychoanalyst wants to know: What are the unconscious drives behind the neurosis?

Our age wishes to have actual experiences in psychic life. It wants to experience for itself, and not to make assumptions based on the experience of other ages. Yet this does not preclude its trying anything in a hypothetical way—for instance, the recognized religions and the genuine sciences. The European of yesterday will feel a slight shudder run down his spine when he gazes at all deeply into these delvings. Not only does he consider the subject of this research all too obscure and uncanny, but even the methods employed seem to him a shocking misuse of man's finest intellectual attainments. What can we expect an astronomer to say when he is told that at least a thousand horoscopes are drawn today to one three hundred years ago? What will the educator and the advocate of philosophical enlightenment say to the fact that the world has not been freed of one single superstition since Greek antiquity? Freud himself, the founder of psychoanalysis, has thrown a glaring light upon the dirt, darkness and evil of the psychic hinterland, and has presented these things as so much refuse and slag; he has thus taken the utmost pains to discourage people from seeking anything behind them. He did not succeed, and his warning has even brought about the very thing he wished to prevent: it has awakened in many people an admiration for all this filth. We are tempted to call this sheer perversity; and we could hardly explain it save on the ground that it is not a love of dirt, but the fascination of the psyche, which draws these people.

There can be no doubt that from the beginning of the nineteenth century —from the memorable years of the French Revolution onwards—man has given a more and more prominent place to the psyche, his increasing attentiveness to it being the measure of its growing attraction for him. The enthronement of the Goddess of Reason in Nôtre Dame seems to have been a symbolic gesture of great significance to the Western world—rather like the hewing down of Wotan's oak by the Christian missionaries. For then, as at the Revolution, no avenging bolt from heaven struck the blasphemer down.

It is certainly more than an amusing coincidence that just at that time a Frenchman, Anquetil du Perron, was living in India, and, in the early eighteen-hundreds, brought back with him a translation of the *Oupnek'hat* —a collection of fifty *Upanishads*—which gave the Western world its first deep insight into the baffling mind of the East. To the historian this is mere chance without any factors of cause and effect. But in view of my medical experience I cannot take it as accident. It seems to me rather to satisfy a psychological law whose validity in personal life, at least, is complete. For every piece of conscious life that loses its importance and value—so runs the law—there arises a compensation in the unconscious. We may see in this an analogy to the conservation of energy in the physical world, for our psychic processes have a quantitative aspect also. No psychic value can disappear without being replaced by another of equivalent intensity. This is a rule which finds its pragmatic sanction in the daily practice of the psychotherapist; it is repeatedly verified and never fails. Now the doctor in me refuses point blank to consider the life of a people as something that does not conform to psychological law. A people, in the doctor's eyes, presents only a somewhat more complex picture of psychic life than the individual. Moreover, taking it the other way round, has not a poet spoken of the "nations" of his soul? And quite correctly, as it seems to me, for in one of its aspects the psyche is not individual, but is derived from the nation, from collectivity, or from humanity even. In some way or other we are part of an all-embracing psychic life, of a single "greatest" man, to quote Swedenborg.

And so we can draw a parallel: just as in me, a single human being, the darkness calls forth the helpful light, so does it also in the psychic life of a people. In the crowds that poured into Nôtre Dame, bent on destruction, dark and nameless forces were at work that swept the individual off his feet; these forces worked also upon Anquetil du Perron, and provoked an answer which has come down in history. For he brought the Eastern mind to the West, and its influence upon us we cannot as yet measure. Let us beware of underestimating it! So far, indeed, there is little of it to be seen in Europe on the intellectual surface: some orientalists, one or two Buddhist enthusiasts, and a few sombre celebrities like Madame Blavatsky and Annie Besant. These manifestations make us think of tiny, scattered islands in the ocean of mankind; in reality they are like the peaks of submarine mountain-ranges of considerable size. The Philistine believed until recently that astrology had been disposed of long since, and was something that could be safely laughed at. But today, rising out of the social deeps, it knocks at the doors of the universities from which it was banished some three hundred years ago. The same is true of the thought of the East; it takes root in the lower social levels and slowly grows to the surface. Where did the five or six million Swiss francs for the Anthroposophist temple at Dornach come from? Certainly not from one individual. Unfortunately there are no statistics to tell us the exact number of avowed Theosophists today, not to mention the unavowed. But we can be sure that there are several millions of them. To this number we must add a few million Spiritualists of Christian or Theosophic leanings.

Great innovations never come from above; they come invariably from below; just as trees never grow from the sky downward, but upward from the earth, however true it is that their seeds have fallen from above. The upheaval of our world and the upheaval in consciousness is one and the same. Everything becomes relative and therefore doubtful. And while man, hesitant and questioning, contemplates a world that is distracted with treaties of peace and pacts of friendship, democracy and dictatorship, capitalism and Bolshevism, his spirit yearns for an answer that will allay the turmoil of doubt and uncertainty. And it is just people of the lower social levels who follow the unconscious forces of the psyche; it is the much-derided, silent folk of the land—those who are less infected with academic prejudices than great celebrities are wont to be. All these people, looked at from above, present mostly a dreary or laughable comedy; and yet they are as impressively simple as those Galileans who were once called blessed. Is it not touching to see the refuse of man's psyche gathered together in compendia a foot thick? We find recorded in *Anthropophyteia* with scrupulous care the merest babblings, the most absurd actions and the wildest fantasies, while men like Havelock Ellis and Freud have dealt with the like matters in serious treatises which have been accorded all scientific honours. Their reading public is scattered over the breadth of the civilized, white world. How are we to explain this zeal, this almost fanatical worship of repellent things? In this way: the repellent things belong to the psyche, they are of the substance of the psyche and therefore as precious as fragments of manuscript salvaged from ancient ruins. Even the secret and noisome things of the inner life are valuable to modern man because they serve his purpose. But what purpose?

Freud has prefixed to his *Interpretation of Dreams* the citation: *Flectere si nequeo superos Acheronta movebo*—"If I cannot bend the gods on high, I will at least set Acheron in uproar." But to what purpose?

The gods whom *we* are called to dethrone are the idolized values of our conscious world. It is well known that it was the love-scandals of the ancient deities which contributed most to their discredit; and now history is repeating itself. People are laying bare the dubious foundations of our belauded virtues and incomparable ideals, and are calling out to us in triumph: "There are your man-made gods, mere snares and delusions tainted with human baseness—whited sepulchres full of dead men's bones and of all uncleanness." We recognize a familiar strain, and the Gospel words, which we never could make our own, now come to life again.

I am deeply convinced that these are not vague analogies. There are too many persons to whom Freudian psychology is dearer than the Gospels, and to whom the Russian Terror means more than civic virtue. And yet all these people are our brothers, and in each of us there is at least *one* voice which seconds them—for in the end there is a psychic life which embraces us all.

The unexpected result of this spiritual change is that an uglier face is put upon the world. It becomes so ugly that no one can love it any longer—we cannot even love ourselves—and in the end there is nothing in the outer world to draw us away from the reality of the life within. Here, no doubt, we have the true significance of this spiritual change. After all, what does Theosophy, with its doctrines of *karma* and reincarnation, seek to teach except that this world of appearance is but a temporary health-resort for the morally unperfected? It depreciates the present-day world no less radically than does the modern outlook, but with the help of a different technique; it does not vilify our world, but grants it only a relative meaning in that it promises other and higher worlds. The result is in either case the same.

I grant that all these ideas are extremely "unacademic," the truth being that they touch modern man on the side where he is least conscious. Is it again a mere coincidence that modern thought has had to come to terms with Einstein's relativity theory and with ideas about the structure of the atom which lead us away from determinism and visual representation? Even physics volatilizes our material world. It is no wonder, then, in my opinion, if the modern man falls back upon the reality of psychic life and expects from it that certainty which the world denies him.

But spiritually the Western world is in a precarious situation—and the danger is greater the more we blind ourselves to the merciless truth with illusions about our beauty of soul. The Occidental burns incense to himself, and his own countenance is veiled from him in the smoke. But how do we strike men of another colour? What do China and India think of us? What feelings do we arouse in the black man? And what is the opinion of all those whom we deprive of their lands and exterminate with rum and venereal disease?

I have a Red Indian friend who is the governor of a pueblo. When we were once speaking confidentially about the white man, he said to me: "We don't understand the whites; they are always wanting something—always restless—always looking for something. What is it? We don't know. We can't understand them. They have such sharp noses, such thin, cruel lips, such lines in their faces. We think they are all crazy."

My friend had recognized, without being able to name it, the Aryan bird of prey with his insatiable lust to lord it in every land—even those that concern him not at all. And he had also noted that megalomania of ours which leads us to suppose, among other things, that Christianity is the only truth, and the white Christ the only Redeemer. After setting the whole East in turmoil with our science and technology, and exacting tribute from it, we send our missionaries even to China. The stamping out of polygamy by the African missions has given rise to prostitution on such a scale that in Uganda alone twenty thousand pounds sterling is spent yearly on preventatives of venereal infection, not to speak of the moral consequences, which have been of the worst. And the good European pays his missionaries for their edifying achievements! No need to mention also the story of suffering in Polynesia and the blessings of the opium trade.

That is how the European looks when he is extricated from the cloud of his own moral incense. No wonder that to unearth buried fragments of psychic life we have first to drain a miasmal swamp. Only a great idealist like Freud could devote a lifetime to the unclean work. This is the beginning of our psychology. For us acquaintance with the realities of psychic life could start only at this end, with all that repels us and that we do not wish to see.

But if the psyche consisted for us only of evil and worthless things, no power in the world could induce a normal man to pretend to find it attractive. This is why people who see in Theosophy nothing but regrettable intellectual superficiality, and in Freudian psychology nothing but sensationalism, prophesy an early and inglorious end for these movements. They overlook the fact that they derive their force from the fascination of psychic life. No doubt the passionate interest that is aroused by them may find other expressions; but it will certainly show itself in these forms until they are replaced by something better. Superstition and perversity are after all one and the same. They are transitional or embryonic stages from which new and riper forms will emerge.

Whether from the intellectual, the moral or the aesthetic viewpoint, the undercurrents of the psychic life of the West present an uninviting picture. We have built a monumental world round about us, and have slaved for it with unequalled energy. But it is so imposing only because we have spent upon the outside all that is imposing in our natures—and what we find when we look within must necessarily be as it is, shabby and insufficient.

I am aware that in saying this I somewhat anticipate the actual growth of consciousness. There is as yet no general insight into these facts of psychic life. Westerners are only on the way to a recognition of these facts, and for quite understandable reasons they struggle violently against it. Of course Spengler's pessimism has exerted some influence, but this has been safely confined to academic circles. As for psychological insight, it always trespasses upon personal life, and therefore meets with personal resistances and denials. I am far from considering these resistances meaningless; on the contrary I see in them a healthy reaction to something which threatens destruction. Whenever relativism is taken as a fundamental and final principle it has a destructive effect. When, therefore, I call attention to the dismal undercurrents of the psyche, it is not in order to sound a pessimistic note; I wish rather to emphasize the fact that the unconscious has a strong attraction not only for the sick, but for healthy, constructive minds as well —and this in spite of its alarming aspect. The psychic depths are nature, and nature is creative life. It is true that nature tears down what she has herself built up—yet she builds it once again. Whatever values in the visible world are destroyed by modern relativism, the psyche will produce their equivalents. At first we cannot see beyond the path that leads downward to dark and hateful things—but no light or beauty will ever come from the man who cannot bear this sight. Light is always born of darkness, and the sun never yet stood still in heaven to satisfy man's longing or to still his fears. Does not the example of Anquetil du Perron show us how psychic life survives its own eclipse? China hardly believes that European science and technology are preparing her ruin. Why should we believe that we must be destroyed by the secret, spiritual influence of the East?

But I forget that we do not yet realize that while we are turning upside down the material world of the East with our technical proficiency, the East with its psychic proficiency is throwing our spiritual world into confusion. We have never yet hit upon the thought that while we are overpowering the Orient from without, it may be fastening its hold upon us from within. Such an idea strikes us as almost insane, because we have eyes only for gross material connections, and fail to see that we must lay the blame for the intellectual confusion of our middle class at the doors of Max Müller, Oldenberg, Neumann, Deussen, Wilhelm and others like them. What does the example of the Roman Empire teach us? After the conquest of Asia Minor, Rome became Asiatic; even Europe was infected by Asia, and remains so today. Out of Cilicia came the Mithraic cult—the religion of the Roman army—and it spread from Egypt to fog-bound Britain. Need I point to the Asiatic origin of Christianity?

We have not yet clearly grasped the fact that Western Theosophy is an amateurish imitation of the East. We are just taking up astrology again, and that to the Oriental is his daily bread. Our studies of sexual life, originating in Vienna and in England, are matched or surpassed by Hindu teachings on this subject. Oriental texts ten centuries old introduce us to philosophical relativism, while the idea of indetermination, newly broached in the West, furnishes the very basis of Chinese science. Richard Wilhelm has even shown me that certain complicated processes discovered by analytical psychology are recognizably described in ancient Chinese texts. Psychoanalysis itself and the lines of thought to which it gives rise—surely a distinctly Western development—are only a beginner's attempt compared to what is an immemorial art in the East. . . .

And now we must ask a final question. Is what I have said of the modern man really true, or is it perhaps the result of an optical illusion? There can be no doubt whatever that the facts I have cited are wholly irrelevant contingencies in the eyes of many millions of Westerners, and seem only regrettable errors to a large number of educated persons. But I may ask: What did a cultivated Roman think of Christianity when he saw it spreading among the people of the lowest classes? The biblical God is still a living person in the Western world—as living as Allah beyond the Mediterranean. One kind of believer holds the other an ignoble heretic, to be pitied and tolerated if he cannot be changed. What is more, a clever European is convinced that religion and such things are good enough for the masses and for women, but are of little weight compared to economic and political affairs.

So I am refuted all along the line, like a man who predicts a thunderstorm when there is not a cloud in the sky. Perhaps it is a storm beneath the horizon that he senses—and it may never reach us. But what is significant in psychic life is always below the horizon of consciousness, and when we speak of the spiritual problem of modern man we are dealing with things that are barely visible—with the most intimate and fragile things—with bowers that open only in the night. In daylight everything is clear and tangible; but the night lasts as long as the day, and we live in the night-time also. There are persons who have bad dreams which even spoil their days for them. And the day's life is for many people such a bad dream that they long for the night when the spirit awakes. I even believe that there are nowadays a great many such people, and this is why I maintain that the spiritual problem of modern man is much as I have presented it. I must plead guilty, indeed, to the charge of one-sidedness, for I have not mentioned the modern spirit of commitment to a practical world about which everyone has much to say because it lies in such full view. We find it in the ideal of internationalism or supernationalism which is embodied in the League of Nations and the like; and we find it also in sport and, very expressively, in the cinema and in jazz music.

These are certainly characteristic symptoms of our time; they show unmistakably how the ideal of humanism is made to embrace the body also. Sport represents an exceptional valuation of the human body, as does also modern dancing. The cinema, on the other hand, like the detective story, makes it possible to experience without danger all the excitement, passion and desirousness which must be repressed in a humanitarian ordering of life. It is not difficult to see how these symptoms are connected with the psychic situation. The attractive power of the psyche brings about a new self-estimation—a re-estimation of the basic facts of human nature. We can hardly be surprised if this leads to the rediscovery of the body after its long depreciation in the name of the spirit. We are even tempted to speak of the body's revenge upon the spirit. When Keyserling sarcastically singles out the chauffeur as the culture-hero of our time, he has struck, as he often does, close to the mark. The body lays claim to equal recognition; like the psyche, it also exerts a fascination. If we are still caught by the old idea of an antithesis between mind and matter, the present state of affairs means an unbearable contradiction; it may even divide us against ourselves. But if we can reconcile ourselves with the mysterious truth that spirit is the living body seen from within, and the body the

outer manifestation of the living spirit—the two being really one—then
we can understand why it is that the attempt to transcend the present
level of consciousness must give its due to the body. We shall also see
that belief in the body cannot tolerate an outlook that denies the body
in the name of the spirit. These claims of physical and psychic life are so
pressing compared to similar claims in the past, that we may be tempted
to see in this a sign of decadence. Yet it may also signify a rejuvenation, for
as Hölderlin says:

> Danger itself
> Fosters the rescuing power.[1]

What we actually see is that the Western world strikes up a still more
rapid tempo—the American tempo—the very opposite of quietism and
resigned aloofness. An enormous tension arises between the opposite
poles of outer and inner life, between objective and subjective reality.
Perhaps it is a final race between ageing Europe and young America;
perhaps it is a desperate or a wholesome effort of conscious man to cheat
the laws of nature of their hidden might and to wrest a yet greater, more
heroic victory from the sleep of the nations. This is a question which history will answer.

In coming to a close after so many bold assertions, I would like to
return to the promise made at the outset to be mindful of the need for
moderation and caution. Indeed, I do not forget that my voice is but one
voice, my experience a mere drop in the sea, my knowledge no greater
than the visual field in a microscope, my mind's eye a mirror that reflects
a small corner of the world, and my ideas—a subjective confession.

---

[1] *Wo Gefahr ist,*
   Wächst das Rettende auch.   (Hölderlin.)

E
The Voices of Science

SIGMUND FREUD

Psycho-Analysis

I have already insisted that the eighteenth-century Enlightenment and many of us, its heirs, have taken natural science as the exemplar of how the human mind ought to go to work on all questions it asks itself. There is a very strong world-view—call it Enlightened, positivist, naturalistic, materialist, secularistic, humanist, none of these names are more than sect names—which gives, in the works of its various practitioners, whole varied sets of answers to the questions of man's condition. I propose in this subsection to give a few samples of these scientific faiths, or prescriptions for our mental security. I begin with the greatest and most influential, that of Sigmund Freud (1856–1938). Once more, no one of Freud's writings shows him whole. For the relatively little-known piece I give here I claim only that it is his own attempt to put in his own words in his maturity (in 1926, when he was 70) a brief outline of his work. This account of psychoanalysis was written by Freud for a supplement to the Encyclopaedia Britannica. A few minor changes made by the editors of the Encyclopaedia are noted in footnotes to this extract from Volume XX of the English translation of the standard works of Freud. You will note the scientist's austerity and simplicity of style—an interesting contrast with the essay of Jung's above.

SINCE PSYCHO-ANALYSIS WAS NOT MENTIONED IN THE ELEVENTH EDITION of the *Encyclopaedia Britannica,* it is impossible to restrict this account to its advances since 1910. The more important and the more interesting portion of its history lies in the period before that date.[1]

From Sigmund Freud, *Complete Psychological Works.* Translated from the German by James Strachey in collaboration with Anna Freud. Vol. XX (1925-1926), The Question of Lay Analysis (London: The Hogarth Press, 1959), pp. 263-270.

[1] [This paragraph was omitted in the *Encyclopaedia Britannica.* It is explained by the fact that Freud was writing a contribution to the three supplementary volumes issued in 1926, which were merely intended to bring the eleventh edition, published in 1910-11, up to date.]

PREHISTORY

In the years 1880-2 a Viennese physician, Dr. Josef Breuer (1842-1925), discovered a new procedure by means of which he relieved a girl, who was suffering from severe hysteria, of her many and various symptoms. The idea occurred to him that the symptoms were connected with impressions which she had received during a period of agitation while she was nursing her sick father. He therefore induced her, while she was in a state of hypnotic somnambulism, to search for these connections in her memory and to live through the "pathogenic" scenes once again without inhibiting the affects that arose in the process. He found that when she had done this the symptom in question disappeared for good.

This was at a date before the investigations of Charcot and Pierre Janet into the origin of hysterical symptoms, and Breuer's discovery was thus entirely uninfluenced by them. But he did not pursue the matter any further at the time, and it was not until some ten years later that he took it up again in collaboration with Sigmund Freud. In 1895 they published a book, *Studies on Hysteria,* in which Breuer's discoveries were described and an attempt was made to explain them by the theory of *"catharsis."* According to that hypothesis, hysterical symptoms originate through the energy of a mental process being withheld from conscious influence and being diverted into bodily innervation (*"conversion"*). A hysterical symptom would thus be a substitute for an omitted mental act and a reminiscence of the occasion which should have given rise to that act. And, on this view, recovery would be a result of the liberation of the affect that had gone astray and of its discharge along a normal path (*"abreaction"*). Cathartic treatment gave excellent therapeutic results, but it was found that they were not permanent and that they were not independent of the personal relation between the patient and the physician. Freud, who later proceeded with these investigations by himself, made an alteration in their technique, by replacing hypnosis by the method of free association. He invented the term "psycho-analysis," which in the course of time came to have two meanings: (1) a particular method of treating nervous disorders and (2) the science of unconscious mental processes, which has also been appropriately described as "depth-psychology."

SUBJECT-MATTER OF PSYCHO-ANALYSIS

Psycho-analysis finds a constantly increasing amount of support as a therapeutic procedure, owing to the fact that it can do more for its patients[2] than any other method of treatment. The principal field of its application is in the milder neuroses—hysteria, phobias and obsessional states; and in malformations of character and sexual inhibitions or abnor-

---

[2] [In the *Encyclopaedia Britannica:* "for certain classes of patients."]

malities it can also bring about marked improvements or even recoveries. Its influence upon dementia praecox and paranoia is doubtful; on the other hand, in favourable circumstances it can cope with depressive states, even if they are of a severe type.

In every instance the treatment makes heavy claims upon both the physician and the patient: the former requires a special training and must devote a long period of time to exploring the mind of each patient, while the latter must make considerable sacrifices, both material and mental. Nevertheless, all the trouble involved is as a rule rewarded by the results. Psycho-analysis does not act as a convenient panacea (*"cito, tute, ju-cunde"*) for psychological disorders. On the contrary, its application has been instrumental in making clear for the first time the difficulties and limitations in the treatment of such affections. For the moment it is only in Berlin and Vienna that there are voluntary institutions which make psycho-analytic treatment accessible to the wage-earning classes.[3]

The therapeutic influence of psycho-analysis depends on the replacement of unconscious mental acts by conscious ones and is effective within the limits of that factor. The replacement is effected by overcoming internal resistances in the patient's mind. The future will probably attribute far greater importance to psycho-analysis as the science of the unconscious than as a therapeutic procedure.

Psycho-analysis, in its character of depth-psychology, considers mental life from three points of view: the dynamic, the economic and the topographical.

From the first of these standpoints, the *dynamic* one, psycho-analysis derives all mental processes (apart from the reception of external stimuli) from the interplay of forces, which assist or inhibit one another, combine with one another, enter into compromises with one another, etc. All of these forces are originally in the nature of *instincts;* thus they have an organic origin. They are characterized by possessing an immense (somatic) store of power (*"the compulsion to repeat"*); and they are represented mentally as images or ideas with an affective charge. In psycho-analysis, no less than in other sciences, the theory of the instincts is an obscure subject. An empirical analysis leads to the formulation of two groups of instincts: the so-called "ego-instincts," which are directed towards self-preservation, and the "object-instincts," which are concerned with relations to an external object. The social instincts are not regarded as elementary or irreducible. Theoretical speculation leads to the suspicion that there are two fundamental instincts which lie concealed behind the manifest ego-instincts and object-instincts: namely (*a*) Eros, the instinct which strives for ever closer union, and (*b*) the instinct of destruction, which leads towards the dissolution of what is living. In psycho-analysis the manifestation of the force of Eros is given the name *"libido."*

[3] [In the *Encyclopaedia Britannica* this sentence was transferred to the end of the article.]

From the *economic* standpoint psycho-analysis supposes that the mental representatives of the instincts have a charge (*cathexis*)[4] of definite quantities of energy, and that it is the purpose of the mental apparatus to hinder any damming-up of these energies and to keep as low as possible the total amount of the excitations with which it is loaded. The course of mental processes is automatically regulated by the *"pleasure-unpleasure principle"*; and unpleasure is thus in some way related to an increase of excitation and pleasure to a decrease. In the course of development the original pleasure principle undergoes a modification with reference to the external world, giving place to the *"reality principle,"* in accordance with which the mental apparatus learns to postpone the pleasure of satisfaction and to tolerate temporarily feelings of unpleasure.

Topographically, psycho-analysis regards the mental apparatus as a compound instrument, and endeavours to determine at what points in it the various mental processes take place. According to the most recent psycho-analytic views, the mental apparatus is composed of an *"id,"* which is the repository of the instinctual impulses, of an *"ego,"* which is the most superficial portion of the id and one which has been modified by the influence of the external world, and of a *"super-ego,"* which develops out of the id, dominates the ego and represents the inhibitions of instinct that are characteristic of man. The quality of consciousness, too, has a topographical reference; for processes in the id are entirely unconscious, while consciousness is the function of the ego's outermost layer, which is concerned with the perception of the external world.

At this point two observations may be in place. It must not be supposed that these very general ideas are presuppositions upon which the work of psycho-analysis depends. On the contrary, they are its latest conclusions and are "open to revision."[5] Psycho-analysis is founded securely upon the observation of the facts of mental life; and for that very reason its theoretical superstructure is still incomplete and subject to constant alteration. Secondly, there is no reason for surprise that psycho-analysis, which was originally no more than an attempt at explaining pathological mental phenomena, should have developed into a psychology of normal mental life. The justification for this arose with the discovery that the dreams and mistakes ["parapraxes," such as slips of the tongue, etc.] of normal men have the same mechanism as neurotic symptoms.

The first task of psycho-analysis was the elucidation of nervous disorders. The analytic theory of the neuroses is based on three cornerstones: the recognition of (1) *"repression,"*[6] of (2) the importance of the sexual instinct and of (3) *"transference."*[6]

(1) There is a force in the mind which exercises the functions of a

[4] [The word is in English in the original. This seems to be the only instance in which Freud himself used this English equivalent of the German *"Besetzung."*]

[5] [In English in the original. In the *Encyclopaedia Britannica* the phrase is preceded by the words "in every respect."]

[6] [In English in the original.]

censorship, and which excludes from consciousness and from any influence upon action all tendencies which displease it. Such tendencies are described as "repressed." They reman unconscious; and if one attempts to bring them into the patient's consciousness one provokes a *"resistance."*[6] These repressed instinctual impulses, however, have not always become powerless. In many cases they succeed in making their influence felt in the mind by circuitous paths, and the indirect or substitutive satisfactions of repressed impulses thus achieved are what constitute neurotic symptoms.

(2) For cultural reasons the most intense repression falls upon the sexual instincts; but it is precisely in connection with them that repression most easily miscarries, so that neurotic symptoms are found to be substitutive satisfactions of repressed sexuality. The belief that in man sexual life begins only at puberty is incorrect. On the contrary, signs of it can be detected from the beginning of extra-uterine existence; it reaches a first culminating point at or before the fifth year ("early period"), after which it is inhibited or interrupted ("latency period") until the age of puberty, which is the second climax of its development. This diphasic onset of sexual development seems to be distinctive of the genus Homo. All experiences during the first period of childhood are of the greatest importance to the individual, and in combination with his inherited sexual constitution form the dispositions for the subsequent development of character and disease. It is wrong to make sexuality coincide with "genitality." The sexual instincts pass through a complicated course of development, and it is only at the end of it that the "primacy of the genital zones" is attained. Before this there are a number of "pregenital" organizations of the libido—points at which it may become "fixated" and to which, in the event of subsequent repression, it will return (*"regression"*). The infantile fixations of the libido are what determine the form of any later neurosis. Thus the neuroses are to be regarded as inhibitions in the development of the libido. There are no specific causes of nervous disorders; the question whether a conflict finds a healthy solution or leads to a neurotic inhibition of function depends upon quantitative considerations.

The most important conflict with which a small child is faced is his relation to his parents, the *"Oedipus Complex"*; it is in attempting to grapple with this problem that those destined to suffer from a neurosis habitually come to grief. The reactions against the instinctual demands of the Oedipus complex are the source of the most precious and socially important achievements of the human mind; and this holds true not only in the life of individuals but probably also in the history of the human species as a whole. The super-ego, too, the moral agency which dominates the ego, has its origin in the process of overcoming the Oedipus complex.

(3) By *"transference"* is meant a striking peculiarity of neurotics. They develop towards their physician emotional relations, both of an affectionate and hostile character, which are not based upon the actual

situation but are derived from their relations to their parents (the Oedipus complex). Transference is a proof of the fact that adults have not overcome their former childish dependence; it coincides with the force which has been named "suggestion"; and it is only by learning to make use of it that the physician is enabled to induce the patient to overcome his internal resistances and do away with his repressions. Thus psycho-analytic treatment acts as a second education of the adult, as a corrective to his education as a child.

Within this narrow compass it has been impossible to mention many matters of the greatest interest, such as the *"sublimation"* of instincts, the part played by *symbolism,* the problem of *"ambivalence,"* etc. Nor has there been space to allude to the applications of psycho-analysis, which originated, as we have seen, in the sphere of medicine, to other departments of knowledge (such as Social Anthropology, the Study of Religion, Literary History and Education) where its influence is constantly increasing. It is enough to say that psycho-analysis, in its character of the psychology of the deepest, unconscious mental acts, promises to become the link between Psychiatry and all of these other branches of mental science.

THE EXTERNAL HISTORY OF PSYCHO-ANALYSIS

The beginnings of psycho-analysis may be marked by two dates: 1895, which saw the publication of Breuer and Freud's *Studies on Hysteria,* and 1900, which saw that of Freud's *Interpretation of Dreams.* At first the new discoveries aroused no interest either in the medical profession or among the general public. In 1907 the Swiss psychiatrists, under the leadership of E. Bleuler and C. G. Jung, began to concern themselves in the subject; and in 1908 there took place at Salzburg a first meeting of adherents from a number of different countries. In 1909 Freud and Jung were invited to America by G. Stanley Hall to deliver a series of lectures on psycho-analysis at Clark University, Worcester, Mass. From that time forward interest grew rapidly in Europe; it expressed itself, however, in a very forcible rejection of the new teachings—a rejection which often showed an unscientific colouring.

The reasons for this hostility were to be found, from the medical point of view, in the fact that psycho-analysis lays stress upon psychical factors, and from the philosophical point of view, in its assuming as an underlying postulate the concept of unconscious mental activity; but the strongest reason was undoubtedly the general disinclination of mankind to concede to the factor of sexuality the importance that is assigned to it by psycho-analysis. In spite of this widespread opposition, however, the movement in favour of psycho-analysis was not to be checked. Its adherents formed themselves into an International Association, which passed successfully through the ordeal of the World War, and at the present time (1925) comprises local groups in Vienna, Berlin, Budapest, London, Switzerland,

Holland, Moscow and Calcutta, as well as two in the United States. There
are three periodicals representing the views of these societies: the *Inter-
nationale Zeitschrift für Psycho-analyse, Imago* (which is concerned with
the application of psycho-analysis to non-medical fields of knowledge), and
the *International Journal of Psycho-Analysis.*

During the years 1911-13 two former adherents, Alfred Adler, of
Vienna, and C. G. Jung, of Zurich, seceded from the psycho-analytic
movement and founded schools of thought of their own, which, in view
of the general hostility to psycho-analysis, could be certain of a favourable reception, but which remained scientifically sterile.[7] In 1921 Dr. M.
Eitingon founded in Berlin the first public psycho-analytic clinic and
training-school, and this was soon followed by a second in Vienna.

[7] [The last clause was omitted in the *Encyclopaedia Britannica*.]

JOHN LANGDON-DAVIES

Science, the New Religion

The New Age of Faith *(1925) by the English publicist John Langdon-Davies (1897–   ) is no doubt a now pretty well forgotten best seller and book-club success. But it says with clarity and firmness something that seems most pertinent to our purpose in this book—that there is in the minds of many, a religious faith in science.*

The pillar of faith in Science as religion rests even in our age of existentialism, Freud, and alienation, on a simple belief in Evolution as Progress. The natural scientists have explained for us the long, slow but reasonably well-understood processes that have produced homo sapiens *on a planet that earlier could do no better than trilobites or dinosaurs. The social scientists continue to try hard, but with less success, to explain that now man is here on earth, there is a process of* Cultural Evolution *which will result in a peaceful, righteous, happy society on a planet that once could do no better than produce aggressive, unhappy, if affluent, societies in a few small areas, leaving the rest of its surface to equally aggressive and unrighteous but far from affluent ones. And—this is very important —this Cultural Evolution will, must, get its job done in no time, just a few seconds in terms of the time scale of* organic *evolution. An absurd faith? But did not one of the greatest exponents of an earlier faith, the patristic theologian Tertullian, write* certum est quia impossibile est *(it is certain because it is impossible), a dictum commonly and effectively simplified into: I believe* because *it's absurd? It is true that we are now employing a terminology somewhat different from that of natural science, but these believers in Evolution-Progress are priests, not scientists. The reader who wishes to sample a fine contemporary statement of their doctrines will find one in Leslie A. White,* The Science of Culture: A Study of Man and Civilization *(New York: Farrar Straus, 1949), and again in effectively condensed form in a work edited by two disciples of Professor—I nearly wrote, Reverend—White, M. D. Sahlins and E. R. Service, eds.,* Evolution and Culture *(Ann Arbor: University of Michigan Press, 1960).*

John Langdon-Davies, *The New Age of Faith*, (Garden City, N. Y.: Garden City Publishing Co., 1925), pp. 13-27.

IN THIS BOOK TWO RELATED QUESTIONS ARE DISCUSSED; FIRST, WHAT HAS science to tell us about human society? and second, how far will human beings listen to what science has to tell them? The second of these two questions is really the more important, because unless human beings are willing to follow the dictates of organized common sense, as we have been taught to call science, it does not really matter at all, so far as social progress is concerned, how many truths are dug up by diligent scientists: the truths may glitter like diamonds in the light of the scientist's brain, they will be as invisible as a black cat in the dark room of ordinary human striving.

It is common sense, for example, that too much candy is bad for children, but the chances are that the emotional check of fear will stop a child's overeating long before any knowledge of physiology. Common sense about physiology, it is true, is behind the parent's sharp "don't eat any more, or I'll—," and it is just possible that society may say, "I am a child, or rather a large group of children and I will appoint a number of scientists, specialists, experts and busybodies to be my foster parents, armed with organized common sense to tell me what is good for me"; it is unlikely, but it is possible; and a small number of people exist who think it would be desirable. And so we shall consider in this book what would be likely to happen if those foster parents were appointed. We will also examine the potential foster parents' claim to a great and good scientific knowledge about social needs and aspirations.

And again we will ask if organizing common sense does not sometimes end in organizing it away altogether; if the self-styled scientists, who want to save society, have not in some instances every sense except common sense; and in other instances no sense at all. We shall have to look into each of these questions.

But first of all, why "The New Age of Faith"? Because we are going to deal only with the problems of the present day; with the question, can science save our present social life; with the needs, aspirations, difficulties and perplexities of A. D. 1925:—and no other age has been so noticeably an age of faith as the twentieth century. The distinguishing feature of our age is that we take more things on faith than any other age has ever done. True, we do not all of us believe with the fervour of our ancestors in God or the Devil; for in the direction of orthodox religion, the sun seems to be nearing a very red western horizon; but in spite of this we believe in more things, for which our reason cannot account, than did any monk in a medieval cloister. Moreover our faith is not merely a Sunday one; it is called into action in all the petty uses of our daily lives, and never more so than at the moments when our ancestors could afford to be most rational.

Look, for instance, at the medieval farmer going to market on his mare; he knew well enough the forces which propelled him thither: he knew not only how to control them but why certain acts would produce certain results: thus, if he wanted to go faster he had but to use the same sort of stimulus which would appeal to any boy, had often appealed to himself, indeed, as boy and man; namely, the stimulus of the stick. And because humanity is animal the farmer understood, emotionally as well as intellectually, the reaction of the mare to the stimulus: he understood that he got to market faster because mare and boy alike do not want an unpleasant stimulus repeated. Further than this there was free will also; if the mare chanced to be a donkey, and valued her obstinacy more than she feared its consequences, she could choose to endure a second and similar stimulus rather than mend her pace. No mystery here, no exercise of faith on the part of the farmer; for it has never been free-will but always determinism, which has seemed a mystery to mankind and in need of an explanation.

Now, compare with this picture, our own fate to-day: we are in a Ford car; we want to go faster, our foot presses the mechanism and we shoot forward; why? Honest folks say, "heaven knows"; meaning that they shoot forward in response to an act of faith: less honest folk will be learned and mechanical; use long names and clothe their ignorance, more or less considerable, behind them; admit, if pressed, that behind such long words looms the unknown and for them unknowable. Unless, in short, we understand the mechanics of motor cars in general, and of Ford cars in particular, we do not really know why the stimulus produces the result, we know nothing about the connections between our foot and the force it controls; or at least what we do know of this connection is precisely what was once believed about the connections between a prayer and the deity: —pressing down the lever is a prayer to an unknown force, made in the perfect faith that the force must answer the prayer.

All that has happened, indeed, is that the faith has increased to a certainty; for while the old prayers were not very often answered, and the forces to which they were offered had free will and used it, our new gods, though still unknown it is true, are gods in chains. And this is the triumph of faith, so to enslave the god, that the god is bound to obey. This is perfect faith, the faith which presses down a lever to command an unknown force, knowing that the force, however unknown, must obey. And this faith is present everywhere in our New Age of Faith; it permeates every detail of our lives, producing its own type of outlook to life itself and forcing, as we shall see, even science and scientists to bow beneath its yoke. Let us, then, consider a few more examples.

Once upon a time the housewife could get first, light, then, heat from a simple enough source, her tinderbox; nothing more easily to be understood than this; no need for faith, nor for the mental attitude which a constant exercise of faith produces. But look at the same good lady to-day; what housewife understands the forces which she sets free, when she presses a button and summons electricity out of the gloom? What percentage of the population can follow the force or forces all the way from the glowing electric stove to the distant dynamo and beyond? Plainly a larger percentage has to take it all on faith; and the pressing of the electric button is just such another prayer as the pressing of a Ford car control.

True there was a greater amount of superstition of a sort in the older age of faith: the housewife, for instance, believed in fairies, who would do her work while she slept, in exchange for a few little kindnesses on her part; a belief which declined hundreds of years ago, as Bishop Corbett tells us in his great poem:—

> "Farewell rewards and fairies,
> Good housewives now may say;
> For now foul sluts in dairies
> Do fare as well as they. . . ."

But even if the fairies did not exist, at least the idea of them was more rational than the idea of the electric laundry washer, which fills their place:—what is electricity? We take it on faith, whereas we took the fairies on illusion.

The farmer, too, greased the post against which the mare had grazed her leg, in order that the graze should heal more rapidly: this was superstition, no doubt, but the farmer was wrong only because in some way or other he imagined that the post was human and its matter susceptible to kind treatment; whereas to-day heaven, literally, only knows what the physicist thinks the post is made of, and though we need not consider the physicist superstitious when he talks of atoms and electrons, it is only by faith that we can accept his statements. This, therefore, is an age of faith; not necessarily, however, of superstition, for faith and superstition are not the same.

Science has done more than this towards undermining our reason however; for it has taken the very ground from under our feet, and substituted a nightmare myriad of atomic solar systems, so much the reverse of solid, they tell us, that if the central sun in each were as big as the old-fashioned one, which still gives us light, in spite of the scientists, the outer planets within the atom would be as far away as, or farther away than, Neptune. What chance of justifying that view of this grassy bank except by faith!

Of course somebody's reason comprehends it, discovers its truth indeed, but not our own; and we cannot forget that somebody's reason has discovered a number of things, which did not turn out satisfactory in the long run: faith in our brother's reason, indeed, is in no way different from faith in God: it may be the wrong brother, just as it may be the wrong god.

In short, if we think for a moment of the world in which we live; a world of X-rays, or radium and radio, of telephones and telegrams, of magnets and magnetos, of light and heat, as they are now conceived, of atoms, protons and electrons, of finite and unbounded space, of every sort of unknown and invisible force;—how many of us can see such a world as credible by logic and reason alone? How much of all this must we not rather take on faith? Some people it is true can claim all these as the daily companions of their intellectual walks abroad, just as Enoch could claim to "walk with God" and therefore presumably, to know him otherwise than by faith; but we can most of us make no such claims. Ninety-nine men out of every hundred approach science and its works in the same spirit and through the same gateway as their ancestors approached God and His. This is why we may call the twentieth century a New Age of Faith.

And the name is not merely an idle whim; it is used deliberately to underline something, to emphasize certain tendencies, which need to be underlined and emphasized. Men are to-day more than ever in danger of thinking that they use their reason; that they are guided and actuated by rational processes; that the days of blind faith and unsupported guesses are over, and that now society moves more and more towards scientific deliberateness and a spirit of "organized common sense." Now the truth is that even the modern attitude towards science is irrational to a degree which it would be hard to overestimate. What has happened to produce this result?

In the first place, we know that when white men have first appeared among savages, the latter have often mistaken them for gods and worshipped them and their attainments. Now among us to-day the gap in intellectual attainment and knowledge between the average man and the scientific specialist is far greater than the similar gap between a white explorer and a savage; and the average man has taken a leaf from the savage's book—to use a metaphor strictly impossible, seeing that the savage is unlettered—and exalts the scientist onto a high pedestal, whence he must receive the barbaric homage of people who do not really understand or appreciate either his achievements or his possibilities.

In the second place, men are born worshippers and only become reasonable and rational after a long discipline; but the modern passion for democratic education has given countless masses the implements with which to approach science without the discipline to approach it intelligently. And so the halls of science have been thronged with hosts who are only fit to worship and wonder, not to criticise and understand.

And in the third place, life itself, for all our wealth and comfort, has become so unsatisfying, and the future, unconsciously at least, so menacing, that we need a new religion for moral support, and have found it in science.

It is because these three tendencies are so important for the understanding of the relations between science and society that it seemed worth while expressing them in the title of this book: for many of the phenomena which we shall observe will be more clearly understood if we start by emphasizing the humanistic side of science. Too often people put science outside the universe of human emotions and desires, and raise it up on a pole like a cold-blooded super-reptile, even as the serpent in the wilderness was raised up; a rational entity apart and above. Just below, but still reptilian in coldness of blood and lack of emotion, are placed the scientists, a strange group of statues, immovable above the flood of human futility and emotionalism. Science and scientists in this sense are companion in this: they simply do not exist.

Science, it is true, is the child of reason; but it has to enter into the popular mind by the gateway of emotion: unless it has what the movie public calls a heart appeal, it might as well not exist. This is a painful and unpalatable truth, which scientists in particular will find it difficult to accept: nevertheless, when we study science in its social aspects, we must begin by accepting its limitations; we must not hope to find pure reason; we can at best hope not to find pure prejudice. Science, as we have said, is like an explorer suddenly come among savages; it is surrounded by men born to worship, and worship it must force itself to accept. "There is one science, and Haeckel is its prophet," has always been the typical formula used by the super-faithful in face of opposition.

There is another characteristic of the New Age of Faith, which must be mentioned in these introductory sentences, and that is the amazing humility of the average man in the presence of science or scientists. Humility is the very hall-mark of religion: religion began, so students of social origins tell us, with the birth of humility; when the savage stopped commanding mountains to move, and in a humbler spirit begged some deity to move them for him. Just such a humility characterizes the New Age of Faith, a humility born of the average man's sense of his own ignorance and insufficiency joined to an admiration of the priest of science, which comes from quite a different cause. The priest of science, like all other priests the world over, tends in most cases to be ill paid for his services; his office has its drawbacks. Among more primitive races the priesthood was hedged about with so many restrictions and pains and penalties, that it took a man of character and idealism to accept them all; with us the restrictions and pains and penalties are less picturesque than with savages, but they exist, usually in the form of low salaries or no salary at all; and as the average man thinks first of all of his salary, he has a great admiration for the scientist, who is willing to work for so little. Thus, humility and admiration on the part of the average man have set a considerable halo about the head of the scientist; and halos are dangerous above all to the reason as they are apt to obscure clearness of vision with their haze. Moreover the man in the street assumes that no one who professes and calls himself a scientist could possibly be anything else but noble and wise; for otherwise how would he be willing to undergo the penalties, the low salary, the long education?

Alas! the man in the street, like man anywhere else, seldom learns by experience, or he would know by this time that charlatans covet halos so much that they will always pay a heavy price for the privilege of wearing one. Moreover the art of eating one's cake and having it is known even to the priests of the lowly Toda tribe in India, who enjoy the privileges of their office and yet avoid the penalties often in a most ingenious manner: thus when complete segregation from women is demanded of them, and they are enjoined to "turn their back on every woman," they obey the letter of the law and receive their dulcineas wearing their garments back to front. Hence it does not follow that a Toda priest is a man of high ideals and truly called to his vocation; and the New Age of Faith also is remarkable, for the enormous number of pseudo-scientists masquerading in borrowed plumes, having sworn to turn their back on the lucrative and easy Error, yet entertaining her with clothes reversed and thereby preserving a semblance of scientific truth. We shall examine these gentlemen of easy virtue later. We have them always with us because of the working of the laws of supply and demand, just as Billy Sundays and Bryans supply a demand for a religion adulterated in order to make it palatable. . . .

The New Age of Faith. Such then is the subject matter of our book; the interplay between science, a body of ascertained truth, and man, who wants that body to contain something different from what it does contain. Man wants practical results to-day; science offers a method which holds some promise of results in a distant future: man, being a baby, will not be happy till he gets what he wants, and to stop his crying pseudo-scientists dish up a meretricious substitute for the truth. If man eats too much of it, he is likely to be sick; and at any rate he will be better for a purge. This book is a purge.

We begin with the collapse of an idol: the idol is the one worshipped by scientists a generation ago; it had an optimistic look about it, until it fell off its pedestal; but now, though glued together as well as possible, it has a pessimistic look. We begin by discussing why this should be and we then describe the different ways in which man has hoped hitherto to control his destiny: can we find any hope, we ask, of his controlling it in the future by scientific knowledge of heredity, eugenics, and biology in general?

In the next part we attack various authors who have misled the public about the facts of science on these subjects, and then in the final part we state the cold facts for which science can really vouch, offering them as a basis for the understanding and solution of the social problems dependent on them.

An so in the end we ask once more if man can save himself through scientific knowledge from what looks sometimes like an inevitable doom. Whatever we may think about this problem, we will probably decide that man must first be saved from the pseudo-scientists.

So much by way of introduction; one thing remains to be said. Though facts are facts, more or less, even on scientific subjects points of view are individual and subjective. If they are not precisely individual, they are conditioned to a large extent by the atmosphere in which a man has lived; it will therefore not be irrelevant to remind the reader that this is a book written by a European for Americans to read.

Now, there are certain broad lines along which all Europeans tend to think differently, or perhaps it would be more accurate to say, feel differently, at the present time, from all Americans: that is not of course anything more than a generalisation, crude indeed, but with a vital truth in it. Though it would horrify Dr. Lothrop Stoddard, for example, it is nevertheless true that in some ways an Englishman might even find Spain and the Spanish view of life less foreign to him than America and the American view of life. How is this so?

In one of his remarkable essays Miguel de Unamuno, who is never tired in other places of contrasting Spain and Europe, says: "If I am to tell you the truth, it hurts and wounds me to see men marching as confidently as if they marched on solid ground, some confident in the prejudices and anti-prejudices of their religious beliefs, others slaves of science, other slaves of ignorance, slaves all of them. I would have them doubt, I would have them suffer, above all I would have them despair, I would have them be men and not mere partisans of the party of progress."

In those words we have perhaps, the expression not of a Spaniard in contrast to a European, not of the average man anywhere—he is uniformly optimistic in all latitudes—but of the European post-war intelligentsia as contrasted with the American. Though we may not wish you to share such an outlook, we do sometimes wish that you could understand why some people have it. That you cannot, is because Europe is poverty-stricken and disillusioned, while America is prosperous and optimistic. And the same contrasted plight may cause misunderstanding between the readers and writer of this book, also. Let us see how.

When the contemporary scientist turns his attention to the problem of human social destiny, he tends to a feeling of depression and gloom; but in America especially, that pseudo-science, which exists only to give the paying public what it wants, is, in some quarters, noticeably optimistic. One American club secretary, for example, described the address of a popular lecturer as having "a fine spirit of optimism about it that charmed the members, while it appealed to their solid business sense in no uncertain way" and the possession of this businesslike optimism made of its owner, "a regular fellow, with a he-man's grasp of modern problems."

If we in Europe were also prosperous and happy we would certainly voice something of the same idea; in fact we did so during the latter part of the Victorian age, when we were convinced that everything was for the best in the best of all possible worlds; but as we are not prosperous and happy to-day, we can revenge ourselves by pointing out the mote in our brother's eye.

This mote would seem to be the application of business methods and ideals to science: optimism appeals to solid business sense, therefore by all means let us have optimism at the expense of scientific accuracy and common sense; that is the salesman's attitude to science.

Optimism, of course, has its place, and that place is business, for the salesman must believe in his product so that he may convince everybody that it is better than all rivals; but in science only the pseudo-scientist deals in such methods. The real scientist is first concerned with the truth, and scarcely at all with its effect upon people's nerves and prejudices; and since he builds for all eternity and not for time, he would rather admit present ignorance, than have a false truth inevitably discovered in the distant future.

And the public must learn to wait for the truth until it has been discovered, though it is often so much more easy to read the scientific romances of the Sunday magazine section. Moreover, the fact that distracted Europe once, not so long ago, had very much the optimistic club secretary's outlook on science, suggests that that outlook is not in itself a sufficient safeguard against future discords; and therefore there is something to be said for a devil's advocate of a less certain and dogmatic belief in progress; of the need for reserved judgments and admitted ignorance on many matters; and of the point of view expressed once more in the works of Miguel de Unamuno: "And since man is naturally intractable, and does not habitually thirst for the truth, and after being preached at for four hours usually returns to his inveterate habits, these busy inquirers, if they chance to read this, will return to me with the question: 'Well, but what solutions do you offer?' And I will tell them, once and for all, that if it is solutions they want, they can go to the shop opposite, for I do not deal in the article. My earnest desire has been, is and will be that those who read me should think and meditate on fundamental things, and it has never been to furnish them with thoughts ready-made."

To quote this at the beginning of so small a book must be humbly, as an ideal attempted, and not as a task accomplished.

ALEXIS CARREL

The Remaking of Man

In Man, the Unknown *(1935) I resurrect another now-forgotten best seller. Its author, Alexis Carrel (1873–1944) was a French biologist who came to the United States in 1905 and joined the Rockefeller Institute in 1909, where he had a distinguished career in research, winning a Nobel Prize in 1912. His ideas on man's fate were firm, and for a scientist mildly unorthodox. But he is an interesting example of the scientist turned philosopher-preacher-publicist. His enthusiasm for eugenics is now pretty much dated, and his whole tone is very far from that of Kenneth Keniston. Here is a Utopia indeed.*

A CHOICE MUST BE MADE AMONG THE MULTITUDE OF CIVILIZED HUMAN beings. We have mentioned that natural selection has not played its part for a long while. That many inferior individuals have been conserved through the efforts of hygiene and medicine. But we cannot prevent the reproduction of the weak when they are neither insane nor criminal. Or destroy sickly or defective children as we do the weaklings in a litter of puppies. The only way to obviate the disastrous predominance of the weak is to develop the strong. Our efforts to render normal the unfit are evidently useless. We should, then, turn our attention toward promoting the optimum growth of the fit. By making the strong still stronger, we could effectively help the weak. For the herd always profits by the ideas and inventions of the élite. Instead of leveling organic and mental inequalities, we should amplify them and construct greater men.

We must single out the children who are endowed with high potentialities, and develop them as completely as possible. And in this manner give to the nation a non-hereditary aristocracy. Such children may be found in all classes of society, although distinguished men appear more frequently in distinguished families than in others. The descendants of the founders of American civilization may still possess the ancestral

From Alexis Carrel, *Man, the Unknown* (New York: Harper & Brothers, 1935), pp. 296-308, 321-322.

qualities. These qualities are generally hidden under the cloak of degeneration. But this degeneration is often superficial. It comes chiefly from education, idleness, lack of responsibility and moral discipline. The sons of very rich men, like those of criminals, should be removed while still infants from their natural surroundings. Thus separated from their family, they could manifest their hereditary strength. In the aristocratic families of Europe there are also individuals of great vitality. The issue of the Crusaders is by no means extinct. The laws of genetics indicate the probability that the legendary audacity and love of adventure can appear again in the lineage of the feudal lords. It is possible also that the offspring of the great criminals who had imagination, courage, and judgment, of the heroes of the French or Russian Revolutions, of the high-handed business men who live among us, might be excellent building stones for an enterprising minority. As we know, criminality is not hereditary if not united with feeble-mindedness or other mental or cerebral defects. High potentialities are rarely encountered in the sons of honest, intelligent, hard-working men who have had ill luck in their careers, who have failed in business or have muddled along all their lives in inferior positions. Or among peasants living on the same spot for centuries. However, from such people sometimes spring artists, poets, adventurers, saints. A brilliantly gifted and well-known New York family came from peasants who cultivated their farm in the south of France from the time of Charlemagne to that of Napoleon.

Boldness and strength suddenly appear in families where they have never before been observed. Mutations may occur in man, just as they do in other animals and in plants. Nevertheless, one should not expect to find among peasants and proletarians many subjects endowed with great developmental possibilities. In fact, the separation of the population of a free country into different classes is not due to chance or to social conventions. It rests on a solid biological basis, the physiological and mental peculiarities of the individuals. In democratic countries, such as the United States and France, for example, any man had the possibility during the last century of rising to the position his capacities enabled him to hold. Today, most of the members of the proletarian class owe their situation to the hereditary weakness of their organs and their mind. Likewise, the peasants have remained attached to the soil since the Middle Ages, because they possess the courage, judgment, physical resistance, and lack of imagination and daring which render them apt for this type of life. These unknown farmers, anonymous soldiers, passionate lovers of the soil, the backbone of the European nations, were, despite their great qualities, of a weaker organic and psychological constitution than the medieval barons who conquered the land and defended it victoriously against all invaders. Originally, the serfs and the chiefs were really born serfs and chiefs. Today, the weak should not be artificially maintained in wealth and power. It is imperative that social classes should be synonymous with biological classes. Each individual must rise or sink to the level for which he is fitted by the quality of his tissues and of his soul. The social ascension of those who possess the best organs and the best minds should be aided. Each one must have his natural place. Modern nations will save themselves by developing the strong. Not by protecting the weak.

Eugenics is indispensable for the perpetuation of the strong. A great race must propagate its best elements. However, in the most highly civilized nations reproduction is decreasing and yields inferior products. Women voluntarily deteriorate through alcohol and tobacco. They subject themselves to dangerous dietary regimens in order to obtain a conventional slenderness of their figure. Besides, they refuse to bear children. Such a defection is due to their education, to the progress of feminism, to the growth of short-sighted selfishness. It also comes from economic conditions, nervous unbalance, instability of marriage, and fear of the burden imposed upon parents by the weakness or precocious corruption of children. The women belonging to the oldest stock, whose children would, in all probability, be of good quality, and who are in a position to bring them up intelligently, are almost sterile. It is the newcomers, peasants and proletarians from primitive European countries, who beget large families. But their offspring are far from having the value of those who came from the first settlers of North America. There is no hope for an increase in the birth rate before a revolution takes place in the habits of thinking and living, and a new ideal rises above the horizon.

Eugenics may exercise a great influence upon the destiny of the civilized races. Of course, the reproduction of human beings cannot be regulated as in animals. The propagation of the insane and the feeble-minded, nevertheless, must be prevented. A medical examination should perhaps be imposed on people about to marry, as for admission into the army or the navy, or for employees in hotels, hospitals, and department stores. However, the security given by medical examination is not at all positive. The contradictory statements made by experts before the courts of justice demonstrate that these examinations often lack any value. It seems that eugenics, to be useful, should be voluntary. By an appropriate education, each one could be made to realize what wretchedness is in store for those who marry into families contaminated by syphilis, cancer, tuberculosis, insanity, or feeble-mindedness. Such families should be considered by young people at least as undesirable as those which are poor. In truth, they are more dangerous than gangsters and murderers. No criminal causes so much misery in a human group as the tendency to insanity. Voluntary eugenics is not impossible. Indeed, love is supposed to blow as freely as the wind. But the belief in this peculiarity of love is shaken by the fact that many young men fall in love only with rich girls, and vice versa. If love is capable of listening to money, it may also submit to a consideration as practical as that of health. None should marry a human being suffering from hidden hereditary defects. Most of man's misfortunes are due to his organic and mental constitution and, in a large measure, to his heredity. Obviously, those who are afflicted with a heavy ancestral burden of insanity, feeble-mindedness, or cancer should not marry. No human being has the right to bring misery to another human being. Still less, that of procreating children destined to misery. Thus, eugenics asks for the sacrifice of many individuals. This necessity, with which we meet for the second time, seems to be the expression of a natural law. Many living beings are sacrificed at every instant by nature to other living beings. We know the social and individual importance of renunciation. Nations have always paid the highest honors to those who gave up their lives to save their country. The concept of sacrifice, of its absolute social necessity, must be introduced into the mind of modern man.

Although eugenics may prevent the weakening of the strong, it is insufficient to determine their unlimited progress. In the purest races, individuals do not rise beyond a certain level. However, among men, as among thoroughbred horses, exceptional beings appear from time to time. The determining factors of genius are entirely unknown. We are incapable of inducing a progressive evolution of germ-plasm, of bringing about by appropriate mutations the appearance of superior men. We must be content with facilitating the union of the best elements of the race through education and certain economic advantages. The progress of the strong depends on the conditions of their development and the possibility left to parents of transmitting to their offspring the qualities which they have acquired in the course of their existence. Modern society must, therefore, allow to all a certain stability of life, a home, a garden, some friends. Children must be reared in contact with things which are the expression of the mind of their parents. It is imperative to stop the transformation of the farmer, the artisan, the artist, the professor, and the man of science into manual or intellectual proletarians, possessing nothing but their hands or their brains. The development of this proletariat will be the everlasting shame of industrial civilization. It has contributed to the disappearance of the family as a social unit, and to the weakening of intelligence and moral sense. It is destroying the remains of culture. All forms of the proletariat must be suppressed. Each individual should have the security and the stability required for the foundation of a family. Marriage must cease being only a temporary union. The union of man and woman, like that of the higher anthropoids, ought to last at least until the young have no further need of protection. The laws relating to education, and especially to that of girls, to marriage, and divorce should, above all, take into account the interest of children. Women should receive a higher education, not in order to become doctors, lawyers, or professors, but to rear their offspring to be valuable human beings.

The free practice of eugenics could lead not only to the development of stronger individuals, but also of strains endowed with more endurance, intelligence, and courage. These strains should constitute an aristocracy, from which great men would probably appear. Modern society must promote, by all possible means, the formation of better human stock. No financial or moral rewards should be too great for those who, through the wisdom of their marriage, would engender geniuses. The complexity of our civilization is immense. No one can master all its mechanisms. However, these mechanisms have to be mastered. There is need today of men of larger mental and moral size, capable of accomplishing such a task. The establishment of a hereditary biological aristocracy through voluntary eugenics would be an important step toward the solution of our present problems.

Although our knowledge of man is still very incomplete, nevertheless it gives us the power to intervene in his formation, and to help him unfold all his potentialities. To shape him according to our wishes, provided these wishes conform to natural laws. Three different procedures are at our disposal. The first comprises the physical and chemical factors, which cause definite changes in the constitution of the tissues, humors, and mind. The second sets in motion, through proper modifications in the environment, the adaptive mechanisms regulating all human activities. The third makes use of psychological factors, which influence organic development or induce the individual to build himself up by his own efforts. The handling of these agencies is difficult, empirical, and uncertain. We are not as yet well acquainted with them. They do not limit their effects to a single aspect of the individual. They act slowly, even during childhood and youth. But they always produce profound modifications of the body and of the mind.

The physical and chemical peculiarities of the climate, the soil, and the food can be used as instruments for modeling the individual. Endurance and strength generally develop in the mountains, in the countries where seasons are extreme, where mists are frequent and sunlight rare, where hurricanes blow furiously, where the land is poor and sown with rocks. The schools devoted to the formation of a hard and spirited youth should be established in such countries, and not in southern climates where the sun always shines and the temperature is even and warm. Florida and the French Riviera are suitable for weaklings, invalids, and old people, or normal individuals in need of a short rest. Moral energy, nervous equilibrium, and organic resistance are increased in children when they are trained to withstand heat and cold, dryness and humidity, burning sun and chilling rain, blizzards and fog—in short, the rigors of the seasons in northern countries. The resourcefulness and hardihood of the Yankee were probably due, in a certain measure, to the harshness of a climate where, under the sun of Spain, there are Scandinavian winters. But these climatic factors have lost their efficiency since civilized men are protected from inclemencies of the weather by the comfort and the sedentariness of their life.

The effect of the chemical compounds contained in food upon physiological and mental activities is far from being thoroughly known. Medical opinion on this point is of little value, for no experiments of sufficient duration have been made upon human beings to ascertain the influence of a given diet. There is no doubt that consciousness is affected by the quantity and the quality of the food. Those who have to dare, dominate, and create should not be fed like manual workers, or like contemplative monks who, in the solitude of monasteries, endeavor to repress in their inner self the turmoil of the secular passions. We have to discover what food is suitable for human beings vegetating in offices and factories. What chemical substances could give intelligence, courage, and alertness to the inhabitants of the new city. The race will certainly not be improved merely by supplying children and adolescents with a great abundance of milk, cream, and all known vitamines. It would be most useful to search for new compounds which, instead of uselessly increasing the size and weight of the skeleton and of the muscles, would bring about nervous strength and mental agility. Perhaps some day a scientist will discover how to manufacture great men from ordinary children, in the same manner that bees transform a common larva into a queen by the special food which they know how to prepare. But it is probable that no chemical agent alone is capable of greatly improving the individual. We must assume that the superiority of any organic and mental form is due to a combination of hereditary and developmental conditions. And that, during development, chemical factors are not to be separated from psychological and functional factors.

We know that adaptive processes stimulate organs and functions, that the more effective way of improving tissues and mind is to maintain them in ceaseless activity. The mechanisms, which determine in certain organs a series of reactions ordered toward an end, can easily be set in motion. As is well known, a muscular group develops by appropriate drill. If we wish to strengthen not only the muscles, but also the apparatuses responsible for their nutrition and the organs which enable the body to sustain a prolonged effort, exercises more varied than classical sports are indispensable. These exercises are the same as were practiced daily in a more primitive life. Specialized athletics, as taught in schools and universities, do not give real endurance. The efforts requiring the help of muscles, vessels, heart, lungs, brain, spinal cord, and mind—that is, of the entire organism—are necessary in the construction of the individual. Running over rough ground, climbing mountains, wrestling, swimming, working in the forests and in the fields, exposure to inclemencies, early moral responsibility, and a general harshness of life bring about the harmony of the muscles, bones, organs, and consciousness.

In this manner, the organic systems enabling the body to adapt itself to the outside world are trained and fully developed. The climbing of trees or rocks stimulates the activity of the apparatuses regulating the composition of plasma, the circulation of the blood, and the respiration. The organs responsible for the manufacture of red cells and hemoglobin are set in motion by life at high altitudes. Prolonged running and the necessity of eliminating acid produced by the muscles release processes extending over the entire organism. Unsatisfied thirst drains water from the tissues. Fasting mobilizes the proteins and fatty substances from the organs. Alternation from heat to cold and from cold to heat sets at work the multiple mechanisms regulating the temperature. The adaptive systems may be stimulated in many other ways. The whole body is improved when they are brought into action. Ceaseless work renders all integrating apparatuses stronger, more alert, and better fitted to carry out their many duties.

The harmony of our organic and psychological functions is one of the most important qualities that we may possess. It can be acquired by means varying according to the specific characteristics of each individual. But it always demands a voluntary effort. Equilibrium is obtained in a large measure by intelligence and self-control. Man naturally tends toward the satisfaction of his physiological appetites and artificial needs, such as a craving for alcohol, speed, and ceaseless change. But he degenerates when he satisfies these appetites completely. He must, then, accustom himself to dominate his hunger, his need of sleep, his sexual impulses, his laziness, his fondness for muscular exercise, for alcohol, etc. Too much sleep and food are as dangerous as too little. It is first by training and later by a progressive addition of intellectual motives to the habits gained by training, that individuals possessing strong and well-balanced activities may be developed.

A man's value depends on his capacity to face adverse situations rapidly and without effort. Such alertness is attained by building up many kinds of reflexes and instinctive reactions. The younger the individual, the easier is the establishment of reflexes. A child can accumulate vast treasures of unconscious knowledge. He is easily trained, incomparably more so than the most intelligent shepherd dog. He can be taught to run without tiring, to fall like a cat, to climb, to swim, to stand and walk harmoniously, to observe everything exactly, to wake quickly and completely, to speak several languages, to obey, to attack, to defend himself, to use his hands dexterously in various kinds of work, etc. Moral habits are created in an identical manner. Dogs themselves learn not to steal. Honesty, sincerity, and courage are developed by the same procedures as those used in the formation of reflexes—that is, without argument, without discussion, without explanation. In a word, children must be conditioned.

Conditioning, according to the terminology of Pavlov, is nothing but the establishment of associated reflexes. It repeats in a scientific and modern form the procedures employed for a long time by animal trainers. In the construction of these reflexes, a relation is established between an unpleasant thing and a thing desired by the subject. The ringing of a bell, the report of a gun, even the crack of a whip, become for a dog the equivalent of the food he likes. A similar phenomenon takes place in man. One does not suffer from being deprived of food and sleep in the course of an expedition into an unknown country. Physical pain and hardship are easily supported if they accompany the success of a cherished enterprise. Death itself may smile when it is associated with some great adventure, with the beauty of sacrifice, or with the illumination of the soul that becomes immersed in God. . . .

The day has come to begin the work of our renovation. We will not establish any program. For a program would stifle living reality in a rigid armor. It would prevent the bursting forth of the unpredictable, and imprison the future within the limits of our mind.

We must arise and move on. We must liberate ourselves from blind technology and grasp the complexity and the wealth of our own nature. The sciences of life have shown to humanity its goal and placed at its disposal the means of reaching it. But we are still immersed in the world created by the sciences of inert matter without any respect for the laws of our development. In a world that is not made for us, because it is born from an error of our reason and from the ignorance of our true self. To such a world we cannot become adapted. We will, then, revolt against it. We will transform its values and organize it with reference to our true needs. Today, the science of man gives us the power to develop all the potentialities of our body. We know the secret mechanisms of our physiological and mental activities and the causes of our weakness. We know how we have transgressed natural laws. We know why we are punished, why we are lost in darkness. Nevertheless, we faintly perceive through the mists of dawn a path which may lead to our salvation.

For the first time in the history of humanity, a crumbling civilization is capable of discerning the causes of its decay. For the first time, it has at its disposal the gigantic strength of science. Will we utilize this knowledge and this power? It is our only hope of escaping the fate common to all great civilizations of the past. Our destiny is in our hands. On the new road, we must now go forward.

LANCELOT LAW WHYTE

The Search for Understanding

*Lancelot Law Whyte (1896–　　) is a well-known English scientist, inter-
ested, as many scientists are, in the questions of man's condition. In this
first chapter of his* Accent on Form, *Whyte sets very clearly and soberly
in historical as well as psychological perspective the kind of master problem we are concerned with in this book.*

*Curiously, there is an undertone of cybernetics theory running through
this chapter. The notion of man's capabilities as having been implicit in
his condition all along, somewhat connotes the new biological discoveries
of the triggering mechanism in the genetic cell. And the particular way
Whyte puts his theory of the human faculty for progressive discovery
rather suggests the programming aspects of automation.*

*Perhaps the familiar interpretation of creation in terms of cause and
effect may give way to a new concept whereby the universe may be seen as
one vast control and communications process, equipped with feedback
mechanism and with its programme set at the moment of creation. In this
view the old argument of whether the solar system is running down will
lose its meaning, since the important question will not be energy itself but
the means of communication by which energy is transferred, or the proces-
sing of information and goal direction. This concept, strangely enough, is
more consonant with the mystic writings than with the traditional pragmatic
scientific approach. If all things exist in one giant programme, and come
into being in time because of a built-in triggering mechanism, and all units
of the machine are permanent, then the favorite apocalyptic phrase "was
and is forevermore" begins to take on meaning. Whyte may consider this
speculation rather a liberty on his thinking, but it should not be surprising
to find that modern scientists may soon construct a world-view based on
the principles of cybernetics.*

Lancelot Law Whyte, *Accent on Form*. Edited by Ruth N. Anshen, *World Perspectives*, II (New York: Harper & Brothers, 1954), pp. 1-13.

Mankind Is Capable of Acquiring Understanding
But Is Still Abysmally Ignorant

WHAT KIND OF UNIVERSE IS THIS INTO WHICH WE ARE BORN?

Is it the creation of an intelligible God, whose purpose in putting us here we must try to discover?

Or is the universe an assembly of atoms following laws of chance, and mankind an accident?

Or does the universe display an order in which every part is harmoniously related to the whole, if we could but see it?

No one knows the answer to these questions. Nor do we know how much it is possible for man to know.

The mystery of the existence of the universe may forever lie beyond human comprehension. We are part of a cosmic process which cannot be compared with anything else, since it is unique.

Yet it may be useful to pose absolute questions and to consider what kind of answers might be given to them. The human mind has advanced because men dared to ask questions that seemed strange because they pointed toward new problems. No limit can be set today to what the human mind may achieve tomorrow. Speculations on the nature of the universe may prove as fertile as the first attempts of Homo to fabricate a tool.

Moreover no one can live without either conscious convictions or unconscious working assumptions regarding himself and the universe. A latent metaphysic molds every human life. Those who claim they have none still work on rules of some kind. We are all conditioned by our experience.

I have tried to express here my picture of the universe and of man. It is based on scientific knowledge interpreted and adjusted in the light of a personal judgment. For science is incomplete and its present ideas are unlikely to be final.

The first step is to discover what meaning we can give to the question: What kind of universe is this?

We can ask of science: Do such fundamental laws of nature as are already known tell us anything about its basic character? Do the known laws go so deep as to reveal the actual form of the order of nature?

The answer is that we cannot be sure. The known laws are in many respects imperfect and incomplete, and beneath them may lie some deeper and more general order than that which has already been discovered.

So let us put our question in a narrower form and ask: What can science say about the fundamental laws of the three realms of matter, of life, and of mind, or about their relations?

The answer is: nothing *fundamental* yet, on any of these points. There is no satisfactory theory of the fundamental physical particles, of biological organization, or of mental processes, or of their interrelations.

This may be regarded as rather disappointing fifteen generations after the foundation of exact science by Galileo and Kepler. Many particular facts and partial rules are known, but no truly fundmental principles have yet been discovered, if by that we mean principles which throw a clear light on particles, organisms, or minds, or on their relations. The known laws are probably only special cases of deeper laws still to be identified. On these great issues science is as yet silent, and no living person knows anything for certain. So far we know nothing fundamental about the universe into which we are born.

There are moments when the depth of human ignorance is frightening. We then find ourselves looking into a bottomless abyss and we have to call on our last reserves of courage. What is cancer, that murders the body of a friend; or psychosis, that can destroy the mind; or death, that is for the individual the apparent end to everything? Other moments are less horrible, but perhaps lie even heavier on the conscience and will. When the gravest decisions have to be made, how little knowledge we have of the proper criteria to use! In every realm the deeper our need, the more profound our ignorance proves to be.

I remember two occasions on which this sense of human ignorance came to me with special force, once in a personal and once in a social situation.

The first was when a close friend revealed features which I felt to be nearly psychotic. The friend seemed to be living in a world so far from reality that I was scared. Circumstances prevented me from passing on the responsibility to a psychiatrist. I became occupied with the problem: How did this condition develop? What roles had heredity, parental influence, and personal experience played? I collected what I thought might be the most relevant facts, but I was still unable to gain enlightenment and I fell back on the question: How far could scientific knowledge be of help? From this I reached a further question which startled me: In the entire history of mankind had anyone yet recorded and interpreted the reasonably full story of one human being, showing how all the main physical and mental characteristics had developed?

I realized that if the proper study of mankind is man, this question was of unique importance. But the answer was: No. This had not even been attempted, in fact we had not the knowledge which it would require. There were some rather detailed studies of genius; there were stories of "identical" twins; there were medical and psychological case histories;* and there were some fairly detailed conventional biographies. But what I wanted was not yet feasible. All the biological and human sciences put together did not let us understand even the main features of the story of one human person. The art or science of biography had scarcely begun. For example, we had no idea how a set of genes actually influenced the development of adult anatomy and physiology; nor did we know why one child was generous and courageous and its brother or sister mean and cruel.

So I could achieve neither intuitive nor scientific understanding of my

---

* Perhaps the psychobiological studies of the American psychologist Adolph Meyer come nearest to what I was looking for.

friend. . . . But it did not matter. By divine fiat, good luck, or organic vitality—how can I claim to know which?—my friend's life grew richer and the frightening symptoms passed away.

The other occasion was in London during the winter of 1941-42. Europe had fallen; the most hideous mania in the history of the West had seized power; the outlook for Britain was grim; the spiritual values of Western civilization had for long been declining and then in wartime were nearly forgotten.

I asked myself, was there any rhyme or reason in this? Was it indeed the decline of the West? Was there any philosophy of history or any scientific interpretation of the biological and social development of man that could throw light on these crises of civilizations? No, there was not. Toynbee, for example, neglected the biological background of human development and the profound impact of science. The human race was here even more ignorant than in relation to physical and mental disease. No man had ever lived who could estimate the significance of his own culture in the over-all story of mankind. One could not even hope for any assurance in a period so short as one lifetime. . . . This situation led to no happy ending; the frightening symptoms are still present.

On both of these occasions I had felt the vast hopelessness of human ignorance. And yet my mind rebelled at the idea that anything that could happen was completely beyond comprehension. I never doubted that there existed an order of nature which included man and was progressively accessible to human intelligence. It followed that all human distress occurred within the natural order and must in some manner be transformed, though not necessarily removed, by a deeper understanding of that order. The point was to discover in any situation the *optimum line of development,* even if that was only to relax and to seem to do nothing. What mattered was to reduce the unnecessary frustrations and to enrich life, even if that could only be done by accepting the inescapability in every individual life of bitter experience.

Later I came to realize that it was no good taking particular historical situations too seriously. It was ridiculously early to condomn man as a failure. Homo sapiens was the kind of species that could not live properly in accordance with its capacities without a way of thinking appropriate to the particular stage of development which it had reached at any time. The present attitude of the West was the result of a long development through the Renaissance, the Reformation, the Enlightenment, and the growth of science and technology, and the modern world had not yet found a system of convictions appropriate to an age of science. A naïve reliance on an incomplete and unbalanced science was no substitute for what Christianity had meant to an earlier time. To the biologist or anthropologist the malaise of the twentieth century was in no way surprising. Homo sapiens was a biologically immature species that had not yet fully developed the latent capacities of its brain, and might be going through a crisis which was an inescapable phase of its social development. We should try to understand rather than to condemn without proper trial.

If one is able to accept this long view, it is human understanding rather than human ignorance which is astonishing. The remarkable fact is not that no man has ever lived who has possessed the kind of fundamental knowledge we so badly need, but that the race has managed to achieve any understanding at all, and how much it has gained.

Here the facts are certainly extraordinary. The interbreeding species Homo sapiens, marked by an average hereditary equipment similar to our own and by characteristic social habits, emerged from its ancestral Homo stock between four hundred and one hundred thousand years ago, and may only have developed the faculty for articulated speech around fifty thousand years back. Making allowance for prior types of Homo that disappeared we can regard it as certain that *neither five hundred thousand years ago, nor at any earlier time, was there either on the earth or elsewhere in the solar system any organic species possessing any knowledge based on the units of thought which we call ideas.*

At that time there was no articulated speech, or spoken sounds broken up into meaningful units; no thought communicated by dividing it into distinct and significant parts and separating it from immediate organic situations; no systematic conceptual understanding. Many highly complex systems of symbolic communication were already in use, for example in the dance of bees and the song of birds. But these did not involve units of thought detached from immediate activities. There was as yet no germ of intellectual understanding of the relatedness of things in an objective world. The potentiality for this was already present, say four hundred thousand years ago, in the hereditary equipment of the emerging species Homo sapiens, but what was to prove the outstanding characteristic of mankind had not yet been manifested.

Then very slowly, though perhaps in minor rushes and relapses, starting from this absolute ignorance and without the guidance of any conscious aim, the human species began its incomparable adventure of discovery and self-discovery. Discovery of external nature went hand in hand with the discovery of human faculties, the arts of action developing in parallel with the art of thought, the entire process resulting in the progressive maturing of capacities which had been latent in the human hereditary make-up. From prehuman gabbling, gesture, and dance there developed—perhaps starting rather abruptly a hundred or fifty thousand years ago—first language, then script, and finally the culture that blossoms in Newton and Beethoven.

This is no less than a miracle. For this cumulative process of the realization of human potentialities took place without conscious design, as part of the pervasive continuity of natural process. In some sense which has still to be made clear natural law guided the development of man. This flowering of latent capacities must have been implicit in the condition of man all along, though it required a favorable environment to bring it out.

We may consider this a miracle, but it simply proves the richness of the "unconscious knowledge" and biological assets of the species, or of the laws which governed the process.

I shall call the essence of this characteristically human process which works mainly cumulatively and unconsciously, *dis-covery,* including under that term the simultaneous and interacting aspects of the external discovery of nature and the internal discovery of the latent capacities of human nature. All creation, imagination, and invention are aspects of this dis-covering of the new.

This historical fact of human discovery is more astonishing and more significant than human ignorance. For without the fact and the experience of past discovery we could not even have the idea of ignorance. Our awareness of our ignorance is evidence of our faculty for discovery. The abyss is not bottomless, we have made a start.

Even when human ignorance was still absolute there was present in organic nature a formative process, a surplus vitality, a creative, exploratory, or inventive instinct which, when the time came, would shape in human brains and minds ideas that would bring enlightenment. This organic faculty for achieving understanding from ignorance is the one unchallengeably favorable fact about man. He can grown in understanding.

This fact is neither trite nor trivial. None of the world religions has adequately recognized the supreme importance of this human faculty for progressive discovery. Science does, and on this account alone can speak with authority when these long issues of the human past on this planet are in question. In his ability to grow in understanding man seems to touch the divine, and yet here it is unconscious processes which provide the foundation, and science which takes up the service and protection of this great faculty. What irony that the unconscious and science should be the servants of the noblest element in man!

We know very little about the unconscious mental processes which provide the basis for the creative, imaginative, and inventive faculties. Like many other organic processes they work, and perhaps even work best, without our knowing how. But it is clear that no arbitrary accidents or merely occasional *tours de force* can account for the inexorable continuity which, transcending all rhythms and setbacks, has led from the earliest members of the species to where we are now. And since the individuals who achieved the myriad steps knew little or nothing about what they were doing, the main credit must go to unconscious processes.

In retrospect we can observe that in its scarcely conscious search for understanding the species invented for itself one supremely valuable kind of instrument: *ideas.* Their value was not discovered as the result of any deliberate investigation. Ideas arose as a residue of barely conscious mental processes, doubtless associated with processes occurring in the brain, but not yet understood. All we can say is that some kind of formative process in the brain shapes new forms of activity and response within the plastic records of past experience, and that in certain circumstances these new unified forms or clarified patterns become the object of our attention, that is, become conscious as "ideas."

This view of ideas implies that man makes them for himself, though by methods of which he is unaware. Plato's conception of eternal Ideas or universal intelligible Forms was different. He imagined that the Demiurge, or Skilled Workman who made our world, desiring that all created things should be as like Himself as possible, took from His own real world the Models (or Forms, or Ideals) representing the generic idea of everything, and used them to make Copies in the world of appearances. Thus the transient world of phenomena came into existence.

Plato's image has been of great importance for the human mind, for it contained the fertile thought that within every changing appearance there lies an unchanging factor, in medieval language the form that makes every particular thing what it is. But today we who accept the outlook of science enjoy an even more powerful image: we see the creative process not in some divine act in the past, but in the continual daily working of our own minds, even the humblest. For every person over one or two years of age and not mentally defective is perpetually shaping new patterns of thought, new little ideas or hunches, every day of his life. We have brought the formative process back into nature and into ourselves, and here we are wiser than Plato. Mankind forges its own instruments for the voyage of discovery.

But the major instruments, the new *primary* ideas, take a long time to perfect, much longer than an Egyptian pyramid for example. The largest pyramids may have taken some twenty years to build, but *in the two thousand five hundred years or hundred generations of Western thought only some ten or twenty primary ideas have been produced!* I am here leaving aside ideas related to subjective experience such as God, Beauty, Goodness, and Justice, and considering only those ideas which serve directly as instruments for understanding the universe. Here are some of those which seem to me most important. Where possible I have added the name of a person who either gave precision to the idea or greatly extended its use.

NUMBER	*Pythagoras*
SPACE	*Euclid*
TIME	
ATOMS	*Democritus*
ENERGY	
ORGANISM	*Aristotle*
MIND	
UNCONSCIOUS MIND	*Freud*
HISTORICAL PROCESS	
STATISTICS	
(FORM)	
(STRUCTURE)	

These twelve ideas can be regarded as covering all the primary insights which the Western mind, and that means human systematic reason, has yet had into the nature of the universe. These are the main instruments of intellectual understanding which the race possesses today. Each has gradually grown clearer and more definite and has been stabilized by persistent use. If we had to send a summary of scientific knowledge by radio to a distant star these would contain the nucleus of the most reliable information.

ERWIN SCHRÖDINGER

The Not-Quite-Exact Sciences

Erwin Schrödinger (1887–   ), Nobel Prize winner in 1933, is an Aus-trian physicist. He is interested in some of the wider aspects of the science he practices so skillfully, but he is no apostle or preacher. The essay that follows seems to me a very temperate and reasonable statement of the kind of "relativism" a scientist true to his training has to embrace. But I incline to the belief that to deny to science complete "objectivity" as Schrödinger does is really another way of saying that science does not aim at Truth, Reality, etc.—all needing capital letters—which is itself a way of saying that science cannot be a religion.

THERE IS A WELL-KNOWN SAYING OF ZOLA'S, THAT ART IS NATURE SEEN through the medium of a temperament—*L'art c'est la nature vue au travers d'un tempérament.* Can the same be said of science? The question is an important one, because it affects a fundamental claim which is nowadays frequently put forward in the name of science. Unlike painting and liter-ature and music, which are subjective ways of apprehending reality and, therefore, liable to alter with the alteration of the cultural environment, science is said to furnish us with a body of truth which has not been molded by the human temperament, and is accordingly objective and stable. How far is this true?

Before answering the question directly it will be necessary to make a distinction between two groups of sciences. On the one hand we have what are called the "exact" sciences and, on the other, those that deal with the human spirit and its activities. To the latter group belong such sciences as history, sociology, psychology, etc.

From Erwin Schrödinger, *Science and the Human Temperament.* Translated by Dr. James Murphy and W. H. Johnston (New York: W. W. Norton, 1935). Re-printed by Dover Publications under the title *Science Theory and Man* (1957), pp. 81-105.

This essay is expanded from an Address to the Physics and Mathematics Section of the Prussian Academy of Science, February 18, 1932, and freely rendered by Dr. James Murphy.

Now it is obvious, I think, that the body of truth which these humanist sciences put forward cannot claim to be entirely objective. Let us take history as an instance. Although we demand of the historian that he will keep to the objective truth of the events he describes, yet if he is to be something more than a mere chronicler, his work must go beyond the discovery and narration of bald fact. Therefore, the selection which he makes from the raw material at his disposal, his formulation of it, and his final presentation must necessarily be influenced by his whole personality. And indeed we gladly forgive the subjective intrusion of the historian into the material he is dealing with, provided we feel the touch of a strong personality weaving for us an interesting human pattern from the bald events of history. Indeed, it is here that scientific history begins, while the work of the conscientious chronicler is looked upon as merely furnishing its raw material.

Similar remarks apply to all those sciences that deal with human life and conduct. One and all, the presentation of their truths must necessarily show the active influence of the human temperament. Of course there is always the ideal of maintaining the greatest possible degree of objectivity in the procedure of these sciences, and a work in this branch of study will be considered scientific or otherwise insofar as it remains faithful to or falls away from the objective ideal. Yet there is not one of those humanist sciences that has not a certain artistic element in it. And in so far as they have this they come under Zola's description. The object with which they deal is always *vue au travers d'un tempérament*.

Let us now turn to the "exact" sciences. From the procedure followed in these sciences everything subjective is excluded on principle. Physical Science belongs essentially to this category. From all physical research the subjective intrusion of the researcher is rigorously barred so that the purely objective truth about inanimate nature may be arrived at. Once this truth is finally stated it can be put to the test of experiment by anybody and everybody all the world over, and always with the same result. Thus far Physics is entirely independent of the human temperament, and this is put forward as its chief claim to acceptance. Some of the champions of Physical Science go so far as to postulate that not only must the individual human mind be ruled out in the ultimate statements of physical research, but that the human aspect as a whole must also be excluded. Every degree of anthropomorphism is rigorously shut out; so that at least in this branch of science man would no longer be the measure of all things, as the Greek Sophists used to maintain.

Is that claim entirely true? To a greater degree than in the case of any other science it is true. But I think it goes too far. We may readily grant that a physical experiment, say, for simplicity's sake, a counting of stars, is independent of the question whether it is carried out by Mr. Wilson in New York or Fräulein Mueller in Berlin. The result will always be the same, provided of course that the requisite technical conditions are fulfilled.

The same is true of all established experiments in Physics. The first and indispensable condition that we demand of any process of experiment before it can be admitted into the regular procedure of physical research is that it will invariably reproduce the same results. We do not consider an experiment worthy of scientific consideration or acceptance unless it can fulfill this condition. Now, it is from the immense mass of individual results accruing from such reproducible experiments that the whole texture of Physical Science is woven. And these classical results are the only raw material allowed to be used in the further development of scientific truth. Therefore, as no other source of knowledge than that of exact experiment is admitted here, it would seem at first sight that Physical Science is wholly within its rights in putting forward its claim to be the authentic bearer of absolutely objective truth. But in estimating that claim certain further considerations must be taken into account.

The legitimate data of Physical Science are always and exclusively those arrived at by means of experiment. But consider the number of experiments which have actually furnished the data on which the structure of Physical Science is based. That number is undoubtedly very large. But it is infinitesimal when compared with the number of experiments that might have been carried out, but never actually have been. Therefore, a selection has been made in choosing the raw material on which the present structure of science is built. That selection must have been influenced by circumstances that are other than purely scientific. And thus far Physical Science cannot claim to be absolutely independent of its environment.

Let us take some of the factors that come into play when a selection has to be made from the experiments that offer themselves as possibilities if somebody wishes to undertake a work of research in some new direction. Obviously there is first and foremost the question of what experiments are practical in the circumstances. Certain experiments demand complicated and expensive apparatus, and the means of securing these are not always at hand. No matter how promising these experiments may be, they have to be set aside by reason of the high expense which they would entail.

Another group of possible experiments is set aside for entirely different and more subjective reasons. They suggest themselves to the mind of the scientist, but for the moment he finds them uninteresting, not only because they are not related directly to the undertaking that he has on hand but also because he may think he already knows the results to which they would lead. And even if he feels that he cannot exactly forecast such results, he may find them of secondary importance at the moment and thus neglect them. Moreover, there is the consideration that if he were to take all such results into consideration he would not know what to do with their immense number. Add to this the fact that our minds are not of infinite compass in their range of interests. Certain things absorb our attention for the moment. The result is that there must always be a large number of alternative experiments—and very practical experiments too—which we do not think of at all, simply because our interest is attracted in other directions.

All this leads to the inevitable conclusion that we cannot close the door to the entry of subjective factors in determining our scientific policy and in giving a definite direction to our line of further advance.

Of course it goes without saying that any advance which we undertake is immediately dependent on the data here and now at our disposal. And these data represent results that have been achieved by former researchers. These results are the outcome of selections formerly made. Those selections were due to a certain train of thought working on the mass of experimental data *then* at hand. And so if we go back through an indefinite series of stages in scientific advance, we shall finally come to the first conscious attempt of primitive man to understand and form a logical mental picture of events observed in the world around him.

These first observations of nature by primitive man did not arise from any consciously constructed mental pattern. The image of nature which primitive man formed for himself emerged automatically, as it were, from the surrounding conditions, being determined by the biological situation, the necessity of bodily sustenance within the environment, and the whole interplay between bodily life and its vicissitudes on the one hand and the natural environment on the other. I mention this point in order to forestall the objection that from the very start a compulsory element might be attributed to the overpowering sway of objective facts. This is certainly not true, the origin of science being without any doubt the very anthropomorphic necessity of man's struggle for life.

It often happens that a certain idea, or group of ideas, becomes vital and dominant at a certain juncture and illuminates with a new significance certain lines of experiment which hitherto have been considered uninteresting and unimportant. Thirty years ago, for instance, nobody was particularly interested in asking how the thermal capacity of a body changes with the temperature, and scarcely anybody dreamed of placing any importance on the reaction of thermal capacity to extremely low temperatures. Perhaps some old crank, entirely devoid of ideas, might have been interested in the question—or maybe a very brilliant genius. But once Nernst put forward his famous "third law of thermodynamics" the whole situation suddenly altered. The Nernst theorem not only embodied the surprising prediction that the thermal capacity of all bodies at an extremely low temperature would tend toward zero, but it also proved that all chemical equilibria could be calculated in advance if the heat of reaction at a certain temperature were known, together with the thermal capacity of the reacting bodies, down to a sufficiently low temperature.

Much the same sort of thing has taken place in regard to the so-called elasticity constants. The physicist had hitherto ignored the significance of the numerical value of these constants and left the whole question to the interest of the practical engineer, the bridge-builder, and the seismologist.

But when Einstein and, after him, Debye, put forward a general theory for the lowering of the thermal capacity of bodies at low grades of temperature, whereby the temperature at which the lowering of the thermal capacity first became manifest is shown to be related to the elastic properties of the material in question, this absolutely novel and unexpected connection aroused a new interest which led to widespread experimental researches in this domain, extending it, for example, to crystals in the various crystallographic directions, etc., etc.

Another instance, which now appears almost as an example of tragic neglect, is the experiment in the diffraction of light which was carried out by Grimaldi (1613-1663). This Italian scientist discovered that the shadow of a wire formed by intercepting a beam of light coming through a slit from a distant source does not show the characteristics that might have been expected; that is to say, it is not a simple dark band across a light field. The dark band is a complex affair. It is bordered by three colored stripes whose respective widths become smaller toward the outside, while the inner part of the shadow is traversed by an odd number of light-colored lines parallel to the borders of the shadow. This experiment, which was carried out long before Huygens' wave theory and Newton's corpuscular theory of light were put forward, was the first experiment of its kind to prove clearly and definitely that rays of light do not travel strictly in straight lines and that the deviation from the direct line is very closely connected with the color or, as we should say to-day, with the wave-length.

In our day this is considered a fundamental fact not only for the understanding of the propagation of light but also in our general scientific picture of the physical universe. If we were to express the significance of Grimaldi's experiment in contemporary terms, we should say that Grimaldi had made the first demonstration of that indeterminacy in Quantum mechanics which was formulated by Heisenberg in 1927. Until the time of Young and Fresnel, Grimaldi's observations attracted little or no attention and nobody attached any great importance to them. They were regarded as pointing to a phenomenon which had no general interest for science as such, and for the following one hundred and fifty years no similar experiments were carried out, though this could have been done with the simplest and cheapest material. The reason for this was that, of the two theories of light which soon afterward were put forward, Newton's corpuscular theory gained general acceptance against the wave theory of Huygens, and thus the general interest was directed along a different path. Following this path, other interesting experiments were carried out which were of practical importance and led to correct practical conclusions, such as the laws of reflection and refraction and their application to the construction of optical instruments. We have no right to-day to say that Newton's corpuscular theory was the wrong one, though it was the custom for a long time to declare it so. The latest conclusions of modern science conform neither to the corpuscular theory nor to the wave theory. According to modern scientific conclusions, the two theories throw light upon two quite different aspects of the phenomenon, and we have not been able up to the present to bring these two aspects into harmony with each other. The interest which was taken in the one side of the question for a long time absolutely submerged any interest that might have been taken in the other. Referring to the history of experimental research into the nature of light, and various theories that arose at one time or another from this research, Ernst Mach remarks "how little the development of science takes place in a logical and systematic way." A very similar—or rather the reverse—case occurred with the theories relating to the constitution of matter. In the case of matter, the corpuscular theory was the one to hold the field up to very recent days, because it is much more difficult to bring forward experimental confirmation of the wave theory in regard to matter than was the case in regard to light.

Following Kirchoff we have become accustomed to admit that science is ultimately concerned with nothing else than a precise and conscientious description of what has been perceived through the senses. The dictum of this eminent theorist has often been quoted as a prudent warning to all those who engage in the construction of theories. From the epistemological point of view it undoubtedly contains a good deal of truth; but it is not in accord with the *psychology* of research. It is completely erroneous to believe that anybody attaches any interest whatsoever to the quantitative laws that are discovered during experimental research—*if we take these laws by themselves,* such as the fact, for instance, that the vapor pressure of some organic compounds or the specific heat of the elements depends in this way or that way on temperature. Our interest in any investigation of this type is due to some further consideration which we intend to attach to the result, that we try to get hold of. And here it is immaterial whether this anticipated consideration, or line of thought, be already existent in the shape of a clearly defined and elaborate theory or whether it be still in the embryonic stage of being a mere vague intuition in the brain of some genius in experimental research.

The psychological truth of what I have said becomes manifest the moment we are faced with the difficulty of explaining to the layman just *why* one is carrying out this or that investigation. When I speak of the layman here I do not mean the term to apply just to those people who do not give their minds to the consideration of impractical things, either because they are not interested in them or because they are overwhelmed by everyday matters. I mean the term to extend much wider. In the circle of a learned society which unites representatives of the various branches of science and literature in order to coöperate in research work, every day one finds one's self a layman in the sense quoted above. Each of one's fellow-members finds himself to be a layman in the same sense. For after having attended a lecture given by a colleague he frequently cannot help asking himself (disrespectful though it may sound): what, in the

name of Providence, is the fellow making such a fuss about? That attitude
is of course not really meant offensively. But it is a very good illustration
of the point that I am making, namely, that quite a special trend of interest
is needed in order that a man may readily admit the extreme importance
of some—and the unimportance of others—of the multitudinous questions
that can be put to nature. In the case just mentioned (let us say it was
your own lecture) it may happen that a colleague comes up to you and
says: "Look here, do tell me why that particular thing interests you. To
me it seems quite immaterial whether, etc., etc. . . . ." Then you will endeavor
to explain. You will try to show all the connections your theme has with
others. You will try to *defend* your own interest in the matter. I mean that
you will try to defend the reason *why* you are interested. Then you will
probably notice that your feelings are much more ardently aroused in this
discussion than they were during the lecture itself. And you will become
aware of the fact that only now, in your discussion with your colleague,
have you reached those aspects of the subject that are, so to speak, nearest
to your heart.

In passing, I may say that here we meet one of the strongest arguments
in favor of bringing together the representatives of the remote branches of
science or of literature into associations for collaboration in research work.
These associations are helpful and recuperative in compelling a man to
reflect now and again on what he is doing and to give an account of his
aims and motives to others whom he considers his equals in a different
province of the realm of knowledge. Therefore, he will take the trouble to
prepare a proper answer to their questions. For he will feel himself
responsible for their lack of comprehension and will not haughtily look
upon it as their fault instead of his own.

But though it be granted that the special importance of an investigation
cannot of course be grasped without knowing the whole trend of research
that had preceded it and had attracted attention to that particular line of
experimentation, it might still be seriously questioned whether this fact
really points to a highly subjective element in science. For on the other
side it might be said that scientists all the world over are fairly well agreed
as to what further investigations in their respective branches of study would
be appreciated or not. One may reasonably ask whether that is not a proof
of objectivity.

Let us be definite. The argument applies to the research workers all the
world over, but only of *one* branch of science and of *one* epoch. These
men practically form a unit. It is a relatively small community, though
widely scattered, and modern methods of communication have knit it into
one. The members read the same periodicals. They exchange ideas with
one another. And the result is that there is a fairly definite agreement as
to what opinions are sound on this point or that. There is professional
enthusiasm about any progress that may be made, and whatever particular
success may be achieved in one country, or by one man or group of men,

will be hailed as a common triumph by the profession as a whole. In this respect international science is like international sport and also, as nothing immediately utilitarian is expected from either, they both belong to the higher and detached realm of human activity.

Now, the internationality of science is a very fine and inspiring thing; but it just renders this "*consensus omnium*" slightly suspicious as an argument in favor of the objectivity of science. Take the case of international sport. It is perfectly true that we have conditions which secure an objective and impartial registration of how high So-and-So jumped or how far So-and-So threw the discus. But are not the high jump and the discus-throwing largely a question of fashion? And is it not the same with this or that line of experiments in physics?

In public sport we are acquainted only with certain kinds of games that have been developed, largely because of some current interest or because of racial tastes or climatic conditions; but we have no grounds for saying that these furnish a thoroughly exhaustive or objective picture of what human muscular ability is capable of. And in science we are acquainted only with a certain bulk of experimental results which is infinitesimally small compared with the results that might have been obtained from other experiments. Just as it would be useless for some athlete in the world of sport to puzzle his brain in order to initiate something new—for he would have little or no hope of being able to "put it over," as the saying is—so too it would, generally speaking, be a vain endeavor on the part of some scientist to strain his imaginative vision toward initiating a line of research hitherto not thought of. The incidents that I have already quoted from the history of science are proof of that point.

Our civilization forms an organic whole. Those fortunate individuals who can devote their lives to the profession of scientific research are not merely botanists or physicists or chemists, as the case may be. They are men and they are children of their age. The scientist cannot shuffle off his mundane coil when he enters his laboratory or ascends the rostrum in his lecture hall. In the morning his leading interest in class or in the laboratory may be his research; but what was he doing the afternoon and evening before? He attends public meetings just as others do or he reads about them in the press. He cannot and does not wish to escape discussion of the mass of ideas that are constantly thronging into the foreground of public interest, especially in our day. Some scientists are lovers of music, some read novels and poetry, some frequent the theaters. Some will be interested in painting and sculpture. And if any one should believe that he could really escape the influence of the cinema, because he does not care for it, he is surely mistaken. For he cannot even walk along the street without paying attention to the pictures of cinema stars and advertisement tableaux. In short, we are all members of our cultural environment.

From all this it follows that the engaging of one's interest in a certain subject and in certain directions must necessarily be influenced by the environment, or what may be called the cultural milieu or the spirit of the age in which one lives. In all branches of our civilization there is one general world outlook dominant and there are numerous lines of activity which are attractive because they are the fashion of the age, whether in politics or in art or in science. These also make themselves felt in the "exact" science of physics.

Now how can we perceive and point out such subjective influences actually at work? It is not easy to do so if we confine ourselves to the contemporary perspective; because there are no coördinates of reference within the same cultural milieu to show how far individual directions are influenced by the spirit of the milieu as a whole. At the present moment practically one culture spans the whole earth, and so the development of science and art in different countries is to a great extent influenced by one and the same general trend of the times. For that reason it is best to take historical instances to elucidate what I have said, because in the past organic cultures were confined to much smaller territories and there was a greater variety of them at the same time on this planet.

Grecian culture is a classic example of how every line of activity within the one cultural milieu is dominated by the general trend of the culture itself. In Hellenic science and art and in the whole Hellenic outlook on life we can immediately discern a common characteristic. The clear, transparent and rigid structure of Euclidian geometry corresponds to the plain, simple, and limited forms of the Grecian temple. The whole structure of the temple is small, near at hand, completely visible within the range of the onlooker's eye, losing itself nowhere and escaping the eye nowhere either in its extension or form. This is something quite different from Gothic architecture. So, too, in the case of Greek science the idea of the infinite is scarcely understood. The concept of a limitless process frightened the Greek, as is evidenced in the well-known paradox of Achilles and the tortoise. The Hellenic mind could not have interested itself in the Dedekind definition of the irrational number, although the idea of the irrational was already present in the synoptic form of the diagonal of the square or of the cube.

Greek drama, especially that of the earlier epochs, is absolutely static when compared to ours. There is little or no action. We are presented with a tragic situation and the action is limited to the decision which a human being makes in certain definite circumstances. So also in Greek physics the dynamic is missing. The Greek did not dream of analyzing motion in its single subsequent phases, of asking at any moment for the cause of what would happen in the next moment, as Newton did. The Greek would have found this sort of analysis petty and incompatible with his esthetic sense. He thought of the path along which a body moved as a whole, not as something that develops but as something that is already there in its entirety. In looking for the *simplest* type of motion the rectilinear one was excluded because the straight line is not perceptible in its entire range—

rectilinear motion is never completed, can never be grasped as a whole. By observing the star-strewn heavens the Greek was helped over his difficulty in regard to the concept of motion. He concluded from this that a circular path uniformly traversed is the most perfect and natural movement of a body, and that it is controlled and actuated in this movement by a greater central body. I do not think that we are warranted to-day in laughing at this naïve construction of the Greek mind. Until a short time ago we have been doing a very similar thing ourselves in the quantum theory of the atom. *Faute de mieux,* we have contented ourselves with similar naïvetés and the steps that we tried beyond them have emphasized rather than liquidated the fiasco of the Newtonian differential analysis.

Let me now turn to another instance. The idea of evolution has had more dominant influence than any other idea in all spheres of modern science and, indeed, of modern life as a whole, in its general form as well as in the special presentation of it by Darwin (namely, automatic adjustment by the survival of the fittest). As an indication of how profound the idea was, we may first recall to mind the fact that even such a clear-sighted intellect as that of Schopenhauer was incapable of grasping it (indeed he violently rejected it because he considered it to be in contradiction to his own, equally profound, conception that "Now" is always one and the same instant of time and that the "I" is always one and the same person)—while, on the other hand, Hegel's philosophy, by embodying that idea, has prolonged its life up to our day—far beyond its natural span. Moreover, Ernst Mach has applied it to the scientific process itself, which he looked upon as a gradual accommodation of thoughts to facts through a choice of what we find most useful to fit in with the facts and a rejection of the less appropriate. In astrophysics we have learned to look on the various types of stars as different stages in one and the same stellar evolution. And quite recently we have seen the idea put forward that perhaps the universe on the whole is not in a stationary stage, but that at a definite point of time, which is relatively not very long ago, it changed from quite a different condition into a steadily expansive stage which, according to the results of Hubble's extraordinary observations, seems to be its present stage. (These observations show that the spectral lines of very distant nebulæ are appreciably shifted to greater wave-lengths and that this displacement is proportioned to the distance of the nebulæ. This points to immensely great velocities on the part of these systems moving away from us, so that it would appear as if the whole universe is in the process of a general expansion.) We do not consider this hypothesis as mere empty phantasy, because we have grown accustomed to the evolutionary idea. If such ideas had been put forward in a former age they certainly would have been rejected as nonsensical.

All this shows how dependent science is on the fashionable frame of mind of the epoch of which it forms a part. When we are in the midst of a general situation ourselves it is difficult for us to see general resemblances. Being so near, we are apt to perceive only the marked distinctions and not to notice the likenesses. It is just as when we first see the several members of the same family one after another we readily perceive the resemblances, but if we come to know the family intimately then we see only the differences. So too when we live in the midst of a cultural epoch it is difficult to perceive the characteristics that are common to various branches of human activity within that epoch. Let us take another example to illustrate this. A German father looking at the drawings of a ten-year-old son will mark only the individual qualities and will not readily perceive the influence of a general European type of drawing and painting. But if he looks at the drawings of a young Japanese boy he will readily recognize the influence of the Japanese style as a whole. In each case the naïve attempt of the boy is controlled and molded even in its smallest detail by the artistic tradition amid which he lives.

ARCHIBALD VIVIAN HILL

The Humanity of Science

Archibald Vivian Hill (1886–   ), still another Nobel Prize winner (1923), is an English physiologist who has long been a professor at Cambridge University. The reader should note that in this urbane essay Professor Hill does not subscribe to the thesis later announced by C. P. Snow (see p. 296) as to the two worlds of humanism and science. I make no attempt here to decide between them, but I think it obvious that such gap as there may be would be less obvious, less wide, to a physiologist like Hill than to a physicist like Snow.

THE WORD "HUMANITY" BRINGS TO MIND AT ONCE THE SUPPOSED CONFLICT (or at least the supposed contrast) between the humane studies so-called (namely, literature, language, history, and art) on the one side, and science on the other. That conflict, I think, is a complete illusion—as false as the common idea that professors all have long beards, look like nothing on earth, and are absent-minded in their personal habits—as absurd as the notion that no mathematician can do arithmetic—as ridiculous as the libel that women, as a class, drive motor-cars any more dangerously (if that were possible) than men. The truth is that science can be, and should be, and often is one of the humanities.

In a recent series of broadcast talks on various aspects of science the speakers emphasized not only the useful side, the practical side of their researches, but even more the intellectual side, the joy of discovery, the wonder and delight of the knowledge so acquired of the world inside and around us.

Humane culture does not reside only in the limited past of recorded history. The methods of science may be used to reveal the details of primitive cultures far older than Greece or Babylon. Nor is there need to wait five hundred years before the ideas and discoveries of the science of to-day become a respectable branch of the humane study of the future. Natural Science is an essential part of a decent education, as essential as

From Sir John Boyd Orr, Professor A. V. Hill, Professor J. C. Philip, Sir Richard Gregory, Sir A. Daniel Hall, Professor Lancelot Hogben, *What Science Stands For* (London: Allen & Unwin, 1937), pp. 30-38.

literature, history, art, and language; it can offer to the human spirit just as fine a discipline, just as delicate and sympathetic a view of the world. The phrase, "humanity of science," is a claim that science has an equal part with other studies in humane culture. In A. E. Housman's words, "Let us insist that the pursuit of knowledge"—scientific or otherwise, I would add—"like the pursuit of righteousness, is part of man's duty to himself."

In the dictionary "humanity" is first defined as "the quality or condition of being human."

About twenty-eight years ago, during my studies at Cambridge, I read a number of interesting papers in the *Journal of Physiology* by a certain Joseph Barcroft. I had not realized then the "quality or condition of being human" of those who write scientific papers; I supposed that the author of those papers was a learned, respectable, and elderly gentleman. I recall very vividly the astonishment with which one day I suddenly realized the identity of a friendly and humorous young man who demonstrated to us in our classes. Sir Joseph Barcroft, as he now is, recently told how to get scientific people to work together in teams; he is quite as human as he was in 1908; but I find no difficulty to-day, after twenty-eight years, in realizing that he *is* the author of his papers—indeed, I cannot imagine any-one else as their author! That is because I have learnt, what it has been one of the chief purposes of these talks to show, that the scientist at work is a human being like the rest of us.

Another, an acquired, meaning of the word "humanity" is "kindness or benevolence." Here we may seem to be on more debatable ground, in talking of the humanity of science. The world unfortunately is filled with war and rumours of war. The fruits of science, it appears, may be used chiefly to injure, to exterminate, fellow men. Bombing aeroplanes and poison gas are regarded by many as the most significant products of a scientific age. But science can scarcely be blamed for the misuse which non-scientific people (that is, most of the world) make of certain scientific discoveries. Are we, for example, to forbid long-range prediction of the weather because, if it is successful, it may become easier for some dictator to prepare for an attack on a neighbour? Are we to say that attempts to find out the mechanism of the human ear must be abandoned because the ear may be used in hunting submarines or locating enemy aircraft? Shall we stop research workers from studying, and so possibly from pre-venting, plant diseases, because if they succeed too completely or too sud-denly an economic crisis may result from over-production of food or tobacco? Are the embryologists' "organizers," which control the develop-ment of animals, to be excommunicated because conceivably some day knowledge of them may lead to the control of cancer—and so result in over-population and war? I have no doubt of your answer, at least to this last question: but how—I ask you—is the scientist to know *which* of his dis-coveries will be misused by wicked or thoughtless men?

We must not take too seriously, then, the war-hysteria of the present time: let us think of things in their proper historical perspective and try to realize what science has actually done. Who would like to think of disease as due to evil spirits? Who wants hundreds of women to die in childbirth of puerperal fever as they did before Pasteur? Who would like to return to surgery before the days of anaesthetics and antiseptics? Who would abolish the transport and machinery by which fresh and healthy food is brought to us cheaply from the ends of the earth? Who that goes on a long journey would like to return to an age when it might be months before he could hear of friends at home? Who indeed, in days to come, would be altogether happy to return to 1936, when one-eighth of all the deaths are due to cancer, and common prejudice against scientific methods of producing immunity still permits diphtheria to kill many hundreds of children annually? Are the inhumane uses to which science can be put by non-scientific people to be held an objection to the innumerable humane things which science has done, or might do—anyone can think of them— for the betterment, the greater health and happiness and wisdom of men?

I said intentionally and provocatively, "by non-scientific people"; after all, it is government by Parliament or dictator which decides on the use or abuse of any particular discovery: and the number of dictators, or Prime Ministers, or even Members of Parliament, who have acquaintance with science, is still—to put it mildly—insignificant. You cannot blame the inventor of safety matches if a naughty boy uses one to set fire to a haystack!

Another aspect of science which this title might suggest is the degree to which the developments of science are caused by, or directed to, the human needs, the social ideas, the material environment of the time. It is easy for the partisan of any particular political faith to find in history, whether of human thought or of human action, the workings of his pet principles. I doubt personally whether the lives of Newton, Faraday, Clerk Maxwell, or of Leeuwenhoek, Pasteur, or Pavlov, give support to any particular political creed, unless it be that of tolerance. It is true, all the same, that political, economic, and philosophical ideas, and the human needs of the moment, provide a bias for the work which scientific men do. To take a rather flippant example, one has often heard it said that modern theories of molecules, atoms, and electrons have been given a very distinct bias by the modern habit of playing ball games. Certainly my own work in physiology has been directly influenced by an early interest in athletics. On a more serious plane, Pasteur's discoveries in bacteriology, which have had so great an influence in medicine, were prompted largely by the diseases of silkworms, sheep, and wine which were impoverishing French agriculture. Lord Kelvin's researches were part of the technical and industrial developments of his day. The Royal Institution, where Davy, Faraday, Dewar, and Sir William Bragg have worked, was founded by a movement to improve the condition of the poor. In England in the sixteenth century the expansion of trade and ideas led to the foundation of the Grammar Schools, which are now our Public Schools. In America to-day the same spirit is building universities and research institutions, endowing science, and constructing a two-hundred-inch mirror for an astronomical telescope.

We scientists, therefore, are not unaffected by social and economic things, any more than we are uninfluenced by the work of others, often in very different fields from our own. The chain of technical events, for example, which is leading to television, has led equally to a knowledge both of the upper atmosphere and also of the workings of nerves and ears. Just as we derive our bodily and mental inheritance, through our parents, from unnumbered others in the past, so the scientific discoveries of to-day are the products, not only of our own efforts, but of the ideas and experiments, the successes and more often the failures, of all those who have preceded us. In this sense the "humanity of science" implies that science is a product of human society; and that its progress depends upon all those ideas, movements, and facilities which are current at any moment in society.

The word "humanity" has one very special sense, pertinent to this talk, namely that of mankind as a whole. Compare the nationalism of politics with the internationalism of knowledge. Of all the interests of mankind there are none so clearly and obviously international as science and learning.

One need not go back far into history for examples. Shortly after the War there was an International Congress of Physiology at Edinburgh. An attempt was made from abroad to exclude the Germans, our late enemies, from attendance. It was made perfectly clear by a number of British physiologists—people who had taken their part to the full against Germany during the War—that if the Germans were excluded they themselves were not coming. The Germans came, and friendly scientific relations were restored. Similarly, when recent political events in Europe produced a crop of exiles from universities and learned institutions, it was their scientific and other academic colleagues who came at once to their rescue. This chivalrous international tradition, this feeling that science and learning are common factors in humanity, is a very ancient and respectable one; and it is one of the few possible antidotes to the excesses of nationalism at the present time.

Do not imagine that this kind of internationalism implies any lack of affection for one's own country. I am myself an unrepentant internationalist in science, but I very much prefer, perhaps for that very reason, the free democratic institutions of our own country to any of the dictatorships. That preference, however, does not hinder my faith, some would call it a religious faith, in the international spirit of science and learning; or diminish my anxiety to co-operate with genuine scientists in whatever country. Mankind is afflicted to-day by political and economic terrors of his own making. Science has saved him already from many of the worse terrors of the world in which he finds himself. May not the example of science, with its spirit of friendly co-operation, lead gradually to a more reasonable view of international relationships, and so make its greatest contribution of all to human welfare?

F

Inventing the Future

RENÉ JULES DUBOS

Utopias and Human Goals

René Jules Dubos (1901–   ) is a French-born bacteriologist, a natural-
ized American citizen in 1938, and now with the Rockefeller Institute for
Medical Research. The chapter on "Utopias and Human Goals" from his
very interesting little book Mirage of Health *makes a fine contrast*
with the thesis of Messrs. Murray and Keniston with which we began this
book; and the attitude reflected in Mirage of Health *makes an equally*
suggestive contrast with that of his fellow Frenchman and fellow research
biologist, Alexis Carrel, whom we have just heard from (see p. 436). It
would hardly be necessary to write a book entitled Mirage of Unanimous
Agreement.

Arcadias and Utopias

THE ANCIENT PROVINCE OF ARCADY LIES IN THE HEART OF THE PELOPON-
nesus, all but isolated from the rest of Greece by mountains. In the legend it
was the domain of Pan, who played the syrinx on Mount Maenalus, and
of rustic people celebrated for their musical accomplishments and their
rustic hospitality, but also notorious for their ignorance and low standards
of living. Yet it was this unfavored land, poor, rocky, chilly, devoid of all
the amenities of life, affording adequate food only to goats, which was
transformed through the alchemy of art into the myth of Arcadia. From
Vergil to Nicolas Poussin, "I, too, dwelt in Arcady" has symbolized the
golden ages of plenty and innocence, of unsurpassable happiness enjoyed
in the past and enduringly alive in memory.

    While the Greco-Roman civilization placed its land of dreams in a
remote and not easily accessible Arcadia, Chinese Taoism found it in any
place where man could achieve identification with nature—in romantic
mountain paths, isolated fishing villages, or mist-bathed landscapes. According to Lao-tzu and his Taoist followers, joy and bliss were possible only

From René Dubos, *Mirage of Health* (New York: Harper & Brothers, 1959), pp.
216-236.

in a world of primitive simplicity. Men could achieve health and happiness only by merging themselves with their environment and living in accord with the laws of the four seasons, by participating with other living creatures "in the mysterious equality and thus forget themselves in the Tao."

The Taoist's withdrawal from conflict and his attempt to identify himself with the physical and social environment constituted a philosophy of health. Avoidance of travel minimized the transfer of new pathogens from one community to another. Life without aggressive behavior and in accordance with the rhythms of the seasons made it possible to reach a state of harmony with the environment. This way of life was not designed to solve the difficulties arising from social contacts and conflicts. Rather, it attempted to prevent or at least to minimize the emergence of new problems by creating a stable world in which new stresses, but also new experiences, were ruled out.

While the Arcadian bliss and the contented intimacy of the Chinese Tao are rarely attainable in real life, they constitute eternally the stuff of human dreams. As a substitute for the Arcadias of the past, men never tire of imagining for the future new types of social order free of the defects and vices found in all actual societies. But utopias differ profoundly one from the other despite their common basis of illusion, because each is colored by the value judgments of its originator. Utopian ideals vary all the way from a desire for nirvana to the longing for exciting experience; from the passivity, indolence, and tolerance of Goncharov's oblomovism to the ceaseless activity and creative endeavor of the Faustian universe.

Propounders of utopias have not even been able to agree on the value that they attach to life. Plato considered that life without health was not worth preserving for the sake of either the individual or the community. He saw no virtue in encouraging the survival of a fellow man threatened by continuous sickness. The state physicians of his *Republic* were to watch with care over "the citizens of goodly conditions, both in mind and body" but persons who were defective either mentally or physically were "to be suffered to die." This attitude is a far cry from the ethics of modern utopias. Life, it is now taught, must be preserved at all cost, whatever the burden that its preservation imposes on the community and on the individual concerned. Whether this lofty ethical concept will retain acceptance if put to the acid test of social pressure still has to be proved. Western man may rediscover wisdom in Plato's social philosophy when the world becomes crowded with aged, invalid, and defective people. He may once more rationalize himself into the belief that happiness is not possible in the absence of usefulness to the social group and that survival under these conditions is therefore not worth having.

Designers of utopias must also formulate judgments of value regarding the type of human beings they want to foster. The society best suited for producing athletes, warriors, and men of action is not necessarily the best breeding ground for artists, scholars, philosophers, and mystics. In addition, many trivial factors, conscious or unconscious, influence the community in determining the defects that it will tolerate and the level of physical and intellectual adequacy to which it aspires. Most Western societies today regard as unacceptable certain smells or skin blemishes which were a matter of course a few generations ago and are still accepted as the normal state by many primitive or semicivilized peoples. Modern man looks with dismay on the fact that syphilis, malaria, yaws, intestinal disorders, etc., are so common in some areas of the world as not to be regarded as diseases. Yet he accepts as part and parcel of a normal life baldness, poor eyesight, chronic sinusitis, and other bodily defects which might be regarded as handicaps or even as repulsive traits in other cultural contexts.

Clearly, health and disease cannot be defined merely in terms of anatomical, physiological, or mental attributes. Their real measure is the ability of the individual to function in a manner acceptable to himself and to the group of which he is a part. If the medical services of the armed forces seem more successful than their civilian counterparts in formulating useful criteria of health, this is due not to their greater wisdom but rather to the fact that their criteria are more clearly defined. On the whole, effective military performance required attributes less varied and less complex than the multifarious activities of civilian life. But criteria of adequacy change even in the military world. The soldier of past wars who marched or rode his way to victory through physical and mental stamina might not be the most effective warrior in the push-button operations of future conflicts.

For several centuries the Western world has pretended to find a unifying concept of health in the Greek ideal of a proper balance between body and mind. But in reality this ideal is more and more difficult to convert into practice. Poets, philosophers, and creative scientists are rarely found among Olympic laureates. It is not easy to discover a formula of health broad enough to fit Voltaire and Jack Dempsey, to encompass the requirements of a stevedore, a New York City bus driver, and a contemplative monk.

One of the criteria of health most widely accepted at the present time is that children should grow as large and as fast as possible. But is size such a desirable attribute? Is the bigger child happier? will he live longer? does he perceive with greater acuity the loveliness or the grandeur of the world? will he contribute more to man's cultural heritage? or does his larger size merely mean that he will need a larger motorcar, become a larger soldier, and in his turn beget still larger children? The criteria of growth developed for the production of market pigs would hardly be adequate for animals feeding on acorns in the forests and fending for themselves as free individuals. Nor are they for man. Size and weight are not desirable in themselves, and their relation to health and happiness is at most obscure. In his essay *On the Sizes of Things or the Advantages of Being Rather Small,* Boycott concluded, in fact, that an animal about as big as a medium dog has the best possible size for our world!

Curiously enough, the assumption that human beings should grow fast and large has never been examined closely as to its validity and ultimate consequences. Its only certain merit is that weight, size, and a few other physical traits can be measured readily, provide objective and convenient characteristics on which to agree, and can be on the whole readily achieved. There is no evidence, however, that these criteria have much bearing on happiness, on the development of civilization, or even on the individual's ability to adapt to the complex demands of modern technology. While high humidity usually enhances the development of orchid plants, it is not particularly favorable to the development of the flowers; *Grevillea robusta,* which provides valuable timber under the relative drought conditions of Australia, yields but valueless wood when caused to grow rapidly as a shading plant on the coffee plantations of the tropical Guatemalan highlands. For man, similarly, mere size has never been the determinant factor of his survival and success, either as an individual or as a species. Large size is likely to prove even less of an asset in the world of the future, and may even become a handicap. The specifications for man's body and mind may have to be reformulated in order to meet with greater effectiveness the exigencies of the mechanized world.

Arcadias are dreams of an imaginary past, and utopias the intellectual concepts of an idealized society. Different as they appear to be, both imply a static view of the world which is incompatible with reality, for the human condition has always been to move on. "Man has never sought tranquillity alone," wrote Sir Winston Churchill. "His nature drives him forward to fortunes which, for better or for worse, are different from those which it is in his power to pause and enjoy." Prehistory and ancient history show that men have never been able to forget their nomadic past and to rest quietly in the corner of the earth they had made their own for a while. Not satisfied with changing their geographical environment, men also crave for changes in their social atmosphere. Their utopias have never been able to keep pace with their fundamental restlessness, with their eternal dream of a New Jerusalem.

From Biological Adaptation to Social Evolution

Fossil remnants of prehistoric man have been found in greatest profusion in East Africa. It seems that Ethiopia, Kenya, Tanganyika, and neighboring countries have provided conditions well suited for the evolutionary changes through which the human race achieved the diversity which permitted it to colonize the whole world. On the one hand, much of East Africa consists of highlands with a moderate climate varied enough to produce the stimuli required for the evolution of an all-purpose ancestor of man. On the other hand, this region offers a large variety of geological strata, topographical configurations, climates, fauna, and flora to which early man could gain easy access. Within a few hundred miles are to be found high peaks, rich plateaus and lands below sea level; torrential waters, immense lakes, and gentle seas; tropical forests, alluvial plains, and deserts of sand. Thus, even short migrations provided for man in this area the opportunity to gain experience with and achieve biological fitness to a wide range of physical environments. And he did not have to travel far to reach the lands where he was to embark on his cultural destiny. From the Abyssinian mountains, the Blue Nile opened for him a channel to the luminous and fertile deltas of the Near East which became the cradles of his civilizations.

As he moved into new lands and new climes man underwent adaptive biological changes in response to the various environments that he encountered. To a large extent this biological phase of evolutionary history seems to have been completed by the end of the Pleistocene epoch. Physical man was then essentially a fait accompli. But, while the size of his brain, his physiological reactions, and even his fundamental instincts have probably changed little since that time, the social structures that he has developed have continued to evolve. It is clear that the collective evolutionary course of mankind has now set the human species apart from the rest of the animal world. The present phase of human evolution differs qualitatively from the purely biological phase because passive submission to the environment has been replaced by an active creative process. Evolutionary changes which were once the slavish expressions of natural forces have become increasingly self-directing. They affect not so much the body and the mind of man as the type of life that his social organization makes possible. Their effectiveness is based on the ability to acquire and transmit information in a manner that gives to the social body the cumulative experience and knowledge of each of its members.

All these new aspects of human activities are identified with the invention of tools and the development of social groups. Communal life, in villages and then in cities, created new environmental problems that stimulated new adaptive processes. This major change occurred only some ten thousand years ago. At the rate of three generations per century, this lapse of time is far too short to have allowed adequate play for the usual mechanisms of biological adaptation. Rather, it was through the development of social practices that man met the countless and unexpected new challenges that he encountered in the course of his migrations and social upheavals. Religious beliefs, empirical wisdom, and eventually scientific understanding played dominant roles in helping him to resist threats originating from nature or, more often, from his own activities. Whereas other living things survive through adaptive changes in their bodies and their instincts, man strives to impose his own directional will on the relations that he has with the rest of the world. Consciously, though often not wisely, he decides on the kind of life he wishes to have; then he acts to render possible this way of life by shaping the environment and even attempting to alter his own physical and mental self.

Social Changes and Ecological Equilibria

Modern man believes that he has achieved almost complete mastery over the natural forces which molded his evolution in the past and that he can now control his own biological and cultural destiny. But this may be an illusion. Like all other living things, he is part of an immensely complex ecological system and is bound to all its components by innumerable links. Moreover, as we have seen, human life is affected not only by the environmental forces presently at work in nature but even more perhaps by the past.

Any attempt to shape the world and modify human personality in order to create a self-chosen pattern of life involves many unknown consequences. Human destiny is bound to remain a gamble, because at some unpredictable time and in some unforeseeable manner nature will strike back. The multiplicity of determinants which affect biological systems limits the power of the experimental method to predict their trends and behavior. Experimentation necessarily involves a choice in the factors brought to bear on the phenomena under study. Ideally, the experimenter works in a closed system, affected only by the determinants that he has introduced, under the conditions that he has selected. Naturally, however, events never occur in a closed system. They are determined and modified by circumstances and forces that cannot be foreseen, let alone controlled. In part this is because natural situations are so complex that no experimental study can ever encompass and reproduce all the relevant factors of the environment. Furthermore, human behavior is governed not only by biological necessities but also by the desire for change. When surfeited with honey man begins to loathe the taste of sweetness, and this desire for change per se introduces an inescapable component of unpredictability in his life.

It is the awareness of these complexities which accounts for the clumsiness of the scientific language used in reporting biological events. The scientist emphasizes *ad nauseam* that what he states is valid only "under conditions of the experiment." As if apologetically, he is wont to qualify any assertion or general statement with the remark, "All other things being equal—which they never are . . ." Because things are never the same, almost everyone admits that prediction is always risky in political and social fields. But it is not so generally recognized that the same limitations apply to other areas usually regarded as falling within the realm of the so-called exact sciences, for instance, the epidemiology of disease.

Many examples have been quoted in earlier chapters to illustrate the unexpected and far-reaching effects that accidental circumstances have exerted in the past on the welfare of man. The introduction of inexpensive cotton undergarments easy to launder and of transparent glass that brought light into the most humble dwelling, contributed more to the control of infection than did all drugs and medical practices. On the other hand, a change in fur fashion brought about a few years later an outbreak of pneumonic plague in Manchuria; the use of soft coal in English grates caused chimney sweeps to develop cancer; Roentgen's discovery endangered the lives of scientists and physicians exposed to X rays in the course of their professional activities. Likewise oil and rubber may in the future come to be regarded as having been the indirect causes of disease and death. In addition to the human beings killed or maimed in automobile accidents, many are likely to suffer, directly or indirectly, from the air pollution brought about by the widespread use of oil and rubber. Furthermore, neuroses peculiar to our time may someday be traced to the speed and power that rubber and oil have made possible, as well as to the frustrations caused by crowded city streets and highways.

Human goals, which condition social changes, profoundly affect the physical and mental well-being of man. And, unfortunately, the most worthwhile goals may have results as disastrous as those of the most despicable ambitions. Industrial imperialism was responsible for an enormous amount of misery among children during the early nineteenth century. But, as we have seen, the present philosophy to assure the survival of all children and to protect them from any traumatic experience also is likely to have unfortunate consequences by interfering with the normal play of adaptive processes.

Philosophical and social doctrines have been the most influential forces in changing the human ways of life during historical times. The high regard in which the human body was held by the Greco-Roman world certainly played a role in the development of hygiene and medicine during the classical times of Western civilization. In contrast, the emphasis on mystical values and on eternal life, the contempt for bodily functions, which characterized certain early phases of the Christian faith, probably led to the neglect of sanitary practices during medieval times—even though it did not necessarily decrease the enjoyment of sensual pleasures by normal men and women. Today, as in the past, the relation that man bears to his total environment is influenced by values of which he is not always aware. A civilization that devotes page after page of its popular magazines to portraying the rulers of the business world is bound to produce men very different from those taught to worship Confucian wisdom, Buddhic mysticism, or Blake's poems—even if that worship often does not go far beyond mere lip service. To feel at ease among the neon lights of Broadway demands a type of body and mind not conducive to happiness in the mists of a Taoist moonscape.

Technology is now displacing philosophical and religious values as the dominant force in shaping the world, and therefore in determining human fate. What man does today and will do tomorrow is determined to a large extent by the techniques that expert knowledge puts at his disposal, and his dreams for the future reflect the achievements and promises of the scientists. From them he has acquired the faith—or rather the illusion—that society can be planned in a manner that will assure plenty, health, and happiness for everyone and thus solve all the great problems of existence.

As modern technological innovations are the direct outcome of scientific research, scientists can no longer afford to stand aloof from social problems. Knowledge can grow without regard for ethical values, but the modern scientist cannot help becoming involved in ethics, since science can no longer be dissociated from the applications of science. In the past the social effects of science were slow in manifesting themselves. Today they are immediate and reach every aspect of the life of every man, for good and for evil. The scientist has convinced society that his efforts deserve to be generously supported because he has become one of its most effective servants. As a penalty for his dependence on public support and for the influence that he has gained he cannot escape being made responsible for his activities, even if their results are different from what he had hoped. In the present decade he has to deal with the consequences of the release of man-made radiations. He may soon acquire the knowledge that will permit him to control the behavior of people and the genetic endowment of children to be born, a power frightening in its unpredictable potentialities for evil.

To discover, to describe, to classify, to invent, has been the traditional task of the scientist until this century; on the whole a pleasant occupation amounting to a sophisticated hobby. This happy phase of social irresponsibility is now over and the scientist will be called to account for the long-term consequences of his acts. His dilemma is and will remain that he cannot predict these consequences because they depend on many factors outside his knowledge or at least beyond his control—in particular on the exercise of free will by men. The scientist must therefore avoid pride of intellect and guard himself against any illusion or pretense as to the extent and depth of what he knows. He must also develop an alertness to the unexpected, an awareness of the fact that many surprising effects are likely to result from even trivial disturbances of ecological equilibria. Fortunately, the scientific method is well suited for the cultivation of this alertness to the advent of the unpredictable. The scientist cannot predict the remote consequences of his activities, but he can often provide techniques for recognizing them early. One of the few encouraging indications that science has come of age is the fact that extensive studies on the potential danger of radiations were initiated as soon as it became apparent that the forces unleashed by knowledge of the atom would find a place in the technology of war and peace.

To become worthy of his power the scientist will need to develop enough wisdom and humane understanding to recognize that the acquistion of knowledge is intricately interwoven with the pursuit of goals. It has often been pointed out that the nineteenth-century slogan, "Survival of the fittest," begged the question because it did not state what fitness was for. Likewise it is not possible to plan man's future without deciding beforehand what he should be fitted for, in other words, what human destiny ought to be—a decision loaded with ethical values. What is new is not necessarily good, and all changes, even those apparently the most desirable, are always fraught with unpredictable consequences. The scientist must beware of having to admit, like Captain Ahab in Melville's *Moby Dick,* "All my means are sane; my motives and objects mad."

Health, Happiness, and Human Values

It is often suggested that a moratorium on science would give mankind the opportunity to search its soul and discover a solution to the problems that threaten its very survival. Although no one is naïve enough to hope that stopping the clock would bring about the solution of ancient human problems, many believe that a scientific status quo might prevent or retard the development of new threats. This static formula of survival is not new; indeed, it has been used with much biological success by social insects. Certain species of ants and termites had completed at least fifty million years ago the highly stratified and efficient type of colonial organization which they still exhibit. They have solved many of the problems which are the subject of endless discussions and conflicts in most human societies. Their queens, warriors, and workers all are produced as needed by genetic and physiological control; they have functions which are clearly defined and regulated in terms of the welfare of the colony as a whole. Even problems of eugenics have been solved in these insect societies by confining reproduction to a certain caste and promptly eliminating all abnormal and diseased individuals.

The very survival and wide distribution of highly organized insect societies which have not changed in fifty million years is evidence that living things can achieve a more or less stable equilibrium with their environment and that, beyond a certain degree of adaptation, change is no longer necessary for biological survival. It is conceivable, therefore, that human societies also could stop evolving and thus avoid the dangers inevitably associated with the adaptive problems bound to arise from any change. In fact, this has happened on several occasions in many parts of the world.

Before their contact with the white man the Eskimos, the Polynesian Islanders, and certain nomadic tribes had worked out stable societies with an acceptable degree of physical health and happiness. As pointed out by Arnold J. Toynbee, however, the human beings in all these societies were degraded by specialization and by limitation of their activities to a level far below that of the ideal all-round men evoked in Pericles' funeral speech. These "arrested" societies resembled in some respects the societies of bees and ants. Their stability may have resulted in the avoidance of many new adaptation problems but proved incompatible with the growth of their civilizations, indeed, with the very growth of man. It was the awareness of this limitation which had estranged D. H. Lawrence from the Polynesian Paradise:

There they are, these South Sea Islanders, beautiful big men with their golden limbs and their laughing, graceful laziness. . . . They are like children, they are generous: but they are more than this. They are far off, and in their eyes is an early darkness of the soft, uncreate past. . . . There is his woman, with her knotted hair and her dark, inchoate, slightly sardonic eyes. . . . She has soft warm flesh, like warm mud. Nearer the reptile, the Saurian age. . . .

Far be it from me to assume any "white" superiority. It seems to me, that in living so far, through all our bitter centuries of civilization, we have still been living onwards, forwards. . . . The past, the Golden Age of the past—what a nostalgia we all feel for it. Yet we don't want it when we get it. Try the South Seas.

The fact that, except for a few arrested societies, man has been living and struggling forward in a great life-development shows that utopias and all static formulas of society are out of tune with the human condition. It is the desire for change which has set man apart from the rest of the living world, by leading him to a life of adventure away from the environments to which he was biologically adapted, and it is this desire that will continue to generate the creative forces of his future. The Athenians symbolize for us the most brilliant achievement of mankind because, according to Thucydides, "They go on working away in hardship and danger all the days of their lives, seldom enjoying their possessions as they are always adding to them. They prefer hardship and activity to peace and quiet."

Once his essential biological needs are satisfied, man develops other urges which have little bearing on his survival as a species. When he no longer needs to struggle for his loaf of bread he is wont to crave an unessential savory, then to long for some artistic expression. When he has established all kinds of direct and indirect contacts with the surrounding world he begins to worry about the next television set and soon longs to explore the rest of the universe. Indeed, it is probably the most distinguishing aspect of human life that it converts essential biological urges and functions into activities which have lost their original significance and purpose. Eating habits are now determined by acquired tastes and by social conventions rather than by nutritional requirements. The acts of love are performed for pleasure rather than for reproduction. "If all our women were to become as beautiful as the Venus de' Medici," wrote Charles Darwin in Chapter XIX of *The Descent of Man and Selection in Relation to Sex,* "we should be for a time charmed; but we should soon wish for variety, and as soon as we had obtained variety, we should wish to see certain characters a little exaggerated." Thus, man desires change for change's sake, without regard to any biological need. This desire expresses itself in the most ordinary manifestations of life, like the choice of food, and in the most sophisticated occupations, like the various forms of art. It affects the newest technological developments, like the hoods of motorcars, as well as the most ancient occupations, like hunting. Now that highpower rifles are available, sportsmen are returning to the use of primitive weapons. In 1957 forty thousand adults registered for the right to hunt with bow and arrow in the state of Michigan alone.

It is important, indeed, that there be available opportunities for change, for when they are lacking man is apt to satisfy his thirst for change by acts of violence or destruction. Dostoevsky's sniveling hero in *Letters from the*

Underworld could not find satisfaction in the order and comfort of the "Crystal Palace" world in which he lived; he chose an antisocial way of life because it was the one form of freedom of action still available to him. "Well, gentlemen, what about giving all this commonsense a mighty kick . . . simply to send all these logarithms to the devil so that we can again live according to our foolish will?" "Man only exists for the purpose of proving to himself that he is a man and not an organ-stop! He will prove it even if it means physical suffering, even if it means turning his back on civilization." Many forms of delinquency among our overfed teenagers probably come from their unspent creative energy.

Mankind behaves like the restless, sleepless traveler who turns in his berth to one side and then to the other, feeling better while changing position even though he knows that the change will not bring him lasting comfort. This restlessness is commonly identified with the concept of progress. In reality, however, the only certain fact is that human history is increasingly governed by the search for variety, at times for the sake of creation, more commonly just for recreation, but in any case unrelated to the forces which determine the evolution of biological traits. Progress means only movement without implying any clear statement of direction. At most it can be said that, despite so many disheartening setbacks, the activities of man seem to have on the whole a direction upward and forward which tends to better his life physically, intellectually, and morally.

The desire for progress may be nothing more than man's declaration of independence from the blind forces of nature. To paint the Last Supper, to write a poem, or to build an empire demands the expenditure of a form of energy and produces a type of result which does not have an obvious place in the natural order of things. In fact, as we have seen, certain of man's ideals and goals threaten to have consequences unfavorable for the human species. The cultivation of refined or esoteric tastes may interfere with the play of adaptive mechanisms and render man more vulnerable to some of his ancient plagues. The very mastery of nature may release dangers that cannot be controlled. Changes in the social order which increase the richness and variety of life can also, especially if too rapid, upset the ecological equilibria on which depends the continuation of the human species.

Awareness of dangers is not likely to deflect the course of mankind, for man does not live by bread alone. "All man wants," wrote Dostoevsky, "is an absolutely *free* choice, however dear that freedom may cost him and wherever it may lead him." True enough, most men run almost mechanically like clocks from their birth to their death, motivated only by their biological needs of the moment and by the desire to feel socially secure. But their very passivity makes them of little importance for social evolution. The aspect of human nature which is significant because unique is that certain men have goals which transcend biological purpose.

Among other living things, it is man's dignity to value certain ideals above comfort, and even above life. This human trait makes of medicine a philosophy that goes beyond exact medical sciences, because it must encompass not only man as a living machine but also the collective aspirations of mankind. A perfect policy of public health could be conceived for colonies of social ants or bees whose habits have become stabilized by instincts. Likewise it would be possible to devise for a herd of cows an ideal system of husbandry with the proper combination of stables and pastures. But, unless men become robots, no formula can ever give them permanently the health and happiness symbolized by the contented cow, nor can their societies achieve a structure that will last for millennia. As long as mankind is made up of independent individuals with free will, there cannot be any social status quo. Men will develop new urges, and these will give rise to new problems, which will require ever new solutions. Human life implies adventure, and there is no adventure without struggles and dangers.

Envoi

Men naturally desire health and happiness. For some of them, however, perhaps for all, these words have implications that transcend ordinary biological concepts. The kind of health that men desire most is not necessarily a state in which they experience physical vigor and a sense of well-being, not even one giving them a long life. It is, instead, the condition best suited to reach goals that each individual formulates for himself. Usually these goals bear no relation to biological necessity; at times, indeed, they are antithetic to biological usefulness. More often than not the pursuit of health and happiness is guided by urges which are social rather than biological; urges which are so peculiar to men as to be meaningless for other living things because they are of no importance for the survival of the individual or of the species.

The satisfactions which men crave most, and the sufferings which scar their lives most deeply, have determinants which do not all reside in the flesh or in the reasonable faculties and are not completely accounted for by scientific laws.

"Reason," wrote Dostoevsky, "can only satisfy the reasoning ability of man, whereas volition is a manifestation of the whole of life. . . . Reason knows only what it has succeeded in getting to know . . . whereas human nature acts as a whole, with everything that is in it, consciously, and unconsciously, and though it may commit all sorts of absurdities, it persists." Exact sciences give correct answers to certain aspects of life problems, but very incomplete answers. It is important of course to count and measure what is countable and measurable, but the most precious values in human life are aspirations which laboratory experiments cannot yet reproduce. As Haeckel pointed out, Richtigkeit—correctness—is not sufficient to reach Wahrheit—the real truth.

Homo sapiens as a biological machine may not have changed much since Pleistocene times, but mankind has continued to evolve, developing a new kind of life almost transcendental to its earthly biological origin. It is a paradoxical attribute of many human beings that their behavior is often governed by criteria and desires that they value more than life itself. To comprehend the biology of mankind, the story of human evolution, it is helpful to remember Aristotle's saying: "The nature of man is not what he is born as, but what he is born for." Indeed, some men in all ages have been guided by the faith that "he who would save his life first must lose it." Alone among living things, men are willing to sacrifice the purely biological manifestation of their existence at the altar of a higher form of life—conceived in the soul rather than experienced in the flesh. Even the least religious of thinking men believes in the deep symbolism of what Paul wrote of human nature: "It is sown a natural body; it is raised a spiritual body. . . . The first man is of the earth, earthy: the second man is the Lord from heaven."

Because man is a spiritual body he is more concerned with a way of life than with his physical state. Balzac, on his deathbed, projected Herculean labors and pleaded with his physician to keep him alive six weeks longer in order that he might finish his work. "Six weeks with fever is an eternity. Hours are like days . . . and then the nights are not lost." Marcel Proust, also on the day before he died, wrote of those obligations of the artist which seem to be derived from some other world, "based on goodness, scrupulousness, sacrifice."

"Work is more important than life," Katherine Mansfield confided to the last pages of her *Journal*. Searching for a definition of health that would satisfy her body riddled with tuberculosis and also her tormented soul, she could only conclude: "By health, I mean the power to live a full, adult, living, breathing life in close contact with what I love—the earth and the wonders thereof—the sea—the sun. . . . *I want to be all that I am capable of becoming,* so that I may be . . . there's only one phrase that will do— *a child of the sun.*"

The sun is not merely a source of warmth, of light, of food, of power. It is also the symbol of human aspirations. Like Icarus, who soaring upward to heaven plummeted to the sea and died when his waxen wings were melted by the sun, man deliberately exposes himself to dangers and even to destruction whenever he tries to escape from his biological and earthly bondage. Wherever he goes, whatever he undertakes, he will encounter new challenges and new threats to his welfare. Attempts at adaptation will demand efforts, and these efforts will often result in failure, partial or total, temporary or permanent. Disease will remain an inescapable manifestation of his struggles.

While it may be comforting to imagine a life free of stresses and strains in a carefree world, this will remain an idle dream. Man cannot hope to find another Paradise on earth, because paradise is a static concept while human life is a dynamic process. Man could escape danger only by renouncing adventure, by abandoning that which has given to the human condition its unique character and genius among the rest of living things. Since the days of the cave man, the earth has never been a Garden of Eden, but a Valley of Decision where resilience is essential to survival. The earth is not a resting place. Man has elected to fight, not necessarily for himself but for a process of emotional, intellectual, and ethical growth that goes on forever. To grow in the midst of dangers is the fate of the human race, because it is the law of the spirit.

MARSTON BATES

Man and the Balance of Nature

Marston Bates (1906–   ), Professor of Zoology at the University of Michigan, has had a wide research experience in various parts of the globe, both on land and on the oceans. The following passage from his The Forest and the Sea *is an honest facing of the difficulties a trained scientist confronts when he tries to place man—ethics and all—in Nature. I suggest that the ecologist's concept of homeostasis, like the physicist's concept of equilibrium, ought to lead the scientist to the kind of position as to planned social, economic, and political action suggested by the familiar Hippocratic "Do no harm"—don't interfere too radically and too rapidly with Nature. In politics, this would imply a conservative position. Note also that the position of another biologist, Dr. Dubos, in the preceding passage, also has conservative implications. Incidentally, Professor Bates's reading suggestions, on pp. 263–268 of his book, are an admirable prospectus for the reader who wants to go further in many directions.*

THE PROBLEM OF MAN'S PLACE IN NATURE, THEN, IS THE PROBLEM OF the relations between man's developing cultures and other aspects of the biosphere. The understanding of these is greatly handicapped by the way in which we have come to organize knowledge. To be sure, man with his varying cultures and cultural traits forms a special phenomenon which requires special means of study and the accumulation of special sorts of information. But still, man has not escaped from the biosphere. He has got into a new, unprecedented kind of relationship with the biosphere; and his success in maintaining this may well depend not only on his understanding of himself, but on his understanding of this world in which he lives.

This makes the split between the social and biological sciences particularly unfortunate. Economics and ecology, as words, have the same root; but that is about all they have in common. As fields of knowledge, they are cultivated in remotely separated parts of our universities, through the use of quite different methods, by scholars who would hardly recognize any-

From Marston Bates, *The Forest and the Sea* (New York: Random House, 1960), pp. 250–262.

thing in common. The world of the ecologists is "unspoiled nature." They tend to avoid cities, parks, fields, orchards. The real world of the economists is like Plato's, it is a world of ideas, of abstractions—money, labor, market, goods, capital. There is no room for squirrels scolding in the oak trees, no room for robins on the lawn. There is no room for people either, for that matter—people loving and hating and dreaming. People become the labor force or the market.

More and more, in all areas, we tend to separate the study of man from the study of nature. The separation is one of the basic lines of division in the way we have organized knowledge, in our pattern of specialization. The natural sciences and the social sciences exist in practically complete isolation from one another. Man's body, curiously, has been left with the natural sciences while the social sciences have taken over his mind—at a time when we are most aware of the artificiality of the body-mind separation.

Our third great division of basic knowledge, the humanities, has long since forgotten about nature. Joseph Wood Krutch can well remark: "There are many courses in 'The Nature Poets' in American colleges. But nature is usually left out of them." Surely there is some way of putting all of these things together, of achieving a more balanced view of ourselves and the rest of the natural world. The matter, I think, has some urgency.

Ours has been aptly called the age of anxiety, and this is curious. We should be able to look about us and feel a certain self-satisfaction. We have learned to develop and direct tremendous power; we can create the kind of conditions we find comfortable; we can produce large quantities of a great variety of foods; we have achieved a surprising degree of control over disease and physical pain. In almost any way we assess man's relations with his environment, he seems to be doing well when compared with the past, even though there is still obvious room for great improvement.

Yet, despite this abundance and progress, almost all attempts to look at man's future are gloomy. I can't think of any recently written image of the future that sounds very attractive, even when the author was trying hard to look for glories. The glories mostly turn out to be bigger and better gadgets, faster trips to a dismal Mars, or better adjusted husbands and wives who no longer take to drink. Usually the author looking into the future doesn't pretend to like his 1984 or his brave new world: but looking about him, this is what he sees coming.

Our anxiety about the future, when we analyze it, turns largely on three related things: the likelihood of continuing warfare, the dizzy rate of human population growth, and the exhaustion of resources. But these don't look like insoluble problems. Surely men who can manufacture a moon can learn to stop killing each other; men who can control infectious disease can learn to breed more thoughtfully than guinea pigs; men who can measure the universe can learn to act wisely in handling the materials of the universe. Why are we so pessimistic?

Chiefly, I suspect, because we have come more and more to doubt our ability to act rationally. Reason seems to be a property of individual men, not of the species or of organized groups. Somewhere we have lost the faith of the Eighteenth Century French philosophers in the perfectibility of man, and the rather different faith of the Nineteenth Century in the idea of progress.

Maybe the anthropologists are right when they say that culture acts as a thing in itself, sweeping along according to inexorable laws, no more under man's control than rodent evolution is under the control of the mice in the fields. The difference between men and mice, then, would be a matter only of awareness, of self-consciousness. We can study the laws of cultural evolution—or organic evolution—but we can't change them. We can foretell our doom but we can't forestall it.

I don't believe this, and I doubt whether the extreme culturists really believe it either. If they believed what they say, I think they wouldn't talk so much. They are like the disciples of Karl Marx who say they believe in the inexorable dialectic of history, but continually try to give history a push in the right direction. Man can't change the laws of cultural evolution or organic evolution—true enough, no doubt—but understanding the laws and acting with the laws, he can influence the consequences. He has in his hands a certain measure of control over his destiny, but this control depends on understanding, and on the spread and proper use of knowledge.

The great immediate threat, of course, is the misuse of nuclear power, the danger of catastrophic war. The long-term threat is the cancerous multiplication of the numbers of men: a new human population the size of the city of Detroit every month, year after year. The thought is dizzying. And then the thought of a nuclear blast capable of killing last month's millions in a few seconds is hardly reassuring. It looks as though, as a part of nature, we have become a disease of nature—perhaps a fatal disease. And when the host dies, so does the pathogen.

How, in the face of our power, in the face of our danger, do we develop a guiding philosophy?

No single man, no single field of knowledge, holds the answer to that. But all men and all knowledge can contribute to the answer. Insofar as man's relations with the rest of nature are concerned, I think we must make every effort to maintain diversity—that we must make this effort even though it requires constant compromise with apparent immediate needs. To look at this, it may be most convenient to sort out the arguments into those that are primarily ethical, those that are primarily esthetic, and those that are essentially utilitarian.

Albert Schweitzer remarks in his autobiography that "the great fault of all ethics hitherto has been that they believed themselves to have to deal only with the relations of man to man." This is particularly true in the Western, Christian tradition. The present material world, in the philosophy of this tradition, is unimportant, no more than a transient scene for the testing of the soul's fitness for eternity. The material universe is completely man-centered. Nature, insofar as it is noticed, is only a convenience—or a temptation—with no positive value in itself.

Animals are unimportant because they have no souls. God may notice the sparrows, but this is an example of His omniscience rather than of His preoccupation. Even Christ gave no thought to the Gadarene swine. The first arguments against bear-baiting, cockfighting and the like were not that they were liable to cause injury and pain to the animals, but that they were liable to demoralize the human character, leading to gambling, thievery and the like.

For a considerable part of humanity, however, this world has direct religious significance. Many primitive religions have various forms of nature worship, of animism and totemism. But in some of the great religions, particularly Buddhism and Hinduism, attitudes toward nature—toward animals in particular—have an ethical basis. For many millions of Hindus it is a sin to kill any animal. With the Jains, this is carried to an extreme to avoid possible injury even to the tiniest of insects.

We deplore the Hindu attitude toward cattle as uneconomical—which it certainly is—and a handicap to the development of India. In countries within the Western tradition, however, attitudes toward animals often cannot be explained on practical or rational grounds. I suspect that a visitor from Mars, observing our treatment of dogs, cats and other domestic pets, would conclude that they were sacred animals. Horses in some Western subcultures are also treated as sacred animals. The horror of eating horse meat—or dog meat—seems not too different from the Muslim horror of eating pig or the Hindu horror of eating any animal.

There have always been individuals within the Christian tradition with a love of nature, with a kind feeling toward animals. St. Francis of Assisi rightfully is their patron. In modern times this has grown into a cult of great emotional force, leading to the development of a variety of formal organizations for the prevention of cruelty to animals, for the protection of wildlife, which reaches an extreme in the anti-vivisectionist groups. This attitude is most highly developed in the industrialized regions since it goes along with economic security and relative leisure. It is a characteristic of "affluent societies." It is reassuring in the sense that kindness and tolerance and sympathy—whether for slaves, for children or for animals—seem to gain force and spread with economic development.

This kindness and sympathy for animals might well be classed as an ethical attitude. Curiously, along with the cult of kindness to animals, we have a parallel development in the same societies and circumstances of the cult of the sportsman, in which killing becomes a good in itself. As hunting ceased to be a necessity, it became a luxury for men; and hunting as play, hunting as sport, has long characterized classes of men with the leisure to indulge in it. Hunting is sometimes thought to represent a basic "instinct" in human nature, and certainly there is something elemental and primitive in the thrill of the chase. Intellectually, I have abandoned hunting as a sport since, when a boy, I watched the agonies of a raccoon I had wounded. But often enough, hunting for some worthy "scientific" purpose, I have felt my intellectual pretensions slide away and I have become lost in the purely emotional absorption of getting my game.

The sport of kings and noblemen has now become the sport of millions, of anyone with an automobile and a rifle or shotgun. It is recreation. But also a philosophy has developed whereby this killing of deer and ducks and quail is supposed to inculcate virtue. Krutch quotes the propaganda slogan of a gun company: "Go hunting with your boy and you'll never have to go hunting for him."

I get lost in the ethical issues involved in these problems. Intellectually I sympathize with the teachings of Buddha, that all life is sacred. But practically, I see no way of acting on this. There is no logical stopping place before the end reached by the people of Samuel Butler's *Erewhon*. They became vegetarian out of respect for the rights of animals. But as one of their learned men pointed out, vegetables are equally alive, and equally have rights. So the Erewhonians, to be consistent, are reduced to eating cabbages certified to have died a natural death. Monkeys, deer, cows, rats, quail, songbirds, lizards, fish, insects, molluscs, vegetables—where do you draw the line between what can be properly killed and eaten, and what not? It so happens that I don't like decayed cabbages and I do like rare roast beef—which leaves me, as usual, blundering around in a quandary.

The ethical question is difficult. We have drifted in the modern world into a position of ethical relativism which leaves us with no absolutes of good and bad, right and wrong. Things are good or right according to the context, depending on the values of the society or culture. Yet one feels that there must be some basis of right conduct, applicable to all men and all places and not depending on any particular dogma or any specific revelation. Science has undermined the dogmas and revelations; and it provides, for many working scientists, a sort of faith, a sort of humanism, that can replace the need for an articulated code of conduct. But our scientists and philosophers have so far failed to explain this in a way that reaches any very large number of people. This, it seems to me, is one of the great tasks of modern philosophy, which the philosophers, dallying in their academic groves, have shunned.

When some thinker does come forth to provide us with a rationale for conduct, he will have to consider not only the problems of man's conduct with his fellow men, but also of man's conduct toward nature. Life is a unity; the biosphere is a complex network of interrelations among all the host of living things. Man, in gaining the godlike quality of awareness, has also acquired a godlike responsibility. The questions of the nature of his relationships with the birds and the beasts, with the trees of the forests and the fish of the seas, become ethical questions: questions of what is good and right not only for man himself, but for the living world as a whole. In the words of Aldo Leopold, we need to develop an ecological conscience.

It is someimes said that the esthetic appreciation of nature is relatively new, that the Greeks, for instance, did not admire landscapes. The matter can be argued and I don't know that anyone has made a careful study of changing attitudes, or of differences in attitude among the great civilizations. Within our own civilization, it looks as though the conscious appreciation of the beauties of nature had its roots in the so-called Romantic Movement of the Eighteenth Century. We can see this most plainly in literature, in landscape painting and in landscape architecture. It is less clear in the other arts, though Lovejoy plausibly equates it with the love of diversity and the search for new forms that characterize Western art generally in the last two centuries.

It looks as though man's esthetic appreciation of nature increases as the development of his civilization removes him from constant and immediate contact with nature. The peasant hardly notices the grandeur of the view from his fields; the woodsman is not impressed by stately trees, nor the fisherman by the forms and colors on the reefs. In part, this is the general problem of not seeing the familiar, of not appreciating what we have until it is lost.

The reasons behind the conservation movement, from this point of view, are similar to the reasons for preserving antiquities, for maintaining museums of art or history or science. Nature is beautiful, therefore it should not be wantonly destroyed. Representative landscapes should be preserved because of their esthetic value, because of their importance in scientific study, and because of their possibilities for recreation.

I have often wished, as I saw a tropical forest being cleared, that this beautiful place could somehow be protected and preserved for the future to enjoy. The idea, to the people involved in the clearing, seems absurd. The forest is an enemy, to be fought and destroyed; beauty lies in the fields and orchards that will replace it. This was the attitude of our ancestors who in the end effectively cleared the great deciduous forest that once covered the eastern United States, leaving only accidental and incidental traces. How we would love now to have a fair sample of that great forest! But the idea of deliberately saving a part of the wilderness they were conquering never occurred to the pioneers. Nor does it occur to pioneers now in parts of the world where pioneering is still possible.

There must be some way in which one nation can profit by the experience of another nation; some way of saving examples of the landscapes and wildlife that have not yet been devastated by the onrush of industrial civilization. In Africa there is a danger that the national parks will be regarded as toys of colonial administrations, and fade with the fading of those administrations. And the colonial powers, even with the experience of loss in their homelands, are not always too careful about the preservation and maintenance of samples of the natural world under their care.

In tropical America we have the effect of the Spanish tradition. The Romantic Movement never crossed the Pyrenees. Spanish thought and art remain essentially man-centered. Some of my Spanish friends have suggested that the relative failure of science to develop in that tradition may be a consequence of this indifference, on the part of most of the people, to the world of nature. The correction for this might be deliberate attempts to foster nature study in the school systems. Whatever the cause, the conservation movement has not made great headway in the parts of the world dominated by Spanish culture.

In the United States, we have a National Park system, and various sorts of reservations and wildlife refuges under national, state and private auspices. This is largely the consequence of the dedicated efforts of a few people, and we are still far from the point where we can sit back and congratulate ourselves. Conservation interests fall under different branches of government and efforts to form a coherent and unified national policy have not been very successful; we still have no Department of Conservation with cabinet rank. The struggle for financial support is always hard. And there is a constant, eroding pressure from conflicting private and governmental interests.

Ugliness—by any esthetic standard—remains the predominant characteristic of development, of urbanization, of industrialization. We talk about regional planning, diversification, working with the landscape—and we build vast stretches of the new suburbia. The ideas so forcefully developed by Patrick Geddes, Lewis Mumford and others like them, fall on deaf ears. We need an ecological conscience. We also need to develop ecological appreciation. The Romantic Movement, despite its two hundred year history, has not yet reached our city councils or our highway engineers.

Practical considerations are—and perhaps ought to be—overwhelmingly important in governing man's relations with the rest of nature. Utility, at first thought, requires man to concentrate selfishly and arrogantly on his own immediate needs and convenience, to regard nature purely as a subject for exploitation. A little further thought, however, shows the fallacy of this. The danger of complete man-centeredness in relation to nature is like the danger of immediate and thoughtless selfishness everywhere: the momentary gain results in ultimate loss and defeat. "Enlightened self-interest" requires some consideration for the other fellow, for the other nation, for the other point of view; some giving with the taking. This applies with particular force to relations between man and the rest of nature.

The trend of human modification of the biological community is toward simplification. The object of agriculture is to grow pure stands of crops, single species of plants that can be eaten directly by man; or single crops that provide food for animals that can be eaten. The shorter the food chain, the more efficient the conversion of solar energy into human food. The logical end result of this process, sometimes foreseen by science fiction writers, would be the removal of all competing forms of life—

with the planet left inhabited by man alone, growing his food in the form of algal soup cultivated in vast tanks. Perhaps ultimately the algae could be dispensed with, and there would be only man, living through chemical manipulations.

Efficient, perhaps; dismal, certainly; and also dangerous. A general principle is gradually emerging from ecological study to the effect that the more complex the biological community, the more stable. The intricate checks and balances among the different populations in a forest or a sea look inefficient and hampering from the point of view of any particular population, but they insure the stability and continuity of the system as a whole and thus, however indirectly, contribute to the survival of particular populations.

Just as health in a nation is, in the long run, promoted by a diversified economy, so is the health of the biosphere promoted by a diversified ecology. The single crop system is always in precarious equilibrium. It is created by man and it has to be maintained by man, ever alert with chemicals and machinery, with no other protection against the hazards of some new development in the wounded natural system. It is man working against nature: an artificial system with the uncertainties of artifacts. Epidemic catastrophe becomes an ever present threat.

This is one of the dangers inherent in man's mad spree of population growth—he is being forced into an ever more arbitrary, more artificial, more precarious relation with the resources of the planet. The other great danger is related. With teeming numbers, an ever tighter system of control becomes necessary. Complex organization, totalitarian government, becomes inevitable; the individual man becomes a worker ant, a sterile robot. This surely is not our inevitable destiny.

I am not advocating a return to the neolithic. Obviously we have to have the most efficient systems possible for agriculture and resource use. But long run efficiency would seem to require certain compromises with nature—hedgerows and woodlots along with orchards and fields, the development of a variegated landscape, leaving some leeway for the checks and balances and diversity of the system of nature.

Ethical, esthetic and utilitarian reasons thus all support the attempt to conserve the diversity of nature. It is morally the right thing to do; it will provide, for future generations, a richer and more satisfying experience than would otherwise be possible; and it provides a much needed insurance against ecological catastrophe. "Unless one merely thinks man was intended to be an all-conquering and sterilizing power in the world," Charles Elton has remarked, "there must be some general basis for understanding what it is best to do. This means looking for some wise principle of co-existence between man and nature, even if it be a modified kind of man and a modified kind of nature. This is what I understand by *conservation*."

In defying nature, in destroying nature, in building an arrogantly selfish, man-centered, artificial world, I do not see how man can gain peace or freedom or joy. I have faith in man's future, faith in the possibilities latent in the human experiment: but it is faith in man as a part of nature, working with the forces that govern the forests and the seas; faith in man sharing life, not destroying it.

SIR CHARLES GALTON DARWIN

The Next Million Years

Sir Charles Galton Darwin (1887–   ) is an English physicist, grandson of the famous naturalist. I find his little excursion into our field of cosmological-philosophical-ethical studies, The Next Million Years, *a fascinating example of what seems to me the logical world-view that bases itself on a rigorous scientific naturalism. I use "logical," of course, not in the sense good logicians use it, but merely to indicate a kind of consonance between what goes on in the head and what wells up in the emotions of the thinker. The thesis of Darwin's book is that, since man has in the 100,-000 years or so he has been on earth shown the full range of his capabilities, his "human nature," it will take about a million years to develop a new, different, perhaps "better" species. (Or merely better adapted—but adapted to what?) Meanwhile, the next million years will be much like the last five or six thousand we know from history, full of the ups and downs of human societies and human individual lives, fascinating, varied, uncertain, harsh, and exalting to those who experience them, but to the eye of the historian they may appear as a single piece, as life in a long geological era looks to the geologist. We are a long way from Condorcet and Herbert Spencer. Back, perhaps, at Lucretius, who would surely have enjoyed Sir Charles's book?*

BEFORE COMING TO THE DETAILS IT MAY BE WELL TO REMIND THE reader once again of the operation of the law of large numbers in connection with probabilities. In the events of the world one cannot of course actually give numerical values to the odds as one can in a game of chance, but I can use the analogy to show what I mean. If I said that the odds were two to one on such and such a state of the world as compared to some rival state, I should not mean that it was twice as likely that the favoured state would be happening all the time; I should mean that in the course

From Charles Galton Darwin, *The Next Million Years* (Garden City, N. Y.: Doubleday & Co., 1953), pp. 168-181, 197-208.

of the ages it would prevail for about two-thirds of the time, and the rival state for one-third. Now there can be no doubt that most things in the world fall under the category of large numbers—the mere fact that there are even at the present time two thousand million individuals guarantees this—so that probabilities become certainties in the sense that very probable things will be happening most of the time, while less probable things will still happen, but only for a small part of the time. But there may be occurrences so rare that the law of large numbers cannot be applied to them at all; for example the discovery of the New World in the fifteenth century was a unique thing, because there were no other new worlds to discover. Or again there is the unlikely, but possible, chance that there should be a collision of the solar system with another star, which would destroy all life on earth. If any such rare event should occur, it would upset all predictions, and there is nothing more to be said about it.

There are no doubt readers who will dislike many of the things I am forecasting and who will try to evade them by the hope that one of these rare unforeseeable chances will entirely alter things, and lead to a condition of the world more to their liking. It is possible, but it is much more likely that such things will be unfavourable than favourable. Whereas small changes produced by chance are as likely to be beneficial as detrimental, when it comes to large changes, the probability is that they will be unfavourable. I have already cited an example of this from the science of genetics, where, by means of X-rays, changes can be induced in the genes of the cells of animals. If the change is small, it may benefit the animal, but if it is large it is almost invariably deleterious, and often lethal. The balance of the natural forces in an animal is so delicate, that any large change in one feature upsets it entirely; only if there were compensating large changes in other features could the condition of the animal be improved, and there is practically no chance of these other changes happening to occur simultaneously. A similar principle must apply to the delicate balance of interactions which go to make up the life of the human race. Thus anyone who hopes that some rare, large, unforeseeable occurrence may better the fate of humanity is almost certain to be disappointed, for it is enormously more likely to worsen it. The best hopes of benefiting humanity are to be based not on this, but on the working of small changes and the law of large numbers, by which there is at least some prospect little by little of improving the condition of the world.

In what follows I shall divide up the principal activities of humanity under the headings of population, economics and so on, and consider each briefly in turn. It may be well to repeat that the views I put forward on these subjects are not intended to be exclusive. It is to be expected that there will be many happenings that contradict them; I am only claiming that such happenings are likely to occur a good deal less frequently than the conditions described here.

Population

The central feature of human history must always be the pressure of population. Man, the wild animal, will obey the law of life and will tend to multiply until he is limited by the means of subsistence. This is the normal condition of the world, and it carries the consequence that the final check on population is by starvation. There will be a fraction of humanity, a *starving margin,* who have got to die simply because not enough food can be grown to keep them alive. The death may be directly due to intermittent famines, or to diseases caused by malnutrition, or it may be due to warfare; for when a country is dying of starvation and sees, or thinks it sees, a neighbouring country with plenty to eat, it would be beyond most human nature to accept certain passive death instead of possible active death. The central question for humanity is the problem of the starving margin.

To those of us living the life of Europe at the present time this is a shocking fact, implying a condition so unfamiliar that there are many who may not willingly believe it. This is because of the quite exceptional history of the nineteenth century, during which, in spite of enormous increases of population, many countries had no starving margin at all. The disbelief may be helped by the fact that the population of some countries has recently started to decrease. Such decreases have occasionally happened before too, but, as I have argued earlier, they constitute an entirely unstable state of affairs, in that the nations which are decreasing in numbers will die out, and will be replaced by the starving margins of the others.

On the time-scale I am considering, the action of starvation can be treated as if it were uniform and continuous, but it is fortunate that it would not appear so to the individual, for famines are not like that. Since man can never aspire to the real control of climate, there will always be fluctuations in the harvests he can produce. For some years there may be a sequence of good harvests, and starvation will be forgotten by everyone, but after that a few bad harvests will fatally redress the balance. So it would be wrong to imagine that the starving margin suffers a life of continuous grinding misery, but rather one of misery alternating with a precarious prosperity. Even so there are many at the present time who will regard this state of affairs as very dreadful, but . . . it has always been the normal condition of life of the Eskimos, who have the reputation of being the most cheerful race on earth. So, as far as concerns the individual, the starving margin would not be in a state of continuous misery, but rather of misery alternating with happiness, which after all is not very far below the state of the rest of the world. For history regarded on the long-term scale, however, these fluctuations of prosperity disappear, and the fact has to be faced that it will be starvation that limits the numbers of the human race.

The effects of over-population will be a chief feature to be considered in the later sections of this chapter, but here the question arises of what the total population of the world is likely to be, and the answer is immediate. Whatever food the efforts of mankind may produce, there will always be exactly the right number of people to eat it. It all comes back to Malthus's doctrine and to the fact that an arithmetical progression cannot fight against a geometrical progression. If at any time some discovery, usually an agricultural one, should make a greater supply of food available, then, reckoning on the long-term time-scale, instantaneously the population will rise to the new level, and after that things will go on as before, but now with a larger starving margin in the larger population. It is by no means evident that the world will be any the better for it, but the point is not whether it is a good thing, but whether it will happen, and the answer is that undoubtedly it will. The social sense of any community, and its immediate practical interest, will not tolerate living in contact with the sufferings of its own starving margin, if it is in any way possible to relieve them. The relief will all too frequently involve bad agricultural practice which will ruin the land in the long run, but short-term necessity will always prevail against long-term prudence. What is the good of telling a man that he must die now for fear that his grandson may be short of food a century hence? So all over the world there will be immediate pressure to produce more food, and the forecast of the future numbers of mankind is the same thing as the forecast of the future of agricuture, but unfortunately it will all too often not be the ideally best agriculture.

I do not know how far it would be possible at the present time for an agricultural expert to forecast the total amount of food the earth could produce, but I am certainly in no way qualified to do so myself. I shall therefore, though only very tentatively, set down a few considerations on the subject. In the state of wild nature animals and plants have learnt to live even in the most unfavourable sites, which they have been driven to occupy through the intense pressure of natural selection. This suggests that the total amount of living matter of all kinds on earth can never be very different from what it is now. It is true that new ice ages or pluvial periods, which we cannot foretell, might bring rain and therefore fertility to the present deserts of the earth, but even if there were no compensatory loss of fertility elsewhere, this would hardly even double the area available for life. So it may be assumed that the total living matter of the earth is roughly constant, and all that man can hope to do is to convert more of it to his own use. This he does by promoting the growth of particular types plant at the expense of the rest; it does not increase the total amount of living matter, for there must be less vegetable life in a wheat field, than in the same field when it is let to run wild. Now under the pressure of his needs man has already exploited to a very great extent the more fertile soils in many parts of the world, but he has only succeeded in replacing the wild plants by food plants through the liberal use of fertilizers. There are still no doubt a good many parts of the earth where this has not yet happened; in particular this is true of the New World where the pressure of population has not yet become at all severe. But on the whole to develop further food supplies means devoting inferior lands to agriculture, and such lands will call for an even greater use of fertilizers. So the possibility of greater supplies of food may be assessed by the available supply of fertilizers.

It may then be that the future numbers of humanity will depend on the abundance in the surface of the earth of the chemical elements which are necessary for life. Most of them are abundant enough to raise no difficulty, either because they occur in practically unlimited quantities, or because only small quantities are needed. Two only deserve comment, nitrogen and phosphorus. The supply of nitrogen in the air is quite unlimited, but it is not easily available to plants by natural processes, and to supply it in sufficient quantities for agriculture demands a considerable amount of mechanical power. This method of getting nitrogen is of course already common practice, and provided enough work is done to win it, there seems no reason to think that nitrogen need ever run short. The question of phosphorus is far more serious, though less of it is needed. At the present time it cannot be said to be actually in short supply, though even now it is commercially very profitable to mine fossilized phosphorus deposits, and they are used even in the soils which are naturally fertile. There are great tracts of land, in particular in Africa, which are permanently deficient in phosphorus, and these can never be raised to the fertility of the more favoured regions, unless large quantities of it can be supplied to them. So it may well be that the future numbers of the human race will depend on the abundance of phosphorus in the earth's surface.

I have so far only considered extensions of the methods of ordinary agriculture as the way to increase food supplies, but there remains the possibility that wholly new methods might be discovered. All existing animals depend on the vegetable kingdom for the supply of the constituents of their bodies, but man might aspire to free himself from this limitation. It may well be that some day it will be found possible to synthesize from their component elements some of the exceedingly complicated molecules which make up the important proteins. The essential first step is to do this on the laboratory scale, but even if this was accomplished it would be a very different thing to make them in bulk, and it would constitute a problem of chemical engineering very far beyond any that has yet been dreamed of. It is perfectly open to anyone to disagree, but I simply cannot believe that there will ever exist factories capable of turning inorganic materials directly into food, so that they should be able to do it on a scale which could supply the diet of thousands of millions of mankind. Unless it could be done on this scale it would not have any material effect on the numbers of humanity.

There remains the possibility that new types of vegetable should be converted into food fit for man. I have already touched on the possibility that man might some day make grass into an article of human diet, which is in effect only to say that he might discover a more efficient way of eating it than through the medium of beef. But it is to be remembered that the ox has to graze most of the time in order to get enough protein even for its own body, and this shows that only a small fraction of the grass could be really useful to man. The process of directly extracting the protein might be more efficient than making the ox do it, but it would hardly be hundreds of times more efficient. And it is at least possible that, when the plant-breeder had modified the grass into being rich in proteins, he would find it demanded fertilizers on such a large scale, that it would be more profitable to use them instead for growing wheat.

A quite different suggestion that has been made, is that food supplies could be increased to an enormous extent by the cultivation of the vast areas of the ocean. The prospects do not look at all good. We know that every spring the plankton grows so fast that in a few weeks it has stripped the upper layers of the ocean bare of some of the chemical salts needed for life. To get large food supplies out of the sea would therefore demand much more than the mere harvesting of the plankton, though this would itself be a formidable task indeed. Either it would be necessary to expend an enormous amount of power in churning up the ocean, so as to make available the salts from the unimpoverished depths, or else fertilizing chemicals would have to be poured into the sea on a quite fantastic scale.

I shall not pursue such conjectures further, since, when unmade discoveries are admitted to be possible, the subject becomes so uncertain that it is hardly a profitable field for close argument. Nevertheless, I shall risk saving what appears to be the most probable forecast of the future numbers of mankind, though I need not say, I recognize that it may be completely upset by some unforeseen discovery. In view of the fact that it is only the existing vegetable kingdom that can be exploited, I do not believe there will be any revolutionary changes in agriculture but only steady improvements; the improvements will, so to speak, be described by increases in percentages, not by multiples of the present yields. The world will be covered by a population of the same sort of density as is now found in its richer agricultural districts, in countries such as China, India or much of Europe; but, in reckoning this, allowance must be made for differences of climate and of the natural fertility of the soils. In effect this will mean no great increase in the populations of Europe and Asia. The soils of Africa are for the most part not so good, but there is room for some increase there. There should be great increases in the Americas, and considerable ones in Australia and in some of the large Pacific islands. As I have pointed out short-term necessity is often likely to interfere with really good cultivation, but even if this good cultivation could be assumed, it may be estimated that the population of the world is never likely to be more than about three to five times its present numbers.

Golden Ages

The conditions of population pressure must be expected to be the world's normal state, but it is not of course a constant state, for there have at intervals been what may be called *golden ages,* periods when for a time a part of the world could forget about the starving margin. There has tended to be a certain warping in the proportions of history, as given to us by historians, perhaps because it has been chiefly during golden ages that there has been sufficient leisure for anyone to become an historian. At all events the great histories of the world have been written in such periods; Herodotus, the father of history, wrote during the commercial boom of Athens, Tacitus in the great days of imperial Rome, Gibbon at the height of the eighteenth century Age of Reason, and however much they were depicting less favourable times, their views were inevitably coloured by the conditions that they saw round them. Now we are living in or perhaps at the end of a golden age, which may well prove to have been the greatest golden age of all time, and we too are apt to be warped by the feeling that it is a normal time.

Many readers may be shocked at first at the thought that the past century, an epoch so often decried for its many faults, should have been the greatest of golden ages, but I think it can be justified. In past golden ages the prosperity was usually at the expense of other peoples; for example, Rome prospered by looting the east and enslaving the barbarians of the west. Our golden age came about with comparatively little harm to others; it was mainly through mechanical discoveries which made possible transportation on a great scale, so that vast new areas of the world could be opened up for agriculture. It is true that this was done largely at the expense of the American Indian, and his treatment often does not make a pretty story, but still it was a case of many hundred millions prospering at the expense of a few millions, and so the proportion of suffering inflicted to benefit received must have been far smaller than in most of the previous golden ages. The chief benefit was of course to the white races of the Atlantic seaboard, who for more than a century have been able to forget about their starving margin, but it has by no means been limited to them, for many of the other races have benefited too, as is witnessed by the great increases of population of India and Africa, though in these parts of the world they have not been so easily able to forget their starving margins. We are again becoming very conscious of the world's population problem, but now there are no frontiers or unknown parts of the world into which to expand, and so our golden age is probably near its end.

In the future there will of course be other golden ages, but it can hardly be expected that the balance between good and ill will often be as favourable as it has been in the recent one. It might be that, either by conquest or by commercial exploitation, some region should gain mastery over other regions, to such an extent that it could relieve the starvation of its own margin at their expense. The conquering nation would flourish and call it a golden age, forgetting that its prosperity was at the expense of the peoples it had overcome; it would be very unlike the colonial exploitations of our own age, which, even if they are open to criticism in some ways, have in most cases increased the populations of the colonies. Another possibility that might create a new golden age is that some discovery should make available a vast new source of food, and that consequently there would be enough food for perhaps double the previous population of the world. At once there would be a golden age, but after a very few generations the result would be even more desperate than before, for there would be a starving margin of people now twice as great. This in effect is not unlike what has been happening recently, but the present age has had an advantage, never likely to be repeated, in that it started at a time when the civilized world had frontiers over which it could expand, and now it has abolished all frontiers by expanding over the whole earth. Unless there should be a catastrophe to the world beyond all thinking it can never contract to such an extent that there would again be frontiers, and it is only if this happened that it could have the chance of again exploiting the vacant places of the earth, so that only under these conditions could there be another golden age, which in any sense would match the present one. . . .

Civilization

It will make a fitting end to my essay to consider the future of civilization; whether it will endure, permanently rising to still greater heights, or whether it is destined to decay after a period of efflorescence, as has happened to so many civilizations in the past. Though we should all agree rather vaguely as to what we mean by civilization, different people may regard very different aspects of it as the central feature. To some it may mean principally great developments in art or literature, to others well-equipped cities and houses, to others a good system of law, to others deep learning, and to others good social conditions. I do not dispute that all or any of these may be involved, but countries could be named, which everyone would concede were civilized, yet which have conspicuously lacked some of these excellences. So for want of a general definition the best way I can describe what seems to me to be involved is by citing an example from the past, the civilization of China.

The Chinese Empire has been civilized for over three thousand years, and until very recent times has enjoyed a very fair measure of isolation. Broadly speaking, during all that time it has retained the same general characteristics. It has been ruled by a succession of dynasties rising and decaying in turn. During the periods of decay, the provinces have often been practically independent, conducting warfare with one another, until at length a new strong hand has arisen to control them. In its forms of government it is true that China seems never to have produced anything like European democracy, but this lack is offset by the creation of a highly organized civil service, not merely centuries but millennia before anything of the kind existed in Europe. All the time the general character of the civilization has been preserved, now in one place, now in another. Sometimes it has been advanced by important new discoveries, such as the invention of printing. All the time there has been a liability to famines, which have killed off millions. The perpetual presence of a margin of starving humanity has set a low value on human life, and has made for callousness in regard to the sufferings of the people. This has led to much cruelty, of a kind we are unfamiliar with now, though it could have been matched anywhere in Europe a few centuries ago. There have been golden ages, when the arts have flourished as nowhere else on earth, and deep learning has been achieved, which we only do not reverence so much as do the Chinese, because it has taken rather a different colour from our own; but even in this we have to concede that the Confucian philosophy has lasted far longer than any of the philosophies of the West. It would seem that in its constancy of character, both in its virtues and in its defects, the Chinese civilization is to be accepted as the model type of a civilization to a greater degree than any of the other civilizations of the world.

In the manner in which it has retained its individual character permanently the Chinese civilization seems pre-eminent, but of course others too have survived for quite long periods. The Roman civilization, though it died in the West, was preserved in a modified form for nearly a thousand years longer in the East. In the same loose sense the Mesopotamian civilization was preserved by the Arabs at Baghdad, until it was overthrown by the Turks, and even so it survived in Egypt and in Spain. There have not been a great many different civilizations in all, so that it is not very safe to generalize; but admitting that some have disappeared leaving no heirs, still the general conclusion must be that in the main there has been at least some survival, if not in the place of origin, then elsewhere. However, that may be, our present civilization is in an incomparably stronger position, for it is dominated by the Scientific Revolution, which, as I have tried to show, makes it basically different from all previous civilizations.

The Scientific Revolution has introduced ways of thinking, which can claim a quality of universality, because they are objective and nearly independent of aesthetic tastes. Even now the community of scientists is quite international, so that they can discuss together the matters that concern them without any thought of national or racial differences. This has never been true of ideas in art, philosophy or religion. For example, the learned of Europe and the learned of China each reverence their own classical literature profoundly, but neither values very highly the classics of the other; whereas in their own subject the scientists of the whole world cannot help valuing the same things. If he is thinking, say, about an electric current, an educated Central African will go through the same processes of thought as an educated Englishman, and no difference in their aesthetic tastes will make any difference between them in this. The Scientific Revolution has changed the world materially in innumerable ways, but perhaps the most important of all is that it has provided a universality in methods of thought that was wanting before. So there is an even stronger reason to believe that the new culture cannot die, than ever held for any of the old civilizations; it has only got to survive in one part of the earth for it to be recoverable everywhere. Even the old civilizations survived for the most part, and it can be regarded as certain that the new culture will be inextinguishable.

A much more difficult question to answer is the question whether civilization will be retained within the same races, or whether there will have to be a perpetual renewal from more barbaric sources. Western Europe, which largely provided the barbarians who recreated the Roman civilization, is itself at the present time in imminent danger of committing suicide. Must civilization always lead to the limitation of families and consequent decay and then replacement from barbaric sources which in turn will go through the same experience? The new developments in birth-control make the threat a great deal more formidable, but in the long run I do not think that it is to be feared. There are already many people with a natural instinctive wish for children, and this wish is sometimes strong enough to outweigh the economic disadvantage which undoubtedly at present attaches to having a family. Such people will tend to have larger families than the rest, and in doing so will at least to some extent hand on the same instinctive wish to a greater number in the next generation. As I have already argued, the limitation of population is an unstable process, which cannot persist. It is very conjectural how long the transformation will take, but as the change that is needed in the balance of human sentiments is very slight, it seems likely that the new balance will not take very long to be established, perhaps thousands of years, but not hundreds of thousands. The first nation or race which can keep its civilization, and at the same time superpose on it this change in the balance of instincts, will have the advantage over all others, both the civilized races that lack the instinct, and the barbarians who have not needed it for their survival. This nation will in consequence dominate the world.

In the establishment of permanently civilized races the most important control will be this small change in the balance of human instincts, because it will have become inherent in the race's nature, and will not need to be taught to each succeeding generation. But it will be helped, and might be much accelerated, if creeds should arise working in the same direction. In the history of mankind creeds will continue to be of very great importance. Among the most important there will always be the creeds, which, without undue fanaticism, inculcate a strong sense of social obligation, since it is only through such creeds that life is possible in crowded communities. There will also no doubt often be fanatical creeds to disturb the peace of the world, and there will be others to comfort the world. I shall not attempt to conjecture what the tenets of these last will be; their main function is to act as a solace to their believers in the very bleak world I have described. It is only this that makes the world tolerable for many people, and this will be much more true in times of real hardship, than in periods of relatively easy prosperity like the present.

The detailed march of history will depend a great deal on the creeds held by the various branches of the human race. It cannot be presumed with any confidence that purely superstitious creeds will always be rejected by civilized communities, in view of the extraordinary credulity shown even now by many reputedly educated people. It is true that there may not be many at the present time, whose actions are guided by an inspection of the entrails of a sacrificial bull, but the progress has not been very great, for there are still many believers in palmistry or astrology. It is to be expected then that in the future, as in the past, there will be superstitions which will notably affect the course of history, and some of them, such as ancestor-worship, will have direct effects on the development of the human species. But superstitious creeds will hardly be held by the highly intelligent, and it is precisely the creed of these that matters. Is it possible that there should arise a eugenic creed, which—perhaps working through what I have called the method of unconscious selection—should concern itself with the improvement of the inherent nature of man, instead of resting content with merely giving him good but impermanent acquired characters? Without such a creed man's nature will only be changed through the blind operation of natural selection; with it he might aspire to do something towards really changing his destiny.

To conclude, I have cited the past history of China as furnishing the type of an enduring civilization. It seems to provide a model to which the future history of the world may be expected broadly to conform. The scale will of course be altogether vaster, and the variety of happenings cannot by any means be foreseen, but I believe that the underlying ground theme can be foreseen and that in a general way it will be rather like the history of the Chinese Empire. The regions of the world will fall into provinces of ever changing extent, which most of the time will be competing against one another. Occasionally—more rarely, than has been the case in China—they will be united by some strong arm into an uneasy world-government, which will endure for a period until it falls by the inevitable decay that finally destroys all dynasties. There will be periods when some of the provinces relapse into barbarism, but all the time civilization will survive in some of them. It will survive because it will be based on a single universal culture, derived from the understanding of science; for it is only through this understanding that the multitudes can continue to live. On this basic culture there will be overlaid other cultures, often possessing a greater emotional appeal, which will vary according to climate and race from one province to another. Most of the time and over most of the earth there will be severe pressure from excess populations, and there will be periodic famines. There will be a consequent callousness about the value of the individual's life, and often there will be cruelty to a degree of which we do not willingly think. This however is only one side of the history. On the other side there will be vast stores of learning, far beyond anything we can now imagine, and the intellectual stature of man will rise to ever higher levels. And sometimes new discoveries will for a time relieve the human race from its fears, and there will be golden ages, when man may for a time be free to create wonderful flowerings in science, philosophy and the arts.

Epilogue

Can we do anything about it all? The picture I have drawn of the future that humanity may expect is certainly very different from the hopes of the optimistic idealists of the past and the present. Such people may argue that many unforeseen wonderful things have happened in the past, and that it is idle to speculate about what other wonderful things the future may hold in store. They are forgetting that we are living in an entirely exceptional period, the age of the scientific revolution. I have called it a golden age, and I would remind them that during the course of history man has assigned the epoch of the golden age at least as often to the past as to the future.

Anyone who disagrees with my forecast must try to get beyond a vague optimism, which merely expresses the confidence that "something will turn up". In particular he must find a really solid reason which shows how the threat of over-population will be avoided; the observation that it has been avoided in some countries during the last four years is not enough. Let him then give the fullest rein to his imagination, let him suppose that anything is permissible, but let him follow out the consequences to their conclusion. I will venture to say that if he does so he will find that one or other of two alternatives is the result. Either he will come to general conclusions not so very different from mine; he will find that his utopia, however pleasant it may be in other ways, in the long run will suffer from many disagreeable features of the kind that I have been considering. Or else he will find that his imagination has gone so far out of the realms of reality that it contradicts the physical or the biological laws of nature.

Nevertheless for all of us it is intolerable to think of the future unfolding itself in complete predestined inevitability for the eternity of a million years. There are two things we must do; one is to know, the other to act. As to knowing, in my introductory chapter I described an analogy in mechanics, and I suggested that it should be possible to discover a set of laws, like the laws of thermodynamics, which would place absolute limits on what can be done by humanity. Biological laws cannot be expected to have the same hard outline as physical laws, but still there are absolute laws limiting what an animal can do, and similar laws will limit man not only on his physical side, but also on his intellectual side. If these could be clearly stated, we should recognize that many attempts that have been made at improving man's estate were hopeless.

It is for others, better versed than I am in the biological sciences, to work out these laws, and it is in all humility that I put forward the basis, on which, it may be, that they could be founded. The first principle is that man, as an animal, obeys the law of variation of species, which condemns human nature to stay nearly constant for a million years. The perfectibility of mankind, the aim of so many noble spirits, is foredoomed by this principle. The second is that man is a wild animal, and that doctrines drawn from the observation of domestic animals are quite inapplicable to him. The third principle is the non-inheritance of acquired characters, a principle familiar in animal biology, but all too seldom invoked in connection with human beings. If these, and any further principles as well, or any alternatives to them, were accepted, it might sometimes be possible through them to show up the absurdities of bad statesmanship, and certainly it would be the part of a wise statesman to work within their limitations, because only so could he hope to achieve success.

What action can be taken about the future of the human race? I am afraid that the answer must be very little indeed, and this is for the simple reason that most human beings do not care in the least about the distant future. Most care about the conditions that will affect their children and their grandchildren, but beyond that the situation seems too unreal, and even for those who do think about the more distant future, the uncertainties are too great to suggest any clear course of action. For example, consider the inevitable fuel shortage that is to come so soon. I know that my sons will not suffer from it very seriously, and I know that the fifteenth generation of my descendants will get no coal at all. Am I likely to refrain from putting coal on the fire on a cold evening by the thought that it may make one of my fourteenth descendants suffer for it? Such matters are so unreal to our minds, that it is not to be expected that they will ever be given much weight. Life is always precarious, and it is so hard to be sure of keeping alive for even ten years, that it is not surprising that no one should care much about what is going to happen even as short a time ahead as a century. In hardly any of the affairs of the world will man really be interested in the more distant future.

Still for the sake of the distant future something can be attempted more profitable than has been usual hitherto. Attempts at improving the lot of mankind have all hitherto been directed towards improving his conditions, but not his nature, and as soon as the conditions lapse all is lost. The only hope is to use our knowledge of biology in such a way that all would not be lost with the lapse of the conditions. The principles of heredity offer an anchor which will permanently fix any gains that there may be in the quality of mankind.

In final conclusion I had better declare my personal inclination. I do care very much about the future of the world, and I want most intensely my own descendants to play their part in it. However bleak the future, I am not content with the thought that it should be a world in which I have had no continuing part. No matter whether in the long ages to come life is to be a joy or a misery—and certainly much of it will be a misery—it will be an adventure that is well worth while.

RODERICK SEIDENBERG

Another Distant View

Roderick Seidenberg (1899–   ) is an American professional architect who has made his own interesting voyage into distant times in a book called Posthistoric Man. *Seidenberg, unlike Sir Charles Galton Darwin, thinks mans' fate in the remote future will be very different indeed from what it is today. But Seidenberg hardly can be said to arrive at a Utopia, for the essence of a Utopia, it seems to me, is that it should represent the fruition, the achievement, of what we now—perhaps only in our noblest moments, it is true—want and understand. But Mr. Seidenberg's posthistoric man will be as unlike us as are the ants or bees or any other fully "socialized" animal. He differs radically from Darwin, not so much in his conclusions as in his assumption that human culture is an instrument of evolutionary change that can alter the course of, in a sense supersede, the biological evolution of* homo sapiens. *Here in a contemporary form is another old chestnut, or crux of discussion of man's fate: Nature or Nurture?*

THE WORLD IS IN TRANSITION—WHICH IS BUT TO SAY THAT IT IS MOVING toward a new principle of integration. In the interim it is torn by a conflict of past and future values—or drifting in the void of their mutual clash. If society once drew strength and sustenance from the inner sources of being through the revelations of saint and mystic, it seems destined to abandon this well of inspiration in focusing wholly upon the external manipulation of its affairs and the purely mundane solution of its problems. The rift is not recent: it was already mirrored in the Christian ethos according to which the free will of the individual endowed man with a choice between damnation and salvation; between the hell of an atomistic, earthbound existence, limited and finite, and the mystically illumined vision of the eternal within. But in accepting the major promise, man hoped also to avoid the minor cost: it was the tragedy of human nature that man sought

From Roderick Seidenberg, *Posthistoric Man: An Inquiry* (Chapel Hill: University of North Carolina Press, 1950). Also available in paperback, Beacon Press, 1957, pp. 226-238.

the eternal for himself instead of in himself. "Exorbitantly heartened by the truth that God is in him, and by the false conclusion that his ego is immortal, the willful individual went the way—not of the Christian ideal but of his all-too-animal human nature. The fires of the Christian world had *energized* him, but its values could not *aim* him. European genius abondoned the perpendicular Gothic spire and the deep Divine Comedy to launch into horizontal adventures: to discover and control the horizontal periphery of life."[1]

But in that release science came of age, and the world of the machine was set in motion. The rift deepened, and behind the conflict of values a new mode of social cohesion emerged. While the individual will of man, released from the protecting panoply of the Divine Will, moved impetuously toward chaos, another principle asserted itself. A vast system of external control, nurtured by man's earthbound intelligence, implicit in the logic of his machine, and inherent in the very necessity of his social relations, emerged in ever clearer form until its widening influence has encompassed his world. Thus, aware of the logic and necessity of his outward compulsions, while still sensitive to the inward power of his inherited values, modern man finds himself torn asunder by conflicting tensions. In this dilemma he has sought escape from his predicament without sacrificing the belief in his own power, responsibility, and freedom in the face of the inevitable by seeking refuge in a countervailing sense of guilt and failure. But behind this desperate rear-guard action lies an ominous sense of fatality; a tragic awareness that perhaps the high promise of mankind is passing in a movement of overwhelming scope and finality.

For the problem of social integration will not long remain suspended in midair between a resolution that we have left behind and one that we fear to accept. It is certain to be resolved, sooner or later, under the impact of historic forces in which the individual will find himself galvanized and directed by an outward compulsion, in the very degree in which his inward response has failed him, toward a unity beyond himself. If Western society is moving away from, rather than toward, the ideal of the Christian synthesis attained in the Middle Ages, the general trend of history as reflected in the transition from the guidance of the instincts to that of intelligence must inherently favor this wholly extroverted mode of social integration. How far this transition has progressed is indicated by the extent to which man no longer feels called upon, by an act of inward freedom, to accept the necessity of a higher principle of unity. But in thus finding his own inward compliance an irrelevant gesture, he has alienated himself from that mystic communion in the "Whole" which endowed his humblest act with a sense of participation in a supramundane order. In this surrender man has renounced his inward freedom: he has abandoned, for better or for worse, his citizenship in the *Civitas Dei* for that of the secularized state or, at the farthest, that of the world community. And though doubtless he

---

[1] Waldo Frank, *Chart for Rough Water* (New York: Doubleday and Company, Inc., 1940), p. 118.

has brought to his new allegiance the emotional overtones that once sanctified an earlier obeisance, he is discovering to his comfort or humiliation—as the case may be—that his feelings and attitudes are meaningless gestures in the arbitrary finality of events.

That he may retrieve his lost position is not impossible: that society as a whole may attain an inward freedom to which at best it distantly aspired under a more propitious dispensation seems unlikely and improbable, however, in view of an undeniable drift in a contrary direction. The salvation of mankind is not to be achieved by mystic and saint alone; and the hope that man might control the course of events in harmony with spiritual values he has never yet attained is denied in the very momentum of history itself. But in saying this it does not follow that humanity is doomed to sink, irretrievably, into chaos and confusion. Man has survived in the past and is likely to survive in the future. Indeed, he gives every evidence of moving in a contrary direction toward increasing cohesion and unity on the basis of what appears to be an irreversible principle. But, in viewing the future condition of man on this reckoning, it would seem that we are menaced as much by the threat of survival in terms of an arbitrary, dehumanized collectivity as by the danger of collapse and disintegration in the structure of our values. The challenge to the soul of man is thus seen to be a threat both from within and without; but in fact these threats represent obverse aspects of a single encompassing movement that promises to engulf the soul under an ever more stringently deterministic scheme of things. If man is not threatened, his soul is; and therein lies the profound dilemma of our entry into a future different from our past.

The dilemma is heightened by the fact that we are aware, however subtly and unconsciously, that our entry into the future will not so much be conditioned by us as we are certain to be conditioned by it. Thus we are left standing awkwardly on the threshold of a new dispensation, reviewing our inner resources against the overwhelming drift and pull of outward trends, uneasy in the knowledge that our response to the challenge of the future is limited to our heritage from the past. If the consciousness and the will of man represent indeed an eddy, as it were, in the cold determinism of matter, then the challenge behind the looming impasse of the future resolves itself into a choice between the creation of a society of transfigured members held together in the higher communion of their spiritual kinship with the Whole, with the Cosmos, which is God—and a barren collectivity of dehumanized individuals seeking mere continuity of existence in the sluggish stream of evolutionary development. Either the spiritual force at our command is equal to this basic challenge, and man will attain unity in a society of potential persons, or the "ravening" atomistic individual of the world must seek survival in the arbitrary, mechanical collectivization of the herd. Such, it would seem, is the fateful choice before us.[2]

[2] This theme is eloquently and deeply argued in the works of Waldo Frank; see particularly *Chart for Rough Water*.

Fateful choice! Are not these the words that have ever accompanied the inspired admonitions of prophet and seer? Yet all their exhortations, from a time when Ikhnaton, Lao-tse, Isaiah, and Plato might already have spoken of a venerable past, failed to win man to the paths of wisdom. Are we to expect preachments deeper in their mystical sources, more divine in their authority, than those of Christ? If we failed to understand the dialogues of Socrates, the parables of Christ, are we to be saved by the insight of latter-day prophets lost in the "undergrowth of being"? The tragedy of man is the tragedy of numb idealism, of his vague, perplexed, indeed all too humble aspirations. Only in the deep imagination—in the illumination—of saints and geniuses of the spirit has man beheld far-off visions of himself projected against an illimitable firmament; in the world of his own closed horizons his hopes and aspirations have driven him only toward mundane ends in a spirit of animated complacency. The testimony of history supports the suspicion that man seeks indeed escape from freedom! The high road of the mystic may lead to spiritual freedom; the low road of mankind points only toward a predestined fate. And thus, conceivably, though man may have within him the spark of divinity, he will stumble on, unillumined, in the plateau regions of existence.

The spirituality of man is rooted in the freedom of the will. The unique and infinite worth of the person rests upon this premise; and though in turn this doctrine represents a central pillar of the democratic dogma, since it expresses the equality of man in his incommensurable value, it is equally the kernel of a conflict in the modern world in the relation between the State and the Individual. Thus, it is interesting to note, during the nineteenth century virtually every free and noble-spirited writer from Tolstoy to Thoreau, from Kropotkin to Emerson, rose in defense of the Great Tradition and the integrity of the individual against the steady encroachments of the state. But today it is no longer the state alone that is in conflict with the implications of these doctrines: it is a wider system of things wherein the state itself, in its supreme and sovereign aspects, is being drawn into the orbit of larger, world-wide agglomerations. Nor will the totalitarian pattern that has crept upon the state fail to emerge in these larger spheres of international scope. In this ubiquitous system of things the welfare of the individual rather than the salvation of the person is affirmed; and even the welfare of the individual is necessarily defined in the concrete terms of the welfare and security of the average—that is to say, of society as a compact and indivisible unit. As the gravitational force of the mass increases, that of the individual decreases, relatively as well as actually, until a final condition of solidarity and conformity is attained. At this level the individual is no longer sheathed in a halo of unique and infinite worth: he has only such relative values as may be ascertained in the language of statistical averages—those basic averages and percentages upon which the emerging system of the future is inherently predicated. But in this mechanization of society and dehumanization of the individual we cannot fail to see the eclipse of the spiritual structure of man.

The historical analysis of this transition reveals the machine as a primary agency in the transformation of society. The hope that society might absorb the benefits of the machine while avoiding the evils of mechanization has thus far proved illusory; and the gloomy predictions of certain nineteenth-century philosophers concerning the inevitable impact of the machine upon our civilization have been answered, not by the course of events, but by the words of twentieth-century prophets who, attacking mechanization as the basic cause of our plight, assure us that under proper guidance and control the machine and its technology, directed toward balanced and humane purposes, will become the open-sesame to a new era for mankind. For they believe that the machine will in time be "tamed" to its proper function, and that ". . . the mass man, with his mass thinking and mass ethic, whose projection in the world of the crashing wheel was toward chaos, may tend to disappear."[3] But a deeper comprehension of the nature of the machine as an integral, and indeed perhaps inevitable, concomitant of the transition from the guidance of instinct to that of intelligence sustains the conviction, apparent in the cumulative drift of industrialized civilization, that the hope of retaining the machine while avoiding the consequent mechanization of society is wholly wishful and fallacious. For the logic of the machine, repeating always its fixed and predesigned patterns, is a mass logic; and collectivism, as Karl Marx perceived, is inherent in its laws and implicit in its operations. Thus man is called upon to pay a price for his adventure into the richer potentialities of the material realm by a corresponding externalization of his own nature.

The communal impulse in man, of course, long antedated the advent of the machine: indeed, it was the norm of primitive social life, being itself a kind of biologic mechanism whereby man triumphed in his collective strength over his adversaries and his environment. But that earlier collectivism, which arose out of a wholly innate and primal social impulse, made coherent and explicit through the instruments of symbol and language, differs, as we have seen, from its modern surrogate. For it arose out of the instincts, in unconscious or preconscious patterns of behavior, whereas the collectivism of today is born of the inherent but nonetheless deliberate acceptance of the dictates of intelligence in the conscious organization of society. If, in time, out of the rich soil of man's heritage, his traditions, his myths, and his beliefs, purified and etherialized, bore fruit in the high conception of a communal society of autonomous souls, united in their spiritual bondage to God; if man attained, however imperfectly, a form of religious communality in response to an innate need of divine guidance, he has long since abandoned that vision. This highest social version of the Christian ethic was at once the crowning expression of the primitive community and the nearest approach to the *Civitas Dei* Western man appears to have achieved; but it gave way after the anarchic interim of the "unleashed ego" and the "atomistic individualism" of modern society to a new collectivism, no longer of the spirit, but of the conscious mind—an

[3] Garet Garrett, *A Time Is Born* (New York: Pantheon Books Inc., 1944), p. 234.

organized collectivism in place of a collective organism. And in that contrast the hopes and ideals, the means and the ends, of two worlds are seen in final and decisive opposition.

If the communal life of early man appears to us an inherent phase in our primitive development under the guidance of the instincts, its counterpart in the highly organized collectivity of modern society seems no less inevitable under the guidance of our intelligence. And just as language, myth, and symbol were the agencies of co-ordination in the primitive, localized community, so the machine constitutes today the effective instrument of collective integration in the social structure not merely of the community but of mankind as a whole. As myth and symbol epitomize in poetic form distillates of feeling and emotion, so the machine, epitomizing the principle of intelligence, acts as a pure and primary crystal of organization—an external agency, unifying, co-ordinating, crystallizing the structure of human society. In this contrast of inner and outer modes and agencies of attaining social cohesion man will necessarily come upon new procedures, new concepts, new values, and new attitudes. For he will have come upon a new age.

And thus we may ask ourselves whether he will establish a new synthesis of values, awaiting only his own high courage and direction, in which the future will be seen in time as the fulfillment and enrichment of the heritage of the past; or is man emerging through a hitherto undisturbed surface into another dimension, into a new form of existence—indeed, into a new and perhaps final phase of human evolution? In these pages an attempt has been made to state that question not in the light of contemporary events, however inviting to speculation, but rather in terms of a basic morphology of man's twofold approach to the problems of life: the primal approach through instinct, and the secondary but ultimately dominant approach through intelligence. If the conclusions arrived at in the course of this argument appear to support unequivocally the notion that man is entering upon a new phase in his development, different in direction from his past, that is not to say that our own response to this vista of the future is likewise unequivocal. If our logic can pierce, ever so haltingly, into the future, our hearts cannot. It was the belief of the ancient Egyptians that the heart was the seat of thought; it will be the mark of the future that man will distinguish between thinking and feeling as he learned, long ago, to distinguish between his dream world and his waking world. The dissociation of feeling and thought will alter our sense of reality, opening up to us a new world, more rigid, impersonal, and arbitrary than that of the past: plainly, its values will be alien to our values, its vistas alien and unfamiliar to our vision. The character of this new dispensation will patently be in harmony with those factors and forces most deeply involved in bringing it about—and perhaps the least of these will be our own spiritual aspirations, our own inmost sentiments, our hopes and our fears.

By the same reasoning it may seen vain and futile to attempt to project ourselves into that future which will belong, in any event, not to us, but to our far-off descendants. Our faculties are certain to fail us in piercing that future, if only because our fantasies and visions are so often a response of the heart. Nor would the very terms of our language, rooted in the past, prove adequate where thought and imagination are balked. Nevertheless, it is clear that we may venture upon certain basic, if abstract, generalizations. Thus, noting the inherent, obligatory, and accelerating trend toward increased organization in every aspect of life—a process tending toward the final crystallization of society—we perceive that the world of the future will be characterized by a wholly new type of universal collectivism arising out of an inexorable principle of social integration. The impact of the machine in effecting this transformation of society is clear and undeniable. But to assess more fully the significance of such profound changes in the structural fabric of society, and the role of the machine in bringing them about, it became necessary to inquire into the abstract meaning of organization itself. And here the interpretation of organization as a modulus of the triumph of intelligence over instinct provided a clue, not only to the nature of the historic process but to the function of the machine in effecting a decisive change of direction in the further evolution of human society. For if the future is indeed subject to prediction, the past must already reveal—if not its incipient form—at least the evidence of an inexorable principle, a law of historic determinism, upon which its course might be predicated. Such a principle seemed clearly affirmed in the slow but inevitable dominance of intelligence over instinct; it remained necessary to establish on this basis the peculiar potency of the machine in precipitating and accelerating this inherent drift.

Through the vehicle of analogy we arrived at an interpretation of this phenomenon in accordance with a thesis first enunciated by Henry Adams: namely, that the stages in the course of human evolution may be comparable to changes of state in a purely material system as expressed by the Rule of Phase in thermodynamic theory. The transition from an earlier, instinctual stage to a later, universally organized condition of society under the dominance of intelligence seemed to suggest some such *change of phase;* and on this basis it became apparent that the machine as a pure and archetypical form of organization itself—served as a primary crystal in effecting the structural transformation of society. If such an interpretation led to the conclusion that human society was moving inexorably toward a condition of total crystallization in its structural edifice, the trend of history, revealing mankind entering ever wider orbits of co-ordinated relationships, certainly seemed to support rather than to deny this implication. The analogies suggested by such an approach to the interpretation of the historic process seemed justified and strengthened, moreover, by the profound transformation in status of both the individual and society under the impact of the machine. For the depersonalized emergence of the individual as an atomic constituent of the social mass—defined in terms of averages and percentages—clearly suggested those mass aggregates amenable to thermodynamic interpretation on the basis of statistical mechanics.

Behind these generalizations dealing in wide perspective with a new phase in human evolution, we come upon intimations of more detailed aspects of the future. By and large the direction of man's psychic orientation, at least within the span of history, has moved from a more subjective, introverted position to an increasingly objective, extroverted one: doubtless his expanding command of the outer world weakened and narrowed the domain of his inner responses. The final depersonalization of the individual, implicit in the future condition of man, must complete this vast process of externalization to a degree perhaps difficult to conceive in terms of our own dichotomic natures. For the very source of inner values in the instinctive approach to life must gradually atrophy; and our sensibilities, drawing strength from the emotions, must inevitably become blunted and wither away. Meanwhile the patterns of behavior developed under the guidance of intelligence alone will spread and proliferate until the whole range of life will have become encompassed. But that is not to say that mankind will henceforth have done with all contrary tendencies: at critical moments in the course of events leading ultimately to a condition of social fixity, movements of opposition will arise, remotely analogous perhaps to those reactions called for in the physico-chemical domain by the principle of Le Chatelier.[4] But it is amply clear, in any event, that the drift toward increased externalization is in harmony, if not indeed synonymous, with the explicit depersonalization inherent in the dominant forces of the future. And without fear of carrying the logic of the argument to some *reductio ad absurdum,* we may perceive that the trend of events must ultimately approach a condition of stable equilibrium in which the individual will be a rigidly fixed component of the mass in an objective continuum of society and its environment.

The inevitability of these aspects of the future touches upon the nature of human freedom. For we may perceive that freedom, seen against a backdrop of inevitability, can hardly be a matter of choice in direction: at best it may remain a factor in the dimension of time. Thus the retardation traditionally exercised by the conservative—the conservator of values, forever betrayed by the reactionary—may express an intuitive sense of the fleeting character of our values and our world; a fear that human freedom, like the hourglass, has only its appointed run. Conceivably freedom is an illusion arising out of the infinite range of combinations in the patterns of instinct and intelligence available to the individual in his every action. If

---

[4] Significantly, Alfred J. Lotka warns us that the principle of Le Chatelier can only be applied to biologic phenomena on the basis of more or less remote analogies. A careful reading of Lotka, however, would seem to indicate that a wider principle than the one enunciated in the domain of thermodynamics by Le Chatelier may be implicit in biologic phenomena, but its formulation remains to be established. See Lotka's *Elements of Physical Biology,* pp. 281ff. It is interesting to note that Lawrence J. Henderson in his book *Pareto's General Sociology* (Cambridge, Mass.: Harvard University Press, 1935, p. 47) relies upon the very interpretation of this principle by W. D. Bancroft which Lotka assailed as unjustified and inapplicable to social phenomena.

instinct alone functions as the activating agency there can be no freedom; in the functioning of intelligence alone there is likewise no freedom of action. Thus freedom may be a purely *historic* reality—unknown in the remote past and destined to evaporate in the remote future. Only in the interim of subtle and balanced reactions may we taste to the full the peculiarly human sensibility of freedom; and from this point of view we may understand why Lao-tse was concerned *not* to build a bridge across the stream separating his village from one so close the barking of the dogs could be heard! For this paradoxical wisdom embraces a profound thermo-dynamic principle: the principle, namely, of retarding the flow of entropy. The slowness, not the speed, of man may be his saving—temporarily.

The life span of man's evolution may thus conceivably be subject to his choice and his will; it is questionable to what extent he can affect its direction. Even his knowledge, which constitutes the fulcrum of his actions, is no longer his individually: it belongs in its massed volume and extent to the community as a whole. Thus the momentum of society becomes less and less contingent upon the pace or the direction of its component individuals; while, contrariwise, that of the individual will inevitably come to depend ever more stringently upon the dicta of society. The conclusion thus descends upon us that man's course is set in all but the dimension of time; and that even here the determining factors of his development will allow him no final escape. For the process of crystallization, which constitutes an inherent aspect of this all-embracing determination, is a converging, cumulative, essentially irreversible process that approaches a condition of stable equilibrium as its limit. And the ultimate stabilization of human relationships toward which man is drifting implies a gradual reversal and slowing down of the tempo of his history: in place of an accelerating rhythm of change he will experience a gradual abatement and exclusion of all change and variation, until at length he will find himself in an ever more securely established milieu—in a period of unchanging continuity. He will have passed through the transitional, historic phase of his evolution, and attained at length a posthistoric stage.

In the course of his development he has been constrained from time to time to abandon his most cherished myths. Thus he has abandoned his animism; his Ptolemaic astronomy that assured his position in the center of the universe; his faith in a hereafter that endowed him with eternal life; his belief in the supreme and infinite worth of his person that assured him a position of isolate dignity in an otherwise meaningless and impersonal world; and even perhaps his faith in a God whose attributes, under the impact of man's rationalistic scrutiny, became ever more abstract until He vanished in the metaphysical concept of the Whole. The shedding of these inestimable illusions may be merely stages in his diminishing stature before he himself vanishes from the scene—lost in the icy fixity of his final state in a posthistoric age.

DENNIS GABOR

The New Golden Age

With Dennis Gabor's "Inventing the Future" we come a full circle from where we started. This Professor of Applied Electron Physics at the University of London too regrets the "lost vision" of Utopia; but he seems to find it again, and in those very gadgets that alarm, or at best bore, our humanist intellectuals. So little dies off and disappears completely in the long slow course of our cultural history! And Utopia, Progress, Evolution (in a teleological sense) are still young gods; I conclude that they are far from dead.

I BELIEVE THAT IT IS A VERY SIGNIFICANT FACT THAT NO OPTIMISTIC Utopia has been written for the last thirty years. Utopian literature did not die, as one might think, in 1914; it survived the first World War by about a decade. Some of H. G. Wells' best utopian works date from this time, and I recall with particular pleasure the *Daedalus* of the young J. B. S. Haldane, sparkling with optimism, and belief in salvation by science. But after Aldous Huxley's incomparably brilliant anti-utopia *Brave New World* (1931), no more utopias were written, only dreary science fiction and George Orwell's horrible nightmare *1984*.

Working against Leisure

If we cannot get encouragement from the men of letters, can we perhaps get it from our fellow-scientists? No more utopias were written for the last generation, but we have now scientific forecasts from two distinguished physicists, *The Foreseeable Future* by Sir George Thomson (1958), and *The Next Million Years,* from Sir Charles Darwin (1952). Thomson's is a cautious application of the scientific method, neither very encouraging, nor disturbing, but Darwin's is a profoundly depressing book. His thesis, is, briefly, that we are not moving towards a Golden Age, because the present is a Golden Age, and the next million years will see a sort of statistical fluctuation around a level rather lower than the present. I have no

From Dennis Gabor, "Inventing the Future," *Encounter,* London, May 1960, pp. 13-16.

wish to give a rival forecast of the next million years, but I want to give my view, for what it is worth, of the near future. My thesis is, briefly, that from a purely material point of view a "Golden Age" is at hand—but that there are immensely strong forces at work to prevent us entering it for the next few generations—and that there is nobody to show us the way to it.

The plain fact is that science and technology have immensely enlarged the set of "possible worlds." Until quite recently, the majority of people had to work hard to keep a leisured minority. We are now for the first time in history faced with the possibility of a world in which only a minority need work, to keep the great majority in idle luxury. Soon the minority which has to work for the rest may be so small that it could be entirely recruited from volunteers, who prefer the joys of a useful and even of a dedicated life to idleness.

Men have always envied the leisured classes, but it now appears that the dream of leisure for all is turning into a nightmare. Indeed, to think of the privileged classes of the past is enough to make one doubtful. The aristocracies of the past had two great psychological satisfactions which would be denied to a leisured majority: they could command human service, and they believed themselves to be *élites*. Yet for the averagely gifted members of the privileged classes life became bearable only by hard drinking!

The leisured society of the future is still mostly below the horizon, but it seems to me that our contemporary world has already developed several very strong defence mechanisms to prevent it from becoming a reality.

The first defence mechanism is Parkinson's Law: "Work automatically expands so as to fill the available time." Though this great law was first formulated in this country, if we want to see it in action we must look to the United States, the most advanced and richest industrial country, where "to-morrow is already here." In the United States in 1957, for the first time in history, the "white-collar workers" have outnumbered the "blue-collar workers"; there are now more paper-pushers than tool-pushers. It is only surprising why they do not outnumber them 3:1 or 4:1. Not very long ago the great majority of mankind had to work in agriculture; even in the U.S. in 1900 the proportion was 31 per cent. To-day less than 12 per cent are sufficient to produce so much food that a great fraction of it goes daily down the drains, that millions are on a slimming diet, the producers of canned foods advertise that their food has *less* calories per weight than that of their competitors. Or look at the car industry, where less than a million workers produce so many cars that they can be sold fast enough only by employing all the means of high-pressure salesmanship to make customers change them long before the cart starts showing signs of wear. These are very clear manifestations of Parkinson's Law. But looking at it this way, the growth of paper-pushers is not a tumour; it is the healthy reaction of a society in which people have been brought up to work, not only for earning money, but also because they want to feel useful, and want to keep their self-respect.

A second, perhaps even more important defence mechanism is the recent strong increase of the birth rate, particularly noticeable in the United States, but also in Britain and in France. This is quite a different phenomenon from the overpopulation of poor and ignorant countries. It is again an expression of our healthy and virtuous civilisation; people have more babies not because they cannot help it, but because they love having children. Nevertheless, apart from the very different motivation, it looks dangerously like Malthus' Law, on which Darwin based his pessimistic outlook; the law that a population tends to increase up to the starvation limit. I am inclined to take a less serious view of this, as may be seen from my putting Malthus' Law on the same level as Parkinson's Law. I do not believe that in highly civilised countries the population need grow up to the starvation level, but it looks to me as if it had a tendency to grow up to a level sufficient to ban the nightmare of leisure for everybody.

A third defence mechanism, and a very strong one, is, of course—Defence. All I need say about it is that much of the effort in all industrial countries goes into making the most devilishly ingenious products of the human mind, which at best will never be used, at worst might destroy all of us.

Our contemporary world has a fourth defence mechanism ready against a too easy life, and I am glad to say that at least this one is wholly laudable. It is aid to the under-developed countries of the East. It is not on a large scale, and it will not last long, as these countries are already making very determined efforts to raise themselves to a higher technological level; but while it lasts it will be good for them, and good for us.

These four, as I see it, are the chief defence mechanisms of our society against the nightmare of a leisured world, for which we are socially and psychologically unprepared. I do not feel competent to give an opinion on the question whether mankind can or cannot be conditioned to bear leisure without boredom, and without losing that magnificent spirit by which a poor animal, almost toothless and clawless, has raised itself gradually to the status of modern man. For my part, I should be satisfied with a compromise, because man in the past has shown rather too much fighting spirit. But I can see little sign of any preparations to meet this problem in our Western civilisation, and none at all in the Soviet Union where the official creed is, of course, to deny the existence of the problem altogether.[1] This may well be a great danger, because they are making such great strides in

[1] The official attitude of Marxists is, I believe, well illustrated by the following quotation from the late Frédéric Joliot: "There are those who object to the view of progress which depends upon shorter working hours on the grounds that then people will not know what to do with their leisure, and will let themselves lapse into idleness and immorality. Such fears are groundless, because the time saved on working hours will open up to the individual a culture rich enough to induce him to work spontaneously during his leisure at the things he enjoys, and even attain the supreme joy of creative achievement in the realm of art and of science." (*Quelques réflexions sur l'énergie, Physique et Chimie*, Paris, 1958.)

To believe this one would have to believe first either that in future *everybody* will be exceptionally gifted, or that the less gifted members of the old leisured classes were driven to drink by a bad conscience.

their industrial development that they may well take the step from poverty to plenty in one generation, instead of the two or three of the Western countries, psychologically completely unprepared and with all their dynamism still in their blood.

It is a sad thought indeed that our civilisation has not produced a *new vision,* which could guide us on into the new "Golden Age" which has now become physically possible, but only physically. All we have is the pedestrian dream of the trade unions of the 35-hour week, the 24-hour week, and so on. But even this is not certain, because work which is not necessary to sustain life may have to come back as *occupational therapy.* This reminds me of the pathetic picture of the dog in the old physiological laboratories, climbing endlessly up a moving ramp. The dog will never get anywhere, but at least it will keep in fine fettle.

The Lost Vision

Who is responsible for this tragi-comedy of Man frustrated by success? If the intellectuals at the other side of the fence say that the fault is ours, of the scientists and inventors, we are not in a position to deny it. But instead of bowing our heads in shame, I think we ought to return the accusation, and ask: "Who has left Mankind without a Vision?" The predictable part of the future may be a job for electronic predictors, but that part of it which is not predictable, which is largely a matter of free human choice, is not the business of machines, nor of scientists, not even of psychologists, but it ought to be, as it was in the great epochs of the past, the prerogative of the inspired humanists, of the poets and writers. And for more than a generation we receive from these quarters little else but more or less polished expressions of despair and disgust.

Some thirty years ago the French critic Julien Benda wrote a famous book, *La Trahison des Clercs,* in which he accused the *"clercs,"* the writers and thinkers (who by their vocation had the duty to uphold the ideals of freedom, justice, and the dignity of the individual) of "treason" by embracing dogma of one sort or another, or the creed of extreme nationalism. Today we are faced with a new treason of the *clercs*—oh, nothing as crude and criminal as the treason of the French intellectuals Barrès and Maurras—no treason by commission, but only by omission: by not giving us a vision for which to live.

Until such time when our *clercs* change their mind, and come up from their depths of comfortable and complacent despair, we shall have to muddle through, from invention to invention. And if we want a measure of hope, we must not turn to the intellectuals; we must look at the present and into the past.

In the present we can see more simple happiness of the Common Man than has ever existed in the world. Even uniformity can have its delights. Some years ago I saw in the *New Yorker* the following cartoon: a suburban row of houses, as far as the eye can see, and through every gate steps a

young man, who has just arrived with the commuter's train. A little dog
with wagging tail runs out to greet every young man, behind every dog
runs a little toddler, and behind every little toddler, on the doorstep, stands
a smiling young wife. This is stereotyped happiness, but unique and wonderful for those who live it. Worse things can happen to humanity than this
scene repeating itself through a hundred generations!

This is what we can see in the present. Looking into the past, we can
see our ancestors, men with much the same capabilities as ours, miserably
sheltering under dripping trees from the cold pelting rain. The journey which
led from these poor savages to the distinguished audience following my
remarks seems to me worth while. It will be for another in another historic
epoch before another audience, to draw the balance of splendours and
miseries and to decide whether the rest of the journey was necessary.

POSTSCRIPT

THE TRADITION OF THE
ENLIGHTENMENT

The Tradition of the Enlightenment

I DARE NOT CALL THESE WORDS A CONCLUSION. BUT I SHOULD LIKE TO TRY to start a conscientious reader on the way to clearing up in his own mind and for himself some of the stimulating confusions the contents of this book should have bred. Or at least, I should like to start him on the way to clarifying some issues sufficiently so that the confusions can be put up with.

What the thinker tries to organize by means of thinking never gets organized in its entirety so long as the thinker keeps trying to "test" that organization "empirically"; or—our language here can never satisfy the professional philosopher—it cannot be wholly organized as truth so long as we try to verify the truth of our ideas by what common sense and natural science are at bottom in agreement to call "facts." Francis Bacon long ago put it clearly in the *Novum Organum* (Book I, aphorism 10): *The subtilty of nature is far beyond that of sense or of the understanding.*

The thought has occurred to less confidently rationalist or empiricist thinkers than Bacon. Here are two very different contemporary expressions of this never-to-be-forgotten (but often so forgotten) commonplace.

Definition is ordinarily supposed to produce clarity in thinking. It is not generally recognized that the more we define our terms the less descriptive they become and the more difficulty we have in using them.[1]

I realize that if through science I can seize phenomena and enumerate them, I cannot, for all that, apprehend the world. Were I to trace its entire relief with my finger, I should not know any more. And you give me the choice between a description that is sure but that teaches me nothing and hypotheses that claim to teach me but that are not sure.[2]

More crudely put: the human brain just can't hold the universe. It is absurd to try to understand, *and expect others to understand as we do,* the status system in the United States, the meaning of Marxism-Leninism, the ways of God to man, and of man to God, the state of Nature, the future of democracy.

Absurd, and absolutely necessary. For any foreseeable future, and in spite of the popularizers of logical positivism, men are going to spend millions of hours at this essential human task of asking questions they cannot answer to the universal satisfaction of the race, cannot even answer in the

[1] Thurman Arnold, *The Folklore of Capitalism,* quoted in Marston Bates, *The Forest and the Sea* (New York: Random House, 1960), p. 130.
[2] Albert Camus, *The Myth of Sisyphus* (New York: Vintage Books, 1960), p. 15.

justified hope that inspires the scientist to believe he can find the causal agent or agents of cancer, or clear up the difficulties in the structure of the atom as it is now pictured. I am willing to be quite dogmatic on this point. Metaphysics is an essential thing.

Here we face another and related problem. The statement that questions about man's condition—questions like those we have encountered throughout this book—cannot be given answers universally accepted as correct, or "true," has of course to be tagged as itself a metaphysical position, a statement on man's condition, put most simply as a form of *relativism,* or *skepticism.* And it is crystal-clear from the historical record that relativist and skeptical philosophies, though held with determination by some thinkers, go somehow against the grain of most human thinking-and-feeling. Here again I must risk being brief and dogmatic: Over the centuries, Western thought has in the balance held relativism—especially the ethical relativism of "one man's virtue is another man's vice"—disreputable, and no true description of the universe and man's place in it.

Now orthodox Christianity, and indeed any transcendental organization of human sense-experience which holds that such organization is superior to, master of, prior to, more complete than such sense-experience, has minimal trouble with this most human dilemma of relative-absolute. The statement, "Those whom God hath joined together let no man put asunder" from the Anglican Book of Common Prayer solves, for the true believer, the problem of divorce, at bottom because God—any god—is well above sociology, social psychology, and in our squabbling human sense, above ethics. Job came to understand this very well indeed, though I'm afraid J. B. never will.

For to the historian of ideas one of the basic sources of the kind of difficulty Professor Murray brings so clearly to our attention is the gap left for many Westerners of the faith I have called Enlightened between their age-old desire to know the Truth and the rigid—yes, I mean rigid—relativism of the natural science they have espoused as a guide to all human activities. Of course many Enlightened manage to forget the gap, or bridge it after a fashion. The religion of the Enlightenment is young, lusty, growing —its warring sects in their fecund variety give good evidence that this is so. But the gap remains, and it will have to be attended to, or our pessimistic and alienated intellectuals will continue to be more numerous than is socially desirable (yes indeed, the high-minded intellectual is a fine antiseptic—but you can easily get too much of any antiseptic).

In brief: science has to be relativistic and skeptical; the scientist never can believe that he has mastered Nature; he cannot actually believe that his "laws" exist wholly outside his mind; indeed, Professor Gabor's provocative phrase, "inventing the future," comes naturally to a scientist because he knows—or should know—that he *invents,* does not merely *discover,* his laws; the scientist must shy away from all the absolutist implications given to the terms he uses by outsiders—or misguided scientists—when they are hypostasized, and capitalized, as Evolution, Force, yes, even as Nature, even as the Expanding Universe.

Now a great many very intelligent people can, apparently, accept happily a world-view essentially relativist and skeptical of ultimates, can take nature as the scientist shows it to them, minus an initial capital—and minus any moral purpose recognizable to us humans, minus any interest in us, and certainly not wholly to be conquered by us, even when we follow Bacon's injunction to conquer by obeying her. *Her?* The hypostasizing habit is deepseated indeed, surely not just a matter of Latin gender. Still, a great many people can now once more see nature with Lucretius:

> *natura videtur*
> *libera continuo dominis privata superbis*
> *ipsa sua per se sponte omnia dis agere expers.*

> Nature is seen to be free at once and rid of proud masters,
> herself able to do what she does by herself without the gods.

Clearly many of those whose work we have been reading have happily adjusted themselves to the world of science.

The Stoics, the Epicureans, a great many others in the great days of later Graeco-Roman culture did very well without the consolations of "religion." Our modern existentialists, however, though their basic position is singularly like that of these Graeco-Roman rationalists, take things much harder. We come to what is surely near the heart of the modern difficulty. Epictetus and Lucretius were no democrats, and they had never been exposed to a systematic doctrine of Progress. We moderns are almost all democrats, and we have all been brought up to believe in Progress, and we cannot help but show the effects of this upbringing. We must want to make converts of the many, must want all men to agree with us, must want to raise the many to the best that has been thought and planned. We want, as the Christians have always wanted, to raise the many to the heights of the few, to achieve the standards of an aristocracy for a democracy.

But we want to do this without the transcendental world-view of Christianity, without the authoritarian traditions of Christianity, without the certitudes of Christianity, without the slowly developed Christian way of filling by ritual, by skilled cure of souls, by first-rate blah-blah (remember the references to Stuart Chase, pp. 309 and 320) the horrid gap between what we want to be and what we are. We want to eliminate entirely from this world what our Christian predecessors called evil, and which we too find evil. But our world-view that Nature is All (pardon my capitals) surely gives us no reason to hold that evil is not just as natural a part of man's condition as is good: we make ourselves, but out of materials that long experience has shown cannot be used very differently from the way they have been used. And they are very uneven, as well as limited, materials.

I do not for a moment think that the many can come anywhere near seeing the universe as, for instance, Mr. Bridgman sees it (see p. 328). I single him out because he states very clearly the aristocratic individualism implicit in what I shall call extreme scientific rationalism. Read carefully his last pages. He holds so firmly to the fine scientific concept of flux as bearable, indeed enjoyable, that he can suggest that it is possible that "in the predawn of history the human race took a fork in the road which committed it to the use of the mechanism of words with their static [and absolutist?] meanings instead of a fork which might have allowed it to reproduce more faithfully the fluent character of things as they are." But the fork was taken a long long time ago, and I should guess we should have to have Sir Charles Galton Darwin's brand-new species before we could do a great deal in our abstract thinking to be more faithful to "things as they are."

For things as they are—our culture, our institutions, as well as "nature" —somehow include several billion human beings utterly unable to change, by the kind of effort we call thinking, the basic beliefs their society has taught them. Their lives, their cultures, can indeed be changed, as we who have lived through the last fifty years know well, and as what is happening in Africa today illustrates with particular clarity. But they cannot be changed as those of a few, a very few, aristocrats of a sort, can be changed—by hard thinking of the kind we have here sought to gather from so many sources. To change the behavior of the many, the thinking of the few has to be transmuted into a faith, emotion-charged, dogmatic, quite unlike the thinking of Mr. Bridgman—or indeed, quite unlike much of the thinking illustrated in this anthology. I repeat, it is inconceivable that the many should ever, in a measurable time, be capable of assuming the mental stance of the scientist *qua* scientist, or of acquiring a consistent world-view like his.

This fact ought to allay some of the worst fears of our alienated intellectuals. There may be, as Dr. Dubos suggests (p. 468), a kind of homeostatic balance in even our disturbed society, a balance maintained by the unthinking many. And certainly it is no cynicism but rather the opposite, to suggest that, on the empirical evidence held so dear by the Enlightened, it is fortunate for social stability that the billions of the human race do not use their minds on matters that have exercised you and me in this book. Think of our existing conflicts of ideas and ideals multiplied, as the law of probability would have it, many thousands of times!

And yet the troubled in soul are many, and their trouble may be seeping down further and more rapidly than I have admitted. Some months ago I talked on this "alienation of the intellectuals" to a group of fourth-year medical students, insisting that most Americans, not intellectuals, were not alienated, nor even disturbed. One of the group, specializing it is true in psychiatry, said firmly that anyone who had any experience of clinics knew well that a very great number, an unusual number, of ordinary people are disturbed, worry themselves sick nowadays. I felt I had to remind him that for millions today his profession has taken over the cure of souls, that he is in a sense preparing for the priesthood of science, that priests have always had to know that man is born to trouble. I need hardly say that I made no impression on him, and after all, he had had clinical practice, and I had not.

Grant then that we all need a new faith, a faith not in flux, not in the relativism of natural science—*a faith that Truth is to be found, not just invented*. But finding the Truth, the way of religion, is very different from inventing the truth, the way of science. The social scientist, even with the aid of history, has difficulty understanding the genesis and growth of the higher religions of the past. For one thing, they are few—Taoism, Confucianism, Buddhism, Zoroastrianism, Judaism, Christianity, Islam, their variants, and perhaps the still somewhat inchoate religion of Enlightenment —too few to make a good set of case histories, and most of them too little known sociologically. But one factor does seem to me clear: A great charismatic evangelist must precede and call forth the evangel. I do not mean just a Billy Sunday or a Billy Graham; I mean a Moses, a Christ, a Buddha, a Mohammed. It is hard indeed—I write now as a naturalistic historian—to distinguish such in their beginnings from the cultist, the faddist, the minor prophet. And, unpleasant though it may be for some of us to face the prospect, the most likely, perhaps merely the least unlikely, candidate for such a place as founder of a great religion in our time would appear to be Karl Marx.

Such a founder, but a gentler one, may be amongst us now, though not, I feel sure, in an academic chair. Until he comes, we shall have to put up with the present multiplicity of world-views. Few of these world-views are genuinely and fully relativist, skeptical, or cynical. Their holders hitherto in our free West, where this "multanimity" is greatest, have got along together in part because our early modern experience with the Wars of Religion has led to a kind of pragmatic acceptance of the impossibility of imposing unanimity in these matters by authority; in part because many Christians, though not giving up their views about Truth, have come to accept toleration of differences as part of God's scheme for this world now; in part because a strong current in the world-view of Enlightenment, much buttressed by Darwinian emphasis on the role of variation in organic revolution, has held that such differences of opinion are in themselves good and necessary; finally, in part because the legacy of four hundred years has made an amalgam of these attitudes a living force in our democratic tradition, alive in our culture—dare one say—in what Jung calls our "collective unconscious"?

Some of the intellectual buttresses for this attitude of acceptance of multanimity in matters of ultimate beliefs have indeed weakened in our century—especially those depending on the world-view of Enlightenment. These historical "forces" well stated by Mr. Heilbroner (see p. 352) have made it hard for some intellectuals to maintain the faith of Enlightenment with its high estimate of ordinary human beings as moral and political animals. All over the West the intellectuals are, in fact, trying to amend, remold, develop that faith, a process that on naturalistic-historical grounds one has to say is itself a sign of life and health. Were our intellectuals *not* alienated, were they saying what their great-grandfathers have said, then indeed we should feel, with Spengler, Toynbee and their like, that this is the Downfall of the West.

Men—intellectuals anyway—cannot agree on ultimates, and yet they cannot accept the resulting chaos of beliefs as quite "natural." They witness, they experience, the relative. Yet something in them yearns for the absolute. Philosophical ways out, Hegel's dialectic of thesis-antithesis-synthesis and many another system that accepts process or change as reconcilable with permanence, indeed *as really* permanence, will not do. Yet most of us survive the difficulty, and live with it. The late Albert Leon Guérard was fond of telling a story about a doctor's oral at Stanford in which a professor who believed in the flux badgered the candidate into taking a pretty dogmatic and absolutist position and then remarked, "Well, Mr. X, you *are* an absolutist, aren't you!" The candidate refused to be browbeaten. "Yes, sir," he replied, "I suppose I am—relatively." I should guess that that candidate is not very much alienated, even now.

For we are all relativists, or at least pluralists, when we confront the "is"; blond is blond, brunet is brunet, and the twain not only meet, but produce a confusing continuum of shades in between. Yet in the "ought to be" we are all absolutists, or at least monists, of a sort. Cecil Rhodes seems to have held that the whole human race ought someday, not so far off, to be all English-speaking, preferably blond and blue-eyed. There are those who think the whole human race ought, and very soon, to become good democrats.

You not only can, but must, have it both ways: you must accept the incredible variety of existing things, human and inhuman, including most emphatically the variety of human appraisals of good and bad, right and wrong, beautiful and ugly; and you must accept the human inability to accept this variety in the spirit of the Benthamite "push-pin is as good as poetry"—or any other assertion of full emancipation from this ranking, this ordering of the human condition. Do not believe the man who tells you he believes in nothing. The chances are overwhelming that in mid-twentieth-century America he means that he does not believe in Christianity, and does believe in a generalized democratic Enlightenment; but of course he may believe in Sartre, or Freud, or Wittgenstein, or Zen Buddhism, or Marxism-Leninism; he may even believe in Science.

This much at least should be clear at the end of our long investigation: those who wish to diminish the variety of philosophical or religious beliefs in our present Western culture must first recognize that that variety has existed for a very long time. In what we may call the engineer's meaning of planning and achieving change we are still extremely ignorant of how to bring about wholesale rapid and persisting change in this variety of beliefs. The miracles of hidden persuaders, brain-washing, Madison Avenue? Of course, these are real, but they are also limited and specific. The chemists can do miracles—temporary ones—with the pigments of human hair; they cannot do the same for the pigments of the human eye, nor even, beyond some innocent synthetic tanning, for those of the human skin. A good deal of the human brain (soul?) seems quite beyond the best or worst Madison Avenue or the Kremlin can do. George Orwell looks now like a prophet indeed, but not like a good predictor. 1984 is further off than it was a decade or so ago.

And second, at least in an open or democratic society, the most ardent seeker after more agreement on ultimates amongst us, be he Christian or Enlightened, must accept the impossibility, in such a society, of bringing about such agreement by what we may call in shorthand force—force exerted by government or by society or by lesser groups. The price we pay—at least for the foreseeable future—for democracy would seem to be multanimity, and even a degree of alienation. There is always the possibility that the price may be too high, beyond our resources. But there is equally a possibility that we can pay it; we have certainly paid large installments already.

Reading Suggestions

OBVIOUSLY THE BEST WAY TO READ PHILOSOPHY IS TO READ THE PHILOS-
ophers. Still, philosophy is a formal academic discipline, it has a vocabulary
and methods of its own, and it has had a long history. An introductory
manual is a necessity. I recommend for the beginner one of Bertrand Russell's earlier books, still deservedly in print, *Problems of Philosophy* (1912)
now available in a Galaxy paperback. A useful if less polished example of
the "problem" or "analytical" approach to philosophy is Max Rosenberg,
Introduction to Philosophy (New York: Philosophical Library, 1955). The
historical approach seems to me a necessary complement, and here I come
back to Bertrand Russell, *A History of Western Philosophy* (1945), now
available in a Simon and Schuster paperback. Russell's bias is toward the
tough-minded, but he has a fine gift of exposition. Two old, detailed, and
distinguished Germanic manuals of the history of philosophy are now available in translation in Dover paperbacks: W. Windelband, *History of
Ancient Philosophy,* and H. Höffding, *History of Modern Philosophy.*
   What is now called "intellectual history" or "history of ideas" casts its
net more widely than the history of formal philosophy, being concerned as
well with "climates of opinion," with ideas as they penetrate to the intellectual classes, or even further. Here there is a classic, A. C. Lovejoy,
The Great Chain of Being, in a Torchbook paperback. Lovejoy's collected essays, *Essays in the History of Ideas,* Capricorn paperback, are useful as guides to this particular approach to the study of ideas. There are a
number of textbooks or manuals for the student: Crane Brinton, *Ideas and
Men* (New York: Prentice-Hall, 1950), which attempts a historical study
of the "Big Questions" of man's condition in our Western culture from the
Greeks and Jews to the present; J. H. Randall, Jr., *The Making of the
Modern Mind* (rev. ed., Boston: Houghton Mifflin, 1954), by a professional
philosopher, which deals with the period since the end of the Middle Ages;
J. Bronowski and B. Mazlish, *The Western Intellectual Tradition: From
Leonardo to Hegel* (New York: Harper, 1960), which gives fruitful emphasis to the relations among general intellectual history, the history of science
and technology, and conventional history. Three very interesting books
about man's cultural history really belong in this category: H. J. Muller,
The Uses of the Past, in New American Library paperback; H. B. Parkes,
Gods and Men: The Origins of Western Culture (New York: Knopf, 1959);
and Erich Kahler's *Man the Measure* (New York: George Braziller, 1961).

Dr. Parkes's book has a "List of Books," with brief critical descriptions, which can serve the reader as an admirable guide to the study of Western culture through the Middle Ages. A further volume, continuing into modern times, is promised. A good anthology, with a useful introduction, is F. LeV. Baumer, *Main Currents of Western Thought* (New York: Knopf, 1952).

To revert to the analytical approach, some study of logic and epistemology is essential. As a readable approach to traditional (dare I say, old-fashioned?) logic, I suggest R. W. Holmes, *The Rhyme of Reason* (New York: Appleton-Century-Crofts, 1939). Symbolic logic clearly can't be made easy or for most of us interesting; but it is important, and Susanne K. Langer's *Introduction to Symbolic Logic,* 2d ed., in a Dover paperback, displays her great gift of clear exposition. For the problem of knowledge as it seems to moderns, an essential is C. K. Ogden and I. A. Richards, *The Meaning of Meaning,* a Harvest paperback. If you keep your critical instincts awake, I can recommend an interesting *oeuvre de vulgarisation* (the French is necessary, because of the bad connotations of corresponding terms in English), Stuart Chase, *The Tyranny of Words,* a Harvest paperback.

The best introduction to what the social or behavioral sciences have achieved is Clyde Kluckhohn, *Mirror for Man* (1949), a Premier paperback. Stuart Chase, *The Proper Study of Mankind* (rev. ed., 1956) is a bit too optimistic, but most useful.

As for the philosophers themselves, the above should certainly provide a reader with an all-too-rich set of choices. For the beginner a bit in awe of them, I make a perhaps unorthodox suggestion: Plato (Jowett's familiar translations will do, preferably in the two-volume edition of Raphael Demos, *The Dialogues of Plato,* New York: Random House, 1937), at least the *Republic, Apology, Phaedo, Timaeus;* Pascal's *Pensées*—there is a Dutton Everyman paperback, with an introduction by T. S. Eliot; William James, at least *Pragmatism,* a Meridian paperback, and *The Will to Believe,* a Dover paperback; Nietzsche, *Beyond Good and Evil,* a Gateway paperback in a good new translation, and the *Birth of Tragedy* and the *Genealogy of Morals,* also in new translation in an Anchor paperback. I have chosen these philosophers because they are born writers, who come through as stylists even in such relatively bad translations as those Oscar Levy made of Nietzsche. After them, you can tackle any, even Kant, with due patience. A cut-and-dried but certainly very representative list is given in Bertrand Russell's above-mentioned *Problems of Philosophy.*

There seems to me no royal road—no first-rate introduction—to what non-Western men have thought and felt about the matters we are here concerned with. And though I feel that a lot of pious nonsense is produced to further the rise of a "world-consciousness" in us poor white provincials, and to diminish our shocking ethnocentrism, the fact remains that the serious student of man's condition in the mid-twentieth century has got to do what he can to understand what goes on in the heads and hearts and endocrines of Asians and Africans. There are worse introductions to this than straightforward history. You can get the "facts" and good reading suggestions from M. Savelle, editor, *A History of World Civilization,* 2 vols. (New York: Holt, 1957). This is a collaborative American textbook, uneven, and hardly addressed to the general reader, but it does go into Indian, Chinese, and Japanese civilization in good detail, and surveys our physically One World in the twentieth century. For the primitives or non-civilized—there would appear to be some still—one must go to anthropology. Here there is a masterly introduction in the late Alfred Kroeber's *Anthropology,* rev. ed. (New York: Harcourt, Brace, 1948). A good approach to the most important of these non-European cultures is afforded by volumes of the American Foreign Policy Library published by the Harvard University Press, especially J. K. Fairbank, *The United States and China* (rev. ed., 1958), W. N. Brown, *The United States and India and Pakistan* (1953), E. O. Reischauer, *The United States and Japan* (rev. ed., 1957), and E. A. Speiser, *The United States and the Near East* (1947). The reading lists in each of these books are up-to-date and critical. Still another approach is through studies in the history of religions, an immense field indeed, which has in the last few hundred years especially interested positivist or Enlightened scholars, many of whom have felt rather superior to their subject. Of these positivist studies I have an especial weakness for the bluff, lively, but by no means egregiously hostile *Treatise on the Gods* of the late H. L. Mencken (New York: Knopf, 1930). There is a lot of information in a much more prejudiced treatment, S. Reinach, *Orpheus: A History of Religions,* new enlarged ed. (London: Peter Owen, 1960), which contains the famous definition of religion as: *a sum of scruples which impede the free exercise of our faculties.* John Murphy, *The Origins and History of Religions* (New York: Philosophical Library, 1952), is even more detailed, and much more detached and scholarly. W. L. King, *Introduction to Religion* (New York: Harper, 1954), is both sympathetic and scholarly.

Two famous contemporary books by leading exponents of transcendence of ethnocentrism have to be tackled. There is the great ten-volume *Study of History* (New York: Oxford University Press, 1934-1956) of Arnold Toynbee, and the excellent two-volume condensation of it by D. C. Somervell (New York: Oxford University Press, 1947-1957); or better perhaps in this connotation, Toynbee's *An Historian's Approach to Religion* (New York: Oxford University Press, 1956). Then there is F. S. C. Northrop, *Meeting of East and West,* a Macmillan paperback. Both these writers seem to me excessively high-minded, but perhaps only the high-minded can make ours something nearer One World.

Finally, my Section IV, which deals with only a very few representations of what I call current "Whither Mankind" books, could be vastly expanded. Any "quality" periodical nowadays is bound to have articles and reviews

that add to this already immense literature. Much—most—of it is probably
"alienated," but it is clearly a sign of our times. I shall content myself here
with what seems to me a remarkable cross section of such writing in English. This is the Harper series edited by Ruth Nanda Anshen under the
title "World Perspectives." The separate volumes can be located in any
major library under the name of the editor; Harper & Brothers, (49 East
33d Street, N. Y. 16) will gladly supply a complete list for any inquirer.
The editor's introduction to each volume may suggest to the unwary reader
a certain definite, almost monolithic approach, but the series actually
covers the full range of our contemporary many-mindedness, from "materialism" to "idealism," from the godless to the god-inspired.